BE READY WHEN THE SH*T GOES DOWN

BE READY WHEN THE SH*T GOES DOWN

A Survival Guide to the Apocalypse

FORREST GRIFFIN

AND ERICH KRAUSS

with Illustrations by Jason Lee

wm

WILLIAM MORROW

An Imprint of HarperCollins*Publishers*

BE READY WHEN THE SH*T GOES DOWN. Copyright © 2010 by Forrest Griffin and Erich Krauss. All rights reserved. Printed in the United States of America. No part of this book may be used or reproduced in any manner whatsoever without written permission except in the case of brief quotations embodied in critical articles and reviews. For information address HarperCollins Publishers, 10 East 53rd Street, New York, NY 10022.

HarperCollins books may be purchased for educational, business, or sales promotional use. For information please write: Special Markets Department, HarperCollins Publishers, 10 East 53rd Street, New York, NY 10022.

Designed by Richard Oriolo

Library of Congress Cataloging-in-Publication Data has been applied for.

ISBN 978-0-06-199825-6

10 11 12 13 14 OV/RRD 10 9 8 7 6 5 4 3 2

Dedicated to my friend, Big John Grantham

CONTENTS

PARENTAL WARNING: ORTBIYAAMBTA—1435

N ow that I am a famous author, it has come to my attention that there is no rating system for books. There is a rating system for movies, CDs, and even video games, but absolutely nothing for books. I am sure the reason for this is that kids today are far too lazy to read, even when the subject matter is filthy. In any case, this has to change. When I did the promotional tour for my *New York Times* bestseller, *Got Fight?*, I cannot count how many eight- and ten-year-old kids came up to me and had me sign their copies. Of course I signed their books because it put money in my pocket, but it was very inappropriate for kids that age to be buying my book. Having lost some sleep over the whole matter, I felt the need to come up with a rating system and apply it to this book.

As you can see above, I have given this book a rating of ORTBI-

YAAMBTA—1435, which is an acronym for Only Read This Book If You Are A Male Between The Ages of fourteen and thirty-five. Simple and to the point, am I right? The reason for such a harsh rating is due to all the dirty language, which includes but is not limited to "ass clown," "ball juggler," "cum catcher," "dick sucker," "eel stroker," "felcher," "goo-gargler," "hippie," "ignoramus," "jack-off," "kitty-kicker," "loser," "motherfucker," "narcissist," "ogler," "penis," "queef," "rubber," "stupid," "teetotaler," "urethra," "vagina," "wannabe," "X-ray-glasses-wearing-peeper," "yodeler," "zelcher" (like felcher, only with a Z . . . Don't ask). Notice how I used one swearword that starts with each letter of the alphabet. Genius, am I right? (Note: I do not want to get e-mails saying that I did not use every one of these words in the book. They are all printed above, so yeah, they have all been used.) Anyway, I figure that if you are fourteen, you have probably heard most of these swearwords before, so reading the book won't corrupt your mind too terribly. Your parents might still see you as their little angel, but we both know the truth. Fourteen is the new thirty. If you are under fourteen or over thirty-five, you have most likely heard these words, but the context in which they are used might either give you nightmares about the "bad man" or cause uncontrollable vomiting, depending on which end of the spectrum you fall. In any cause, you've been warned—now go buy your copy! Just don't read it if you're not the right age.

ACKNOWLEDGMENTS

I would like to thank Lucas Rakofsky for not suing me for passing his ideas off as my own . . . which, by the way, I have been doing for years . . . At least that is what he says.

I would like to thank Chuck Norris for saving America. I have a Total Gym that I've never actually used, but I'm sure it's phenomenal. It's also an excellent clothes rack.

I would like to thank Ben & Jerry for making it so damn hard to make weight. Fuck you, Ben, and fuck you, Jerry.

I would like to thank myself for teaching all of you how to survive the apocalypse. You should thank me as well.

I would like to acknowledge my freshman English teacher, not because she changed my life for the better, but rather because she gave me a B for my apparent incorrect usage of commas. That was bullshit. Nobody with a life has thought as much about commas as I have. If you, want to connect two, thoughts without having to start a new sentence, and rename the subject, use a comma. I mean is, that so fucking hard (comma) bitch! . . . Telling me I don't know how to use commas. I used eight commas in this paragraph, and I did an excellent job.

I would like to thank the chief medical adviser for this book, Anthony Rakofsky, who happens to be allergic to peanuts. As a matter of fact, he is allergic to nuts of any kind. Despite his help on this book, when I start my new utopia in the aftermath of the apocalypse, I will ban people like him from breeding. Seriously, how are people who are allergic to nuts still alive? Talk about pampering the weak! Personally, I have Gladsens syndrome, which is an immune deficiency. Although this too is a pretty big weakness and makes me terrified to shake people's hands, I am bigger and manlier than Anthony, so I will be exempt from any of the postapocalyptic rules or restrictions that I create in my kingdom.

I would like to thank Tucker Max, author of *I Hope They Serve Beer in Hell*, for making me look like a good guy in comparison.

I would like to thank my mother, again. I thank her for everything good I do from now until the day I die. Everything bad I do, like this book for example, I blame entirely on bad sitcoms, violent video games, and heavy-metal music.

I would like to thank Bill O'Reilly and Bill Maher for making me the angriest person on the planet.

I would like to thank yoga instructors for being totally and completely insane. Seriously, yoga will not cure cancer or make your erection stiffer (we all know the only way to get a stiffer erection is to allow your penis to get repeatedly stung by bees).

I would like to thank my management, Zinkin Entertainment, for making it seem reasonable for companies to pay enormous amounts of money for me to do nothing.

Thanks to Zakk Wylde and Eric Hendrikx for supplying the Vehicle of Death section.

Thanks to Frank Scatoni and Raffi Nahabedian.

And finally, I would like to thank coffee for helping me find my inner rage.

A very special thanks goes out to contributing editor Bret Aita for outstanding work. I've never met Bret and don't know what a contributing editor does, but Erich told me he's doing a phenomenal job.

CAUTION

Do not under any circumstances burn this book for heat. It is preferable that you die of hypothermia before you destroy this book.

WARNING

This book was written for idiots by idiots.

NOTE

This book was not tested on animals. It was tested on migrant day laborers. Hey, fuck you, they signed the waivers. No, they couldn't read English, but whose fault is that?

WARNING

To protect the innocent, the names, dates, and places in this book have all remained real. Only the facts have been changed.

WARNING

It is important that you understand that absolutely no research went into this book. Well, that isn't entirely correct. Erich spent about twenty minutes on the Internet, but that was mainly to get the correct spelling of names, which I am pretty sure he still got wrong.

WARNING

There are only four warnings, one caution, and one "note" in this book. There should obviously be a lot more. Please do not sue me.

MONEY-BACK GUARANTEE

In the event of the apocalypse, if the information in this book does not save your life, Forrest Griffin will personally refund every penny you spent on its purchase, including the tax. (Disclaimer: Money must be collected in person, *after* the apocalypse. In the event that you are dead, your family members are not allowed to collect the refund, even if they bring your corpse to Forrest's house in a wheelbarrow.)

FORREST, WHAT THE FUCK ARE YOU THINKING?

So a lot of you are picking up this book and thinking, "Forrest, you're a fighter, and not a particularly good one, what the fuck do you know about surviving the apocalypse?" Or perhaps you're muttering quietly to yourself, "Why should I take advice on surviving the end of the world from a guy who gets hit in the head on a regular basis?" Or maybe you're saying, "Sure, Forrest is the guy I want helping me battle it out in a nuclear wasteland, but he's not necessarily the guy that I want teaching me about water purification." Fine. I can sort of understand your skepticism, so let me explain.

I've learned many lessons during my time on this planet, but at the age of, oh, let's say elevenish, I learned a very important one. If you read my last book, you're probably thinking this has something to do with the time I shit myself while bungee-jumping at Dollywood, but you're wrong. Although that little experience clued me in to the fact that you probably shouldn't eat Mexican food an hour before you dive off a fifty-foot tower, the lesson I am talking about is one of the biggies.

The event that changed my perception of the world and, even more importantly, the people in it, occurred on a beautiful spring afternoon in Augusta, Georgia. School had just let out for the day, and I was heading home with my five best friends in the world. All of them were traveling on their bikes, and I was on foot because my bike had a broken chain. Being fatherless at the time, I had every intention of going to one of my friends' fathers to get the needed repairs, but fathers have a tendency to help out their own kids first. In any case, I was huffing it on foot.

Everything was as right as rain as we made the journey from the schoolhouse to our neighborhood. I kept a decent pace, and my friends did tricks on their bikes to ensure I never fell too far behind. We were telling jokes, laughing, and making plans for the upcoming weekend. But just as we turned onto the street that led to all of our homes, I noticed the face of one of my friends change. It went from the happy-go-lucky face of a typical eleven-year-old to the panic-stricken face you see in horror movies just before a person gets mutilated by a chain saw. At first I thought he was grimacing for my benefit because he was looking in my direction, but then I noticed that he was actually looking over my shoulder.

That's when I heard the snarling, growling beast. Still running, I looked behind me and saw the biggest fucking dog in the world, foaming at the mouth and sprinting in our direction. This rabid rottweiler turned our casual trip home into the Tour de France. All of my friends lifted their asses off their seats and stood up on their pedals, pushing with all of their strength. At first our scattering confused the irate and rapidly approaching dog, which I later named Cujo. He went after the bikes first, but as my friends pulled ahead, he decided to conserve his strength and turn on me.

It was just like one of those documentaries you see on the Discovery Channel where a lion storms into a pack of wildebeests. At first the lion just sort of runs around, but then he quickly hones his laser sights on the weakest, most pathetic creature in the group. In this particular case, I was the pathetic creature because I wasn't currently in possession of a bike.

I sprinted for home, and with the insane mutt having been momentarily distracted by my friends, I had approximately a ten-yard lead, but I could hear the rapid clicking of his long-nailed paws drawing nearer. By the time I could see my house in front of me, my fear had risen to an unimaginable level. If I hadn't pissed just prior to leaving school, my pants would have been soaked. I made this high-pitched piglet squeal that I had never made before and have never made since. Each time one of my feet touched pavement, I was certain it would be the last. Eleven years old and this was it, the end of my life.

In my terror, I peeled my eyes away from my home and turned them on my group of friends, hoping they would somehow save me or at the very least offer me some type of reassurance that everything would be all right. Never in my life had I needed the support of another human being so badly, and I knew that if there was anyone I could count on being there for me, it was my trusted amigos.

Instead of seeing the support I so badly needed, I saw something that will be forever etched into my frontal lobe. My blood brothers, *mi hermanos*, my partners in crime were pointing at me, laughing their asses off. And I am not talking about smiling or even chuckling—each and every one of them was bent over the front of their handlebars, mouth wide open, laughing from the belly. The kind of laughter you get when someone you absolutely hate trips in the school cafeteria and stomach-surfs on their food tray down a flight of stairs, except it was *Look at Forrest get chased by that rabid dog!*

I sprinted across my front lawn, and surprisingly I made it to the front steps. I leaped up them in a single bound and skidded to a stop on the front porch. With trembling hands, I threw open the screen door and reached for the knob. The killing machine was right behind me now, but I had made it. I'd escaped a brutal mauling that if videotaped would have undoubtedly been played over and over again on the nightly news, perhaps even led to stiffer dog laws in the United States, until . . .

The fucking door was locked.

Cujo lunged, but with the screen door having already swung shut on my backside, he bounced off. The instant he landed, he came right back at me. Although my face was pressed firmly against the wooden door, I could feel his hot breath on the back of my legs. For a brief instant I thought that perhaps I was protected, but that's when Cujo put those fantastically long claws to use and began tearing into the metal screen mesh. I tried reaching into my pocket to get at my keys, but there wasn't enough room. I was literally sandwiched between the door and the screen.

In less than a minute I not only felt Cujo's claws tearing into my skin, but I could also feel his wet nose. His game plan became overwhelming apparent—he was attempting to tear a large enough hole into the screen to get his head through, and once he managed that, my legs and butt cheeks would essentially become Alpo.

The fear became so great that something snapped in my mind. I don't want to say I blacked out because I was still awake, but my body somehow started working on autopilot. When my mind refocused, I was clinging to one of the thick, circular pillars that traversed our porch, seven feet off the ground. To this day, I have no recollection of making the four-foot journey from the door to the pillar or even climbing the pillar. To be quite honest, I don't even see how I could have covered that distance without getting mauled.

In any case, I was clinging with all my strength to this pillar and the rabid rottweiler was angrier than ever. It was just like one of those Tom and Jerry cartoons where Tom is clinging to something several feet off the ground, and a pit bull is jumping toward him and snapping its massive jaws.

After what seemed like an eternity, but in reality was probably closer to ten minutes, my mother pulled into the driveway. She saw me clinging for dear life to the pillar, screaming and crying, and then she saw the dog at my feet, leaping into the air in an attempt to reach my flesh. Like a soldier who rushes blindly into the battlefield to save a comrade, my mother exited her car, grabbed a thick branch off the ground, and then stormed up onto the porch. She arched that stick back like a baseball bat and then swung for the hills.

The branch connected with the top of Cujo's head. Unfortunately, my mother's weapon of choice consisted of 90 percent mildew, causing it to evaporate upon impact and cause no harm to the dog whatsoever. It did, however, make Cujo realize that it had a much more accessible meal. It turned on my mom, and while she swung her half-size bat to keep the dog at bay, I leaped off the pillar, pulled my keys from my pocket, and sprung open the front door.

I don't know how my mom did it, but she managed to fight off the dog and back up through the front door. Once we were both inside, we slammed the door and fell to the floor in exhaustion, both of us dripping blood. My wounds most likely required stitches by today's standards, but due to the fact that we didn't have medical insurance, my mom broke out her kick-ass first-aid kit, cleaned the gashes with some peroxide, and then threw butterfly bandages on those suckers. The dog had clearly been rabid, and at the very least we should have been given some antibiotics, but somehow we both avoided dying horrible deaths.

The attack left me with some decent-size scars on my legs and ass, but instead of reminding me of the horrors of that day, they remind me of the important lesson that I learned. The lesson is this: When the shit goes down, even your best friends in the world will abandon you, and most likely do so while laughing their tits off. Whether it's a dog attack or the apocalypse, no one is going to save your sorry ass but you, so you better be fucking ready.

I've spent the last twenty years making sure I'm ready, and now I'm going to make sure that none of you get swept up in fallout. Now you might be thinking, "Forrest, by teaching everyone your secrets, aren't you making it harder for you yourself to survive when the end of the world comes?"

The answer is no, I'm definitely not. Because we both know that if you're reading a book by me, clearly learning from books isn't your thing. So yeah, I'm not that worried. Besides, worst-case scenario, I've got my mom to protect me and I'm pretty sure not even this book will save you from her.

BE READY WHEN THE SH*T GOES DOWN

YOU **MUST** PASS THIS TEST . . . THIS TIME I MEAN IT!

A s I've mentioned in all of my high-profile television and radio interviews, my previous book, *Got Fight?*, spent nine weeks on the *New York Times* bestseller list. So what's the problem? Everything that becomes popular too quickly becomes unpopular just as quickly. The clothing brand No Fear ring a bell? No, probably not—see my point. This is not because the product sucks in any way[1]—it is because of you, the consumer. When an army of nerds is seen toting a certain product between the chess club and front lawn of the high school where they receive their afternoon beatings, normal people get turned off from purchasing the product.

---

[1] Of course I am referring to my book, not the No Fear clothing brand, which sucks huge donkey cock—and I mean that in a bad way.

Personally, I want my books to be read by only the cool crowd,[2] so I am going to have to be a lot more selective this time around as far as whom I allow to purchase a copy. In the test below, you will find three types of questions.

The first type question will rate your manliness. I know what you are thinking—"If I passed the manliness test in your last book, *Got Fight?*,[3] can I go ahead and skip this test?" The answer is no. After all, a lot can happen in a year. A woman could have removed your balls and placed them in her purse[4] or you could have finally gotten around to buying that two-hundred-dollar pair of jeans you always wanted. You must prove to me that you are a man now, not sometime in the distant past.

The second type of question will judge your worth as a human being. Essentially, do I even want you surviving the apocalypse? Remember, I have knowledge you need, and I want to make sure you are worthy of receiving it before I slip you my large baton (of knowledge).

The third type of question will judge your Forrest Griffin Survival IQ. It has nothing to do with trying to stuff various-shaped blocks into various shaped holes. In my world, I am only concerned with stuffing one object into one hole. That's right—the object is *knowledge* and the hole is your *brain*! But before I give you this injection of knowledge, I must ensure that you have the necessary cunning, craft, and ingenuity to properly receive it. If you are not ready and I give it to you anyway, it could blind you or kill you or both. Both would be the worst.

This test is more important than the SATs or that test you took after watching the Kmart employee theft video (by the way, I scored a hundred percent on my employee theft test at Food Line—try to top that, bitches!). It will determine whether or not you are allowed to read the book that will help you outrun the death that scorches the face of the earth in the not-so-distant future. So, I highly recommend reclining in your chair, sipping on your chamomile tea,[5] and really thinking each question through before answering.

Tip: If you get stuck on a certain question, answer based on how you think I might react in such a situation. Pretty much all the questions below

---

[2] You know, the people who devour those awesome *Twilight* books.
[3] Did I mention that it was on the *New York Times* bestseller list for nine weeks?
[4] Or a man could have placed them in his fanny pack, which would be much worse.
[5] Anyone that drinks chamomile tea does not deserve to survive the apocalypse. Decaffeinated tea defeats the purpose of tea—it is the same as drinking Near Beer.

FORTUNE COOKIE WISDOM

I want it known that although I have placed Fortune Cookie Wisdom boxes throughout this book, in no way am I racist against Orientals . . . or Asians . . . or whatever they are called these days. They are good at math and have small penises—what's not to like? The reason I use the term is that after consuming a cheap, lousy, Chinese dinner of overfried, MSG-filled dog, the fortune cookie often gives you a pearl of wisdom that makes the meal not so bad. Hopefully, the fortune cookies in this book will make it not so bad, as it contains too much MSG and has the same consistency as fried dog meat.

P.S. My mom, who is as liberal as they come, still calls Asians "Orientals." It is a throwback from a different era and she can't help herself . . . and she loves their rugs.

were situations I found myself in over the course of my filthy life, and my reaction is always the correct reaction, even if it seems like a terrible reaction upon first glance. If you think how I behaved was strange, stupid, or perhaps slightly homoerotic, not only will you flunk the test and fail to be buttered with my hot knowledge, but I will also come to your house and steal one of your lovely pets. If you do not have a pet, I will shit underneath your couch, close all the doors and windows, and turn the heater all the way up.

(Note: If you do not pass the test in this book, you can still purchase a copy; you just aren't allowed to read it.)

FORTUNE COOKIE WISDOM

While shitting under the couch is horrible, it is nothing compared to the upper-decker, which is where you shit in the upper lid of a toilet. Every time you flush, it smells more like shit. Although I have never personally given an upper-decker, in college, me and a couple of friends went to a party, and the two girls who owned the home where the party was being held turned out to be real bitches, so my two friends both shit in the upper lid of their toilet. I was the lookout guy. And no, I didn't ask if they both shat into the upper lid at the same time. I don't want to know those kinds of things. It raises far too many questions.

1. **You step into the octagon with Anderson Silva and things don't quite go as planned. How do you react?**

   a. Remember that the last time you were in this situation you started crying in front of millions of people (e.g., Keith Jardine). Instead of repeating the experience, you immediately bolt from the cage, all the while singing Flock of Seagulls' "And I raaann . . ."

   b. Fight Anderson Silva in the parking lot, except this time you use some type of weapon such as a billy club, baton, or bazooka.

   c. Quickly invent some injury that prevented you from fighting to your full capability, such as glaucoma.

   d. After you wake up, get in the referee's face for stopping the fight.

   e. Throw your hands up into the air and pretend you won. When they announce that Anderson won, begin shouting, "I was robbed!"

   f. Remain in the ring and take your defeat like a man.

ANSWERS

   a. +8 points. Excellent answer. It will cause every reporter and fan to ask you, "What the hell were you thinking?" for the next several months, but at least no one will see you cry . . . again.

   b. -8 points. Bad choice. Anderson Silva is a master with nunchucks as well. Most likely he will claim your weapon and beat you to death with it.

   c. +4 points. I am not a big fan of fighters who make excuses, but if you cite glaucoma as being the reason for your loss, you get the +4 points for originality. However, if you made up a more generic excuse such as a slipped disc, broken foot, or busted hand, subtract ten points . . . Remember, all fighters are injured to some degree during the training process. Why? Because a part of their training consists of actual fighting.

   d. -5 points. After suffering such a terrible loss, the last thing you want to do is get beat up by Mario Yamasaki. It would be a career killer.

   e. -5 points. An excellent way to look like an even bigger jackass.

   f. -2 points. Now I know that I said this was the proper way to handle a loss in my previous book, but I am now retracting that statement in an attempt to make myself feel manlier. If you chose this answer, fuck you! You think you are better than me? You try getting beat by Anderson Silva and then sucking it up for a postfight humiliation interview.

2. Which way is north?

    a. Toward the mountains.

    b. Over by that lake.

    c. Down by the stream.

    d. Toward that mangrove forest.

ANSWERS

    a. -5 points. No, stupid, the mountains are in the south.

    b. -5 points. The lake is in the southeast. Either your compass is broke or you have eaten too many paint chips.

    c. +8 points. Correct. You score big!

    d. -8 points. While you were trying to answer this question, I made a voodoo doll in your likeness and I'm currently sticking pins into its genital region.

3. You get completely wasted in a bar and at the end of the night you somehow end up in a cougar's apartment, getting it on. While the two of you are engaged in hot, sweaty, sloppy sex, she cocks her head back from the doggie-style position and says in a sweet and maternal voice, "Honey, you ain't been in me for the last five minutes." How do you react?

    a. Despite her intense disappointment, you down a Powerade and attempt to get back into the game.

    b. Curl into the fetal position and began to weep.

    c. Robe quickly, make small talk for approximately five minutes, and then spend the next four days hoping that you never see her again.

    d. Ask her why the fuck it took her five minutes to speak up.

    e. Apologize and then spoon with her for the rest of the night.

ANSWERS

a. -5 points. I am not a big fan of quitters, but you got to know when you
    are defeated. If you couldn't keep it up when you thought you were the
    biggest stud this sweet lady had bedded in her short fifty-five years,
    you most certainly won't be able to keep it up while she is doing her
    nails, texting her friends, and playing tennis on the Wii. If you chose
    this answer, you are either a sadomasochist or are overly determined
    to achieve something you probably shouldn't have attempted in the
    first place.

b. -5 points. Absolutely pathetic . . . While you're at it, might as well
    have her change your diaper and take your temperature with a rectal
    thermometer. (Come to think of it, that might actually get me excited
    again . . . I am sure Freud would have something to say about that;
    after all, that woman was old enough to be my mother.)

c. +8 points. This is the correct answer because it's how I reacted. I
    really truly hoped that I would never see her again, but just like my
    hopes to strut into the octagon and give Anderson Silva a critical
    beat-down, it didn't work out for me. Not long after this emasculating
    experience, I saw her at a restaurant while I was eating with a group of
    friends. I sank so low in my chair only my forehead could be seen over
    the top of the table—not an easy thing when you're six three. (Note to
    self: Never tell anyone about this traumatic experience.)

d. +5 points. Who allows you to beat on their backside for five minutes
    without saying anything? Who does that? Unfortunately, a combination
    of the alcohol and the humiliation of her statement shut down my two
    remaining brain cells and prevented me from asking this question. If
    you should find yourself in this exact situation and have the gall to
    inquire about the meaning behind the delay, please e-mail me the
    answer. I still want to know . . . It is more like a *need*, really . . . The
    more I think back on that experience, the more horrible it becomes. I
    remember I had that drunk sweat going, and I was literally drenching
    her back. It was super gross.

e. -5 points. Do you really want to smell mothballs, talcum power, and
    Chanel No. 5 all night? Yeah, didn't think so.

f. God, this is really confusing. I can't remember what answer goes with
    what question.

4. Early in your MMA career you agree to fight Dan "The Beast" Severn. Instead of trading strikes, he repeatedly takes you down and lies on top of you. He has on his trademark black underroos, his mustache is tickling your neck, and his barrel chest is squashing your innards. In an attempt to get under his skin and turn this into an entertaining fight, what do you whisper into his ear?

    a.   You looked thinner on TV.

    b.   Magnum PI called, and he wants his mustache back.

    c.   You look like a fat Freddy Mercury, anyone ever tell you that?

    d.   You better hurry this up—you've got that seventies porno to make later.

    e.   Hey, do you and Don Frye share the same mustache because I have never seen the two of you together.

    f.   If you let me up, I will give you a shirt for Christmas that reads MUSTACHE RIDES 5 CENTS.

(P.S. No need to check Sherdog.com. Yes, I lost that fight.)

ANSWERS

    a.   +3 points. I said this to him and meant it. The dude was huge, and when you fit all that mass into those tiny shorts, it is kinda disturbing.

    b.   +5 points. If you watched the fight, you know just how boring it was. I had my head pinned up against the cage for the majority of it, giving me plenty of time to think up remarks. I felt this was one of the better ones. As a matter of fact, I think it even made me crack a smile.

    c.   +5 points. Although I have been told that Tank Abbott used this insult while commentating on one of Severn's fights, I came up with it all on my own and whispered it to him while he was lying on top of me. Scary to think that Tank Abbott and I have the same sense of humor.

    d.   +8 points. Not sure when I said this to him in the fight, but I thought it was more original than my other rips.

    e.   +5 points. Another good one. Seemed to upset him too.

    f.   +6 points. I didn't say this, but it would have been funny. The first time I saw that shirt it was on the back of a sixty-year-old woman in Juárez, Mexico. Thinking she had a great sense of humor, I went up to her to ask her about her shirt, but she didn't speak a lick of English. Obviously, she didn't have a clue what her shirt said.

5. **You are heading into the desert to escape the aftermath of the apocalypse, and you get to bring one person with you on your journey. Which one of the following would it be?**

    a. Stripper

    b. Doctor

    c. Wilderness Man

    d. Plumber

    e. Prostitute

    f. A Navy SEAL

    g. Little Person

ANSWERS

    a. -5 points. Stripper: Despite what you might be inclined to believe, a stripper has very little value in the desert. Come to think of it, a stripper has very little value period. This is due to the fact that while she was growing up, her father told her she had very little value. I know what you are thinking, "But, Forrest, what if I want to go out with a bang!" If that's your goal, you should have picked a prostitute. A stripper is like a car that starts but won't actually take you anywhere (except to the ATM). In addition, she is going to find a way to talk you out of your water, shelter, food, and any dignity you have left.

    b. +5 points. Doctor: Although there are no medical instruments or supplies in the desert, doctors are smart people who are fairly good at improvising. If you picked a doctor, I give you +5 points. However, if the doctor is a psychiatrist, subtract 15 points. Unless, of course, you are a stripper. If you are a stripper and selected a psychiatrist to wander with you in the desert, give yourself +15 points. The two of you will have plenty of time to work out your daddy issues.

    c. -4 points. Wilderness Man: The majority of you most likely chose a wilderness man, but I must now inform you that this is a terrible choice. By nature, a wilderness man is a loner. You need him more than he needs you, and he will ditch you the first chance he gets. In addition, they are notoriously bad conversationalists.

d.   -8 points. Plumber: If you picked a plumber, hit yourself upside the head with a lead pipe. This question was supposed to be a gimme, but apparently you managed to fuck it up.

e.   -4 points. Prostitute: Unlike if you were to bring a stripper, you will probably get laid frequently with a prostitute companion. While this might seem appealing, you must remember that prostitutes don't fuck for free. You are going to have to take care of this person. That means feeding them, clothing them, and putting up with their bullshit. You will also spend most of your days foraging for medicinal plants to soothe your burning loins.

f.   +10 points. Navy SEAL: Navy SEALs might not be as familiar with surviving off the fat of the land as wilderness men, but they are as tough as nails and great improvisers. They also often have a hero complex, so there is a good chance that they will take you under their wing and save your ass from dying a horrible death. This was the correct answer.

g.   +5 points. Little Person: This was another correct answer. Little people are great entertainers, and they are small enough that you can carry them around in a backpack. They can also be quite useful—you can send them up trees to steal eagle eggs, into caves to scout for dangers, or even down into small holes in the earth to flush out furry animals. (Unfortunately, the word "midget" has gone the way of the word "Oriental." Midget used to be a socially acceptable way to describe people who were, well, midgets. Now you have to call them "little people" or "vertically challenged" or something crazy like that. I long for the day when I can say the word "midget" again without being judged or called a size-ist.)

6. A good buddy of yours sets you up with a woman who works at his office. You go out on a date, things go well, and at the end of the night you go back to her place. Just before you are about to get it on, she says, "I have to confess something. I have herpes." How do you react?

a.   Use a condom.

b.   Run from her house, get in your car, and speed away. Even if you are in your own home, leave immediately. No kissing your dog good-bye, no stopping to take a leak. You just hightail it the fuck out of there.

  c. Have sex with her, but pour Scope on your genitals afterward to kill whatever you may have picked up.

  d. Ask her if she's into blow jobs or anal.

  e. Ask if she has a younger sister that doesn't have herpes.

  f. Put an arm around her and spend the next four hours listening to her problems, most of which revolve around the fact that she has HERPES.

  g. Tell her it is okay because you have syphilis.

ANSWERS

  a. -15 points. You are an idiot . . . If you don't know why this is a terrible decision, there is no point in me telling you. Chances are, you will bring a hair dryer into the shower at some point in the very near future.

  b. +8 points. Good job, you are not a complete moron. When this happened to me, I think I may have made a few minutes of small talk, but I was out of there pretty damn quick. As you could imagine, I was irate at my friend. In addition to setting me up with a girl who had the gift that keeps on giving, he also set me up with a promoter who wrote me a bad check and a roommate who went completely nuts and called the cops on me. Yeah, I really need to start choosing my friends more wisely. I'm telling you, this chick roommate was a fucking nutcase. I had a girl over one night, and I guess she could hear us laughing and talking and humping. Not sure why that would piss her off, but it did. Instead of asking us to quiet down, she kept turning off the a/c. It was Georgia in the middle of summer, so it was hot as fuck. To avoid my bed turning into a swimming pool, every time she turned it off, I would turn it back on. The next morning, she called the cops on me. They busted into the house like some sort of domestic disturbance was going on. I talked my way out of it, but I had to live with the bitch for another few months. The surprising part is when she moved out, she actually left me money for the bills.

  c. -5 points. I actually heard this on one of those sex talk shows. The guy shaved his pubic region, had sex with a prostitute, and then dunked his nuts into a glass of Scope because he was worried about catching something . . . I'm talking Scope, ladies and gentlemen. (As a side note, Bigger John had a friend in college who used to not only wash his junk with alcohol after sex, but also pour it into his pee hole.)

d.   -5 points. Although you can't see me, I am shaking my head, thinking about how stupid you are.

e.   +5 points. Terribly inconsiderate, but worth a try.

f.   +3 points. I am giving you a few points for this because I am really trying to be a better human being.

g.   +0 points. Good, you found your soul mate.

7.   You're driving home from the gym, and suddenly you realize that you have to take a shit. Not wanting to drop your payload in the Starbucks crapper for fear of getting eighty-sixed for life, you convince yourself that you can make it to your personalized porcelain palace. After ten torturous minutes, you pull into your driveway and breathe a sign of relief. You run into the house and straight for the bathroom, but you quickly realize that it is much more difficult to keep your glutes flexed while running. Your turd stops playing peekaboo and makes a mad dash for freedom. Not wanting to admit to yourself the finality of the situation, you drop your TapouT trunks and leap toward the toilet, realizing this will be a wet one. While in midair, you fire-hose everything in sight. I'm talking the floor, the bathroom curtain, and the fluffy horseshoe toilet mat that your wife adores (I never knew what purpose they served, but now I know). After a few minutes of just kind of looking at the holocaust caused by the in-flight shit storm, you dig deep and begin the cleanup process. You wipe everything down and go through two cans of Lysol, but you still have that damn fluffy toilet mat to deal with. Instead of burning it in the backyard, you toss it into the washing machine. Forty minutes later, it comes out as fluffy and fresh-smelling as the day it was purchased. However, being a stupid man, you're not quite sure if you can put a fluffy toilet mat in the dryer. Wanting to put the whole situation in the past, you toss it on top of the dryer and walk away. An hour later, your wife brings the toilet mat into the living room and demands to know why it is sopping wet. What do you tell her?

a. I couldn't find a sponge, so I used it to wash the car.

b. I have no idea what you are talking about. Didn't know we even had a toilet mat.

c. Oh, the toilet mat. Yeah, I shit on that and tried to clean it up.

d. Is that a new dress? Damn, you look beautiful today.

e. Did you know the capital of Peru is Venezuela?

ANSWERS

a. -5 points. Lying to women about things that transpire in their household is just plain stupid. She might pretend to buy your excuse, but a few minutes later, she will go out and check for clues. If the car is not washed and the driveway is dry, expect another global shit storm. Later that night, when your defenses are down, she will break you. Like a preschooler, you will have to admit that you accidently shit on her fluffy toilet mat.

b. -5 points. Total ignorance can sometimes work. After all, women do not have that much faith in men's intelligence. If you can't remember her birthday, why in the hell would you notice a fluffy toilet mat, right? But be prepared for the topic of the wet, fluffy toilet mat to come up at social gatherings. *Oh, Margaret, I forgot to tell you, the strangest thing happened the other day. I came home and our toilet mat was sitting on top of the dryer, sopping wet.* Chances are, a husband of one of your wife's friends will have shit on a toilet mat at some point in time, and then the cat will be out of the bag.

c. +8 points. This is the correct answer. In my particular case, I was watching TV when my wife came into the room. Without missing a beat, I told her I shit on the toilet mat and then tried to clean it up. She stood there for some time, waiting for further explanation, but I gave her none. I simply began channel-surfing. Of course it led her to say things like, "Forrest, you are a disgusting human being," and "There is no fucking way I am going to take care of you when you get old," but at least I was spared the monthlong inquisition.

d. +5 points. Telling your wife she looks beautiful is an excellent distraction. However, the cause of the soggy toilet mat will eventually pop back up. If you use this time to come up with a more clever excuse, give yourself the five points. If you use the time to drink beer and watch football, you get zilch.

FORTUNE COOKIE WISDOM

This gem of wisdom is designed for my female readers. You all know that men are inherently disgusting—and I mean *disgusting*. But it is even more important to realize that as men get older, they get even more disgusting. More ear hair, more nose hair. In fact, my stepfather actually combs his nose hair into his mustache. This is true. So, however gross your fella is now, know that when he's retired, sitting on that porch and watching that sunset, he will be approximately ten times more disgusting than he is now. In my case, I keep a rag by the bed to spit luggies in. Do I jerk off and spit luggies into the same rag? Yes, I fucking do. Is that disgusting? It most certainly is. But just wait until I get old.

e. +5 points. If your wife is the argumentative kind, this might actually work because of course she will know that Venezuela is a separate country, not the capital of Peru. She will take at least ten minutes to berate you and tell you what an idiot you are. In the meantime, she will forget that she was supposed to be berating and yelling at you about the toilet mat. Excellent diversionary tactic. However, if your wife is not the argumentative kind, subtract 5 points, as it will only piss her off. If you wife is somewhat sane, you must stroke her ego or the tactic simply won't work. For future reference, in addition to making a remark about her beauty, I will also accept:

1. You know (sigh), I was thinking about you while you were gone.

2. I just realized how much care and love you put into decorating the house.

3. I don't know how you do it (dramatic pause). I simply don't know how you do it.

8. What type of animal do you own?

a. Grizzly bear

b. Tiger

c. Dog

1. Standard-size mutt that weighs between fifteen and thirty pounds

2. Tiny rodent that weighs less than fifteen pounds

3. Big dog that weighs more than thirty pounds

d. Cat

e. Hamster

f. Horse

g. I do not own an animal.

ANSWERS

a. +8 points. We obviously can't all have grizzly bears, but how awesome would that be? If you are one of the select few, you should write your own book on being manly . . . The downside to owning a grizzly bear as a pet is that oftentimes they will kill and eat you. It would be the same as a mouse owning a cat as a pet. Not a smart idea, but still ultramanly.

b. -5 points. You would think that having a tiger would be ultramanly, but it's not. Unfortunately, there are a lot of feminine men who have already chosen tigers as pets, especially here in Las Vegas. If you think about it, what real man wants a big pussy? Sorry, buddy, should have picked a grizzly bear.

c. Dogs are pretty standard for guys to own, so we have to break this one down further do decide if you are manly or unmanly in your choice of pet.

   1. 0 points. If you have an average-size dog, you are pretty much average in every way. Yes, I base your self-worth on the size of your dog.

   2. -5 points. Although Chuck Liddell and Mickey Rourke are two of the toughest people I know, they both own small dogs, which costs them points on my manliness scale. If you own a big dog and think that you are manlier than these two individuals, you are wrong. I once watched Chuck jump off a fifteen-foot balcony in a bar in Mexico, just to give a waitress a tip. And Mickey Rourke starred in *9½ Weeks*—can't get any manlier than that. Assuming, of course, you don't watch the last fifteen minutes of the film, where he exposes his weaknesses and cries.

   3. +5 points. Before you shoot your wad thinking that you just scored 5 points, there is a catch. If your big dog just sits around at the foot of your chair, farting and chewing on its own limbs, subtract 10 points (do not count the original 5 points I gave you for owning a

big dog). In order to score points with a big dog, it has to be trained to help you out in some way. For example, fetch the paper, kill birds and other dogs, urinate on people you don't like, or play poker.

d.   -5 points. I want to make something very clear—I do not own cats; my wife does. I admit that I pet them from time to time, and if her copy of *Cat Fancy* is open on the table, I may read an article or two. But in no way does that mean I own a cat. Sure, I may bring the cats to Starbucks with me and spend exorbitant amounts of money on their vet bills, but I only do that to make my wife happy. I may have even personally picked out one of the cats from the shelter, but that was just to ensure that we got the manliest cat possible. So what I am saying is that if your wife owns a cat, that is totally cool. However, if you personally own a cat, subtract 5 points.

e.   -150 points. If you are over the age of seven and own a hamster, you are a very, very disturbed human being. I have taken away so many points that it is impossible for you to pass this test, so you might as well quit and go watch Freckles run laps on his wheel.

Confession: While I may be an adult male with no bizarre sexual proclivities, I do in fact own a hamster (it's name is Marzipan—I know, very nice). However, my hamster was a rescue. That's right, in the Las Vegas valley, people foreclose on their homes all the time, and when they move back to Wisconsin or wherever the fuck they are from, they just leave their pets to fend for themselves. One day, my wife and I saw what looked liked a crazy rat running around my yard. Eventually, it came close enough for us to see, and my wife, being a Good Samaritan, began screaming at me to catch it. I ran upon it, but I didn't realize how fast those little fuckers could move when terrified. After several minutes, I had it cornered up against the house, and I reached out to grab it. Not wanting to get taken, it swiped at my fingers with one of its harmless, microscopic paws, and I literally jumped back five feet, thinking it was going to kill me. Needless to say, it didn't score me any manliness points with the old lady. Anyhow, I ended up catching the eight-ounce hamster, and we nursed it back to health. Now I keep it in my closet, literally and figuratively. Once in a while I set him loose around the house in his little ball to torture the cats. Yeah, I'm pretty much a hero.

f.   +8 points. This is another one of those tricky answers. In order to score big points for owning a horse, you must ride it on a regular basis. And I'm not talking about riding up and down the block—you must ride to do manly shit, such as to get across your property to fix a fence or back and forth to work. What kinds of job allow you to

commute to work on a horse? A fucking lot of them. You could be a
bartender in an Old West saloon, gunfighter, or a border patrolman.
All of these are ultramanly jobs. Another stipulation is that you
have to wear the proper attire while riding a horse. No biker shorts
allowed. You have to wear chaps, a cowboy hat, and boots at all
times. However, if you do not wear pants under your chaps, subtract
10 points as this is way too Village People to be manly . . . Come
to think of it, I want you to strike the chaps part. They are most
definitely a no-go. A certain member of the Village People gave chaps
various implications, making them unwearable by the majority of the
population. From now on, chaps may only be worn in biker bars that
cater to special clientele . . . and by "special clientele" I mean people
who are into crazy sex and bondage stuff.

g. -4 points. If you do not own some kind of pet, you are not manly. After
all, being a guy is about controlling shit. And since women hate being
controlled, you must fulfill this requirement on creatures that don't
talk back. The more pets you control, the manlier you become. Unless,
of course, you own cats. Please do not be that person who has fifteen
cats. That is just kind of sad.

9. When you go to the gymnasium, what is it about you that stands out the most?

a. Your matching clothes.

b. Your body odor.

c. Your perfume or cologne.

d. Your jewelry.

e. Your makeup.

f. Absolutely nothing.

ANSWERS

a. -5 points. Unless you are in the military, do not color coordinate your
gymnasium attire. It causes me to laugh and distracts me from my
workout.

b. -5 points. I know what you are thinking: "But Forrest, it has been
scientifically proven that women like the musky order that emanates
from a guy's ripe armpit or crotch." While this might be a hundred
percent true, the gym is not a place to pick up women. Real men pick

up women at truck stops and on street corners, not gymnasiums (by the way, real men do not train at health centers, fitness clubs, or even gyms. Real men only train at gymnasiums). When working out, I do not want to catch a whiff of your mating scent. **PLEASE WEAR CLEAN CLOTHES TO THE GYMNASIUM.** I am not opposed to bathing, either.

c. -8 points. I cannot count the number of times I have gagged while doing cardio due to some floozy's perfume or some douche bag's cologne. You're at the gymnasium, not Club Pure.

d. -6 points. This is just hazardous to your health. Not only does it increase your chances of losing an ear or finger in one of the weight machines, but it will also increase your chances of getting mugged in the parking lot . . . By the way, what gymnasium do you work out in? Is the parking lot well lit, and generally what time will I find you there alone?

e. -5 points. Do I really need to explain this one . . . oh, and before I forget, if you can talk on the phone or read a book while doing cardio, you aren't really doing cardio.

f. +8 points. Good, you're a normal human being like the rest of us.

10. **You are getting ready to head into the desert again, but this time you get to bring one person of faith with you. Which religious background would you choose?**

a. Muslim

b. Scientologist

c. Buddhist

d. Christian

e. Southern Baptist

f. Mormon

g. Hindu

h. Atheist

i. Jewish

j. PENCIL IN YOUR OWN ANSWER HERE. (This choice is reserved for risk takers, as you will either lose or gain major points, depending upon your answer. However, with most people not being nearly as smart as they think they are, I must reserve this option

FORTUNE COOKIE WISDOM

As far as the standard IQ test goes, scoring a 100 means you are about average, scoring under 80 means you are mildly retarded, scoring over 120 means you are intelligent, and scoring over 130 means you are a genius and can join MENSA. If you are wondering what MENSA is, it is a group of socially awkward individuals that are very intelligent, but haven't yet figured out how to use their intelligence in any practical way. Do I say this because I am jealous? Perhaps a little. As I mentioned in my last book, I took a legitimate, sit-down, two-hour IQ test my freshman year in collage, and I was dismayed to learn that my IQ was 84, just five points above being mildly mentally retarded. Remember, this was back in '98 before all this politically correct bullshit, so the sheet of paper that deciphered the scores actually said the word "retarded." Now it says "disabled" or some shit, which probably would have made me feel a little bit better. I remember the people who gave the test tried to give me a pep talk, telling me that it really wasn't that bad, but I was mortally depressed for two days. I mean, I actually tried really hard on the test. So take it from me, never, ever take an IQ test, especially if you are concerned that you might be dumb. Trust me, you are. But as long as you don't take the test, you can always pretend (and just for the record, an IQ test is not that dumb test you download off the internet. A real IQ test takes approximately four hours).

for those who have taken an IQ test and scored over a hundred. If you have taken an IQ test and scored under a hundred [as I did] or never taken an IQ test, you are restricted to picking from one of the choices above.)

ANSWERS

    a.   +4 points. Muslim: These guys are headquartered in the desert, so they probably have a good idea on how to survive there. However, if they are fundamentalist Muslims, do your best not to piss them off. For example, do not joke about their faith or use their religion in any type of multiple-choice quiz.

    b.   -4 points. Scientologist: From what I gather, most Scientologists live in Hollywood, so they probably know nothing about surviving in the desert. Unless they can call that spaceship down to rescue your ass or you enjoy a good yarn of science fiction, they are terrible traveling companions.

c. +2 points. Buddhist: There is only one reason to bring a Buddhist—if you want to die a cheery death.

d. -4 points. Christian: I don't know any Christians that come from the desert, and they always think they are right. They will undoubtedly lead you on a mission to civilize a group of savage squirrels. With that said, I think I might be Christian. I know for a fact my wife is.

e. -8 points. Southern Baptist: They hate everyone and love guns. You would think this would be ideal, but if are unlike me and actually have melanin in your skin, you will most likely get a decent tan while wandering across the desert, causing the Southern Baptist to lynch you.

f. -4 points. Mormon: Having a Mormon traveling mate is good because they come from the desert, but it can be very difficult to ride a ten-speed on sand and you will be forced to give 10 percent of your animal skins to the church.

g. +4 points. Hindu: Not only are they familiar with living on harsh terrain, but they are also used to fasting. Chances are, they will eat very little. Good choice! Just do not murder cows—it tends to really piss them off.

h. -8 points. Atheist: All the atheists I have ever met have been super negative. In addition to this, they also tend to be super lazy. I mean, if they are too fucking lazy to find themselves a belief system, what makes you think they are going to collect firewood. Terrible choice.

i. +4 points. Jewish: It is said that Jewish people wandered the desert for forty years, but once they got out, they all went straight to Hollywood. There is a chance that some of that desert survival knowledge got passed on through their genes, but I doubt it. The reason I awarded you with positive points is that they will undoubtedly teach you how to maintain your beard.

j. PENCIL IN YOUR OWN ANSWER HERE: If you wrote the word "Amish," your risk taking paid off big-time! Go ahead and give yourself 25 points. Amish people are the true survivalists. Having renounced all technology, they have learned how to survive without drilling for oil or making major motion pictures. Give them an ax and a bucket, and they'll make butter, log cabins, and horse-drawn carriages. If you're hanging with one of these guys, no matter what conditions you may find yourself in, you will most likely do all right. Your life will never progress beyond *Little House on the Prairie* and time will probably go pretty fucking slowly, but at least you will live! However, if you penciled in anything other than Amish, the results of your IQ test obviously got mixed up with that of someone much smarter than you. Go ahead and subtract 15 points . . . You might also want to think seriously about taking your own life.

11. What is your favorite magazine?

   a. *Fight* magazine

   b. *Martha Stewart Living*

   c. *Sports Illustrated*

   d. *Muscle & Fitness*

   e. *GQ*

   f. *Playboy*

   g. *Hustler* or another hard-core porn mag.

   h. *Cat Fancy*

ANSWERS

   a. +8 points. A good magazine because I am often in it. Sometimes, they even let me put on my Big Boy pants and write my own articles.

   b. -5 points. You've been putting off that gender reassignment operation, but I think it's about time to open that door.

   c. +0 points. For the most part, this magazine is reserved for fat has-beens dreaming of their high school football days and living vicariously through some millionaire's numbers. Oh, and by the way, if you collect sports cards, you should burn the cards along with yourself . . . or feed them to your hamster.

   d. -5 points. You might not be full-blown gay, but you are definitely peeking over the fence. I mean, even the chicks in this magazine look like dudes.

   e. -8 points. Not only have you fallen over the fence, but you've also rolled down a hill, slipped into a creek, washed out to sea, and swallowed by an overly gay whale.

f.   +0 points. You would think that a magazine with a half-naked chick on the cover would be megamanly, but it is not. Once you open it, all you see is articles and stories and advertisements. And in the few naked pictures it does contain, the women are covering most of their junk. If you want to be a real man, you must look at porn mags that actually offend your girlfriend.

g.   +8 points. Now this is what I am talking about.

h.   -4 points. For the second time, I do not subscribe to *Cat Fancy*. My wife does.

ACTUAL RANDOM CONVERSATION IN THE GRIFFIN HOUSE

JAIME: Forrest, for the tenth time, they are never going to put you on the cover of *Cat Fancy*.

FORREST: Sure they will. Don't they have somewhat famous people on the cover from time to time?

JAIME: No, they don't. They just have cats on the cover.

FORREST: But what if I am holding our cat?

12. When does cannibalism become okay?

a.   When you are hungry.

b.   When your buddy Joe actually begins looking like a giant pork chop.

c.   Anytime. Even now, before the apocalypse. Might as well get used to the taste.

d.   Never. You should die before you consume human meat.

ANSWERS

a.   +5 points. I sometimes get hungry between brunch and lunch, so I know how badly it sucks. I will accept this answer.

b.   -5 points. If your buddy starts looking like a giant pork chop, you waited far too long.

c.   -5 points. I am sorry, but I cannot accept this answer. Why eat humans now, when there are so many unwanted dogs and cats?

d.   -8 points. Next thing you'll tell me is that it is "wrong" to piss in the community pool. Go get a job, you fucking hippie.

13. From the last question, you learned that it is perfectly okay to eat human meat when you are hungry. However, I must now propose a moral question. At what point is it okay to turn your traveling mate into food?

    a. The instant he dies of natural causes.

    b. When he is looking kinda sick.

    c. Shortly after you poison him.

    d. When he trips or falls.

    e. When he goes to sleep.

    f. Anytime he turns his back.

ANSWERS

    a. -5 points. Seriously, when have you ever waited for a chicken or cow to die of natural causes before you ate that son of a bitch. Personally, I have no interest in consuming roadkill. We have butchers for a reason.

    b. -2 points. Although this is a better answer than the last, you still probably waited too long. Human meat has an uncanny ability to "turn" quickly.

    c. +8 points. This is an excellent answer, but it is extremely important not to use a type of poison that will linger in his system. So instead of using an actual poison per se, you might want to use some type of club or heavy rock.

    d. +5 points. People become very vulnerable when they trip or fall, making it an excellent time to turn them into food. If you feel guilty about this, just remember that you saved them from having to conjure that fake, awkward laugh people always make when they trip or fall.

    e. +5 points. Killing someone in their sleep is the best because they don't feel a thing. Or is that when they die naturally? In any case, they won't put up much of a fight.

    f. +5 points. All survivors know not to turn their back on someone. Chances are, this guy is going to get you killed somewhere down the road. Might as well eat him now.

TEST RESULTS

So now I am going to ask you to tally up all your points. If you scored sixty-five points or higher, you are allowed to proceed. Just do so at your own risk. But regardless of score, the following people are not allowed to read my book:

DICKHEAD REPORTER

All reporters are not dicks. As a matter of fact, I owe a lot of my success to this hardworking, underpaid group of people who spread the aware- ness of my awesomeness to others. However, there are a few reporters who need to cram their head in a blender. A perfect example is the reporter who interviewed me a few days after I defeated Quin- ton Jackson and received the UFC Light Heavyweight title belt. It was the biggest moment of my life, and I felt on top of the world. In an attempt to sink my ship, he said, "What do you say to the people who think Quinton won, that he got robbed?" I replied, "What do you say to someone who has never tried, never bled, never had the guts to really go for something they really wanted? What do I say to those who sit behind a desk and talk into the microphone and criticize the deeds of others? I say . . ." and I hung up. A second later, I did a victory dance for my wife because it was one of those rare times when I had the perfect comeback. Seriously, I now tell this story with more excitement than I do the one about winning the title belt.

Another time I had a perfect comeback was shortly after I got my ass kicked by Anderson. I was signing autographs at the Olympia, and some muscle head (and I could tell immediately I didn't like him because his shirt was too tight, he had tattoo sleeves on both of his arms, and he had actually shaven his arms so that you could more clearly see the tattoos and the rippling veins in his biceps). He strutted up to me with his chest puffed out and said, "Yeah, bro, I just got to know, why did you run out of the ring after the Anderson fight?"

He was a pretty big guy, so I stood up. "That is a good question," I said, and waved him close as if I were going to tell him a secret. "You see the thing is, your mom—now I'm sure you've heard this—gives the best fucking blow jobs, and she was waiting in the locker room to suck my dick. I was so excited, I just had to get back there and get my dick sucked. I mean, your mom is an absolute pro."

As the words came out of my mouth, I could see him get physically tense. Instead of waiting around for a rebuttal, I walked past him and went over to sign an autograph for a kid. The meathead just stood there for close to a minute, mad-dogging me, and I just smiled at him. As he walked off, he continued to stare at me. I tried to nail him one last time by giving him the universal dick-sucking sign, you know, where you motion your hand toward your mouth and stick your tongue into your cheek, but he had already turned around. Anyway, if you're a douche bag like that reporter or meathead, please do not read my book.

ARMCHAIR QUARTERBACK

On almost a daily basis I have someone on the street come up to me and tell me how to fight. Now I realize that people like to get involved in the sport, and I also realize that there are a lot of fighters out there who are probably better than me, but to have someone who couldn't run twenty meters without vomiting tell me to "keep my hands up" is pretty fucking annoying. It's good advice, but very, very annoying. If you are the type of person who likes to tell other people more knowledgeable than you how to do their job, please do not read my book. I mean, if I walked into McDonald's, I wouldn't tell you how to flip a burger.

INTERNET WARRIOR

This is a message to Fraghead237. Fuck you! I know you thought you were so clever romoshopping me in a tutu and having me dance around a giant dick, but I just wanted to let you know that my private investigator just discovered where you live. I am coming to your house later today to stab you in the neck.

P.S. I am just kidding because I have the strange feeling that you are my target audience. Well, I am not kidding, but you are still my target audience.

PEOPLE YOU SHOULD ENCOURAGE TO READ MY BOOK

LUMBERJACK: There is a reason the Village People didn't include a lumberjack in their soiree—they are simply too manly. In my book, anyone who swings an ax for a living can automatically read my book. This includes serial killers and mohels who use an ax or an axlike instrument to perform their Brith Milahs.

WILDERNESS MAN: Anyone who wears a dead animal on their head is allowed to read my book. The only stipulation is that the animal must have some sort of tail. Personally, I don't think that is too much to ask. You will be hard-pressed to find an animal without a tail. And even if you do find an animal without a tail, you probably won't want to wear it on your head. This includes frogs, apes, sloths, various sea urchins, and, of course, humans.

PIRATE: There are many forms of pirates, but not all of them get an automatic thumbs-up to read my book. If you are a pirate and want to skip all the annoying tests, you must carry a sword . . . and the sword must be constructed from steel. Your flesh sword does not count.

PREPARE NOW, PART I: HOW TO BE TED KACZYNSKI WITHOUT ALL THAT UNABOMBER CRAP

As you may have learned from my first book, I was once a Webelo—that's right, not a Boy Scout, but a Webelo. Pretty low on the survival skills totem pole, but at least it was a step up from the Cub Scouts. Anyhow, before I was ejected from this society for chucking a can of soda at my scoutmaster's head, we went on a few camping trips. These consisted of about twenty of us kids, and five or six parents, all of whom were stupid enough to get duped into taking care of twenty boys in the wilderness. I would like to say that I learned all sorts of practical knowledge on these outings that I could pass on to you, but of course the parents ended up putting up the tent and doing all the merit-badge-worthy tasks we kids were supposed to do. However, I did learn a few lessons from these experiences, the most important being that the wilderness sucks. If you have a house with hot water, you should probably stay there because the wild will do everything in its power to make you absolutely miserable.

On the second day of one of these little adventures into the great unknown, the parents gathered up all the kids, brought us down to a luke-warm creek, and expected us to bathe. That's right, twenty half-naked kids, five adults (also half naked), bathing in a creek with bars of soap. Did I mention that it was in a fucking creek? I immediately felt molested. The only cool thing to come out of the mass bathing ritual was that my step-father, Abe, taught all the kids how to change in nature using a towel. We thought it was the coolest thing, and for the next few days every kid spent at least two hours a day changing and rechanging their shorts (kids are fucking weird).

The absolute worst part about camping was taking a dump. I was excited when we first got there because there were outhouses, which meant I didn't have to dig a hole, but when I ventured into one of these portable shit houses, I learned that the words "cleanliness" and "wilder-ness" do not go together. I made the mistake of looking down into the hole, and it looked like a shit monster had been murdered in there. There was shit everywhere—I mean, how do you get shit on a wall? There was a toilet seat, yet shit somehow ended up on the wall. It was just like that scene from *Slumdog Millionaire* where they shit off the piers.

Fearful of getting consumed by the shit monster, most of us kids resorted to pooping in the woods, and with all kids being inherently lazy, we didn't bother to dig holes. We just shit on the ground and then ran off. So by the end of the three days, everyone had spent seventy-two hours tra-versing a shit field, and we all stunk like walking death. The entire expe-rience made me realize one thing—I fucking hate the wilderness. If you are like me and spend a good portion of your life trying to avoid all things outdoors, this book will do you well, because, when doomsday comes, the outdoors will be your new home.

Before I tell you how the world will end, there are some things that you need to do to prepare yourself. Since you are currently reading a book on the apocalypse written by a professional fighter who's suffered some pretty serious head trauma, I'm assuming that you have some mental impair-ments of your own. You're not a full-blown moron, but you have trouble with simple things like walking without tripping, wiping your butt, counting, and, most importantly, reading. I will not judge you because I am well versed in moron, and we're in this together. However, it is quite possible that it will take you several years to read this book from start to finish, making it important that we start your training before I supply you with the various end-of-the-world scenarios and tell you what to expect. Just trust me that all this stuff will come in handy.

IS THAT AN ASSAULT RIFLE IN YOUR PANTS? (WELL, IT SHOULD BE)

Learning how to defend yourself is not something that happens overnight. It takes a lot of practice, which means you must start your training now. While numerous accountants, stockbrokers, housewives, and other regular people will survive the apocalypse by blind luck, the majority of those who dodge death's bullet will be survivalists who predicted the coming-of-the-end and received the proper training. These people will have at least basic knowledge on how to shoot and kill with their hands, and unless you are on a level playing field, there is a good chance that you will become their future food source.

To avoid such an outcome, I've included some very basic knowledge on how to defend yourself. You don't have to become an expert marksman or a professional fighter, but at the very least, you must be able to shoot a

DICK IN A BOX BY BIGGER JOHN

Both Forrest and I are firm believers in being armed at all times. Back before I got replaced by a bunch of Vegas douche bags, I used to corner Forrest for his fights. When he went to Sacramento to fight Tito the first time, I went with him. We were hanging outside with all the fighters, and suddenly Tim Sylvia comes up to us and starts making fun of Forrest for the thick leather coat he had on.

"Dude, what the fuck you wearing that huge jacket for?" he said. "Are you a moron? It's eighty-five degrees out here."

Without batting an eye, Forrest said, "It's not a jacket, it's a holster."

"Excuse me?"

"I said it's not a jacket, it's a holster." And with one quick movement, Forrest pulled the Glock 40 from the inside pocket.

Now I am not trying to call Tim a pussy or anything, because I honestly think he is one of the toughest heavyweights we've seen in the sport of MMA, but you should have seen the look in his eyes when Forrest pulled that gun. Instantly he knew he was dealing with someone on a whole different level of crazy.

Hating to get left out of anything, I decided to add to the effect and pulled the Glock 40 I had in my belt holster underneath my shirt. Tim immediately tried to grow back his balls by talking about his favorite guns, but I will never forget the look on his face. It was priceless . . . Anyhow, I guess the moral to this story is that you should always remain strapped, even if it requires you to wear a thick leather jacket in eighty-five-degree weather.

target at close range and understand how to properly apply a choke hold. Note from the HarperCollins legal team: Keep in mind that the apocalypse hasn't hit yet. Every state has its own laws about who can legally acquire a gun and how that gun must be carried. I'm not saying you should break any of those laws so that you can buy or use guns, and if you're not eighteen (or twenty-one in some states), then this section doesn't even apply to you.

HOW TO STAND WHEN FIRING
YOUR GUN IN AN INCREDIBLY SAFE
AND RESPONSIBLE WAY

There is no such thing as a proper shooting stance. It is important that your stance is balanced and stable, but the exact foot positioning is entirely up to you. Some people like to stagger their feet, while others prefer to keep their feet square. My only suggestion is to establish a shooting stance that feels comfortable and familiar. For example, I shoot from my fighting stance, which involves placing my left foot forward and my right foot back. I could just as easily shoot from a square stance, but being a professional fighter, my fighting stance feels very comfortable and natural. If Lyoto Machida shot guns, I am sure he would shoot from a karate horse stance. And if Royce Gracie shot guns, he would shoot from a butt-scoot stance. See what I am getting at? If you choose a shooting stance that is not familiar, it can take you a moment to establish it when shit goes down, and the last thing you want to be focusing on in a shoot-out is the positioning of your feet.

To learn what feels most comfortable, practice drawing your gun and aiming. This can be done on the firing range, or, if you're like me, while traversing the desert in your underwear. Whatever position your feet naturally gravitate to, adopt that as your shooting stance. Once you've got your feet positioning down, make sure to square your shoulders, put a slight bend in your arms, and keep your head up and straight.

Quick Draw

The Old West quick draw is fun to practice in abandoned warehouses on unsuspecting vermin (and by *vermin* I mean rats, not homeless people).

To assume my shooting stance, I step my left foot back and my right foot forward. With my feet spread roughly shoulders' width apart, I bend my arms and keep my head up. It is very important to notice that I am not leaning backward away from the gun, which is a mistake a lot of people make when first learning how to shoot.

While creeping around an abandoned warehouse, I am surprised by a very large rat. Immediately I spread my feet apart and grab the grip of my gun.

I place my left hand on my abdomen to ensure I do not shoot my fingers off.

I quickly jerk my gun from my holster. Instead of extending my arm straight, which would take too much time, I keep my elbow back and simply level the barrel with the ground. This last step is very important—if your gun is not level, there is a good chance that you will shoot yourself in the foot. Note: To state the obvious, do not actually shoot the vermin.

GET A FUCKING GRIP (OR WHY RAP VIDEOS ARE NOT A GOOD WAY TO LEARN ABOUT GUNS)

Back when I was playing high school football in Georgia, a few idiots on my team unfortunately decided to do a drive-by shooting one night. As they crept by the house, both the driver and the passenger opened up. Being a complete genius, the driver extended his arm out his window, turned his gun sideways, and attempted to shoot over the top of the vehicle. Instead of riddling the house with bullets, he shot though the roof of the car. A bullet entered the back of the passenger, which prompted him to turn his gun on the driver. A shouting match ensued. A few hours later at the hospital, the police showed up and rightfully arrested both of them. Please, attend to this lesson and learn how to shoot like a normal human being.

How you grip a gun is another matter of debate, but there are a few general rules everyone can agree upon. First off, you want to establish a two-handed grip. If one of your hands is injured or holding something of importance, it's possible to establish a single-handed grip and still aim accurately, but a two-handed grip will give you far better results. In the illustrations below, I demonstrate a single-handed grip, as well as the two-handed grip that I always use.

FORTUNE COOKIE WISDOM

If you talk too passionately and too much about guns, it may lead people to believe you have a tiny penis.

Single-Handed Grip

To establish a single-handed grip on my gun, I grab the grip with my right hand. If you are left-handed, you want to grab it with your left hand. Notice how the web between my thumb and index finger is positioned as high up on the grip as possible, my thumb is positioned by the safety, and my finger is not on the trigger. The only time you want to actually place your finger on the trigger is when you are about to shoot. If you are running or walking with your gun drawn, always keep your finger off the trigger to prevent an accidental discharge. All law enforcement officers are taught this during training, but apparently no one mentioned it to Kiefer Sutherland. In the few episodes of *24* that I have seen, he is always running with his finger on the trigger. Although I find this extremely annoying, I keep praying that he will accidently shoot that sniveling computer cunt Chloe O'Brian.

Double-Handed Grip (Not to Be Confused with the Similarly Worded Masturbation Technique)

This method of gripping a gun is often employed by law enforcement officers and competitive shooters. To begin, I grip the gun with my right hand just as I did when performing the single-handed grip, except now I run my right thumb down the length of the barrel just below the slide. Next, I wrap my left hand around my right hand, and then run my left thumb down the barrel just beneath the slide. This grip, I assume, gives me optimal control of the gun and allows me to quickly shift from one target to the next. In addition to this, the forward positioning of my thumbs helps me quickly line up my sights on new targets.

The Gangster Grip

If you feel the best way to hold a gun is sideways, you're either an idiot or a wannabe gangster. The only reason you should ever hold a gun sideways is if you have a severe shoulder injury that prevents you from holding a gun straight. *But it looks super cool*, you say. No, it doesn't. In addition to making you look like a complete retard, it will be next to impossible to hit the broad side of a barn.

IT'S NOT JUST POINT AND CLICK

Most guns have two sights, one on the front of the gun and one at the back. If you are shooting at something more than fifteen feet away, it is in your best interest to line up both sights on your target. However, this process can take a few seconds, which can get you killed when in a close-range shoot-out. If an aggressor is within fifteen feet, hold your gun level and place your front sight on the center mass of your target. Unless your gun is cocked upward or downward, there is a good chance that you will hit what you are aiming for. Then again, Bruce Willis and Arnold Schwarzenegger never do this, and they seem to hit people from twenty or thirty meters away, which is amazing accuracy. So maybe you should stop reading this book and start watching more action movies. As a matter of fact, I think you can get a lot out of a movie if you watch it fifty thousand times, which is what I did with *Good Will Hunting* when I was living in that shitty one-room apartment back in my college days. Unfortunately, instead of learning how to shoot a gun, I learned how to freak out my family members by having imaginary conversations with the characters in the movie and referring to them as my friends.

When firing, do not pull the trigger: squeeze the trigger. The smaller the squeeze, the more fluid you will become at shooting your gun. And once you have shot a round, slowly release your pressure on the trigger. Although this might seem simple, it is very difficult to accomplish, especially when someone is shooting back at you. To avoid this rookie mistake, learn to steady your nerves by shooting as often as possible.

WHEN YOUR GUN GOES LIMP

There are three types of malfunctions that can prevent your gun from firing. Having a gun is great, but having a gun that doesn't fire sucks. To avoid having to use your gun as a boomerang, I recommend practicing how to deal with all three types of malfunctions.

TYPE ONE: This malfunction is usually caused by not properly seating the magazine into the well. You'll know when it happens because as you attempt to fire a round, you hear your gun click but no shot is fired. To solve the issue, you remove your finger from the trigger, release your support hand from the gun, smack the bottom of the magazine with your palm, tilt the gun to the side, rack the slide back with your free hand, and then reestablish your two-handed grip on the gun and again squeeze the trigger. To simplify, TAP, RACK, ROLL.

TYPE TWO: This type of malfunction is often referred to as a "Brass High" or "Stovepipe" because it is caused by a shell casing getting stuck in the ejection port, which locks the slide into the back position and prevents you from firing off any more rounds. While this is different from a type-one malfunction, it is remedied in the exact same way: TAP, RACK, ROLL.

TYPE THREE: A type-three malfunction is often referred to as a "Feedway Stoppage" because you have two rounds competing for the same space in either the chamber or receiver. To remedy this issue, use the steps below.

1. Remove your finger from the trigger (pretty fucking obvious, but you would be surprised).

2. Release your support hand from the gun and then use it to pull the slide back until it locks.

3. Release the magazine, grab the slide again with your free hand, and rack it three times. If the magazine doesn't eject, you might have to pull it free.

4. Insert a new magazine.

5. Reestablish your two-handed grip on the gun and begin firing.

It is important to mention that this type of malfunction takes considerably longer to fix than the previous two. If you are in a gunfight when a type-three malfunction occurs, there is a good chance that you will get shot if you remain out in the open. To prevent this, move for cover as you fix your weapon or beg for mercy.

If you choose the latter, here are some of the things you might want to say:

a. I was just kidding; my gun wasn't even loaded.

b. Hey man, these aren't even real bullets.

c. I thought we was just playing, dog.

d. Don't shoot! I'm pregnant!

WHAT TO DO WHEN BEING CHASED BY TINA TURNER

During the apocalypse, a lot of shoot-outs are going to occur on the road as you are attempting to go from point A to point B.[6] Sometimes these will occur while you're driving a semi loaded with gas and being chased by Tina Turner wearing earmuffs. Obviously, while driving, it is a good idea

---

[6] It's good to be prepared for this type of encounter, but as of yet, I have not found a firing range that allows you to shoot out of a moving vehicle. Occasionally I do this in the desert, and I've found that my aim is absolutely horrible. But I haven't given up hope because they make it look pretty easy in the movies.

to wear your seat belt at all times. In addition to there being numerous obstacles in the road, a lot of people will use their vehicles as battering rams in an attempt to disable your vehicle.

However, anytime you are parked, you want to remove your seat belt, which is something I learned while in the police academy. If you're right-handed like most people, you will most likely wear your gun on your right hip. This is the exact location where your seat belt locks, and it can make it very difficult to get to your gun. Not wearing your seat belt will help you get to your gun quicker, but if you're a douche bag like me and habitually lock your seat belt every time you get in the car, it is good to get into the habit of removing your gun and placing it underneath your left thigh.

Another reason not to wear your seat belt while your car is parked is that it makes it too difficult to exit your vehicle when shit hits the fan. In most cases, attempting to start your car and drive away takes too much time. By the time you put your vehicle into drive, your aggressors will have already showered it with bullets. A much better option is to quickly bail out of your car and use it as cover.

DICK IN A BOX: MR. & MRS. GRIFFIN BY JAIME

One night not long ago I woke up at two or three in the morning, and I noticed that Forrest was not in bed next to me. I figured he was either jerking it on the Internet downstairs or he had gone to the store to get some sweets. I called his name, and when I didn't get an answer, I went downstairs to check on him.

I couldn't find him anywhere, so I went into the garage. I was horrified by what I found. The car was gone, the garage was wide open, and the door leading into the house was unlocked. I instantly lost my mind. I thought, "This motherfucker left me here by myself, and someone could have murdered me." I was shaking mad, and so I decided to get a little revenge by faking a crime scene. I dumped the contents of my purse onto the floor and knocked everything off the tables. Once the setting was perfect, I hid behind a cabinet in the living room. In case someone broke in before Forrest returned, I armed myself with my .38.

Ten minutes later I heard Forrest come in. I almost let out a laugh, but then I heard his grocery bags drop to the floor and the familiar sound of him chambering his Glock 40. It was at this point that I realized faking a crime scene might not have been the smartest move. Not wanting to say anything for fear of startling him, I remained utterly quiet. I heard him creep up the stairs, and then I heard him slowly open each of the upstairs doors. He never yelled, never gave up his location. He moved in and out of each room, clearing them like an assassin.

Suddenly I heard his footsteps back downstairs, moving toward me, and that's when I shouted, "I am right here, I am right here." I came out of hiding with my .38, and he came into the room with his Glock 40. It was like a scene straight out of *Mr. & Mrs. Smith*. Needless to say, he was not thrilled by my antics, but eventually he realized that he was in the wrong and apologized.

Luke Rebuttal

Jaime told me that story shortly after it happened, and her tone was quite different. It was almost gleeful. When Forrest cleared the house like a trained killer, it actually turned her on. Forrest was just as aroused. Although I wasn't there, I know for a fact that he was excited about the fact of possibly getting to shoot an intruder. I wouldn't be surprised if later that night, they had the best sex of their lives.

Never have I met two people more paranoid or heavily armed. Between the two of them, they must have more than fifteen guns in their house. And they are not just handguns. Forrest has a .22 rifle with a built-in silencer, as well as an AR-15. That's fucked up. Who needs an automatic weapon for home protection? In addition to having his own personal armory, he is always going on and on about reactionary gaps. For example, the gate that surrounds his neighborhood is a reactionary gap because it gives him time to arm himself against a possible intruder. The wrought-iron bars on his windows are a reactionary gap, the four locks on his front door are a reactionary gap, his state-of-the-art alarm system is a reactionary gap, and the key lock he has on his bedroom door is a reactionary gap. I don't know how much time

Forrest needs to reach his guns—there is one in every room, for Pete's sake—but I guess the guy likes to be prepared.

I'm not quite sure what's wrong with them. Jaime grew up in a small town in Arizona, and Forrest and I grew up in a suburban neighborhood in Georgia where you left your doors unlocked at night. Neither one of them has ever been held at gunpoint, but both seem convinced that it is only a matter of time until the shit hits the fan. Think I am blowing their paranoia out of proportion? Most fighters are sponsored by companies like Muscle Milk and Condom Depot. Forrest is sponsored by Advanced Armament, which is a company that builds silencers for all types of guns. Instead of getting free protein shakes in the mail, Forrest receives free silencers.

I'm telling you, Jaime and Forrest are meant to be together. Like most couples, they have date night, but instead of going ice skating or to Applebee's, they go to the firing range. They also go to the firing range every Sunday after church. So if you are thinking about trying to break into Forrest's house or carjack him because you found this book repulsive, you are going to get hurt. And Jaime won't be one of those girls who cries after she kills you. As she etches another notch into her belt, you'll hear her whisper, "Fucker, you shouldn't have tried to break in." In fact, that will be the last thing you ever hear because according to Forrest, if Jaime has to shoot a home invader, she will do everything in her power to ensure he is dead to prevent him from plotting any type of revenge. Never have I met two people more perfect for each other. Guns are what tie them together—that and the violent sex they have.

NEWSFLASH: GUNS ARE USELESS WITHOUT BULLETS

Having guns and knowing how to use them is all well and good, but you're not going be able to do shit with them if you don't have bullets to put in them. If you're truly serious about getting ready for our impending destruction, you need to start buying bullets. Now. Seriously, go this second. I'll be waiting right here when you get back. Go now, jackass. Oh, so you think you don't need to go this instant? Now you're too good for this book?

Let's see you try and use your Glock when the only stashes of bullets are in the hands of powerful, tribe-leading overlords with nicknames like "Zeus" and "The Professor."

Go buy bullets now and bury them in your backyard under the old oak tree. And don't tell anyone where they are. Especially not me.

FIGHT, FLIGHT, AND WHAT TO DO WHEN PISSING YOUR PANTS ISN'T AN OPTION

I imagine that cavemen were pretty in tune with their fight-or-flight instinct. If a caveman headed out into a field to pick some berries (not sure if cavemen picked berries or not, but it seems like a very cavemanish sort of thing to do), and suddenly a woolly mammoth came charging out of the bushes, his mind would instantly assess the situation and decide which option would give him a better chance of survival. In the amount of time it takes you or me to step on the brakes at a red light, the caveman would either chuck a spear at the advancing beast or begin running his fucking tits off toward the nearest tree. Although the life of the caveman sucked in pretty much every way imaginable, especially when it came to mating, he had a serious leg up on modern man when it came to interpreting his instincts.

Most of us still have the fight-or-flight instinct buried deep in our brains; we just struggle with its interpretation, which is what leads to panic or making the wrong choice. Luckily, in the civilized world in which we currently reside, we often get a second chance when we fail to interpret our instinctual signals correctly. However, the apocalypse will be the caveman days all over again, so it is in your best interest to start getting acquainted with what your mind is trying to tell you in times of stress.

This can be accomplished by putting yourself in extremely dangerous situations where the only hope of survival is to make the right choice. For example, you can jump out in front of a moving bus. Your brain will undoubtedly send you a shit load of terrifying signals, but you must learn to interpret them correctly. If your instincts tell you to stand your ground and fight the bus, you are probably not making the right assessment. In such a situation, your only chance to live another day is flight.

WHY YES, YOU CAN KILL SOMEONE WITH A PENCIL: WEAPONS OF OPPORTUNITY

A weapon of opportunity is anything around you that you can use as a weapon (no, it couldn't more self-explanatory). For example, as I sit here writing this, I can see several weapons of opportunity. I can use the pen sitting on the table to stab you in the eye, I can use the strap-on lying over in the corner to bludgeon you over the head, and I can even use the hot cup of coffee in my hand (yes, I only type with one hand) to blind you. However, if the cup of coffee in your hand happens to be an iced latte, not only would it be a terrible weapon of opportunity, but it would also make me question your manhood. If you threw that into my face, it would just piss me off. Another terrible weapon of opportunity would be a banana. You starting to see what I am getting at? I would love to have had this idea all on my own, but when I did a seminar at a Marine base, that is what they preached—weapons of opportunity. If you're in a position where you need a weapon, a household object will do. If there is a knife, a vase, a shoehorn around you, turn it into a weapon. Remember, you never want to be in a fair fight if an unfair fight is an option (that line was all mine, I swear!).

Obviously, this type of training will increase your chances of dying a horrible death and never making it to the apocalypse, but if all goes well and you hone your instincts, you will be well prepared for the end of the world. (Just kidding, of course, I don't want you to jump in front of a bus. Besides, there is no way to hone your instincts—that is why they are called instincts.)

To give you an idea of how to properly and improperly read your instincts, I will share a story with you from my drunken college days. I believe I was nineteen or twenty at the time, and I was hanging out in a bar that was notorious for serving minors. After a few beverages, the front doors flew open and cops stormed in, shouting about how they were conducting a raid for underage drinkers. My fight-or-flight instinct kicked in, and luckily I made the right choice. Instead of taking a swing at an officer of the law, I ran toward the emergency exit, kicked it open, and bolted out into the night.

Two cops were standing there, ready to catch anyone who decided to skip out, and I was again presented with a fight-or-flight choice. I could have chosen to tackle one of them, which would have led to me getting beaten with clubs, Maced, kicked, and handcuffed, but again I read my instincts correctly. With a little shuffle of my feet, I avoided their reaching arms and then sprinted down the street with all my strength.

After about four minutes sprinting at full velocity (that was drunk time, so it was probably more like twenty seconds) I was gassed out of my mind. Certain that a full-scale manhunt had been launched to find me (yes, I was drunk *and* paranoid), I began searching for a place to hide. The first location that jumped out was a fraternity house. Figuring that if anyone could sympathize with my predicament, it was a group of drunken assholes, I headed toward it. Huffing and dripping sweat, I opened the front door without knocking, ran into the living room, and then knelt down by the window so I could peer out at the street for cops.

While I was huddled there, three frat brothers walked into the room, each with a plastic cup filled with beer. They looked at me for a second, I looked at them, and then I returned my eyes to the street.

"What the fuck you doing in our house?" one of them shouted.

"Don't worry about it," I returned without even turning around.

"Dude, I said what the fuck are you doing in our house?"

"Your mother will explain it to you when you're a big boy," I said, slightly perturbed.

I heard a cup of beer drop and feet rapidly approaching me. By the time I stood up, all three of them were in my personal space, shouting at me. For the third time that night, I found myself in a fight-or-flight scenario. Outnumbered three to one, my reptile brain was sending me all sorts of messages. I probably should have interpreted the signals the same as I did on the previous two occasions, but for some reason I thought my brain was saying, "Hey bro, fuck this running shit. You need to fight these bitches. You got 'em, bro. Ain't no tang." Apparently, my reptile brain really likes clichés and is a frat-boy douche bag at heart.

There were three of them lined up in front of me, and not knowing their names, I will refer to them as Dickhead one through three. Well, I saw Dickhead One pulling his fist back to hit me, and for some reason my drunken mind gave me the instruction to hit Dickhead One. So, that is what I did. About half a second after my fist bounced off his face, Dickhead Two crashed his knuckles into my cheek. Pissed off that I had just gotten punched, I socked Dickhead Two in retaliation. Immediately after my fist landed, Dickhead Three belted me one. Again, this angered me, so I punched Dickhead Three. A split second later, Dickhead One tagged me, and the vicious cycle began again. I hit Dickhead One, which prompted Dickhead Two to land his second shot. After I hit Dickhead Two, Dickhead Three hit me.

Believe it or not, we went down the line like this for more than four minutes (again, drunk time—I have no idea how long it was in real time). With there only being one of me and three of them, I obviously got the worst end of the deal. It was kind of like I was playing a game of charley horse, except instead of playing with one guy I was playing with three. And instead of slugging each other in the arm, we were slugging each other in the face. Luckily, everyone sort of got tired at about the exact same moment and we stopped hitting each other. Realizing that it was only a matter of time before we all recuperated and the hitting began again, I reassessed my previous interpretation and ran. I bolted straight out the front door and sprinted my way home. Apparently, I didn't learn much from this lesson because twelve years later when I stepped into the cage with Anderson Silva, my reptile brain told me to actually fight him. It wasn't until I regained consciousness that I realized the correct response should have been flight, at which point I fled. It was obviously too late by that point.

The moral here is that when your mind is sending you mixed messages in a dangerous situation, running is probably the safe choice to make. The only time you actually want to fight is when you are matched up with a much weaker opponent and actually have something to gain. For example, either fighting a mentally handicapped person in order to impress your girlfriend or fighting a child to acquire his satchel of sweets is acceptable. But other than these two scenarios, you pretty much want to run.

LUKE

Forrest is one of the few fighters who doesn't have a nickname. But if he did, it would undoubtedly be "Tackleberry." If you don't understand this reference, go rent *Police Academy*.

THE WILDERNESS IS JUST LIKE THE OCTAGON BUT WITH TREES

You never want to bring your fists to a gunfight, but there will come a time during the apocalypse when the majority of ammunition gets exhausted. Granted that might take a long fucking time, but it is important to prepare for it nonetheless. If your goal is to become a badass fighter, there are dozens of exceptional MMA instructional books on the market, all of which are produced by Victory Belt Publishing (Erich is fucking shameless, plugging his own company . . . what a douche). However, the chance that you will encounter a professional fighter during the apocalypse is slim.

The majority of people you have to contend with will most likely be tough sons of bitches—after all, they somehow found a way to live long enough to see all the ammunition dry up—but they probably won't be super dangerous in the hand-to-hand combat department. Although learning how to throw proper strikes and apply fancy submissions will not hurt you in any way, it is not high on your apocalypse-preparation to-do list. When it comes to fighting during the apocalypse, you want to focus on choke holds because they are the only techniques that allow you to turn your aggressor's lights out, permanently.

Below I have included two of the more effective choke holds that can be applied from the standing position. My suggestion is to practice these techniques as often as possible. Simply learning how to apply these choke holds is not enough—you must train them ritualistically. When they are applied improperly, you will fail to sever blood flow to your opponent's brain and quickly gas out your arms, which puts you in danger. Personally, I recommend practicing them on drunk people in your local bar, and once you have them down, work up to moderately sober people. Trust me, applying an effective choke hold is not as easy as Sayid makes it seem on *Lost*.

Standing Rear Naked Choke from Behind

I sneak up behind Erich and wrap my left arm around his neck. If your opponent tucks his chin to his chest in an attempt to prevent you from cutting off the blood supply to his brain, which is probably a good tactic on his part, you can pull his head upward using your opposite hand.

To apply the rear naked choke, I grab my right biceps with my left hand and then position the back of my right hand behind Erich's head. To sever blood flow to his brain and give myself an immense amount of pleasure in getting back at him for constantly editing the shit I say in this book, I squeeze my arms tight.

Guillotine Choke
Off the Tackle

Erich attempts the old-school football tackle, and being a good deal taller than him, I simply place my hand on his head. In addition to stopping his forward momentum, it is quite demeaning.

Before Erich can elevate his head, I step forward and wrap the blade of my left arm across the front of his neck.

To apply the standing guillotine choke, I clasp my hands together, drive his head downward using my chest, and pull my left forearm up into his neck using my right hand.

FORREST FACTOID

Ages ago I was in a friend's bar in Georgia and some dickhead out in the street decided to chuck a beer bottle into the air. Being slightly drunk myself, I charged out there, took the guy down, and mounted him. I had no intention of busting him up—I simply wanted to prevent him from getting more out of hand and wrecking my buddy's bar. After he calmed down, I walked back into the bar like a big hero. The encounter couldn't even be described as a scuffle, but when I looked down, I noticed that I was gushing blood out of my foot. I was covered in blood, and everyone began looking at me like I just got my ass handed to me out in the parking lot. Apparently when we were on the ground, my foot rolled over the beer bottle he had broken.

Learn from my mistake and pain. If you want to be an MMA fighter, you absolutely must learn how to grapple, but taking your opponent down shouldn't be your first choice in an apocalyptic street fight. Unless the natural disaster that eliminated the majority of humanity somehow covered the surface of the earth with soft feathers, I would recommend doing everything in your power to keep a fight standing. Just think about all the rusty nails and jagged pieces of scrap metal that will be littered about. Do you really want to end up with that shit embedded in your backside? I didn't think so.

NOTE: As far as the guillotine choke goes, realize that you have just crammed your assailant's head down toward your legs, and he still has two free hands to completely annihilate your groin with, which is most likely what he will do when he realizes he can no longer breathe and begins panicking. But don't worry, you don't need your groin—there will not be that many women around during the apocalypse anyway. And besides, pee tubes are not that bad.

THE MAN CAVE

Note: The "Man Cave," in today's society, is a stupid term for the room in which you keep your foosball table. During the apocalypse, the Man Cave will actually be a cave you live in. It will protect you from the elements and keep you safe from predators.

When a fifty-kiloton nuclear bomb goes off, everything within a several-mile radius gets completely annihilated. If you are outside the immediate blast zone and you have built a fallout shelter in your backyard, your survival will depend upon your ability to quickly take refuge in it. If you are located ten miles from ground zero, you will generally have about thirty minutes before radioactive fallout reaches your area. If you are fifty miles out, you have about three hours. And if you live a hundred miles out, you have approximately six hours. The good news is if you are quickly alerted to the fact that a nuke went off, and you manage to speedily make it to your shelter, you only have about two weeks until the radiation drops to a survivable level. Granted it will be a frustrating two weeks—most fallout shelters do not have Internet access, which means no porn—but making do with just the bare necessities for a spell is better than dying an agonizing death.

In addition to preventing you from sucking up large doses of radiation and growing a set of hairy eyeballs on the back of your head, a well-constructed fallout shelter will protect you from hurricanes, tornadoes, viral outbreaks, police search warrants, and alien invasions. Sure, most neighborhoods have community fallout shelters, but I highly recommend steering clear of these. There is always that guy who at the last minute begins banging on the door, wanting to get let in. And there is always that old woman who wants to obey said fuck-nut's demand, jeopardizing everyone who was smart enough to show up early. Another problem with community fallout shelters is the smell. While the stench of your own farts doesn't bother you too bad, other people's farts smell horrible, and when you are in a confined space, they can make you physically sick. Personally, I've experienced farts so bad that I would have rather gone out into nuclear radiation than suffer through them. When you add crying babies into the mix, it simply isn't worth it. Just imagine spending two weeks at your local DMV—that is what surviving in a fallout shelter is like. You will be much better off constructing your own shelter.

The first rule with building a fallout shelter is not to tell anyone about your fallout shelter. If you go around running off at the mouth, every neighborhood shit bag will flee to your backyard when shit hits the fan. As a matter of fact, you don't even want to tell all of your so-called friends. Douche-bag friends are like herpes—they tend to follow you around and ruin an otherwise glorious day. Even if they are not colossal douche bags, you still won't have enough supplies to feed all of them. To ensure your own survival, you want to limit yourself to two, maybe three, other people. If you have a lot of children, you only want to take your favorite ones, or at least the ones that you think will have the best chance of helping you survive. However, keeping your fallout shelter a secret during the construction phase poses a problem. To solve this dilemma, I suggest taking everyone camping. Shortly after you get to the campgrounds (before you have to visit the awful outhouse and shit monster), disable their vehicles and leave. While they are out there trying to figure out how to get their vehicles going, race home and build your fallout shelter. As an added bonus, some of your friends or family members might die during their long trek back to civilization, which means fewer mouths to feed.

However, if you do decide to prohibit some of your friends and family members from entering your shelter when shit hits the fan, it is very important to bring some type of radio or noisemaker to drown out their screaming and begging and banging as they perish from radiation poisoning and starve to death. Listening to their whimpering is horribly uncomfortable, and we don't want any of that.

Before building your shelter, you are going to want to purchase plans from a qualified professional. I could have offered you step-by-step instructions, but they would have undoubtedly led to your demise. However, I can offer a few tips in this area. The majority of fallout shelters should be built underground, and with limited space in your backyard, deciding upon its location involves some careful consideration. Obviously, you do not want to disturb your workshop, horseshoe pit, barbecue area, or the dirt patch where you and your buddies swill beer, so you will most likely want to backhoe your wife's rosebushes and tulip garden. In addition to this, you will want to build at least two rooms. The first room will be your general living area, and the second room will be the "jail" or "time-out" room where you lock annoying family members. The spare room will also serve as the toilet.

THE LIGHTS JUST WENT ON AT THE STRIP CLUB . . . YOU AIN'T GOTTA GO HOME, BUT YOU CAN'T STAY HERE (AKA GET THE HELL OUT OF DODGE)

Having a fallout shelter in your backyard can save you from dying from radiation poisoning or a rapidly spreading virus, but it will do very little to help you survive for the long term. After the initial shit storm passes, you'll want to be prepared to get as far away from metropolitan areas as humanly possible. Sure, large cities are packed with food, ammunition, and every other luxury you could ever want, but if you survived, chances are others did too, and it will quickly become a battle of "who can get what first."

People will undoubtedly band together to form militant groups, and if the government is still around, there is a high probability the lawmakers will declare martial law. Every day you spend mulling around town, your chances of getting attacked increase. I'm not saying that you should bug out if a storm passes through your area, but if you're listening to your portable radio in your shelter and you hear chatter about how entire cities have been laid waste, your best chance of survival is to find an isolated area in which to lay low (much like you do when a girl you "know" is pregnant). It is much easier to get out of town during times of chaos than waiting for a lockdown or full-blown revolution to occur.

If you live in a town that has just a few hundred inhabitants, remaining in your home can be a lot safer. But even then it can be beneficial not to actually stay indoors. Remember, there will be a lot of people on the move, and when traveling through your area, they are going to need supplies. They will raid the stores first, but when all resources have been depleted,

---

NOTE FROM ERICH

I asked Forrest to write up some of his thoughts and send them to me. This is the text message I received about an hour later. *I just realized that I use the computer so little for actual work that when I sat down to type something, my first thought was "Why am I here, I didn't want to jack off at the computer just yet."*

---

they will begin to go from door to door. With this, I give the same advice I do to upcoming fighters: Be First! Don't sit around and wait to get looted. Get out there and be first by looting your neighbors.

WHERE YOU RUNNIN' TO, BOY?

The first step is to find a safe zone not far from where you live. It could be a national park, a wooded area on the outskirts of your city, or a cabin up in the mountains. Basically, you need to find an unpopulated area that holds no real interest to anyone. The only requirement is that the safe zone has some type of running water, whether it be a stream, a well, or a natural spring. In the case of a nuclear or biological attack, there is a good chance that the water will be contaminated for some time, but this can be remedied by ensuring you have a water filter in your Go Bag, which I will touch upon later (unless I forget).

THE ONLY SHOPPING TRIP THAT WILL EVER MATTER (OR BE EVEN REMOTELY FUN)

Once you have found an isolated spot, the next step is to prep it for a prolonged stay. Personally, I recommend digging a fairly large ditch, lining it with thick plastic, and then filling it with your supplies. Deciding on the amount of supplies you'll need depends on the type of apocalypse that has occurred. With some disasters, it could take as much as six months for things to begin to settle down, so I would recommend being on the safe side and packing as much shit as possible. It seems obvious to me what

LIVE LIKE A LESS-ANNOYING EWOK

If digging a ditch to stash your supplies seems like too much trouble, build a tree house like you did when you were twelve. Although it will be super difficult to haul all your shit up there, it will allow you to play "pirate" and supply you with hours of self-entertainment. It will also give you enhanced visibility of your surroundings. The only catch is that the tree fort must be in the wild. If you can see the roof of your home from your tree fort, your safe zone is not located deep enough in the wilderness. Personally, I like the tree-fort option because I grew up in an urban area, and there was no space for that kind of shit. In fact, I wanted one so bad as a child, I made my mom go out and buy me one of those bed tents, which is basically a tent that fits over your mattress. They are pretty pathetic, but realizing the alternative was no tent at all, I kept mine until I was fifteen. I would have kept it longer, but one day when I invited my friends over, they all began making fun of me. I reluctantly disposed of the tent, and now I can no longer find them on the market. If I could, you bet your ass my wife and I would be sleeping in one.

type of shit you should be stuffing in the hole, but then again, I'm writing this book and you're reading it, so it might not be obvious to you. Here are the essentials:

1. **CANNED FOOD:** I recommend bringing a lot of it. Unless you are morbidly obese, you should be able to survive just fine off three cans of food per day. Multiply that by six months, and you have 720 cans of food. I know the economy might currently be tight, but this is not an area in which you want to skimp. Trust me when I say that you don't want to resort to eating squirrel. Just trust me. And it is very important to have some variety. I know you might love canned peaches, but they'll get pretty fucking gross after eating them for a month straight.

2. **TENT:** As I will cover later, your Go Bag does not include a tent, so it is important that you stash one at your safe zone. There are a lot of tents on the market, but most of them are designed

for weight rather than durability. Seeing that you won't need to carry your tent out of your safe zone, I recommend purchasing one from a military surplus store. Although they tend to weigh more than expedition tents, they are a lot more rugged, and they are also usually camouflage color, which will do wonders to conceal your whereabouts.

3. **SLEEPING BAG:** You're going to want to get a minus-twenty-degree sleeping bag. It might be hot as hell in the summer months, but you will be glad you have it should a nuclear winter set in. To ensure you are warm enough, I would also include several wool blankets (wool retains heat more than most other fabrics when wet).

4. **PROPANE STOVE:** Cooking on a propane stove is a smart move because it gives off very little light and almost no smell. To ensure you don't run out of gas the first week, I recommend bringing at least two five-gallon canisters.

5. **GUNS:** Although your bug-out bag should contain a gun and a healthy amount of ammunition, you can never be too safe. I recommend burying a shotgun or automatic weapon, both of which are burdensome to carry while on the move.

6. **MATCHES:** You should include at least a dozen large boxes of matches, all individually wrapped in plastic. The waterproof kind is mandatory.

7. **BOOKS ON NATIVE PLANTS:** Although you're probably not going to take the time to read up on the local flora and fauna pre-apocalypse, you will have nothing but time on your hands while chilling in your safe zone. This book could save your life should you be forced to remain in the wild longer than you thought.

8. **FIRST-AID KIT:** This should not be your standard first-aid kit containing a few Band-Aids and antiseptic. You want to include gauze, bandages, antibiotics, needle and thread, the whole nine yards.

9. **SHOVEL AND PICK:** These will come in handy for all sorts of things, including making various pitfalls for intruders to fall into.

10. **AX:** Needs no explanation.

11. **FISHING LINE:** In addition to allowing you to catch fish, fishing line is also excellent for setting traps. These traps might not hurt an intruder, but they can be rigged as an alarm system to let you know people are near your camp.

12. **SEVERAL PAIRS OF BOOTS:** Your feet are more precious than you know. You have to take care of them. As far as the type of boot, you want to go with something fashionable. Think *Outlaw Josey Wales* boots. If you are a real man, you can run in cowboy boots with no problem. They will serve no purpose in the apocalypse because I am pretty sure horses will be the first creature to go, but man, they look cool.

13. **A GARGANTUAN SUPPLY OF CREAM PUFFS AND HONEY:** These are among the few foods that never go bad. If you do not like cream puffs, you can substitute anything made by Little Debbie. Although Little Debbie products don't taste the best, no matter what biological conditions should occur, they can never taste any worse. They are so heavily preserved, they already taste nuked.

Once you have filled your hole with all these goodies and any personal items you might desire while living alone in the wild for months and months, fill it in with dirt, cover it with leaves and twigs, and then leave some sort of marking so you can find it again. Personally, I recommend using a large obsidian rock, one which has "no right being in that type of field." And yes, I stole that from *The Shawshank Redemption*.

WHEN THE SHIT HITS THE FAN, YOU'D BETTER HAVE A PLAN: CREATING YOUR ESCAPE ROUTE

The subject of this section is very similar to what your mom explained to you about getting out of the house in case of a fire. I'm basically telling you how to get out of Dodge when the shit goes down. However, creating an escape plan in order to reach your safe zone is not as easy as it sounds. You have to assume that shit is going to be fucked up big-time, which means that the roadways will either be packed with other fleeing people or choked with abandoned and ruined vehicles. In addition to not being able to speedily traverse major thoroughfares such as freeways and even byways, roads will also be very dangerous. These usual transportation arteries will be patrolled by law enforcement, military, bandit groups, and escapees from Jenny Craig Twinkie Rehab Centers. If you disregard my advice and begin humping it down the highway, you're asking for trouble.

To avoid becoming an easy target, you want to chart out a drivable escape route using back roads. Purchase a topographic map of your area, and then simply begin connecting residential streets with power-line access roads to scenic byways. Get creative. Railroad tracks, dry riverbeds, and some hiking trails are often drivable. However, it is extremely important that you practice this route every four or five months in your four-wheel-drive vehicle. The first time is just to see if it is doable, and the follow-up times are to make sure nothing has changed. If you chose a dirt access road as part of your escape plan, and a tree has fallen across that road, it can stop you dead in your tracks. You also want to avoid traveling under any man-made structures such as bridges and tunnels, as these may be purposely destroyed by the military in times of martial law to ensure the containment of specific areas. Also, I would not recommend using any routes that require you to physically swim or immerse yourself in a body of water because many disasters will contaminate the water supply.

AN EXPLANATION

Before we get too far into talking about the apocalypse and all that, I need to clear something up. In my previous book, *Got Fight?*, I had a few of my childhood friends offer some background knowledge on me. Thinking that they would all talk about how great I was, I told them ahead of time that I would not alter or edit their writing. As it turned out, my friends do not view me in the same light as I view myself. In other words, they said some pretty horrible shit.

Thinking that the book would sell five copies, I held true to my promise and included their insights unedited. I did, however, say some pretty horrible stuff in return, especially about my psychopathic friend "Big John." Having only spent an hour and a half working on the entire book, it did not occur to me that people would automatically assume that I was talking about Big John McCarthy, the world-famous MMA referee. I overlooked this fact, and as a result, everyone who read my book now thinks Big John McCarthy is a total nut-bag degenerate. This is not true. McCarthy is actually a very nice person who cares about the well-being of others. Big John my friend cares only about himself and combs the neighborhood in which he lives looking for unwanted puppies to drown. To save McCarthy from this terrible association he has had to endure for the past year, I have included descriptions of both men. In addition to this, I will now refer to my childhood friend as Bigger John.

This is the picture Bigger John sent for the book. Looking huge, am I right?

If you think I was too harsh on my childhood friend Bigger John in my previous book, let me explain the type of person we're dealing with. When I told him about this apocalyptic book, he wanted to include a section titled "When Killing a Man Just Isn't Enough." In John's world, revenge is everything. For example, if someone were to kill his family, simply killing that person would not be enough. He would want to make him suffer, and how would he achieve that? Yep, you guessed it: by raping him. (When Bigger John read this, he wanted to make sure that the reader knew the difference between man-rape and homosexual sex. Man-rape is all about humiliation and dominance. Homosexual sex is about being gay. His words: "You can fuck a man, and depending on your reasoning for doing it, you can still be a real man.") I thought about including the section because I didn't want to anger him, which might provoke him to use his step-by-step instructions on me, but in the end I just couldn't do it. As a result, I have taken to hiding, so you might not see me for a while. Anyway, be on the lookout for the man in the photos, and if you ever see him, by all means, never turn your back on him.

Now as for Big John McCarthy, he was one of the first MMA referees, and he did an insane amount to promote and legalize the sport in the early years. I respect him as a person—not so much can be said about the man on the previous page.

The next step is to develop an escape route on foot. Hoofing it out of the chaos is not optimal, but with many disasters, it will be your only choice. Although you still want to avoid major roads when mapping out this route, you also want to choose the straightest possible line to your safe zone. If the path you choose involves hiking through remote parts of the forest, you may want to stash alternate methods of travel such as bicycles, off-road vehicles, or even a rubber raft to cross a river. However, a word of caution: Do not attempt to use a super-spring pogo stick to make your escape. As practical as this might sound, the pogo stick offers far more danger than it does value. Trying to pogo-stick down a steep embankment of volcanic rock will seldom end in success. Don't feel badly if you already purchased one—I was a rookie once myself.

You can never be too safe. Once you have mapped out both escapes, learn all the ins and outs of your path to freedom. Get to know both routes like the back of your girlfriend's head. This involves traveling them with nothing but the supplies you will have with you, as well as at various times of the year, in order to learn how the terrain and climate will affect you. Although this might arouse suspicion from law enforcement, especially if your route takes you through people's backyards, getting chased will only benefit your training. Find possible sources of fresh water along the way, and search out hiding places and defensible positions.

When I was a child, I loved hiding places, but living in an urban environment, I often had to create my own. I remember for one of my birthdays my mom bought me a shovel (yeah, strange present, I know). The only place to dig was a small dirt patch in the backyard, so that is where I took to digging a hole. In a matter of days, I had dug a ditch well over my little head. The coolest part about it was that I had to maneuver around several water pipes, which I used as a ladder and to store stuff on. I even covered the thing with a piece of plywood that had fallen off my neighbor's fence. It was fucking epic, but needless to say, my mother made me cover it up once we began having plumbing issues. I guess my reason for bringing up this story is that holes are excellent hiding places.

In any case, both of the routes you create should be segmented into several key checkpoints that will allow you to regroup and hunker down for a few days if need be. If the route to your safe zone is more than a few miles, you might also want to stash weapons and supplies along the way.

As with your shelter, tell no one about your escape routes. People have a way of talking, even if it is just to tell others how crazy you are. Keep your mouth shut, plan in secret, and do not leave any maps or traceable evidence behind. Think I am being overly paranoid? Let me tell you a story. At eighteen, I was still living at home with my mom. Shortly after I broke up with my longtime girlfriend, I brought a new girl over to the house. My mom had always told me that I could tell her anything, and so when she asked me how things were going with this new girl, I said, "Great, we had sex on the patio furniture by the pool." I quickly realized by the look on her face that she was not as "cool" as she reported herself to be. She was absolutely not cool with me having sex with random chicks on the patio furniture.

In addition to telling no one about your escape plan, when the piss hits the wind, be very selective about who you bring with you. Personally, I recommend traveling alone, but if you absolutely have to bring that special somebody, make sure he or she is capable of handling themselves in stressful situations. And once you are on the move, do not pick up stragglers. At the onset of the apocalypse, people will be freaked out and desperate. The last thing you need is some desperate cling-on waving down the National Guard when you're almost home free. However, I am sure my sweet, seventysomething-year-old grandma Ruth would disagree with me on this point. She picks up scraggly, obvious-serial-killer hitchhikers on the freeway every chance she can get. Seriously, I have no clue how she hasn't yet been killed.

SURVIVAL IN A BAG (YOUR GO BAG)

Your Go Bag should contain everything you need to get from your house to your safe zone. Remember, you're not going on a two-week camping trip: You're running to save your fucking life. As a result, you only want the bare essentials. If your Go Bag ends up weighing seventy-five pounds, you will need a Sherpa. And a Sherpa will not only slow you down, which makes you vulnerable to anyone chasing you, but he will also have a very difficult time getting over fences and other obstacles (might have something to do with them being very squat people, much like my coauthor Erich, who, by the way, I make carry all my shit). Personally, my Go Bag weighs less than thirty pounds. Here is what it includes:

- **GLOCK .45:** Small, light, and effective.
- **AMMUNITION:** Fifty rounds. While people like Bigger John would suggest including a lot more than fifty rounds, ammunition gets heavy really quickly. The goal is to reach your safe zone as fast as possible, not to see how many shoot-outs you can get into.
- **MULTIPURPOSE TOOL:** Personally, I like Leatherman and Gerber (or anything a manufacturer will send me for free . . . hint, hint). Whichever tool you decide upon, it should come equipped with a knife, a screwdriver, some type of sexual aid, and a pair of pliers, which will come in handy in case you need to hot-wire a car (see chapter 4).
- **MRES:** This stands for "Meal, Ready-to-Eat," and they are lightweight, self-contained, filed rations that you can eat while on the journey to your safe zone. Deciding how many to include should be based upon how long it takes to reach your safe zone. I would recommend planning on three per day, and then adding a couple of extra on top just in case you encounter some unseen obstacle.

Chances are you are either going to be running or walking at a very fast pace along your escape route, and it is very important to keep your energy high.

- **PEANUT BUTTER**—It is high in calories and protein and doesn't spoil. And if I see you dehydrated on the side of some trail with a mouth full of peanut butter, in utter and complete agony, it will provide me with a good belly laugh.

- **WATER:** How much water to bring should be based upon the time it takes to reach your safe zone, as well as if there are any water sources along the journey. In either case, I would bring at least three sixteen-ounce bottles for each day you will be traveling, even if there are available water sources. Water adds serious weight to your Go Bag, but it is something that you absolutely cannot live without.

- **WATER PURIFIER:** These days, water purifiers are small, light, and easy to use. Even though a water source may appear clean, in the wake of a natural disaster or viral outbreak, you can never be too careful.

- **MAP:** Packing that topographic map you bought, which charts out your escape route to your safe zone, is extremely important because you might need to take a detour due to an unseen occurrence. Later in the book, I teach you how to read topographic maps, because trust me, you won't be able to figure it out on your own.

- **COMPASS:** Just like having a topographic map, this navigational tool might very well save you from getting lost and dying a horrible death in the wilderness.

- **WATERPROOF MATCHES:** Fires should be avoided when possible because they can give away your location. However, a small fire could save your life should the weather turn bad. Waterproof matches are just awesome. In fact, why wait until the apocalypse to start carrying them!

- **GOGGLES:** They seem like a very postapocalyptic thing to have, so I threw them in my bag just in case.

FORTUNE COOKIE WISDOM

Bar fighting makes you tough, without a doubt. Even if you win, you are often carted off to jail, where you are usually required to participate in more fighting. And if you really mess a guy up in a bar fight, you get to go to prison, which makes you super tough because you have to spend all your time trying not to get raped . . . As a side note, I am not down with that saying "Anything that doesn't kill you makes you stronger." I am pretty sure getting raped in prison makes you and your bowels a little weaker.

- **GLOVES:** Gloves are an absolute necessity when navigating through a postapocalyptic wasteland. However, they should not be so bulky that you have a difficult time holding and firing your weapon.

- **WOOL SOCKS:** If your feet are fucked, you're fucked. I recommend bringing five pairs of wool socks and putting on a fresh pair every eight hours. If the weather is warm, strap your wet socks to the back of your backpack so they can dry.

- **BOOTS:** The reason I included a pair of boots in your Go Bag is that you might not have enough time to put them on before fleeing your home. The first step is to always get the hell out of Dodge—when you reach a place that is somewhat safe, remove the shoes you are wearing and put on your boots.

- **WOOL BLANKET:** If at all possible, you do not want to stop and sleep while making your escape to your safe zone. However, if the terrain is too dangerous to traverse at night, you might need to bed down for a few hours. While there are some excellent sleeping bags currently on the market, nothing retains heat in wet conditions better than, or is as durable as, a wool blanket.

- **FLASHLIGHT:** You don't need to go crazy and stash a floodlight in your Go Bag. You just need something that is bright enough to show you where you are going. If you find a flashlight that doesn't suck through its batteries in twelve minutes, e-mail me the name of the brand.

- **TOOTHPASTE:** If you have never heard of this handy little device, you are a filthy fuck mongrel. For those of you who have been using a toothbrush your entire life, I just want to reiterate the importance of taking care of your teeth. Later in the book I give instructions on how to pull a rotten tooth, but you want to avoid this at all cost. Granted, a few days without brushing won't do you any harm, but if you are unable to reach your safe zone for whatever reason, you will be very glad you brought some toothpaste.

GET INTO SHAPE, YOU FAT SLOB

As you're fleeing from the apocalypse you're almost certainly going to need to be on foot for some of the time; therefore, it's crucial that you're in Armageddon-ready shape at all times. There are two ways you can get in shape to survive the apocalypse. You could be like me and train in a climate-controlled gym on a treadmill, which is obviously the pussy way out. The only reason I do this is that this type of preparation actually helps speed up the arrival of the apocalypse. Here is my routine: I overconsume food, and then go to the gym to burn off that food on an electric treadmill in an air-conditioned room. I figure that if enough people follow this layout, the apocalypse will be here before you know it, which is a good thing.

However, if you want a more manly approach, simply walk out into the woods and see how far you can go in any direction. You could buy a weight vest to increase resistance, but again, that is pussy. A much better approach would be to simply gather all the shit you would need in a real survival scenario and haul that shit instead. Remember, there will be no CrossFit during the apocalypse. There will also be no trendy diet-and-exercise programs. Having the ability to hike long distances and sprint really fast will be the most important attributes you can possess. Being a good hiker will allow you to travel for long distances to reach sources of food and water, and being able to sprint really fast will allow you to outrun predators. When it comes to jump squats, Thai kicks, and all that nonsense, leave it in civilization.

VEHICLE OF DEATH

While being in shape is good, your own two feet will only get you so far. Remember how I was telling you to chart a drivable escape route to your safe zone? Well, if shit hits the fan big-time, chances are you won't be able to make that drive in your family sedan. In order to make it out of your driveway and over the rubble, you are going to need to build a *Vehicle of Destruction* (VOD). I toyed with the idea of coming up with my own step-by-step instructions on how to build this monster, but realizing I should probably give you something you might actually be able to use, I decided to bring in an expert. Trying to find the perfect expert could have been rough. In addition to his being knowledgeable about automobiles, I also wanted him to be a dirty, mean fucker. You know, the kind of guy who lives out in the mountains like Gargamel and spends all his waking hours dreaming up sinister ways to exterminate his enemies. A guy kind of like me, except he knows a thing or two about cars. Luckily, I knew the perfect man for the job.

Let me tell you about this fucking guy. Certain that it was only a matter of time before the world as we know it crumbled and fell into the fiery pits of hell, he purchased his own mountaintop outside of Los Angeles, on which he built a bunker and a recording studio. The bunker is so him and his family can survive the end of days, and the recording studio is so he can compose the dark symphony of the apocalypse, which will inspire people like you and me to press on. I have never seen this guy's parents, but I am pretty certain one is a Hell's Angel and the other is Thor, god of thunder. The guy is six two, 235 pounds, and one terrifying son of a bitch. I mean, his beard alone is enough to make children cry. It looks like something a plumber would remove from a clogged drain in a crack house.

Seriously, how this guy gets his beautiful wife to mate with him is beyond me, but he's got three kids that resemble him enough to convince me that it wasn't the milkman. Anyway, after reading the lyrics to his songs "Destruction Overdrive" and "The Blessed Hellride," and hearing rumors that he themed a room in his bunker after the movie *The Exorcist*,

I put a silver cross around my neck, armed myself with a Bible and some garlic, and approached him about giving my readership some pointers on constructing a VOD. Who is this mechanical visionary I have brought into our friendly picnic? None other than Zakk Wylde, Ozzy Osbourne's lead guitarist for the past twenty-five years and front man for Black Label Society, the kind of band your mother warned you about. So put on your thinking caps, I am now going to turn you over to the modern-day Viking.

ZAKK WYLDE'S DO-IT-YOURSELF DEATHCORE WARMACHINE

What's going on, brothers and sisters of the Berserker Nation? Here's the situation: You've never been through a catastrophic disaster and you need some advice for gettin' yourself from point A to point B without some *Mad Max* motherfucker hunting your ass down and then killin' and grillin' you like it's the fucking Fourth of July at the Dahmer's house. Don't want your organs to become a shish kebab? Well, you've come to the right place. Before Mr. Dahmer gets hold of your loins, Father Zakk here is gonna open up the Black Label Garage and explain how to build the ultimate postapocalyptic, land survival vehicle, or as I like to call it, **the Deathcore Warmachine** (DW).

Since I brought up *Mad Max*, remember Mel Gibson's black-on-black "Interceptor" from the movie? It was the makeshift car he drove around through the decimated terrain of Australia. His base vehicle was a 1973 Ford Falcon XB GT hardtop coupe with a 351-cubic-inch V8 that was supercharged and modified to put out six hundred horsepower. Cool car, am I right? Wrong. The only part of *that* ride we have any use for in our design is the paint job; at least Mel got the colors right. Nothin' for nothin', the Deathcore Warmachine will run Mel's car right-the-fuck over.

I'm using the exact truck I drive today for our base vehicle, a black Ford F-350 Super Duty. Yes, I suggest you start saving your pennies now so you can go out and buy one.

The F-350 has a 6.4L Power Stroke turbo diesel engine that runs stock at 362 horsepower and delivers 650 pounds of torque. It has a towing capacity of 25,000 pounds and can haul over 6,000 pounds in the bed. Although this is a pretty powerful monster, you are going to want to do some modifications to get it outfitted for Judgment Day.

In order to begin the transformation of your DW, you want to get a turbo supercharger under the hood, increase the intake and exhaust velocities, and install a superchip specifically fine-tuned for increasing the horsepower and torque of your ride. My DW already came with a turbocharger, but we needed a better one. The upgrade kits they make, with all the specialty hardware and fittings, can be installed at your local performance shop (not the oil-change place guys). If you consider yourself a gear head and want to save a few bucks, you can order most of this stuff online and do it yourself. All you have to do is pick up a copy of an auto performance magazine next time you're gazing at porn mags at the liquor store—the performance magazines have tons of ads in the back selling this shit. (While you're at it, you might as well check out the ads in the back of the porno mags, as they also contain some pretty cool gadgets.)

Once all these modifications are complete, take your ride into a performance shop and have a superchip installed. The guys there will check the tuning and program the chip to optimize all the modifications you've made. I know what you are thinking: "This sounds fucking expensive!" Well, it is. All of the modifications will cost you between $7,500 and $12,000, depending on how much of the work you do yourself. But you can't really put a price tag on power.

Why do you need so much power? Suppose you, Forrest, and I are out in the DW hunting down something to eat and we come upon a roadblock caused by a fallen tree or some giant boulders. Instead of Forrest getting out and moving that shit off the road himself, we wrap the DW's heavy-duty winch and cable around that motherfucker (the *tree*, not Forrest), and tow it out of our way. Five minutes later, we're all back to hunting caribou.

Seeing that I'm already talking about killing shit, let's talk about the next round of modifications. Since most living things on the planet will be dead, it will probably take you quite a long fucking time to hunt down a food source. So it is important that your DW is capable of traveling for long distances without having to refuel. To ensure this, you want to install two fifty-five-gallon, heavy-duty drums on the bed of the truck. One drum will serve as your water supply, and since you don't want to drink toxic waste or some bacteria that cause you to shit yourself for a month, I suggest you purchase a filtration kit at your local camping store. Next, you want to install that filter directly to the drum, so you will also need to pick up the proper fittings, a pump, and the appropriate length of half-inch polyurethane tubing, all of which you can find at a pool supply store, or if you are on a budget, you can simply steal them from the next koi pond you come across. I recommend the pool store, though. Those goldfish do some crazy shit.

If you think water is for pussies and prefer beer instead, you'll want to ignore what I wrote in the previous paragraph and turn that first drum into a fermentation tank so you can brew your own beer, which will be great when there's not a bar left on the planet. Just remember, the goal is not to make a nice-tasting beer, but rather a beer that will get you fucking plastered. Luckily, beer is the easiest thing to make on the planet. I mean, you can even make that shit in a plastic bag in prison. There are four ingredients that you need, and these can be purchased online or stolen from microbreweries across the globe:

INGREDIENTS

> Specialty grains
> Malt extract
> Hops
> Yeast

Here's what you do:

1. Put the specialty grains into a large grain bag (like a giant tea bag) and boil it in a pot for thirty minutes to an hour at 150 degrees.

2. Add the malt extract before the boil and add the hops just after, creating a subtle, yet vibrantly bitter taste. Ahhhh yes!!!

3. Next, cool the boiled mix down to about eighty degrees, at which point it is ready to transfer into the tank.

4. Stir in the yeast while the mix is still warm in order to start fermentation. Once you have agitated the mix, you'll need to cap off the container so it is airtight, and then let it sit for about a week.

The second drum you install on the back of the DW will serve as a mixing tank for biodiesel, a clean-burning fuel derived from a hundred percent renewable resources. I strongly recommend this modification because our current fuel reserves won't last forever, and the DW won't do you jackshit if runs out of gas in the middle of the fucking desert.

With the fuel situation sorted out, the next step is to battleproof the DW. I recommend a full metal jacket made from depleted uranium plate metal like they use on the M1A1 Abrams Main Battle Tanks. If you can't get your hands on some of that stuff, any heavy-gauge sheet metal from your local metal shop will suffice. Ideally, you want to reinforce the hood, front wheel wells, and sides of the truck. You will also want to add a firewall between the cab and the truck bed to protect your ass from explosions or impacts from the rear. Next, on the front of the DW you want to install a heavy-duty plow so you can charge and knock shit over. A variety of plows can be purchased for trucks—a grand will get you one of the basic models, and $4,500 will get you a badass plow with a robotic arm and joystick controller for the cab. I recommend going with the joystick plow, as tearing shit out of the earth will be the closest you get to video games in the apocalypse.

Now let's talk about hardware. Not that geeky computer intra-Web shit all those iPhone-carrying twittering twats run around with in their sophisticated world of nonfat soy lattes and Bluetooth wireless whatever-the-fucks. Remember, it's fucking D-Day and all that shit is out the fucking window. I'm talking about the arsenal of weapons we're gonna outfit this motherfucker with in order to keep your heart beating another day.

In addition to stocking your cab with the guns Forrest and friends explained earlier, you want to mount the tripod of a 7.62-millimeter, multibarrel machine gun to the center of the truck bed. This piece of hardware has Gatling-style rotating barrels, and is electronically driven by the small generator running off biodisel fuel. Not sure where to get one? Try the same *Soldier of Fortune* magazine that you used as a kid to buy ninja stars and nunchucks. In fact, get some of those too. You never know when it's gonna come down to hand-to-hand combat.

Once your vehicle is equipped with all the essentials, the last item of importance is the rear seat. While this could serve as another area to store food, equipment, and weapons, you are going to need a place to shag your old lady. Remember, it's all about survival, and without a good spot to bang one out with your girl, your seed-spreading days are over, end of story. To make sure your gene pool survives, install a long, spring-cushioned seat in the back, without any obstacles that will jab you in the nuts or become uncomfortable while taking the skin boat to tuna town. Make sure you have proper height in the back area as well. This can be accomplished by standing on your knees and then measuring the distance from the cushion up to about two inches above your head. With the proper room, you can not only bang your girl doggie style, but also have the space needed to easily get a thumb in her ass and then reach up and give her one of those Dirty Sanchez mustaches. Hey, if it's the end of the world, you ought to be able to stuff her like she's a Thanksgiving turkey and have some fun with it.

Anyhow, that is what I got on the subject. I'm fucking out of here. God Bless.

Strength – Determination – Merciless – Forever

PREPARE NOW, PART II: DON'T FORGET TO PACK YOUR TOOTHBRUSH

Being prepared for the apocalypse is about a lot more than just having the right gear and knowing how to use a compass. You need to get mentally ready, because you're going to have to sacrifice a lot of things that were essential not that long ago if you want to survive. And when I say "essential" I'm not talking about your Xbox 360 or Internet porn subscriptions. I'm talking about your family and friends (though if you're reading this book, video games and porn probably are your family and friends).

Supposing you have an actual family and/or friends, you're going to have to prepare yourself before the shit goes down to make some tough decisions after the sky has started falling. These decisions are not going to be easy; therefore, it's important to get ready now.

NOTE: I like this saying—If you are going to be dumb, you better be tough. And trust me, buddy, you are fucking dumb. But I like you, and I don't want you to suffer, so heed my words well in this section, and you will be as mentally tough as a washed-up porn star's meat-clam.

LOVE, THE GREAT ARCH-NEMESIS

If you're a decent human being, chances are your kids, parents, significant other, and household pet "Scraggels" have grown somewhat attached to you. This is no good because "love" is the arch-nemesis of the apocalyptic survivor.

In every apocalyptic movie I have ever seen, people are always trying to find someone they love, which introduces them to all sorts of unnecessary dangers. If you happen to be away from your family when the shit goes down, the last thing you want is for one of them to set out on a heroic cross-country journey to find your ugly ass. Since you prevented all members of your family from reading this book (and rightly so), *you* will be much more prepared to find *them*. It can help to inform them to stay put in case of a disaster, but once fear sets in, people do crazy things. Unfortunately, the only real way to prevent your family from searching for you postapocalypse is to get them to dislike you now using the tactics below. Although some of these might sound a bit cruel, adopting them may very well save the ones you love from doing something stupid when civilization falls.

1. Stop leaving notes when you go places. Notes attach you to people when you are far apart. It is your way of saying, "Even though I am not with you, I was thoughtful enough to tell you where I was going and when I would be back." For many of you men out there, this will not be a problem because you are already completely inconsiderate. For women, this might be as difficult as trying to quit smoking, but it is an essential part of the distancing process.

2. Purchase your loved ones generic cards for special occasions such as birthdays, Christmas, and Valentine's Day, but purchase

the wrong card for the occasion. For example, if it is your son's birthday, purchase him a Christmas card. If it is Valentine's Day, purchase your wife a "get well soon" card (personally, I bought my wife a "condolences" card, as I find myself deeply sorry for having brought her into my twisted existence). Giving family

members these cards will tell them that you put absolutely no thought into the gesture. In addition to causing them to love you less, it will fuel animosity between you. Build enough animosity, and they'll be glad when you "go missing." This is the best-case scenario.

3. Make your significant other think you are cheating. This can be accomplished by:

   a. **IF YOU ARE A MAN:** Steal strands of long blond hair from a beauty salon and strategically plant it in your underwear. To ensure she finds them, you might want to tie a few into a bow around your junk.
   IF YOU ARE A WOMAN: Start going to the gym.

   b. **IF YOU ARE A MAN:** Spray various types of perfume on your suit while at the mall.
   IF YOU ARE A WOMAN: Soak your panties in Jack Daniel's.

   c. **IF YOU ARE A MAN:** Leave used condoms EVERYWHERE.
   IF YOU ARE A WOMAN: Purchase a box of Magnum XL condoms, and then hand one to your man the next time you have sex. He will quickly realize that this raincoat is not his. However, if Magnum XL is his regular size, you'll probably want to bake him a cake to ensure he sticks around. A man that large has options.

   d. **IF YOU ARE A MAN:** Sprinkle stripper glitter on all your clothes.

    IF YOU ARE A WOMAN: Sprinkle stripper glitter on all your clothes.

e. **IF YOU ARE A MAN:** Sleep with other women.
    IF YOU ARE A WOMAN: Sleep with other ~~women~~ men.

f. **IF YOU ARE A MAN:** Purposely leave the toilet seat up, the cap off the toothpaste, dishes in the sink, and your dirty underwear on all door handles in the house. I know these are little things, but they add up. Just ask my wife. After several years living with me, she cares not if I live or die.
    IF YOU ARE A WOMAN: Leave used feminine hygiene products in plain view in the trash, call your man every fifteen minutes to ask him how he feels, ask to snuggle after sex, replace all his meat with soy burgers, and never wash your feet.

If you followed my advice above, your significant other has most likely left, your kids hate you, and you're currently in your new, one-bedroom apartment, sleeping in a twin bed and weeping into a bottle of Southern Comfort. On the upside, your family will most certainly not come looking for you when the shit goes down. And that was the goal, so consider the whole deal a triumphant success. If you are starting to think that perhaps that's not what you wanted, next time you might not want to take advice from a guy who punches people in the face for a living. Just a thought.

THE POSTAPOCALYPTIC FAMILY UNIT

If you are lucky enough to be with your family when the apocalypse occurs, and all of you somehow survive, consider yourself blessed. However, men, women, and children in our society have inherent weaknesses. Some of these weaknesses will have a negative impact on the family unit during the apocalypse, so it is important that you begin eradicating these now.

FACT: Men Think They Know It All

Men are constantly getting their families into trouble because they are too prideful to admit when they don't know something. While we men secretly realize that there are certain times when it's in everyone's best interest to hand the reins over to our smarter half, we will never do this willingly. It is up to the women to force this transformation. Below I have included some examples of ways to shatter a man's know-it-all attitude:

1. Every time your man listens to your advice, immediately start blowing him.

2. Make sure that your man's beer is chilled at all times. Men tend to listen to the one bearing the coldest beer. This is the only reason we pay attention to Hooters waitresses, I swear.

3. Every time your man admits he does not know something, reward him with a little backdoor action.

4. Every time your man ignores your directions while driving and ends up getting lost, give him " the shocker for men" the next time you have sex. The shocker is the number one way to teach a man a lesson. What is the shocker? It involves your pinkie, a hole, and a whole lot of discomfort. If your man is a real idiot, use your thumb. (Seriously, men are so misguided and ignorant, they actually think they are good in bed. They think this simply because women, not wanting to crush their egos, have told them they weren't horrible. Personally, I just don't ask.)

5. Promise your man sex if he can assemble the IKEA computer desk without any leftover pieces. Trust me, you won't have to deliver. Next time, he will hire a qualified craftsman. Note: Let him know ahead of time that taping the missing pieces to the legs or base does not count. Remember, men will cheat whenever possible, especially when sex is the reward for victory. Note II: I am not trying to come down on other men for being retarded at putting shit together because I am no better in this department. Before I made it in fighting, I was living with my friends John and Amber. I bought a bookshelf, put the four walls of the thing together, and then decided to postpone the rest until a later date. Three weeks later, I came home and learned that Amber had finished its construction herself. I guess she got tired of looking

at it. Note III: Leave shit half finished, and women will usually do the man's work for you. Note IV: Scratch that last note—I forgot this section was supposed to be for women.

FACT: Women Panic

In every household around the planet, a woman jumps on top of a table at least once a day while the man of the household must vanquish the creature that startled her. While coming to the rescue might make you feel manlier pre-apocalypse, it is a good way to get yourself killed post-apocalypse. Don't believe me? Let's take a look. Below is the phrase that currently inspires you to stop looking at porn and come charging out of your office with a broom. However, instead of putting "mouse" into the sentence, we will replace it with something that you will more commonly find postapocalypse. Let's see how large your stones are now.

PHRASE: Eeeek! . . . Honey, I just saw a _____. You must come out here and kill it!

WORD SUBSTITUTION:

- Ravenous motorcycle gang
- Lion
- Crazed chimpanzee
- Nuclear explosion
- Pack of hungry wolves
- Global superstorm
- Volcanic eruption

As you can see, a woman's inclination to panic is a great way to get yourself eaten or killed or both. If you want your family to survive, you must break her panicking habits NOW.

The best way to do this is to get her familiar with the things that cause her panic. Here are some suggestions:

a. Place fake spiders around the house so she gets used to insects.

b. Nail all the doors and windows shut, crack a couple of smoke grenades, and scream "Fire!" Note: Stink bombs and smoke grenades are two different things.

   c. Lock her in a closet with a harmless rat and scream, "Two enter, but only one shall leave!"

   d. Blow horns at odd hours of the day.

   e. When your wife falls asleep in the car, park your front bumper up against a brick wall, scream as loud as you can, and slam your fist into the horn.

   f. Leave a pile of cut-up credit cards on the kitchen table and tell her that they are hers. Note: To avoid losing an eye or testicle, wear protective gear.

If your wife survives these little tests, and she doesn't make you sign divorce papers, she will be one step closer to being ready for the End of Days. Consider yourself a wonderful husband and treat yourself to an all-night drinking binge down at the tavern.

FACT: Children Are Lazy

Remember when there was only one fat kid in every group of children. He was always the jolly sidekick who never got to dance with the hot chicks, so he ended up going gay and being the "IT" guy with the ponytail. Well, not anymore. These days, most kids in the group are fat. They shovel burritos, pizza, burgers, and nachos into their increasingly fat faces, and then huff around the school yard complaining. Why are they complaining? I have no idea. Their parents maxed out all the family credit cards to purchase their precious little muschbags every video game they ever wanted, as well as all the Snackdoos and Tootsie Shit-Pops they could suck down while playing said video games.

I have a perfect example. Back when my little brother Leaf was twelve, I cooked him some bacon on the stove. I fed him his meal and then went to take a shower because I'd gotten grease on my arm (yes, grease splatters require a shower). Well, it turns out that I forgot to turn off the stove, and about ten minutes into my shower, Leaf walks into the bathroom and tells me that the kitchen is on fire. The expression on his face was not alarm, but rather annoyance. I guess he had sat there for several minutes, smelling smoke, and finally found the energy to come down the hall to tell me.

I went sprinting out of the bathroom naked, and by the time I got to the kitchen, the wall was actually on fire.

You can't really blame kids for being disgusting. When I was young, I would have continued to shit in a diaper and have it magically cleaned if I'd had a say in the matter. It's the parents. If your goal is to survive the apocalypse, you are going to have to transform your child into a survivor. I'm not talking about going nuts with it like Sarah Connor, but you are going to have to get your kid into good enough shape that he can run at least a few laps around the track without having an asthma attack.

Here are some suggestions:

1. Have them make their own food, and I'm not talking about making their own PB&Js. I'm talking about forcing them to kill and skin the animals they eat. If they have no problem killing forty thousand people in Call of Duty: Modern Warfare, they should have no problem skinning a chicken. At the very least, it will teach them the value of life.

2. Cancel their Internet. Notice how I said "their" Internet and not "the" Internet. Porn is one of those things that will vanish in the apocalypse, so you got to get it while the getting is good.

3. Build an obstacle course between the television and their Snackadoos and Tootsie Shit-Pops.

4. Glue their cell phone to the ceiling. If they want to text their friends, they have to climb a ladder. Or, if you are really daring, take away their cell phone altogether. Seriously, does a five-year-old really need a cell phone? (Damn it, I can't wait for the apocalypse to restore some order to this planet.)

5. Make your child become an actor and steal all of his residuals. (It won't help them much, but it will make you wealthy without actually having to do anything yourself—just smart advice, really.)

THINGS TO SAVOR BEFORE THEY TURN TO ASH

The nice part about acquiring an apocalyptic mind-set is that it forces you to cherish the things most people take for granted. Below is a list of items that you should savor now, while you still have a chance.

Cleanliness

Personally, I shower approximately six times a day. I shower when I wake up, before each training session, after each training session, and before I go to bed. Obviously, I like the feeling of being clean. Each day I make the most of the fact that sparkling water flows freely from the faucets in our homes. Sometimes, I will let the water run just to hear its soothing melody.

When the apocalypse comes, clean water will be but a fond memory. Although I am sure it will prove very difficult to get used to my own filth, I think I will be able to deal with it. I mean, after a certain point, you stop smelling yourself, right? What will be harder to deal with is the filth of others. You see, in addition to losing clean water, we will also lose Bed Bath & Beyond, which currently does an excellent job at masking the fact that we are all little more than grimy animals. Without all the sweet-smelling perfumes and home wax kits, everyone's situation downstairs will get a lot more unruly. Instead of resembling a neatly manicured lawn, the post-apocalyptic bush will actually resemble a bush. The tidy landing strip all guys currently enjoy will transform into a damp woodland area. Personally, I have no desire to excavate such a landscape, for it is only a matter of time until you run into something horrible. What is the worst thing you can encounter? I have no idea because I wasn't an adult during the seventies, but I can certainly guess. Just think of what you would find beneath a mangrove forest—white aphids, small pieces of gristle, or perhaps something that smells like week-old crab Louis. If you do not take advantage of all the benefits a clean body supplies, you will regret it down the road.

Coffee

Coffee is a wonderful elixir that contains magical properties. And unlike most magical elixirs, it can be found on just about any street corner. While it has been proven that coffee in general reduces wrinkles, enlarges your genitalia, and grows hair in all the right places, certain coffees are superior to others. Who is king of this mountain? Starbucks, of course. Personally, I consume about eight Ventis a day. I know what you are thinking: "Forrest, don't you feel ashamed supporting that type of corporate monster?" No, I do not. Starbucks claims to help developing countries with free trade, and on each cup it has the word "recycled" printed on it. If the CEO of the company is off club-fucking baby harp seals on the weekends, I don't want to know about it. Of course, the downside to my current indulgence is that I will most likely go through serious withdrawals when the apocalypse comes. To make a full recovery, I will have to go through six excruciating stages:

STAGE ONE: Forrest is extremely tired. His basic motor skills are drastically reduced, and he has trouble speaking. He is forced to communicate with others through barbaric grunts. (Note from Erich: Forrest already speaks in barbaric grunts. Just listen to any one of his mush-mouth interviews.)

STAGE TWO: Forrest realizes that he is not going to get any more coffee, and extreme anger sets in. His rage overcomes the fatigue, and he attempts to cause extreme harm to a number of small animals. Luckily, without any caffeine in his system, he is unable to actually catch any animals.

STAGE THREE: Without caffeine keeping his digestive system running smoothly, Forrest loses the ability to defecate. He screams at random people. When no one is around, he acts out his rage toward trees, automobiles, and log cabins.

STAGE FOUR: Forrest blames his coauthor, Erich Krauss, for not somehow saving coffee. He searches for him far and wide in order to beat him senseless.

STAGE FIVE: Forrest attempts to find a coffee substitute. He chews bark from various trees and eats bugs that appear similar to coffee beans in shape and color. He gets diarrhea and is finally able to shit again.

STAGE SIX: Forrest adapts to having no coffee.

Drinking Water

Drink as much water as you can. When the apocalypse comes, the beverage of choice will be lukewarm urine.

Television

There will obviously be no television after the apocalypse, so it is very important that you watch all the really good shows now. This will prevent you from having to kill the people who are always talking about the shows you never saw. Here is my recommendation:

1. **LOST:** Everyone can agree on this one. It just has this way of pulling you in.

2. **DAMAGES:** I am getting into it. I never thought I could like a show where the leads were two chicks.

3. **SONS OF ANARCHY:** It is as cheese-dick as can be, but man, do I love it.

4. **TRUE BLOOD:** It is a ridiculous premise, it is a ridiculous show, and it is a glorified soap opera about vampires. I love it, and so will you.

5. **PSYCH:** James Roday is a god. I believe I said this in the first book.

6. **ARCHER:** Although this cartoon probably won't make it to the second season, the main character has become my new alter ego.

SHOWS THAT MIGHT CAUSE THE APOCALYPSE

All the British comedies that are supposedly better than the American versions. British people are just weird and I don't get their sense of humor. However, *Flight of the Conchords* is okay, but I think it comes out of New Zealand. Same difference, right?

Sense of Security

I secretly think that at any minute people are going to storm into my house and try to kill me and my wife. Maybe even harm my wife's poor cats. You're probably a lot less paranoid, so enjoy that sense of relaxation and freedom while you still can. Postapocalypse, someone will always be out to get ya, even when you are trying to take a dump!

A Comfortable Bed

Enjoy a comfortable bed, because postapocalypse, you will be sleeping on a rucksack on rocks—and that is if you are lucky! Don't complain how your mattress is lumpy, too soft, or too firm. Remember, a rucksack on rocks!

THINK YOU'RE READY?

So you think you're ready now? Wow, you're pretty confident. That's good: the apocalypse is going to need people like you. How else am I going to find people dumb enough to walk headfirst into my bear traps so that I can steal their food?

If you want to have even a remote chance of surviving, you better keep reading because you haven't seen shit yet. You might be ready for the inevitable, but you still don't have any idea what that will be (or even what "inevitable" means).

HOW SHIT WILL
GO DOWN

So here we are again, at the crossroads of a looming end-of-the-world scenario. Remember Y2K and that whole deal? The world's computer systems were going to crash, the power grids were going to shut off, planes were going to drop from the sky . . . Instead, everyone just got drunk, screwed their brains out, and then went on with life. Then, according alien-communicator Nancy Lieder, the end of the world was going to come in 2003 as a massive interstellar object known as Nibiru or Planet X collided with earth. The attacks of 9/11 were taken as an omen, and the end of times was nigh. We were all bracing (well, at least those of us that were so utterly pathetic we actually listened to a fat, old, insane woman). Again, the predictions led to absolutely nothing.

Now the next apocalyptic hurdle is looming on fate's horizon—

December 21, 2012. This date is derived from the double-wheeled cycles of the Mayan calendar, which complete their rotations every twenty-five thousand years. Strangely enough, another rotation begins right after this one ends, so I'm not quite sure how that translates into "the end of time." But then again, I just punch people in the face for a living . . . and sometimes in the gut, or the ribs, or balls, or wherever really.

In my opinion, trying to pinpoint the day the world will end is just plain stupid. There have been dozens of predictions over the years, and none of them have held up. Instead of focusing on calendars and wheels and such, we should take a hard look inward. There are nearly 7 billion people currently running around this rock like ants on a rotting pumpkin, and we're not exactly a gentle life-form. Instead of focusing on taking care of our home, we're constantly thinking up new ways to waste our limited resources and create bigger bombs to blow shit up. I don't know about you, but I don't need an ancient calendar to tell me that there is a good chance we will kick our own asses in the near future. There is a high probability that we will do ourselves in. It's not like we lack options. Crashing the global economy because we are too lazy to keep up with the math is a likely scenario, as is developing and spreading a viral pandemic. Can you predict when these events will occur? Most certainly not. But that doesn't make them any less real.

I don't have much hope that humans will get their shit together in time to avoid one of these scenarios, but even if we were to fix our greed and our population problems, we could still get our asses kicked back to the Stone Age by Mother Nature. Earthquakes, tsunamis, tornadoes, volcanic eruptions, asteroids, wildfires, and a stampeding pachyderm of Oprah Winfrey's studio audience are all occurrences that can wipe out hundreds of thousands of people in an extraordinarily brief amount of time. Matters get even worse when you imagine all of these events coinciding in one perfect storm of destruction.

There are also more fantastic possibilities. Throughout the history of man, every notable culture has had its own end-of-the-world prophecy. The Vikings had Ragnarök, the Christians have Armageddon, and even the Hopi Indians of the Southwest had an end-of-time prophecy. In recent years, everyone seems to be all stressed out over the Mayans' prediction, which states that the world will come to an end in 2012. But the very fact that people are stressed out over that one almost certainly means it's not going to happen, so I'm not sweating it.

Regardless of how it happens, there is hope. Unless the earth is smashed into pieces, certain species will always survive. And now that humans have evolved to a semi-intelligent state and can problem-solve, it is likely that come the end of the world, pockets of human civilization will continue to exist. Maybe not always in the manner we are accustomed to, but in some capacity. If you are among the lucky few to survive the Great Purge, the big question is, Do you want to survive? To give you an idea of what type of horrible shit you will have to endure when all hell breaks loose, here are several end-of-the-world scenarios ranging from the plausible to the "you're on crack if you honestly think this is how shit will go down."

WHEN $12 TRILLION JUST ISN'T ENOUGH: THE ECONOMIC APOCALYPSE

I suspect that this book will shortly end up in the dollar bin at your local discount bookstore, but if you're one of the few who purchased it for the full retail price (idiot), chances are you have some money in your pocket to buy frivolous shit you don't really need. You have a nice place to live, a fun little backyard, a deck with a barbecue, and classy furniture. Your cupboards are all well stocked, allowing you to regularly stuff your face to the point where you find it difficult to rise off your designer leather couch. You spend most of your time playing video games and jerking off to Internet porn. You're happier than a pig rolling around in its own feces.

Now I want you to imagine all of it gone. Imagine that you awoke one morning to discover that all the money you have in the bank is worth less than toilet paper and all of your investments are down by a hundred percent? Although it might sound like a paranoid delusion, an economic collapse of this nature could very well happen in our lifetime.

I don't claim to be an economist. In fact, I don't claim to know much about nothin', no how, but the United States has multiple ways to screw

FORTUNE COOKIE WISDOM

I always thought that if enough people thought shit was gold, you could start crapping in a bag and spending it at the grocery store. That's why I bought my house when it cost a bazillion dollars. I knew that it wasn't worth that much, but since enough people believed in that value, I thought I would be fine. What the crash of the housing market taught me is that the only things of true value are those that will help you survive, which translates to food, water, and fertile land. So all those shiny things that we tend to place a shit-ton of value on, such as gold and diamonds, are pretty much worthless because they don't serve a purpose. Take my advice: buy a shit-ton of cows instead of a house. Gold sucks. I can only assume we have attached value to it because we like shiny things, like magpies do. All gold is good for is filling your teeth, and that's just because it is a malleable metal (yes, I've been looking for the opportunity to use the world "malleable").

the economic pooch. I mean, have you ever thought about what a dollar is *really* worth? You know you can get something for it. For instance, a dollar will buy you a bag of chips, a soda, or get you a closer gander at a stripper's meat curtains. We are told that it has value, and everyone in society has agreed to assign it value. But it's just a piece of paper. What is backing up its value?

Well, it used to be the gold, but in 1973 the United States completely separated the value of the dollar from any form of the gold standard. Separating currency from an actual physical asset allows governments to print as much money as they need to fund their pet projects, like running the country. Although this is pretty normal, and in moderation can be healthy for economic growth, flooding printed money into the economy in times of economic stress artificially solves problems without curing the underlying conditions that created the economic stress.

With a sudden overabundance of paper, the value of the dollar drops, while the prices of goods and services go up. This is called inflation, and although most of us are accustomed to this seemingly natural occurrence,

THINGS THAT WILL LOSE THEIR VALUE AFTER THE APOCALYPSE

The majority of things that hold value in our society now will be absolutely worthless come the apocalypse. For example, that shiny iPod you possess, your smartphone, and your day planner will be fucking worthless. Another thing that will lose value are your stuffed animals. I know they are really sentimental, but they will be fucking worthless. Except, of course, for my stuffed animal Mr. Tibbs. He will still be very valuable . . . Won't you, Mr. Tibbs . . . yes you will. Look at you, with your little button nose.

under the right conditions, it could royally fuck us. If we were to take on a large amount of national debt (which we already have), and belief in our government to pay back this debt suddenly became substantially weakened (which it has), inflation could lead to a little situation called "hyperinflation." (I always thought that when you place "hyper" in front of a word, it made that word better. I guess I was wrong.) It is pretty much the same thing as regular inflation, just severely magnified. At that point, money basically becomes paper with photos of really old white guys printed on the front. The worst part? Being so rough, it doesn't even make good toilet paper.

If in a very short period of time money lost its value, prices for living essentials like food and shelter became more than what people could pay, and jobs dried up left and right, our buying power would evaporate. This means that the goods and services currently provided to us by countries around the world would get a whole lot more expensive. Ever been to a third-world country where the exchange rate is like two hundred to one, and you end up paying a couple of hundred pesos or baht for a beer? If the value of the dollar dropped far enough, the same thing could happen here in the United States. Imagine a world where a lap dance or pregnancy test cost $6,000. Terrible . . . simply terrible.

This would inevitably lead to some pretty pissed-off folks walking around. There would also be some pretty pissed-off nations. Such a situation could go beyond a serious economic depression—it could lead to civil unrest and possibly even war. Unlike the collision of the earth with a "backdoor" asteroid, which you will learn about later, there are ways to spot this type of apocalypse. Below I have included some of the things to look out for (I'm telling you, the house of cards is falling, and I can smell the shit hitting the fan . . .).

1. **HIGH UNEMPLOYMENT:** This is pretty obvious. If people don't have jobs, they can't go snorkeling in the Bahamas, pimp out their ride, or buy their stripper girlfriends the breast implants they really, really need. Everyone stops paying their debts, and suddenly banks and other lenders don't have cash coming back in, which prevents them from lending to anyone else. But it is not like the banks are overly eager to lend money because no one has a fucking job. When unemployment gets super high, say 25 percent, start really worrying.

2. **RISING INTEREST RATES IN THE TEN-YEAR TREASURY BILL:** The ten-year Treasury bill is one of the ways the government raises money. It issues these bonds as a kind of IOU to the person or country buying them. In addition to paying back the loan, the bonds also pay interest. Usually the interest rate is quite low because the U.S. government's credit rating has always been strong, which means people believe they will cough up the cash when the time comes. If you see interest rates on the ten-year start to rise, it means that the government is having trouble selling the bonds and is trying to entice buyers. If the rate goes over 5 percent, it's time to start worrying. Because of the high interest rates, the U.S. government will have a very difficult time paying up on the loans. The rest of the world will no longer see the U.S. credit rating as strong, and suddenly finding buyers for U.S. bonds will become a lot harder. If this happens on a global scale, where many countries' debt is sold at exceedingly high interest rates, it could result in a global economic meltdown.

    P.S. It's all happening right now . . . Scared? Not scared enough.

3. **A SHARP RISE IN JOCK ITCH:** Although this may not seem like an economic indicator, it is. The less people have to spend on goods and services, the less they tend to spend on nonessentials.

FORTUNE COOKIE WISDOM

Sorry, but we traded our country for shitty plastic toys. We bought worthless items from China which they made through slave labor, and in turn they used the money to buy U.S. Treasury bonds. So, China has bought our debt, and now they own us. I learned the other day that we are in danger of losing our credit score, and I've been torn up about it ever since because I'm not sure what's brought me more happiness: a stable, democratic government or those really cheap, lead-painted Tonka trucks I buy every time I go to the toy store.

Without a job to go to or cash to spend out on the town, people will spend a lot more time at home. What will be the first thing they cross off their shopping list? That's right: soap. With laundry and personal hygiene becoming secondary to food and shelter, our unclean nut sacks will be spending a lot more time inside equally soiled underwear. The filthier your crotch gets, the more worried you should become. For all practical purposes, you should look at your junk like a Richter scale, but instead of measuring the magnitude of an earthquake, you will use it to monitor your level of filth. If it registers an 8.0 on the Cheese-Sack scale, it won't be long before the shit goes down.

4. **HIGH OIL PRICES:** If gas prices get too high, people can't afford to drive as much, which means they go out less and stop spending money. As a result, fewer things get sold and businesses stop being able to pay their rents or mortgages. People start to get laid off. In addition to this, transporting food and harvesting crops gets more expensive as a result of the rise in the oil prices, causing food to get more expensive. Those who are still employed need to pay more for commuting to and from work, which makes it harder for them to buy food. A vicious cycle, really. Although high gas prices should not cause you to go out and buy a bunch of guns (you should already have done that), when this is coupled with an already crippled economy, it is important to keep your eyes peeled and plan your escape routes.

ECONOMICS 101

For those of you who were completely lost on the last section, I am going to give you a quick lesson on economics. Basically, it all started with the barter system. In the old days, people would trade animal pelts for prostitutes (kill a beaver, get a beaver—that was the motto). Then we came to the New World and traded smallpox blankets to the Indians for their land and pretty much everything else they had. (What a fucking deal that was.) Eventually people stopped accepting smallpox blankets, and with just cause, so we agreed there should be a common united currency. For a while that was gold, but with gold being a pain in the ass to carry around, someone had the bright idea to use paper. They printed the portraits of a bunch of really old dead guys on the cover and called it money (yes, this didn't happen until the late nineteenth century). As this money thing caught on, you could use it to get really cool shit, like Happy Meals and all that great stuff for our bodies and environment. But getting increasingly lazy, we grew frustrated with all the counting, and decided to replace money with magical cards. These cards worked for a short while, but then a group of rebels blew up the buildings that stored all the records of how much everyone owed, leading to anarchy and eventually the apocalypse. The End.

5. **A DRASTIC DIP IN THE AMOUNT OF BLOW JOBS DISPENSED:** This indicator is in direct economic correlation to the increase in unclean genitalia described previously. With human funk being the new perfume and cologne, random afternoon blow jobs or "the shining of the bean" will all but vanish. Think you could endure the sour taste and terrible odor? Imagine going down on a homeless person (I tried to convince Erich that he needed to do this for research purposes, but he wouldn't go for it) . . . Think about it for a while, and then get back to me. If matters get so bad that crackheads stop giving so much as hand jobs because you are too stinky, it is only a matter of time until the world as we know it ends.

Although each of these factors sucks big-time, if they were to all occur simultaneously we would very well be looking at an economic apocalypse. Remember, just because the stock market may be going up, it doesn't mean that the economy is healthy and things are going good. A market propped up by artificial cash injections in the form of bailouts or drastic increases in the money supply is merely an illusion. Many times in history a country has had a strong stock market while the real foundations of its economy were rotting.

NOT JUST A TERRIBLE MOVIE PLOT: THE ASTEROID APOCALYPSE

Asteroids are the shit left over from the creation of the universe—the afterbirth, if you will. But instead of being a nice, runny, warm flow of human mucus and soupy-goodness, these fuckers are made of solid rock. Some are even composed of pure, dense iron. If an asteroid measuring more than two kilometers in diameter is spotted heading toward Earth, it is fancily nicknamed a "Planet Killer." I'm going to repeat that for clarity—PLANET KILLER, meaning no more planet. End of world.

Having trouble wrapping your head around this? Grab your bongs and I'll break it down for you. A collision would be nothing like the ones in the old Asteroid arcade game. Real asteroids are not a bunch of Lucky Charm–colored digital blobs, and when one hits you, most likely you will be dead, soon to be dead, or, if you are lucky, living in a world that makes Dante's third ring of hell look like a slip-'n'-slide party with the UFC Ring Girls. *Who the fuck is Dante, how many rings of hell are there, and who is the third ring reserved for?* Don't worry about any of that. Just trust me when I say that none of it is good news for you.

Now you're probably saying, "Forrest, won't we see an asteroid coming?" First of all, fuck off, it's "Mr. Griffin" to you. But yes, in many cases, we will. Scientists have built really big telescopes, but with most scientists being slightly perverted, there is a good chance the scopes will be pointed at some chick undressing in Iceland rather than at the night sky. Knowing this is a very real probability, they have come up with the term "backdoor asteroid" (see what I mean about scientists being perverted). A backdoor asteroid is one that sneaks past our radar, and if it should be larger than a kilometer in diameter, things will get way out of hand. Here is what you have to look forward to upon impact.

First off, this thing will hit our stratosphere at a shit-ton of degrees, which scientists say is hot enough to burn the pubes off a groundhog six feet below the crust of the earth. (There's another fantastic turn of phrase: "crust of the earth." Sounds like what was in the jockstrap I put in Bigger John's pillow case right after the first Tito fight!) With 70 percent of the earth's surface being covered by water, this flaming ball of molten death will most likely land in the ocean somewhere. It won't hit the surface and cool off—like a fat-fingered proctologist, that thing is going to hit the bottom of the ocean and keep on going, burrowing its way deep down into the earth. In addition to displacing all that water, it will also displace rock, gravel, and Davy Jones's locker itself. All this matter and water will shoot up into the atmosphere, where it will be scorched by the now-incendiary skies. Eventually, though, it has to come down, and when it does, it won't do any good. The shit will "literally" be going down.

Let me illustrate this for you using a more practical, real-world scenario. Let's say you have to squeeze out one of those double-fist-size, rock-hard balls of Indian clay from your nervous butt hole. You know what I mean, the kind of turd that actually makes you hesitate for a moment when you realize what is coming. The one where you have to mentally prep for the inevitable pain and perhaps even the humiliating Groan-Out-Loud. Well, imagine letting one of those go in a public restroom equipped with those taller toilets. You know the kind, where your butt is like two feet from the surface of the water. When that petrified shit ball hits the surface, it will displace the water below with such force that you will receive a dose of toilet water straight up your chocolate starfish.

In the case of a real asteroid, the toilet is earth, the toilet water is the ocean, the compressed mass of fecal ore is the asteroid, and your colon is so far in outer space it might as well be Uranus (drumroll, please). How-ever, instead of cool, soothing shit water (which can actually feel quite good if your sphincter is burning from last night's chimichanga), a hail-storm of molten earth and boiling water will fall back to the earth's surface in a radius of a fuck-ton of miles (yes, a fuck-ton is bigger than a shit-ton). Quite literally, a rain of fire.

If you think that being up in the mountains, far away from the point of impact, will help keep you safe, think again. Next comes a scorching, five-hundred-mile-per-hour wind, burning everything in its path. These winds, created by the overheated atmosphere, would carry the falling debris and spread this fiery cheer over hundreds of miles, instantly ignit-ing trees and man-made structures. Then tsunamis created by the impact would rise up to a hundred and fifty feet and sweep outward from ground zero and extinguish some of the flames once they reach land. Yes, I know you are thinking the same thing as me—good ol' Mother Nature has the same sense of humor as a small boy watching a snail drag its bubbling, dying corpse of slime across a pile of rock salt.

The impact will also give us fantastic earthquakes. These things will shake the earth much like a frustrated babysitter shakes a crying baby.[7] Millions of people living in densely populated urban centers such as New York City, Beijing, Mexico City, and São Paulo will be crushed under moun-tains of cement-and-steel infrastructure. But none of that really matters because the world will already have caught on fire, and not in the way Lance Bass hoped. No *Project Runway* here, buddy! Just a massive wildfire that will make Smokey the Bear put a bullet in his furry head.

Am I just telling you horror stories to keep you up at night? Am I blow-ing this whole asteroid thing out of proportion? Let me give you this bit of news. It is estimated that the likelihood of an asteroid hitting Earth is six thousand to one. And that number is not in our favor—I'm talking six thousand to one that such an event *will* occur. It's simply a matter of when and how big it will be. But don't give up all hope. After all, the odds were much worse when Han Solo went into that asteroid field, and he somehow

---

[7] Yes, I too was once a babysitter. Think that's funny? Fuck you. I babysat my brother Leaf when I was fourteen, and he would often cry for hours upon hours. Of course I didn't shake him, as that would be a horrible thing to do. But I did scream at him for a while to make him stop. Probably not the best tactic now that I look back on it, but, man, it sure did work.

pulled out alive. However, I strongly suggest taking my advice below, as it will dramatically increase your odds of surviving an asteroid attack.

Hints for surviving an asteroid attack:

1. Stay away from asteroids.

2. Dig a hole deep into the bowels of the earth and then never come out.

3. Build a spaceship and then fly away just prior to impact.

4. Develop a machine that can turn you into a cockroach. Those nasty little fuckers can live through anything, including the heel of my boot.

5. Sorry, just kidding. There ain't shit you can do about this one. It's a fucking asteroid.

THE REASON EVERYONE IN THE 1950s WAS SCARED SHITLESS: THE NUCLEAR APOCALYPSE

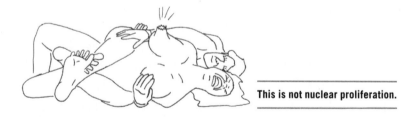

This is not nuclear proliferation.

Have you ever seen a country really, really, insanely pissed off? France totally doesn't count, by the way. I'm talking about a country that's actually a threat. If a country got totally fucked over, say, as a result of an economic collapse, there is no telling how far they would go. Don't believe me? Just look at that crackhead prostitute who hangs out on the corner of Las Vegas Boulevard and Flamingo. She will do some pretty crazy shit for five bucks, or so I've heard, and she can get all the clean water and food she wants down at the shelter. (Note: Do not look at her too hard or you won't be able to eat your lunch. However, it is great if you are trying to cut weight. As a matter of fact, if you are way overweight, you might want to consider bedding her, as it will permanently reduce your appetite.)

People will do just about anything when desperate, and that includes scorching the tits off Mother Earth. But how will these types of countries get their dirty hands on an atom bomb? It's called "Nuclear Proliferation," son. Now I am sure you've heard that term bandied back and forth during your lifetime, but it isn't what happens when a fart follows you back to the dinner table while on a date, and it's not what happens when a stripper's HHH breast implant explodes during an oil wrestling match at a dingy, riverside bar on the outskirts of Meth Town USA.

Nuclear proliferation is a term used to describe the spread of nuclear weapons or nuclear technology to countries that are not on the "cool" list. For example, if the USA and Russia, both of which are recognized nuclear states, were playing a game of football, and a little Guatemalan kid suddenly ran out on the field, snatched up the ball, and then went skittering into the locker room, nuclear proliferation would have occurred. Of course, the football would have to be a nuclear weapon and the Russians would actually have to learn how to play football, but you catch my drift.[8]

This is a very real scenario. When the Soviet Union fell in 1991, not only did the world lose the sense of fear that came from watching *Red Dawn*, but many of the Soviets' weapons that had been stockpiled over the course of the cold war simply disappeared, as did some of their key scientists and the materials necessary to develop a nuclear weapon system. Much of this junk has never been accounted for, and it could have found its way anywhere. If one of these nukes ended up in the hands of a pissed-off dictator whose country has been leveled by a global economic collapse, what would stop him from kicking off a massive fireworks display that will end civilization as we know it?

In addition to a nuke possibly sitting in the basement of a dilapidated shack in some third-world country that hates the Western world, cyber-

---

[8] If you are one of those nerds who read this sentence and thought, "Well, in Europe, 'football' means soccer, and the Russians aren't half bad at that," if you are thinking anything along these lines, do the world a favor and run your head into a brick wall. This book is distributed in America, and that's my freakin' target market, so "football" means fucking football. Get it! Oh, and fuck you. I seriously doubt you could come up with a better analogy.

terrorism is another threat we face. Cyber-terrorism could arise when a fanatical group wishing to cause harm to a specific nation (America, it always has to be America—I guess it's because we're the poster child for Fat and Happy) ends up procuring a really smart computer nerd, convinces him to hack into a country's nuclear weapons launching system, and then drops a payload on an unsuspecting nation. This is a very real scenario, which is why security is so tight at Comic-Con. Think about it: it wouldn't be that hard for a terrorist cell to stake out a *Star Trek* convention or sign up for *Avatar* language lessons. After the meeting in the parking lot, they jack the smartest geek in the group. The terrorists know he won't put up much of a fight, as years of playing Halo in a windowless room and emerging once a year for his annual nerd fest have made him exceedingly doughy.

While nerd-kind is highly intelligent and keen with problem solving, they have a nagging inferiority complex. By repeatedly telling the geek how smart he is, combined with the conversion speech the Emperor used on Luke Skywalker and providing him with seventy-two virgins while he is actually alive, the terrorists could win the geek's loyalty and have him hack into any computer system on the planet.

Apocalyptic Movies You Must See

1. *The Stand*: Best apocalyptic movie of all time. And I don't want to get a bunch of letters telling me that I am wrong because it was a miniseries. A miniseries is a movie, shithead, it's just a really long one broken up into parts.

2. *Carriers*: This movie was recommended to me by Stephen King in *Entertainment Weekly*. My big problem with this flick is that the main characters wear these flimsy surgical masks in an attempt to avoid a virus that has wiped out a large majority of the population. Obviously, such masks would do absolutely nothing to save them. The reason I recommend this movie is that (spoiler alert, asshole) nearly all the characters die before the end. Other than their deaths, everything in the movie is totally unrealistic.

3. *28 Days Later*: As I mentioned in my last book, this movie reinvented the zombie genre simply by making the walking dead capable of running super fast. Although much of this movie was unrealistic, it accurately portrayed how quickly viruses can spread and how dangerous they can

be. I know this because of all the advanced medical training I've received during my frequent trips to the ER.

4. *28 Weeks Later*: Same as the first movie, only bloodier and starring the guy who picks fights with everyone in *Trainspotting*.

5. *Escape from New York*: This movie gives us very little information about the apocalypse itself, but New York does become a prison, which I am pretty sure is what it is presently becoming. Other than perhaps a little foreshadowing, the best part of this movie is Kurt Russell's mullet.

6. *Mad Max*: I think this movie is very realistic about how homoeroticism will manifest when the shit hits the fan. Seemingly overnight, people will transform from businessmen into gay, leather-clad barbarians. Personally, I know for a fact that I will be wearing a leather leotard and tights minutes after the first bomb lands.

7. *The Road*: Not sure if this movie was very realistic, but it was depressing as shit. It made me question whether or not I even want to survive the apocalypse.

8. *Planet of the Apes*: I don't know if it is actually an apocalyptic movie because we haven't outlined the parameters of what can be classified as apocalyptic, but monkeys overtaking everything sounds pretty fucking apocalyptic to me. In any case, while the original is good, the remake is fucking unwatchable, except for that female ape/Mark Wahlberg love-story side plot . . . Did I say that out loud? I meant the movie is just terrible; forget I ever said anything about that side plot. Would you excuse me? I'm just gonna go throw on that DVD for a few minutes . . .

9. *Star Wars*: Not actually an apocalyptic movie, but it is awesome.

Back when I was a kid, they used to show a movie called *The Day After*, and it scared the living shit out of everyone. It wasn't filled with the special effects they have now, but you got the point. A nuclear blast would seriously fuck some shit up. However, today, people seem to be so blasé about the possibility of a nuclear war. To snap you back to reality, here is a likely scenario of what you can expect:

One afternoon, you are sitting on your front stoop, sipping on your gin 'n' juice, trying to recall where you stashed your blunt. Your hoes are upstairs in your tiny studio apartment, drinking cheap champagne and gettin' it on, and you're contemplating going up there and joining them in the mix . . . If only you could find your damn blunt! (Sound familiar? Yes, I stole it from a Snoop Dogg horror movie.) Suddenly a really old, creepy man who happens to work at the cemetery wanders by, looks at you, and says in his grave, old-man voice, "A storm is a-brewin'." Then he hobbles off.

As you watch the geezer zigzag down the street, you hear what sounds like a siren wailing in the distance. Seconds later, there comes a terrible roar from above, and you look up to see what appears to be a trail of fire streaking across the darkening sky. Your eyes track it until it disappears over the horizon, and just as you are lulling yourself back into relaxed contemplation, a deafening *BOOM* rocks your eardrums and a bright white flash blinds you. As you regain your vision, you see a ball of flame gather up into a familiar amalgam of orange and black. Within seconds it is there, the classic calling card of the end of the world—the Mushroom Cloud.

You immediately forget about your blunt and go sprinting upstairs hoping to get one last romp with Laticia and Uganda, but it is too late. Immediately after the nuke hit, the air around the detonation rose to twenty thousand degrees Fahrenheit. The blast proceeded to suck up all the air underneath and around the detonation, and then a split second later it pushed it all back out in a shock wave. You see, a nuclear explosion contains so much energy that it actually creates an electromagnetic pulse that radiates in all directions, flattening everything in its path.

Just as you are removing your pants, you see your blunt lying on the floor and pick it up. You take a hit, but it is not the type of hit you were hoping for. That's right, you take a nuclear blast straight to your face. I would go into gory detail about what the shock wave does to your body, but there might be kids reading this book, simply because I have warned them not to (which was my ploy all along), so I will skip right to the end, which is where you, your house, your bitches, and of course your blunt all get vaporized. That's absolutely correct, vaporized. Remember that episode of the original *Star Trek* where they turned people into little cubes of dust. That's you.

Nuclear bombs are fucking terrifying. And it's not just the big fancy explosion and the super-awesome shock wave. When the atomic bomb exploded over Nagasaki in 1945, it shot radioactive fallout sixty thousand feet into the atmosphere. That shit didn't just come straight back down—

it got sucked up in prevailing wind currents and traveled long distances before eventually finding its way back to earth. That's why if you are anywhere near a blast zone and survive, they tell you to "shelter in." In idiot terms, that means stay the fuck inside. Do not go outside to look at the pretty sky. Get into your fallout shelter as quickly as possible and then wait for the radiation to subside. If you ignored my advice and did not build a fallout shelter, you're most likely screwed. But you should at least give survival a shot by sealing up all the door frames and window ledges with duct tape, shutting off any outside source of ventilation, and then going down into the basement. If you do not have a basement or fallout shelter, crawl under your desk like they used to tell kids to do during the Cuban missile crisis in the early sixties. This will in no way save you—I just think it is an amazing way for you to die. On the upside, the desk will most likely fall on you and serve as your coffin.

What happens next is wholly dependent upon your location in relation to the blast. If you are living in the target city, the one that has been struck, you are smack-dab in the thick of some mayhem. Since you had the foresight to purchase this book, I'm going to give you a tip: save some of the money you would normally spend on booze and your Internet porn subscriptions and go buy yourself a radiation dosimeter that tracks the level of radiation, which is measured in rads.

At the very least, you want to get a radiation badge, which looks much like a credit card. Anything measuring more than one hundred rads is considered "hot" (saw it on *Fringe*, so it has got to be legit). If the area in which you are residing is registering hot, no one is coming for you. The First Responder teams, such as the Chemical Biologic Incident Response Force (CBIRF), label zones that measure a hundred rads or greater as No Go Zones, and they ignore that part of town altogether. Chances are you will be stuck there for several days. In cities that have a population greater than 7 million, such as Los Angeles and New York City, the No Go Zone will produce anywhere from one hundred to two hundred thousand fatalities within the first twelve hours. Those who do survive but did not construct a fallout shelter will most likely be soaked with a heavy dose of radiation, which is evidenced by severe burns and sickness.

ANIMALS KNOW WHEN IT'S BETTER JUST TO DIE

If you do not have the money to purchase a radiation detector, just go down to your local pet shop and pick up a shit-ton of canaries. Apparently, they die super quick from radiation and will let you know when to get the hell out of Dodge (yes, I stole this from *Close Encounters of the Third Kind*).

Outside of the No Go Zone, you have the Fallout Zone. If you managed to seal up your doors and windows or get into your fallout shelter quickly enough, you might have a glimpse of hope at truly surviving. Some degree of radiation sickness should be expected. If you purchased a radiation dosimeter like I suggested, you can always test yourself to see how fucked you are. If you don't have one, you can gauge your level of sickness by your symptoms. Minor radiation poisoning can lead to throbbing headaches or light skin burns. Significant doses are said to be able to cause genetic mutations. I don't think this means that overnight you will grow a dick out of your forehead, but it does mean that you'll have a stronger likelihood of having deformed babies should you decide to procreate and bring a child into a jacked-up, godforsaken, post-nuclear-war world. If you ever wondered where all the deformed creatures come from in movies such as *Total Recall*, you got your answer. It's sick fucks like you who want to get your groove on after sucking down large amounts of radiation. You've probably spent many a dark and lonely night thinking about that three-titted girl.

To avoid having to name your child "Thing" or "It," I would highly recommend remaining indoors for at least four days. But be warned, once you do venture outside, you will have to work your way through a gauntlet of dead bodies, rubble, and all sorts of shell-shocked and desperate people who may be completely fucked in the head. As I mentioned in the escape route section, stay off the main roadways and keep to lesser-traveled paths. However, be on the lookout for any Red Cross or other medical units.

If you manage to link up with a unit trained specifically to handle major crisis, you will be sorted out in what is called the DIME system—Delay Treatment, Immediate, Minimal, and Expected (yes, the government loves acronyms). If you see yourself being marked with a green tag, you are basically fine and won't receive much attention, but you can breathe a sigh of relief because you've just advanced to the next round: post-nuclear-war survivor. If you get marked with a yellow tag, you have minimal injuries and will most likely survive. In my personal opinion, the yellow tag is the worst because you will be waiting around for hours and hours, bored out of your mind. If you get a red tag, you are in the immediate category and will receive priority treatment because they think they can save you. If you get a black tag, you have been labeled as "expected"—as in "expected to die" (there simply is no nice way to say that). You won't receive shit, except maybe some morphine for the pain, which at this point may not be such a bad thing.

Going out in a nuclear blast during the end of the world isn't a shameful death, unless of course you were doing something unmentionable during the actual impact. For example, if you were trying to figure out if the chick you were jerking to online was actually a dude, and then you noticed the Adam's apple at the precise moment the bomb hit, I'm afraid your death isn't as heroic as you may have hoped. In fact, once in the afterlife, expect to be the laughingstock of the next world.

If you get released from a medical unit with a clean bill of health or you do not link up with such a unit, it is important to remember that a shit load of people will be fleeing the city. They will attempt to find refuge in towns and states that cannot support an instantaneous mass immigration of this kind. Survivors will be competing for resources, and this will undoubtedly piss off the locals. In a short period of time, refugee camps will be established. Personally, I advise avoiding them at all cost. You want to go solo instead. Just strike it out on your own and live like the wolf—El Lobo. Howling at the moon in your anguish. Always hunting. Always yearning.

However, if this does not work out for you or you get corralled by law enforcement officers, you're going to have to learn how to survive in a refugee camp. It will become a dog-eat-dog world very quickly, and I feel it is my duty to give you some much-needed pointers. How do I know so much about refugee camps? Well, I used to watch that HBO prison show *Oz* all the time, until it got super-duper gay. And there is a strong chance that I watched too much of it, as I am now using words like "super-duper."

FORTUNE COOKIE WISDOM

The apocalypse isn't all doom and gloom. Sure, everyone is dead, the world is in chaos, and all those near-extinct species are now extinct . . . well, most every species is extinct. But you must think of the many benefits. There will be no more reality TV, which is the lowest form of entertainment. Even lower than curling (a pathetic sport that is somehow still in the Olympics). The obvious exception is *TUF* because it is a show where people with actual skill compete against one another for an actual goal. (It did wonders for me. Without *TUF*, you would not be reading this book and, consequently, dying a horrible death in the apocalypse . . . Oh, and that show where they compete to make the best cake is pretty legit too.)

In addition to no more reality TV, the roads will be far less crowded, which means fewer instances of road rage. In fact, most cases of road rage will be me kicking unoccupied vehicles. There will also be no lines anywhere—try to wrap your head around that. Of course, there will be nothing left to actually do, but at least you won't have to wait in line to do it. So your family and friends may have died, but there will be no traffic. Come on, that's a fair trade.

LIKE SUMMER CAMP, ONLY DIFFERENT: HOW TO TOUGH IT OUT AS A REFUGEE

Refugee camps are designed for the unwanted, and so the majority of the time they are constructed on very inhospitable terrain. If you are in Louisiana, expect to be placed in the swamps. If you are in Nevada, expect to be placed in the middle of the fucking desert. If you are in Arkansas—well, anywhere in Arkansas is pretty fucking shitty.

Since they placed you in the crappiest part of the state, there will be no permanent structures. Although tents will be erected overnight, most of them will fall over in the first storm. You will most likely have to sleep outside, but instead of being out in nature with a good deal of breathing room, you will be packed into these camps tighter than a pedophile's shit in San Quentin. Basically you're going to be like the aliens in *District 9*, except without the cat food. (Though come to think if it, you'll probably be pretty hungry, so it won't take long for cat food to become a desired luxury . . . and yeah, I mean you will be selling your body for a can of cat food.) All night there will be the obligatory sobs and anguished wails (kind of like what I hear from my wife during and after sex). To avoid going mad, you are going to have to train yourself to stay hard. I don't mean walking around 24/7 exclaiming, "I am the owner of a boner!" I mean you want to have to stay emotionally tough. You can't let things faze you, no matter how terrifying they may be.

Food will be scarce, and so you must get used to taking things from people who are less aggressive and dominant than yourself. Just like in fighting, survival is based on who really wants it. There are many ways to

develop this mental toughness prior to an actual scenario. For instance, I find it helpful to take things from small children and babies with little or no remorse. It's just a good way to get started. Next time you see a child relishing an ice-cream cone, walk by and simply snatch the dessert from the child's clutches. It also helps to scream as loudly as possible to scare the living shit out of him. This adds to the power of your action. Even if you are in training and trying to eat healthy, snatching ice-cream cones, cotton candy, Popsicles, etc., is great practice. You don't even have to eat

it: just drop the tasty treat on the ground in front of the child. This not only helps you forge your emotional toughness, but it does the same for the child. Children need to experience more of these types of life lessons if they're going to make it. Trust me, you're doing that kid and yourself a favor. It's a win-win . . . Although, it can be kind of difficult explaining that to the parents and the judge.

The next step to becoming refugee-camp tough is to start punching people. I obviously have a bit of a head start in this department, but you too can cultivate your ability to strike another for personal gain so long as you start now. For example, it is okay to take practice swings at those who are weaker than yourself, so long as it is done in the name of your post-apocalyptic training.

Even with this toughness, though, refugee camps are just going to suck, so again, my advice is to stay on your own and avoid refugee camps. In a postapocalyptic world, trust no one. When things begin to settle down and you have the urge to rejoin society, the dosimeter in your Go Bag will come in handy for determining whether or not you will be accepted back into life with others. Measure yourself before you try to reintegrate with any kind of organized group or law enforcement types, as they will most certainly measure you before allowing you to mingle with their constituency. If you are registering above a hundred rads, you will be treated like the redheaded stepchild of mankind. Even if you are below the necessary amount of radiation, your new friends might attempt to give you a "cleansing," which is a whole new joy of this modern world to look forward to.

Hints on Surviving a Nuclear War

1. Avoid living near major metropolitan cities, military bases, or the White House.

2. The Emergency Alert System, which replaced the Emergency Broadcast System in 1997, broadcasts emergencies over the radio, television, and even satellite radio. Keep one of these channels open at all times.

3. Purchase a battery-powered radio for those times when the power goes out.

4. Have at least fourteen days of emergency supplies in your fallout shelter.

5. Build an underground home. In addition to help protect you from fallout, it will dramatically cut down on your electric bill.

6. In case you are not at home when a nuclear attack occurs, purchase a radiation suit and store it in the back of your car.

7. If you are exposed to fallout or radioactive dust, remove all of your clothes before entering your fallout shelter.

8. Avoid vacationing in North Korea or the Middle East.

GIANT SPIDERS ARE SCARY AS SHIT

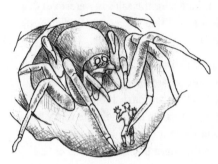

If you think the notion of giant spiders is crazy, you haven't watched enough post-nuclear-war movies. These documentaries have taught me one thing—be very wary of giant insects that have grown to prehistoric stature after ingesting large amounts of radiation. Personally, I cannot think of anything more terrifying. Spiders are all over the place, and in the animal kingdom they are ruthless. While radiation has a tendency to deform and kill humans, it seems to make spiders and other insects larger and more powerful. When all jacked up on green nuclear waste, the little fuckers that you've been smashing for years are going to be the size of minivans, and they will come looking for revenge.

Next time you capture a spider in a jar, grab a magnifying glass and take a good look at it. They are hairier than a female Armenian power lifter, and they have eight eyes that surround their body, allowing them to see in all directions. They are perfect killing machines. If you desire to see their ruthlessness firsthand, throw a more docile insect into that jar. When viewing the spectacle through a magnifying glass, you will most likely shit your pants at the savagery. Instead of tearing its food to pieces, the spider drives its fangs into the flesh of its victim and injects a poison. This poison doesn't kill the poor little buggy, oh no, it liquefies its innards while it is still alive. I recommend watching this horror show very closely, and then I want to hear you tell me you are not afraid of giant fucking spiders.

P.S. Once you're finished studying your future foe, use your magnifying glass to burn that little bastard-fuck to a crisp. At the very least, fill the jar with water or gasoline. Just murder the fucking thing 'cause that's one less spider we will have to deal with postapocalypse.

Apocalyptic Movies You Should Never See

1. *Armageddon*: I really wanted to like the movie because an asteroid impacting Earth is such a feasible scenario for the apocalypse. If scientists spot an asteroid heading toward Earth, our only chance of survival could very well be to send out a mining crew to blow the thing up. If such a thing actually occurred, I am sure the sales of Aerosmith CDs would shoot through the roof. However, I find the movie so ridiculously stupid, it actually makes me angry.

2. *Deep Impact*: Sounds like it should be porn, but unfortunately it's not. This came out around the same time as *Armageddon*. Why do theme movies always seem to come in pairs? In any case, the movie was actually worse than *Armageddon*. Morgan Freeman is president and that's about the only thing I remember beyond the fact that it's about an asteroid. Hopefully, the real apocalypse doesn't have this much drama or bad acting. I'm banking on a whole lot more action and explosions.

3. *Waterworld*: I don't know if there is enough water to cover the whole world, but if there is, I hope I am the first one to develop gills. But even with gills, this movie will still suck.

IT AIN'T BEDROCK, IT DAMN SURE AIN'T FRAGGLE ROCK–IT'S RAGNARÖK, MOTHERFUCKERS

Before I go into the story of Ragnarök, I just want to clarify something. Things will get real nerdy-sounding real fast. Just so you are aware, the story of Ragnarök is where all the Hobbit shit, Dungeons & Dragons, and some of the canned metal tunes came from. I am going to use names like Midgrade the Realm of Men, and Asgard (not Assguard—ASGARD, but don't worry, ass guards will be covered later in the book, as you will probably need one in the apocalypse). If you think I've been listening to techno all day while playing PC games in my basement, you're wrong. That's what you've been doing. I've been in the library, reading up on all this shit . . . well, at least my coauthor has. So if anyone is a nerd, it's him . . . and you . . . especially you.

This is the real story of how the Vikings viewed the end of time. And when I say "Vikings," I am not referring to the ones with "lifebars" or "Hit-

Points" or "damage points" or who-the-fuck-cares points. The kind of Vikings I'm talking about are the raping, pillaging, looting, and killing kind. So put aside your initial reaction to flush my head in a toilet or Saran Wrap me to a flagpole and listen, because even though the nerds of the world jacked up this story to make themselves feel like they could slay anything from the safety of their computer keyboards, the truth is that this story is all about cutting people and hacking them to death with hatchets and axes and tearing things in half and stuff. It is a story from the manliest men to ever exist. Anyway, check it out.

So Ragnarök is going to come after mankind has been fighting for three solid years in winter conditions. I'm talking hard-core war for three years straight in the freezing cold. By this time, a lot of us will be dead or starving or really fucking beat down. During this massive battle, mankind kinda loses its mind. People get sicko-pervo on each other. The prediction says that fathers will start trying to kill their own sons, while mothers will try to hook up with their sons. And sisters and brothers will start getting it on as well. Sounds like some pretty isolated people wrote it, right? Apparently, the Vikings had some deep Freudian issues (maybe this is where the realm of Nerdgard started to relate to them, I don't know).

At any rate, there will be no rules whatsoever, so if Ragnarök really does come to fruition, just go crazy and do whatever the hell you want. But whatever you decide to do, just make sure you dress warm. According to the ancient texts, three straight years of winter wasn't enough. With the onset of Ragnarök, another winter will set in, except this one will be so freakin' cold that they actually give it a name—Fimbulverr. Sounds like what you did with your stinky pinkie the other night, if you know what I mean.

Once this winter comes, we start to meet the bad guys in all of this. Two brother wolves, Skoll and Hati, turn up after chasing shit around the universe for an eternity. Their main target had been the sun and the moon, and about the time of Ragnarök, they finally catch up to them. Being stupid dogs, instead of turning them into their chew toys, they decide to eat the sun and the moon outright. If they were my mutts, I would either give them a swift kick to the ribs for their insolence or send them to Michael Vick for a little obedience training. But that's just me.

While the two stupid dogs are feasting, a huge earthquake shakes the shit out of the entire earth, causing trees and mountains to fall. Unfortunately, the quake breaks the chain that had been holding back another wolf named Loki, who carries the nickname "the Trickster." What a douche. Sounds like a freakin' DJ at some lame-ass techno club. "Hi. I'm Loki, but you can just call me DJ Trickster."

So now there are three wolves on the loose. Either the Vikings liked wolves a great deal more than they should have, or they just couldn't think up any more characters for the stories.

As all this is happening, an insanely giant sea serpent slithers onto dry land. As a matter of fact, this thing isn't just insanely giant—it is super-insanely giant. So giant that it causes a tsunami to sweep across the globe. This serpent has another one of those jacked-up names—Jormungand. I know, a little much, right? But what do you expect—they were fucking Vikings. (Man, there seems to be a kraken or a krakenlike monster in everything these days.)

Now, this is where things start to get weird. The giants are another race of creatures in this whole sordid affair, and they have a creepy ship called Naglfar, which is apparently made from the fingernails of dead men. That's got to be a shit load of fingernails. I mean, can you imagine how gross that fucking ship would smell? Anyway, as these giants come sailing into the picture, the Serpent Jormungand and a great wolf named Fenrir decide they are buddies and join together to form one rank of evil and strife. They march side by side.

If you look to the north, you can see that Fenrir's mouth is so gaped that his top jaw scrapes the heavens of our earth while his lower jaw, wrought with jagged teeth, drags across the trembling ground. To the east, DJ Trickster is streaking toward you in a flaming rocket ship made from every condom ever used throughout the history of fucking. (Okay, I made the used-condom-rocket-ship part up, but after the warship made from fingernails, I didn't feel I was reaching.) Everywhere you look there are monsters and death, but suddenly from the west appears one shining ray of hope, one dream of salvation—the gods. Badass gods. Not only are they super pissed off, but they get their rocks off on beating the asses of supernatural beings. It's fun for them, and they don't mind dying in battle. For them, dying

FORTUNE COOKIE WISDOM
Valhalla is the coolest place ever. The realm where dead Vikings battle all day and feast and fuck all night.

in battle is fucking awesome! One god, Heimdall, sounds one of those classic horns to alert the other gods to what is transpiring on earth. And they spring to action.

Unfortunately they don't actually "spring" into action. There ends up being a lull because the gods have to have a meeting to talk about shit. Personally, I hope it is one of those Council of War meetings where everyone sits around a big table and feasts on hunks of bloody meat and drinks from barrels of ale, just like in medieval times. Hopefully it's not like the usual shit when government officials get together and take forever to make an important decision, and then don't commit to that decision when it is finally made. I say this because during the meeting, Odin, who's the head of all gods, gets on his horse, which happens to have eight legs (could be from nuclear radiation, so watch out for the giant spiders), and rides to a magical spring to get advice from Mimnir, which might be a mermaid or some shit (this wasn't made all that clear in the Cliff's Notes). She isn't pleased with his presence. "Get the fuck out of here and go to the battlefield," she says. "What are you, a little kid? I thought you were king of the damn Aesir gods!"

Ashamed, he goes and assembles all the other gods (finally), as well as all the dead Vikings that live in Valhalla—the place where good Vikings who die in battle end up so they can die in battle later on with Odin at Ragnarök.

While all these gods and dead men are waking up and having their coffee, all the bad guys join up. Jormungand, the scaly, poison-spitting schlong; Fenrir, the big bad wolf; a fellow named Surt, who is the sentinel for the Realm of Fire—(when he's not fighting at Ragnarök, Surt is a part-time bouncer at Club Savage; he enjoys sushi, long walks on the beach, and good conversation)—as well as the Fire Giants and Ice Giants. They all merge into one battalion and start marching to the battlefield, which is called Vigrid. During the hike, they cross Bifröst Bridge. Now, this is a rainbow bridge, which I find a little weird. I mean, either they took a break to star in a Skittles commercial or they were heading to a Nordic Gay Pride parade. Either way, a little out of character for the manliest monsters around.

Then the action starts. Approximately 432,000 dead Vikings, all wearing golden helmets, along with the gods, meet the Legions of Evil in mortal combat at Vigrid. Although this apocalypse has yet to happen, the ancient texts give us a play-by-play for all the primary characters. Odin, the All-Father and King of the Aesir gods, engages the wolf Fenrir in battle first. Basically, the wolf wins by swallowing him from the get-go. Who the fuck made this pussy king? He's supposed to kick some major ass, but instead he gets eaten alive by a giant dog. But then again, I guess being a god and all, he is probably as old as dirt, and so it would be like an eighty-five-year-old man dragging his old bones across the junkyard in an attempt to fight a pit bull. Pretty disappointing.

The next fight on the Ragnarök card is in the bantamweight division—Loki vs. Heimdall. The bout is billed as DJ Trickster versus the Blower of the Magic Horn. For a while it looks like "good" will get the upper hand on "evil" as Heimdall employs his magic horn in sinister ways, but after the two roll around for a while, they end up slapping each other to death. Neither one wins.

Then Thor, who has my vote for the most badass Viking god, takes on the serpent Jormungand. Thor uses his strength and his giant hammer, and Jormungand uses his serpent fangs. Thor beats the crap out of Jormungand, but our hero ends up dying a few minutes later from the venom he ingests. Come to think of it, this bout sounds a little fishy as well. Thor is said to have a "Great Hammer," and he fights an extremely large and thick snake who "he has met before." Then he ends up dying by getting injected with secretions from that snake. And here I was thinking Thor was such a macho guy.

Just when things begin to look bleak for the forces of good, a true badass emerges—Vidar, Odin's son. Pissed off that Fenrir ate his father, he steps on the mutt's lower jaw, grabs his upper jaw, and tears the fucking thing in half. Now that's what I'm talking 'bout.

Unfortunately, this victory means very little. In the final throes of battle, the giant flamer Surt rains fire on all nine of the Vikings' worlds. Pretty much everyone dies—all of mankind, the gods, the giants, and animals. Even the Elves and Dwarves die, meaning there is no hope for Mini-Me, the Keeblers, Time Bandits, or Urijah Faber. This is it. All worlds burn and sink into the seas.

This kind of begs the question How do I survive when everyone is wiped out? Sorry for the obvious, but you just don't. If the Viking story of Ragnarök, the great battle between the Aesir gods and the legions of the underworld, does in fact come to pass, we are all pretty much fucked. But if you have any gumption whatsoever, any balls at all, you will fight to the death, because that's pretty much all you'll be able to do. After all, it could mean the difference between dying by a blade or being porked to death by a depraved Fire Giant. You get to pick. If you choose the former, I have included some tips below on how to take on one of the more common foes of Ragnarök.

HOW TO KILL A SUPERNATURAL WOLF

(Editor's Note: Delete following section—offensive and homoerotic potty talk. Childish—reader will hate.)

When Ragnarök comes, you're gonna want to know how to fight and kill a super-natural wolf. Luckily, the super-badass wolves will already be fighting some of the gods, so you will most likely be pitted against one of the lesser wolves, such as Papsmear and Queernir. Despite being enormous and, for all intents and purposes, mythical, they will act the same as all dumb dogs and charge you. If you follow my step-by-step instructions below, there is a good chance that you will step off the battlefield victorious. You will die a horrible, fiery death a short while later, but that is inevitable.

Step 1: As the wolf charges you, dive off to the side to avoid its gaping jaws and stank breath, and then quickly roll underneath it so that you are gazing up at its underbelly. Unless the mutt has been fixed, you should see an engorged set of red balls swinging above your head like bells in a tower.

Step 2: Remove your rope from your homemade utility belt, lasso that set of nuts, and then climb up the rope. Once you reach the top, cling to the punching-bag-size scrotum and shimmy around to the backside. Do not cling to the front of the scrotum, as the animal will have a tree-trunk-like torpedo whipping around. Ever been hit upside the head with a rubber dildo? No? Yeah . . . uh, me neither. But anyway, supposing you had been hit upside the head with a rubber dildo, this is a thousand times worse.

Step 3a (option one): Remove a pipe bomb from your homemade utility belt and cram it up the wolf's anus like a suppository.

Step 3b (option two): This option comes into play when you are not armed with a pipe bomb. Lacking the option of turning the wolf inside out, you are going to have to kill it using your blade. Luckily, all supernatural wolves have the same weak spot, which is located between the dick and the balls—not the "taint," which is between the balls and ass. I don't have a word for the spot you are looking for, and I certainly hope you don't either, as it would mean you spend far too much time talking about dicks and balls. Unless, of course, you are a woman, and then it's totally cool.

Anywho, the wolf's massive schlong will most likely be guarding this spot, and the only way to gain access to it will be to arouse the wolf to erection. I have no information as to how to do this either. My only advice is to be creative. Once the animal is showing lipstick, the artery will be exposed and ready to slice. Cut deeply and strongly, and you will be victorious.

Note to Reader: If you actually wasted your time reading multiple paragraphs on how to kill a supernatural wolf, which, I remind you, is a creature that will never exist, I would like to give you a call sometime. Not to be your buddy or pal: I simply want to know if people like you truly exist.

P.S. Is there even a word for a person who has a wolf genital fetish?

AIN'T NO CONDOM TO PROTECT YOU FROM THIS: THE VIRAL APOCALYPSE

It starts off as a slight tickle in the throat, a little lump when you swallow, maybe a little soreness. You get congested and your nose begins to run. Sneezing follows shortly thereafter. Within a day, you develop a dry, hacking cough and your breath shortens. The moment you realize you're in trouble is when playing video games becomes impossible because of the energy required. By the end of the second day, you have severe nausea and are puking and pissing out of your backside, which is blistering sore from the continuous wiping. Your headache turns to fever and you lose all body strength.

Day three brings the lesions. They start off small, but they get bigger and deeper as you scratch them. Soon they cover your entire body—they're in your mouth and all over your genitals. You cover yourself in toilet paper and pretend to be one of those lepers from the movies about the Middle Ages or a mummy from ancient Egypt. Either way your prognosis is not good. You lie immobilized in a pool of sweat, blood, and various excretions. Your cough settles deeply in your lungs, and bright green mucus oozes from your encrusted nostrils and stinging eyes. It dries in the back of your cottony throat. Your fever rises and, as you lie there, you swear you can smell your brain cooking in your skull.

The coughing continues, but it is no longer an upper-respiratory hack. It is deep, and every hack is painful. Golf-ball-size globs of phlegm force themselves out of your lungs, Day-Glo and streaked with red. Sometimes you are unable to spit them up, and so you end up swallowing them. You feel like you could drown in your own fluids at any moment. Just as you think that matters couldn't get any worse, your skin deteriorates and begins to fall away. Your veins and arteries can be seen through thinning, waxy layers of epidermis, which cling like rice paper to your body.

There is no remedy. No cure. There is nothing for the pain. In fact no one is coming to help you at all, for you are in quarantine, and there are millions like you—this is more than an epidemic. This is a Viral Apocalypse!

ONLY YOU CAN PREVENT THE VIRAL APOCALYPSE

You probably can't do shit to prevent the viral apocalypse unless you're a scientist working in an underground bunker doing viral research on monkeys, but you can at least have some common courtesy, which is something most people know absolutely nothing about. You see, microscopic viruses would have a much harder time turning into a global killer if people covered their mouths when they coughed and sneezed. And I'm not talking about covering your mouth with your hand: What good does that do? Sure, you might have not blown your nastiness directly into my face, but you proceeded to touch and infect everything within a ten-meter radius.

The worst is when people don't wash their hands thoroughly after taking a dump. When I have friends over at my house, I find myself listening intently after the flush to hear how long the sink runs, just to make sure things are straight. Many of my sick-fuck friends need monitoring, believe me. So, in conclusion, I never want to hear these words come out of your mouth: *Oh yeah, I feel like shit. I have a terrible fever, but I'm a real trouper and came to work anyway.* Fuck you! If you are sick with the plague, lock yourself in your basement and stay there until you rot.

Did my description terrify you? Well, unless you actually shit yourself, you are not nearly scared enough. If you actually did shit yourself, then hopefully it's because you were reading this book in the bathroom, where it's supposed to be read. If you weren't reading it in the bathroom and you shit yourself, don't even think about using the pages to wipe with. This is your mess and I'll be damned if I'm gonna help clean it up.

One of the most plausible end-of-the-world scenarios is an incurable viral pandemic. The virus could come about naturally through mutations in the animal world and then get passed to humans, or it could be created accidently by scientists or on purpose by domestic or foreign bioterrorists. Thankfully most of the stuff we catch these days is either curable bacterial strains or viruses that our bodies can fight off and develop immunities to. Currently, just the pathetically weak die from flu viruses. No one gives this much thought because it is usually just the elderly and children, both of whom are pretty much useless in society. But this won't always be the case.

Now, we've all seen the zombie movies where a virus spreads rapidly through humanity, causing horrible death and then reanimation. Although these movies are ridiculous because the zombies somehow survive with missing limbs, which could never actually happen (I hope), these cinematic masterpieces are very realistic in that it is quite feasible that a man-made, incurable kind of virulence will be released into the general public. What sinister minds could do such a thing? Who are these mad scientists who are laboring to kill us all with the next crushing bug?

The principal cause of a man-made viral threat lies in the genetic alteration of existing viruses for use in biowarfare. Now, of course I would never suggest that our illustrious government would be involved in something that was declared a violation of international law, but there are plenty of

FORREST FACTOID

Chicken eggs are one of the main incubators for viral research. Who knew? I thought they were just for slinging at passing cars or pasting houses with! But it makes sense when you think about it. Eggs are really just abortions in a candy shell, right? Ever open an egg and find that little black dot floating inside? That means it's actually been fertilized! Once I cracked open an egg and found blood. Yep, that cured me of eggs for a while. I've heard that if you go organic with eggs, you also run the risk of discovering a partially developed chicken fetus. If you ever encounter something as tremendous as this, I suggest you invite some buddies over one night, buy a bunch of beer, make sure everyone gets tore the fuck back, then go out to pick up some burritos for the crew. While driving home, slip that slimy little fetus into one of the burritos, mix them up, and then distribute them to your friends once you get home. As everyone digs in, break out the video camera and pan around slowly for the lucky winner. It's kind of like Russian roulette, except no one knows they are playing except for you.

groups and governments that don't adhere to these agreements—or didn't, as in the case of the Soviet Union. Remember how I told you that when the USSR fell, a shit-ton of nukes kinda disappeared. Well, so did a crap load of weaponized biowarfare agents. One of these agents was a genetically engineered strain of smallpox, which has been one of the deadliest diseases in the history of man.

This nasty little viral infection was responsible for killing an estimated 500 million people in the twentieth century, and some experts believe it has been around since approximately 10,000 BC. So this stone-cold killer has been wreaking havoc on humans for thousands of years. How does it do its dirty work? Well, it is caused by a virus called "variola" that is transmitted through inhalation or direct exposure to infected bodily fluids. The virus gets into the nose, throat, and respiratory system, and then heads for the lymph nodes, where it sticks and festers. Open sores pop up on your skin and in your mouth and throat, making drinking orange or grapefruit juice extraordinarily uncomfortable. In some cases, the lesions can combine into large patches that slip off the underlying skin in large peels, much like slippery fruit roll-ups. They can cluster on the soles of your feet and on your palms, making hopscotch, masturbation, fire walking, bitch slapping, and giving foot jobs all but impossible. Did I mention that pus can dribble out of your penis? Yeah, that can happen too.

Sounds pretty terrible, doesn't it? The good news is that smallpox was declared "eradicated" in 1979. The bad news is that the virus had become so rare, we widely discontinued the vaccine around 1970, making all the people born after that date extremely susceptible to the infection. This wasn't considered a big deal because the nasty little fucker had been exterminated. I guess at the time no one thought that there could be a group so hateful they would pour resources into bringing it back from the dead. If the USSR's former stash found its way into the hands of a group that hated Americans, and this group somehow found a way to release it into the population, it could wipe out a large portion of our country. Smallpox only kills around 30 percent of the people who get infected with it, but when you are talking about nearly 300 million people scampering around the land of the free, that is a lot of graves you will have to dig.

What is disturbing is that there have been other strains of the "pox" virus discovered in the wild, as well as strains developed in the laboratory, that can infect both animals and humans (great thinking!). This includes cowpox, monkey pox, and . . . man, I feel ashamed to even say it . . . mouse pox. I mean, really? Mouse pox. I wouldn't be surprised if in the near future some scientist will have to write an apology letter to the world explaining how sorry he is for introducing squirrel pox. This is how I imagine the letter would go:

Dear World,

I am very sorry for inventing squirrel pox. I was working on a project to enlarge male genitalia, got sidetracked, and ended up fucking around with the smallpox virus. One thing led to another; I ended up developing this terrible virus that could wipe out a large portion of the world's population, and then decided to inject it into various squirrels to see what happened. But the last thing we want in this time of crisis is to be pointing fingers, am I right?

If you for some reason come into contact with a squirrel and get the disease, it follows the usual progression of smallpox: fever, nausea, and the pustulelike bumps that turn to lesions. But after the lesions explode, you go through what I like to call a "turning" process. You get big puffy cheeks, grow a bushy tail, and patches of fur pop up in random places. For all intents and purposes, you turn into a giant squirrel. If you have a family member who happens to get infected with this virus, I strongly recommend strapping them down to a bed or tree to prevent them from sprinting across the road at the precise moment a car is coming. Anyway, sorry for this mishap. And good luck!

Yours truly,

Richard

Personally, I feel this is the worst type of apocalypse. I would much rather get vaporized by a mushroom cloud or eat the hot dust of a super-volcano than slowly rot in my bed. To avoid dying a horrible death, take my advice below.

1. Stay away from people. They are disgusting creatures. (I know what you are thinking: "So Forrest, you are telling us to avoid human contact with anyone but our most significant loved ones, but you roll around with sweaty men for a living?" Well, that's only because I haven't yet found a way to make a living without rolling around with sweaty men . . . Do as I say, not as I do.)

2. Wear a body condom wherever you go. If you don't have a body condom, just slip into one of those large plastic bags that dry cleaning comes in and fit a rubber 1970s swim cap on your head. Personally, I tried to go with the full-on contamination suit. Unfortunately, this was short-lived. In addition to my sponsors telling me I couldn't do appearances in a plastic jumpsuit, Dana White informed me that the Nevada State Athletic Commission turned down my request to wear one in the cage. Despite these minor setbacks, I am hoping to get contamination suits into the new fall fashion line. Will you help me on this crusade?

3. Become a homeless person and live in a trash can. Apparently, homeless people can survive pretty much anything.

4. Kill every single person on the planet . . . and pigs. Those little fuckers are nasty germ carriers.

THE HOT NEW THING TO BE AFRAID OF: SUPER-VOLCANO APOCALYPSE

Seventy-five thousand years ago on the island of Sumatra, the human race was brought to the very edge of extinction by one of nature's most powerful and devastating forces. I'm not talking about Cain Velasquez's right cross, though that tends to be pretty powerful and devastating as well. I'm talking about the eruption of a super-volcano. It's exactly what it sounds like—a really big volcano. Although these things are very rare, they fuck shit up beyond all recognition when they blow.

Regular volcanoes like Mount St. Helens and Mount Vesuvius are usually shaped like nipples or penises (whichever you prefer), and as magma boils inside, pressure builds, until one day they erupt and spew

molten rock out of their blowhole. Super-volcanoes, despite being exponentially larger, do not have the traditional cones. Instead, they are largely hidden beneath the surface of the earth. If the shape of regular volcanoes can be described as a nipple or penis, super-volcanoes should be described as a giant, yawning butt hole. The magma of super-volcanoes bubbles underneath the ground in gargantuan reservoirs, held at bay by a massive blockade of rock known as a caldera. Over hundreds of thousands of years, pressure builds in the depths. When the pressure reaches a critical threshold, the magma blows through the caldera, spewing shit into the atmosphere.

To help you better understand this phenomenon, let me use another third-grade fecal analogy. Say there is a morbidly obese man who gets a bad case of diarrhea, but that diarrhea can't squeeze itself out of his swelling anus because he lost an anal bead in his rectum. As the obese man continues to gorge himself, the diarrhea burbles in his great bowels, creating an insane amount of pressure. Then one fateful afternoon while he is loading up his shopping carts at Food 4 Less, the pressure becomes too great, the anal bead becomes dislodged, and gallons upon gallons of explosive shit hurtle into the atmosphere of his tremendous trousers. This is exactly what happens with a super-volcano. The only difference is that there are no feces of any kind involved—but there is a ton of hot magma and ash.

When the butt hole in Sumatra blew seventy-five thousand years ago, it shot so much ash into the atmosphere that the sun was actually blotted out. The ash came down like snow, covering the ground a foot deep more than twenty-five hundred miles from the eruption. The catastrophic event wiped out the majority of the human race living at the time, leaving only a few thousand survivors to struggle through a seemingly never-ending winter. Although there is no evidence of any kind to support this theory, I believe the survivors were forced to turn to incest and cannibalism.

The next blast will most likely come from Yellowstone National Park, which is home to a caldera more than eighty-five kilometers wide and forty-five kilometers tall. Scientists have discovered that this super-volcano erupts every six hundred thousand years, and with the last blast having

THINGS FORREST HATES

- People who smoke.

- People who drive.

- People who breathe.

- People who have been brainwashed by a certain diet and talk badly about the things you eat.

- People who used to be addicted to alcohol and now think that everyone who occasionally uses alcohol is somehow an addict who needs their help.

- People who bash everything that is fun, such as eating bad food or drinking alcohol.

- Fat people who order a cheeseburger and a Diet Coke. (In fact, so many fat people drink Diet Coke, Forrest used to think that diet soda made you fat. Turns out it is just a strange coincidence.)

- Close talkers. Even worse still, close talkers who follow you around as you try to walk away from them.

- Anyone who talks about themselves in the third person. Forrest Griffin hates that.

- Salespeople who refuse to give you refunds.

- People who wear spandex shirts out to the bar.

- People who use too much gel. Unless, of course, the gel is Rogaine.

- People who are balding. Completely bald is totally cool, just not those who are currently going through the balding process.

occurred 640,000 years ago, we are overdue. This baby has got to come out, and Mother Earth is pushing like a son of a bitch. Since 1923, the earth over the caldera itself has swollen and risen more than two feet. It is not a matter of *if* this thing will blow, but rather a matter of *when*. If it should erupt in our lifetime, let me give you a little preview of what could happen.

First, a series of earthquakes will rock the area around Yellowstone, shattering the seal on the caldera and allowing all that magma to eject. It is estimated that falling ash and lava will extinguish all life within a six-hundred-mile radius, and do so with approximately one thousand cubic kilometers of lava. Ash will get ejected into the atmosphere, and when it comes down it will cover lands as far away as the Gulf of Mexico. In a very short period of time, all the farmlands of the Midwest will be covered in ash and destroyed, which will be a major blow to the national and global food supply.

Tens of thousands of people will die pretty much within the first few minutes from hot ash and molten rock. How terrible would this type of death be? Think back to those occasions when you nuked a microwavable burrito too long, and when you went to pick it up, you got that napalm-like cheese-and-bean goo all over your fingers. Now imagine the cheese and beans from a really big burrito dripping on your entire body. Now times that pain by fifty thousandish, let's say. That is pretty much what you are looking at. Luckily, you will be seared into oblivion almost instantaneously, so pain really won't be a factor.

If you manage to avoid hot shit falling on your body and killing you, all is still not a bushel of canned peaches. The ash and debris flung into the atmosphere will very likely block out all the sunlight and drive the world into a state of nuclear winter. When the super-volcano in Sumatra blew its load into the sky, the overall temperature of the earth dropped by just over twenty degrees. Just as with all the ash covering the ground, this will dramatically reduce the world's food supply, which in turn could lead to starvation, extreme bitchiness, and eventually nuclear war.

Hints for surviving the hot blast of a super-volcano:

1. Build an island in the middle of the ocean, kinda like they did in *Waterworld*. Do not leave your island or let Kevin Costner star in any movie made on your island.

2. Get on the boat with Bilbo and Frodo and sail to Valinor.

3. Volunteer on a Russian space station.

4. Kill yourself.

THE END OF THE WORLD ISN'T JUST FOR PAGANS: A SINNER'S GUIDE TO REVELATION

The Christian Bible has its own version of the apocalypse. A lot of people refer to this as "Armageddon," but this is the incorrect word. In fact, Armageddon is the name of the actual place in Israel where the final conflict between Good and Evil will supposedly take place. The end-of-the-world prophecy in the Bible is referred to as Revelation or, according to Apostle John, the Book of Revelation. How did Apostle John know what he was talking about? Well, he saw a bunch of crazy shit go down in these two "visions" he had. Anyone who is named John and has regular visions is undoubtedly Irish, so I have a tendency to believe him. After all, we all know that God favors the Irish and gives them holy visions regularly. I could get deeper into it, but I would be saying too much.

When John goes into one of his more intense visionary states, he hears voices beckoning him up to heaven to meet God. During one such vision, John finds twenty-four old dudes kicking it with some animals, one of which happens to be a lamb. John of course attempts to kick the lamb because he never managed to catch the one that ate his rose bushes down on earth, but the old men quickly stop him. They tell John that the lamb symbolizes Jesus. Now, I don't know if John thought this was a little weird, but I certainly do. If you are the Son of God, you can choose whatever form you want. I would have picked something cooler, like a lion, a giant eagle, a marmoset, or a Tyrannosaurus. Obviously, Jesus never won the "If you were an animal, what would you be?" game.

Anyway, this all-powerful lamb is the one picked by God to learn and divulge the true sequence of the end of the world. The lamb does this through the cracking of the Seven Seals; potentially more evidence of John's heritage, as Seals could be interpreted as those on bottles of whiskey, tapped kegs, or ancient clay jugs of wine. With the cracking of

FORREST FACTOIDS

Forrest Griffin is only to be referred to in the third person omniscient . . . he will also accept Grand Master G.

Forrest has an elevator in his single-story trailer for obvious reasons.

Forrest Griffin only drives barefoot.

Attaining a bachelor's degree takes seven years in Forrest Griffin time.

Forrest Griffin doesn't get knocked out—he just chooses to take naps at odd times.

Forrest Griffin reuses condoms.

Forrest Griffin wears a parachute at all times, just in case.

Forrest Griffin doesn't know his pets' names—he simply refers to them as pets 1 through 4.

Forrest does calisthenics before sex.

Forrest uses car keys instead of Q-Tips. In an unrelated matter, Forrest gets a lot of ear infections.

Forrest Griffin can communicate with trees simply because of his first name. (However, trees have nothing to say. They just bitch a lot about not being able to walk.)

Babies hate Forrest because they know . . . cats love Forrest because they know . . .

each Seal came a vision of how the world will end. How did John see these visions? Apparently, he saw them through the lamb's eyes. I know, sounds a little Ragnarökish, but I am not going to be the one to talk smack. I mean, what if, right?

The vision for the First Seal is that of a king riding a white horse. I thought it was odd that this dude would ride on a white horse and not a white pony. Does this mean that he will prefer heroin to cocaine? I don't know, but this king is also quite the conqueror, so probably not. If he were truly riding the white horse, he'd just doze off in the middle of his sentences and most likely wouldn't do much tooling around. But his drug of choice means little because it is believed that he represents the Antichrist or false prophet. The one who says he is God. Few people will believe him at first, but he will actually be able to work miracles, like making Eddie Murphy funny again. I don't know about you, but if someone pulled that out of their hat of tricks, I would be a believer. This guy ends up fooling a ton of people into following him, and for a moment he becomes more popular than Oprah.

The cracking of the next Seal leads to the vision of a rider on a red horse. This too is quite strange because I have never actually seen a "red" horse. I have seen brownish-red horses, but not actually one that is fire-engine red. I suppose in a supernatural dream it is important to suspend disbelief at some points. Well, this rider is almost as bad as the first one because he brings massive wars and conflict. A lot of people who are really into this story feel that the rider on the red horse is currently among us. If you think about it, it makes sense. In the past hundred years, we've seen World War I, World War II, the Korean War, the Vietnam War, the cold war, Desert Storm, the wars in Afghanistan and Iraq, *Dancing with the Stars*, Halo, *Are You Smarter Than a 5th Grader?*, and countless other raging battles. The signs are all there, so what comes next in Apostle John's visions should interest us all.

When the Third Seal is broken, John sees a rider on a black horse. This horseman brings with him Famine—which reminds me, I'm starving right now! I'll be right back . . .

. . . Okay, back. When I wrote the word "famine" I knew I needed to go out and get some Quiznos. That shit rules when you are hungry. I don't think they'll have Quiznos around when all this biblical shit goes down, so I recommend getting the good grinds while you can. Anyway, the world experiences a bunch of famine, which is a pretty realistic scenario. Other than the "seeing through the lamb's eyes" part, I'm still on board.

With the breaking of the Fourth Seal, the rider on the pale horse emerges. For some reason, the pale horse is different from the white horse. I don't know about you, but I have always considered white a pretty pale color. Perhaps the pale horse is translucent like one of those weird shrimp that Japanese people eat while the little fellas are still alive (when I said "little fellas," I was referring to the shrimp, not the Japanese). Perhaps this means that the fourth and final horseman is actually riding an invisible, giant shrimp or sea horse. Now that I think about it, all this horseman stuff is kinda strange. If John is actually seeing into the future, why is he still seeing people riding horses? Shouldn't he be seeing people driving cars or hovercrafts or light cycles or something? Anyway, the rider of the pale horse brings Pestilence. After looking up that word, I discovered that it means plaguelike sickness or infectious diseases. We've covered how this concept could be a real-deal apocalyptic scenario, so things are starting to look rather grave.

The cracking of the Fifth Seal shows that all the people who had died in God's name will be really pissed off, and they'll begin bitching and moaning to be avenged. Not very "godly," if you ask me. I mean, isn't a part of martyrdom being satisfied with the fact that you gave your life for God? Vengeance just seems a little out of place here. But looking back in history at how some of these folks were killed—being skinned alive, boiled in water and oil, burned at the stake, and one unlucky sap getting his guts ripped out and wrapped around a drum while a bunch of people beat on the thing—I guess you can't really blame them. Under the conditions, a little payback seems to be in order.

When the Sixth Seal is cracked, John sees earthquakes and all sorts of other natural disasters causing havoc on the earth. Basically, shit starts getting really bad. The lamb quickly cracks the Seventh Seal, hoping things will get better, but that's when angels come in and start blowing on their trumpets, which happens to be the most annoying instrument ever created. (That's why they use them in the military to get your ass out of bed at 0500 hours . . . Or is that a bugle?) Instead of things getting better, they get a whole lot worse. Over the course of seven trumpets being blown, all hell breaks loose.

To start with, one-third of all forests and plant life is wiped off the face of the earth, one-third of all the oceans and rivers and well water becomes poisonous, and one-third of the sky goes dark. Pretty bad, I know, but things only get worse. An army consisting of 200 million people starts killing everyone they can find. John must have been a really fast counter to know it was 200 million. I would never have been able to figure that out. I would have said something more like, "A huge fucking army kills a shit load of people." Instead, John seemed to know exactly how many, and that they kill one-third of all human beings (again with the thirds!).

Somewhere in the middle of all these crazy visions, John seems to get hungry and, finding nothing to eat around him, ends up scarfing down a small book. It is described as being sweet when he first starts munching on it, but then it gives him a stomachache. Even if I was really hungry, I don't think I would eat a book, though this book is pretty fucking amazing, so I'm sure it tastes good too. Speaking of which, did I already go over Quiznos and how good it is? I'm sure those twenty-four old dudes watching him trip out were getting pretty hungry as well. With that many people, they could have ordered a six-foot sub. There are usually never enough people to get a six-foot sub. Obviously a missed opportunity there.

So he eats the book. Apparently this leads to another vision because he sees 144,000 people on top of the holy Mount Zion, and they are all hanging out with that lamb. In addition to this, they all have God's name written on their foreheads. Note to Self: If shit goes down, grab a Sharpie and make sure to write God's name on your forehead. Hanging out with a lamb on top of a mountain will be a lot better than what is going on down on the earth. Don't believe me? Let me keep going.

The Ark of the Covenant suddenly shows up in heaven—that's right, the funny box that Indiana Jones discovered, the one that melted all those Nazi guys' faces off. Seriously, I always wondered what happened to that thing after the last scene in the movie when it ends up in the gigantic warehouse. Clearly what happened was that Indiana Jones later broke into that huge U.S. government warehouse, stole the Ark, and brought it up to heaven. Indiana Jones certainly had his thinking cap on. After seeing the damage it could do, hiding it in heaven was a really smart move. I am not sure how having it turn up in heaven helps or hurts the situation, but that is what the Bible says. From what comes next, it leads me to believe it is a bad omen.

Satan is cast down to earth, which I think is a pretty dick move. I mean, if you've already got the guy, why not kill him! There's no point in unleashing him back into the world just to meet up with him in a later battle. I guess it's like fighting a guy you know you can beat down at will. Every time you knock him down, you let him back up just so you can beat him again and really show your dominance. In any case, that is what will happen. Satan immediately starts killing everyone, and then a monster comes out of the ocean and starts doing the same. Eventually Satan, who is on land, makes mankind worship the sea monster, kind of like two guys in prison ping-ponging some unfortunate jailhouse bitch. To make matters worse, the angels are given Seven Bowls, and each bowl is filled with God's wrath. That's right, God's wrath, which apparently has not yet started.

Sores start to pop up on the bodies of everyone who worships the devil and the sea monster, even if they were forced into doing so, and every drop of water on earth turns to blood. Yeah, that blows. The sun burns the living hell out of the earth, everything is blacked out, and another earthquake hits and levels all the mountains and sinks all the islands (that means no more Pure Cane sugar. Fucking hell! I despise the taste of sucrose in my coffee). But instead of simply calling it quits there, both Good and Evil begin to prepare for the final battle at Armageddon.

Then God gets bored again and decides to let Satan out . . . again. Maybe he's been real good and he can come out of his room now. Of course a tiger can't change its spots, and Satan goes back to waging war and torturing folks. So God has to round him back up again and put him in the lake of fire. It is about this time that God has had enough of the bullshit and decides to have Judgment Day, where he condemns Satan, all of his followers, and every evil fuck in the world to eternal damnation. He just picks them all up and dumps them in the lake of fire for good. Once accomplished, he remakes the earth to be a nice, chill place to hang out. The end.

With all that said, I am sure you are wondering how you can survive such an apocalypse.

Hints for Surviving Armageddon

1. Be kind to other people.

2. When in a public restroom, do not urinate all over the seat. That is a ticket straight to hell.

3. Do not cut people off on the freeway, and if you are in the fast lane, go fast.

4. Do not pick on people who are smaller than you. Unless, of course, they deserve it.

5. Give to people less fortunate than you.

SURVIVING THE
INITIAL SHIT STORM

I f the shit went down and you followed my instructions, you survived the initial death toll by taking refuge in your fallout shelter, boogied out of town using your escape route, and now you're chilling out in your safe zone, swinging in a hammock and sipping a warm beer. Assuming you didn't get caught by a demon wolf named Loki while you tried to escape, you fucking made it, buddy! Now, if you didn't take my advice, you are probably lost in the forest and scared as hell because you can hear the "bad men" off in the distance, shouting about how they want to have another go at ya (ah, yes, the characters from *Deliverance* are gonna make you squeal like a pig).

This scenario is much more likely than you actually having followed my step-by-step instructions, so you are definitely going to need some

additional skills to survive (and perhaps some anal lube). I strongly recommend that you find a cave or something, break out your flashlight, and
keep reading. These coming pages may very well save your life, or give you
something to read while you're taking shit. Either way, a job well done on
my part.

MARTIAL LAW

With an estimated global population of nearly a shit-ton of people, it is safe
to say that unless Ragnarök turns out to be more than just my favorite fairy
tale or an asteroid obliterates our planet into pieces, mankind will not get
totally wiped out during the apocalypse. There will be small pockets of
people who survive. They might be forced to live in some pretty inhospitable conditions, but they will still survive. The United States government
realizes this, and because the physical and mental state of these people
will be in question, they developed something called Continuity of Government, or the COG Plan.

There exists a specific directive to this plan called NSPD-51, which
states that in case of a "disaster," the U.S federal government has the
authority to seize all the functions of both state and local governments
(don't worry, I played no part in researching any of this). All that power is
transferred to the Executive Branch of the government (the Office of the
President and his cabinet of advisers . . . and no, the President doesn't keep
his advisers in an actual cabinet, except for maybe Bush, because those
guys were undoubtedly never around). In addition to this, members of the
Legislative Branch (House of Representatives and Senate) and the Judicial
Branch are demoted to advisers (serving wenches). In other words, they
lose all real power and are subjected to the will of the Executive Branch.
(Note: We gathered this information from a separatist camp in Montana.
They also told Bigger John he needed more guns.)

It is important to remember that these actions can only be undertaken
in case of a "disaster" or "Catastrophic Emergency," which is defined as
"any incident, regardless of location, that results in extraordinary levels of
mass casualties, damage, or disruption severely affecting the U.S. population, infrastructure, environment, economy, or government functions . . ."

(Note from Forrest: Blah, blah, blah) So, if any of the disasters we have covered actually transpire, you can pretty much expect the Executive Branch of the government to claim all power, eliminating all the checks and balances currently in place. For all practical purposes, our country would become a dictatorship.

Before I go any further, I want to be clear that I am not passing judgment on this concept. I understand why it is an essential contingency. If one of the scenarios I described earlier were in fact to occur, it would be pandemonium. While nobody wants to see the Executive Branch with any more power, this would actually be necessary in case of an emergency. The President would need the ability to make decisions in a streamlined and succinct manner, without all those checks and balances that we call democracy. Just think of what things would look like if Thor was battling it out with a giant snake in the middle of your neighborhood. The madness would be multiplied by a thousand because of comic book fans alone. Some type of plan must exist to bring those nerds back under control. However, it is more than a little scary to think that that the amount of power we are talking about here has already been quantified and assigned to a specific entity. It is even scarier to think of how that power might be used. And, if you give it some thought, it is even more scarier (yeah you heard what I said) to think that there is someone out there whose only job is to think about how to keep the government running if shit like this goes down— and that we're paying him a full-time salary.[9]

Immediately after the disaster, martial law would almost certainly be declared. Martial law is simply a nice way to say that you are now living in a society completely controlled and regulated by the government. If you're wondering what this world would be like, just think of the book *1984*, only with less stuff. (What? You didn't read *1984*. You're an idiot.) Your value in the society is suddenly based upon what you can do to further this government's efforts or goals. For example, if it were my dictatorship, your worth will be based upon how good of a training partner you are for me, and if you bring me delicious treats and coffee. Basically, if you treat me like Sean Connery in the 1975 movie *The Man Who Would Be King*, and give me gold

---

[9] And it is super-duper scary when you learn that you had a one-night stand with a chick that used to be a man. Trust me, that shit is fucking terrifying.

and jewels like one of those natives, you'll be OK, so long as you don't get all uppity when you realize I am not actually a god, chop off my head, and throw it off a cliff (that part of the movie fucking sucked). Personally, I am not too worried about my place in the new system, as I possess some skills. However, I'd be a little concerned if I were you. I mean, I imagine your most valuable skill is being able to jerk it while simultaneously playing an online game of Call of Duty.

Disagreeing with the government's overall game plan is no longer an option—if you do not follow their orders, you risk imprisonment or execution (arguing with them is much like arguing with Greg Jackson between rounds—it just ain't gonna happen). And if you are deemed undesirable due to your health, age, intelligence, etc., you may end up being expendable. Of course, all of this only applies to extreme cases, such as if 90 percent of the human race was suddenly wiped out in the blink of an eye or if we had a major collapse of the U.S. economy. Either way, this is all important stuff to consider.

Life under martial law would be a life of regimentation. You would work the job you were told to work, and for as long as you were told to do it. You would be compensated however the government saw fit. The government would institute curfews and regulate the information that reaches the general public. Food and medical supplies would be rationed according to your value and status in the new social structure. I know, this system failed in both North Korea and Russia, but the government would still try it thinking they could succeed. After all, we're talking about the government.[10]

Again, I am not saying this would necessarily be a bad thing for a society in the midst of a major disaster situation. It may actually help maintain order and keep us all from raping and killing each other.[11] Maybe even allow us to regroup and start rebuilding in a practical and efficient way. Deciding whether or not to adhere to the new structure of power boils down to one question: Do you trust the government to use that kind of

---

[10] Again, I am personally going to be just fine, as I am a naturally born hoarder. Back when I was a kid, I used to steal ketchup packets everywhere I went, and then suck them down in the privacy (pronounced with an English accent—*priv-a-see*) of my room. If you are smart, you instinctively know hoarders are survivors. Just look at squirrels—they hoard everything, and they've been around longer than sharks (not sure if that is true—might want to look that shit up).

[11] Seriously, if we didn't have a government right now, I would have killed half a dozen people because of road rage.

power honestly and in your best interest? If the answer is yes, you trust the government will do what is best, then you should fall into line and do as you are told (and you can sleep tight tonight, Santa is going to bring you lots of presents this year for being such a good boy). But if you answer is no, you don't trust the government, then you'd better prepare yourself for life on the lam.

Personally, I will want to go it on my own. It's not that I distrust the government—I simply don't want to be milling around among the masses when shit goes down. It's going to be hard to bring my perfect utopia to fruition, and having a bunch of other assholes around is only going to make things more difficult. I don't want to be told what to do or how to live. I would rather forge a new life on my own. If you are like me[12] or if you distrust the government, there are a few things that you must prepare for.

First things first, you must view law enforcement officers and military personnel working to implement this master plan as threats. Their job is to ensure that everyone alive is accounted for under their new system, and it is your job to elude that system and find an isolated spot in which to build your new utopia. They're not going to want a bunch of freethinkers lurking around because it may cause harm to their design, and this is understandable. But it won't be good if they manage to capture you. I'm not advocating going up against them or even trying to dismantle their operations, but if you want to live your own way, you will need to avoid them at all costs. For all intents and purposes, the government will have the mind-set of Spock, and we all know his beliefs—The Few Must Be Sacrificed For The Many.[13] It is the same as the phrase "For the Greater Good." If you're one of the Many, all is well, but if you have some sort of affliction[14] or can't pull your weight, sorry buddy, you are one of the "Few" and the "Greater Good" will sacrifice your ass. If you fall into this category[15], you will become one of the hunted. Most of those hunting you will be organized, armed, well nourished, and trained for this type of situation. To elude them, you must be trained even

---

[12] A Real Man.

[13] I actually did not know this because I am not a nerd. I figured you were most likely a nerd, and I wanted to make you feel at home.

[14] We already established the fact that you are a nerd, so you obviously have a laundry list of afflictions.

[15] Seriously, we're still on this. You are a nerd, which means you are one of The Few. Deal with it! Step away from World of Warcraft for a moment and open your fucking ears.

better, which is where the techniques offered later in this book will come in handy (also, watch *Rambo*. That is where I got 90 percent of the information in this book. The other 10 percent I got from my mother).

As I mentioned earlier, the best way to avoid the ensuing madness and the rigid social structure that will be hammered out of the rubble and mayhem is to get on the move before the "organizers" step in and start running the show. Of course, you want to remain sheltered until the event causing all the death subsides, but get on the move shortly thereafter. If you wait too long, there is a good chance that the government will limit the mobility of the general populace by setting up checkpoints and possibly even camps to facilitate their containment efforts. The trick is to get the hell out of Dodge and then find a location that has clean water, vegetation, and possibly even a healthy amount of wild game. In other words, head to Montana. Just make sure your plot of land is not desired by the government, as that will undoubtedly lead to a confrontation which you are not going to win.

MANLINESS AND THE APOCALYPSE

I know this book is about the apocalypse, but I felt compelled to address manliness in today's society, or the lack thereof. After the apocalypse, this lack of manliness is going to be a real problem, so it's important that we start addressing this issue now. If you take a hard look around, you'll notice that men's hairy nutsacks have gone the way of the appendix. That's right, the vast majority of men have essentially become eunuchs. What are the signs? Well, the fact that tattoos and tanning beds have replaced the good old-fashioned workbooks and callused hands as indicators of manliness is a good start. Even professional fighters, who are supposed to be ultra-manly, have gone soft. After all, it's kind of hard to be a real man when you play more video games than twelve-year-old boys in China. I am not saying that fighters are not tough, because many of them are very tough. But there is a difference between being tough and being manly. You can be tough as hell, own a pit bull, and even ride a motorcycle, and still not be manly.

If you want to be a real man, at the very least you must learn how to

APOCALYPSE MANLINESS TIPS

1. Refer to groceries as supplies. Example: I am going out for supplies.

2. Start every sentence with: "There are times in a man's life where he's got to stand for something . . ."

3. When in doubt, do what Ted Nugent would do. You can start this pre-apocalypse.

fix shit—and I am not talking about your cable. Every guy, both manly and unmanly, knows how to rig his cable box. I'm talking about big shit. Today, most fighters don't have a clue how to fix their plumbing or heat and air—they don't have the slightest clue what Freon is or what it does.

How did this happen? Well, a lot of it had to do with the digital age. Due to all the technological advances, men have forgotten how to hunt women. Instead of chasing women in bars, they pick them up on the Internet, send text messages, and, when all their electronic attempts to get laid fail, they look at Internet porn. The day the great chase became skewed, the lion inside of men died. I know what you are thinking, "Forrest, I still hunt women, it is just a different kind of hunt." No, you are wrong. Typing into a search engine is not hunting, and I don't care if you spend two hours a day on the MILF Hunter website. We have been coddled by technology, and as a result, we have lost the manliness that our fathers earned at a young age.

Men have gotten lazy—plain and simple. Blue-collar workers have always been a little lackadaisical, but now even construction workers have gone soft. Sure, they might be able to lay tile, but they don't know how to lay brick. Sure, they might be able to construct a wall, but they don't know how to fix a water heater. Back in the day, the men who worked with their hands knew how to do everything.

If you fall into this sackless category, don't beat yourself up too bad—you're not alone. I do not work on my car or fix shit after I break it. I am not out there doing ultra-manly things, like vandalism. Just like you, I seek out help when something goes wrong. Most guys call their fathers when shit suddenly stops working, but not having one of them, I call my mother. Yes, my mother is manlier than me. Back when I was a kid, she did all the traditional guy stuff. She went out and worked all day, and then came home and repaired anything that had broken around the house during her absence.

With that shit all taken care of, I assumed the traditional woman's role. In other words, I cooked and cleaned. I probably would have learned how to do all the hard stuff when I struck out on my own, but there was no need to tinker in front of the water heater for nineteen hours, trying to figure out the gizmos inside. If my mom couldn't give me step-by-step instructions over the phone, I could find the answers on the Internet. And if those answers were too complicated, I could use the Internet to find someone to interpret those instructions or simply come out and do the repairs himself.

However, technology is not entirely to blame. There are two other factors contributing to our lack of manliness—the hormones in our meats and women. Yes, I said it, women are to blame for the downward spiral of man, but not for the reasons you might think. Becoming more independent, women have stopped wanting as many kids, and so a large percentage of our female population takes birth control pills, which are chock-full of estrogen. Well, that estrogen doesn't just disappear. With every flush, it gets put back into our water supply, which in turn finds its way into every man on the planet. Did you know that when it rains, you are actually being doused with estrogen? I know this might seem like a cheap way out, but all that womanly DNA (I know estrogen is probably not DNA, but not having the slightest clue what estrogen actually is, that is what I have decided to call it) has got to be having some negative side effects, am I right?

I know the lack of manliness in our society might not seem like that much of a problem now, but it is getting worse every year. We have to think about future generations. When all fathers are just as dumb as their kids, nothing will ever get accomplished. I mean, when fathers come home from an eight-hour workday and start playing video games and surfing on the computer instead of fixing the washing machine, the entire foundation our society is built upon will begin to crumble.

If you are as worried as I am and want to attempt to fix the problem, do not run out and try to sleep with fifty women. Again, manliness is not about the number of women you can bed. If you truly want to become manly for the sake of the next generation, you should start by going out and getting a manly job. What is a manly job? Well, any type of work that endangers your health is a good place to start.

The manliest job I ever had was working on a road crew. We would uncover these massive septic tanks, and being the new guy, I would have to go down in there to remove any of the debris that had fallen into it. So I would head down into the shit pit in a pair of boots and waders, shovel rocks and raw sewage into a metal bucket, and then someone up top would pull the bucket up. Of course, rocks and human feces would fall out of the bucket and rain on my head, which was the part that made the job manly. The first time I crawled out of the pit, a fellow worker named off thirty diseases I could contract from this type of work, the most permanent one being hepatitis. So, yeah, I kinda of have a hint of what it is like to be a real man.

If you get a dangerous job and still feel somewhat unmanly, I have included a list of things you can do to make your balls drop further.

1. Marry a destitute woman that has a lot of children you have to take care of.

2. Do anything wilderness oriented—hunting, fishing, wildernessing. But I don't want to see you out there looking at your phone or GPS system. Get a compass, camp, and learn how to navigate by the stars.

3. Learn how to fix your vehicle. This is perhaps the most frustrating thing on earth, which in turn will add large amounts of manliness points. Personally, I learned how to fix a car in the most manly situation possible—on the side of an active freeway, with semis damn near killing me.

4. Grow a beard. If you are like me and your Irish curse prevents you from growing a beard, get some wicked back hair.

5. Wear boots . . . for a purpose. If you wear steel-toed boots, you better get a job where heavy shit frequently falls on your feet.

6. Eat meat you cooked and caught yourself. Don't be a pussy by shooting a deer and bringing it to a processing plant. Clean that shit yourself.

7. Get a gun. However, if you get a gun and don't learn how to use it, you lose manliness points.

8. Wear slippers around the house and possibly even a smoking jacket. I know, doesn't seem too manly, but it is.

9. Wake up early. I'm talking before 5 A.M.

10. Milk things. If that "thing" is your girlfriend or wife, you get extra points.

11. Sports are relatively manly. I mean, the little bit of manliness I have, I learned from football coaches.

Now, I know a lot of you are probably pretty disturbed right now and want to correct your lack of manliness. Some of you will take my advice above, but others will undoubtedly think that taking directions is the unmanliest thing of all, and attempt to strike out on this mission alone. To prevent you from steering in the completely wrong direction, I have included a list of things that you might feel are manly but are actually very unmanly. I only do this because I care.

1. Beating your woman is not manly. When angry with your old lady, the manliest thing you can do is step out for a pack of smokes and then never show back up. That is what my dad did.

2. As I already stated, getting tattoos is not manly. Unless, of course, you are a sailor or legit biker.

3. Muscles are not manly. Don't be a pony show, as my old boss used to say.

4. Do not wear jewelry. I know pirates used to wear earrings, but they did that for a reason. They had no home, no family, and lived on a ship with a bunch of thieves. Their two gold earrings were to pay for their burial when they died in battle. Whoever stumbled upon their battle-torn corpse would use one gold earring to pay for their burial, and then keep the other for themselves. Unless you plan on dying in battle, do not wear earrings.

FORTUNE COOKIE WISDOM

Manliness isn't like on the show *Mad Men*—that is a re-creation of what we think it would have been like. The manliest thing we have going today are Old Spice commercials, which I actually think might hold the key to regaining our manliness. That's right, commercials are the best shot we have at regaining our manliness. Yeah, we're fucked.

I know all of this might seem like a lot of work, but for the sake of those who will follow us, please make your best effort to become a real man. And don't set aside time for it like you do for the gym—you have to make manly things a way of life. Start a local petition in your area to outlaw estrogen pills. Of course, a large part of the estrogen we ingest could be eliminated by eating organic, but altering yourself in such a manner isn't very manly, so stick with the petition and contacting your congressman. I feel if all of us men band together, we might have a chance of getting estrogen eradicated from our water supply. Unfortunately, that will probably mean a lot more kids running around, but taking care of kids is pretty fucking manly . . . So long as you actually take care of them.

BOB'S USED CAR LOT OF THE APOCALYPSE

You don't need to read this section if you followed my instructions and built a Vehicle of Death, but I realize that shit happens. If you're a woman, you most likely stood in front of the car that you planned to convert for a long time, confused by all the parts under the hood. Eventually you started crying, kicked the bumper in anger, and then cried even harder because you hurt your foot. A few minutes later, you went inside and ate a box of bon bons[16], never again to visit your little pet project. If you are a man, you most likely used the project as an excuse to get away from the missus. Although you spent approximately nineteen hours a day in the garage, you never actually worked on the damn thing because you were too busy drinking beer, looking at porn, and telling your buddies who came over how cool your Vehicle of Death would be when it was finished.

---

[16] Bon bons are delicious.

In either case, you don't have a monster of a ride to plow through all the mayhem that's choking the streets. All you have is your family sedan, and under the current conditions, that won't get you out of your neighborhood. Of course, I told you to have a backup escape route, one you could negotiate on foot, but if you were too lazy or teary-eyed to work on the Vehicle of Death, you probably never got around to doing this either. So you are in a bit of a pickle, but luckily Uncle Forrest is here to bail you out . . . Again.

Below, I offer instructions on how to hot-wire a car, but since we're not at the apocalypse yet, keep in mind that hotwiring cars is still illegal. I'm not suggesting that you go out and do this now. But once the shit hits, all bets are off and you'll do what you need to. Before I get into the actual act of hot-wiring, though, I feel it is important to talk a little bit about the type of vehicle you want to commandeer. The most important thing to remember is that shortly after the apocalypse happens, survivors are going to go gas crazy. Gun battles will break out at every gas station in America, and the winners will most likely suck the pumps dry. So whatever car you commandeer, it is important that it has enough gas in the tank to get you where you are going. If you chose a safe zone several hundred miles away, you will want to stick with vehicles that run off diesel. With the majority of cars running off regular gasoline, diesel will be a lot more available, especially when all the truckers fall asleep due to the lack of meth. And if you can't find any diesel at gas stations or the pumps have stopped working, you can always siphon from the generators in machine shops.

VEHICLES YOU SHOULD COMMANDEER

1. **SEMIS:** Whether or not to commandeer (notice how we said "commandeer" and not "steal") a semi requires careful consideration. If you know exactly where you are going and want to haul a ton of shit needed to survive for the long term, it's obviously a good choice. Once you have the semi, all you have to do is back up to the loading ramp at Costco and begin stocking up on the Cheetos and diapers. Just make sure that you steal

a cool big rig, like the one with the clown face from *Maximum Overdrive*. (Seriously, I better not see you driving around a basic, piece of shit International.)

However, a semi is not something you want to be cruising around in, looking for a place to set up shop. They are not very fast, so outrunning marauders is usually out of the question unless the truck that you pick happens to be Optimus Prime, in which case you have to worry about having Shia LaBeouf around and that will pretty much suck.

Despite what they show in the movies, semis really aren't that great at smashing through blockades, either. Big rigs have their cooling systems in the front of the truck, so if you ram something with it, don't be surprised to break down on the side of the road a few minutes later. I know what you are thinking, "But what about Mad Max, he rammed all sorts of shit." Yes he did, but if it were real life instead of fiction, a few minutes later, the pursuing gang of gay motorcyclists would pull him from his ride and ram *him* in a ditch in the desert.

Another weakness of big rigs is their tires. Although they have a lot of them, they are large and easy to shoot by people in pursuing vehicles. If you've ever watched an episode of *COPS*, you know that most vehicles can drive just fine with one of their tires blown out. Not the same can be said for semis, due to their length. Lose a couple of back tires and you'll go careening all over the road, lose control, crash into a ditch, and then . . . well, you know what happens then. To top all of this off, semis are a fucking bitch to drive because they have 20,000 gears.

2. **SCHOOL BUSES:** School buses are better than either semis or RVs if you are traveling with a group of people because they have a ton of windows to shoot out of. If you don't have guns or are running low on ammunition, you can simply throw things out the window, including the more annoying members of your crew. I mean, that would get pretty much anyone to stop chasing you, am I right? Just picture it. You are chasing a yellow school bus packed with helpless survivors, eager to claim your spoils.

Suddenly they begin chucking old people and whiny teenagers out of the bus windows. Would you still chase them? I sure as hell wouldn't. (I bet you're starting to see why I landed this book deal. I have all sorts of useful wisdom to impart.) In addition to having more windows, school buses are also a lot easier to modify than either a semi or an RV. You can deck it out with barbed wire, skulls, and all sorts of other menacing-looking ornaments. And with a bright orange bus, you will never have any difficulty spotting your ride in a crowded parking lot. The downside is that school buses suck gas big-time and tend to have governors installed to prevent angry bus drivers from doing a hundred and ten on the freeway and producing one of those gruesome scenes from the driver's ed video, *Red Asphalt*. If you chose to commandeer one, I suggest loading the back with multiple barrels of petrol and removing the governor from the engine.

3. **TRUCKS:** If you do not have people or a ton of shit to haul, a truck is an excellent choice. They get decent gas mileage, do well off-road, and if you install a snowplow or steel grille on the front, they are decent for ramming shit. However, there are a couple of things you must do to make a pickup a safe traveling vehicle. First, store several guns and some ammunition in the cab. Second, knock out the back window and store backup ammunition at the front of the bed. Remember, if you have ammunition, you never want it to be too far away from it. Third, properly tie shit down in the back. Although it is the apocalypse, you're still in America. If you want to pack a mountain of shit in the back of your truck and then tie it down with dental floss, move to a third-world country. Lastly, always bring a pet monkey so that he can drive the car while you shoot out the window at pursuers. It is also possible for you to drive and the monkey to shoot, but I have discovered that monkeys have lousy aim. Quite possibly the monkey will shoot you.

4. **HUMMERS:** Despite all the negative shit I said about these gaudy, overpriced vehicles and their owners in my last book, a Hummer is actually a good vehicle to commandeer during the apocalypse

for obvious reasons. They are roomy, rugged, have massive gas tanks, and do exceptionally well off-road. However, if you steal a Hummer with the three-piece rims that Snoop Dog talks about when he raps, you have made a huge mistake.

VEHICLES NOT TO COMMANDEER

1. **TRACTORS:** Although tractors are super cool because they allow you to destroy all kinds of things such as scoreboards, barns, and other vehicles, they are not very practical. They burn a shit load of gas and top out at just a few miles an hour. Unless you are looking to dig a pit of death for people to fall into, avoid hot-wiring heavy machinery.

2. **SPORTS CARS:** While it might seem like a good idea to commandeer a sports car because they can go super fast, you don't have to be Einstein to figure out why they are a terrible postapocalyptic vehicle. First off, it is difficult to fit two big bodies into one of these sleek pieces of machinery, let alone all the extra shit you would want if you go through the effort of obtaining a vehicle. There is no room for an extra gas tank, your various weapons, or a stockpile of ammunition. In addition to this, having the ability to maneuver through various types of rugged terrain will be much more important than speed. With abandoned vehicles and bodies littering the streets, as well as all the damage to the pavement caused by the thousands of accidents that occurred as people attempted to flee, having a low-clearance vehicle is just about the stupidest thing you could choose. I know why a sports car jumped into your mind in the first place: you want to look cool. Well, a sports car will not make you look cool.[17] If you were a douche bag before you climbed into a sports car, you will still be a douche bag once you're behind the wheel. However, if you absolutely insist on commandeering a sports car, stick with American-made vehicles. They have more

---

[17] It will make you look dead.

clearance, more torque, larger tanks, bigger trunks, and handle much better off-road. (Just remember, you're still a douche bag.)

3. **ELECTRIC CARS**: Do I really need to explain this one?

BE FAST, BE FURIOUS

This is obviously something I had to research, and I really wish I had done it sooner. If I had known how easy it was to hot-wire a car, I never would have fought my ass off with Stephan Bonnar to win that crappy Scion. If you are working at Taco Bell or cleaning the diapers of the elderly in order to purchase the vehicle of your dreams, quit your job right now. To have the vehicle of your dreams, all you need is a flat-head screwdriver, a pair of pliers that can strip electrical wires, and a box of Kleenex. The first two tools are to steal the car itself, and the Kleenex is to wipe the jizz off the dashboard when you realize how much easier your life just got.

Before you pre-cum in your shorts thinking about your neighbor's Mercedes and how good you will look sitting behind its wheel, it is important to mention that not all cars can be hot-wired. Many of the cars that came off the conveyer belt in the past half a decade are armed with kill switches. You poke, prod, or talk dirty to them, and they shut down completely, much like most of the women I have met. Unless you are a professional car thief, stick with older models. This shouldn't be a problem because the only time you should consider stealing a car is when you need transportation in a postapocalyptic world. (Please ignore what I said above about quitting your job and stealing a car . . . That was bad advice, and I really don't want to get sued over this book as I did with the last one. Remember stealing = bad until martial law is declared.)

1. **STEP 1**: Check all doors to see if the car is locked. If the doors are locked, smash one of the back windows. Despite what you see in the movies, do not smash one of the front windows. This will deposit shards of broken glass all over the front seats that will surely end up in your ass cheeks. Unless, of course, you like the thought of shards of glass slowly embedding themselves in your colon.

2. **STEP 1A:** Check driver's-side visor to see if the owner of the car has left their keys there. I've never quite figured out who is a big enough moron to actually do this, but it seems to happen with such frequency in the movies that it must be true, though the people who do it are probably the people whose e-mail passwords are 12345. (Fuck, now I have to change my email password . . . and my PIN.)

3. **STEP 2:** Locate the hole where you stick in the keys. This device is referred to as the ignition tumbler, but with these words being too intricate for either you or me, I will just call it the vagina of the steering wheel. Once located, pry off the plastic covers surrounding the vagina.

4. **STEP 3:** Remove the flat-head screwdriver from your utility belt and jam it into the vagina. If your screwdriver is short, you will most likely need to slide it in all the way up to the hilt. Personally, I do not have this problem because I carry a large screwdriver.

    Once you have penetrated the vagina, grip the screwdriver's handle with both hands and twist like a mother. (In case some of you forgot we were talking about hot-wiring a car, do not attempt to perform this procedure on your girlfriend; it will not win you any brownie points . . . but who am I kidding, we all know you do not have a girlfriend! . . . Oh, yeah, that's right, that Australian girl you are seeing, the one you met while on vacation with your parents last May. The one none of your friends will ever get to meet because she lives so far away. I read ya.) Anyway, if you have a strong grip and are lucky, the ignition switch will turn and the car will start. This is the best-case scenario because you won't need to fuck around with wires and risk getting electrocuted. From that point on, starting the car will be as simple as turning the screwdriver.

5. **STEP 4:** If you are attempting to hot-wire a car at this moment and are currently reading step four, you are a loser. You rolled the dice and shit the bed. Although God has completely given up on you, do not give up on yourself.

    Release your grip on the screwdriver, reach underneath the ignition tumbler, and locate the panel that has five to eight wires attached to it. This is where things get a little tricky—you want to locate the positive and negative wires that go up into the steering column. Different cars use different colored wires, but most of the time they are both red. Once located, pull them from the steering column, strip about an inch of the plastic coating off the ends, and then twist them together. It is important to mention that these wires are hot, which might lead to a small shock. (Translation: Ignore the fact that all your muscles have tightened up, urine is dripping down your leg, and spit is flying from between your clenched teeth.) Completing this step supplies electricity for your ignition components so the engine is able to start.

6. **STEP 5:** Return to the assortment of wires and locate the ignition wire, which in many cars is brown. Again, strip approximately an inch of the plastic coating off the tip.

7. **STEP 6:** Lightly touch the ignition wire to the two red wires you already twisted together. In most cases, the car should start. Note: This is the part of the process where it is quite possible to receive a rather strong electrical shock. To avoid this, do not hold the metal tip of the brown wire. Hold farther up, where the plastic is still intact. After you have gotten the car started, separate the brown wires from the red wires so they are no longer touching.

8. **STEP 7:** If you still can't get the car running, throw a tantrum and vent your frustration about your incompetence.

9. **STEP 8:** Your tantrum alerted a motorcycle gang to your presence. Run!

(INSERT MILDLY AMUSING BLOWJOB JOKE) OR HOW TO SIPHON GAS

Unlike the Vehicle of Death I told you to build, most cars you find on the street will not have an extra gas tank built into the back. As a result, you won't get very far unless you learn how to siphon gas. Luckily, I offer step-by-step instructions below. When I am finished, you will be able to siphon better than an underage runaway on Hollywood Boulevard pulling for his next fix of China White. While this knowledge might be able to save you from getting stranded in the middle of a desert, it can also get you in trouble. There are several objects on which you do NOT want to practice your siphoning techniques. Below is a brief list of do's and don'ts.

Okay to Siphon
- Cars
- Boats
- Lawn mowers
- Generators

Not Okay to Siphon
- Curdled milk
- Kerosene lamps
- Drano
- Toilets
- Spittoons
- Animals (especially not raccoons and cheetahs)
- Bottles of glue
- The curious penis dangling through the hole in your bathroom stall at the freeway rest stop.

Step-by-Step for Siphoning Gas

STEP 1: Obtain some type of rubber hose that is smaller in diameter than a garden hose and larger than a catheter. DO NOT use a catheter.

STEP 2: Slide the hose deep into the gas tank's shaft.

STEP 3: Position a receptacle below the car's gas tank.

STEP 4: Stroke the rubber tube with one hand, place your opposite hand on the base of the tube, wrap your lips around the tip, and begin sucking. The goal is to feel the fluid rising in the tube, and then quickly remove your lips before it blows. (If you get a mouthful, do not swallow. You're not trying to impress anyone here.)

STEP 5: Move out of the way and allow the tube to spit its precious fluid into the opening of the receptacle you placed on the ground.

STEP 6: Allow gravity to pull gas from the tank into the receptacle.

STEP 7: Clean yourself up with Kleenex.

STEP 8: Never tell anyone what you have done. Not ever.

BRONCO BUSTIN' FOR DUMMIES

Horses will be an excellent source of postapocalypse transportation because they can go where vehicles cannot. They can climb mountains, move gracefully through dense forests, traverse deserts, and swim across rivers. They also run off grass rather than gasoline, which, unless there is a nuclear winter, will be much more readily available. The most difficult part will be finding a horse. All the domesticated horses will probably get eaten pretty quickly, so you will have to locate and catch a wild horse. Before I give you step-by-step instructions on how to accomplish this, I must mention that breaking a horse is actually quite cruel. Although old westerns make it seem like a very natural process, anytime you steal an animal from its natural habitat, shatter its will, and then make it serve you, it's a pretty dick move. But hey, if you need to get around, you need to get around.

Step-by-Step for Breaking a Horse

STEP 1: Find a wild horse: Thanks to the white man, wild horses are pretty scarce. The best place to find one is at wild-horse refuges, which are scattered around the United States. The problem is that these refuges are the same places where we have corralled all the Injuns, so you must be careful not to get scalped!

STEP 2: Move toward the horse: When you spot a wild horse, you do not want to spook it. Running toward it waving your arms and shouting is a bad idea. You want to move toward the animal slowly and speak softly to it. It doesn't matter what you say, so long as you speak softly. For example, you can say, "Nice girl. You're a nice girl, aren't you? I am your friend, that's right. I want to be your friend and take care of you." Or you can say, "Hey shit stick, I am going to steal your freedom and make you my slave. If you disobey me, I will stab you with my spurs. Don't worry, I will still let you eat grass—not the fresh grass you have now, but rather shitty, dried cubes of hay that taste more like cubes of shit. But be grateful that I will feed you at all. You are a dumb animal and I can kill and eat you anytime." Both are just as effective so long as you talk softly.

STEP 3: Obtain control of the horse: Pull up beside the horse and begin rubbing its neck. Do not pat the horse as you would a dumb child—stroke it nicely, as you would a cat or some other creature you care about. While stroking, slowly place a rope around its neck. If the horse finds this arousing, like David Carradine, quickly move on to another horse.

STEP 4: Shatter the horse's horseliness by treating it like a pimply-faced junior high school student; this can be achieved by sliding headgear onto its face. Such gear is often referred to as a halter, but it looks nothing like the sexy little tops women wear. Next, grip the bottom portion of this headgear and begin to walk. The goal here is to teach the animal to move when and where you want. To break its will, feel free to write insulting things about it on the stalls of the boys' locker room; however, do not attempt to stuff the horse in a trash can or flush its head in a toilet as you would a junior high weakling that you are tormenting for sport. You want to be demeaning, but not totally abusive.

STEP 5: Continue to be mean and annoying: Jab your finger in the horse's side until it moves away from your prodding. Repeat on all sides of the horse until it submits to your every command.

STEP 6: Continue to dress the horse as if it were a child you hated: But instead of forcing it to wear a pair of footed pajamas, put a saddle onto its back. Remember, horses are against God, which is why they are always naked. You must help them find the Lord.

STEP 7: The Bridle: The bridle is much like a ball gag, but instead of putting it on your spouse, you use it on a horse. It consists of a headset, a bit that goes into the horse's food hole, and reins that you can use to steer the animal into places it does not wish to go. Just like getting the ball gag into your partner's (or sometimes repulsive prostitute's) mouth, it can be difficult to place the bit into a horse's mouth. If it refuses to open its chops, slide your finger into the various corners of the animal's hay cave. The horse will find this very annoying and eventually open wide. Once you've accomplished this, slide in the bit and strap it in place.

STEP 8: Mount the horse: Mounting a horse is nothing like mounting a woman. Although both are oftentimes unenthusiastic about being mounted, horses are much larger animals than women. They also have hooves that can annihilate a healthy pair of testicles. With only one remaining testicle, I am very careful to avoid hooves and high heels. As a result, I attempt to mount both of these magnificent creatures very rarely.

To reduce your risk of injury, mount the horse very slowly and then just sit there. Do not stand up on the horse or lie back to get a suntan. Once it is comfortable with your presence, force it to move forward by pressing your legs into its sides. For some reason, horses understand this as the "move forward" command.

STEP 9: Turning. Moving in only straight lines sucks because eventually you will run into something. As a result, the next step is to teach your slave horse to turn. If you want to turn left, press your left leg into his side and pull on the left rein. To get it to move to the right, press your right leg into its side and pull on the right rein. To get it to stop, pull back on the reins. In addition to this, you must learn all the proper terminology, such as "whoa" and "Easy, boy" and " 'smatterchew." This will make you sound like a real cowboy.

STEP 10: Throw a tantrum because you can't get the horse to do what you want.

STEP 11: Your tantrum alerted Injuns to your presence. Run!

THE FLAT ORIGAMI: HOW TO READ A MAP, AND MAYBE EVEN FOLD THEM

First off, let me start by telling you that the wilderness sucks. There are no showers, stores, washing machines, or shitters. All the wilderness offers is dirt, trees, animals, and insects.

In order to spend as little time as is humanly possible under these terrible conditions, it is important to know where you are going. This can be tough because there are also no street signs in the wilderness. Occasionally there is a ribbon tied around a tree or an *X* etched into a rock, but following these will either confuse you more or lead you into the mouth of a grizzly bear den. Unlike when you were a child and hid under the kitchen sink, no one will come looking for you if you get lost.[18] You are totally and completely alone, and to avoid certain death, you must learn how to read a map. And I am not talking about Hollywood Star maps that show you how to get to the houses of various celebrities, though those are super cool, especially if you are a stalker. I'm talking about topographic maps, like the one shown above. Trust me, there is no need to go all Christopher Columbus and attempt to discover Australia for a second time.

How to Do Lines

Topographic maps are filled with a bunch of wavy lines. While at first glance it might appear as though the mapmaker left the map in the backseat of his car where his idiot son had at it with a Magic Marker, these lines are actually there for a reason. The most important lines to familiarize yourself with are the brown ones, as they represent contours, which is a fancy way of saying "points with the same elevation." What is nice about these lines is that they allow you to visualize a three-dimensional image from a two-dimensional drawing. On the next page, there are blank boxes where you can test your hand at conjuring up these three-dimensional images as well as actual topographic maps for you to study. Obviously, this is an important

---

[18] Personally, I was not able to hide under the sink as a child because my mom got those damn cabinet locks. Probably had something to do with the fact that I constantly tried to drink the Windex. It's not that I liked the taste, I just thought it was a pretty color.

skill to have because it tells you what stands in front of you and the easiest way to get around obstacles. If *Butch Cassidy and the Sundance Kid* had been in the possession of a topographic map, they never would have had to jump off that cliff.

Draw image here

If your three-dimensional drawing came out looking like rolling hills, you can now consider yourself an adequate map reader. If it ended up looking like a pair of breasts, you are more of a pervert than a mapster.

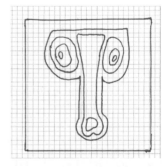

Draw image here

If your three-dimensional image looks like an outcropping of granite coming off two small hills, congratulations! You can now consider yourself an expert map reader. If it came out looking like morning wood, you have dicks-on-the-brain, and that is totally your business, my friend; I don't judge.

Legend (Not Just a Great Movie)

In addition to learning how to read contour lines, you must also familiarize yourself with the legend at the bottom of the map. In this area, the map will show the symbols used to describe certain information on the map. At left, I list some of the more common ones.

Sample Map

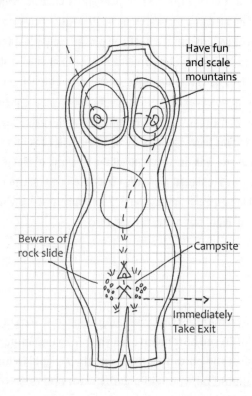

HOW MUCH I HATE THE OUTDOORS

As you are probably guessing by now, I don't much like the outdoors. Well, when I was thirteen, my mother decided we were going to have a bonding experience. Instead of taking me to Disneyland or somewhere cool, she decided to take me white-water rafting. There were seven or eight of us on the oversized inner tube, and being a large kid, I was put in charge of the left side of the boat by the guide. He told me my job was to make sure we didn't get stuck on any rocks, and I was more than excited to take on this task, as it made me feel like I was wearing my big boy pants.

About ten minutes into our adventure, sure enough, we get stuck on a rock. I had wedged my paddle down between the side of the raft, so I tried to push us off the rock using my hands. Of course, my hands slipped off, and my entire torso dunked into the water. Immediately the current swept my head and life vest underneath the boat and pinned me there. I felt no need to panic—to free myself from this predicament, all I needed to do was slide the lower half of my body into the water, push myself away from the boat, and climb back in. However, as I attempted to put this game plan into effect, my mother, who was sitting on the opposite side of the boat, began to panic and grab a hold of my legs. She was trying to pull me back into the boat with all her might, but she was fighting against the strength of Mother Nature and losing terribly. This presented a problem because I couldn't go out of the boat and I couldn't go back into the boat. I was simply stuck with my head and chest pinned under this shitty blowup raft.

Grids

It is important to remember that your map is just one part of a much larger map—the world! To see how much area your map encompasses, you want to visit the scale at the bottom of the page. If your goal in having a map is survival, as it should be, you will usually want one that is 1:24,000. This means that every one inch on the map represents two thousand feet of actual land. Knowing this, you can measure how many inches you have to

After about twenty seconds fighting to free my legs from my mother's death grip, I realized that I would soon pass out. Not knowing what to do, I kicked my mother as hard as I could in her chest and face. As you would expect, this caused her to release her hold, allowing me to follow through with my initial game plan. I slide out of the boat, pulled myself out from under the raft, and then hopped back into the boat. At the time, I did not even care that I had come close to death. The only thing that I cared about was the fact that everyone on the boat was now staring at me with open mouths.

I was exhausted and totally out of breath, but since I had daddy issues, I didn't want to look like a jackass in front of the guy who had given me some authority (yeah, I could have been a stripper), so I breathed slowly out of my nose and pretended that I was looking around at the scenery. A few seconds later, I grabbed my paddle and focused my gaze downstream. I should have probably checked on my mother, who had just received a mule kick to the chest and face, but I figured she was probably okay because she had a life vest on. To this day, neither one of us have every brought the subject up. It was akin to farting during sex in that you and your partner just move on and pretend that it never happened. In any case, the moral of the story is that the wild will try to fucking kill you any chance it gets, and I fucking hate it.

go on your map, and know how many feet you have left to reach your target area on land. For a carry-along measuring tool, you should now measure your penis and convert it to feet using the scale above. Once this is accomplished, all you will need to do is place your johnson on the map to know exactly how far you have to travel to reach your destination. Even if your pecker can only be used to measure six-thousand-foot increments, it may not be as useless as your past girlfriends have told you.

POSTAPOCALYPTIC
DIET-AND-EXERCISE PROGRAM

The human digestive system is not designed to handle processed foods and large amounts of sugar. It is not designed to handle foods that are vitamin fortified, a practice that only began about seventy years ago. If you want to be healthy during the apocalypse, you should eat the same foods our distant ancestors ate, such as nuts, twigs, and berries. It is also extremely important to eat for your body type . . . No, no, fucking no!

If you plan on trying to maintain your specialized, trendy diet in a postapocalyptic world, you are a filthy mouth-breather and will most likely die a horrible death, which is fine because you deserve it. Eat whatever you can find that isn't rotten or spoiled. Eat untreated shoe leather if that is what you have on hand. The human body will adapt. Don't baby your body; it wants to live. It will take whatever calories you give it and turn them into energy. Remember, no one cares if you are ripped when you are fucking dead. If you are thinking, "How will I maintain my daily workout regimen without proper meals?" then you are an even greater idiot. The postapocalyptic exercise program will consist of RUNNING FOR YOUR FUCKING LIFE from syphilis zombies, as well as building shelters and hunting. Basically, staying alive will be all the workout you need. I swear, every time I talk to you it is like I am dealing with my brother's kids!

The Apocalyptic Standard Body Mass Index Chart

Frail: You are weak and fragile. Although you are considered attractive in our current society, after the apocalypse, a large bird or gust of wind will most likely carry you away. Note: Postapocalypse, vomiting up food will be punishable by decapitation and being cooked on a spit.

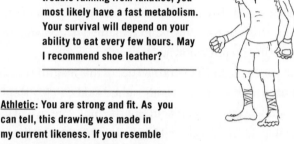

Skinny: You are thin and quick. Although you will probably have no trouble running from lunatics, you most likely have a fast metabolism. Your survival will depend on your ability to eat every few hours. May I recommend shoe leather?

Athletic: You are strong and fit. As you can tell, this drawing was made in my current likeness. If you resemble me, you have an excellent chance of surviving any type of natural disaster. Trust me, we'll be just fine.

Fat: You are one of the jolly folk. If you somehow survive the initial shit storm, your long-term survival will depend upon your body type. As we have all learned from the UFC, there are certain fat guys who are extremely athletic and agile. If you are this type of fat, you might actually have a leg up on those who are athletic because you can survive on your man tits and the medicine ball you call a stomach for a good deal of time. However, if you are the type of fat guy who has trouble getting out of his chair, you most likely won't last a week. But seriously, if you're that kind of fat, do you really want to survive in a world without Cheetos?

Morbidly Obese: You are morbidly obese. You have to pay for sex and most likely cannot see your genitals, so what is the point in surviving the apocalypse? Might as well end things now before getting licked to death by your fifteen cats.

HUNTING

Hunting will be a pretty big deal after the apocalypse, but despite how manly I come across, I am not an avid or expert hunter. I've only been hunting three times, and on two of those occasions absolutely nothing happened. I just sat around in the woods, bored as shit. The only time something eventful happened was when I was twelve. My stepfather Abe took me out into the woods to train me to be a man, and I pretended the best I could that I really wanted to shoot me a deer. When a deer did in fact cross our path, my hand remained frozen and my stepfather put that beautiful creature down.

Once the life had drained out of this magnificent creature, we dragged it back to the car. Yes, that's right, I said car. My stepfather did not own a truck—he owned a Lincoln Continental. The two of us spent the next half an hour stuffing a giant, bloody deer corpse into the trunk. When we were finished, did I look like a shell-shocked kid who had watched his parents be murdered while he hid under the bed? Yes, I most certainly did. To make matters worse, we took the deer home and my stepfather proceeded to skin and gut it. My job was to clean up afterward. So, as you would guess, the only knowledge I took away from the whole situation was how to fit a very large body into the trunk of a car and clean up a bunch of blood and guts. This would have been very useful if I had turned out to be a mafia hitman (which might actually have happened when looking at the trauma I went through that day).

The only living thing that I ever shot was a duck, and even that disturbed me greatly. We were out in the marshlands, and I shot one out of the sky. Immediately the dog took off after it, and I was paranoid as hell that it would bring the duck back half alive and I would have to break its neck or something. I mean, imagine how terrible that would be. You get shot, a dog picks you up in its filthy mouth, you get dragged around through the mud, and then dropped at someone's feet, only to get your fucking neck broken. Horrible. Simply fucking horrible.

So, as much as I would like to give you advice in the hunting department, you are going to have to get this knowledge elsewhere. I am going to retreat the darkness of the closet and weep to myself for the next half an hour or so . . . Thanks so much for making me bring these painful memories back to the surface.

THE SCENT OF A WOMAN
(HOW TO CATCH A FISH)

As I mentioned, you don't want to get picky with your diet. While making the trek to your safe zone, it is important to constantly be on the lookout for anything edible. If you are in the desert and happen to wander by a small creek, hunting for fish is an excellent way to get a decent meal.

The easiest way to catch a fish is with a fishing pole (you've probably noticed by now that I have a tendency to state the obvious). However, the chance that you managed to escape the city with a fishing pole is probably pretty slim. Your first instinct will most likely be to sharpen a stick or try to construct a homemade hook, but if you're like me, both will lead to some type of horrible accident where the testicles are torn or stabbed.

Your safest and most surefire approach is to catch fish with your hands. I know what you're thinking—"that's complete bullshit"—but it is completely true. Here is how you do it:

1. Locate a small creek no more than seven feet in width, and walk its length until you find an area that is stagnant. As a rule of thumb, you want the water to be three or four feet deep.

2. Remove all your clothes. This might seem silly, but remember, at night all you have keeping you warm is a small fire or a crappy lean-to shelter packed with leaves. If you get your clothes wet, you will most likely freeze. According to my coauthor, Erich, who taught survival school for years, if your clothes do get wet, the best way to stay warm is to perform a specialized method of naked spooning, which he attempted to show me despite our clothes being perfectly dry.

3. Wade over to the bank of the creek. Due to the eroding forces of water, there will usually be a cavernous region directly

underneath the bank. When an invading force is in the water, fish will often retreat to this area and burrow their heads into the walls. Once in their hiding places, instead of bolting when a threat approaches as they do when in open waters, they will generally remain motionless.

4. Dip a hand into the water and move it very slowly across the wall of the creek underneath the bank. Believe it or not, this can be very nerve-racking, and your first reaction when coming into contact with slimy flesh is to jolt your hand away. Of course, this will cause the fish to quickly vacate, so you must maintain your cool.

5. There are two methods of capture once you have found a fish. The advanced method is to slide your hand slowly up its body until your fingers are in its gills, apply pressure to trap the fish, and then calmly pull it out of the water. While this is the most surefire method, it requires a very light touch and steady hand. If you're an amateur, the best approach is to use speed. The instant you touch the fish, jam your hand into its body and pin it up against the wall of the creek. Next, dip your opposite hand in and use both hands to pull it out. However, fish are very, very slimy, and without a firm pinch on their gills, you will most likely lose about 50 percent of your catches.

6. Once you have a fish, throw it at least ten feet away from the bank to ensure that it won't flip-flop back into the water.

7. After catching all you can eat, hold each fish down and kill it by bashing its head with a rock. For the morons out there, I must once again state the obvious: Do not obliterate the fish with a large boulder.

8. With fish, you can consume everything but the guts. This means the head and the bones. As a matter of fact, the bones are the best part. After slowly roasting them over the fire for half an hour, they taste just like crackers. Shitty-tasting crackers that

have the consistency of porcupine, mind you, but still better than bulrushes or cattails, both of which taste like piss.

9. Throw a tantrum because you can't catch a fish.

10. Your tantrum has alerted a starving bear to your presence. Run!

8 EASY STEPS TO MILKING A COW

If you don't come across a creek while fleeing to your safety zone, you are going to have to find an alternate source of food. Raiding convenience stores and supermarkets is a bad plan because all of the other survivors will have the same idea. If someone made it there before you, there is a good chance he or she will be ready to defend their food supply with either weapons or booby traps. A much safer option is to eat off the fat of the land. This is where cows come in.

Currently, there are more than 1.3 billion cows in the world, and a large percentage of those are in the United States. They are perhaps the stupidest animal in creation and have absolutely no defense mechanisms to speak of (bulls are different, obviously). Basically, a mentally challenged person could go around killing one cow after another with a wooden club—that is how easy they are to hunt. Although cows will be the primary food source for apocalyptic survivors, without our beef being slaughtered and shipped all over the world, the remaining cows will last a long fucking time. Good news for us!

While it is possible to skin and eat a cow, if your goal is to make it to your safe zone alive, this will most likely take too much time. Milking a cow is a much better option. It is extremely quick and can provide that extra energy you need to make it those last few miles to safety. Below I offer step-by-step instructions on how to steal this precious life-juice from these dumb animals:

STEP 1: Locate a somewhat attractive cow.

STEP 2: Sit next to the cow and wash its udders with a warm cloth, much like they do in massage parlors.

STEP 3: Place a bucket underneath the udders to catch the milk. If you do not have a bucket, simply open your mouth and place your face underneath the udders. This is known as "udder-to-mouth."

STEP 4: Begin the milking process by squeezing one of the cow's teats between your forefinger and thumb. Next, squeeze your other fingers around the teat, forcing the milky goodness to flow. Note: It is okay to whisper sweet nothings into the cow's ear, as it often gets them in the mooooooood. However, never look up into the cow's eyes because chances are it will be looking down at you. If your eyes meet, it gets a little awkward. Instead of getting all personal, you want to keep the whole experience very distant, like you would when visiting your friendly neighborhood glory hole.

STEP 5: Let go of the teat.

STEP 6: Again squeeze the teat. When it feels soft and flabby, the cow has given you all she's got to give.

STEP 7: Throw a tantrum because the cow is not cooperating.

STEP 8: Your tantrum alerted a bull to your presence. Run!

MILKING ALTERNATIVES

Although cows are by far the easiest animals to milk, if you like to live on the wild side or have no other choice, there is a broad assortment of other animals that also produce drinkable milk. Luckily, you can find many of these animals in your local zoo. But before you go charging down there with a bucket and eager lips, it is very important that you realize milking these wild creatures can not only be extremely time-consuming, but also extremely dangerous.

Great Ape

Jane Goodall taught us two things about great apes: they can be very violent, but they can also be very nurturing. If you walk up to one in your everyday street clothes and attempt to suckle from its teat, chances are it will tear off your arms, rip your body in half, and then use your torso as a toilet. I mean, if there were such a thing as rape in the animal world, uninvited suckling at the teat would probably be it.

If you value your life, you must get the ape to offer you her teat. This can be accomplished by dressing up in a monkey outfit and hanging out with the other great ape toddlers. The goal is to make the mother feel utterly sorry for you, so you are going to want to fail at everything monkeylike. For example, keep falling out of the trees, show yourself to be incompetent at peeling bananas properly, hit yourself in the face when you attempt to pound on your chest, and miss every target you aim at with your feces.

Once you are recognized as the complete loser of the group, the mother will eventually come to you, cradle you in her arms, and put her hairy teat directly into your mouth. The problem is getting away from the mother once she has adopted you. As we have all learned from nature documentaries and the end of *Trading Places*, ape males are real pricks. They are always huffing, sprinting at trees, and bitch-slapping bushes. They are constantly showing off, and the chicks hate them for it. After she's fed you, there is a good chance that the female ape will want to mate with you, simply because you are smaller and less violent than a real male ape. Do not try to fight this. Instead, just grin and bear it. The good news is that a man cannot impregnate a female ape because they have incompatible chromosomes. I actually looked that shit up. (I'm sorry about this—I don't know why they let me write a book, let alone *books*. Will I ever run out of material? Not if they let me talk about milking apes.)

Kangaroo

Kangaroos kick really fucking hard, they have a long, whiplike tail, super-sharp claws, gnarly teeth, and they can run up to forty miles per hour. Needless to say, these attributes make milking one extremely difficult, but not impossible. Every animal has a weakness, and with the kangaroo it is her pouch. Whenever I feel like hanging out in a kangaroo's pouch, or a Roo-Hammock as I like to call it, I just gather up all the needed items, which include four feet of nylon rope, a Snickers bar, a kerosene lantern, and a roll of duct tape (duct tape works for everything, don't it?). I would tell you how to use these items to make your entry into the pouch, but that is self-explanatory. Once you are all wrapped up in the warm flesh-blanket, you have direct access to the teat and can suckle away for hours.

Giraffe

You would think that a giraffe would be an easy animal to milk because of its height. I mean, it seems like you should just be able to walk underneath one, turn your head up, and begin sucking out milk as if it were coming from a beer bong. As it turns out, giraffes do not like other animals to be directly underneath them, suckling on their teats. Instead of standing there and letting you get your fill, they have a tendency to bolt. I thought it might be possible to kind of run underneath them as they scurried about, breathing out of my nose as I suckled with my mouth, but they are a good deal faster than I imagined. A healthy giraffe can run up to thirty-seven miles per hour!

I almost wrote this animal off as a practical source for milk, but a lightbulb went off in my head and I decided to use a motorcycle. This actually works really well. The goal is to drive directly underneath the giraffe, stand up on your seat, suckle for a brief moment, sit back down, steer, and then stand back up for another quick hit at the teat. It takes a little while to get full, but giraffe milk fucking rules. (For fuck sakes, why aren't people stopping me? I really didn't think I could get away with this much simply for being semi-famous. In addition to being allowed to put complete nonsense into this book, *Revolver* magazine, which is a pretty big magazine, allowed me to write an article on the sexist animal. Just how far do I have to go before someone stops me? I am crying for help here, people. Why can't anyone hear my screams?)

Animals That You Should Not Attempt to Milk

- **LIZARDS:** If they have nipples at all, they are too small to find.
- **PENGUINS:** They keep slipping from your hands as you try to suckle.
- **SLEEPING BEARS:** Not down with being milked in any way, shape, or form.

- **HUMANS:** I am still researching this one.
- **WOLVES:** Very, very dirty animals. The milk from their one protruding red udder strangely tastes like piss. Other times, it is just waaaaay too salty.
- **RED ANTS:** A really bad experiment on my part
- **LOCUSTS:** Do not, under any circumstances, attempt to milk a swarm of locust.

THE FORREST GRIFFIN SURVIVAL EXPERIENCE

I know I'm sending you mixed messages. I tell you I hate the wild, and then I go on and on about all these survival tactics. You are probably starting to wonder if you can trust this hot knowledge I am giving you. Well, although I personally don't like spending time in the outdoors, I have been cast ruthlessly into the wild on several occasions and survived.

The most traumatic of these experiences was just before my twenty-first birthday when I was in the police academy. In the evening after class, I went back to the dorms and discovered the doors were locked. I tried my key card several times, and each time it did absolutely nothing. A few seconds later, I read a sign on the door that said CLOSED FOR SPRING BREAK. Somehow, I missed the fact that they were shutting the dorms down for the entire week. I was homeless, and to make matters worse, all of the friends I felt comfortable calling were out of town. Not knowing what to do, I returned to my Mazda 626 and just kind of sat there, and not comfortably I might add. I got the car because I'd seen it sitting on some guy's front lawn. When I knocked on his door to inquire about it, his exact words were, "If you can get that blankety-blank-blank off my fucking lawn, you can do whatever the fuck you want with it." I had it towed away, and then my stepfather fixed it up. He took the choke off our lawnmower, drilled a hole into my dashboard, and slapped that sucker in. So, I basically had a 1920s automobile. When I started it, I would have to throttle it up for several minutes using the choke, which proved to be a real panty dropper while on dates.

Anyway, I was fucking homeless, sitting in my piece-of-shit ride. With nowhere to go, I drove to the grocery store, purchased a box of Little Debbie treats and a cheap bottle of wine, and then sat on the curb out in front of the dormitory for the next eight hours. When it started getting cold, I purchased a ticket to an all-night movie theater so I would have somewhere warm to sleep for a few hours. I spent that entire week in that Mazda 626, subsisting on cheap wine and Little Debbies, so don't you tell me I don't know how to fucking survive.

HOW TO FIGHT A WILD ANIMAL

I included this section because it seems like every time I do an interview, a reporter asks me how I would fight a certain type of animal. Sure, they open with the canned "Who is your next opponent?" and "How is your training going?" questions, but it always comes back to me fighting animals. Unfortunately, I know very little about engaging animals in hand-to-paw combat. I do, however, know quite a bit about being viciously attacked by animals.

The most violent animal beat-down I have received came from a giraffe. This happened as a teenager, when a buddy and I decided to pay a visit to the zoo (I know, sounds super gay, but I swear we weren't holding hands or any bullshit like that). As we were cruising around, checking shit out, I saw a giraffe with his head reaching over the chain-link fence separating him from the outside world. He was chewing on some cud, just kind of staring blankly out at freedom. Without thinking, I ran toward the fence, climbed up it, and threw my arm around his big-ass neck. The goal was to have my buddy snap a picture of the two of us, but before he could even pull out his camera, the ferocious giraffe attacked. In one swift movement, it placed a fairly large chunk of my head into its rancorous oversize mouth, which prevented me from leaping off the fence. I, of course, screamed bloody murder, but my friend was absolutely no help. He instantly fell on the ground in a fit of laughter.

I'm quite sure the evil giraffe could have crushed my head like a grape, but realized that it would be put down if he did. Fighting the overwhelming urge to end my life, he released my head from his death grip after a few moments, and my hat fell on the opposite side of the fence. After being viciously attacked by the brutal giraffe, I wasn't going to attempt to retrieve my favorite hat. I walked away with a bruised face and feeling very insignificant.[19]

Since that day, I've had numerous other very close calls with some of

---

[19] Giraffes are evil, evil animals that should be avoided at all costs. Unless, of course, you are trying to milk them from a motorcycle like Evil Knievel would.

the more ferocious members of the animal kingdom. When I was fifteen, I spent a summer in North Carolina, and in order to get from my house over to a friend's house, I had to cross a river. This gave me two choices—I could walk two miles to a bridge or I could ignore a series of "No Trespassing" signs, hop a chain-link fence, and swim across the body of water. Inherently lazy, every day I chose the swim.

Then one afternoon, right before I was about to enter the water to make my way across, a group of people sitting on a deck on my side of the river began screaming and shouting at me. Ignoring them, I began walking toward the bank, but now they were not only screaming and shouting, but also waving their arms madly in the air. After taking two steps into the water, I got really pissed off and began walking down the muddy bank toward them.

"What the fuck is your problem?" I shouted at the group of middle-aged men and women. "I had to hop a fence, big fucking deal. Give me a fine, I don't care. I was just trying to cross the river, man!"

As with most people in North Carolina on a summer afternoon, they were all drinking beer. "Sorry about all the yelling," one man said as he pointed in the direction I had come from. "Just look over there at your footprints."

I did as the man said and followed my footprints, and about two hundred yards back, drifting in the water where I had been preparing to enter the river, was an eight-foot alligator. Although it might not have been as big as the alligators you see on the Discovery Channel, an eight-foot alligator is pretty fucking huge when you see it in the wild. I almost shit my pants. The people informed me that they had posted the NO TRESPASSING signs and put up the chain-link fence for a reason—this little area was a wildlife refuge and was filled with alligator nests (not sure if alligators have nests or not, but that is what I was told).

The next close call I had occurred in South Africa. I went there with my friends Rory and Numo, and wanting to see what the real Africa was all about, we decided to visit a lion refuge. Unlike zoos where all the animals are confined to cramped cages, this place let all the animals run free. (What's up with that? Freedom is for people.) This obviously ruled walking around the park out of the question, but supposedly it was safe to drive.

Both Forrest and his cat are easily amused by paper bags.

Forrest's thoughts: "I bet these birds taste delicious." Jaime's thoughts: "I hope Forrest isn't thinking about eating these birds."

Forrest and Bigger John at Forrest's wedding. Moments after this photo was taken, Bigger John attempted to propose to Forrest.

Proper postapocalyptic attire.

You have absolutely no proof that they're gay.

If you see a strong resemblance, that's because they are related—and I'm talking about the two guys *and* the monkeys on the shirts.

I really had no idea that coming down would be the hard part.

After Forrest's third arrest for road rage, this is the only vehicle he can legally drive.

Why yes, Forrest is this cat's biological father.

Me, postapocalypse.

Bonding with my brother.

Alternate cover shot #1:You talkin' to me?

Alternate cover shot #2

Forrest's thoughts: "This is the happiest day of my life."

Luke's thoughts: "I can't believe he is doing this."

John's thoughts: "I give it a year, tops."

Leaf's thoughts: "When did he even start *liking* girls?"

Bigger John: "Does this mean Forrest really isn't going to take me to Vermont and marry me like he promised?"

This isn't actually me—I just cut it out of a magazine.

Please, no one tell him Santa doesn't exist.

Postcoital

Walking cats is harder than you think.

Someone let the monkeys out of the cage.
Randy Couture, Some Guy, Stephan Bonner, Ron Frazier, Mike Pyle, Tim Credeur, Jay Hieron

The only threesome my wife will let me have.

Forrest trying to get the deer drunk so he can have his way with them . . . His most lascivious fantasy come true.

Don't worry mom, I can't get any uglier.

Forrest convinces Erich you can survive off dirt. To Forrest's amazement, Erich loves it. . . . Yeah, you are reading a book by these two guys. How is that working out for ya? . . . And yes, we went forty miles into the desert to take this picture. If you are wondering about the sprinkler head to my left, I want to let you know that confused me also.

FORTUNE COOKIE WISDOM

Beware of anyone who drinks excessive amounts of Mountain Dew. Back when I was a police office, anytime I broke into a meth laboratory or pulled someone over who was trafficking drugs, I found a shit-ton of empty Mountain Dew containers on the floor of their trailer or backseat of their car.

I figured we would be in an armor-plated Range Rover or something, but they packed all three of us into a shitty little Yugo. I was fighting heavyweight at the time, and Rory is a pretty big dude as well, so we were quite literally sitting on top of one another.

The driver cranked up the engine and drove over to the front entrance gate, and that's when I realized that visiting a lion refuge in South Africa might not have been the best move. The guy who opened the gate had one eye, one arm, and his face had deep scars from where a lion had mauled him. Immediately I thought, "This guy's only job is to let you in and out of the park. What the fuck happens to the people who actually go inside?"

I bit my tongue and didn't say anything, and at first everything was cool—I could see a shit load of lions off in the distance, but none of them charged the vehicle or anything like that. It was actually an enjoyable experience.

Then the Yugo started to overheat. Outside it was 112 degrees, and once the driver shut off the air conditioner, the confines of the car quickly became an oven. I asked if we could roll down a window, and the driver immediately began shaking his head.

"You don't want them to smell you," he said.

Great.

When the car didn't cool, the driver turned on the heater. Other than cooking our nut sacks in our underwear, it did nothing to solve the overheating problem. After another few hundred yards, steam began pouring from the hood and the driver pulled over. "I can not drive anymore," he said.

I figured that they had some sort of system worked out for when one of the cars broke down, but apparently that wasn't the case because no one came by to lend a hand. There was no roadside assistance of any kind. We just sat there in the car, waiting. And with each moment that passed, the lions became more and more curious and began inching their way toward us.

Figuring it was only a matter of time until the lions ripped off one of the flimsy doors to the Yugo and ate my ugly ass, I made my friend Numo get out and piss in the radiator. And yes, if the lions had attacked him, I would have locked all the doors and watched the feast transpire, but that's only because you're not supposed to disturb animals when they are eating. Park rules, you know.

Luckily, my quick thinking paid off, the engine cooled, and we were able to get the hell out of Dodge. As we were leaving the park, I noticed that the guy who let us out had all of his body parts intact. If they had a marketing guy, he needed to get fired. Yeah, let's have the guy who looks like he was mauled by fifty lions let everyone into the park. That will do wonders to soothe the nerves of our guests.

But the more I thought about it, the more it made sense. In South Africa they don't make you sign waivers before participating in dangerous shit, and sticking a guy who had obviously been attacked by lions at the front gate was their disclaimer—their way of letting you know that what you were about to do was pretty fucking stupid.

So as you can see, I am far from the Beast Master. Come to think of it, the only fight I ever won with an animal was against an ex-girlfriend's cockatoo, but all I had to do was open the door and chase it outside with my superior, broom-wielding prowess. With my current track record, the best advice I can give on fighting animals is to simply not do it. If you fight an animal and lose, there is a good chance that you will get eaten. This even applies to dogs. I still have a scar on my right arm that constantly reminds me that even these much smaller creatures are fierce opponents.

ANIMALISTIC ATTRACTION

 Seeing that we are already on the topic of animals, it is time to talk about a very hard truth: after the shit hits the fan, there probably won't be that many people left to mate with, so you are going to have to get creative. What do I mean by "get creative"? What else could I mean? Have sex with animals, of course.

Although it might seem simple to grab the nearest animal and give it a good shagging, most four-legged creatures will not willingly allow you to simply mount and penetrate them. They will undoubtedly put up a fight, and taking a hoof or paw to the face can suck big-time. It is also extremely important to ravish an animal that you personally find sexy. To avoid having to go through this type of decision making postapocalypse, I suggest that you put some thought into the animal you would most like to lay pipe to right now.

As far as women go, they all want to have sex with dolphins. Don't believe me? Just look at any woman's house. What do you see all over the place—that's right, dolphins. I think the reason for this . . . strike that . . . The reason for this is that women love a giant phallic symbol. Dolphins even feel like penises. They are basically a big blue penis, like the schlong of that dude in *Watchmen*.

In fact, a lot of women go so far as to tattoo dolphins on their lower back and ankles. If you see a chick with a dolphin tattoo, there is no doubt she is into cock, and will be willing to bone down. However, watch out for chicks with butterfly tattoos. The butterfly represents ~~lesbianism~~ feminism, and chicks who go so far as to get a butterfly tattoo are most likely into carpet munching and scissoring and all that. The same can be said for guys who get gorilla or ape tattoos—they like to have sex with other men. It is a fact.

Personally, the animal I find the sexiest is undoubtedly the deer. I love the way they move, with that little come-hither tail of theirs and those big glossy eyes. When you creep up on one in the forest and she pops her head up, all nervous like, and your eyes meet, you can tell she is flirting with you. If you are wondering when these amorous feelings first started, I can pinpoint it exactly. It all started the first time I saw *Bambi*—and I say first time because there were many. In fact, certain spots on my VHS copy of the movie are pretty much worn out. And yes, you guessed it: those spots are the scenes in which Bambi's mother makes an appearance.

If you go back and watch *Bambi* today, you will realize what I realized at the age of five: Bambi's mother is fucking hot. She is one hot piece of tail, literally. As a matter of fact, if you don't want to fuck Bambi's mom, you're gay.

If you find my attraction to deer a little disturbing, do not worry—I can't actually catch them. That is a part of what makes them so attractive. Now, they do have tame deer that you can visit in the petting zoo and feed, but those deer are all fat. What kind of sicko do you think I am? I am not into fat deer—I am not into any kind of fat animals. If I wanted to hump a hippo, I would hump a hippo. But I don't. And don't worry, sheep are not beautiful creatures. They are ugly. They are the ugly, fat, drunken sorority girls that won't leave you alone at a party, and who wants them? Certainly not me.

Now that I have shared with you some of my inner feelings about the animal world, I would like you to sit back in your chair and think about what animal you find the sexiest. Is it some kind of tropical bird? Do you find the lioness as she glides across the plains strangely alluring? Or do you find a creature of the sea the most tantalizing? I'm being serious: sit back and give it some deep thought. It is very important to think about this now so that when you spot that animal postapocalypse, you can immediately commence with the fulfillment of your needs . . . no . . . of your desires.

Serious Note to Reader: Unfortunately for you, I like tests, and this was one of them. If you actually made it through my bit on animal fucking, you failed. I mean, who would keep reading a book that talks about humping animals? I know after the apocalypse there will be no laws against that shit, but come on, where is your pride? You should be ashamed of yourself. Deeply, deeply ashamed. However, you have to admit that deer are kind of sexy. If someone held a gun to my head and insisted that I fuck some type of animal, it would most certainly be a deer. (Erich, I told you to hold that gun to my head . . . just do it and close your eyes; this will only take a second.) I mean, those eyes are so big and glassy. You can get lost in those eyes . . .

HOW TO PREVENT MUD BUTT (AKA SWAMP ASS)

Properly wiping your backside shouldn't be your primary concern when trying to escape town and make it to your safe zone, but if you let matters get too carried away back there, you will develop a condition often referred to as Mud Butt. Trust me, this is very uncomfortable.

Personally, I have never shit in the actual woods. I've shit my pants more than a few times, but according to Erich, this has no bearing on the apocalypse. When it comes to shitting in the woods, he is undoubtedly the expert. He insisted that we include a "shitting" section in the book, which I found a little odd. After listening to a few of his stories, you gotta wonder if his goal is to actually teach people how to shit or simply to make them feel better about themselves because they have not shit all over themselves in the wild. If you are like me[20], you will probably agree that Erich has some bizarre fascination with fecal matter. After all, he has German blood. If you were to hack into his computer, there is no doubt that you would find some *shizer* videos in a secret file. Anyway, here is the section on shit:

For the longest time, I thought the best way to wipe your ass in the woods was with whatever you could find—leaves, weeds, bark, small animals—but then Erich proceeded to tell me half a dozen of his wilderness shit stories, the worst one being the time he hiked the Machu Picchu trail in Peru. He was up at fourteen thousand feet and decided he had to take a dump. He found a nice field filled with grass, dropped his drawers, made his deposit, and then broke off a handful of grass to wipe his ass. Although the grass was green, it was not as fresh as he'd first thought. It basically turned to dust in his hand.

Being a dirty, filthy mongrel, he wiped with it anyway, and ended up with shit on his mitt. Not far from the field he heard a small babbling creek, but it was located down a steep embankment of shale. Being a genius, he attempted to scale down the slope and ended up slipping and sliding all the way down. By this point, shit had migrated from his hand to select parts of his torso. He attempted to get at the water, but the stream was completely encased in thornbushes. After a full five minutes tangling with the bush, he gave up. He climbed back up the slope of shale, again slipping and sliding, and by the time he reached the top, he had shit on his torso, legs, and face. With no other option, he was forced to hike another eight miles literally covered in shit and with an ass full of prickly grass particles.

---

[20] It is good to be like me.

Learning from his mistakes, I have devised the ultimate way to shit in the wild. All it requires is a single, somewhat healthy leaf:

Get a leaf.

Fold leaf once.

Fold leaf twice.

Tear semi-circle off corner of leaf.

Unfold leaf and stick thumb through hole.

Stick thumb up ass.

Slide leaf up thumb to remove fecal matter.

Use severed piece of the leaf you tore off to dig shit out from under fingernail.

Display your somewhat clean thumb.

WHY YES, I DO SPEAK SIGN LANGUAGE

If you are traveling with a group of people, you want to develop hand signals. Although they make you look like a sock puppeteer when you do them alone, they make you look like some type of commando when other people are around, even if the people have no idea what the hand signals mean. But beware, sometimes hand signals have more than one meaning. To prevent you from getting confused, I have included some of the more popular hand signals below and the various meanings they have.

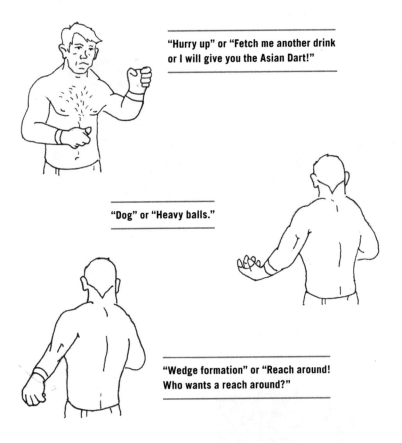

"Hurry up" or **"Fetch me another drink or I will give you the Asian Dart!"**

"Dog" or **"Heavy balls."**

"Wedge formation" or **"Reach around! Who wants a reach around?"**

"I understand" or "Look at my awesome hand puppet."

"Live long and prosper" or "Hope you die a horrible death."

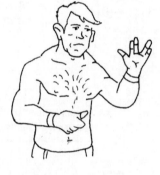

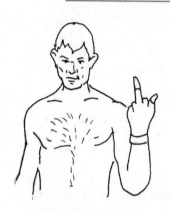

"Fuck you" or "Wanna spin on my finger?"

"Gas leak" or "Twist my nipples while I check your oil . . . ohhh, yeah, creamy cheese delight."

"Move up" or "Put it in here."

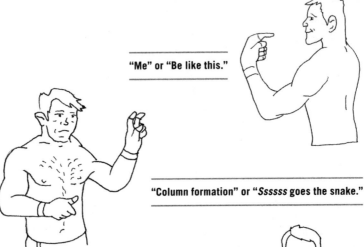

"Me" or "Be like this."

"Column formation" or "*Sssss* goes the snake."

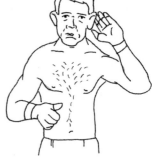

"Listen or hear" or "Can you still see the cauliflower?"

"Hostage" or "Is that the ghost of David Carradine?"

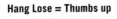

Hang Lose = Thumbs up

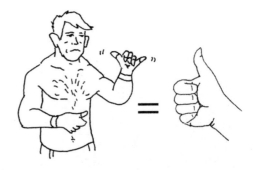

THE MOST DANGEROUS PEOPLE OF THE APOCALYPSE

It is pretty obvious that while making the escape to your safe zone, you want to avoid well-armed, unsavory people. However, there are less obvious people who will pose an equal amount of danger. I have included the list below.

Note to Reader: Erich predominantly wrote this section. I tell you this not because I am a nice guy or because I don't want to take credit for the ideas of others—I obviously have no problem with that (see *Got Fight?*). The reason I tell you this is that I want to absolve myself of the forthcoming ill will directed at hippies. You see, Erich was kidnapped by a clan of nomadic hippies as a small child and was forced to live among them. This explains his lack of hygiene, as well as his passion for "roughing it." When I met Erich, he was sleeping on a pile of clothes and trash that looked like the pit of a hamster's nest, in the closet of a million-dollar house. Gallon jugs of urine and water, which he drank from regardless of what they actually contained, surrounded him. I asked him why he lived in such a manner, and he simply replied, "I am preparing." That is when I knew I had found a writer for my apocalypse book.

Why does Erich, who seems to despise hippies, choose to live like them? Well, I can only liken it to Hitler hating the Jews but being part Jewish. At heart, Erich wants to be a hippie, but he can't do it because it is frowned upon in our society. Erich yearns for the apocalypse so he can be freed from these shackles—free to live like a filthy hippie. And I am not talking about the hippies that secretly have money or families with money, and will reach a point where they will quit being hippies and convert to yuppyism. Erich hates those hippies even more than the others—he sees them as fakers hidden under dirty dreads. After the apocalypse, Erich will show the world what being a hippie is really about.

Hippies

Hippies themselves are not very dangerous. As a matter of fact, the majority of them
will not try to hurt you in any way, even if it
means their very survival. This should dis-
gust you, but it is not why you should fear
them. Hippies are primarily dangerous
because of their hugs. I am not sure why, but
hippies seem to love giving hugs. When they
approach you, hug ready, you are immediately thrown off by their odd smell, which is

a mixture of patchouli and garbage. My guess is they wear patchouli in an
attempt to cover up the smell of garbage emanating from their bodies, but
it doesn't work out like that. It simply produces two distinct smells that
shatter your senses and leave you terribly discombobulated. Like trying to
cover the smell of a meaty man-shit with some bathroom spray. While you
stand there stunned, they wrap their arms around your body, forcing you
to come into contact with their gross body hair.

Although it is possible to live through such an embrace, the majority of
the time one of their hippie buddies will begin playing their terrible music
on either an acoustic guitar or bongo drum. When subjected to their smell,
hugs, gross body hair, and terrible music all at the same time, a victim is
likely to suffer intense seizures. To avoid such an outcome, if you see a hippie approaching you postapocalypse with his arms outstretched, you want
to bolt. Luckily, hippies eat only seeds, nuts, and herbs, and this combined
with massive amounts of weed smoking makes them very slow runners.

The other dangerous aspect about hippies is their compassion. They
love to go against "the man" and save things. This will be even more common postapocalypse because there will be no one there to dissuade them
with billy clubs, tear gas, and, my favorite, rubber bullets. In a matter of
days after the shit goes down, the hippies that have survived will gather in
massive groups, and after several weeks of odiferous lovemaking, someone in the group will get the bright idea to save something, causing their
masses to begin to wander. Within a couple of days, there is a good chance

they will find their way into the city zoo. And guess what? They will release all the starving animals, thinking they are doing a good deed. Unlike normal people, the hippies will not just release the cute, cuddly animals. In their world, a pee-bug is just as important as a panda, and all the cages will be flung open with glee. Despite the angry and ravenous state of the wild animals, they will not feed on the hippies because they are too smelly. As the lions and tigers and packs of wolves go stalking down the street in search of less gamy game, the hippie mass will continue to wander.

Eventually they will find their way into the city prison. Again, they will do this "good deed" of theirs and release all the inmates. And of course the inmates will not kill the hippies because they are simply too smelly. The butt-hungry killers will head out into the streets to find something non-smelly to fuck and/or kill, and the hippie mass will continue its wandering.

After a few more days pass, they will stumble into a science laboratory where testing is done on animals. They will do yet another "good deed" and release the starving, genetically altered, Ebola-infected chimpanzees, all of which are crazed and enraged with syphilis and hungry for vengeance and human flesh (this might actually cause the apocalypse—see *28 Days Later*). Fortunately, these creatures will be so tortured that there is a good chance they will kill the hippie mass, but the damage will already have been done. If you happen to find yourself on the streets of a city where a hippie mass has been, you have zero chance of survival. As a result, avoid San Francisco and most towns in Oregon.

Fat People

Obviously, most fat people cannot move very quickly; thus, most of them will not survive the apocalypse. But there is currently a shit load of fat people, and some will manage to avoid the various pitfalls by blind luck. It will be like the ultimate fat camp—they will learn to survive on nuts, berries, fruits, and vegetables for the first time in their lives. After making this switch, they will feel extremely powerful and have amazing energy supplies. Will they realize the errors of their ways and be changed by their newfound diet? Most certainly not. They will be ready to consume anything in sight, including you.

The majority of overly fat survivors will not last long, but there will undoubtedly be at least a couple who make it past the first few weeks, and they will be very dangerous. Not so much out in the open—fat people are like slow-moving zombies in that they are easy to get away from. The places you must be careful of are confined spaces. Although fat people are extremely large, they are kind of gooey, and they can fit themselves into some pretty tight places, like closets and underneath beds. They are also extremely patient. After all, they are not concerned with what concerns normal-weight people. They care nothing about warmth because all their extra adipose keeps them toasty at night. They can't see their penises, so sex is out of the question. And all the entertainment they need is wrapped up in a Twinkie. Their sole focus will be to get more food, so they will cram their bodies into tight places and wait for weeks for someone to walk by. If you happen to wander past one of their hiding places, you are pretty much doomed. They will leap out at you, wrap their gelatinous arms around your body, and then drop on top of you and smother you with their colossal boob-belly mass. The worst part is they will not even wait until you are dead to begin feasting. For this reason, avoid all confined spaces. If you absolutely must enter a building, check all the cupboards, cabinets, and broom closets before settling in.

Children

Children of the apocalypse must be avoided at all costs. The more innocent a child looks, the more dangerous he or she will be. While adults are scrounging for flashlights, food, and batteries, children will scrounge for candy. After three weeks of eating nothing but Snickers, Kit Kats, and Ho Hos, they will be spun out big-time. They will hit the streets in their Big Wheels looking to dish out some pain, cackling the Mario Brothers' theme  song. Armed with toy military helmets, BB guns, wrist rockets, and pocket-knives, they will be like extremely smart and crafty gremlins.

How much harm could they do? A fucking lot. Remember, these little wrecking machines did not grow up playing with sticks in the backyard.

They have been playing Halo and Call of Duty since the day they were born, and they can shoot the ball sack off an eagle soaring two hundred yards overhead. These are not real kids you are dealing with—they are American kids, spoiled rotten and used to getting what they want. If the picture is still blurry, imagine the little tribe of parentless kids from *Thunderdome*. It will be exactly like that, except the postapocalyptic kids in the real world will not be singing songs and cheering. They will be beating your head in with Tonka toys and screaming at you to give them candy.

And if for some reason they do not choose to kill you, they will undoubtedly try to talk you into taking care of them. With their upturned eyes, they will play the guilt card and make you share your food, shelter, and clothing. Bear in mind, these are not actually your children. If they are your children, you should probably take care of them . . . probably.

Surviving on your own is hard enough, but when you add a bunch of hungry mouths into the picture, things get really difficult really quick. If you should encounter a rug rat in the wasteland, you only have one choice: Run! (Note: This form of orphan trickery can also happen pre-apocalypse. If some woman claims that you are the father of her child, she is lying. Screw genetic testing, it is all bullshit. Many of my friends have fallen for this very con.)

FILTHY FUCKING STREET URCHINS

The Homeless
Although you want nothing to do with hippies, fat people, or children, when the world as we know it ends, befriending a homeless person may very well save your life. Why? Because they are survivors, that's why. I know what you're thinking: "If 99.8 percent of the human population gets wiped off the face of the planet, there will only be

two homeless people left." Wrong. They will be everywhere. After a lifetime of subsisting on leftovers, they can eat a super-flu for lunch. After sleeping on the winter streets of New York and the summer streets of Vegas, they consider a huge natural disaster only a mild inconvenience. An economic collapse—get the fuck out of here. Looting and rioting is a carnival to homeless people. I'm telling you, every last homeless person will survive the end of the world, and if you manage to convince one to become your traveling mate, you will be as right as rain.

Your new homeless friend will teach you how to turn week-old cheese into a fantastic new cologne, divulge his secret recipes for cooking rat, and show you how to turn garbage into a fine sorbet. If the two of you get close, he may even demonstrate how to light a cigarette without igniting your breath, give you clues on how to break your phobia about masturbating in public, teach you how to filter coffee using your underwear, and show you how to build a fort under a bridge, in back alleys, or in the bushes. I'm telling you, homeless people are the ultimate urban warriors. But beware, gaining access to their secret society is not easy, so I recommend starting now. This can be achieved by volunteering down at your local shelter or just being kind and compassionate to those less fortunate. Just think of it as an investment. Personally, I have been volunteering at a shelter here in Las Vegas. Do I care about doing good deeds? Most certainly not. My only goal is to trick the homeless into allowing me into their inner circle when the shit hits the fan.

HOW TO FIGHT IN THE THUNDERDOME

Mad Max Beyond Thunderdome is obviously more than just a movie—it is a guide to know what shit will be like postapocalypse. Based upon this very real depiction of the near future, martial arts and the UFC will continue to grow in popularity. The only difference is that they will undoubtedly add some weapons in the mix and the rules will change. Instead of fighting in the Octagon, you will fight in a Thunderdome-type arena. And instead of striking your opponent with your fists, you will stab each other with swords and spears and shit. You might even have to fight a lion or two (if it was good enough for the Christians, it will be good enough for the apocalypse).

To prevent you from dying a quick death in this type of sporting event, I am going to give you a few tips. Most important, join one of those geeky medieval knight clubs to learn how to wield ancient weapons of death. The only downside is that any friends you currently have will disown you, and you may become brainwashed into thinking that covering your body in tinfoil will provide adequate protection in armed combat. While wrapping yourself in tinfoil does wonders to prevent the government from reading your mind, it provides absolutely no protection when being struck with heavy, sharp objects. Being involved in a medieval club might also lead you to believe that it is a good idea to wear a giant steel cup and leave your legs completely exposed. While this is a great fashion ensemble,[21] you might want to protect your femoral arteries. I know the Spartans like to keep their legs glistening in the sun for other men to gawk at, but you are not as fast and quick as a Spartan (and hopefully not as close to your comrades).

At the very least, you want to cover your legs in heavy leather. If you chose to go bare legged and someone stabs your femoral artery, you will bleed out very quickly. And dying from a leg wound is a pussy way to check out, especially when fighting in the Thunderdome.

WHEN YOU'RE ALL BUSTED UP

While making your way across the rubble to your safe zone, you want to do everything in your power to avoid injury. The best way to accomplish this is simply not to panic. Granted, there will be some pretty freaky shit going on, such as people with half-burned-off faces staggering toward you, animals that are all freaked out and confused, and perhaps even groups of half-crazed individuals on the hunt for human flesh. You might even see that giant spider with its eight legs, huge fangs, and million fucking eyes (woo, scared myself there). No matter what stands before you, do not panic.

---

[21] *Ensemble*. Definition: A slab of metal forged into a giant steal cup. Usage: You kicked me in the groin, but thank goodness I was wearing my ensemble.

MY WORST INJURIES

The worst injury I ever had was when I fought in South Africa. This was back in 2001 before MMA really took off, so the promoter offered me absolute shit. I basically fought for the trip. My opponent was a guy who had wrestled in the Olympics, and a few seconds into our fight, he picked me up and slammed me down on my shoulder. Being a Mickey Mouse event, we were in a boxing ring rather than a cage, and instead of a thick pad underneath the canvas, they had a tiny layer of foam on top of steel. The instant I landed, my shoulder popped out. I felt immediate pain, and when I glanced over at my shoulder, I saw what looked like the tit of a fourteen-year-old girl sitting on top of my deltoid. I would have quit right then, but my opponent began hitting me. I managed to get up, and we tussled for another few moments. As I was throwing punches and kicks, I kept looking over at my shoulder—as if staring at my injury would somehow make it go away.

Anyhow, my opponent got tired, I kneed him in the face, we went back to the ground, and I ended up on his back with one hook in. In some pretty serious pain at this point, I wanted to end the fight as quickly as possible. Genius me, I wrap my bad arm around his throat, grab my wrist with my other hand, and pulled my limp arm up into his throat until he tapped in submission. The second the referee separated us, I began rolling around on the canvas, screaming in pain. Although this was in no shape or way funny, the commentary of the South African announcer was. In his weird accent, he goes, "And the American with an interesting celebration . . . I think he is pretending he is on fire. Maybe it is a stop, drop, and roll type thing . . . Wow,

If you lose your head, there is a good chance that you will injure yourself by stepping in a hole, tripping over shit, or even running into stuff. Just keep your head and be cool. If you have to run, then run. But look where you are fucking going. If you have to jump over a fence, look on the other side first. This is all very common knowledge, but common sense seems to fly out the window when people get scared.

he is really getting into this . . . His face is all clinched up and everything."
Yeah, MMA has come a long way.

I received my second worst injury while working out with Bigger John in the
gym. My shoulder was still fucked up from my fight in South Africa, and he
had this notion that doing floor presses would somehow be better for me
than doing bench presses. I hadn't done bench presses in years, and I had
never done a floor press, but not thinking clearly, I decided to take John's
advice. So, I laid on the floor, he hefted the bar up to me, and then spotted
me on his knees (and yes, it was the gayest looking thing in the world). After
about five repetitions, John leans forward to spot me, and I see a massive
chunk of Copenhagen dip fly from his mouth in slow motion. I had two
hundred pounds in my hands, and I did my best to squirm out of the way, but
there was absolutely no avoiding it. That massive piece of saliva soaked dip
landed right in my eye socket. Immediately my entire head started burning,
and I begin shouting at John to take the weight. Instead of following my
instructions, he began shouting back at me in his brutish voice.

"Fuck that, son, you got another rep or two in you! You got two more reps
easy, son!"

I started screaming, trying to throw the weight off of me, but he held it in
place. Without any options, I did my two reps, John took the weight, and I
went running to the bathroom. After washing out my eyes, we finished our
workout . . . And yes, I am still emotionally traumatized by that event.

However, even if you are calm and collected at all times, there is still
a chance that you will injure yourself somewhere along the way, so I have
included some basic medical skills in this section. It is important to note
that I am not a practicing physician, and there is a good chance that by following the procedures listed below, you will die a horrible death. With that
said, let's get started.

Mending a Broken Leg

If you injure your leg postapocalypse, chances are you will have to do your own diagnosis to discover if it is broken. To begin, examine your leg for any cuts, bruising, obvious deformities, or protruding bones. If all looks well, feel up and down your leg for any gaps or bumps in the bone; also move your leg as you normally would to check if it has full range of motion. If you discover that the bone is in fact broken, check the pulses around the bone to ensure that an artery hasn't been severed or compressed from the swollen tissues or broken bone. If the pulses feel fine, you have a chance of surviving.

Surgery is out of the question, so the only real option is to brace your leg. Although this will be tremendously painful, begin by aligning the broken bone to the best of your ability. This might require some elbow grease. Once you regain consciousness, place a rigid object underneath the leg, such as a rolled-up newspaper or a flat board. Next, wrap an Ace bandage or duct tape around your leg to secure the stabilizer in place.

The next step is to attempt to survive with a broken leg. If you are already in your safe zone, you should have enough supplies to last you through the healing process. If you are in the middle of nowhere, you are going to have to fashion yourself a pair of crutches and attempt to make it to a location where there is food, water, and shelter. Good luck with that!

Broken Ribs

A broken rib hurts like a motherfucker, but unless it's protruding into your lungs, the injury is not life-threatening. To help reduce the pain and aid the healing process, it can be beneficial to brace your chest by heavily taping the rib cage. However, the most important thing you can do is to breathe normally. It might be excruciatingly painful to do so, but constantly taking short, shallow breaths can eventually lead to pneumonia, which will be much more likely to kill you than a broken rib.

Broken Fingers and Toes

Broken fingers and toes are easily treated using the "buddy taping" method. This is where you place the broken finger or toe next to a healthy finger or toe, and tape them together so they are side by side. In case you didn't get this, I am not talking about taping a finger to a toe or vice versa. If your finger is injured, tape it to the finger right next to it. For the best results, do not tape your fingers or toes completely straight. Make sure they have a slight bend.

Major Broken Bones

There are certain bones that will most likely lead to death when broken. For example, pelvic fractures are usually the result of serious trauma, like a high-speed car accident or when you get thrown off a twenty-foot cliff. For these types of injuries, you will want to perform surgery on the back of your head using a bullet. Either that or suffer an agonizing death.

Your Teeth

Your mouth can be a real motherfucker, especially when you fail to clean its contents for six months. That's why I had you include toothpaste in your Go Bag. If you blew through that tube and forgot to pick another one up while pillaging homes, it is only a matter of time until your mouth turns against you. The shitty thing is that your mouth rarely gives you signs to let you know trouble is coming. One evening you go to bed feeling fine, and the next morning you are crying like a baby, unable to chew your eggs. If this happens to you, the first step is to locate the cause of the pain, as it could be the beginning of a cavity, an abscess, or even the dreadful scurvy that plagued British sailors.

Cavities are pretty easy to spot, at least when they have progressed to the point where they are causing you pain. Just grab a mirror and look for the tooth that has started to turn black. Unfortunately, you won't have a dentist around to shoot you full of Novocain and give you a filling, so you will have to cowboy the fuck up and be a man. Yep, I'm talking about yanking that rotten tooth out of your head. Here is how you do it:

STEP 1: Locate the rotten tooth.

STEP 2: Apply some type of pliers around the tooth; a Leatherman tool works great for this.

STEP 3: Depending upon the location of the rotten tooth, you want to pull either straight up or straight down. You may need to employ a slight rocking motion to loosen it.

STEP 4: Once the tooth pulls free, pack the hole with a piece of alcohol-soaked cloth.

STEP 5: Place the tooth on a necklace, and then brag to anyone who will listen about how you yanked that very tooth from your skull. Skip the part where you cried like a big fucking pussy and wet yourself.

If you search all of your teeth and none of them appear to be rotten, you may have a disgusting abscess hiding in your mouth. The warning signs are fever, swollen red tissue, pain when chewing, and a permanent bad taste in your mouth. Abscesses are much like zits in that they are enclosed pockets of pus. However, if you ignore the abscess hoping it will go away like an annoying pimple, it will most likely continue to grow, destroy surrounding tissue, and possibly even kill you. To avoid such an outcome, you must drain the abscess by sterilizing some sort of cutting instrument, either with alcohol or over an open flame, and then lance that bad boy so the pus and blood can drain. Once the opening is empty, pack it with some type of clean material, such as pieces of a boiled sheet. To prevent infection, you want to put fresh material into your mouth every day, as well as rinse the abscess with anything cleansing you may be able to scrounge: hydrogen peroxide, mouthwash, alcohol, urine, or drip some of that boiling water right into the hole.

Scurvy is also relatively easy to spot: look for spots on your skin, spongy gums, and random bleeding. Ignore these warning signs too long, and your teeth will begin falling out like a meth addict's. Luckily, scurvy is not hard to cure. It is caused by a lack of vitamin C in your diet, so all you have to do it is eat more fruits and vegetables such as oranges, lemons, tomatoes, potatoes, and green peppers.

Excuses for Leaving Others Who Are Injured

If you ignored my advice to travel alone, you are going to need to come up with excuses to leave your traveling mates should they get injured. Although this might seem like it would be very easy, it can be difficult to be quick-witted when someone is clinging to your shirt collar and begging you to save their life and not abandon them. To spare you the added brainpower, I have come up with some canned excuses that I will allow you to use.

1. "Shhhhh, buddy. You're all right. You're gonna be just fine. No, I ain't never gonna leave you. I will be right here by your side, guarding your back. However, I am going to go fetch you some water from that creek we saw a few miles back."

2. "Dude, do you have my wallet? . . . I think I dropped my fucking wallet. Hold on, I'm going to look for that shit really quick."

3. "You hear that! . . . Holy shit, we're saved. That is the Red Cross out there. I hear them shouting for survivors. Hold on, buddy, this is your lucky day. I'm going to round them up real quick. I'll be back in a minute with a stretcher."

4. "I've got to go take a shit."

HOW TO SPOON FOR WARMTH

Assuming you don't abandon your injured buddies while you're traveling on the long road to nowhere, spooning is an excellent way to conserve body heat and stay warm. If it is just you and one other person, you will want to rotate every hour so that both of you get a chance to warm your chest and back. If there are more members of your group, you can either spoon in a circle so that everyone is pressed tightly together, or spoon in a straight line, in which case you will want to treat it as a game of musical chairs where the people on the ends rotate into the line every hour. Below I have illustrated the proper way to spoon, as well as the improper way to spoon.

Proper Way to Spoon   **Improper Way to Spoon**

NO, YOU CAN'T INVITE YOUR FRIENDS—THEY WILL TRASH OUR UTOPIA

Congratulations! If you are reading this portion of the book, you made it to your safe zone and spent the last six months chilling out while the world burned around you. You survived when billions of others did not, and you owe your success entirely to me. Please, take a moment to think about this and thank me in your own way. If you can think of nothing original, let me give you some hints on what might be appropriate reciprocation:

1. Build a large Forrest Griffin shrine, but do not decorate it with lame shit like flowers and wreaths and such. If you feel it absolutely must be decorated, use skulls and animal bones and patches of fur.

2. Name one of the wild animals
    you have adopted over the
    past six months after me.
    However, do not name it Griff or
    Griffmeister or the Griffinator.
    You must name him either
    Forrest or Griffin. I will also
    accept Forrest Griffin. However,
    it cannot be one of the animals
    you are currently husbanding.

3. Search me out in the
    postapocalyptic world and
    become a blind follower of my
    cult. I would promise to make
    you my right-hand man, but I
    will most likely already have
    held a six-day gladiatorial event in which the best men in the
    land fought for this honor. However, I can guarantee that I will
    make you a jester or minstrel. At the very least, you can get a job
    as my castle janitor.

4. Sacrifice your life in my honor. This can be done by slitting your
    wrists, beheading yourself with an ax, or simply jumping off a
    cliff or out of a very high tree. However, if you attempt to sacrifice
    your life in my honor and fail, you will have disgraced me. (P.S.
    Please fax or e-mail me a map of your food stash before you take
    the plunge so things don't go to waste . . . I promise I won't make
    a beeline for it once I receive your e-mail, and I further promise
    I won't use a large hunting knife to dispatch you should you
    change your mind about offing yourself in my honor.)

5. Use my name to describe something really cool. For example,
    when telling people about the time you surfed a tsunami or
    battled a supernatural wolf, say, "It was so utterly Forrest." I will
    also accept, "I Griffined the shit out of that wave and wolf."

Up to this point, your primary goal has just been to survive. But you have been there and done that, right? If you're thinking it's time to get to the good stuff, you are absolutely correct. Currently, you are standing at a crossroads and have a very important decision to make. Do you want to live a life of solidarity and continue to eat nuts and berries to survive, or do you want to be a part of something greater?[22] If you decide you want to strike it out alone like Captain Apollo did in the last episode of *Battlestar Galactica* (sorry if I ruined the ending), or just perch on top of a mountain for the rest of your days and reminisce about all you have lost, that is fine by me. You will get bored as shit and most likely get eaten by a bear. But if you feel that it is your destiny, so be it. However, if you want to be a part of something greater, then you must create your own utopia, which will require some work. Again, Uncle Forrest is here to tell you how to get it done.

Things are going to get pretty complicated pretty quickly, especially when you begin adding people to your circle, but it is important to take things in steps, with the first one being finding a place to build your new utopia. Your safe zone might be good for you, but chances are it's not enough to support life on a large scale. If you have trouble envisioning what this new utopia should look like, just picture the Thunderdome. Of course you will want to remove the midget and his pigs, add a whole bunch of hot chicks, some personal servants, and a church whose fellowship worships your awesomeness. You will probably also want to remove Tina Turner from the picture, as she will undoubtedly challenge your power, and seeing what she put up with from Ike, you don't want to be messing with that bitch. In any case, you get the picture.

THAT CASTLE AIN'T GONNA BUILD ITSELF

Once you find the location of your new utopia, the next step is to get yourself a kick-ass castle. You've worked hard all of your life, am I right? You broke your back doing manual labor for years while chasing the American Dream. But after all that anguish and toil, everything got ripped right out from underneath you, putting you back to square one. The good news is

---

[22] Such as being my manservant.

that there is no more American Dream, and you can do things completely different this time. You can start the (insert name of your country here) Dream. You do not have to play by the rules because there are no more rules. The apocalypse came and wiped them all out.

The trick now is to dream big. How big? I'm talking castle big. I'm not talking about going out and building yourself a castle. You worked hard all your life, remember, and that would involve far too much work. But just because you can't build a castle yourself doesn't mean you won't get one. Here is what you do:

STEP 1: Discover a plot of land that will serve as the holy ground of your new utopia. I recommend picking something far away from cities or developed areas in order to limit outside influences. It's best if this plot of land has some type of structure on it. The structure doesn't have to be in good shape—it simply has to be large enough to house several hundred people. Some suggestions would be country schoolhouses, warehouses in the middle of nowhere, some type of missile silo, or even a large network of caves. Whichever location you decide upon, the main thing is that there be running water and a food source nearby. Of course, the food source could always be another group of people.

STEP 2: Rig up a bus into a Vehicle of Death and begin rounding up survivors. By this point, most people will be lonely, scared, and desperate to be a part of some type of society. How you get them to join you is easy: tell them that you have created a safe community where they no longer have to worry about dying on a daily basis. Even if that is not true, people will most likely believe you. Why? Because they want to believe. You will be surprised how many people get on the bus. However, you probably don't want to force-feed them all matching glasses of Kool-Aid when they first get on, as this will probably freak them out.

STEP 3: Begin designing your awesome castle. If you are considering moving into a preexisting castle, you are missing my point entirely. In addition to wanting life to be easy, you also want to be remembered through the ages. Create a legacy. When people visit England and Wales, what do they do? They visit castles and talk about how great the creators of those castles were, even though they did no actual work. Erecting a stone castle is perhaps one of the most difficult things to do. If you can somehow convince hundreds of people to dedicate years of their lives to building you a castle, you will be remembered for thousands of years as being totally awesome. Not wanting to be outdone by guys in medieval times, I would recommend building a castle that resembles Hogwarts. In addition to being massive, that place is also filled with all sorts of magic. How cool would that be?

The one thing to keep in mind is that you do not want your castle to be cooler than my castle. If it is, and you follow my instructions on how to command your followers to build it for you, then I will most likely bring my army over and destroy it. And you will be able to say nothing because I saved your life with the information in this book.

STREP 4: Start a religion that worships you as some type of god. In the next section, I give detailed instructions how to accomplish this.

STEP 5: Order your followers to build you a castle. Not wanting to step out of line with the great leaders of the past, you want to make sure not to overpay your workers. If you are truly a great leader, you will not have to pay them at all. However, you may want to be like the Indians of Central America and feed them coca leaves (or, if you like to stay with the times, cocaine or meth), as it does wonders to boost productivity and morale. You might also want to throw them a goat or pig every now and then to ensure they do not starve. After all, a dead worker is an inefficient worker.

BECOME A DOG (I MEAN GOD. SORRY, MY DYSLEXIA KICKED IN)

Let me begin by saying that starting your very own religion is not an easy thing to do. There are currently only five commonly recognized world religions—Hinduism, Buddhism, Judaism, Christianity, and Islam—and each of them has its roots buried in thousands upon thousands of years of tradition and development. Back in the day, starting these religions wasn't all that difficult because the people of the long-long ago were about as smart

as the clay-and-stone tablets the laws of their religions were etched upon. Spending their waking hours growing food, preparing food, avoiding the plague, and courting farm animals, the majority of people had no time left over for things as ridiculous as arithmetic or that fancy book learnin'. They might have been able to weather some pretty terrible shit, but they had a serious chink in their armor: anything outside of their dimly lit perspective became a giant mystery.

Anyone who had ever learned how to read, count, or wash their genitals had a serious leg up, and the peasants viewed this small number of "learned" people as superior. How did the educated wield their power? Well, they used it to interpret, disseminate, and enforce the confusing traditions of religion. Seriously, these guys had it easy. The most educated dude in the mix probably wasn't half as "Smart as a Fifth" Grader© today, and they were given free rein to write the book on The Truth. And like all people of power should, they used the blind faith of the masses for their own designs. Sure, they used religion as a way to give purpose and meaning to the community, but they also used it to organize and control its members.

Your goal in creating a new religion is to establish that same type of power, but it won't be easy. You could always burn all the books and wait for the next generation of brainless followers, but then you would be old, and what's the point of having power when you are old? You got to take advantage of that shit while you are young enough to enjoy it. The trick will be coming up with a religion that people actually buy. Unfortunately, the mob is a lot more educated than the one that existed in the long-long ago. The amount of knowledge that has been amassed during the past twenty thousand years of human civilization is staggering, and there are currently 750 million people sharing that information on social networks on the Internet. You need to consider that your flock will have some degree of technical familiarity even if there is nothing to be technical about anymore. They will understand the basics of math, science, and reading and writing, which wasn't the case in ancient times. You must keep this in mind when creating your religion, as you will most likely be asked to explain and defend your system of beliefs to those who challenge your authority.

Luckily, in a postapocalyptic world people will be looking for a new set of rules. With the old religions obviously having failed them, they will want a new leader, and that is where you casually step into the picture. As long as you are an alpha-type survivor with the skills and the knowledge to maneuver successfully through the devastation, which will be the case since you are the proud owner of this book, it will be easy to rise to the status of leader. Once there, you should be able to use your charisma to get people to follow any somewhat moderate belief system you dream up. I mean, if Scientology can get half of Hollywood *allegedly* (I had to put that in there because these guys have rocking lawyers) believing their crazy bullshit, you should be just fine.

Before you get all giddy and begin rounding people up, there are a few things to consider. First, are you going to shoot for the stars or be more realistic in your goals? In other words, are you going to start a religion or a cult?

The smart theorize that the difference between the two is how they interact with general society. If your system of beliefs teaches its members how to live in the world, along with other people, regardless of your system's place in society, and it offers them guidelines on how to do so, then you are most likely the proud owner of a religion. If your belief system is intent on separating its members from their social system, and it encourages them to interact only with other members of your system, then you may be the leader of what is commonly referred to as a cult. If you find this confusing, let me simplify. For example, if you take your girlfriend to parties and home for the holidays, and she actually initiates sex with you, then her name is Religion. If your girlfriend lives in the basement, receives sunlight only through specialized tanning bulbs, and a tin bucket in the corner serves as her only toilet, then her name is Cult.

Before you decide which one to start, there is more to factor in to the equation. Another key difference between a religion and a cult is that religions usually require their members to worship a higher power that is above mankind and its limited comprehension. A cult, by definition, will many times ask its members to worship the messenger, as he is seen as either divine or an incarnation of a divine figure. There are of course inherent risks with whichever strategy you decide to pursue. For instance, if you are just the messenger, others will be able to proclaim messages from that source as well, and thus sects or spin-offs can occur and rival yours, even though they use the same basic belief structure that you created. When you leave things up to interpretation, they will eventually get interpreted. Next thing you know, people are attacking your gates and demanding that you release all your serving wenches from captivity—all that hard work straight out the window!

The only real way to establish a belief system where you are free from external risks is to become the sole appointee and sole messenger of The Truth. This automatically points you in the direction of creating a cult, but that's pretty much how almost all "religions" started out anyway. (Don't tell this to the Catholics—they tend to get all bent out of shape over it.)

Whatever route you take, you will most likely want to be at the center of the action. This can be accomplished by setting yourself up as the sole heir to The Truth from the get-go, which is a lot like trying to get kinky with a chick in bed. If you want her to dress up as the University of Georgia bulldog while you go at her woof-woof style, you got to do that shit within the first few months in the relationship, while things are still new and exciting. If you wait until three years in before exposing your fuzzy-fucker fantasies, she will probably freak out. It is the same with your religion. You've got to establish yourself and your intentions from the beginning to give your religion a foundation. That way, if others proclaiming The Truth pop out of the woodwork later on, you have recourse to arguing that your words are the Real Deal.

However, when establishing yourself as the supreme dispenser or speaker of The Truth, you do run into some risks as well. Many of these are what I call Internal Risks. That is, they are derived from inconsistencies in your actions or weaknesses in your resolve. For instance, if you proclaim that homosexuality and premarital sex are wrong, and then go around screwing all of your altar boys, you've just created a contradiction. This is why any religion that preaches abstinence from things such as sex, pursuit of money, desire for material goods, alcohol, and other such "vices" end up having their fair share of hypocrites, which in turn creates dissension and ultimately turns people away from that religion. In the case of a fledgling religion, it is essential for its founder to maintain actions consistent with the beliefs of the system he espouses. Therefore, I suggest that you pick your codes well so you are sure you can stay true to them. In other words, don't be full of shit.

It has been said in business that the three most motivating factors in selling a person on something are sex, greed, and fear. When it comes to religion, I would throw guilt into the mix as well. If your goal is to control the masses, you must control and define each of these aspects of human nature. Of course, you must also deliver to your followers a sense of satisfaction through the realization of purpose. Luckily, this will be quite easy in a postapocalyptic world. With everything they ever knew or loved burned to a crisp, it will be very easy to convince people that they were chosen to live for a greater purpose. It is your job to give them that purpose and to enhance their experience and feeling of value within the new community. For all practical purposes, assume the roll of strip club owner, and view your flock as an abused group of eighteen-year-old girls searching for a daddy. Give them the attention and purpose they are searching for. If you blank out on how to accomplish this, just remember the words "You are the chosen ones" goes a long way with smaller groups of people who have been through a lot of trauma.

The one thing you don't want to do is make your religion easy to follow. You want to ask your people to give up EVERYTHING. If you design your religion like a four-minute abs video and proclaim it is so easy that anyone can follow it, people will be deterred. For some reason, people like to suffer. They are completely content thinking that in the *next* life they will get theirs, which does wonders for allowing you to get yours in the here and now. During the three long months I spent working as a personal trainer, I scientifically proved that the more people pay for something, the more perceived value that something has. That is why we were thinking about charging five hundred dollars for this book. If HarperCollins had gone for it, you would have undoubtedly thought that it contained the formula for shitting golden apples. I thought it was a great idea, but at least we managed to con twenty-five bucks out of you for a book worth no more than a half-used pack of butt napkins.

This is the same thing you want to accomplish with your religion. Don't underestimate the power of fraternities or of military hazing. You must ask people to give up all their possessions. You must ask them to give you all of their food. Even if you can't eat that much food, you can always burn it or piss on it and give it back to the hungries worshipping at your feet . . . Yes, definitely go with the cult option now that I think about it.

Heed my words—do not attempt to create a system that is altruistic, which means it is actually good for the people. There are simply no incentives. If you create a religion totally in your favor, your flock becomes your personal slaves. In addition to doing all the things you hate, such as foraging and farming and going to the bathroom alone, they will bring you free sandwiches and give you regular blow jobs. It is a pretty sweet deal—just take a look back at all the heads of England's various churches in the long-long ago. Those guys were all fat off eating turkey legs and getting blow jobs (I have no proof for this statement, but it seems right). If you invent a religion that attempts to break the class system and get rich people communicating with poor people, the repercussions for being discovered as a fraud will be the same as for any other fraud—they will torture you to death by making you watch *The Hills* on mushrooms. Might as well get something out of the whole deal.

It's also important to know what your people are thinking, not because you care what they think but because it's another way to wield power. This can be achieved by adding confession to the rituals and system of your religion. These sessions should be recorded or transcribed and filed away for future reference. People often hold out in confessions, so it is important that all of the clergy in your new cult are also trained hypnotists. Once you have the members' deepest, darkest secrets, your flock will feel somewhat trapped. They will fear you. It would be like if I told someone about the time I slept with a post-op tranny. I would never tell anyone that. But if I did, you would have something over my head.

If a member of your group gets uppity, you leak the secrets you have on them to the rest of the group. Eventually, it will get out that that dissension leads to horrible punishment. Of course, if exposing their darkest moments is not enough to keep members from getting uppity, there are other ways to deal with their disobedience.

Why does any of this matter? The castle, dummy. Remember the castle. If you don't have a group of blind followers, who in the heck is going to build it for you? I sure as hell ain't.

MIX-AND-MATCH RELIGIONATOR CHART

I'm not gonna lie: starting your own religion is not easy. It takes at least a solid weekend of work with intermittent breaks to fight off the nomadic hordes. If you start to get frustrated and feel like calling it quits, remember that a sage once said, "Don't be a quitter 'till you hit her in the shitter." Your new system doesn't have to be perfect. As a matter of fact, it can be downright insane. Use a mix-and-match Religonator Chart like the one I've laid out below—it really is that simple. The religion you end up with might not exactly fit your needs and desires, but at least you will end up in power and have control.

This chart contains some of the more, how do you say, fantastic beliefs held by a few of the world's religions, as well as a column for what I like to call the "wild card" beliefs. To build you very own religion, circle one belief from each of the major religions, and to add that individual touch, top it off with two beliefs from the wild card column. Once you have made your choices, blend them together and create an almost ridiculous story line and a group of laws. Just go nuts with it and have some fun. Next, write the main story line on a really old scroll, scratch each law onto a stone tablet, and deposit both of these items somewhere in the desert. Just make sure to remember where you put them because later you will need to "find" them in the midst of a vision or dream.

Christian
- Baby born by virgin.
- Leader rises from the dead.
- Walking on water.

Catholic
- Consume the body and blood of your fallen leader on a weekly basis.
- Encourage young boys to hang out with old, asexual men.

Judaism
- The parting of entire seas.

Hinduism
- Good begets good, bad begets bad.
- Cows are sacred.

Scientology
- Aliens provide purity and clarity to humans. (Or some shit like that. Seriously, if they can get away with this kind of shit nowadays, what with modern technology and plenty of other religious options out there, you can get away with just about anything. *Allegedly.*)

Wild card
- Baby born by man virgin.

FORREST FACTOID

Don't be afraid to go crazy with your proclamations about your new faith. After the earthquake that claimed two hundred thousand lives in Haiti, Pat Roberts claimed that the Haitian people brought the death and mayhem upon themselves by worshiping the devil. If you can say something as fucked up as that and still have people follow your advice, you can say pretty much anything.

HOW DAVID KORESH DID IT
(CREATING YOUR GODLIKE PERSONA)

Getting your belief system set up is a good start, but it's not enough on its own. Now that you have a set of "values" in place, you need to make sure you have the presence to match. I know you've never been one to care much about your appearance, especially after the apocalypse (okay, let's be honest: things weren't great for you before the apocalypse either), but you might want to think about trying a few things to appear your holiest at all times.

Wildman Crazy Hair Doesn't Inspire Confidence (i.e., Nick Nolte)

Anytime you introduce a set of beliefs and ask people to follow them, you must become the focal point of excitement for those whom you wish to entice with those beliefs. Essentially, you must become the life of the party. Although I have never seen you personally, I imagine you have let yourself go a little, especially now that the apocalypse has hit. You have greasy skin, your drawers smell like a battle-field, and you always have goop caked in the corners of your eyes. Clean yourself up! You don't have to look overly proper, but you do have to look presentable.

My suggestion is to start with your hair. If you have hair, part it on the side so that you have that big wave traversing your forehead. A good head of hair works really well for telling your flock that you have what it takes to lead them to the promised land. However, if you are looking a little more like Matt Lindland these days, do not try to hide the fact that you are bald-ing by growing more hair around the sides and back. This is a clear-cut sign of weakness. Instead, shave your head bald. Even if you have a bulbous-shaped head, you will look wise and a trifle spooky. Spooky is good, trust me.

FORTUNE COOKIE WISDOM

If you truly want to be remembered as a legend, you will want to die as a martyr at the apex of your life. It will leave people with an iconic image of you—young, strong, and virile. If you hang around too long, you will undoubtedly be remembered as that fat, bloated, old guy hustling on the Vegas Strip for a couple of dollars so you can pay your child support. With this in mind, I still have to admit that martyrdom just isn't for me. Seventy-two virgins sounds well and good, but I cannot be responsible for teaching that many girls how to get it on. Personally, I need a girl with a little experience. Not a Vegas prostitute, but not an amateur either. Now if they offered an endless supply of coffee . . .

You Need to Sound Smarter

Another thing you can work on is your accent. When you have a foreign accent, it creates an illusion of superiority and knowledge. The goal is to choose an accent that best represents your belief system. If you are trying to create a religious community that has Hindu or Buddhist roots, you may want to speak like a Vedic Indian or wise Asian. If you base your belief system on a military concept, Texan, German, and Russian accents will help create an effect of power and militaristic credibility. The only accents you do not want to use are Canadian, Swedish, and of course French. Choosing one of these accents will get you stoned to death or burned at the cross. If you are not sure what accent to take on, just switch it up every few years like Madonna.

Whatever you do, do not use your regular voice. Employing an accent creates the "faraway effect," which is where people perceive anything remote from their lives to be more valuable than the things that are around them every day. This is the reason why everyone thought Pride was so good, because that organization was far away in Japan. But when those fighters came over here, and some of them didn't do that well, it shattered the illusion.

Another helpful hint is to speak using only cryptic phrases. Let me give you an example:

DISCIPLE: Forrest, I am hungry. Can I have a piece of meat?

FORREST: My son, we can only know these things in the end.

Crazy Eyes (aka Forrest Whittaker)

Another critical characteristic you need to develop are crazy eyes. Every religious or political leader that has attained the loyalty and blind allegiance of a group or a country has had them. Just think about David Koresh. He wore glasses to accentuate his crazy eyes, and people actually burned to death for him.

Practice in the mirror by staring at yourself for a really, really long time. As a matter of fact, stare at yourself until you are no longer comfortable doing so, and then stare some more. Eventually, you will automatically begin to make strange faces and your eyes will begin to take on the necessary look of intense commitment that your beliefs require. Although your crazy eyes will dissuade nonbelievers from getting near you, they will have the opposite effect on those who are searching for spiritual guidance. To them, the crazier your eyes get, the more they will believe that you have "seen the light."

NOTE TO READER: In no way are we condoning the actions of David Koresh, Jim Jones, or those guys who started that Heaven's Gate shit. We are simply pointing out that a couple of the techniques they used worked quite well, actually. We want you to use those techniques for good. That is what I will be doing.

Not Shaving for Five Years Finally Pays Off: Your Facial Hair

Another thing you may want to incorporate into your leadership getup is facial hair. Most wise men of religious or political movements have either had distinct mustaches or beards. If you are like me and cannot grow an adult beard, that is even better. The scruffier your beard or mustache, the more wisdom people will think you possess. The two looks I would recommend choosing from are the Fu Manchu beard of the Eastern master or the long beard of the mountain philosopher.

Jesus Was a Snazzy Dresser

Your attire will put the finishing touches upon your new persona, but it is important to make the right choice. Instead of picking something you look good in, ask yourself what you are trying to achieve. A long robe lets your fledgling converts know that you are a man of deep thought. Clothing yourself in animal skins lets them know you are a man of nature. Wearing a turban lets them think that you are without vices, and wearing a militaristic uniform gives off an aura of invincibility and power. It is totally up to you,  but just make sure whatever dress you chose to adopt is readily available, as you will most likely want to outfit all members of your group in similar clothing. This strips away their individuality and creates greater cohesion in the community. Remember, you want your group as a whole to have identity, not the individuals in the group. Dressing everyone the same also makes it easy to identify outsiders and kill them.

FORTUNE COOKIE WISDOM

It can also be beneficial to worship some type of crazy idol. I was going to suggest a dead dude on a cross, but apparently that has already been used. Just go crazy with it to see how far people will go. Personally, my religion is going to worship wind chimes. The reason for this is obvious—wind chimes are moved by God's life breath. Fortunately, I will be the only one who can hear God's voice when the wind chimes speak. I will interpret what he is saying and then share that knowledge with my people. The downside to this, of course, is that a community filled with seven thousand wind chimes will probably get pretty fucking annoying. Man, I hate the sound of those things. Reminds me of old people, for some reason . . . So, on second thought, my religion will most likely worship trees. They have been around longer than humans, and they don't even bother trying to communicate with us, which means they are super wise. The downside to this is that trees will be sacred, which means everyone will have to live in mud huts or some shit. However, I will be able to live in a giant hollowed-out tree because that is how I divine with the gods. Yeah, that's a lot better than listening to wind chimes all day.

Putting Everything Together

Below are few examples of how you can put everything together.

FORTUNE COOKIE WISDOM

As the head of your new religion, you'll quickly find that there are real benefits to human sacrifice, as it's a great way to get rid of people trying to usurp power. Ancient Mayans routinely practiced human sacrifice to appease their various gods and to commemorate the coronations of their leaders. In one such sacrificial ritual, they would paint a victim blue, cut under their breastbone with a flint knife, reach into the gaping hole they created, and extract the still-beating heart Indiana Jones style. After the event, the victim would be flayed and his skin turned into a cape, which the priest would wear while performing a ritual dance.

MATING POSTAPOCALYPSE

If you are planning to start a new society, there is going to have to be some funny business happening at the back of the cave when the sun goes down.

Today's mating rituals are confusing and involve many factors, most of which I do not understand. Postapocalyptic mating rituals will be much more primal and focus on immediate survival. Personal hygiene will play a much smaller role in mating, which is good news for most of my readers. In addition, bow-staff skills will have a much greater relevance attached to them. But that doesn't mean that all those Napoleon Dynamite losers will be able to get mates all of a sudden. Females will look for a big, strong, tough animal with good genetics that she can control enough to provide her and her young with food and shelter. Women will be attracted to a protector and a provider, plain and simple.

However, there will still be some similarities between pre-apocalyptic and postapocalyptic customs. For example, today women want a man with a nice house, and postapocalypse they will want a man with a nice shelter that doesn't leak and is not too exposed to the wind and temperature changes. Today they want a man with a good job, and postapocalypse they will want a good hunter . . . Wow, now that I think about it, all those socially inept weirdos that never get women because the only women tough enough to stay with them are lesbians will be the most-prized bachelors. (You hear that, Erich? There is a chance for you.)

What will men be looking for postapocalypse? Well, in my opinion men should be looking for tough, strong women who are clean and healthy enough to avoid sickness and such. Women that have a little fat (ample ass and tits—okay, that sounds a little harsh when I actually see it on paper, but this doesn't make it any less true) so they can survive during child-birth and the lean winter months. After all, when calories become scarce, it will be great to be fat—not to the point where you can't move, but fat in the sense that you can't see your abs. On second thought, men should probably simply look for any woman that doesn't run from them. Oh, and doesn't have a dirty baby maker.

THE ORIGINAL POWER GEL BY ANTHONY

Female patients often ask me if it is safe for them to swallow their husband's ejaculate during oral sex. The answer is YES! In addition to being completely safe and great tasting (not based upon personal experience, but rather on thousands of hours of research conducted with loose women around the world), it is great for your health. Human male ejaculate is only 10 percent sperm. Among other things, it contains vitamin C (which boosts your immune system), calcium (which makes you grow strong bones), protein (helps you build muscles), zinc (helps prevent a number of health problems), and fructose sugar (a nice energy boost to start your day). If you are still skeptical, I understand completely, but at the very least it can serve as an excellent exfoliant. Ancient Egyptian women routinely allowed their men to blow on their face, and they were renowned for having nice skin.

If you shy away from swallowing because you think it tastes icky, just have your man drink pineapple juice and eat fresh fruit a few days prior to your journey south. This won't make his jizz taste like a lollipop, but it should calm your gag reflex. Seriously, swallowing a mouth load of jizz is a very healthy, natural thing to do, and all women should get accustomed to doing it. It really isn't that bad—just ask Bigger John.

BIGGER JOHN GETS A TASTE OF HIS OWN MEDICINE
BY BIGGER JOHN

Back when I was twenty-seven, I was seeing a former dancer from the Athens area, and she was giving me a blowjob in her parent's house. She asked me to give her some kind of signal or sign to let her know when I was about to blow, but there was no way in hell I was going to do that. Well, I guess she felt the tide rising, and just as the volcano blew, she removed her lips from my pole. I of course let out a tremendous sigh of pleasure, and the next thing I know I have a mouthful of my own cum.

Now, the only reason I am telling this story is because I am sure it has happened to many men. And it is kinda manly knowing that I can blow a load that far—there ain't no dribble dick here, son. But despite being impressed with my distance, I was totally grossed out. I ran to the bathroom, threw up several times, and then grabbed a random toothbrush on the counter and brushed my teeth. It was a pretty rough experience. But truth be told, it was the idea of it that grossed me out more than the actual taste.

POCKET PUSSY

Not one for political correctness, I am going to talk about a controversial topic—the pocket pussy. All men have tried to build one at some point in their life, and all men have experienced horrible repercussions due to their botched experiment (some men may have tried to build a pocket anus. I am not judging, but you are extremely homosexual). Men will be a lot more desperate postapocalypse due to the loss of the Internet, and to prevent them from attempting to construct makeshift devices out of old car parts and rusty nails, I have included a proven pocket pussy blueprint below. Trust me when I tell you this contraption was not designed in haste or developed in some pervert's basement. It was masterminded by Alexander the Great himself, and passed down through the ages by the Freemasons. How did I come across this knowledge? . . . *What travels in the moonlight by way of the eastern pass* . . . enough said.

Supplies

- One latex glove.
- Three pieces of string, approximately twelve inches long.
- Lubricant: whatever is available. (Note: motor oil is precious and should not be used on your dick.)
- Towel.
- Water.

STEP 1 (TOWEL AND GLOVE SETUP): Fold your towel in half and then lay it on the ground. Make sure that the height of the towel is not shorter than your johnson. Next, place the glove at one end of the towel with the cuff approximately three to four inches outside of the towel.

    HINT: Before rolling up the towel, you may want to wet it to make it feel more humanlike. Up to you.

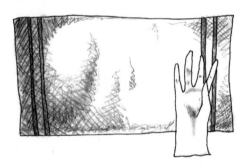

STEP 2 (ROLLING THE TOWEL): Roll up the towel. When done properly, the cuff of the glove should protrude three or four inches from the end.

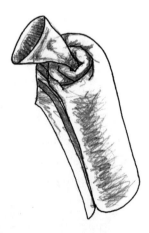

STEP 3 (FOLDING THE GLOVE): Fold the cuff of
the glove over the towel. This is when the
contraption will begin to resemble a vagina.

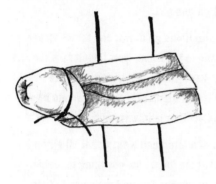

STEP 4 (TYING THE TOWEL): Place three strings approximately two to three
inches apart across the towel. Next, tie the first string to the desired
tightness or looseness.

STEP 5 (ADDING LUBRICANT): Tie the second two strings. Now that your
pocket pussy is complete, add the desired amount of lubricant. Have
fun!

   NOTE: Make sure to remember to change gloves between uses. This
pocket pussy is a onetime deal!

How to Make a Pocket Anus

See instructions above, just add shit.

DICK IN A BOX BY BIGGER JOHN

The sad truth is that when the apocalypse comes, there won't be all that many women left, and so you'll have to get comfortable sharing. Personally, I will not have a problem with this because I am the king of group sex. Unfortunately, it is not "the good kind." In other words, it always ends up being me and two or three other dudes on one girl.

In 2006, I had ten different group sex situations go down, and for whatever reason, each time there was another man in the room. Now I need to make it very clear that I did not set it up this way—that's just how the cookie crumbled. It got so bad there for a while that Adam Singer accused me of not being able to get hard unless there was another man watching.

My whole deal is that I am a horny son of a bitch and want to get laid, and if there happens to be another guy around at the time, I am not going to let him get in the way. Luckily, all these little experiences I've had are going to help me when shit hits the fan. During the apocalypse, every sex situation will most likely be a group situation due the minimal number of women left on the planet, and I will be the first to jump into the mix. If you're nervous about having this type of encounter, I can offer you some advice to make it a little easier.

First off, instead of seeing the other guys in the room as invading your turf, view them as teammates. Anytime you're with a chick, you get nervous about something, such as if you are going to cum too fast or be able to get a stiff enough erection. But when there are other guys present, and you see them as your brothers, your friends, your teammates, they can offer moral support if anything should go wrong. They can provide you with the confidence you need to correct any problem you may be having and get back into the game.

When you acquire this mind-set, you don't see a massive cock as a threat. You simply see it as more cock to get the job done. For example, when playing a game of football, you want the biggest linebackers possible. As long as you have the team mentality, the same thing goes with group sex.

To give you an idea of how a mostly male, group sex situation should transpire, I will share with you one of my funnier gang bang stories. It involved a nurse and my childhood friend Dustin, who now happens to be a sergeant in the army. Well, anytime Dustin and I tag-teamed a girl, he liked to take the role of director, which was fine by me. So on this particular occasion, we were sitting around the living room, and he says to the nurse, "Why don't you take off John's pants." Sure enough, she takes off my pants. Next he said, "Why don't you start sucking on John's cock." Being the truly wonderful woman she was, she began sucking on my cock. Next thing I hear is, "John, lose the shirt." Without thinking, I removed my shirt. A second later, I realized that he had not been referring to my shirt, but rather the shirt of the nurse. It was pretty damn funny, but what really blew my mind was that the nurse was actually able to laugh with my cock still in her mouth. She could suck a dick and laugh at the same time. What a talented girl.

WHO'S THE BOSS

Once you have effectively set yourself up as the Bringer of the Light and established yourself as the top male of the group, the next step is to create a hierarchy, starting at the bottom floor—your laborers. This job will be filled with the people who have pre-apocalypse skills that are no longer valued postapocalypse. This includes but is not limited to lawyers, writers (yes, Erich will be one of my laborers), bureaucrats, plumbers (buckets will be our new toilets), nuclear engineers, astronauts, pilots, bankers (you will own everything of value), and computer scientists. If you happen to be among this group, sorry, buddy, but you are finally going to have to get your hands dirty. And what the fuck are you doing reading my book—you are smarter than this.

Ironically, the people who had jobs that were considered menial pre-apocalypse will most likely have skills that are extremely valuable postapocalypse. This includes but is not limited to professional fighters, artists (someone has to build your statues and paint your murals—aka, keep record of your greatness), wilderness guides, archers, gunfighters, farmers, and carpenters. You don't necessarily have to put these people in a position of power (you want to control as much of it as you can), but you definitely want to make them feel superior to the laborers. This can be

FORREST FACTOID

I was hanging out with the late Evan Tanner a while back, bitching about how people can be so damn critical. Suddenly Evan gets all quiet, and he says to me, "Jesus of Nazareth walked the earth, did nothing but good, and they crucified him for it." That was some pretty heavy shit right there. Needless to say, I quit my bitching.

accomplished by giving them nicer houses, more food, and perhaps assigning each one their own slave laborer. Could you imagine how good it would make a carpenter feel to have his own rocket scientist as a slave?

Your middle class will be made up of people who have skills that neither gained nor lost value postapocalypse. This group will exist solely of strippers and prostitutes.

Lastly, you want to assemble your group of lieutenants. This is where a lot of leaders go wrong. Instead of picking their most loyal subjects to serve in this role, they pick the most ambitious. Although ambitious people often prove to be excellent advisers and will go to great lengths to corral your people into a tightly knit group, they will almost always attempt to overthrow you when you are at your weakest. And since they have a lot more interaction with the people on a daily basis, they can often raise a fairly decent-size army to help them with their task.

To avoid such an outcome, assign all ambitious people to horrible jobs such as pig farming or butt wiping, and fill your lieutenant positions with the dumbest members of your lot. (In other words, follow the path of George W. Bush, not Julius Caesar.) They might not be great advisers, but do you really need an adviser? Hell no, you don't. You also don't need senators or congressmen or anyone else who tells you what is best for your flock. After all, they are your flock. For all intents and purposes, they are your cattle. Before you found them, they were dirty, scared, and confused. They will of course forget this fact, but whipping them back into shape is easy. All you have to do is stage a famine or crisis or war, or make terrible decisions that lead you to a real famine or crisis or war. Anytime people feel threatened, they tend to come together and place blind faith in their leader. Just look at the faith we placed in George W. Bush after 9/11. Enough said.

THE ETCHING ON THE STONE TABLET

One of the nicest aspects about starting your own religion is that it allows you to create laws almost at will. All you have to do is claim that they are of divine origin or suggest that they must exist in order to remain in Divinity's favor. No matter the absurdity of the law you make, no judge in his right mind will attempt to overrule it or say it is unconstitutional. After all, it would be the same as saying God is unconstitutional, and if you have structured your laws correctly, such a crime is punishable by death.

I know it might seem like a good idea to have an anarchistic society, but it simply won't work. Without laws, society cannot function because there is no order. However, I am not saying that you should go crazy with laws. And you especially don't want to make all the laws in your own favor. You want to create certain laws that help solve issues that commonly arise in the community, such as who is allowed to join your group and who isn't, and how to deal with those who cause harm or bring disorder. But there have got to be some benefits to sitting at the helm of this whole thing, and my suggestion is to get a little creative. I am not saying you should enact a law as self-fulfilling as making all women visit you in your bedchambers the day they turn sixteen (if you are thinking, "Damn, that would be sweet," then yes, you are indeed a pedophile), but you definitely want to pass laws that make your life easier or at least less annoying.

Once you create these laws, no matter how absurd, you must enforce them with an iron fist. Personally, I am not one for hurting others, except perhaps for punching people in the face or trying to break their arms with submission holds . . . oh, and maybe once in a while trying to crack a rib with a solid Thai kick, and then also getting real joy out of delivering a stout punch to the liver so the recipient pisses blood for a week . . . but besides all that, I'm not really a guy who likes to dispatch punishment. However, when creating a society, your new utopia, it is absolutely necessary to create consequences for insubordination. You don't want to get all crazy with things, like burning someone at the stake for not bowing the proper number of times when worshipping your awesomeness. You must be fair when doling out punishments in order to keep order and faith in your system. In other words, the punishment needs to fit the crime.

There is always the good old "eye for an eye" type of justice. If someone steals, they get their hands cut off. If someone lies repeatedly, they get their tongues cut out. If someone screws another man's woman—well, you get the picture.

Many smaller groups simply ostracize their members, exiling them to a life on their own, and in a postapocalyptic world this would undoubtedly be a scary proposition. (Note: Ostracize means to shun or ignore, not make your people dress up and act like ostriches. Just letting you know as these things can sometimes get confusing.)

Below I have included some of the laws that I will enact in my postapocalyptic community, as well as the punishment people who break those laws will receive.

1. **LAW**: Men can't dye their hair.

   PUNISHMENT: Public stoning. If you are wondering why not death by hanging, beheading, or crucifixion, let me tell you. First off, stoning seems like a pretty terrible way to go, especially if the people can't throw that good and it takes them a while to put you out of your misery. Second, it makes everyone the killer. If you kill someone by beheading, the blame lies solely with you and the executioner. If you get everyone to partake in the festivities, they all have blood on their hands.

2. **LAW**: Women are not allowed to flirt with men they do not plan to have sex with.

   PUNISHMENT: They must become strippers.

3. **LAW**: You must pitch in by your own free will on community projects, such as building schoolhouses, temples to worship me, and of course my castle.

   PUNISHMENT: While everyone else in the community does man's work, you have to serve them lemonade in a pink dress and hold the bucket for them when they need to relieve themselves. Oh, and you must eat your meals out of the same bucket.

4. **LAW:** Don't wear white after Labor Day.
   PUNISHMENT: Uppity bitches will make fun of you.

5. **LAW:** Stupid people must use condoms. And yes, this includes me.
   PUNISHMENT: They have babies they have to take care of.

6. **LAW:** No ostentatious showing of wealth. (I made this law because I just learned the word "ostentatious" and had to use it in a sentence in order to remember it.)
   PUNISHMENT: Have to extirpate all their wealth (not sure if I used "extirpate" correctly).

7. **LAW:** No hurting coffee plants in any way.
   PUNISHMENT: Death on the spot. However, stoning is not allowed because it may damage one of the plants.

8. **LAW:** Women are not allowed to use their left foot during the full moon. (I would get more into this, but it is very personal.)
   PUNISHMENT: None at all, but I am begging you not to do it. (The begging is a part of it all.)

9. **LAW:** Women cannot use words such as "small" or "tiny" or "microscopic" or "babylike" when referring to a man's genitalia. It hurts a guy's feelings.
   PUNISHMENT: That man is the only lover you may take for five years.

10. **LAW:** All pets must be properly maintained.
    PUNISHMENT: Must spend a week in an animal's cage, getting treated as you treat your animal.

11. **LAW:** No driving and texting at the same time.
    PUNISHMENT: Chances are there will be no working cell phones or vehicles, but you don't want to mess around with this one anyway. Punishable by stoning.

12. **LAW:** No smoking in public places.
    PUNISHMENT: Death by stoning.

If you have trouble coming up with your own laws, the Ten Commandments are a pretty good place to start. Currently, I follow approximately six and a half of them. In case you have forgotten what they are, let me refresh your memory:

1. *You shall have no other gods before me.* In the case of the apocalypse, that God will be me, Forrest Griffin. (Just kidding, real God. Please don't smite me. It was a joke.)

2. *You shall not make yourself a carved image—any likeness of anything that is in heaven above, or that is in the earth beneath, or that is in the water under the earth.* This is the wild card commandment. I'm not quite sure what it means, and I am sure others won't either. Basically, I will define it to suit my immediate purpose. For example, if I catch someone shitting on my lawn, I will shout, "You shall not make yourself a carved image."

3. *Remember the Sabbath day.* Although the Sabbath is currently every Saturday, I like to sleep in on the weekends. I also feel four times a month is a little extreme. As a result, my Sabbath will be every other Wednesday.

4. *Do not take the Lord's name in vain.* I'm actually a firm believer in this one. Although my last book contained about six thousand swearwords, I didn't take the Lord's name in vain once.

5. *Honor your father and mother.* Basically, this means honor your father and then, if you have any goodwill left over, throw it to your mother. I never understood this—mothers birth you, feed you from the teat, raise you, shower you with warmth, and do everything in their power to protect you even after you become a filthy adult. Seems a little unfair to me. After all, fathers are the ones you run and hide from when they get home from work.

6. *You shall not murder.* This is a good one, but I feel it needs a little more clarity. In my religion, it will strictly state, *Do not murder me, Forrest Griffin.*

7. *You shall not commit adultery.* Everyone should abide by this, unless, of course, the chick is super hot and freaky. Just don't get caught.

8. *You shall not steal.* Again, this one needs to be defined. You will not steal from me, Forrest Griffin. However, you may steal from others and give to me, especially if the thing you stole was a warm cup of coffee.

9. *You shall not bear false witness against your neighbor.* I am not quite sure what this one means either, but I assume it has something to do with sleeping in your neighbor's bathtub, which is not a good idea.

10. *You shall not covet your neighbor's house; you shall not covet your neighbor's wife, nor his male servant, nor his female servant, nor his ox, nor his donkey, nor anything that is your neighbor's.* Basically, this is most awesome commandment of the lot. It is solely designed to keep the elitists in a position of power. However, it is kind of worded strangely. It seems to get all sexual there with the neighbor's wife part, but in the same sentence they mention male servants, oxen, and donkeys. Most likely, there were some pretty sick fucks back in the day. I mean, who wants to covet a donkey? A deer, on the other hand . . .

YOU GUESSED IT–A SERIOUS SECTION IN A DICK-JOKE BOOK

How did society get to this point? How are all these intelligent people running around, believing in religions that are based on ideas and concepts and beliefs that cannot be proven. I know, I know. You just gotta have faith. I have been hearing that all of my life, but if I have faith that tomorrow morning I will awaken with the athletic endowments of LeBron James, it just ain't going happen.[23] The fact of the matter is that faith cannot make morons into astronauts, so why will it make the concepts of any religion any more true? That's why when I talk at schools I do not tell the kids that they can do anything. Instead, I say, "If you work really, really hard, perhaps you can be the first one in your family to graduate high school. No, you cannot be an astronaut—sorry, that is not really an option for you.

---

[23] I do that every night, and wake up disappointed every morning.

NAKED ETIQUETTE

Around the time I was working on this section of the book, I got a workout in at the Las Vegas Health Club and then hit the showers. About halfway through, the hairy man showering next to me asked some random guy in the locker room if he would be so kind as to soap up his back. I looked over and saw this hairy man hand a complete stranger a little washcloth and then turn around. You could tell the guy who had been asked to perform this service was in complete shock, and not knowing exactly how to behave, he did as he was ordered. He quickly soaped up the guy's back, handed the washcloth back, and then scurried out of the locker room. I had to use all my willpower not to scream at the hairy man next to me, "What the fuck are you doing?" It bothered me to such a degree that I felt it was necessary to include a few Naked Etiquette laws.

Naked Etiquette Law 1: If you are naked in a public place such as a locker room, speaking to other people is strictly forbidden. Do not talk to me, and do not look at me. Keep your mouth shut and your eyes glued to the wall in front of you. However, I will accept talking while in the sauna, even if you are naked. This helps pass the time and has a less "rappish" feeling associated with it.

Naked Etiquette Law 2: This law is very similar to the first law, but I felt I needed to get very specific just so there was no confusion. Even if you are half naked, which tends to occur when you are at a urinal, talking is strictly forbidden.

Naked Etiquette Law 3: Shaking hands in any place where urination or defecation commonly takes place is strictly forbidden . . . Come on, people, get your head in the game.

Let's work on maybe getting a bachelor's degree or maybe a trade you are really good at. Baby steps, kids."

The thing that gets me is that the people who try to spread religion usually aren't the smartest among us. Just look at any late-night evangelist—every single one of these guys would get creamed in a third-grade spelling bee. But with all of that said, I too have recently found religion.

Does that make me a hypocrite? Yes, probably does, but I have certainly been worse things. I believe in God because when I pray to Him, when I say, "Please take away my fear, my anxiety, my pain," it seems to happen. So when I think about it, I guess faith is not really that blind after all. There really does seem to be something there. I mean, if I do something good and selfless, it feels good. When I do bad things, it feels bad. Sure that could be programmed into me by society, but it could also be God, so I'm going with that one. Besides, now that I am going to church, I will get to go to heaven. In your face, old, agnostic ways!

However, I have to admit that being a nonbeliever was a whole lot easier. I used to be a militant agnostic, which is where you think, "I don't know, and neither do you." Agnosticism appealed to me because its whole belief system could be summed up in that one statement. And what comeback did people have? Since they were unable to prove any of their beliefs here on earth, it all came back to faith. What helped sell me on religion is Pascal's Gambit. Now, I have an interesting take on this idea because I learned about it in Sunday school as a kid, and my brain has taken a LOT of abuse since the fifth grade, but I didn't bother to look it up because I like my personal recollection. Pascal's Gambit is basically this: if you follow the basic tenets of any moderate religion, you will have a better life, you will be more adjusted to society, and you'll help move things along for the betterment of all. You will also be happier, and if there is in fact a God and a heaven, you will get to meet Him and go there because you followed the rules.

On the flip side, you have the atheist's gambit. (And just so you know, I am most likely making this all up, even though in my head I honestly feel it is something someone told me at one point at time.) The atheist's gambit states that religion is restrictive and destructive. To prove this point, all you have to do is look at one of the hundreds of wars that have been fought over religion, such as the never-ending battle raging between Pakistan and India (seriously, why can't the Buddhists and Confucianists just get along!). If you abolished all the religions, the majority of wars would simply end. Sure, the leaders could find other methods to rally their people to fight for their selfish causes, but they would never be able to mobilize the same number of them. So the atheist's gambit basically states that without religion, people will stop all the fighting. They would start living for the moment and stop focusing on getting theirs in the next life.

Personally, I find Pascal's Gambit to be more attractive. After all, I am not killing anyone in the name of religion. If you use a little common sense, it should be easy to figure out that killing people in the name of your religion is probably pretty wrong. As a matter of fact, anytime you use religion to justify a bad action, it is wrong. All religions have done it, even the Mormons. Back in the long-long ago, they used to kill other settlers and take their shit, and it was done in the name of religion. I have no intention of killing people and taking their shit, so I think I am pretty much okay. Sure, it is rough to believe in God and heaven when you see millions of people die before they've even had a chance in life, like all the kids who lost their lives in the Southeast Asian tsunami or over in Haiti when they had that massive earthquake. I mean, I would understand if God smote me down tomorrow because I am a dirty fucker, but all those kids . . . How do you explain that? The answer I have come up with is you don't. If you look too deeply into anything, contradictions are going to pop up. It is just a fact of life. You just got to do what feels right, and recently for me, it has been to find faith that there is in fact a higher power . . . anyway, back to the death and mayhem!

A Note from Forrest

I know this whole section is a little heavy for this kind of book, whatever kind of book it is. But I like to rant about God because I am afraid to die. I want to know what is next, and I think that by ranting about religion, I will somehow see The Light. The good news is that I know for a fact that I am going to heaven; you heathens are fucked.

The other reason for all this religious stuff is that I want to get my book sold in Christian bookstores. Ya, probably not gonna happen. Apparently, you can't cuss in Christian books. It's probably in the Bible somewhere that you can't use profanity, but if this were really important to God, he would have made it one of the Ten Commandments. So it probably isn't any more important than "it is God's will that you should be sanctified, that you should avoid sexual immorality" (from the Bible, p. 418). By the way, from that passage I just quoted, do you get that it's wrong to have premarital sex, because I didn't get it no matter how many times sister Mary-Joy explained it to me . . . Look up Thessalonians 4:3.

GIVE THEM THE GAMES!

I like to think that I learned lots of things from the movie *Gladiator*, but honestly, I probably only learned one: win the hearts of your people, and you will win their allegiance. That said, this lesson clearly didn't work out that well for Emperor Joaquin Phoenix, but then again, he did spend most of that movie whining about Russell Crowe, so he wasn't exactly a winner to begin with. Let's just say winning the allegiance of your people is a very important concept to remember when building your new utopia. I know you want to get your castle built as quickly as possible, but it can't be all work and no play for your people. You must keep them entertained. Back in Roman times, they used to accomplish this by hosting massive gladiatorial events where armed combatants fought with each other, condemned criminals, and even the most insane wild animals. While these events did wonders to keep people entertained, they were extremely expensive and did little to help the state acquire more riches.

If you learn anything from my book, I hope it is that it is wise to kill two birds with one stone whenever possible. I know what you are thinking: "How could hosting such barbaric tournaments ever help the state?" In order to answer this question, I must ask one in return. What is the number one burden of every society throughout the history of mankind? If you answered drug addicts or criminals, you are absolutely wrong. The number one burden has and will always be the elderly. Due to my infinite wisdom, I have devised a way to not only entertain the mob, but also solve the problem of what to do with elderly, a problem that will inevitably arise after the apocalypse.

Before you start imagining all sorts of horrible shit about me, let me be very clear. In no way, shape, or form am I suggesting we arm the elderly with swords and shields and let them have at each other. That is a disgusting

FORTUNE COOKIE WISDOM

Oftentimes in life when confronted by two choices, the harder of the two is most likely the right answer . . . Also, he who falls asleep with itchy butt wakes up with stinky finger.

thought, and I look down on you for even entertaining it. What I am suggesting is much more humane: MMA for the elderly. That's right, it came from my mouth first, mixed martial arts for the elderly. Surprised you haven't already seen it on Spike TV or pay-per-view? I am as well. It is absolutely genius. Not only do you provide sports entertainment for all your hard workers, but you also help the elderly to pull their own weight and remain active members of society. Now, before you scoff at this idea, just remember that Randy Couture and Mark Coleman have been proving this to be a viable concept for years now. To turn it into a resounding success, all you will need to do is structure the organization correctly. The first step to doing this is developing training camps.

MMA FOR THE ELDERLY

Back in Roman times, the majority of their gladiators were either criminals or paid volunteers. This is perfect! After the apocalypse comes, Walmarts will no longer exist, which means every elderly person will be out of a job and sign up for The Games on their own accord. Each "student" will receive food and housing, as well as all the training they need to turn them into fine-tuned, partially mobile, semi-asthmatic, fighting machines. The setting will be that of a peaceful retirement community. All you have to do is make a few small adjustments. For example, replace their naps with rigorous sparring sessions, their pinochle tournaments with takedown drills, their hour of *Ricki Lake*[24] with conditioning routines, and their kite-flying lessons with hill sprints. Other than these few small alterations, it will be retirement paradise. No longer will their existence be a burden on the state. They will have purpose! Forget about helping an old person across the street—turning them into an MMA fighter will help them in life.

---

[24] Does anyone actually watch *Ricki Lake* anymore?

Once you have developed half a dozen camps, immediately begin initiating rivalries. For example, steal all the walkers and wheelchairs in Camp A, and then blame it on Camp B. Next, steal all the pudding from Camp B and blame it on Camp A. Pretty soon, they will hate each other and begin shouting at each other from across the street (yes, in my imaginary world these camps are apparently right across the street from each other). In addition to building up the fights, such tactics will also create unity in each camp. However, it is important that you let everyone know right off the bat that sooner or later members from the same camp will have to fight each other, and there can be no excuses like, "We are gin partners, there is no way we can fight each other." If they get uppity about this, just threaten to return things to how they used to be, which is where they got pampered all day by nurses and got to sleep nineteen hours a day. That will get them back into line.

Before you begin hosting events, it is important to alter the rules from what they are today. The first thing that needs to be addressed is the length of the rounds. Currently, MMA fights consist of five-minute rounds, and it will take both contestants in a geriatric MMA fight that long to hobble out to the center of the cage. To resolve this issue, you can either triple the time of each round or start both combatants in the center of the cage. If you want the contests to be entertaining, I strongly suggest the latter.

The second thing that needs to be addressed is the use of weapons. I'm not talking about guns or knives or anything like that, but rather wheelchairs and oxygen tanks. Obviously, some of the warriors are going to need these devices to simply make it to the ring, and you must decide before the action begins if they will be allowed to use them in combat. For example, will it be allowable to run over your opponent's leg with a wheelchair or bludgeon your opponent with an oxygen tank? Personally, I recommend outlawing any such actions, and handling the foul much like groin kicks or eye gouges are handled today. Give the contestant who got run over or bludgeoned five minutes to recover, and then remove one point from the perpetrator should he prove to be a repeat offender.

Another issue to address is the use of eyeglasses or spectacles. Remove these from the contestants, and it would turn the stare-downs into squint-downs. Personally, I recommend allowing the combatants to wear eyeglasses because not only will it allow them to find their target, but it

WAYS TO KNOW IF YOU ARE A FUCKING FIGHTER

1. You might be a fighter if you have an orthopedic surgeon on speed dial.

2. You might be a fighter if you've ever given a stripper ringworm.

3. If you've ever worn Tapout shorts on a first date, you might be a fighter.

4. You may be a fighter if you play more than nine hours of video games a day.

5. If you take your shirt off at the office, you may be a redneck. If you take your shirts and pants off while at the office, you may be a fighter.

6. If you bleed on a daily basis, you may be a fighter . . . If you bleed on a daily basis and have a tendency to lose limbs, you may be a lion tamer.

7. If you feel comfortable using another man's toothbrush, you might be a fighter.

8. If your favorite thing about a one-night stand is getting to use the chick's body wash, you might be a fighter.

9. If you get into a bar fight in a grocery store, you might be a fighter.

10. If you've ever attempted to pay for a Subway sandwich with an autographed picture of yourself, you may be a fighter.

11. If you use more Icy Hot than deodorant, you might be a fighter.

12. If you've ever said, "He didn't hurt me, I just slipped onto his fist," you may be a fighter.

will also dramatically improve the entertainment value of the match. After all, can you think of a more entertaining display of dominance than the classic Smashing of the Glasses? I certainly can't.

Next you must assess protective gear. In order to keep the event from turning barbaric, the wearing of adult diapers must be allowed. Inform the combatants that they can be worn either under their fighting shorts or in lieu of the traditional trunks—much like sumo wrestling diapers have been worn for centuries.

Another essential piece of protective gear is the groin cup. However, when you are talking about pitting the elderly against one another in combat, this poses a unique problem, as their balls are much longer than younger MMA fighters. We all know that the cup size, thankfully, is not based on the size of one's package, but rather on the actual size of the pubic area itself (but always stick with a medium or large, okay?). But when dealing with the elderly, the container of the cup needs to be extra bulbous in order to effectively hold the elongated testicles. To get an idea of how large, place an orange in a stretched-out tube sock and hold it up by the cuff. You will see what you are up against here. Luckily, the manufacturing of mouthpieces will not be necessary for obvious reasons.

Strength is also something you must consider, as old people do not have a lot of it. Although many of them will be vicious in their attempts, most will be lacking the physical strength to cause any type of damage to their opponent. To remedy this situation, it will be necessary to enlist the participation of what I like to call "the Enhancer." The Enhancer will be a neutral person armed with some type of striking object, say a branch or some type of thick stick. If one opponent is obviously trying to throw another, and it is deemed that the attempt is technically sound, but failing due to a lack of strength, then the Enhancer would proceed to knock the other person over with his stick. Another example would be if a fighter delivered a Thai kick that barely produced any force; in this case the Enhancer would of course administer a sound thwack to the spot where the weak kick had landed. Thus, the Enhancer's entire job will be to upgrade the force of the strikes to a realistic, true fight level.

Once all the rules are in place, the next step is to increase the level of the Spectacle itself. This means that you are going to want it all—the grand fighter entrance, the ring girls, the works! First off, you want to make sure that the fighters are pumped up before heading to the ring. This can be accomplished by turning their hearing aids up to the maximum level, and also making sure that the fighter's entrance song properly represents him. May I suggest some produce a good polka by Lawrence Welk? This will get both the fighter and crowd revved up for sure. To ensure that the fighters make it to the cage before the song ends, I suggest having them ride down to the cage on Rascals. If you paint the rascals with flames or shark teeth, this might actually be pretty cool and entertaining as well.

So as you can see, the concept of MMA for the elderly is really quite exciting when put to paper. And just remember, if you can entertain your herd, they will always follow. If the elderly get bored with MMA for the elderly, you can always introduce them to a new assortment of games. One suggestion would be jousting on Easy Glides. Just get creative and go crazy. The world is your oyster! And to answer your question, no, I don't think it was a waste of time for Erich and me to sit around for hours and figure out the best ways for old people to fight each other.

DE-EVOLUTION

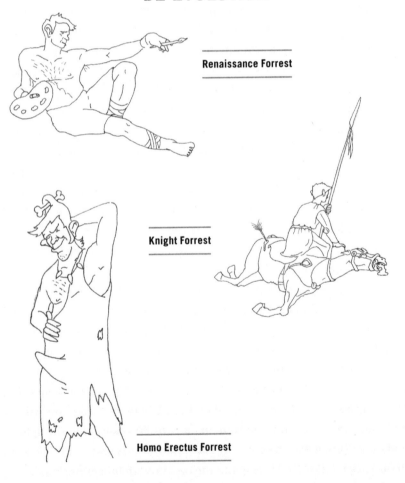

Renaissance Forrest

Knight Forrest

Homo Erectus Forrest

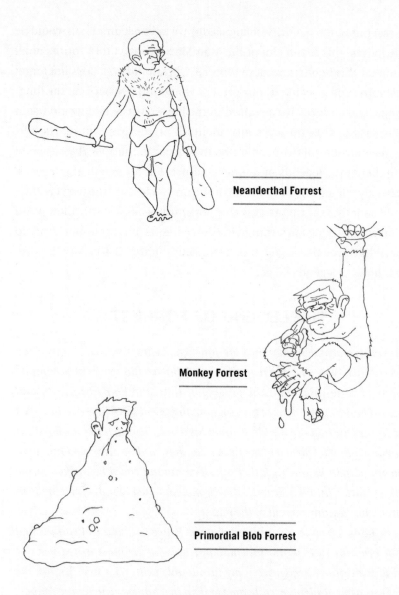

Neanderthal Forrest

Monkey Forrest

Primordial Blob Forrest

There are archaeologists who believe that human civilization has not evolved in a progressive fashion, but rather got knocked back to a Stone Age type of existence numerous times due to apocalyptic events such as the eruption of super-volcanoes and asteroids impacting the surface of the earth. It makes sense if you think about it. If a disaster was severe and it cast the small pockets of human survivors into a desperate struggle for the bare essentials, the majority of knowledge we have accumulated would be lost (why yes, this is the plot of the Mad Max movies. I told you, I got all the info for this book from these films . . . Oh, and *Rambo*. Let's not forget *Rambo*). In such a scenario, our present would quickly become the long-long ago, and children being raised in the barren wasteland would begin writing passages like the one above about our mysterious culture. The personal recollections of the people who lived prior to the apocalypse would end up being the legends of the new culture. For all practical purposes, the apocalyptic survivors would be the future ancients to the next civilization. Personally, I see this as a great opportunity because it will allow me to pass on whatever legacy I want to my descendants. It is my opportunity to immortalize myself as a god, much like Zeus, Jupiter, Osiris, and the like. Here is how my legend will go:

THE LEGEND OF FORREST

My legend is one of death. In the long-long ago, before the Great Hunger and Not Very Much Water, I was a revered general that led the armies of the Empire to many victories. But with the passing of time, the Emperor fell ill, and instead of handing the reins of his kingdom to his evil son Chubaka, he asked me to be the Guardian of his lands upon his death. Through the employment of magic, Chubaka learned of his father's wishes, and he murdered him with his sword of light before his father's final command could be ratified in the People's Court. Chubaka claimed the throne, and I was condemned to die in the arena for the amusement of the masses.

The name given to me in the arena was Bruce Lee, and as I vanquished one foe after the next in mortal combat, I became the most feared warrior in all of the Games. Recognizing my formidable skills as a swordsman, the supreme master, Raden, recruited me to fight in a tournament against supernatural beings that wished ill upon humanity. I fought through a gauntlet of strange fighters with the powers of the Scorpion, the Reptile, and one who could freeze his opponents with a single conjured blast of ice. I called upon the great Force, the fantastical energy that connects all life, and suddenly I was filled with the power of a hundred men. I slew each of the supernatural beings as if they were mere children and the world was, for a time, safe.

I became rich from these conquests, and I enjoyed the spoils of my victories. I continued to spill the blood of many men and dwarves, increasing my hit points daily. But with wealth came great responsibilities. As a member of Wu-Tang Clan, I saw it as my duty to protect the city and its inhabitants from evildoers, and when a crime wave fell upon us, I reacted. Using my vast fortune, I designed never-before-seen weapons, all of which mimicked the vicious fighting nature of the bat. I created a suit that allowed me to glide through the air, a belt equipped with various doodads of destruction, and I traveled from crime scene to crime scene in a black chariot that allowed me to race forward at great speeds across paths of smooth rock.

As my wealth and arrogance grew, I took greater risks. One afternoon I was approached by a stout, shiny-headed man who wished to wager for my beloved "chariot." Thinking that no mortal could defeat me, I agreed to a race. We flew like the wind down a stone path, our machines screaming with power, but alas, the man with the chromelike dome defeated me. Being a man of my honor, I bestowed upon him a pink contract for my beloved chariot, and retreated to the caves of Mordor to grieve. I cast aside all my earthly possessions, all my wealth, even my honor. All I brought with me was a single golden ring, my precious.

When I emerged many years later, it was to a strange and wondrous world. The gears of change had been busy in my absence, and there now existed boxes that could transport images and sounds across great distances. One day the leaders of every country appeared on these boxes, and their message was earnest: beings from another world were descending upon us. They traveled in ships the size of cities, and they had made their intentions clear: the moment they arrived, they would exterminate the entire human race.

I was earth's only hope, but realizing that the Empire had betrayed me by casting me into the arena, they could not ask me to fight for them. Instead, they employed trickery and sent Colonel Sam Trautman, a dear old friend who I had served under in the great war on the planet Avatar. He assured me that I would be under his command, and if I went to battle, I would get what I truly desired, which was for my country to love me as much as I loved it!

Knowing we were outnumbered fifty thousand to one, Trautman and I commandeered an enemy craft, a metallic hawk that flew faster than lightning itself. We took to the sky, but we did not attempt to engage the enemy forces, as we were just one and they were many. Instead, we flew our stolen craft directly into their mother ship, pretending that we were one of their own. It was there that we learned that the bowels of their ships were actually flesh and blood. Instead of driving a stake down into the heart of that ship, which would do little because of its massive size, I released a virus that traveled not just throughout the mother ship, but also throughout all the enemy vessels. In a matter of minutes, I had saved the planet!

But alas, there was not enough time for me to fly my foreign bird away before the enemy ships exploded, so I was forced to travel into a strange device they called the Stargate, and it transported me to a different universe. I was set down on a small desert planet, and the primitive inhabitants mistook me for a god. They showered me with jewels and women, but after many years of basking in these luxuries, I left my tribe of Ewoks and searched the sky far and wide for a passageway back to my homeland. Alas, I found it, another Stargate in all that sky, in all that dark. I gripped destiny's hand, and together we flew through the passageway, and in a matter of moments I once again recognized the stars around me.

But something was amiss. A massive mountain of pure rock was hurtling toward my homeland from the heavens. I knew that if this monolith impacted my world, it would surely destroy it with great floods, earthquakes, volcanic eruptions, and firestorms. The Great Danger lay just below my machine, and so I brought the craft down upon the chaotic surface. A team of my comrades had already arrived on the rock, led by a man named Bruce Willis. They had drilled a deep hole into the core of the object and were preparing to blow it to bits with an explosive device. When the timing device failed to operate, it became clear that one of us had to stay behind and manually detonate the weapon. Someone had to lay down his life for our home world. I told the others to go. Leave me behind and I would carry out this final task. I only asked them to tell my wives that I loved them all.

After my comrades had flown away into the darkness, I pressed the button that would reunite me with my ancestors of yore, including the great warriors Jackie Chan, Chuck Norris, and Dwayne Johnson. The subsequent explosion decimated the rock on which I had chosen to die, but alas, I did not perish. I was hurled into a cloud of rock and debris, and with my godlike strength,

I clung to a small fragment of stone as it spun wildly outward. Once I was clear of the discharge, the ride smoothed and I realized I was heading toward my home planet. I rode that rock down as a returning conqueror, steering it to its destination. I managed to maneuver my horse of stone toward a vast blue ocean, took the deepest breath I've ever taken, and then hit the water. The force of the impact pushed me down hundreds of feet. My world faded to black.

I awoke to find that I had grown webbed feet and gills, and that I was breaking underwater. As my vision cleared, my eyes were met with the strangest sight. A small yellow square sponge and an enormously obese pink starfish were staring at me with wide eyes. Once they realized I was all right, they burst into hysterical laughter and ran away cackling at the top of their lungs.

I had no idea where I was. In fact, it came as quite a surprise when I wandered outside and realized I had been in a dwelling made from a giant, hollowed-out pineapple. At any rate, I seized the opportunity and swam desperately toward the surface hundreds of kilometers above.

I swam for a great many days, and when I finally stood on solid land, my entire country stood before me, and the president himself bestowed upon me the Medal of Valor, our highest honor. I settled in with my wives and my dog, Boba Fett. We've lived in harmony ever since, but I will stand prepared, as I always have, to once again defend my lands, my women, and you, my children of the corn.

EPILOGUE

Most kids don't give death much thought, but around the age of ten or eleven, I became obsessed with it. With a single terrifying dream, I transformed from a happy-go-lucky runt into one terrified son of a bitch. Before you make a judgment call about my manliness, let me give you the details of this nightmare. I was at my biological father's house down by the coast, and somehow I fell off the edge of a pier that stretched out over a sandy beach. Except instead of the pier being seven feet high, it was more than a thousand.

I'd had falling dreams before, and like most people, I would always wake up just prior to impact. Not this time. My body slammed down into the unforgiving surface and I died. I could feel my body broken in fifty places, and assuming that this little accident had really happened, I figured that in a matter of seconds my brain would shut off and my spirit or whatever would head toward a bright light. That's not what happened. I remained utterly lucid. I could feel hundreds of shattered oyster shells digging into my back. I could hear seagulls crying and waves breaking in the distance. I could smell the ocean air. I was just as coherent as I had been before making this great fall, but I was utterly paralyzed. I couldn't move my body, blink, or communicate. For all intents and purposes, I was fucking dead.

I lay there for a great long while, and eventually people came and scooped up my broken body. They carried me away, brought me to a funeral home, and I was placed in a coffin. Next thing I know, I am in the ground, and I could hear dirt being shoveled onto my box, putting me into the ground for all eternity. I tried to scream, "I am still alive!" but no words came out of my mouth. All I could do was lie there and listen to the voices of my family grow more distant.

Despite my being placed underground, there was still light in the coffin. I should have realized that this meant I was dreaming, but I was too terrified by that point. Logic had been shut off and all I had left was my horror. I'm not sure how long I lay there, but pretty quickly there came noises around me. That noise was the maggots burrowing into my rotting flesh, consuming my body. Their numbers grew with each passing minute, and soon I was engulfed, my arms and legs and torso being removed bit by bit.

My life was not the same for a great long while when I awoke from that dream. For a week or more I walked around in a daze, and just when I began to feel that perhaps I could leave it in the past, I had another similar dream. My death was exactly the same—I fell off that skyscraper pier and crashed down into all those oyster shells, but this time, instead of putting me in a coffin and burying me, they loaded me onto the metal shoot of an incinerator. My head had been propped up on something, so I could see down the length of my body. As my feet entered the fire, searing pain shot through me. My entire family stood around me with grim faces, and I tried to scream at them to pull me out of the fire, but just as with the first dream, I couldn't move or make a sound.

When I awoke from that one, I knew there would be no going back to my haphazard, blissful childhood. While other kids thought about the upcoming weekend and all the fun stuff they had planned, I thought about death. No matter where I was or what I was doing, anytime my mind drifted, I would think, "Forrest, you are going to die, and you know exactly what will happen. Nothing. You will be stuck in a body you can't use, and maggots will eat you. You will see and feel every horrible thing to come." I got paranoid about everything, especially getting onto the school bus. I would break out in sweat every time I had to climb those stairs because I was certain that the bus would crash and I would die. At night, instead of passing out the instant I hit the bed like normal, I would just lie there in a twilight sleep, reliving those terrible dreams over and over. And when I did fall asleep, I always woke up scared.

For seven or eight months, I lived in a constant state of fear. In my first book, *Got Fight?*, I told a story about that time in my life. I was in a locker room before basketball practice, and this jock who had made it his life's purpose to fuck with me began making fun of my attire. I guess he thought my shirt was too tight and my shorts too short. He had been on my ass for a while, and realizing that his mother had recently died, I said, "Does it make you feel better, picking on me? Does it take your mind off the fact that the maggots are eating your mother right now?" I'm sure a lot of people thought I was the asshole of the century for saying something like that, but that's where my mind was at this time in my life. I thought about maggots all day and all night, and about the fact that it was only a matter of time until I heard them eating my flesh.

The horror became so unbearable, I went searching for answers. I was in Catholic school at the time, so I talked to the priests. In fact, my desperation had reached such extreme levels, I thought about becoming a priest. I would do anything it took to avoid the terror I had experienced in my nightmares. The priests I tried gave me the heaven run-around as usual, but nothing they said was real or tangible. Those fucking nightmares were more real that heaven, and so I didn't buy into anything they said. I was stuck with my misery.

There was a time there when I thought that ending up in a loony bin might be a very real possibility for me, but then one night while I was rehashing the nightmare over and over, it took a different turn. Just as all the other times, I was lying in a coffin and could hear the maggots eating my body, but strangely the terror had left. Instead of panicking at the thought of my decomposition, I focused on the maggots, and I could feel my energy or life force or whatnot inside of them. I felt my energy burrowing through the ground, and then a bird scooped that energy up. Before long, I could feel myself take the form of a muscle in a bird's wing. I was soaring through the skies, and it felt wonderful. At the same time, I could feel another part of my (I want to say "chi," but that is lame) energy being absorbed into the roots of a tree. In a matter of just a few hours, as I was lying there in bed, the terror left me. Just like in *The Lion King*, I came to terms with the great cycle of life. I didn't see a bunch of dancing and singing wild animals, and Simba never made an appearance, but I was over-fucking-joyed, to say the least.

I don't want to say that I accepted death, because I didn't and still haven't. I realize that one day my life will have run its course and I'll die, and end up as the muscle in a bird's wing. Although I have always liked muscles and want to experience the exhilaration of flight, I want to delay this day as long as possible. Deep down in my heart, I am still that eleven-year-old kid sitting in the darkness of his room, listening to Nine Inch Nails and burning himself with a lighter. I think about death more often than I should, but the results are much more positive than they once were. The idea of death makes me thankful that I am alive right now, allows me to enjoy each day, and makes me realize that I have to do whatever I can to hang on to life.

The downside is that when you focus on trying to stay alive, it causes you to take a much harder look around you and you see the possible dangers. And when I look around me these days, what I see looks bleak. Personally, I see a giant neon sign blaring in the sky, and its message is very simple: people have gone too far. Just like every person's life runs its course, so does every society. When a forest gets old, it develops a massive amount of undergrowth that threatens all the life within it. To keep the forest from withering and dying, Mother Nature sends in our happy friend fire, which wipes out the excess brush and undergrowth, puts nutrients back into the soil, and allows the forest to start the life process over again. But when you stop Mother Nature from doing her job and beat back all the flames, then, when another fire eventually comes, it is catastrophic.

It wipes out not only the underbrush, but also the entire forest, leaving nothing but a charred moonscape.

I don't know how close our society is to having run its course, but to me it looks like there is a lot of fucking underbrush choking the life out of us. Eventually there will be a correction; a massive reset button will be pushed. It's just a matter of time. When you get to the point where there are too many people using too much of our resources, it puts a burden on the earth, and good old Mother Nature is going to implement a correction. We can beat back the flames all we want, but eventually that fire is going to find its way through our meager blockades and cleanse the surface of the earth. With my mind focusing so heavily on death, it makes me think about that fateful day, and I personally want to be one of the ones who survive, which is the reason I wrote this book. I want to feel what it is like to be the muscle in the wing of a bird, but not just yet. I want to be a part of a tree rustling in the wind . . . just not yet.

APPENDIX

Believe it or not, I actually read quite a few books, and one of my favorites is Stephen King's *On Writing*, which teaches you how to write books good . . . or is it write books *well*? In either case, with only two books under my belt, I am not so ostentatious to think that I could teach you how to write a book. I can, however, give you an idea of how to sell a book concept. To illustrate this, I have included the proposal we sent to HarperCollins to get this book picked up. If you're not a quazi-celebrity and your goal is to get a publisher to give you actual money (personally, I requested them to deliver the cash in actual sacks with dollar signs printed on the front of them), I suggest you select your words more carefully, make the proposal make sense, and pretend you actually know something about the subject you are writing on, but hopefully this will give you a good idea of where to start.

P.S. You should watch *Where the Buffalo Roam*—it made me want to be a writer of words.

FORREST GRIFFIN'S SURVIVAL GUIDE TO THE APOCALYPSE

Forrest Griffin and Erich Krauss

Authors of the *New York Times* Bestselling *Got Fight?*
(currently No. 5 on Advice, How-to, and Misc.)

" . . . and that's one of the nights when I learned that if you're going to pay a stripper to punch you in the face, you'd better make sure that she's not wearing any large, gaudy rings."

—FORREST GRIFFIN

"Everyone should carry a gun, especially if you have a small penis like me. The second amendment was not designed to protect yourself. It was written—and I read this in my NRA magazine, so you know it's not biased—to protect us from the Government. They are crazy and oppressive and will one day lead us into the apocalypse."

—FORREST GRIFFIN

Why is Forrest Griffin, the former Light Heavyweight Champion of the Ultimate Fighting Championship (UFC) and *New York Times* bestselling author of *Got Fight? The 50 Zen Principles of Hand-to-Face Combat*, writing a book on how to survive the apocalypse? Seriously, why the hell not? Most children dream about a sparkly world filled with unicorns and stardust where everyone is kind and friendly to each other. Some of those children even grow up to write terrible books about magic and wizards and little boys named Henry (or is it Harry? Fuck, I always forget that shit . . . I know I just jumped from third person to first person, but I figured that you, as an editor, would put two and two together. If you didn't, put down my proposal now and back away from it slowly. You are mentally challenged, and under no condition will you be allowed to publish *my* book.)

Fortunately, Forrest did not fantasize about little boys named Henry. While getting his face rearranged by bullies in school, he dreamed about the near-extinction of mankind and all of the fantastic repercussions that come with it. Think about it: with grooming and personal hygiene no longer a prerequisite to social acceptance, you can let your mutton-chops grow and live out your secret sexually twisted fantasy of becoming Wolverine, which in turn would allow you to dry hump a broad assortment of four-legged creatures with impunity. You could kill squirrels with your bare hands, practice throwing knives all day, and never have to say "excuse me" after farting.

But most important, you could drive down the freeway without worrying that a 125-pound douche bag will somehow grow balls of steel and cut you off. And if one of the four remaining 125-pound douche bags should cut you off, there would be no one stopping you from pulling out one of the six forty-five caliber handguns protruding from your home-made utility belt and dispensing some vigilante justice. Once the douche bag is good and dead, you could strip naked, paint yourself in his blood, and go sprinting down the road singing any one of Madonna's top hits. Most important, you wouldn't be judged or arrested for any of these actions, which is what currently tends to happen. (Note to Editor: My agent said that the intro had to be dramatic, a real ball-grabber. How am I doing?)

Sure, there might be other authors who claim to be able to write a perfect apocalyptic survival guide, but none of them are destined to be a postapocalyptic leader. This is not a joke—it has already been written. When Forrest was fifteen, his mother informed him that while he was in the womb, she had crazy dreams about him walking over a barren wasteland of a thousand corpses, followed by a group of lost souls. She truly believed that this meant he would lead mankind into a new age. Of course, she told him this after the first Terminator movie had come out, which led him to believe that his mother had trouble deciphering between "dreams" and the "movie she had just seen."

He proposed his doubt, but she held fast. (Note to Editor: This actually really pissed me off. I was like, "Mom, why do you have me taking piano lessons then? Why not have me learning something more valuable, like how to be a ninja or a Jedi warrior?" And it wasn't like I was even good at the piano. The first day, my teacher said, "I can't rightly take your money because I know for a fact that you will never play the piano." Maybe my mom kept me going because it was free, I don't know . . . but you could imagine how humiliating this was for the future post-apocalyptic leader.)

Unlike John Connor in the Terminator movies, Forrest did not depend on his mother to teach him how to traverse a soiled planet. To prepare himself physically, he joined the secret society of the Webelos (if you read my last *New York Times* bestseller, then you know I was quickly ejected from this survivalist society for chucking a can of soda pop at my scout master's head, but we will leave this fact out of this book so that the reader thinks I was a super-badass boy scout).

To make himself mentally tough, he purposely got rejected by every hot girl in high school and let everyone, including smaller children, severely pummel his face on a regular basis. To train his skin to handle the darkness of a nuclear winter, he spent all his free time in his bedroom with the lights out, listening to Nine Inch Nails and softly weeping to himself.

When he grew into a man, his mother's words were not forgotten. He became a police officer and learned how to shoot to kill. And to ready himself for the inevitable day when all the ammunition has been exhausted on roaming bands of marauders, he became a professional fighter and learned how to kill with his mitts. (I know what you're thinking—*really, you became a cop and a fighter solely because you wanted to prepare yourself for the apocalypse?* If it's going to help sell this book for half a million bucks, then yes, it's a hundred percent true.)

To complete his training, he teamed up with author Erich Krauss, a survival expert who spent ten years of his life living in the Amazon rainforest and other godforsaken terrain. (Seriously, this guy is fucking crazy. He sleeps in a closet, pisses into an old milk jug, and lulls himself to sleep with visions of the downfall of man. I was kidding about a lot of the other stuff, but I'm being serious about this . . . Krauss is nuts; I was also being serious about the half a million bucks.)

Having spent the last four months riling up each other in the deserts outside of Las Vegas (really, it was more like a couple of hours a week, but who's counting?), they have completed the outline to their manifesto—*Forrest Griffin's Survival Guide to the Apocalypse.* In its pages you will learn to prepare yourself pre-apocalypse, such as constructing your getaway bag, which should include an assortment of weapons to help you get out of the city, as well as an assortment of sexual toys that will help you kill time once you're sitting in the middle of the fucking desert. It will teach you how to handle the various types of apocalypses, including viral, nuclear, economic, and natural disaster. It will inform you on how to do all sorts of really smart survival-type thingies.

And did I mention zombies? Yeah, it will have all sorts of methods for killing zombies with your hands. And for the readers who think the death of 99.9 percent of all people is somehow a bad thing, it will look at the upside of living in a barren wasteland, such as being able to leave your most humiliating stories behind you. Forrest will reveal his most traumatic moments, including the time he had sex with a post op. In case you are not hip with the lingo kids, a post op is a man who has had his junk removed, his Adam's apple shaven down, the whole dealeo. If he didn't believe that the apocalypse was coming and all you fuckers would die, would he admit that? I think not. (Public Service Announcement: Be aware of post ops—some can pass as women for two or three nights of sexual intercourse before you realize something is amiss.)

If you still doubt Forrest's future role as the Messiah of all mankind, he only has two words for you—ketchup packets. Even before he learned of his mother's visions, he had a hoarding mentality and would constantly steal ketchup packets. If you're smart, then you instinctively know that hoarders are survivors. Just look at squirrels—they hoard everything, and they've been around longer than sharks (not sure if that is true—might want to get your fact checker to look that shit up).

For now, all you need to know is that when the world ends, Forrest will be King, so bow down, bitches. Blow off one lesson as stupid or idiotic, and you could end up as a whore to a leather-clad motorcycle gang that travels the desert looking for oil. Seriously, Forrest is going to fill that empty head of yours with some knowledge. And let me tell you, he's got some knowledge to spill. That summer in the Webelos, he didn't spend all his time jacking off. He picked up some *skills*. There is no escaping the coming of the end. When that day arrives, tucking that small pecker of yours between your legs and clicking your heels together won't bring back your loved ones or all your shiny toys. You're in the wasteland, motherfucker, so become a soldier in Forrest's legion and pillage your way into the new age. This is Forrest Griffin's *Survival Guide to the Apocalypse*.

NOTE TO READER

If you are standing in the bookstore, reading the last chapter in an attempt to save a whole bunch of time and some money, please stop reading immediately and go to the checkout line. I say this because I want you to actually buy my book so I get that $38 in royalty money.

PSS. Seriously dude, close the book and go buy it!

PSSS. I'm standing right behind you, and I'm starting to get pretty fucking pissed off. If you read another word without shelling out some cash, I am going to hurt you.

PSSSS. I'm really sorry about getting so harsh before. Totally uncalled for, and I don't blame you if you dislike me now. But I really want you to like me, and I think you buying this book will really help my goal. I am begging you, brother. Please!

PSSSS. I really don't care if you buy this book or not. I hate everyone, my writing sucks, this book sucks, I don't have any friends. I'm going home to sleep for two days.

PSSSSS. I just woke up and I feel much better. Mood swings, you know. Did you buy this book yet?

CARL
LLEWELLYN WESCHCKE
PIONEER AND PUBLISHER OF BODY, MIND & SPIRIT

About the Author

Melanie Marquis is a lifelong practitioner of magick, founder of the United Witches global coven, and organizer of Denver Pagans. She has written for the American Tarot Association, Llewellyn's almanacs and datebooks, and national and international Pagan publications including *Circle* and *Pentacle* magazines. Her books include *The Witch's Bag of Tricks, A Witch's World of Magick, Beltane,* and *Lughnasadh.* She is the coauthor of *Witchy Mama* and the creator of *Modern Spellcaster's Tarot.* She lives in Colorado.

CARL
LLEWELLYN WESCHCKE
PIONEER AND PUBLISHER OF BODY, MIND & SPIRIT

THE MAGICKAL LIFE OF THE MAN BEHIND
LLEWELLYN PUBLICATIONS

Melanie Marquis

Llewellyn Publications
WOODBURY, MINNESOTA

FIRST EDITION
First Printing, 2018

Book design by Rebecca Zins
Cover design by Kevin R. Brown

Text set in Bookman Old Style

Llewellyn Publications is a registered trademark of Llewellyn Worldwide Ltd.

Library of Congress Cataloging-in-Publication Data (pending)
ISBN 978-0-7387-5327-0

Llewellyn Publications
A Division of Llewellyn Worldwide Ltd.
2143 Wooddale Drive
Woodbury, MN 55125-2989

www.llewellyn.com

Printed in the United States of America

This book is dedicated to the past, present, and future generations of the Weschcke family and to the extended Llewellyn family that includes within its wide embrace employees, friends, authors, artists, printers, retailers, distributors, visionaries, seekers, and readers just like you who know it's always possible to learn something new.

Photo Credits

Window display for drugstore advertising Adlerika, a product manufactured in St. Paul. Circa 1930. Credit: Minnesota Historical Society.

NAACP members picketing outside Woolworth's for integrated lunch counters, St. Paul. 4/2/1960. Photographer: St. Paul Dispatch-Pioneer Press. Credit: Minnesota Historical Society.

Spread from *American Cinematographer* magazine, December 1973 issue, pp. 1570-1, "Filming *Isis* Among the Witches." Used with permission.

Photograph of Carl in front of Summit Avenue mansion from *Twin Citian* magazine, December 1966 issue, p. 102, "476 Summit Avenue." Used with permission.

Carl Weschcke's senior portrait and accompanying artwork from St. Paul Academy and Summit School yearbook, Saint Paul Academy Review (SPAR), 1948. Used with permission.

Every effort has been made on the part of the publisher to identify photographers and subjects, but due to the age and frequent lack of written documentation, this was not always possible.

Acknowledgments

The creation of this book would not have been possible without the combined help and efforts of the many people who contributed time, energy, and love toward this project. I would like to thank everyone who has contributed to this book by sharing memories and information that I would not have been able to include otherwise.

My biggest thanks go to Sandra Weschcke and Gabe Weschcke, for without your welcome and your willingness, this book could never have been. Researching for this book was a once in a lifetime opportunity for which I will be forever grateful.

I wish also to express my deepest gratitude to my editor extraordinaire Elysia Gallo, for help with this project that has gone far above and beyond the ordinary call of duty.

A special thanks also to Jean-Louis de Biasi for your information on the Ordo Aurum Solis, to Michael Night Sky for your encouragement and contributions, to Guy V. Frost for sharing your research on Llewellyn George and Ida H. Fletcher, and to Stephen Brewster of Manchester for sharing your and Carl's correspondences and for your help in piecing together a little more of the magickal mysteries that were Carl's life.

I am also grateful for my family and friends, who continue to love me even when I'm writing constantly.

And I am also grateful for you, for picking up this book and choosing to share in the secret of how Carl Llewellyn Weschcke became so much more.

Contents

The Llewellyn Vision Statement:

To be the world's leading provider of works for personal growth and the transformation of body, mind, and spirit.

The Llewellyn Mission Statement:

To serve the trade and consumers worldwide with options and tools for exploring new worlds of mind and spirit, thereby aiding in the quests of expanded human potential, spiritual consciousness, and planetary awareness.

The Magic of Carl

The Twin Cities of Minneapolis/St. Paul is a surprisingly large hub for publishing. Having been in this business since the early 1980s, I knew about Llewellyn Worldwide; however, I knew very little about Carl Weschcke.

Carl was looking to transition away from some of his daily responsibilities and free up time to write. I would find out later this was his real passion. We hit it off pretty well when I joined the company in late autumn of 2005. At that time Carl was still coming into the office every day—in a suit, I might add—and we met regularly to talk about subjects, authors, book projects, and more. I quickly learned that Carl was the living persona of everything that Llewellyn did. He knew about every subject the company published, and not just a little bit. Carl was well-versed in everything from the rune alphabet to the Golden Dawn and Wicca to all forms of divination. The subject he loved the most was astrology, and he talked about that more than any other. I learned over time that he had corresponded with Gerald Gardner and considered Israel Regardie a personal friend. It's safe to say that Carl had probably forgotten more about these subjects than most of us will ever learn.

As I said, astrology was his favorite subject. That was the base for the origin of Llewellyn back in 1901 when Llewellyn George published his first astrology book. Carl took great pride in the fact that books like the *A to Z Horoscope Maker* and the *Moon Sign Book* were still in print. The twelve-book astrology series he created with Noel Tyl was a big success in its day and a milestone he remembered fondly.

The *Moon Sign Book* and the other almanacs were hot buttons for Carl. Each year when it came time to create the new editions, everyone was inundated with messages from Carl. He was a fountain of ideas for content and marketing for each title, and everyone in editorial, marketing, and sales heard from him.

He would dissect every bit of copy from the catalogs to the internet to the back covers of the books. Carl did not invent the infomercial, but he understood the concepts very well. Sell every benefit and take as much space as you need. Unquestionably, he was a natural-born marketer. Whether it be titles, covers, artwork, or copy, there wasn't a thing he didn't have an opinion on. He wasn't just casting stones. He knew the subjects and the markets and had done the work. When he bought Llewellyn in 1960 he did all the work: editor, designer, typesetter, marketing, salesman. In the process he created many of the markets that exist today.

Over time Carl stopped coming into the office in favor of working from his home office a few minutes away. As a prolific writer, there would be dozens and dozens of emails from him every day. All of his emails had a unique date system in the subject line so that he could save and reference every communication. He was a Virgo, after all.

Aside from the daily email exchanges, I would go to his house every Wednesday for lunch. We would discuss a host of things, from book titles and topics to authors and ideas to cultivate. There were times he would have stacks of books ready to discuss or a manuscript all marked up that he wanted us to publish. I never knew what to expect. Sometimes he wanted to discuss current world events, politics, or even currency fluctuations. Always fun, always interesting, always educational.

Sandra was forever trying to keep Carl on a diet. She would prepare him a healthy sandwich and a pickle. He would chase it with a diet cherry Pepsi. Of course, Carl being Carl, he would occasionally eschew the prepared lunch and send me a note asking to pick up a pizza. In order to stay out of the doghouse, he was careful to save some slices for Sandra to have for dinner.

When I say these lunches were educational, I do not necessarily mean in the didactic sense. Sure, Carl was always interested in the practical of how things worked. He would certainly teach things that I would need to know. It's not everyone that knows Futhark and Futhorc. But it was Carl's take on how things worked in the universe that sticks with me. Things do not just happen. You put a thought out to the universe or you put energy into a subject or idea through conversation and it will eventually come back around. For example, I cannot count how many conversations we would have about an author we had not heard from, or hoped to hear from, and not long after they would turn up. Or a book subject that we just could not find anyone to write—shortly thereafter it would present itself, and you had nothing else to do but say *aha!*

Carl did many things in his life. He was a pioneer in this field. He was a fearless publisher who arguably created the New Age market, perhaps not as the sole creator, but he had a significant hand in it. To me, his greatest strength was his belief in potential. Carl always saw the potential in everything. Whether it be a manuscript, a market, or an author, he could see what it could be at its very best.

When we had a manuscript on a subject that we were keen to publish but the author was having difficulty following our direction, some of us would suggest scrapping it and moving on. Carl could see what the book could be or the benefit it could be to the readers, and he would push for it. He never did it in an angry or fist-pounding-the-table way. He did it through words—specifically conversations and debates. He loved to debate on a topic he believed in, and he would never, ever back down if he really wanted it (Virgo).

In his books he wrote a lot about the power of the mind—the subconscious mind, dreams, meditation, and how all these things could lead a person to become their greatest possible self. Literally thousands of pages on the topic because he believed in this potential for everyone.

That was the magic of Carl.

—Bill Krause

Introduction

his is a book about more than Carl Llewellyn Weschcke. Pioneer and publisher in the New Age of body, mind, and spirit for over half a century, Carl was always emphasizing, encouraging, and urging through his words, books, and actions to "become more than you are!" Unlike so many of us who know all kinds of really wise stuff but are prone to coming up a little short in terms of putting those principles into everyday practice, Carl was a person who actually lived up to his own advice. I wouldn't say he completed his quest—for I believe his work and legacy will continue to increase its impact, not to mention the fact that he would have much preferred to live to be 120—but without a doubt, I would say that he succeeded in his quest. It can truly be said that Carl Llewellyn Weschcke became more, much more. For it is impossible to tell his story and the story of the modern rebirth and expansion of interest in occult sciences, witchcraft, Paganism, and the New Age without the stories being intrinsically intertwined.

When Carl first came on the scene as a book publisher in the early sixties, the occult was very much occult, or hidden. At worst, it was demonized or sensationalized in magazines and on TV, and at best it was hidden away in the darkest shadows, something that wasn't typically mentioned unless you wanted to become the topic of the next Sunday sermon or have the neighborhood children avoid your house like the plague come Halloween. Magickal groups and occult societies existed, of course, as they always have, but they were generally hidden, closed off to outsiders, and in short supply. It was difficult for the average seeker to find others of like mind with whom they could learn and practice. Independent study was off the table for most people, as quality occult books were rare and virtually impossible to obtain without investing a great deal of time and money, particularly in the United States. The majority of occult books in circulation were out-of-print "classics" from British publishers and authors who had issued the books decades previously and not again since.

The occult books that did manage to make it into the hands of American readers were often impractical, focusing mostly on abstract spiritual concepts and theories rather than hands-on, user-friendly applications. It was historically general practice amongst many occult and esoteric writers to keep any significantly valuable mystical insights or genuine practices well hidden amidst a sea of overall nonsense, contradiction, and ambiguity, carefully constructed to confuse and frustrate all but the most determined and adept of seekers.

Carl was a different sort of occultist: he felt that anyone with an interest should be invited to the party. He was very passionate in his belief that magick and occult knowledge should be brought into the light, made widely available and accessible to all who wanted it.

He succeeded in doing exactly that. With the books Carl published, the independent study of occult topics such as clairvoyance, astral projection, ritual magick, and witchcraft became not only possible for the average person, but suddenly convenient. Easy to find, affordable, and covering an enormous range of varied subject matter, Llewellyn books helped to create a culture in which solitary magickal practice and independent occult learning could flourish.

It didn't happen overnight, and it certainly didn't happen without a lot of hard work, careful thinking, focused effort, tenacity, and good old-fashioned luck. In this book you'll discover exactly how Carl managed to do what he did, transforming a small mail-order publishing business with only a handful of astrological titles into a thriving worldwide company that has sold millions of books and remains the largest independent New Age and occult book publisher in the world.

There was no blueprint for Carl to follow, no mold or model of a successful occult book publisher in America that he could mimic and improve upon. With vision, love, intuition, imagination, intelligence, business sense, and a working understanding of predictive astrology to guide him, Carl did his best to find his way, and where there wasn't a way, he created a new one, learning from his missteps and triumphs as he went along. He developed new publishing practices and marketing strategies that would forever leave their mark on the book industry while at the same time significantly alter the landscape of magickal practice in America.

Carl's love for learning and mysticism inspired him, and his belief that anyone who wanted to increase their potential had a fundamental right to do so compelled him forward. Through Llewellyn Publications, Carl introduced a new generation of readers to the works of Aleister Crowley and Dion Fortune. He helped bring into the public eye the works of Ophiel, an outspoken innovator and advocate for results-based, practical occultism. He published the works of Raymond Buckland and Lady Sheba, who were among the first witches to make themselves and their previously secret rites and practices publicly known in America. He helped popularize the works of the Golden Dawn and bring to magickal seekers everywhere the methods of the Secret Order G.B.G., the Ordo Aurum Solis, and many other groups and traditions. Not only did Carl bring these magickal technologies and spiritual philosophies to new audiences, in many cases he worked tirelessly to *create* those audiences, offering frequent opportunities for people to engage with the subject matter and with each other, to come together and become involved in ways that provided tangible benefits that were bound to be contagious.

It's impossible to measure exactly how deep or far-reaching the impact that Llewellyn Publications and Carl himself have had on the development of magick in America and arguably around the world. Countless individuals have discovered new abilities of the mind and spirit thanks to a Llewellyn book. Innumerable souls who felt lost and alone have found hope and discovered they are not alone thanks to a Llewellyn book. Some of today's most well-known magickal traditions, rituals, rites, and techniques were pulled out of the shadows and put back into working practice on the pages of a Llewellyn book. Many of today's most exceptional and widely respected magickal teachers, authors, coven leaders, Pagan group founders, and elders took their first steps down their spiritual paths after getting their hands on a Llewellyn book. The prominence and success of Llewellyn has catalyzed thousands upon thousands of witches, magicians, astrologers, fortunetellers, and other alternative occult thinkers out of the woodwork and into the dynamic stream of thriving subcultures, where we can more openly and easily discover new techniques and philosophies, exchange ideas, learn from one another, and grow.

Now this is not to say that this all might not have happened on its own without Carl; in fact, I think he'd be the first to say that it was not his doing, and you'll indeed read his own words to that effect within these pages. But the way it happened certainly did have a lot to do with Carl. Llewellyn was (and is) a driving force in a movement of revolutionary spirituality and evolutionary thinking that is larger than all of us, that is more than all of us; Llewellyn provided (and continues to provide) an ever-growing audience of interested seekers with the materials and information needed to study and master a vast variety of New Age sciences, magickal techniques, spiritual philosophies, Pagan traditions, and occult disciplines independently—no guru or elitist magickal society memberships required.

The more I got to know Carl, the more I realized just how large a role he played in—well, all of it. Throughout his life, he seemed to always be "bringing it," doing his best to inspire, encourage, and spur into action the mechanisms of human evolution that he believed in with all his heart and soul. Not just in his publishing business or through the books he wrote, but also in his day-to-day interactions, Carl had a way of empowering those around him by making them aware of the power that was already residing within themselves. He had a gift for being able to see a person's potential even if they didn't yet realize it themselves, and if he could find a way to help the person become more aware and achieve that potential, he did all he could to make it happen.

I can't help but think of Carl like the wizard behind the curtain, *Wizard of Oz*-style but with a keen self-awareness and command of his own magickal abilities that Dorothy's wizard was initially lacking. Carl was happy behind the curtain. He didn't care about being admired or getting all the credit for his innovations and orchestrations. He never sought any accolades, and on more than one occasion he graciously allowed (or lovingly prodded) others into the spotlight to take credit that was his own rightful due. Though he found himself in it plenty, Carl never really enjoyed the spotlight. His only interest in it was as a means to shine light on the fact that we all have the responsibility and the ability to become more than we are, as he dedicated his life to helping us be.

My wish for this book—which I believe to be Carl's wish, too—is that the previously untold stories, behind-the-scenes perspectives, and never-before-published gems of wisdom that you will find on these pages will inspire you to become more than you are, too!

This is a book about Carl and the light that he became.

Chapter 1

Early Life and Family Ties

Born on September 10, 1930, into a prominent family of Roman Catholics in Saint Paul, Minnesota, Carl Llewellyn Weschcke may seem on the surface an unlikely candidate to become a leading pioneer in New Age and occult publishing, but that's exactly what he did. Like most "normal" boys, Carl grew up doing "normal" things—collecting rocks and stamps, searching for bugs, and exploring the great outdoors. He attended a private prep school for boys and even played sports on the school's team. Carl enjoyed a very typical, very traditional Minnesota upbringing. It just so happened that the Weschcke family had mystical, spiritual, pioneering roots that ran deep.

Carl was the son of two native Minnesotans, Magdalene Tippel Weschcke and Carl Weschcke, whom he was named after. The Weschckes married in 1916 and had four children: Carlola, Dolores, Carl, and Ernest. The couple enjoyed a mutual interest in telepathy, which they practiced while they were dating and later shared with their children, along with discussions of reincarnation, psychic abilities, and meditation.

The Weschckes were never pushy about their beliefs, however. Individuality was accepted, respected, and celebrated, and the children were encouraged to think for themselves and be exactly who they were meant to be. Carl's parents nurtured his philosophical side, and with them he would often discuss his ideas about spirituality as well as practice feats of psychic communication.

However unusual their beliefs, the Weschckes were still a very traditional family in many ways. Magdalene was an extremely dedicated and loving mother, always striving to be thoughtful, focused, and engaged in the care and growth of her children. She was a strong, intelligent, resilient, and selfless woman, putting her family first in everything she did. A talented cook, she often prepared multiple meals to accommodate the varied dietary requests of her vegetarian husband and her children, all of whom ate meat except for Carl, who preferred to share his dad's vegetarian cuisine.

Magdalene's children were her greatest joy, and just as she was devoted to them, so too were they devoted to her. While Carl's mom was arguably a textbook example of what was considered at the time to be the "perfect" housewife, Carl's dad was also very traditional in many ways. He believed in providing for his family and protecting them, and he was willing to do whatever was needed to ensure that his duties were met. In fact, when Carl was only a toddler, a burglar broke into the Weschcke home and confronted Carl's mother, who pleaded for mercy as she shielded her young children. Carl's dad heard her cries and grabbed his gun, sending the burglar stumbling on his way to the local hospital with a pistol shot to the groin.[1] The burglar turned out to be an escaped felon and murderer on the run who had conned his way into the Saint Paul social scene.[2]

---

1   *Minneapolis Star,* "Think Patient Home Prowler."

2   *Star Tribune,* "Deputies Trail Society Bandit."

Carl's dad worked hard to give his family all that they needed, even if it meant working hard at things that weren't exactly thrilling. He found he was a success in business, following in his own father's footsteps to work as an executive in the family pharmaceutical company. He was good at it, and it provided a steady income for the most part, but his deepest passions and interests were decidedly elsewhere.

A naturalist and an enthusiastic horticulturalist, Carl's dad had a love of nature and a curiosity about the ins and outs of plant growing that were insatiable. At only fifteen years of age, he began experimenting with nut growing on the grounds of his family home in Saint Paul, preparing a plot and creating his own miniature backyard orchard of sorts. It was an idea borne of both practicality and entrepreneurship. Explaining how his interest in nut growing was first captured by his fondness for black walnuts, butternuts, and hickories, Carl's dad wrote:

> Because I liked eating these nuts, I thought I would try to grow some for my own consumption and so avoid having to depend on a grocer's occasional supply of those shipped in, always a little stale. Raising nuts appealed to me economically too, since obviously trees would need little care, and after they had begun to bear would supply nuts that could be sold at interesting prices.[3]

The prices that could be fetched from a good nut crop did indeed prove to be interesting, and as the years went by, Carl's dad's passion for nut growing only expanded. He decided to purchase several hundred acres of mixed farmland and wild woods near River Falls, Wisconsin, on which grew a variety of native hazelnut trees so that he would have more space and opportunity to further his nut-growing experiments. The "Hazel Hills" farm was born, and it was here that young Carl spent his summers running through the woods in search of bugs, rocks, fossils, and new adventures.

---

3   Weschcke, *Growing Nuts in the North*, 7.

There wasn't very much obvious potential to the property when Carl's dad first acquired it. Many areas were covered by a tangled mass of overgrowth, and a vast amount of basic landscaping needed to be done right from the start. There wasn't even a house on the property, so Carl's dad decided to build one. The Weschckes retained their house in Saint Paul so that the children could attend school in the city, but for quite some time Carl's dad would spend his weekends and any other free days he could find at Hazel Hills, building with his own hands piece by piece a beautiful log cabin that would become the family's summer retreat. Whenever they could manage it, Carl's mother would bring the children to Hazel Hills so that the family could all be together while Carl's father worked tirelessly to build the new home.

Before the main house was complete, the Weschckes made do with a small makeshift metal dwelling that Carl's dad had quickly put together to provide for only the bare basics of shelter while the more permanent home was being constructed. Devoid of the luxuries of electricity, plumbing, or even running water, the temporary housing wasn't much more than a shack, really, but it was adequate. Over time, the little metal house came to be known affectionately among the family as the "Tin House."

The Weschckes may have had to rough it a bit in the cramped quarters of the Tin House, but they were a resourceful, close-knit bunch, and they managed just fine. Carl's older sister Dolores recalled warm memories of the times spent there, their dad telling stories and singing songs to them all before bedtime. He loved to make the family laugh and would often perform his tunes under the stage name of "Carlos," the mysterious, destined-to-be-world-famous singer that only the Weschckes had heard of.

It wasn't very long before the permanent house was complete, which proved to be infinitely more comfortable and impressive than the tiny Tin House. Carl's dad had brought in enormous pine logs from northern Wisconsin that had to be cut and treated onsite. He had laid the foundation from native stone rock and fitted the giant logs together one by one. He carefully crafted the door handles, hinges, and locks from wrought iron and did all the plumbing and electrical work himself. Electricity wasn't yet available in the area through a public utility, but Carl's dad was quite the inventor, so he found a way. He built his own wind generator, a water turbine, and a steam engine that he had connected to a bank of batteries, and succeeded in being one of the first in the area to have a home that was fully equipped with electricity.

The home Carl's dad had built for his family was well above and beyond what most people would describe as a log cabin, but that is what he called it nonetheless. The house was large and spacious, and Carl's dad had put in a swimming pool, tennis courts, and riding stables to encourage his family to stay active and enjoy activities in the great outdoors. There was even an artificial pond stocked with fish so that the children could enjoy fishing during their summer stays at the farm, as well as a herd of goats that provided milk for the children to drink. Though it had taken a tremendous amount of effort and patience to get it to that point, Hazel Hills was an elaborate and beautiful property.

Carl's dad loved experimenting with the trees on the farm, and he soon created several new hybrid tree species that eventually spread throughout Wisconsin, Minnesota, and beyond. Weschcke hickories and Weschcke butternuts were among the most successful, as was the "hazilbert," created from two different varieties of hazelnuts: the American hazel (*Corylus Americana*) and the European filbert (*Corylus avellana*). The resulting Euro-American hybrids Carl's dad grew were hardier than the ordinary American hazelnut trees that predominated the area. They were better suited to the cool climate and were able to produce more bountiful nut crops with nuts that were nearly twice the size of a typical American hazelnut. The Weschcke hazilberts had greater disease resistance, too, which made for a more stable and reliable nut crop.[4]

---

4   "History of Hazelnuts in the Midwest," MidwestHazelnuts.org, https ://www.midwesthazelnuts.org/uploads/3/8/3/5/38359971/history _of_hazelnuts_in_the_upper_midwest_--handouts_[read-only].pdf.

Carl's dad saw in the hazilbert a golden opportunity, and the Weschckes were soon manufacturing and selling a number of food products made from the nuts, including hazilbert oil, hazilbert flour, and hazilbert butter. The hazilbert butter created by Carl's mother was a family favorite and a best seller. Carl described it as being "like peanut butter, but a lot tastier."[5]

Carl's dad was a dreamer, just as his son turned out to be, and he envisioned that his hybrid hazilberts had the potential to sweep the US and become the new go-to crop, outproducing corn and wheat and requiring far less human labor and resources. Although the hazilbert enterprise never rose to anywhere near those heights, a loyal following of friends, family, and exotic nut enthusiasts all knew that if they had a craving for anything that could possibly be made with a hazilbert, Hazel Hills was the place to find it. In fact, most guests to the Weschcke farm came to expect that at least one jar of hazilbert butter would be thrust upon them at some point during their visit.

Another hybrid tree developed on the Weschcke farm was the result of combined cuttings from an apricot tree and a hybrid species of plum tree. The resulting tree bore an abundant harvest of flavorful, colorful, hardy fruit that Carl's dad named the 'Harriet' apricot in honor of his mother.[6] Soon, orchards of apples, cherries, mulberries, grapes, and figs were flourishing on the farm, as well as several new varieties of spruce and pine trees. "We had just about every kind of tree that would grow naturally in the environment, and some that shouldn't have survived our winters—like the fig in particular,"[7] Carl proudly remembered.

The Hazel Hills experimental farm grew to be one of the best organic nut breeding orchards in the upper Midwest, and to this day the new tree varieties Carl's dad dreamed up and created con-

---

5   Weschcke, "Mrs. Penny's Spirit Rocking Chair."

6   Weschcke, *Growing Nuts in the North,* 81.

7   Weschcke, "Mrs. Penny's Spirit Rocking Chair."

tinue to flourish. In 1956 he was awarded a bronze medal from the Minnesota Horticultural Society in honor of his contributions.[8]

Carl's dad eventually wrote a book about his nut-growing experiments that he self-published under the title *Growing Nuts in the North*. He describes his hands-on work with the trees as "both a physical and mental tonic," and writes:

> *It is a fine thing to have a hobby that takes one out-of-doors. That in itself suggests healthful thought and living. The further association of working with trees, as with any living things, brings one into the closest association with nature and God.*[9]

Hazel Hills was a family enterprise, and the Weschcke children were expected to participate in the work of the orchards so that they could experience firsthand the unique benefits and challenges of farm life. Carl and his little brother, Ernest, often worked together and played together. Carl loved to take Ernest for rides around the farm on the custom tractors and other vehicles their dad had created and crafted. Being the elder of the two, Carl could drive the machinery while the young Ernest sat back and enjoyed the ride, taking in the sights, sounds, and smells of the orchards. Nature was respected and appreciated at the Weschcke household, not only because the nut trees supplied a fair portion of the family's income, but also because of the sheer enjoyment and pleasure that naturally flows from a life that strives for harmony and balance with the great outdoors.

Farm life did have its challenges, and to the Weschckes in particular, creative solutions were required. When faced with a gopher problem, Carl's compassionate father was not content to employ the common method of shooting the creatures like all the neighbors did. He knew that something must be done, but as a vegetarian and animal-lover, he couldn't help but feel pity for the pesky animals even though they relentlessly plagued his precious trees.

---

8   *Minneapolis Star Tribune*, "Horticultural Group Honors 9."

9   Weschcke, *Growing Nuts in the North*, introduction.

In pondering the problem, he came up with an unusual way to solve it:

> It was with the idea of establishing a balance of nature against these animals that I conceived the idea of importing bull snakes. When I first brought some of these snakes to my farm, I loosed them and they wandered off to a neighbor's premises where they were promptly found and killed. Later importations I confined to my basement, where I built an artificial pool with frogs and fish in it....My children were delighted to have the snakes there and made pets of them.[10]

Though nonpoisonous, the snakes can grow to be up to six feet long. It's no wonder Carl turned out to be a bit eccentric—after all, not everyone grows up with gigantic snakes living in their basement as pets!

Not only did the young Carl not mind the snakes, but he also took great delight in simply running around the orchards, exploring his environment. He soon developed what would prove to be a lifelong love and appreciation for nature as a whole and for trees in particular, just as his dad possessed. "He loved trees," Carl reminisced about his father, "and he talked about the tree elementals he felt and sometimes saw. He was a natural pagan and he would sometimes go naked except for a pair of rubber boots and run through the trees during rain storms."[11]

After Carl heard his dad recounting a spooky story about seeing a glowing green light in the woods one night, he was enthralled and eager to have his own mysterious experiences amidst the dense, dark forests surrounding the family home. Carl's dad had been walking back home from a neighbor's house one night when he spotted a glowing green light close to the ground. He was so startled that he ran all the way back to his property without daring to take a closer look. Feeling braver in the daylight, he returned to the same spot the next morning to find an innocent piece of rot-

---

10   Weschcke, *Growing Nuts in the North*, 85.

11   Weschcke, "Mrs. Penny's Spirit Rocking Chair."

ting wood. The glowing light turned out to be nothing more than the phenomenon of natural phosphorescence, but to Carl's inquisitive and curious mind, that sounded every bit as interesting as if the light had indeed been caused by some supernatural activity. "I would always look for rotting wood on my many kid-explorations of the woods as I walked the old stream bed to find agates," Carl recalled. "I never did find any with that green glow. I did find Indian graves, and hoped to see the spirits of the people who lived before. I never did."[12]

Although he may have been disappointed in the lack of phosphorescent wood and indigenous disembodied souls he encountered at Hazel Hills, Carl definitely had his share of mystical experiences as a youth. When asked in an interview in 2009 if he could recount any strange or paranormal occurrences from his childhood, Carl responded:

> Yes—too many to fully describe and many are colored by the view of a young person to whom dreams and psychic experiences were often as "real" as any day-to-day experiences. However, one in particular has always remained in the forefront of my childhood memories. I was perhaps four years old when I came down the stairs to find my grandparents visiting. I was so overjoyed that I levitated from the stairs into the living room. Memory or dream? Other memories are of dream visitors—teachers, guides, or dream characters? When I was perhaps six years old, I was playing outside with a friend. When I was called in for lunch, I told the maid about my friend named "Banana." She informed me that she had kept her eyes on me the whole time, and I had been alone.
>
> Whatever! (a typical Minnesota exclamation) I always had a broad view of life and the universe. I said to my grandfather, we've lived before, haven't we? He merely said "Yes, we believe so."[13]

---

12   Weschcke, "Mrs. Penny's Spirit Rocking Chair."

13   Marquis, "Interview with Carl Llewellyn Weschcke."

Carl absolutely adored his grandfather Charles, a Theosophist who shared his natural thirst for learning and exploring. An early and avid reader, Carl enjoyed looking through his grandfather's unusual books and magazines that often had an esoteric or philosophical slant. Before he started first grade, Carl was already reading journals from the Theosophical Society that his grandfather, who was a leader in the organization, provided him. Carl was also keenly interested in astrology and astronomy and even built his own telescope so that he could study the stars. His interests in the esoteric grew ever stronger as the years progressed, and his grandfather did everything he could to encourage this interest. Carl recalled:

> When I was eleven years old, my grandfather Charles gave me a horoscope. He had commissioned one of the leading esoteric astrologers of the day to prepare this for me as a Yule gift. When I say leading, I do not refer to the popular newsstand astrologers of the thirties, but to Charles Luntz of St. Louis... The horoscope was an impressive document to an eleven-year-old boy. It was typed on heavy vellum paper, and was over fifty pages long. Naturally, my horoscope interpretation very much reflected Theosophical concepts, including comments on my immediate past life and immediate next life. While I can attest that most of the interpretation and prediction in the Luntz horoscope have been verified in my seventy-three years of this life, I can speak with less certainty about that past life and even less about the future one... Of my future life, his prediction is that I am due to return as a female. I can't say whether I look forward to a feminine incarnation or not, but I anticipate the adventure.[14]

The mystical was presented to Carl as if it were nothing unusual, and yet he still had experiences that he found to be entirely unexplainable. One such experience occurred near the Mississippi River, where he liked to play as a boy when staying at the family home in Saint Paul:

---

14   Marquis, "Interview with Carl Llewellyn Weschcke."

I was the kind of kid that loved to explore Nature. In the summer I had a whole forest to explore, but the rest of the year—in the city—I would explore along the cliffs and valleys of the Missis- sippi, about two blocks from our home. One area was a partic- ular favorite: Shadow Falls. There was still a small stream that flowed for about two blocks in length before tumbling down about a hundred feet into a valley that then emptied into the Missis- sippi. In the winter, of course, the stream was frozen and so was the falls. One Saturday afternoon I was doing my usual exploring (the same territory that I walked and climbed many times), and I started walking across the frozen stream about ten feet above the falls—and then I slid toward the edge with nothing to stop me—except at the last minute something did stop me at the very edge, and I gingerly slid my feet to the stream bank and climbed out…I do attribute that kind of action to an instinctive psychic self-protection which I presume we all have, at least in varying degrees.[15]

At the age of fifteen, Carl was to have another very memorable paranormal experience at the family's house in Saint Paul. A great many years later, Carl was still able to recount the story vividly:

I was alone in the family house one evening while my parents were at our summer home in the country. I was reading in bed and was disturbed by a familiar sound. The light switches in our living room were brass and made a distinctive and rather loud noise easily heard in the quiet house. As I was alone, I had to determine the source of the sound. Well, the living room lights were on, and I was more than sure I had turned them off.

Looking through the house, nothing was amiss and the out- side doors were locked.

Back to bed and my novel. Soon a similar sound was heard— and again one I could identify: the sound of the basement light switch. Again, I found that light on when I was more than sure it was off on my previous search of the house.

Back to bed and to sleep, feeling perfectly secure. I was awakened several hours later by the telephone. It was a collect

---

15   Ibid.

call for my mother. I explained that she was not at home and
I would not accept the call. A man's voice intervened over the
operator's... The man said that my Uncle Louis had died in a
Los Angeles hospital, and would I have my mother call to make
arrangements.

I am convinced that those light switches were my uncle's last
attempt at communicating with his sister.

As far as I am concerned, this was a real encounter with the
paranormal, and there was nothing frightening about it... Are
real "ghosts" or true spiritual contacts ever really frightening?[16]

The Weschcke home was always filled with interesting personalities, and everything from telepathy to communicating with the
dead was openly discussed. One interesting personage who was a
frequent visitor to the Weschcke home was Mr. W. W. Allen, who
worked for Carl's dad and grandfather as a lawyer for the family
business. Mr. Allen was not your typical lawyer. He had become a
family friend, and on the many occasions that he spent the night
at the Weschcke home, he refused the guest bed and instead preferred to rest sitting upright in a chair. When questioned about
this odd behavior, Mr. Allen explained that he was working out-
of-body as a type of helper on the "inner planes." Carl recalled
one particularly peculiar instance where his dad and Mr. Allen
were discussing a matter of business that needed the immediate
approval of Carl's grandfather, who was away on a trip at the time.
As Carl describes,

Allen closed his eyes for several minutes, then opened them and
said, "CW approves." Two days later, Dad had a letter from him
remarking on how Allen had mentally contacted him and how
satisfied he was to give his approval... Mr. Allen was an inter-
esting man.[17]

Another unusual friend of the family was Mrs. Penny, who was
one of the nearest neighbors to the Weschckes' home at Hazel Hills.

---

16   Weschcke, "A Really Scary Ghost Story."
17   Weschcke, "Telepathic Communication."

A gifted medium, she kept a heavy rocking chair in her living room that would start rocking (with no one in it and with no breezes blowing) whenever she felt the presence of a spirit. She would talk about the spirits and ask questions, and the chair would rock in reply to spell out an answer.[18]

Other family friends shared with the Weschckes an interest in table tipping, a method used to communicate with spirits of the dead. When in his middle teens, Carl had what started as a nice, quiet evening at home transform into a night he would never forget:

> My parents had some longtime friends, Mabel and Fred Brown, and they were over for dinner one evening. Following the meal, all retreated to the living room and talked about numerous subjects...Mr. Brown asked if we had ever experienced table tipping. We had not, and he suggested we get a table and give it a try. I got out a heavy metal card table and four chairs from the front closet and set them up. Then Mr. Brown, my parents, and myself sat at the four sides of the table and rested our hands on the surface. Mr. Brown talked about his experiences for awhile, and then spoke to the air and asked, "Is anyone here?" The table seemed to vibrate a bit, and then quickly rose up, resting at an angle on just one leg, and then settled back down. I gave up my place to Mrs. Brown so that I could watch everyone. Again Mr. Brown asked a question, and the table responded more quickly and more vigorously by tipping up as before. I saw no motion of hands except to move with the table surface, and I saw no connection between the table and participants' knees. After awhile, I again joined in and I think we "played" for about an hour. I don't recall that any of the answers were impressive, but I was impressed and confident that the phenomenon was genuine, whatever it was. No one was moving the table either consciously or unconsciously by any physical means.[19]

Around this same time, while in his middle teens, Carl purchased a copy of William Seabrook's *Witchcraft: Its Power in the*

---

18   Weschcke, "Mrs. Penny's Spirit Rocking Chair."
19   Weschcke, "Table Tipping and Ouija."

World Today. Although Seabrook was most known for his travel books, he had been a personal acquaintance of Aleister Crowley and many other cutting-edge occultists of the day. The book ignited Carl's fascination with a whole new aspect of occult learning, enchanting him with unexplored worlds of witchcraft and magick. Seabrook's work was sensationalist, yet it still contained some gems of real magick and ritual. Among other obscure but genuine practices, the book makes mention of the "witch's cradle," a sensory deprivation/meditation device that is used as an aid to clairvoyance. Carl was instantly intrigued and began to look into the practice of witchcraft further. He soon came across a magazine article by Seabrook that talked about another sensory deprivation technique using full-face meditation masks to induce psychic visions, and as this was much simpler and more straightforward than constructing a witch's cradle, Carl decided to try a similar method. He began experimenting with blindfolds but found that it didn't really do much for him in terms of enhancing his clairvoyant abilities. He quickly moved onto using candles instead to help him connect with his psychic mind, and with this he found he was much more successful.[20]

Throughout his high school career, Carl continued his enrollment at Saint Paul Academy—the same traditional, all-boys private school he had attended since primary school. Carl's friends didn't always understand his interest in the esoteric and occult, but he was well-liked and respected just the same. Ever since he started at the school in first grade, Carl was known for being a bit of an oddball. He had a quiet nature and preferred to sit under the trees during breaks rather than play sports like most of the other boys. "I was a very shy person as a young boy, and basically reclusive,"[21] Carl explained. Even so, he also had a great sense of humor and a love of fun, which quickly gained him a group of

---

20   Night Sky, "Carl Llewellyn Weschcke."
21   Bahn, "Hubert Humphrey Was a Vampire!"

lifelong friends that he would come to call "the Boys." Carl recalled fond memories of how he had made his first friends, remembering especially vividly a time when he and his friend Bob had worked together to build a model fire station out of wooden blocks, both boys taking pride in their deluxe creation.

While his friends were obsessed with baseball cards and hockey games, Carl spent most of his time reading, studying, and exploring the mysteries of the natural world with the help of a chemistry set and the telescope he had crafted himself. He had a very serious-minded nature, but he also had a penchant for adventure. As he grew into an older teenager with the prospect of graduation looming ever closer on the horizon, Carl felt increasingly compelled to indulge in having good times with his buddies that didn't always meet with the approval of parents or school administrators. When the students had to take a dance class, Carl put his knowledge of chemistry to work and created a super stink bomb that became so infamous among his classmates that it was mentioned to peals of laughter decades later at the forty-year class reunion. On another occasion, Carl had obtained some fireworks to show off to his friends. He stashed them in his mother's car, hoping to shoot them off once nighttime fell. Unfortunately, and much to the chagrin of Carl's mother, some of the fireworks exploded prematurely, leaving scorch marks and a lingering odor of sulfuric smoke in his mother's beloved vehicle!

Despite what might be inferred from the firework incident, Carl had a great love for cars. Being of an entrepreneurial spirit like his father, he made it both a hobby and a business to buy old cars and resell them at a handsome profit. To his friends, it seemed like Carl had a different car nearly every time they saw him. His high school yearbook even included a joke that the only car Carl hadn't been seen driving in recent memory was a current year model![22] One of his favorite cars was a late thirties model Cadillac

---

22   Saint Paul Academy Yearbook, 1948.

that he had inherited from his grandmother. Carl's friend George Millard remembered fondly the days when the two pals would race to school in the mornings at just the last minute, striving to be the one who managed to arrive the latest without actually being late, which resulted in a demerit from the headmaster. George would arrive with less than a minute to spare, thinking surely he was the last to arrive and thus the winner, but then Carl would come racing up and screech to a halt right behind him in his shiny Cadillac, wearing a big grin on his face and appearing out of nowhere, almost as if he had been waiting and hanging back till the very last second so he could secure the victory.

One thing Carl didn't at all care for at school was the athletics. At Saint Paul Academy, the high school students were required to participate in a team sport. Carl chose hockey and played in the position of goalie. While his teammates remember him as a good player who always had his teammates' backs, he was also known for his rather unusual habit of suggesting changes to the game that he considered to be improvements. He never simply accepted anything without questioning it, and if something seemed illogical or nonsensical, he was bold enough to say so. The coach never agreed to his suggestions for improving the game of hockey, but it certainly brought Carl's teammates a laugh whenever his typical reserve cracked in the name of logic and for the sake of progress to reveal a highly outspoken individual with fantastic, grandiose ideas. After a year on the team as goalie, he was moved to the position of team manager, which the coach found to be a much better fit for Carl's executive abilities.

Even amongst his friends, Carl acted as the natural leader of the crew, thus eventually earning himself the nickname "the Baron." While his friends were pretty conventional, Carl was very unusual, always interested in subjects that his pals struggled to understand or appreciate, though they found his ponderings compellingly interesting all the same. "Carl was the prophet of the group," George remembered.

From George Millard, Carl's lifelong friend:

The glue of an eighty-year friendship that endures for all that time possesses an unusually resilient and strengthening quality to persevere. Some energy, natural or extra-natural, must be of essence in the attachments. I believe Carl Weschcke's nature was continually at work energizing the glue, for after our group of friends had all temporarily separated for various reasons, including military service, work, travel and/or geography, Carl kept the group together. For the last several years until Carl's departure from this life, a monthly luncheon at Carl's home continued the bond, with some of the group driving a few hundred miles to attend. Others, who had occasion to visit the Twin Cities from the East or West Coasts, made it a point to coordinate their trip with the lunches. We called the room on Carl's lower level where we would meet for lunch the "Adlerika Bar," and we all miss it.

What energy or spirit did Carl possess to cause this bond? I believe it was because in more than one way, Carl could and did live in two worlds yet was always able to connect. He was able to associate with conventional friends and people while maintaining his own interests. I feel Carl would not object to being called a devotee of some eccentric thoughts, actions, and mannerisms. He was nonconforming, creative, curious, and idealistic. He usually had about five or six hobbies going on at any given time, and he was aware from early childhood that he was different. He was intelligent, opinionated, and outspoken, and he never felt the need for reassurance or reinforcement from society. He was possessed with a mischievous sense of humor, and it was his warm friendship that kept us all together.

Carl's attitude and lively observations of current events, as well as his incredible reading and writing pace, kept all of us bonding with him. He was definitely unconventional in a lot of ways and expressed ideas and thoughts we had not considered. Yet Carl was consistently a very intelligent listener and thinker, and was always interested in considering new scientific and philosophical conclusions or theories. He was always interested in other people's points of view and would happily engage in a lively and intelligent conversation. Any one of our crew would go out of their way to prove how much he meant to all of us.

"The Boys" liked to get away from the city, heading to the Hazel Hills farm or to a property in northern Wisconsin where there was a small hunter's shack and an absence of parental supervision that the friends found ideal for their teenage adventuring. They nicknamed the shelter the "Rabbit Hutch," and though it was small and very basic—a small cabin with one bedroom, a small kitchen, and an open floor plan—it served well as a private clubhouse. The Boys headed to the Rabbit Hutch as often as they could, just hanging out, laughing and talking or relaxing with their dates if they were lucky enough to bring any. Some members of the group found entertainment in engaging in half-hearted battle with the multitude of crows that plagued the property (though more than one of those boys would have second thoughts about their teenage sport in later years). One of the boys even had a set of bright red matching custom jackets made for the crew that featured the slogan "Riddum Brothers Exterminators" emblazoned across the back.

One pastime the boys often enjoyed was attempting to jump-start their cars with a tractor that emitted puffs of smoke that looked like fluffy white donuts hanging in the frigid winter air. On one memorable occasion, the boys had found a small diesel-powered shovel machine in a gravel pit. They managed to jumpstart it using the tractor, then spent a lovely afternoon smashing cans with the machine's shovel. On another occasion, Carl's friends Bob and George decided to pool their money together and purchase an open cockpit biplane for the sum of $400. They hired a World War I pilot to teach them to fly it, with the intention of learning to do acrobatic stunt flights through the Minnesota and Wisconsin skies. Their parents soon got wind of the plan, however, and put a quick stop to it. They had to sell the beloved plane to the Cole Brothers Flying Circus. "The Boys" remained friends throughout their lives.

Before they knew it, it was graduation. In 1948 Carl finished his studies at the Saint Paul Academy and was faced with the intimidating decision of where to go and what to do next.

From Ernest J. Weschcke, Carl's brother:

In the early years, from what I can remember, I was mostly a nuisance to my big brother. We spent some time at Hazel Hills.

One time in particular that I can remember quite vividly was the time that I (probably eight or nine years of age) was riding the old blind workhorse that was at the farm. The horse got spooked for some reason, reared up, and threw me off.

The horse's front legs hit the old metal picnic table, it lost its balance, and then rolled over me—with a Western saddle on it. The horn of the saddle hurt my chest as the horse rolled over on me.

Carl was there to help me as I was hurting very badly. He prepared a bath with Epsom salts to help soothe my pain. And for some reason we had to keep it a secret from Mother and Dad.

———————————

Pioneer Roots

The Weschckes are considered one of the pioneer families of Minnesota. Carl's great-grandfather, Dr. Carl Weschcke, was an innovator and natural leader. Born in Limlingerode in the Saxony province of Prussia on March 4, 1831,[23] Dr. Weschcke immigrated to the United States on February 27, 1860. America was touted at the time as the land of promise, and Dr. Weschcke was intrigued by the prospect of new opportunities and new adventures that might be found away from his homeland. He booked passage on a ship that carried him to New Orleans, but Dr. Weschcke soon traveled north up the Mississippi River, where he came across the small settlement of New Ulm, Minnesota.[24]

New Ulm was a community built largely of German immigrants who were part of the Turner movement, a philosophy encouraging physical fitness and democratic political reform. The Turners believed in the principle of a mind-body connection, their motto being "A sound mind in a sound body." Strong believers in freedom and equality, American Turners were opposed to slavery. Dr. Weschcke was attracted to New Ulm, and finding that the community was without a physician or druggist, he decided to make his home there. For several years Dr. Weschcke was New Ulm's one and only doctor and pharmacist.[25]

Soon after arriving in New Ulm, a crisis struck, and Dr. Weschcke's services were called into special demand. Tensions were rising between the Dakota and the US government. The government had been seizing tribal lands in the Minnesota River Valley and selling them off, forcing the Dakota onto reservations and promising money and provisions that never came in exchange for

---

23   *New Ulm Review*, "Oldest Mayor in America."

24   *Memorial Record of Southwestern Minnesota* (Chicago: The Lewis Publishing Company, 1897), 238–239, and Wellcome, "The Pioneer Doctors of the Minnesota Valley, Second Paper, Dr. Carl Weschcke of New Ulm."

25   Wellcome, "The Pioneer Doctors of the Minnesota Valley, Second Paper, Dr. Carl Weschcke of New Ulm."

their sacrifice. The Dakota watched their homelands diminish until they were left with only a small fraction of their previous territory, and with provisions running low and running out, tensions finally reached a breaking point. In August of 1861 the tribe decided to attack the nearest settlements in retaliation for the continued injustice done to them by the agents of the US government, and New Ulm was amongst the communities that were hardest hit. The attacks lasted for several days, and many men, women, and children of New Ulm were among the dead and wounded.

As the only physician in New Ulm, Dr. Weschcke attended to the numerous injuries as best he could throughout the siege, working tirelessly with the help of only a handful of untrained volunteers. The Dakotah House, a local hotel, was used as a makeshift hospital.[26] One of the volunteers was Pauline Spoerhase, who was employed at the hotel as a cook but quickly took on the role of nurse to assist Dr. Weschcke with the wounded. Medical supplies were running out quickly, and Pauline had to scrape the lint from the hotel linens so that the doctor could use it to staunch the flow of blood from the open cuts of the wounded.[27]

For days Dr. Weschcke refused to leave his post despite being entirely exhausted; he knew the town was depending on him, and as long as his help was needed, he was determined to render his services to the best of his abilities. When reinforcements finally arrived, bringing with them several more physicians, Dr. Weschcke was still reluctant to abandon his duties, as there were still so many in urgent need of care. He continued at his post throughout the six long days and nights of battle until all the injured had been treated.[28] In recognition of his service, Dr. Weschcke was appointed to the post of Military Surgeon for the US Army, where he served until his help was no longer required.

---

26 *New Ulm Review*, "Oldest Mayor in America."

27 Find a Grave, "Pauline Spoerhase," https://www.findagrave.com /memorial/61239678/pauline-spoerhase.

28 *New Ulm Review*, "Oldest Mayor in America."

In 1863 Dr. Weschcke married a Miss Harriet Gaeger, a New Ulm resident originally from Prussia who had immigrated to America with her family as a child. Five years later, in 1868, he opened the Pioneer Drug Store, New Ulm's first.[29] There, he invented many custom medicines and vitamin tonics for stomach ailments and other complaints. Dr. Weschcke's formulations would eventually form the foundation of a Weschcke family business that would continue for several generations.

Dr. Weschcke was also very involved in local politics. He served several terms as mayor of New Ulm, and also served as a councilman and coroner. At the time of his retirement at the age of 73, he had the honor of being America's oldest mayor in office.

Dr. Weschcke and his wife, Harriet, had a large family of seven children, with three sons and four daughters. The sons grew up to follow in their father's footsteps, with one son, Emil, setting up a medical practice in California, and the other two sons, Charles and Ernest, continuing the family pharmaceutical business in Minnesota.[30]

Charles (who would become Carl's grandfather) and his brother Ernest opened their own pharmacy in Springfield, about thirty miles southwest of New Ulm. The brothers built upon Dr. Weschcke's original medicines and set to work developing new patent formulas. As their business and their ideas for new products expanded, the brothers decided to found a pharmaceutical manufacturing firm that they named the Adlerika Company. The company was to be located in the much larger city of Saint Paul.

Tonics and patent medicines were the standard back in those days, and some of the concoctions the Weschcke brothers created became quite popular. One of their patent medicines that became well-known across the country was a stomach tonic called Adlerika, designed to help clear away harmful bacteria from the digestive

---

29   *Memorial Record of Southwestern Minnesota* (Chicago: The Lewis Publishing Company, 1897), 238–239.

30   Ibid.

tract. "Adlerika, the laxative that completely evacuates the bowels, pleasant to take," proclaimed a seemingly self-contradictory ad for the product. "Think your insides are clean? Adlerika will surprise you!" was another slogan that sold countless bottles of the mysterious tonic to legions of optimistic Americans who swore to its benefits. Times were different back then, but a super-powered laxative touted with the ability to clear the intestines virtually instantly is a hard sell in any day and age.

The brothers teamed up with Carl Brainard of the Saint Paul Advertising company and soon developed innovative and aggressive ways to market their products. The Weschckes would regularly advise physicians on the benefits and selling points of Adlerika, and only one or two physicians in each city across the country would be chosen as the exclusive carriers of the popular tonic. This arrangement gave physicians a built-in incentive for selling more Adlerika, as it was in high demand and many people would go to whichever doctor could prescribe it.

The Weschcke brothers were always thinking outside the box for new ways to promote their products. Charles even wrote a book to help sell more Adlerika, encouraging the idea that a tonic for indigestion could be the key to personal happiness. *Overcoming Sleeplessness*, published in 1935, explained the importance of diet and a clear bowel in helping to cure insomnia. Charles also formed a group of singers, and performed songs on a radio program called "Charlie Kent and His Adlerikans." The radio program aired for several months in 1935 and featured old-time songs, hymns, and, of course, ads for Adlerika.[31]

The Adlerika Company continued to grow, and a new branch called Frederick Stearns and Company was opened in Canada. They continued to add new products, including Daru liver pills and Vinol. Vinol was described as an iron-rich vitamin tonic that could

---

31 J. David Goldin, "Charlie Kent and His Adlerikans," Radio Gold Index Database, http://www.radiogoldindex.com/cgi-local/p2 .cgi?ProgramName=Charlie+Kent+and+His+Adlerikans.

improve one's pep and vigor. The brothers were no less creative in marketing their new concoction. One ad for Vinol read:

> *Is Your Daughter Popular? Maybe she needs something to really bring out her charm. She can't be attractive if she's pale, underweight and scrawny. Encourage her appetite with vitamin B-1 and Iron, in VINOL. Your druggist has this pleasant-tasting tonic.*

In 1944 the Weschcke brothers formed a new company by the name of Chester-Kent, and the Adlerika company was eventually absorbed under the new name.

Like his brother Ernest, who was a very serious and intimidating individual, Charles Weschcke was indeed a businessman first and foremost, yet he had another side to his personality that one might not expect from an individual so sharp and shrewd when it came to matters of making money. Though well-off himself and in no way disadvantaged or disenfranchised, Charles was extremely passionate about humanitarian affairs and was a staunch supporter of equality, regardless of one's color or creed. He employed many minorities at his company and was one of the original founding members of Saint Paul's Urban League as well as the Saint Paul chapter of the NAACP, Minnesota's first. His wife, Harriet, was also active in the cause, and they often attended NAACP local meetings as well as national conventions together as a couple.

Just as his grandson grew up to be, Charles was also a great supporter of the creative arts. A personal friend to the painter and photographer Anton Gag, who had, for a time, rented the additional room that topped Dr. Weschcke's Pioneer Drug Store, Charles helped to pay for Anton's daughter Wanda to study at the Saint Paul Institute of Art when she was just starting out, years before she created the best-selling picture book *Millions of Cats.* "I'm to go to art school," wrote Wanda in her diary, "and such charming arrangements! I don't even have to work for my board." Charles simply instructed her to "do the things you were meant to do," feeling that he was predestined to help her in such a way as would benefit the world of art and humanity as a whole. Wanda didn't have the same faith in herself as Charles had, writing in her diary, "He thinks (oh how can he) that I will repay humanity a thousand-fold for what is being done for me."[32] Charles's intuition was correct, of course, and Wanda Gag went on to become a well-known author and artist. At the time of this book's publication, *Millions of Cats* remains the oldest American picture book still in print.

Charles was also very spiritual and kept an open mind to alternative ways of thinking. He was a dedicated Theosophist and served as vice president of the American Theosophical Society for many years. He had a profound interest in astrology, reincarnation, and many other metaphysical subjects, which would eventually spark his future grandson's early fascination with the occult. The Weschckes were pioneers in the pharmaceutical industry and remain an important part of the history of medicine in Minnesota.

32   Gag, *Growing Pains.*

Chapter 2

Carl the Collegiate

Carl wasn't really sure what he wanted to be when he "grew up," but he knew he had an interest in business. He had been thinking for a while of going to Harvard, attending the four-year degree program, then continuing on to graduate studies in business. Now that the time for a decision had come, however, he was having second thoughts about Harvard. Would it be worth attending a full four-year general studies program when he knew his interests lay in the field of business?

After a chance conversation with a family friend, Carl opted to ditch his plans for Harvard and instead enroll at Babson College, an all-boys private college that provided a full curriculum with a focus on business where he could earn his degree much sooner in their three-year program. The school was small and not well-known, but Carl felt confident that it was the right place for him to continue his education. He explained,

> I'd always felt that it was a great waste of time to go through an arts course and then through a business school when I was primarily interested in business. At the same time, however, I

*felt that a straight business education would be rather narrow-
ing, so I'd been looking around for something different. A friend
of Mr. Babson's suggested this school, and told me as much
as he knew about it. From what he said, I was sure that this
was the kind of school that I wanted, something that would give
me a definite business foundation, and yet have some college
aspects.*[33]

The college was located near Boston, Massachusetts, so at the
age of eighteen and fresh out of high school, Carl courageously
packed up his belongings and left the town in which he had been
born and raised in order to pursue his ongoing quest for further
adventure, experience, and knowledge. The campus was beautiful,
with wide expanses of green grass, old trees, and imposing buildings that seemed to radiate a feeling of classic academia. Soon
after classes began, one of Carl's professors instructed the students to write about their career goals, their goals at Babson, and
their first impressions of life at college.

Carl wrote:

> *When I arrived here on campus, I was a little scared, as it was
> something completely new and I didn't know anyone here. How-
> ever I soon met a swell bunch of guys and we are all fast friends
> now and the school has become familiar and even seems rather
> homey. The classes that I have attended so far have all been
> interesting, and I am sure that I am going to like it here.*[34]

Of his career goals, Carl wrote:

> *I have been interested in business as far back as I can remem-
> ber, having grown up in a business atmosphere. My father has
> always been associated with several business enterprises and
> the family's closest friends have been sales managers, corpora-
> tion consuls, and business executives, and conversation around
> the house has been centered around proxy fights, advertising
> campaigns, etc. For several years now, I have kept my own*

---

33   Weschcke, "Myself at Babson."
34   Weschcke, "Myself at Babson."

accounts and have read extensively in the field of general business and finance, and I have for quite some time been determined on entering the business world. However, as yet, I have not decided in what field I would like to specialize.

He mentioned in his paper that he had served as adjutant of the school battalion during his senior year in high school, explaining how this showed that he had leadership qualities. "In fact, I've been told that I have too much leadership quality," Carl admitted.[35]

When classes were a bit dull, Carl would occasionally daydream and doodle. One of his college notebooks featured an idea for a Vinol ad he had sketched out. The drawing included a family and an oversized crystal ball with a fortuneteller, along with the slogan "For a Healthy Future."

He wasn't very social during these years, although he did hold a position on the executive committee of his senior class and helped raise funds for a dorm renovation project. Carl found most of his fun during this time in the world of books, and his magickal studies were continuing to expand and deepen. One day he found a book about witchcraft authored by Gerald Gardner, *High Magic's Aid*, which Gardner had written under the pseudonym "Scire. O.T.O. 4=7." The book discusses, among other things, the topics of witchcraft initiation, old gods of love and laughter, and the passwords "Perfect Love and Perfect Trust." Carl found the book so intriguing that he wrote to Gardner with his questions and comments. "Reading Gerald's book, I finally felt at home," explained Carl. "I bought more of Gardner's books and even wrote to him—and he kindly answered me." There began a correspondence that would last for many years into the future.

One of the first things Carl asked Gardner about was the witch's cradle he had read about years previously in the Seabrook book he had purchased. Gardner was hesitant to answer any of Carl's

---

35   Ibid.

questions regarding the witch's cradle in particular or the use of sensory deprivation to induce clairvoyance in general.

Said Carl,

> *He was more interested if I personally knew Kim Novak, the actress, than in answering my main questions about the witch's cradle and Wicca—because, he said, his answering would violate his oaths. But then he referred me to three people who, he said, could answer my questions without violating oaths. One of these, Margaret Bruce, sent me drawings of the cradle and other objects and explained their use.[36]*

Gardner also put Carl in touch with Charles Clark, who many years later would send to Carl a copy of what amounted to being Gardner's own personal Book of Shadows, which he had typed out himself in the mid to late fifties. These documents eventually became known as the "Weschcke Papers" and were later used by Aidan Kelly to research the development of the Gardnerian tradition of witchcraft.[37] Carl was also studying the works of Dion Fortune, Aleister Crowley, Manly Hall, Rudolf Steiner, Blavatsky, Besant, Leadbeater, and many others. He was enrolled in correspondence courses from the AMORC Rosicrucians and became keenly interested in Kabbalistic work. Though he continued to study just about everything related to magick and mysticism that he could get his hands on, his attentions were diverted away from witchcraft somewhat, and it wasn't until many years later that his fascination with the subject would be renewed.[38]

Carl's interests in magick and the occult were so diverse that he didn't identify with any one particular path or philosophy. He simply tried to learn as much as he could about any idea he came across that seemed to offer the potential to expand his mind and help him grow or otherwise benefit in some way. His personal practices at the time focused heavily on clairvoyance training, working with blindfolds, candles, and other methods to sharpen his natu-

---

36   CLW email to Melanie Marquis, September 11, 2013.
37   Kelly, "Inventing Witchcraft."
38   Night Sky, "Carl Llewellyn Weschcke."

ral gifts. He even fashioned himself a full-face sensory deprivation mask at one point by painting liquid latex onto a hat mannequin and attaching a zipper so that it could be zipped up like a hood to cover his entire face. Carl never liked the idea of being limited to only one discipline, and he never cottoned to dogma that proclaimed to be the only one true way.

In his second year at Babson, Carl had to write a paper for his philosophy class outlining his religious beliefs. He wasn't at all afraid to stand apart from convention, choosing pantheism as the focus of his essay, a philosophy that was considered to be heresy by many as its basis is the belief that the Divine is in everything and that everything is divine. Carl's essay was titled "Why I Am a Pantheist."

He wrote:

> Pantheism allows for an understanding and acceptance of all religions and philosophies. First of all, the viewpoints of the various systems of thought may be broadened through the use of symbolism so that there is no real difference except the position of the observer; secondly, these various philosophies are the result of the development of the soul; and finally their existence, at least for the present, is necessary for the development of the soul.

Carl continued diligently in his university studies, impressing his professors with everything but his occasional spelling errors and frequent typos. He had a roommate in his senior year who didn't much care for Carl's typing skills, either. Carl recalled,

> I had a roommate with whom I was good friends, until he reminded me that I needed to write a senior thesis. This was before the day of computers and even before electric typewriters, and I had a big Underwood mechanical typewriter. Being the kind of guy I am, I wrote the longest thesis on record, typing madly, and heavy-handed, through the night. Tom moved out. He didn't type at all, wrote his stuff longhand, and paid for it to be typed.[39]

---

39   CLW email to Melanie Marquis, December 14, 2011.

The thesis was accepted, and Carl completed his degree in three years, earning a bachelor of science with distinction in business administration and finance in 1951. It was time for him to figure out his next move, so he packed up his belongings and headed back home to Saint Paul to regroup and contemplate his hopes and plans for the future.

Chapter 3

Finding His Way

With his well-earned degree in hand, Carl moved back into his parents' house in Saint Paul and soon started working in the family pharmaceutical business. His parents hadn't pushed him into it at all, but it seemed like a natural and sensible thing to do all the same. He took a position at the Adlerika Company, and finding he was rather good at business, he was soon promoted to general manager. The work was tolerable but dull. It didn't excite Carl at all, and though he stuck with it, he couldn't shake the feeling that there had to be something more for him, some larger way in which he could contribute to the world. It wasn't long, however, before Carl had reason to take a fresh look at his life and count his current blessings.

In the summer of 1952 he received an unexpected letter from the United States government informing him that he had been drafted for the US Army. Carl may not have felt much like a pharmacist or business executive, but he knew that it definitely suited him a lot better than being a soldier. Terrified but resigned to his fate, Carl told his friends the news and announced that they would have to have the party of all parties to give him a proper send-off. The

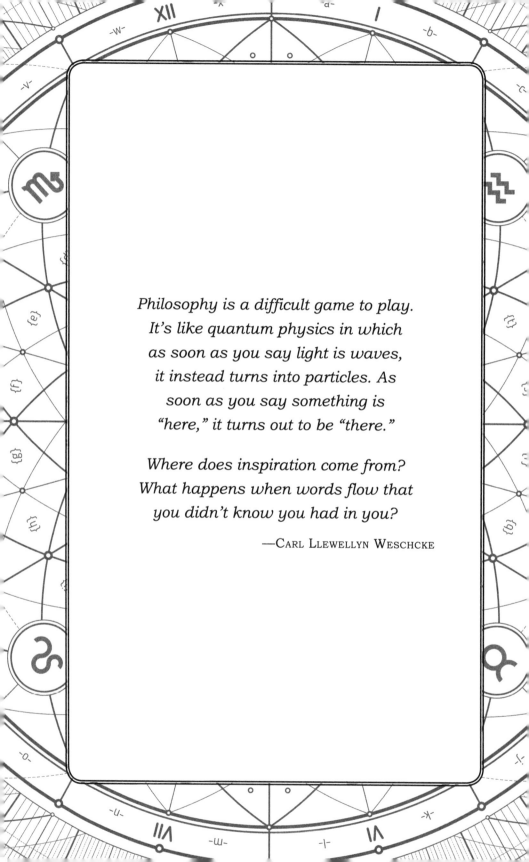

Philosophy is a difficult game to play.
It's like quantum physics in which
as soon as you say light is waves,
it instead turns into particles. As
soon as you say something is
"here," it turns out to be "there."

Where does inspiration come from?
What happens when words flow that
you didn't know you had in you?

—CARL LLEWELLYN WESCHCKE

entire old crew of cohorts that had graduated with Carl from Saint Paul Academy headed out to their clubhouse in the thick woodlands of Wisconsin, picking up an abundant supply of liquor along the way. When they arrived at the Rabbit Hutch, Carl insisted that they must have an actual bar from which he could serve the cocktails. There wasn't a bar, so Carl decided to make one. "Take down the outhouse door!" he commanded. His friends complied with his wishes and soon the door was off its hinges and balanced across a couple of old tree stumps, much to Carl's delight. The party raged late into the night, with Carl serving drinks and thinking this could very well be his last chance to have fun with his buddies in the freedom of civilian life.

A few days later Carl was called in by the army for a physical examination and psychological evaluation. To his extreme gratitude and surprise, the army decided to reject him due to unspecified health reasons. As Carl was young and able-bodied at the time, one has to wonder if it was truly health reasons that kept Carl out of the army or if he had simply revealed so much of his nonconformist, antiestablishment way of thinking that the military had deemed him unfit. Whatever the reason for the rejection, Carl was relieved and glad to get it. He was very patriotic and loyal to American ideals, but the idea of having to go into combat or shoot other people was something that he felt that he personally couldn't handle.

The whole experience reminded Carl to look on the bright side of life, and he gave his best to help the family business thrive. He soon started working as general manager for the Chester-Kent branch of the family business, which eventually absorbed the Adlerika Company. Chester-Kent made not only pharmaceuticals, but also cosmetics, household chemicals, and food products. Chester-Kent was struggling at the time, and Carl was determined to improve it. He tried marketing a few new products, which he hoped could restore the company's profitability. One such product he created was called Yo-Zyme, described as "Yogurt in pleasing tasting tablets." It was made primarily of yogurt, brewer's yeast, and lactose. An early ad for Yo-Zyme proclaimed, "Enjoy pep and vitality with Yo-Zyme,"[40] while another ad suggested that "The years will slip away" with Yo-Zyme.[41]

Carl did well in the world of business and made a fine executive by being flexible, creative, and a natural problem-solver. As enthusiastic and dedicated as he tried to be, however, his heart was simply not in it. He knew it wasn't what he wanted to do forever, so he started to toy with different ideas.

When a small cafe across the street from the Adlerika building was put up for sale, Carl decided that he would like to give restraunteuring a try. He had often grabbed lunch there before the business had closed, and he had fond memories of the place. He didn't like to see it go. Besides, it might be fun to own a cafe, and how hard could it be, anyway? Carl made the purchase, and soon the Wabasha Cafe had opened its doors once more, serving hamburgers and other simple American food fare, hot coffee, and cold pop. Carl did the cooking. If you were one of Carl's close friends, he might even offer you specialty items that weren't listed on the main menu—whether you wanted it or not!

His good friend George Millard recalled Carl making strange-looking concoctions—thick green syrups and odd-smelling liquids—that he would gleefully offer his friends to try along with their hamburgers. These were test formulas for new products he was trying to work out for Chester-Kent. "No thank you!" the friends would refuse. "But this one will really clean you out fast!" Carl would assert, as if that were a good thing. There was one formulation that was reported to give the skin a faint greenish tinge, "but it goes away," Carl would say. Carl and his friends had some good times at the little diner they had come to call the Adlerika Bar and Cafe.

---

40 Yo-Zyme advertisement, *Minneapolis Star*, June 7, 1951.

41 Yo-Zyme advertisement, *Muncie Evening Press*, Muncie, Indiana, January 27, 1954.

From Ernest J. Weschcke, Carl's brother:

I remember when Carl had bought a cafe/coffee shop across from where the Adlerika building was. He did a lot of work on that building along with doing the cooking. Anyway, he felt it to be necessary to do some painting that required a ladder and RED paint.

Well, you can probably guess what happened: he fell off the ladder and of course there was RED paint on him and the sidewalk. Everyone thought he was dead due to the intense RED color on the sidewalk.

———————————

Just a few months after Carl had opened the restaurant, his beloved grandfather Charles passed away. It was a hard loss for twenty-four-year-old Carl, who not only had to deal with the sorrow of his grandfather's death, but suddenly had a whole lot more responsibility in the family businesses to take on as well. Grilling up hamburgers and pushing unapproved test tonics on his buddies had somehow lost its luster. Within less than a year of its opening, the Wabasha Cafe shut its doors again.

Perhaps inspired by his grandfather, who had written wellness books to help support sales of his patent tonics, Carl soon had the idea to write a book of his own. In less than two weeks he had penned a book that he titled *The Science of Feeling Fine*. "I never knew where the information came from—but it did,"[42] said Carl. Dealing largely with the connection between physical health and spiritual health, the book offered basic health advice about diet, sleep, and exercise. In the book's introduction, Carl writes:

> We are beginning to temper the discoveries of purely material science with a philosophy of spirit, and this marriage of spirit and matter will produce an age of peace, art, and health.[43]

He published the book through the Chester-Kent company, printing it himself, trimming and assembling the pages, and stapling it all together with a golden yellow wrap-around cardstock cover. He sold the book to friends and even managed to get a few copies into local retail stores.

The book wasn't exactly a huge hit, to say the least, but Carl had enjoyed writing it, and it sparked in him another idea. It hadn't been too difficult to produce *The Science of Feeling Fine*, and it really didn't look too bad, considering he had never tried to create a book before. Maybe he could make more books. Maybe he could become a publisher.

---

42   CLW email to Melanie Marquis, September 16, 2010.

43   Weschcke, *The Science of Feeling Fine*.

In a bit of manifestation magick, he had special stationary printed up bearing the letterhead "The Baron's Press," in reference to an old nickname he had earned in high school. The idea was yet to congeal into any kind of concrete form, but it was stewing. He even started making notes for a new book, which he intended to be an examination of the work of Aleister Crowley.

Carl had also become very active in the civil rights movement, which without a doubt helped satisfy his need for greater purpose. He poured his heart into it and spent virtually every moment of spare time he had working for the cause. He enrolled in law classes through an extension course offered by LaSalle University so that he could better understand how the law might be used as a tool for securing the equality that he adamantly believed was the natural right of every human on earth.

He continued his work as a business executive, and within just a few short years of joining the company, Carl was promoted to vice president of Chester-Kent. He also took on additional jobs as treasurer for Acme-Northern Industries (manufacturers of the TenderTyme potty chair), vice president of Delta Electric Light Company, and vice president of the Saint Paul Advertising Company. He succeeded and excelled in the role of business executive, but his deepest passions were for his far more meaningful work as a civil rights activist and for his studies into the worlds of magick, which he continued. He became a member of the Theosophical Society, the Fortean Society, and the Society of the Inner Light, which had been founded by Dion Fortune.

While his magickal studies and civil rights work were absorbing and definitely enough to keep him fully engaged in life, Carl knew that he still needed to find a career path that was more satisfying and enjoyable. In addition to his dreams of being a writer or a publisher, Carl considered that perhaps he might want to be a teacher. With that in mind, he enrolled in correspondence courses in philosophy, as he had always had an interest in the subject. He did well in his studies, receiving high praise from his professor for an essay titled "The Mystical Method of Plotinus." Carl wrote:

> *In writing on Plotinus' mysticism, I have selected a subject that interests me greatly. The ultimate conclusion, as I see it, of mysticism, is that man is not limited to the two accepted levels of knowing, perception and reason. Yoga, too, includes this concept of a suprarational means of knowing, and certain schools of modern psychology, not to mention parapsychology, also suggest this possibility. If man were only a passive participant in life, then he could never direct his energies or make the necessary ethical decisions for accelerating his own evolution. It is essential to recognize that the combination of soul and body results from involution, while evolution is the path of return to the source for all creation. The desire of the soul to participate in matter is the instrument by which evolution is accomplished.*

Carl enjoyed philosophy and rather liked the idea of being a teacher, but it wasn't long before the hands of fate would bring his long-held dream of being a publisher back to the front and center.

Chapter 4

A Champion for Civil Rights

The year 1954 was one of great change in America, and it proved to be a year of great change in Carl's life, as well. He was in his mid-twenties, a college graduate, an executive at the family business... and he still had not found his way. His work wasn't enough; it wasn't inspiring. He was young and had plenty of energy to spare. He wanted to live a life of greater purpose, to have a positive impact on the lives of others in bigger and better ways.

While his own world was pretty posh, having the benefit of various trust funds in his name as well as a steady source of income, Carl was aware of and disturbed by the social injustice he saw taking place in the greater Saint Paul community and beyond. It was a time when racism was common, a time when segregated facilities were the rule rather than the exception in many places around the country. Discrimination in all areas of life was typical to the point of being expected, be it on the bus, at the schools, or at the real estate office. In 1954 Carl decided to join the Saint Paul chapter of the NAACP "because of a concern that the individual have

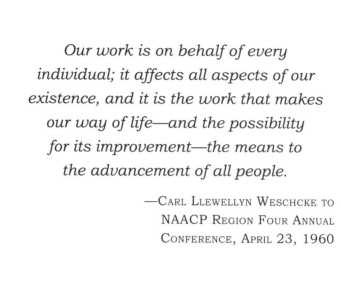

*Our work is on behalf of every
individual; it affects all aspects of our
existence, and it is the work that makes
our way of life—and the possibility
for its improvement—the means to
the advancement of all people.*

—Carl Llewellyn Weschcke to
NAACP Region Four Annual
Conference, April 23, 1960

*We are planting the seeds for the Tree of
Life that will never die because it has been
watered by the love and blood of people
for something bigger than themselves.*

—Carl Llewellyn Weschcke to
NAACP Region Four Annual
Conference, April 23, 1960

*All of us must play a bigger part if
the American Spirit is not to wither
away under the disease of self-
ambition and self-satisfaction.*

—Carl Llewellyn Weschcke to the
Minneapolis NAACP, March 27, 1960

maximum opportunities for employment, housing, and education, according to his ability."[44] A black woman named Bertha whom Carl had hired to work with him at the family business had sold him a membership, and after the first meeting, he was hooked. "I went to a meeting and I saw there was a lot to do—particularly in the areas of employment and housing for blacks,"[45] Carl explained.

There may have been an additional, more personal reason why Carl was prompted to join the civil rights cause at the particular time that he did. He had just lost his grandfather, who had been a part of the civil rights movement in Minnesota for decades, and Carl may have felt compelled to carry on the legacy.

Charles Weschcke had been one of the founding members of the Saint Paul chapter of the NAACP,[46] and in 1919 he had been unanimously elected to the organization's board of directors.[47] In 1921 Carl's grandfather, along with his grandmother, Harriet, had attended the NAACP National Convention as delegates representing Minnesota.[48] Thirty-nine years later Carl would be hosting the 51st NAACP National Convention in his home city of Saint Paul.

In 1954, when Carl first joined the movement, the civil rights fight was rapidly expanding in scope and heating up by the day. On May 17, 1954, the United States Supreme Court made a trademark ruling in the case of *Oliver Brown et al. v. Board of Education of Topeka, Kansas* that determined segregated schools to be unconstitutional. The court issued an order for all public schools to be desegregated, but there was no specific deadline or timeframe given for when these changes needed to be implemented.[49] Despite the legal victory, the pushback against integration was swift and

---

44   *Minneapolis Star,* "Town Toppers."

45   Kelly, "Angels' Voices."

46   *Minneapolis Star* "Town Toppers."

47   NAACP, *The Appeal,* November 29, 1919, 3.

48   NAACP, *The Appeal,* July 2, 1921, 3.

49   "Civil Rights Movement: Desegregation Timeline of Important Dates," "May 1, 1954, Brown v. Board of Education," accessed May 14, 2017, http://www.shmoop.com/civil-rights-desegregation/timeline.html.

hard. Many school districts in predominantly white communities were hesitant or downright hostile to the idea of school desegregation, especially in the South. Black students who attempted to integrate often would be faced with government-sponsored intimidation, threats, and episodes of mob violence. Georgia, Mississippi, and other states were soon seeking to enact laws that would make it a crime to oppose segregation. The NAACP had taken a leading role in obtaining the *Brown v. Board of Education* ruling, and they vowed to continue the fight until segregation was no longer a reality. Thurgood Marshall, special counsel for the NAACP, promised that "any efforts to perpetuate segregation will have to be answered in the courts."[50]

Indeed, the NAACP provided legal services and support for many students who had fallen victim to state-sponsored discrimination in the wake of the *Brown v. Board of Education* decision. A major part of the work that the Saint Paul chapter of the NAACP did at the time Carl joined was to raise money for the national office to help fund these legal battles in support of school integration efforts across the country.[51]

By taking a leading role in the fight for integration, the NAACP became a prime target for those who wanted to continue segregation despite the new law. In Mississippi, the White Citizens' Council was formed just a couple of months after the Supreme Court ruling, intent on standing in the way of school integration.[52] "The ire of the councils is directed against 'agitators' in general and the National Association for the Advancement of Colored People (NAACP) in particular," one newspaper reported, stating that the NAACP was "the only organized opposition" to the White Citizens'

---

50   *Orlando Sentinal*, "Mixing Suits Threatened by NAACP."

51   From CLW personal files circa 1954–1955.

52   "Civil Rights Movement: Desegregation Timeline of Important Dates," "July 11, 1954, White Citizens' Council Formed," accessed May 14, 2017, http://www.shmoop.com/civil-rights-desegregation/timeline .html.

Council movement. The White Citizens' Council maintained that they would stand against integration by "any legal means," but their actions often crossed the boundaries of legality. One merchant who was an NAACP branch president had a group of white men pull up to his store and demand that he come along with them. He was driven to his bank, where he was met by his banker, his wholesaler, and others who extended him credit. He was told that he had to "give up, go bankrupt or get out."[53] It wasn't just the private citizenry who stood opposed to the efforts of the NAACP, either. The governor of South Carolina called the NAACP a "subversive organization,"[54] and even the attorney general elect of Minnesota commented that he wondered if organizations like the NAACP didn't "go out of their way to find trouble."[55]

Violence and retaliation against NAACP members and officials in particular quickly escalated following the Supreme Court desegregation ruling. In July of 1954, the home of an NAACP official in Sulphur Springs, Texas, was shot up after the group had submitted a petition to the local school district requesting for integration efforts to be carried out more quickly.[56] In Baton Rouge, Louisiana, two NAACP lawyers who had unsuccessfully attempted to register thirty-nine black children at a public school found that they were soon facing possible disbarment following a request from the school district.[57] Retaliation against the NAACP wasn't limited only to the South or aimed solely at school desegregation efforts, either. In Benton Harbor, Michigan, the wife of the local NAACP branch president received an alarming phone call from an anonymous caller who threatened to shoot her husband over a suit the group had filed in an attempt to end discriminatory practices in public

---

53   Price, "Using Boycott."

54   *Greenville News*, "Timmerman Doesn't Believe."

55   *Minneapolis Star*, "Lord Asks Chance."

56   Associated Press, "Home of NAACP Official Shot At."

57   Associated Press, "NAACP Lawyers Threatened in Louisiana."

housing. The local police chief chalked the phone call up to "the work of a crank" and took no further actions on the matter.[58]

Beatings, shootings, and even bombings of NAACP activists and their families would become increasingly common in the months and years that followed. It wasn't exactly an easy thing to be an NAACP member in 1954. But Carl was a true believer in civil rights, so he didn't let the potential danger stop him from lending his full energy to the cause.

Despite the many risks and frustrations involved, Carl thoroughly enjoyed his work with the NAACP, and he met many friends through the organization. One such friend was Marjorie Toliver, who was also a member of the Saint Paul branch. The two became more closely acquainted after Carl approached her one day announcing that he had an extra ticket to a concert. He asked her if she would like to go. Assuming that Carl meant to give her the ticket so that she could attend alone, Marjorie gratefully accepted. She was taken aback when Carl then announced the time that he would pick her up to go with him to the concert, but she didn't want to be impolite or hurt his feelings, so she went along with it. The two got to know each other better, and as they worked together for the cause of civil rights, they soon developed a close friendship and camaraderie that would last a lifetime.

Supporting efforts to achieve a fully integrated education system both statewide and nationwide remained an important goal for the Saint Paul NAACP, but it wasn't the only goal. Integrated schools had been common in Saint Paul since the 1860s,[59] and there were additional civil rights crises that were causing major problems for local minority residents. One of the most pressing civil rights issues in Saint Paul at the time was discrimination in the housing market. Housing discrimination was a serious problem that continued in many places across the nation despite constitutional

---

58   *The News-Palladium*, "Police Probe Report Life of NAACP Chief."
59   Green, "Race and Segregation in Saint Paul's Public Schools, 1846–1869."

equal protection laws and due process laws that seemed to promise equal rights for all. Many white realtors and private owners
preferred to sell or rent their properties only to whites, leaving few
housing options open to minorities. Housing applications from
minorities were often rejected for no logical reason, and prospective homebuyers and renters were frequently faced with blatant
rudeness from lenders and realtors acting on racist beliefs and
unfounded fears of increased crime and declining property values.

This was the story in Saint Paul in the mid-1950s, just as it was
in many other cities in the US. Minority families who attempted
to integrate into predominantly white neighborhoods often found
they were treated as outcasts, harassed, or even openly threatened
by neighbors. Most new housing developments were open only to
whites, and the neighborhoods that did welcome minority residents became increasingly overcrowded and isolated.

Exacerbating the problem in Saint Paul, a major flood in 1952
had destroyed a large number of homes in the Upper Levee, an
area that was nicknamed "Little Italy" due to its high concentration
of Italian immigrants. "Little Italy" was a sort of shanty town built
along the Mississippi River, settled in the 1880s to mid-1900s by
Italian, German, and Polish immigrants who made their homes
from scrap lumber and tin. When rising waters breached the levee
and caused major structural damage in what was already considered a rather unsafe place to live due to the frequent flooding,
the city of Saint Paul decided to rezone the area as industrial and
began the process of evicting the remaining residents. With most
renters and realtors refusing to rent or sell to immigrants or other
minorities, many of the families dislocated from the Upper Levee
had no place to go.[60]

Further growth in Saint Paul made the housing crisis even more
critical. The development of new highways divided and effectively
destroyed long-established minority communities and dislocated

---

60   National Park Service, "Little Italy: A Floodplain Neighborhood."

hundreds of families. In 1956 the city of Saint Paul decided on the location to build I-94 and chose to route the new interstate directly through the heart of the black community. The freeway construction completely wiped out Rondo Avenue, the main vein of a prominent minority neighborhood that housed a thriving community of successful businesses and family homes. "Rondo was wonderful; the people were wonderful," recalled Carl's friend and fellow civil rights activist Marjorie Toliver. More than 600 families were displaced by the interstate construction, and the neighborhoods to the north and south of Rondo became even more densely packed and overcrowded as housing choices available to minorities remained extremely limited.[61]

Conditions in the Selby area, just to the south of Rondo Avenue, rapidly deteriorated as displaced minorities flocked to the few areas that were open to them, creating a situation of severe overcrowding. Single-family dwellings were often occupied by multiple families who had no choice but to make room for family members and friends who literally had no place else to go. In 1950 80 percent of Saint Paul's black population lived within the Selby area, and housing conditions were considered substandard at best. With the destruction of Rondo Avenue, the problem became exponentially worse.[62]

Carl was well-to-do and white; he had the means as well as the skin color to procure virtually any property in the city. Many people in his position wouldn't have thought twice about such problems as housing discrimination if it didn't affect them personally. Carl, however, realized that discrimination is everyone's problem, and he couldn't stand idly by and do nothing while hundreds of families in his hometown struggled to find adequate shelter. Carl was a "fixer." When he saw a problem in the world, he had an inclination to take personal responsibility for solving that problem. Being

---

61   McClure, "Rondo Neighborhood."
62   Ibid.

a person who valued the comforts of home very highly and who believed strongly in equal opportunity to achieve one's maximum potential, he felt called by the housing crisis in Saint Paul and was compelled to do something about it.

He didn't have the slightest desire to ever become a lawyer, but he signed up for correspondence courses through LaSalle Extension University and started studying law. He wanted to gain a deeper understanding of how our country's laws and legal system might be used to further the civil rights cause in general, and to achieve a fair and open housing market in particular. He soon became secretary for the Saint Paul NAACP's Housing Committee as well as secretary for the Citizens' Committee for Open Occupancy. He also decided to make civil rights a lifelong commitment, and in September of 1956, right around the time he was turning twenty-six, he became a lifetime member of the NAACP. As part of an effort to raise more funds for the organization, Carl's was the first lifetime membership from Minnesota to be paid in full.

With Carl wholeheartedly pouring himself into the cause, the quest for an open occupancy ordinance to prevent housing discrimination in Saint Paul was intensifying. The goal was to enact legislation at the city and/or state level that would guarantee a fair and open housing market, free from discrimination. The NAACP and other concerned citizen groups in Saint Paul were pushing the city council to adopt an open occupancy housing ordinance, but so far they had not been able to get the city to take any concrete actions on the matter.

On November 27, 1956, Carl spoke before the Saint Paul Ministers Association, urging local church leaders to educate their congregations about the importance of passing the fair housing ordinance and to inspire them to take action and put pressure on local leaders, explaining:

> *Democracy is not merely the distribution of rights but depends on the distribution of responsibilities and duties. We are all interdependent, and my freedom and growth depend on my brother's*

freedom and growth... We must make every person aware that
open occupancy is just as important to him as to his new neigh-
bor. It is only through the extension of liberty, as the business of
every man, that liberty is preserved.

He didn't just offer lofty words but also presented some specific
points of action and strategy that the clergy could employ:

Some of you may be able to speak directly to your people about
the need for open occupancy and the things that they as indi-
viduals can do to help in actual integration. Some of you may
be able to utilize church clubs or have panels such as this to
reach the individual citizen. The time to prevent possible mis-
understandings or misguided fears is now, and the weapon is
understanding and love and the recognition that humanity is a
human unity.

Carl's talk to the Saint Paul Ministers Association was mimeographed and circulated by the Saint Paul Council of Churches, and
the NAACP also made available to the churches a number of educational pamphlets for distribution to their congregations addressing the myths and misinformation that were circulating about the
effects of integrated housing.[63] On December 10, 1956, having
proved himself through his work for the Housing Committee and
the Citizens' Committee for Open Occupancy, Carl was elected to
serve as secretary for the Saint Paul branch of the NAACP.[64]

It soon appeared that success in fair housing in Minnesota
might actually be achieved. At the 1957 legislative session, the
Minnesota State Legislature issued an official declaration stating:

The opportunity to buy, acquire, lease, sublease, occupy, and
use and enjoy property and to obtain decent living and housing
accommodations without discrimination because of race, color,
creed, religion, national origin or ancestry is hereby recognized
and declared to be a civil right.[65]

---

63   McClure, "Rondo Neighborhood."

64   *Minneapolis Star*, "NAACP Names Officers."

65   Minnesota State Law, chapter 953, section 2, 1957.

The declaration also created an Interim Commission to study the issue of housing discrimination. The committee was to report back to the legislature before the 1959 session to recommend whether or not further legislation was required. This seemed like a positive development at first, but it was not enough to make a significant impact on the problem. Discrimination was still happening frequently, and housing options open to minorities continued to rapidly dwindle. In addition, the city government of Saint Paul as well as that of its sister city of Minneapolis seemed to take the state's declaration as an excuse for inaction, and they continued to stall on city-wide housing ordinances while awaiting further cues from the Minnesota legislature.[66]

Carl had begun to take upper-level courses in philosophy through the University of Minnesota's extension program,[67] and his knowledge of law paired with his interest in philosophy gave him insight and inspiration for his civil rights activism. He gave the problem of housing discrimination a great deal of thought, making pages and pages of notes, studying laws, and doing his best to formulate a plan of action that would finally lead to non-discriminatory housing in Saint Paul and beyond. In his personal notes from around this time, Carl wrote the following:

> *To be free is to live according to the law of our being. The craving for improvement indicates the existence of goodness and goodness of our inner being. Our action must respect personality. Personality can grow only in a freedom-pervading social ethics. Equality is a pre-condition of liberty.*

Carl and the rest of the Saint Paul NAACP continued to work tirelessly toward a solution to the housing crisis, writing letters to newspapers and government officials, educating the public, and gaining the support of other concerned citizens groups and equal rights organizations. Near the end of August in 1958, the city of

---

66   *Minneapolis Star*, "55% Prefer Owner's Rights."

67   From CLW personal files circa 1961–1963.

Saint Paul agreed to hold a public hearing on open occupancy, bringing together NAACP members and other civil rights activists, church leaders, and community representatives to speak before the Saint Paul city council. Among the speakers was Marshman Wattson of the American Civil Liberties Union, who spoke about the legal right to open occupancy that should be guaranteed to every citizen according to both federal and state constitutions. Leonard Carter, who at the time was president of the Saint Paul branch of the NAACP, presented evidence of overcrowding in minority neighborhoods in Saint Paul and the severe lack of housing opportunities available to them. Also in attendance were local church leaders, a representative from the Saint Paul Parent-Teachers Association, the director of the Minnesota Labor Committee for Human Rights, and many other concerned citizens and organizations who spoke up in favor of an open occupancy ordinance that would put an end to racial discrimination in housing throughout Saint Paul. Despite the pressure brought on by the hearing, the city council failed to take any meaningful action.[68]

It wasn't long before Carl would have his own private civil rights battle to fight, too. In February of 1959, a friend in France attempted to mail Carl a copy of Marquis de Sade's infamous book *The 120 Days of Sodom*. Reissued by Penguin in 2016, the book is now considered to be a "classic," but at the time the book was extremely controversial and was banned in many places.[69] Before Carl could receive it, the book was seized by US customs officials, who deemed the book "obscene." Carl objected on the basic principle of the matter, calling the seizure of the book "an attempt at thought control."[70] Despite multiple letters to the customs bureau, including one in which Carl enclosed postage and requested that

68   Blodgett, "Saint Paul Holds Hearing on Open Occupancy."
69   *The Guardian*, "'The Most Impure Tale Ever Written.'"
70   *Minneapolis Star Tribune*, "St. Paul Man Protests."

the bureau could at the very least send the book back to its original owner, the book was never returned.

Meanwhile, hope for further fair housing legislation at the state level was fading fast. After the 1957 declaration by the state legislature that nondiscrimination in housing was, in fact, a civil right, the State Interim Commission that was selected to review the problem decided that it wasn't enough of a problem to justify them doing anything further to solve it. The commission issued a majority opinion that since only 2 percent of Minnesota's total population was affected by housing discrimination, no further legislative action was required.

Five members of the commission who had disagreed with the recommendation decided to sponsor a fair housing bill anyway, albeit a rather weak one. The bill would have established penalties for discrimination in the commercial sale of homes or lots, but the law wouldn't have applied to individual homeowners in private transactions. Even with such a severely limited scope, the housing measure was swiftly defeated.[71] There was still one important state-level win for civil rights in Minnesota, however, with the defeat of a proposed amendment that would have allowed employers to require photos of applicants prior to interview, in effect giving employers a loophole for continuing discriminatory hiring practices. The Saint Paul NAACP had strongly denounced and opposed the proposed amendment.[72]

With state-level fair housing legislation defeated for that session, the NAACP decided to strengthen their efforts to obtain action at the city level. The group requested a second hearing on open occupancy to be held in Saint Paul on May 22, 1959, and the mayor of the city agreed. The NAACP made plans to provide transportation for anyone who wished to attend. The chamber was packed. For hours, the council members listened while the NAACP and other

---

71   *Austin Daily Herald*, "Human Rights Bills Have Hard Sledding."

72   Minnesota Historical Research Society, NAACP archives.

concerned organizations presented their demands for an open
occupancy ordinance to be passed without further delay.[73] As secretary of the Citizens' Committee for Open Occupancy, Carl was
asked to speak to the Saint Paul City Council that morning and act
as emcee, introducing the speakers and speaking a little himself,
as the chairman of the committee was unable to be in attendance.
Carl began by reminding the city council and mayor of the fact that
segregation in housing was indeed everybody's problem and not
only the problem of minorities:

> *When individuals are denied the opportunity or stimulus to*
> *self-improvement by the normal incentive of pride in property*
> *ownership, it is not they alone who suffer, but the whole commu-*
> *nity as well is deprived of the contributions which these persons*
> *might otherwise make.*

Throughout his presentation, Carl encouraged the city council
and mayor to take a personal ownership in the problem and to
take the actions needed to ensure equal rights to open housing.

> *Racial discrimination and segregation does not exist in isolation*
> *but is always influenced by the action or inaction of governmen-*
> *tal and legal institutions...If Saint Paul is to maintain its tradi-*
> *tion as an all-American city and America is truly to be the land*
> *of the free, then we must join the other cities and states that*
> *have recorded their belief in the individual dignity and equal-*
> *ity, as well as the absolute right, of all their citizens to partici-*
> *pate fully in our American society...Mayor Dillon and members*
> *of the city council, the Citizens' Committee for Open Occupancy*
> *strongly requests that action to provide fair housing for all be*
> *taken today.*

Over a dozen more speakers presented their cases in favor of
open occupancy, and nearly as many representatives from the
home builders, corporate, and real estate communities spoke
in opposition. The hearing stretched on for a record four hours,
finally ending with the council directing Louis P. Sheahan, a city

---

73   Blodgett, "Saint Paul Holds Hearing on Open Occupancy."

attorney, to look into the legality of a proposed ordinance that would make it a misdemeanor for property owners to refuse to sell or rent to anyone based on their race, creed, or color.[74] The attorney ultimately advised the city that fair housing was the state's problem, and that it was therefore out of their jurisdiction to do anything about it.[75] The Saint Paul NAACP was at a loss for what to do about the housing crisis, but they hadn't given up, and they vowed to continue their efforts until victory was won.

Later that year, on Halloween of 1959, Carl was unanimously elected president of the NAACP's Minnesota state conference of branches.[76] An article in the *Minneapolis Star* reporting on Carl's election illustrates his wide range of activities and interests at the time, mentioning not only that he was a business executive, but also including that Carl was "a writer in his spare time" who was working on a "satire of American mores and habits" as well as a "philosophical study of Aleister Crowley, a little-known British poet who died in 1948." The article also mentions that Carl had an impressive collection of books, which at the time included approximately "5,000 volumes mainly in the fields of philosophy, religion, witchcraft, and magic."[77]

In his new role as president of the Minnesota NAACP, Carl would renew and bolster the open occupancy effort by fostering greater cooperation between groups and individuals statewide that shared the common goal of obtaining a fair housing market. Not only was he involved with the NAACP, but he was also active in the ACLU, the Urban League, and the Metropolitan Housing Association, where he served on the board of directors.[78] The Metropolitan Housing Association was an organization of labor unions, credit unions, and cooperative housing developers founded to provide

74 Blodgett, "Saint Paul Holds Hearing on Open Occupancy."
75 *Minneapolis Star Tribune*, "A Fair Housing Law."
76 NAACP, *The Crisis* magazine, January 1960, 38–39.
77 *Minneapolis Star*, "Town Toppers."
78 NAACP, *The Crisis* magazine, January 1960, 38–39.

low-income housing options for minorities in the Twin Cities area. One of the group's earliest actions was to develop a 30-acre complex of apartment homes that would be open to anyone regardless of race, religion, or national origin.[79]

Shortly after Carl became president of the Minnesota NAACP, he called a special meeting of all the group's board members, branch presidents, and secretaries, and also invited a representative from the United Fair Housing Council. The plan was to host a statewide Fair Housing Conference, and Carl announced that a committee would be formed that very evening to plan the strategy for "welding the conferees together into the common organizational front" as well as create an outline of housing legislation "consistent with NAACP philosophy" that could be pursued at the state and city levels. One of the board members present at the meeting, Curtis Chivers, cut in to suggest that "there may not be much value in attacking the city rulings." Carl disagreed, stating that since the state legislature had declared in 1957 that fair housing was to be considered a civil right, the failure of the cities to secure these rights made the cities themselves "open to suit for the denial of civil rights."

There had also been some squabbling among some of the board members regarding two local organizations and which, if either, group the NAACP should work with in cooperative efforts to secure fair housing. A representative from one of the groups mentioned that their fair housing efforts were organized at a church meeting sponsored by a Catholic interracial council. One of the NAACP board members made a comment that if the churches really supported fair housing efforts, there would be no need to go from house to house giving out literature and pledge cards. Carl quickly put an end to this awkward moment by choosing that particular time to read out a telegram that had been sent to him by Leonard Carter, who by then had been promoted to the highly respected position

---

79   *Minneapolis Star Tribune*, "Housing Group Names Drug Official."

of NAACP regional secretary: "I am sincerely hopeful that a unified program with respect to the housing problem can be achieved as a result of this meeting," Carl read. After a brief moment of silence in which the group took in the words, a couple of the board members muttered comments about how the issue should never have had to come up in the first place. The discussion was ended with it being agreed that any organizations wanting to participate in the NAACP Fair Housing Program should be welcomed.

Later in the meeting, Carl revealed his limitless thinking when it came to finances. With a whopping $23.63 in the Minnesota state NAACP treasury at the time, Carl called for fundraising efforts to enable a budget of at least $1,300 in order to fund the Fair Housing Conference, to rent a space for the creation of a central NAACP office and hire a paid staff secretary, and to further "the immediate goal" of achieving "meaningful legislation to eliminate all synthetic barriers to the housing of one's choice and ability." Carl explained:

> We must challenge the conscience of citizens, legislators, and officials, and we must challenge the validity of any pseudo-legal obstructions to win these rights for all America.

The budget, however seemingly unrealistic and overly optimistic it appeared to be, was unanimously approved.[80]

Even with his new responsibilities as president of the Minnesota state NAACP, Carl remained just as active on the local level and continued to be a leading player in the quest to secure a city-wide open occupancy ordinance in Saint Paul. Although their efforts had so far met with little success, the group received acknowledgment in the NAACP's national member publication, *The Crisis*, which proclaimed:

---

80   Minnesota Historical Society, Minnesota State Conference of NAACP, minutes of a special board of directors meeting, December 15, 1959.

The St. Paul branch has pursued a concerted action to get the
local city council to adopt an "open occupancy" ordinance in order
to combat discrimination in the sale and rental of housing.[81]

The "concerted action" was not yet over, and within months Carl
was back at the podium speaking before the Saint Paul City Council, once again demanding an end to housing discrimination.

The city of Saint Paul was considering the sale of some property to be used as the future site of new housing construction,
and Carl wanted the city to stipulate that any housing constructed
on the property be open to anyone regardless of their skin color.
Since previous attempts to appeal to the morality of the council
had been unsuccessful, Carl took an approach this time around
that focused strictly on the laws. He made his case like a prose-
cuting attorney, clearly detailing state and federal civil rights laws
that were intended to prevent discrimination of the very type that
the city of Saint Paul was negligently allowing to occur. He praised
the city for having already decided to reduce the size of lots on the
property and encouraged the council to do more to benefit the ultimate residents of the area and the city as a whole, saying,

> *We urge that you, by resolution here today, act to further move in*
> *the interest of the public and assure yourselves that this needed*
> *housing will be open to all citizens on an equal basis.*

He then went on to describe the housing problem in Saint Paul
in a way that left little room for argument:

> *Our community is still allowing real estate agents to rent or sell*
> *to people, and bankers to finance such sales, on the basis of*
> *such people's color, religion, or nationality. Saint Paul's Corpo-*
> *ration Council feels that an ordinance outlawing discriminatory*
> *practices in housing is beyond the power of the city because*
> *of the state's declaration of concern that housing be available*
> *without discrimination. Here is an area of action that will clearly*
> *demonstrate Saint Paul's concern for the housing needs of all its*

---

81   NAACP, *The Crisis* magazine, August–September 1959, 433.

citizens. Failure to act may be construed, by some, as condon-
ing known discriminatory practices, and, in effect, racial zoning.
Action by the city would be to open new housing to all people
who can afford it and be in support of the Fourteenth Amend-
ment to the Federal Constitution—that a member of a minority
group shall not be denied equal rights, and the Fifth Amend-
ment—that the privileges of citizenship may not be withdrawn
from any citizen without due process of law.

In addition to the housing crisis, other civil rights battles were still waging across the nation as the fight for school desegregation expanded to become a fight for equal rights and desegregation in every aspect of public life, from riding the bus to ordering a sandwich at the soda fountain. In the South, segregation at lunch counters was still commonplace, with black customers being forced to stand or sit in separate areas away from white customers. Even large variety chain stores like Woolworth's had segregated lunch counters at their southern stores.

In a planned protest on February 1, 1960, a group of four black college students entered a Woolworth's location in Greensboro, North Carolina, sat at the lunch counter, and were denied service, just as they had expected would happen. They refused to leave, and both police and media were soon on the scene. The story quickly became nationwide news. The "Greensboro Four," as they had been nicknamed, remained in their seats at the Woolworth's counter until closing time, then returned the next day with more students to repeat their sit-in protest. By February 5 around 300 students had joined in, effectively shutting down business as usual in downtown Greensboro. NAACP chapters around the country soon became aware of the heavily televised protest and sponsored similar efforts in a show of solidarity.[82] In northern states NAACP chapters held demonstrations at local stores that were still allowing segregation at their southern locations. The Minnesota NAACP

---

82   "The Greensboro Sit-In," History.com, accessed July 9, 2017,
      www.history.com/topics/black-history/the-greensboro-sit-in.

was one of the first to join in the protest, with youth members picketing outside of the Woolworth's store in downtown Minneapolis later that same month. As president of the Minnesota NAACP, Carl was asked by the *Minneapolis Star Tribune* to comment on the local protest. The newspaper reports that Carl praised the "courage and conviction" of the NAACP youth members who had taken part in the demonstration, and he further commented:

> The NAACP in Minnesota must always protest injustice, and call attention to the public that our program is not one of appeasement but one of battle against every sign of second-class citizenship.[83]

When Carl spoke before the Minneapolis branch of the NAACP, he again praised the youths for their bold actions and emphasized the importance of such protests:

> These demonstrations are not merely protests against the racial practices in these stores…They are directed against all forms of racial segregation, including dragging school-desegregation, as they dramatize to the public the entire civil rights struggle. The retaliation by white supremacists, supported by local police, is becoming more severe as students are expelled from colleges, faculty members fired, arrests and heavy fines for so-called trespass and disturbance of the peace, beatings, and threats of more beatings—but the sit-in movement is growing faster than ever because today there is a new generation of the spirit that is determined to fight its own battle for equality and dignity. …Support here in Minnesota for this sit-in protest adds fuel to the fire that will force the national management of these chain stores to temper their business practices with human morality. Our demonstrations will give further strength to a new massing of support and action for our demand for full civil rights now. Our picketing seeks to prod all people out of their complacency and apathy in the face of continued injustice and forcible suppression of simple human dignity.

---

83   *Minneapolis Star Tribune*, "NAACP Hails Those Who Picketed."

By the end of March, the desegregation protests had spread to 55 cities in thirteen states, with civil rights advocates staging sit-ins and pickets at not only segregated lunch counters, but also segregated beaches, hotels, libraries, and other public facilities. Carl called the widespread protests "dramatic proof that simple human dignity is being forcibly suppressed in the South today."[84] Although protesters were frequently arrested and charged with trespassing, disorderly conduct, or disturbing the peace, the concerted efforts finally paid off, and diners and other establishments across the south were beginning to integrate by the summer of 1960.[85]

Soon after the Woolworth's protest in Minneapolis, the Fair Housing Conference was held in downtown Saint Paul, calling on "all people believing that property rights and housing opportunities should not be arbitrarily denied to any individual" to come together and take action. The purpose of the meeting, as Carl told the *Minneapolis Star Tribune*, was "to present a new understanding of the need for civil rights legislation." Local religious leaders, the dean of the University of Minnesota law school, an official from the Federal Housing Administration, civil rights leaders including NAACP national housing secretary Jack Wood, the deputy highway commissioner, and even the Minnesota state governor came together to share ideas and resources in the hope of finally putting an end to housing discrimination. Carl was one of the principal speakers at the event,[86] presenting a plan for action that he titled "An Outline for Effecting Fair Housing in Minnesota." He emphasized that fair

---

84   *The Carolina Times*, April 16, 1960, image 7, "Student Drive Against Segregation at Southern Lunch Counters Has Sparked Nationwide Action," accessed July 17, 2017, http://newspapers.digitalnc.org /lccn/sn83045120/1960-04-16/ed-1/seq-7/ocr/.

85   "The Greensboro Sit-in," History.com, accessed July 9, 2017, www.history.com/topics/black-history/the-greensboro-sit-in.

86   *Minneapolis Star*, "Federal Official," and *Minneapolis Star Tribune*, "Fair Housing Will Be Topic."

housing wasn't just the government's problem or the problem of minorities:

> *The winning of political and economic rights remains the moral problem of every American, for he must choose between the ideals of the American faith and his present indifference to the needs of other people. And he must choose, for it is personal responsibility for individual judgment and action that is the basis of democratic strength.*[87]

The concept of the "American Faith," according to Carl, encompassed

> *the ideals of the essential dignity of the individual, of the fundamental equality of all men, and of the unalienable rights to freedom, justice, and a fair opportunity.*

There were many attendees at the conference that were not members of the NAACP, and Carl sought not only to gain their support, but also to inspire them into action. The NAACP at the time was thought of by many people as a radical political organization, accused of everything from Communism to tyranny. Carl explained,

> *We are not political, but whenever people act in sympathy for others, whenever we are sensible to the demands of love and beauty in humanity, we engage in a moral act that is also a political act seeking to preserve and enlarge individual freedom.*

He called for citizens' committees to put more pressure on city governments to enact fair housing ordinances and to "answer the teachings of race hate by our enemy, and the false information given by the misinformed."[88] Further pursuit of new fair housing legislation at the state level was also in the works.

---

87   CLW, "An Outline for Effecting Fair Housing in Minnesota," presentation to Fair Housing Conference, St. Paul, MN, March 5, 1960.

88   Ibid.

Less than two weeks later, Carl was traveling to Washington, DC, to join the ranks of Roy Wilkins, Martin Luther King Jr., and other influential civil rights leaders from across the nation to take part in the Leadership Conference on Civil Rights. A lobbying group comprised of members from many different civil rights organizations, the Leadership Conference on Civil Rights had spearheaded the drive for every major civil rights legislation beginning with the passage of the Civil Rights Act of 1957.[89]

When Carl attended the conference in March of 1960, the goal was to make integration, voter rights, fair housing, and other civil rights causes a national priority. They were pushing for a comprehensive federal civil rights bill that would actually make a significant impact on the lives of Americans. What they got was the Civil Rights Act of 1960, which established federal inspection of voter registration sites and provided penalties for anyone who attempted to obstruct a person's right to vote or register to vote. It also extended the duration of the Civil Rights Commission, which would remain in charge of overseeing voting practices.

Although it would be several years before more comprehensive civil rights bills were passed, the groundwork laid by the Leadership Conference time and again helped to gain the congressional support needed to make reality the Civil Rights Act of 1964, the Voting Rights Act of 1965, and the Fair Housing Act of 1968, which finally banned discrimination in most housing nationwide.[90]

Less than two months after the Leadership Conference, on May 6, 1960, Carl had the opportunity to speak before the Democratic Party Platform Committee, representing the NAACP and outlining their hopes for greater attention to be paid to the civil rights struggle not just in housing discrimination, but also in areas such as

---

89   "NAACP: A Century in the Fight for Freedom," Library of Congress, accessed July 10, 2017, https://www.loc.gov/exhibits/naacp/the -civil-rights-era.html.

90   Ibid.

the sluggish desegregation of schools and the voter suppression that continued in the South. He urged,

> *We call for a civil rights plank that demands stronger legislation in the next congress and aggressive leadership by the executive branch of the federal government. We must have an end to the philosophy of gradualism that has been used to justify the continued suppression of citizenship function and individual opportunity in the hard-core South. The federal government has the moral obligation to promote voting by its citizens and to extend sanction to those citizens and organizations promoting the registration and voting of persons not now fully participating in the political life of the nation.*

At the time, the southern black vote was only 25 percent of its potential. Carl continued,

> *New civil rights legislation must support the Supreme Court's school desegregation decision and must direct the executive branch to aid in the integration of public school systems with all deliberate speed. We call for the Democratic Party to act with courage in the framing of its platform; to act without fear of reprisals and threats from Southern "hangers-on," we call for you to act for individual opportunity and progress and not for the advocates of apartheid.*[91]

The civil rights cause did indeed make it into the Democratic Party platform that year, and although it was tacked on right toward the bottom of a very long document, when John F. Kennedy accepted the presidential nomination, it was one of the first things he mentioned, stating that "'The Rights of Man'—the civil and economic rights essential to the human dignity of all men—are indeed our goal and our first principles. This is a Platform on which I can run with enthusiasm and conviction."[92]

---

91   CLW, "Presentation Before the Democratic Party Platform Committee," representing the NAACP, May 6, 1960.

92   "1960 Democratic National Convention, 15 July 1960," John F. Kennedy Presidential Library and Museum, accessed July 10, 2017, https://www.jfklibrary.org/Asset-Viewer/AS08q5oYz0SFUZg9uOi4iw .aspx.

Late June of 1960 brought civil rights leaders from around the country to Saint Paul for the 51st Annual NAACP convention. Carl had been named to co-chair the National Convention Committee along with Donald Lewis, and the two had taken charge of making arrangements and preparations for the event. The convention was so large in stature and importance that more than 100 NAACP members had been selected to assist them.[93]

For seven days, goals and strategies for winning important civil rights battles were discussed. Topics at the convention included raising the minimum wage to $1.25 an hour (minimum wage was only $1.00 an hour at the time), supporting nondiscrimination in unions, unemployment benefits, social security protection, and health coverage.[94] Among the speakers was Barbara Posey, a teenage girl who at age fifteen had helped to organize and lead the local NAACP youth council in a successful lunch counter sit-in at a Katz drugstore in Oklahoma City in 1958, a year and a half prior to the Greensboro Four sit-in held at the Woolworth's in North Carolina.[95] Since the event didn't receive as much media attention, it was overlooked and overshadowed by the Greensboro Four protest, but Posey's protest in Oklahoma City was actually the first successful lunch counter integration sit-in of the era.

Addressing a crowd of around 1,000 adult delegates and several hundred NAACP youth members on the day after she turned seventeen, Posey began,

As you travel in America, you notice a cancer, a very old cancer, the cancer of segregation and discrimination as it works to destroy the things that we love best. The cancer is working against every religious and democratic principle that we have been taught and that we cherish.

---

93   *Minneapolis Star Tribune*, "Chairmen Named for NAACP Convention."

94   NAACP, *The Crisis* magazine, November 1960.

95   "Oklahoma City African Americans Sit-In for Integration, 1958–1964," Global Non-Violent Action Database, accessed July 9, 2017, nvdatabase.swarthmore.edu/content/oklahoma-city-african -americans-sit-integration-1958-64.

She went on to state that

> We don't want promises—we want to eat, and we want that bal-
> lot. We want it now, and we plan to get both the ballot and a
> Coke. We plan to attend school and to buy that house in any
> neighborhood that we like.[96]

Other speakers included A. Philip Randolph, chairman of the
Negro American Labor Council, and Orville Freeman, the governor of Minnesota. Workshop topics included strategies for sit-in
demonstrations, plans for expanding the vote, and ways to use
purchasing power as a tool for achieving civil rights. Roy Wilkins
was given an "Outstanding Achievement" award,[97] the same award
Carl would receive just a few years later.[98]

The NAACP drive for fair housing in Minnesota never let up, and
eventually their efforts began to bear fruit. After a long campaign
and countless compromises and negotiations, in April of 1961
Minnesota became the ninth state in the nation to enact a statewide fair housing law to prevent discrimination in the sale and
rental of housing due to race, religion, or national origin. Exclu-
sions were made for owner-occupied duplexes, owner-occupied
rooming houses, and one-family dwellings not financed with public
funds, so the law was weaker than fair housing proponents would
have liked, but it was at least something, at least a start. The new
law wouldn't go into effect until the beginning of 1963, however, so
the Saint Paul NAACP continued to pursue a city-wide open occupancy ordinance that was not only stronger, but also would take
effect more quickly.[99]

Even after the state law was implemented, the problem was far
from over, as it would take many more years for public opinion to
catch up with the new regulations. One realtor, Edward Tilsen,

---

96   Houck and Dixon, *Women and the Civil Rights Movement*, 119–121.

97   *Pittsburgh Courier*, "NAACP Faces Challenge."

98   *Minneapolis Star*, "NAACP Group Will Present Awards to 11."

99   *Minneapolis Star Tribune*, "A Fair Housing Law."

reported getting multiple phone calls threatening "to dispose of me if I didn't stop selling to negroes."[100] Although laws preventing housing discrimination are now well-established, it's a problem that still affects many Americans to this day.

Over the course of the next several years, Carl's life would change forever as he took a leap of faith to pursue his long-held dream of becoming a publisher. However, he remained very active in the NAACP as well the ACLU. He served on the Minnesota ACLU executive committee for three years as secretary-treasurer, and eventually served as vice president of the organization.[101] The ACLU provides legal defense and advice in cases involving potential civil rights abuses, and one of the jobs of the executive committee in Minnesota was to decide which cases the group would enter. At one of the meetings, Carl and the other committee members voted unanimously to take the case and represent a black resident of Saint Paul who had been arrested while doing civil rights work in Mississippi. When the arrest was made, attorneys for the ACLU moved to transfer the case to federal court. While being transported into federal custody, the victim reported that he had been beaten by the Mississippi police.[102]

Other cases in which the Minnesota ACLU lent their legal aid included a book censorship case,[103] the case of a man who had been arrested without due process and imprisoned for eight weeks without a hearing or trial,[104] and a particularly interesting case involving the arrest of the owner of a Minneapolis art gallery for exhibiting a painting—"The Lovers"—that the city police officers had deemed "obscene." Carl was a lifetime member of the Minneapolis

---

100 *Minneapolis Star Tribune,* "Dealers Say Law Is Not Solution."

101 *Minneapolis Star,* "Frank Farrell Named Head of State ACLU" and *Minneapolis Star Tribune,* "State ACLU Elects Karlins as President."

102 Minnesota Historical Society Research Library, ACLU Minnesota branch, MCLU executive committee meeting, May 20, 1964.

103 Ibid., MCLU executive committee meeting, August 5, 1965, and September 2, 1965.

104 Ibid., June 10, 1965.

Society of Fine Arts and felt very strongly about the right of people to create, buy, and sell any art they chose. The gallery had been raided by officers of the Minneapolis Morals Squad, the painting was seized, and the shop's proprietor had been arrested. The Minnesota ACLU offered support and aid to the gallery owner's legal team, and when the matter came to court, the Defense made a motion to suppress the painting from evidence since the arrest of the gallery owner and the seizure of the painting were carried out without warrants. The motion was granted, and with no painting as evidence, the city was forced to drop its claims of immorality against the gallery.[105]

While Carl was serving on the board, the Minnesota ACLU was also heavily involved in reforming and preventing civil rights abuses carried out by law enforcement. One effort was to probe the city and county jails in an attempt to investigate possible civil rights abuses and to put pressure on the precincts to improve conditions.[106] The group also presented a civil rights training course to the Minneapolis police department and to the University of Minnesota campus police. They decided to establish a fundraising branch for the specific purpose of raising money to cover the legal expenses of defendants whose civil rights had been violated,[107] and agreed to help with the Indian Civil Rights Defense Fund, working closely with the Minnesota Chippewa Tribal Council and reviewing cases of police brutality against Chippewas (Ojibwe).[108]

One important focus of the work the Minnesota ACLU did throughout the time that Carl was vice president of the organization was to reform the state's mental commitment laws. At the

105 Ibid., MCLU executive committee meeting, January 27, 1966.

106 Shaver, "MCLU to Probe City, County Jails."

107 "American Civil Liberties Union of Minnesota (Saint Paul, Minn.): An Inventory of its Records at the Minnesota Historical Society," "Historical Note," Minnesota Historical Society Research Library, accessed July 9, 2017, www.2.mnhs.org/library/findaids/00497.xml.

108 Minnesota Historical Society Research Library, ACLU Minnesota branch, MCLU executive committee meeting, June 9, 1964.

time, all anyone had to do to have another person committed for mental health issues was to file a petition. Often, the accused party would be held for observation and examination without a prior hearing, and there was no limit set on the time a person could be involuntarily detained before a hearing was to be held or a decision rendered. Those detained were often subjected to nonconsensual medical examinations and shock treatments as part of the observation and examination procedures, and they were routinely prevented from contacting friends, family, or doctors on the outside. One seventy-four-year-old man had been held at the Veteran's Hospital in St. Cloud, Minnesota, for fifteen months before the Minnesota ACLU secured his release. Before being committed, the man had been given a ten-minute hearing (without prior notice) in which he had been denied a lawyer and was not allowed to present any witnesses.

The ACLU also secured the release of a man who had been detained at a state mental hospital for three years without having been given any sort of hearing whatsoever and without being allowed to seek the advice of a lawyer. After the ACLU learned of the case and requested a hearing with the local court, the man was quickly released.[109] Due in part to the pressure brought on by the ACLU, the Minnesota state legislature eventually agreed, by unanimous vote, to modify its mental commitment laws, securing for accused parties the right to attend their own hearing and the right to consult with a lawyer prior to the hearing. It also put a sixty-day time limit on how long a person could be held for observation before the court reviewed the case, and guaranteed for patients the right to send uncensored letters, the right to be free of restraints, and the right to refuse nonemergency medical procedures.[110]

Carl eventually found that he was spreading himself much too thin, and he started thinking that it might be time to cut back on

---

109 Castner, "The Case for Commitment Law Reform."
110 Newlund, "Passes Both Houses."

his many commitments and responsibilities. Important victories had been won, and now there were plenty of other people to take up the reins of leadership. He was bothered, too, by the potential for "mob mentality" to develop in situations of large-group activism that he realized could be an issue even within a positive cause like civil rights. He had witnessed firsthand how easily a crowd could be swayed by the words and actions of a single individual backed by a grand ideology that invited everyone to hop on board the bandwagon. As Carl described it,

> It was an amazing time when at any time a spark could have ignited a holocaust. I was behind the scenes with a master of crowd psychology [Hubert Humphrey, who was a Minnesota senator at the time and active in the civil rights movement]. He would say a few words, and the crowd would literally surge forward, and then he would raise his hands and say something like, "But we don't want that!" and the crowd would move back. He knew what he was doing and would turn to look and grin.[111]

Though Carl thought Hubert was a great man, he also considered him to be a real-life example of what occult circles refer to as an "energy vampire." He didn't think of it in a derogatory way, but rather as simply another way of existing, which some people happened to be—their own vitality dependent on their natural quality of absorbing emotional energy from others. It's sort of like being a psychic sponge, picking up the extra from the abundant, limitless flow of emotions that most humans never seem to stop exuding. Carl recounted one of his most standout memories of the "energy vampire" who eventually became the thirty-eighth vice president of the United States:

> I remember one time he was giving a speech in downtown Saint Paul. There was the most drained man. He was pasty white. He'd been at it all day. And then he started talking. And you could see him absorbing vitality from the people. The more he

---

111   CLW email to Melanie Marquis, September 10, 2013.

talked, his cheeks got rosy, he got this vibrant energy, bouncing up and down... Hubert was a very interesting person.[112]

Witnessing leaders such as Hubert Humphrey who were able to move a crowd with nothing more than a word or a gesture showed Carl that such power was potentially very dangerous. Even though he was on the right side of it, truly fighting for liberty and justice for all, he realized that many problems could arise whenever individuals give up their individuality to mechanically follow any particular leader, cause, or ideology. It disturbed him to see crowds of civil rights activists eagerly following any command they were given without any pause or question. Although the leaders were good and the cause was just, Carl could see clearly that if that were *not* the case, things could indeed go very, very wrong.

The actions and approaches of civil rights advocates around the country varied widely, and a rift had begun to form between those who thought a peaceful solution was still possible and those who felt that if violent means were necessary to secure equality, then violent means would indeed be pursued. There were many extremely influential and impressive civil rights leaders at the time who were raising their voices louder and louder in demand of fairness and freedom, incidentally gaining devoted followers along the way who looked up to those leaders in an almost religious fashion, ready to follow the next call to action without the slightest delay.

Carl greatly admired Martin Luther King Jr. and his unrelenting optimism and advocacy for a peaceful path to equality, but he realized that here was a man with an almost godlike power. He was fully confident that a person like King was unlikely to ever abuse that power, but the reactions of the crowds when faced with such a charismatic leader concerned him nonetheless. He described King as a "great man" and even wrote him a letter that is still held in the archives of a research library in Boston. As much as he looked up

---

112 Bahn, "Hubert Humphrey Was a Vampire!"

to the man, however, and as much as he agreed with his approach, he acknowledged the fact that King was an individual who "could have ignited a revolution that would have turned into horror" if he had chosen to do so.

Revolution and horror indeed seemed more and more imminent across the country as many minorities and activists were becoming increasingly frustrated with the continued rise in police brutality, assassinations of civil rights leaders, violence at the hands of racists, and the pervasive atmosphere of society-sponsored, government-advocated ill treatment and disregard in general. Though the struggle for civil rights had been waging in earnest since 1954, the goals of the movement were still far from being won. Police brutality and violence at the hands of racist whites was still a common fate for minorities as well as for civil rights activists of every color and creed. People were understandably frustrated and upset, and many had reached a point where they were willing to meet violence with violence, brutality with brutality. Hope for gaining victory through peaceful means alone was seeming more and more futile by the day, and outbursts of violence on both sides of the civil rights fight were becoming more and more commonplace across the nation.

In the summer of 1967 tensions between blacks in North Minneapolis and the local police had reached a breaking point. When a black woman was mistreated by the police at a parade that was meant to be a celebration of the community, a large group of citizens decided that enough was enough. They took their cause to the streets of North Minneapolis, demanding justice in a burst of vandalism, arson, looting, and physical assault. Ten people were injured and thirteen protestors—including several children—were arrested. The Minnesota National Guard was called in, and for several days hundreds of officers dressed in riot gear monitored the area to ensure that no further violence would ensue.[113]

---

113   Marks, "Civil Unrest on Plymouth Avenue, Minneapolis, 1967."

Carl's grandfather, Carl Weschcke, Jr., known as Charles (August 1870–February 1954).

Carl's father, Carl Weschcke III (November 1894–October 1973).

The log cabin built at Hazel Hills, the family farm in western Wisconsin where Carl spent many happy summer days.

Early advertisement
and window display
for Adlerika, the
Adlerika Company's
bestselling product.

CARL WESCHKE, rugged individualist, physical culturist, ath-
lete, vegetarian, successful business man, plant breeder, Creator and Originator of the Hazilbert, which appears destined
to feed a famishing world if the present population growth
and soil depletion continues. Mr. Weschke's work and his
life are a genuine inspiration. His work and the reason for it
is introduced in this issue.

OCTOBER, 1962

"YOUTH PHYSICAL FITNESS" Manual by President Kennedy's Council
On Youth Fitness, Analyzed and Evaluated   Page 8
THIRTY FIRST ANNNUAL THANKSGIVING DAY DINNER
VEGETARIAN SOCIETY OF NEW YORK

NOVEMBER 22, DAIRYLAND RESTAURANT, 266 West 33rd Street (Near
Eighth Avenue). For Reservations See Page 16

Carl's father featured on the cover of *American Vegetarian-
Hygienist*. He was a vegetarian and health enthusiast.

Carl as a young lad.

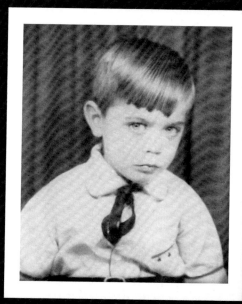

A moody Carl.

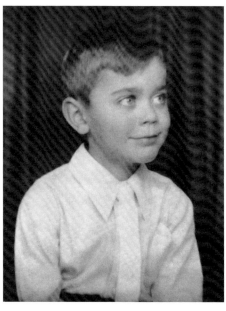

An eager-looking Carl.

Carl monkeying around with who is thought to be his Grandmother Weschcke.

An early indication of Carl's interest in cars?

Carl with younger brother Ernest on a tractor at their farm, from Carl's father's book *Growing Nuts in the North*.

64   GROWING NUTS IN THE NORTH

Electrically operated wagon constructed of native butternut wood known for strength and light weight as well as durability. Author's sons aboard. Photo by C. Weschcke 1941.

CARL LOUIS WESCHCKE

Glee Club
First Lieutenant in Military
Managerial Staff
First Team Hockey
Second Team Football
Now and Then

"Does anyone want to buy a 1908, nine-passenger car for $700?" This is one of the questions with which Carl Weschcke greets everyone. The other question is "Who wants to sell their car for $50?" As you have guessed Carl is interested in old cars. He is particularly fond of large noisy ones, but model T's or electric cars will do. After Carl has managed to purchase another sample of primeval machinery and to sell his present means of conveyance, he is very pleased if his net deficit is less than $10. The only car we have yet to see him drive is a 1948 model.

When Carl is not busy with his old car trade-in service, he has many affairs to take care of in school. For several years he was Sergeants Boyke's Sergeant Friday. In this capacity he kept the military books, and made out the military "D" list. This year he was promoted to a first Lt. and Battalion Adj.

Carl's yearbook page from his high school days at St. Paul Academy

Three Carls in a row: Carl standing between his grandfather and father.

A dashing young adult Carl, perhaps on his way to college.

Llewellyn George, founder of Llewellyn Publications.

A 1906 copy of the original *Planetary Day and Hour Book* by Llewellyn George, which Carl may have used as the basis for *Llewellyn's Astrological Pocket Planner*, first published in 1996.

The 1908 third edition of the *Planetary Daily Guide*, which is now called *Llewellyn's Daily Planetary Guide*.

Early home to Llewellyn Publications in Los Angeles, CA, while still owned by Llewellyn George.

Though he was in full agreement in his frustration with the continued injustices being committed by the local police, the violence and destruction that had ensued in Minneapolis was disappointing to Carl. The incident gave him pause and made him reconsider if his own approach was truly the best. He wondered if a more individual style of activism would serve him better than the type of mass-action group activism he had been fully engaged in for over a decade. He was a respected leader in the civil rights community, and his belief in the importance of equal rights for every human had in no way diminished. His life was pulling him in new directions, however, and he simply didn't have enough time to do everything he wanted to do. He had new dreams to manifest and more goals to achieve, which demanded more attention than he could give without giving up some of his other commitments. He decided it was a good time to shift his focus so that he would have more energy to lend to his other pursuits. He quietly stepped down from the Minnesota ACLU board of directors before his three-year term as vice president came to an end. Years later Carl would describe his feelings on mass action in a way that helps shed light on the thoughts that may have went on behind the scenes in his decision:

> All mass action is political or religiously organized to "bind people together" into an irrational and hence unconscious union that is administered from the top for purposes that are entirely a denial of evolutionary energies...Never give your power over to another, and never let it be subsumed into a crowd no matter how noble the cause seems, because that's the road to dictatorships, to mass terror, and to the loss of humanness.[114]

Carl believed in the rights of individuals to be individuals, and he believed it the duty of each individual to try their best to become their own best selves, to be an agent of change in one's own unique way and to take an active role in their own evolution. He felt that only through individual evolution could the evolution of humanity

---

114   CLW email to Melanie Marquis, September 10, 2013.

as a whole take place, and he had come to believe that individuality could be easily lost in the group-mind, follow-the-leader atmosphere that can pervade any type of mass-action activism.

Carl retained his status as a lifetime member of the ACLU as well as the NAACP, and he continued being active on an individual level, writing letters to newspapers and lawmakers in support of equality throughout the years and decades to come. Though he stepped away from direct involvement in the organized group efforts of the civil rights movement, he remained every bit as passionate about the cause.

Chapter 5

1960s

Several years after he first teamed up with the civil rights movement, Carl's dreams of becoming a publisher began brewing in earnest. Beginning with what he attributed to "a Saturn return" around age twenty-nine, Carl had begun to feel irresistibly drawn toward the world of books, magazines, and the occult like never before. In addition to his custom-printed letterhead for "The Baron's Press," Carl had taken out a subscription to *Publishers Weekly*, at the time a very small trade publication read almost exclusively by publishers and booksellers. He was feeling pretty certain now that he wanted to become a publisher, although he wasn't really sure what steps he needed to take to get there. He figured he could start by doing things that publishers do, like reading *Publishers Weekly* in hopes of learning all he could about the book business. He wanted to prepare himself for success on the road ahead that he hoped to create.

A small ad that Carl happened to spot in the pages of *Publishers Weekly* one day set him on a course that he had not anticipated but that excited him completely. The ad was a listing for a small publisher of astrology books that was up for sale. Carl recounted,

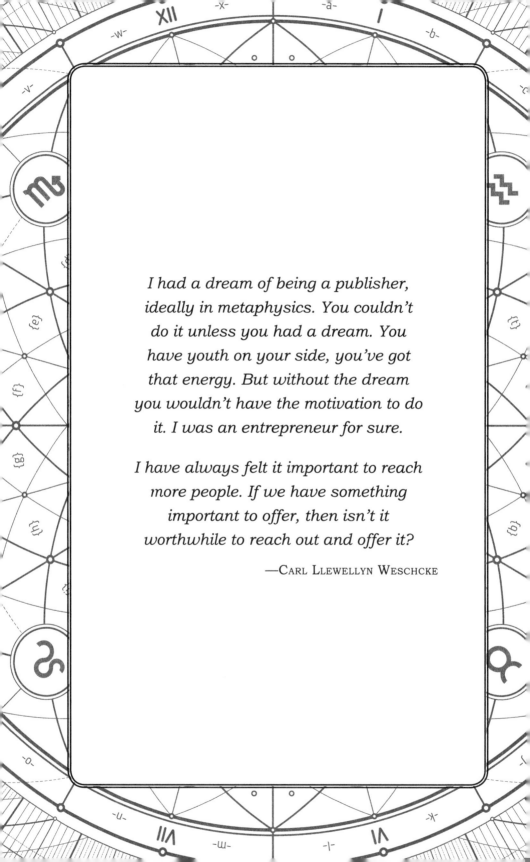

I had a dream of being a publisher, ideally in metaphysics. You couldn't do it unless you had a dream. You have youth on your side, you've got that energy. But without the dream you wouldn't have the motivation to do it. I was an entrepreneur for sure.

I have always felt it important to reach more people. If we have something important to offer, then isn't it worthwhile to reach out and offer it?

—CARL LLEWELLYN WESCHCKE

Until the day in 1959 when I saw that classified advertisement, it had not been in my mind to buy an established publishing company. I had thought to gradually publish one or two books to learn the trade, and then slowly to leave the world of pharmaceuticals for that of books. But that advertisement triggered a response. It was the right moment for it to happen.[115]

Having a lifelong interest in astrology and the occult, this seemed to Carl to be exactly the opportunity he had been dreaming of, and he soon entered into correspondence with Richard Juline, a printer who had bought the business several years earlier from Llewellyn George's estate.

Llewellyn George

Described as a "good-natured, lovable, plump" man,[116] Llewellyn George was born in Swansea, Wales, on August 17, 1876. While in his youth, George and his family moved to America and lived in Chicago for a number of years. He graduated from the Chicago School of Electricity in 1898.

Around this time, George became intrigued with the work of astrologer Professor W. H. Chaney, who had returned to Chicago following an extended teaching tour. An expert astrologer, Professor Chaney was, incidentally, the father of the writer who became known as Jack London, though Chaney had been estranged from his family since before Jack was born. George learned all he could from Professor Chaney, and he was eager to learn more. George soon decided to make a major move. Professor Chaney had spent some time in Portland, Oregon, and it may have been this connection that led George to pack up his life and relocate to the Pacific Northwest.

It wasn't long after settling in Portland that George made the acquaintance of another student of Professor Chaney, a woman

---

115 Night Sky, "Carl Llewellyn Weschcke."

116 Bytheriver, "Llewellyn George."

named Ida Hulery Fletcher. A palmist and astrologer, Fletcher had a dream to open up a school of astrology, a dream which George was able to jump on board with full enthusiasm. By 1901 the Portland School of Astrology was born, and along with it, Llewellyn George's first forays into the world of publishing blossomed naturally into being. George had agreed to teach classes in astrology, but the problem was he didn't have any decent course materials with which to teach. There simply weren't any thorough, detailed, practical, and straightforward astrological study lessons available that George found sufficient, so he had to develop his own. He began creating a series of lessons in astrology, writing the content and rolling them out by hand on a small printing press that Fletcher had procured.

Being a prolific writer and having a driving desire to share all the information he could, George ended up creating quite an abundance of these astrological study guides for his students. As the school became more established, it occurred to George and Fletcher that other astrology enthusiasts who weren't students at the school might also have an interest in the study materials that George had created, so they started making these publications available to the general public, issued directly from Portland School of Astrology Publishing.

In 1905, by which time George was serving as the chief astrologian and principal of the school while Fletcher served as director, the first issue of the *Portland School of Astrology Bulletina* was released, which outlined astrological forecasts for each of the twelve signs of the zodiac. Retitled a few years later as the *Astrological Bulletina*, the publication grew to be quite popular. It did so well, in fact, that the Bulletina Press was adopted as the new moniker for the school's publishing endeavors.[117] A police chief in Oakland, California, was so impressed with the guide that he sang its praises to a local newspaper reporter. The police chief explained

---

117   Frost, "Ida Hulery Fletcher and the Portland School of Astrology."

that he used astrology to help him better perform his duties in law enforcement, consulting the *Astrological Bulletina* to find out the ruling influences of the day so that he could predict what crimes were most likely to be committed and thus take proactive steps to help prevent them. "The chart has never failed me up to the present time," said Chief John H. Nedderman.[118] Such endorsements helped to boost the credibility of astrology in the mind of the general public.

The year 1905 also brought the release of Llewellyn George's *Planetary Daily Guide*, marking the first modern book to offer advanced astrological information in a way that was accessible to nonprofessionals. The *Planetary Daily Guide* was also the first-ever annual produced by Llewellyn. In 1906 George would debut the *Moon Sign Book*. First copyrighted under the title *Better than Magic*, the *Moon Sign Book* included the *Planetary Daily Guide* as well as an abundance of information on how to live in tune with lunar cycles. The book's design incorporated the crescent moon symbol that eventually became the official logo of Llewellyn Publications. George played around with different titles for the book, which quickly became his most popular publication, calling it the *Moon's Sign Book* for a time before eventually settling on simply the *Moon Sign Book*.

Other major titles included the *A to Z Horoscope Maker and Delineator*, first published in 1910. Offering a complete system for casting horoscopes and interpreting them with accuracy, the book helped further establish Llewelyn George's reputation as a trusted authority in the astrological community.

As the publishing arm of the school grew, Llewellyn George made a name for himself in the world of astrology. In 1911 he decided to strike out on his own and open the Llewellyn College of Astrology. He acquired his own printing equipment and continued producing the same publications he had become best known for.

---

118 *Oakland Tribune,* June 11, 1919.

George had learned a lot about the printing trade from his friend L. H. Weston, another astrologer, author, and student of Professor Chaney who had experience as a professional printer. By 1912 George had officially adopted the name of Llewellyn Publications. He produced a number of new astrological pamphlets and books, but the *Astrological Bulletina* and the *Moon Sign Book* continued to be Llewellyn George's signature publications. George's brother Griffeth, known affectionately as Griff, soon made the move from Chicago to the West Coast so that he could assist with the work at Llewellyn Publications.

In 1913 George cofounded the American Astrological Society in New York City. He continued taking pupils at the Llewellyn College of Astrology, and he made his course materials available to the general public through the mail. For just ten dollars (the equivalent of around $250 in 2018), students would receive a complete course in astrology. His main priority to educate and not to profit. Llewellyn George let prospective students know upfront that if they couldn't afford the full price of the course, they could just pay a dollar or two and get the rest to him later.[119]

In addition to books and courses in astrology, Llewellyn George offered a number of interesting products, including a tonic he called Planetary Hair Grower. A newspaper article from 1913 says of the concoction,

> This *Planetary Hair Grower* is no brother to the common unguents and elixirs of the barber shops, but a transcendental and ineffable tonic, of star grease and moon madness all compact.

The official product description stated that the tonic was made from the "purest herbs, etc." and explained that it was carefully prepared under "proper benefic planetary influences at their auspicious times." The Planetary Hair Grower sold for only $1.00 and included full instructions for exactly when to use the tonic for best results, as accorded by the phases of the moon.[120]

---

119 Mencken, "On Astrologer Llewellyn George."
120 Ibid.

Llewellyn George eventually married a woman named Mignon Ruth, who had also lived in Chicago. Widowed, Mignon Ruth had a son from her previous marriage. In 1920, desiring a change of scenery, the George family moved to Los Angeles in hopes of finding an environment more accepting and open to the idea of astrology and its study. There George began writing for the *Los Angeles Times* and contributed to a number of periodicals.

The Llewellyn College of Astrology was reopened in Los Angeles,[121] and George was pleased to find a new steady stream of students eager to take his courses. George had left a mark on the town of Portland that was not forgotten. In honor and remembrance of his legacy, a modern school of astrology that opened in 2013 chose to adopt the original name of the Portland School of Astrology as their own.[122]

In 1927 George founded the National Astrological Association in Los Angeles and served as its president for the first five years. He then started to do a lot of traveling, touring the country, selling his books and pamphlets, and offering astrological lectures to interested groups.[123]

Through his lectures and books, Llewellyn George developed a reputation for his publishing company as well as for himself. His approach to astrology was practical and understandable, and generations of professional astrologers were able to effectively learn their art through his books and study guides.

In 1938 George was awarded with a prestigious honor, receiving the first life endowment from the American Federation of Scientific Astrologers, an organization based in Washington, DC, that incidentally had developed from the National Astrological Association that he had founded in 1927. The organization bestowed upon him the title of "Fellow of Astrology," and he was deemed the "Dean of

---

121 *Detroit Free Press*, "Soothsaying Auto Worker."

122 Portland School of Astrology, "About," "Our Story," http://portlandastrology.org/mission/.

123 Bytheriver, "Llewellyn George."

American Astrologers." George wrote to the organization to express his gratitude, stating,

> I wish to emphasize that I sincerely appreciate the certificate and all it implies, including the title "Fellow of Astrology," as I consider myself a humble student feeling his way toward enlightenment among the stars.[124]

Though Llewellyn George's work did much to loosen the stigma of charlatanry and superstition associated with astrology, such negative opinions of the practice continued to cling in ways that George was not able to idly tolerate. When anti-fortunetelling laws in the forties were threatening the viability of astrology as a profession, George got together with other astrologers and drew up a bill to present to California lawmakers that would have established legitimacy for professional astrology. To gain support for his cause and to bolster his credentials, he became a charter member of the First Temple of Astrology, opened in Los Angeles, and he also founded an organization called Educational Astrology, Inc. George and his colleagues teamed up with lawmaker Everett G. Burkhalter, who presented the bill to the California state legislature in 1943. The bill was soundly defeated.[125] George wasn't ready to give up, however, and continued his campaign to bring an end to anti-fortunetelling laws. Though he never succeeded in that particular quest, he brought the idea of astrology as a credible and legitimate practice and profession into the minds of many.

Llewellyn George passed out of this life in 1954 at the age of seventy-seven, leaving behind seventeen books, countless articles and other publications, and a legacy that brought practical astrology into the twentieth century and beyond. In 1963 the International Congress of Astral Sciences voted Llewellyn George as "America's finest astrological writer."[126]

---

124 Bytheriver, "Llewellyn George."
125 Ibid.
126 Ibid.

Carl had great respect for Llewellyn George's work, and he was excited about the prospect of taking over the reins of the small publishing house. However, the venture was extremely risky. Everyone he asked about it advised him to steer clear. Llewellyn Publications didn't seem like a very lucrative endeavor at the time. The company was publishing only a few titles a year, which were sold almost exclusively through mail order. Sales amounted to only about $40,000 annually, not subtracting any operating costs. But Carl had a good feeling about it, all the same. He decided to trust his intuition about Llewellyn and take the gamble, despite having myriad less-risky investment opportunities to choose from. "My decision was based purely on the fact that it was something I wanted to do," Carl explained. "And once you're on the path, you naturally want to push forward."[127]

Push forward, he did. In corresponding with Llewellyn's current owner, Carl discovered an advantage in his favor. It turned out that Richard Juline had never actually wanted to be a publisher. A resident of Philadelphia who disliked the cold, Juline had bought Llewellyn so that he would have a printing plant in Los Angeles and be able to relocate to a warmer climate. He wasn't interested in the publishing aspects of the business at all; he was really only interested in the physical building and the printing equipment.

Juline was eager to sell, and Carl was eager to buy. They settled on a purchase price of around $50,000. In early January 1961 Carl took a few days off work to travel to Los Angeles to negotiate the terms of the sale and to see what the business involved. Juline would retain ownership of the printing plant, but Carl would take over as owner of the publishing house. A month later, on February 6, 1961, the papers were signed, and Carl was back in LA as the official owner of Llewellyn Publications.

---

127   Sutin, "Father of the New Age."

It took a weeklong stay for Carl to learn what he could from Juline about the book publishing business and to get all the inventory sorted and packed away. Although he loved the California sunshine, Carl's family and his life were in Minnesota, and he had no intention of relocating to the West Coast. Llewellyn Publications was fated to start a new era in Carl's hometown. A freight car was hired, and Carl helped load the boxes of inventory onto the train back to Saint Paul himself.

Carl was living in a small house he had inherited from his grandfather, and he hadn't yet acquired any premises for his new publishing business. When the freight train arrived in Saint Paul, Carl's new and rather massive stock of Llewellyn books was unloaded in the only space he really had for them at the time. The family business office (known locally as the Adlerika building), with its long-established reputation for providing pharmaceuticals and tonics, was now doubling as a storage space for boxes upon boxes of astrology books like the *Moon Sign Book* and the *A to Z Horoscope Maker and Delineator*. The other businesses in the area must have wondered what Carl was up to on that chilly February day as he carried box after box into the small office space on Wabasha Street.

Carl had actually bought all the Chester-Kent stock just a month prior, so the office space as well as the business was his to do with what he liked. With his grandfather gone and his father in his golden years, Carl had resolved to take full responsibility for the company and the debts it had accumulated. His goal was to pay off the debts completely and make Chester-Kent a profitable enterprise once more. His plan was to diversify, selling not only Adlerika, Saxol ointment, Vinol tonic, Yo-Zyme yogurt tablets, and hazilbert nut butter, but also an array of books and other products that would be useful for a student of the occult. He planned to add new subject genres to Llewellyn's list, expanding from astrology into the topics of magick, divination, creative visualization, and more. He also planned to add more hazilbert products and had even experimented with the idea of creating his own line of cosmetics. He hoped to eventually be able to transition over completely to books, but for the time being, Llewellyn Publications would be set up to operate as a division of Chester-Kent.[128] Indeed, many of the early titles Carl published were copyrighted under the name of Chester-Kent or under the name of another family enterprise, the Hazel Hills Corporation—a company Carl's dad had started that specialized in real estate as well as hazilbert nut butter. The Adlerika building wasn't ideal headquarters for a publishing enterprise, but Carl managed to find room for the numerous boxes of books and files, and he organized everything as best as he could, given the limited space.

Llewellyn Publications proved the perfect fit for an ambitious bachelor with an open mind, a pioneering spirit, and a "great love for books." "Purchase of the publishing firm was a natural outgrowth of an interest in the occult Weschcke says he has had 'as far back as I can remember,'" reported the *Minneapolis Star Tribune,* who covered the buy.[129] "I guess I was just born into it," Carl would later say of his occult interest, "the way some kids seem to be born into music or sports."[130]

Carl didn't have any real experience as a book publisher, but he had vision, moxie, and a good head for business. He knew he wanted to grow Llewellyn into something special, something different—a profitable and successful publishing house dedicated to occult learning. Right from the start, Carl began to dream about what Llewellyn could become, what his company could bring to people in terms of education, enlightenment, and entertainment. He wanted Llewellyn to be a force of wisdom, love, and evolution in the world, the premier source for reliable and innovative information on astrology, magick, and other occult arts.

---

128   CLW personal files, February 1961.
129   Cesnik, "Astrology Book Claims New Year Will Be Tense."
130   Armstrong, "Saint Paul Book Firm's Success."

Although Carl and Llewellyn George never crossed paths physically, they shared a special bond. Like Llewellyn George had been, so too was Carl extremely passionate about bringing real astrology to the masses. He wanted to simplify modern astrology and explain it in a way that would be appealing, understandable, and beneficial for everyday people. He wanted to continue the work that Llewellyn George had begun and do his part to empower further multitudes of everyday people in utilizing astrology for genuine benefit. This overwhelming drive and desire to spread knowledge and enlightenment regarding occult subjects like astrology is something both men had in full measure, which allowed Carl to carry on Llewellyn George's legacy in a way that perhaps no one else on earth could do.

Dreamer and visionary that he was, with a college degree in financing, Carl was also very much a businessperson. He planned to keep serving in his executive roles at the Saint Paul Advertising Company and in the family businesses, but his income wasn't nearly great enough to sustain and carry his entire publishing enterprise. He knew that if he wanted to achieve his vision of success for Llewellyn, his business would need to make the money required to do so. This part was tricky. Bookstores were rare, with most books sold through the mail or at large department stores. Getting store space for occult books was virtually unheard of, and metaphysical supply shops were extremely few and far between. Even mainstream book publishers struggled just to break even, much less make a sizable profit.

As Carl explains it,

> The occult world wasn't very active then. People weren't interested in new books on the subject. I believed in it, though, so I went around the country talking to booksellers. I believed there was a need for a more personal type of emotional experience which was lacking in people's lives.[131]

---

131   Sutin, "Father of the New Age."

Carl was a groundbreaker, not only for what he called the "New Age"—the new era of enlightenment and evolution—but also as a pioneer in the publishing industry as a whole, leading the way in showing others how the book business might actually be operated as a business. While many other publishers were satisfied with just scraping by as long as they were able to get a few good books out into the world, Carl had the "heretical" and revolutionary idea that he wanted to make real money while he did it:

> I never saw spirituality and business as a dichotomous problem. Business is like anything else: At any given moment, you make decisions that will influence the course of your life. When starting out, I made some decisions that were outside the norm for the time, such as hiring minorities.[132]

Though he had only a handful of employees throughout the sixties, Carl was providing jobs for people who had struggled to find good employment elsewhere due to their skin color or to being labeled as too weird or free-thinking. He had a knack for recognizing people's unique talents, and he appreciated individuals for their individuality.

Carl never felt the need to conform with convention, especially when conventional ways of doing things weren't very successful. Most publishing houses—even the bigger ones—were operating on subsidies or relying on academic titles to carry the rest of their lists. Carl's idea of having a nonacademic book publishing business dedicated to occult learning that actually made a substantial amount of money seemed like an impossibility at the time, as no one in the country had ever done it before. But that was exactly what Carl aimed to do, so he set about developing a business plan and envisioned a brand-new program of production, marketing, sales, and publicity for Llewellyn Publications.

"Weschcke said he plans to enlarge and improve the entire line of Llewellyn Publications on astrology and the occult," reported

---

132 Ibid.

Jim Cesnik for the *Minneapolis Star Tribune*.[133] Carl knew instinctively that he was going to do things differently; he fully intended to push boundaries and break limits, and he expected to succeed at doing so. He knew there would be risks and very likely mistakes, but he was willing to take the former and make the latter in pursuit of his dream. Bank financing for an occult book publisher at the time was out of the question, so Carl funded everything himself and took the hits when they came. Years later, Carl would tell a reporter that if he'd only wanted to make money, he would have done something else.

While Llewellyn George had successfully pulled astrology out of the shadows of obscurity and superstition for a new audience of readers, that audience was still pretty small, and Llewellyn Publications certainly wasn't a cash cow when Carl acquired it. It was a long-established but still very modest mail-order publisher with only a handful of astrology titles. To take a chance with Llewellyn speaks volumes of Carl's passion for books and for the vision he believed in. Just as he wanted to help people gain the right to achieve their fullest potentials through the civil rights activism in which he was still actively engaged, so too did he long to bring occult and esoteric knowledge to the masses and open gateways of learning into unexplored streets of magick and mysticism.

In Carl's first year of ownership, Llewellyn brought in only $30,000 in sales. "It took awhile for my vision to form," Carl would later reflect. "I recognized that the potential for popularizing astrology and other occult topics was there. But I was a little in advance."[134]

Carl knew there was an audience for his books; he just needed to entice them to come out of the woodwork. The occult sciences were very obscure at the time, and those who were into it generally hid that interest from others. While most people were at

133   Cesnik, "Astrology Book Claims New Year Will Be Tense."

134   Sutin, "Father of the New Age."

least somewhat familiar with terms like "astrology" and "witch-craft," serious interest in such topics was apparent only within the underground of the subculture, with most magickal groups meeting in secret and with solitary individuals privately struggling to glean what they could from whatever out-of-print, outdated occult studies books they could get their hands on.

Carl wanted that to change profoundly. He felt that if anything was worth knowing, it was worth sharing. He was determined to deviate from the longstanding tradition of keeping magickal teachings obscured, hidden, and greedily squandered among the few who would claim ownership of a universal wisdom that is the birthright of all.

Occult books had become increasingly difficult to find, with most titles that anyone had ever heard of coming from British publishers decades previously. Carl knew that if more occult information was readily available, more people would come forward to get it. He wanted to not only publish new titles with a more straight-forward, user-friendly approach, but to also issue reprints of old occult classics that had long since gone out of print and had subsequently become extremely rare and difficult to obtain.

One of Carl's first acts of business was to write to the astrologer Charles E. Luntz, the same man who had cast the eleven-year-old Carl's horoscope so many years earlier at the request of Carl's grandfather. Luntz sent Carl *Vocational Guidance by Astrology*, which had been published twenty years prior and had since gone out of print.[135] Carl also had his sights on resurrecting the works of Aleister Crowley, Dion Fortune, Grant Lewi, and Israel Regardie, and he started making contacts with the publishers, individuals, and organizations that held the rights to occult books that he himself had read and enjoyed. He aimed to expand the Llewellyn catalog by offering not only Llewellyn books, but also books from other publishers. If it was a good occult book that Carl thought might be

---

135 Night Sky, "Carl Llewellyn Weschcke."

helpful to someone, he was willing to help distribute it. Llewellyn's product line quickly shifted from solely astrology titles into the realms of clairvoyance, magick, astral projection, and more, and their customer base slowly began to grow. It wasn't too long before Carl was distributing nearly every English-language astrology book or occult studies book that he deemed to be of any merit.

One new title Carl released very early on in his first year of owning Llewellyn was by a little-known author who called himself Ophiel. Ophiel was the pen name/magickal name of Edward C. Peach. Born in 1904 in Iowa, Ophiel was the son of a housekeeper and a cigar maker. He had studied the occult for several decades under diverse teachers that included Vitvan and Israel Regardie, and was eventually inspired to devise his own system of occult technologies. He realized that within all the various systems of spiritual belief and occult philosophy he had studied, it was the results that mattered, and he didn't feel like a person needed to be an adherent to any particular philosophy or be especially holy in order to experience the positive results that any of these systems promised to afford.

Ophiel's philosophy was that either a technique works or it doesn't. He experimented with different techniques, and in some of those techniques he discovered benefits. During an unexpected episode of astral projection, however, he discovered more than he had ever learned from a teacher—even more than he had ever imagined was possible. Ophiel noticed that the "inner planes" through which he was traveling seemed to be illuminated. He could see the world around him when he was in these altered states, and he recognized that we also "see" when we have our ordinary dreams each night when we sleep. To Ophiel, this discovery meant that there must be a "Light" here, something that illuminates the inner planes to make not only the astral realms but also the physical world visible. His discovery of this "Light" led to more experimentation and exploration, in which he developed brilliant theories and simple methods for understanding how it all works and how to utilize this new understanding of things for real, tangible benefits in this outermost shell of reality known to most of us as our everyday lives.

Ophiel's first question about any occult technique or spiritual discipline was often "Will it give me sex, money, and power?" If the answer was no, then he wasn't interested. He was interested in the benefits, and once he figured out some techniques that seemed to work for himself, he felt led to share what he had learned with absolutely as many people as possible. He knew he was on to something, and he aimed to explain the inner workings of reality and, in effect, show people how to work the system. He was able to simplify the most beneficial magickal teachings and techniques he had learned in his own studies, and he taught the many effective methods he had discovered independently in a way that was easy to understand and put into immediate action for immediate benefits.

Ophiel didn't believe that there was any power in the dogma of any given system, but rather that the power resided within the techniques themselves, which, in theory, could be used by anyone regardless of their personal beliefs. Ophiel had lived a rough life and had struggled, and now that he had finally made good on his years of occult study and figured out how to do such things as travel on the inner planes of reality, he was extremely motivated and compelled to share those teachings and to discover more. Though he was no longer studying with him, Israel Regardie— with whom Carl was in correspondence—lived in California near Ophiel and they were still in close contact. Ophiel entered into Carl's sphere of awareness, and he was exactly the kind of author that Carl wanted; he was the kind of author that had something entirely new to offer people so they could learn and grow.

Ophiel told Carl that he had written some manuscripts about his experiences and that more were coming. As Carl had only very recently acquired Llewellyn, he didn't have a whole lot of money to invest in new authors, but he liked Ophiel and found his writing to be nothing short of revolutionary. He appreciated Ophiel's practical, easy-to-understand, benefits-focused approach, and he wanted to find a way to help this author achieve his goal of sharing his message with anyone who wanted to learn it. Ophiel didn't like the idea of getting only a small percentage from the sales of his work, which was the typical author-publisher setup, so the two struck a deal for an alternative arrangement. Ophiel would pay for the printing cost of his books, and Carl would help produce, edit, and distribute them. Sales of each book were to be split 50/50, whereas with a more traditional arrangement, the author's royalty is usually around 10–15 percent of total sales. The publisher would often be named as Peach Publishing, listed with a Saint Paul address even though Ophiel was still living in California.

Ophiel's first book was released in 1961, titled *The Art and Practice of Astral Projection*. Carl had found a printer in Hong Kong who was willing to print the book for the sum of $1,000, which Ophiel paid for with money he had received from an unexpected settlement. Carl's ad copy he created for the book read, "In the past, the secret of Astral Projection could only be taught in an occult school—but now it is easily and safely learned by anyone." Carl thought the book to be so promising that he suggested to Ophiel that they produce an astral projection correspondence course to further facilitate learning. "One of the discussions we had centered around the concept of students working together to produce a 'map' of the astral world," Carl reflected. He would eventually come to call *The Art and Practice of Astral Projection* "Ophiel's best book," and even decades later he stated that the program of training Ophiel had developed was "one of the very best and important any student can undertake."[136]

In the years to follow, Ophiel and Carl would produce many more projects together. One such project was a joint venture they called the Gnostic Institute, through which they planned to offer a

---

136 Weschcke, "Letter to Janine Chapman."

variety of correspondence courses as well as Ophiel's *Astral Light* newsletter. In the first issue of the newsletter, Ophiel described their vision:

> *We will specialize in Truth teaching of a type that will lead to practical working results and not give out reams of idle talk and discussions that go round and round in a circle and get no place and/or nowhere....much of the Occult is only talk and talk and nothing practical.*[137]

There is little biographical information to be found about Ophiel besides what he himself included in his many manuscripts. Carl described him as a big man who somewhat resembled Captain Kangaroo, while one of Ophiel's students described him as having that "'far-off' look in his eyes, "Like he was half in the material and half in the astral planes simultaneously."[138] It seems strange that there is not a lot of information available about Ophiel and who he actually was as a person, as he seems to have been quite the unusual and interesting character.

Carl described him as being a good friend who was enjoyable to talk to despite being difficult to work with, while other occultists often considered him uncouth. At one point, for example, Ophiel decided that he didn't want to handwrite his manuscripts any-more, so he started sending Carl audiotapes for his secretary to transcribe. The problem was that Ophiel might get up to make a snack, leaving the recorder running, so that the secretary had to sit through long pauses in the recordings to be sure that they didn't miss anything. He was also rumored to have a habit of tak-ing food off other people's plates if he saw that they weren't going to eat it—practical, but a little too unconventional for the "old guard" occultists to bear. Of course, Ophiel was never pretending to be an angel. He dedicated his first book to "Ophiel's mean, violent, and

---

137   Ophiel, *Astral Light.*

138   Mark W., "My Contact with Ophiel," *The Astral Light*, volume 1, number 4, September 22, 1996.

stubborn disposition,"[139] without which, he says, he would have given up long ago. On another occasion he wrote of himself, "I personally am not a sweet loveable type of person. I have no beautiful nature." Despite his personality flaws, Ophiel was certainly, as he himself described, "not an occult faker."[140]

In addition to finding exciting new authors, resurrecting old classics that had gone out of print, and distributing virtually any interesting occult books he could find whose copyright holders were agreeable, Carl also wanted to safeguard success where it already dwelt and do all he could to increase it. The *Moon Sign Book* was Llewellyn's signature title and biggest seller, although it was selling an average of only 2,500 copies a year at the time that Carl purchased the company. Carl immediately saw the potential as well as the need for a massive increase in sales. Speaking to a reporter for the *Minneapolis Star Tribune* at the end of 1961, Carl stated that he anticipated selling 50,000 copies of the fifty-seventh annual *Moon Sign Book* for 1962, foreseeing "steadily increasing circulation as the book is improved and enlarged."[141] Having virtually zero experience as a publisher but still having the confidence to announce to the media that you expect to increase sales twenty-fold in your second year of business is a pretty bold move, but Carl was lacking in neither confidence nor ambition.

Up to the time that Carl had taken ownership of Llewellyn, the readers of the *Moon Sign Book* consisted primarily not of astrology students, as one might expect, but of gardeners and farmers, who relied on the manual to help them choose the best times for planting and harvesting different crops. "Even if you don't have a green thumb, you can't miss having a fine garden and flowers if you follow the signs in the *Moon Sign Book*," proclaimed a classified ad in the Garden Service Directory of the *Detroit Free Press*.

---

139   Ophiel, *The Art and Practice of Astral Projection.*
140   Ophiel, *Astral Light.*
141   Cesnik, "Astrology Book Claims New Year Will Be Tense."

For decades the book had been advertised primarily through classified ads and gardening catalogs, and it was more readily found in gardening supply shops than in traditional bookstores. Generations of farmers and gardeners around the country swore by the *Moon Sign Book* just as many do today, proclaiming that planting by the moon affects moisture content, immunizes plants from insects, and ensures that seeds will grow to fruition. Carl aimed to bring a larger audience to Llewellyn's number one selling annual, so he began a new publicity campaign to launch the first *Moon Sign Book* that would be published under his guidance and direction. The book would still be advertised to the gardeners who had come to rely on it, but Carl also intended to make everyday people who weren't at all involved with agriculture aware of the benefits that astrological timing can bring. What he needed was some good publicity.

Carl decided to make contact with a prominent mathematician, author, and astrologer who was popular at the time. Carl Payne Tobey, whom Carl called "the most well-known astrologer in America today," was indeed a household name among those who had any significant interest in the subject. Carl had admired Tobey's work for many years, appreciating his scientific methods of research and verification and his use of advanced technologies in the quest for more accurate and beneficial systems of astrology. Tobey was invited to contribute some predictions to the *Moon Sign Book*, and newspapers around the country were notified via press releases that Carl himself crafted and distributed. Carl also named Tobey as the vice president and research director for Llewellyn Publications.

A rare planetary alignment that was to take place in February 1962 had sparked new interest in astrology. Many groups and religious sects were talking of end-of-the-world fears and prophecies, with some expecting nothing short of total destruction. Everyone wanted to know what was going to happen, and here was the *Moon Sign Book* that promised to shed some light on the upcoming astronomical occurrence with predictions from one of the biggest names in astrology.

The timing was ripe for publicity opportunities, and Carl had laid the groundwork that enabled him to seize the moment. He had chosen Tobey for his high profile as well as for his expertise. He had carefully selected and forged relationships with news outlets nationwide with whom he could share his articles and press releases regarding astrology, the *Moon Sign Book*, Carl Tobey, and the end-of-the-world prophecies that so many people were talking about. The strategy proved sound, and the groundwork paid off. United Press International syndicated a lengthy piece about the *Moon Sign Book* that was run in many newspapers across the country. The *Medford Mail Tribune* in Oregon hailed the *Moon Sign Book* as "one of the oldest and most widely read publications in the field," while one reporter in Indiana called it "a thought-provoking book," though they were neither moon gardener nor occultist. The *Tallahassee Democrat* agreed with Tobey's prediction in the fifty-seventh annual *Moon Sign Book* that "the life of President Kennedy should be ultra carefully guarded."

According to Tobey's calculations, every president that had been elected up to that point when a Jupiter-Saturn conjunction was occurring in an earth sign had died in office, and a Jupiter-Saturn conjunction that had begun in February 1961, just weeks after Kennedy was sworn into office, was reason enough for concern. On November 22, 1963, Tobey's prediction sadly proved accurate when the president was assassinated while riding in a motorcade through the streets of downtown Dallas, Texas.

The 1962 *Moon Sign Book* also included advice on when to mow, when to go to the dentist, when to bake bread, the best days to call the plumbers, the best days to write a letter, and more. While Tobey provided the intro and the main predictions for the upcoming year, Carl wrote a good amount of the book himself, though he took no credit.

With more press coverage, the visibility of the *Moon Sign Book* and public interest in astrology increased. Carl continued to place classified ads offering the book for $1.50 by mail in gardening catalogs and newspapers in Idaho, Missouri, Montana, and other farming communities in order to retain the book's core audience, but he also sought out new markets in the form of bookstores, department stores, esoteric societies, and students of the occult. He spoke to retail store owners throughout the Twin Cities and even delivered a talk—and complimentary copies of the *Moon Sign Book*—to an organization dedicated to the study and preservation of antiquities. "We have great plans at Llewellyn Publications for helping bring about a new intellectual orientation in our culture," Carl announced to the group. "A revolution that will reestablish man's awareness that there is a pattern to the universe, that there are principles which guide individual life and endeavor."[142]

Astrology was thought of as an old science—and indeed, it's one of the oldest—but Carl was determined to breathe new life into the subject through research, technology, and fresh applications. He dreamed of founding a Llewellyn Research Center, which would serve as a headquarters for magickal and astrological research. Readers would be invited to send in their horoscopes and other personal information in order to compile extensive astrological data that could then be used to check current prediction methods for accuracy and make improvements. There would also be experiments, with readers invited to take part in feats of astral projection, mental telepathy, remote viewing, and other psychic and magickal arts.[143] "I think we should attempt to examine phenomena analytically," Carl once said, "and never let fear or preconceptions take over."[144]

---

142 CLW presentation to the Antique Society, circa 1961.

143 Ibid.

144 CLW email to Stephen Brewster, February 20, 2011.

Carl's research center never quite panned out as he simply didn't have the funds, but he soon found other ways to keep the arts of astrology and psychic development moving forward with new publications and new projects. He joined the American Federation of Astrologers in 1962 and released Luntz's *Vocational Guidance by Astrology*, the first new-to-Llewellyn title to be fully funded, copyrighted, and published under Carl's leadership. The book had been originally published twenty years prior by a Philadelphia-based publisher of comics and popular literature, but had since gone out of print.

Carl had also made contact with the Society of the Inner Light, who held possession of Dion Fortune's works, which were no longer in print. He wanted to bring Fortune's books to a new audience, so he asked the society if he could buy the copyrights to publish new editions of her manuscripts. While her books were rather obscure in America at the time, Carl was well versed in occult literature from around the world and had been a longtime fan of her work.

Dion Fortune was the pen name of Violet Mary Firth, born in Wales in 1890. Firth experienced mediumistic abilities and lucid dreams as a child, and she began writing poetry at an early age. In her early twenties she worked as a psychoanalyst at a clinic in London, and in 1919 she was initiated into the Hermetic Order of the Golden Dawn's outer order of Alpha et Omega, a Rosicrucian order founded in Paris by S. L. MacGregor Mathers in 1906. She adopted a new magickal name based on her family motto "Deo, non Fortuna" (meaning "God, not luck"), and she began writing articles on the occult under the pen name Dion Fortune. The head of her magical order, Moina Mathers, who was S. L. MacGregor Mathers's widow, felt that Fortune's publications were too far out of line, a betrayal of oath-bound magickal secrecy. This caused Fortune to want to pull back from her involvement with the group, and in 1924 she decided to found her own magickal order, which she called the Community of the Inner Light. She acquired a property in Glastonbury to serve as headquarters, and within five years she had cut all ties with the Golden Dawn. The group later became known as the Fraternity of the Inner Light and eventually the Society of the Inner Light, and it continues to this day to preserve and apply Fortune's philosophies in providing a training system for initiation into the Western magickal traditions.

The society agreed to let Carl publish Fortune's occult classics, among which was *The Secrets of Dr. Taverner*. Originally published in England in 1926, the book is a work of fiction about a psychic psychologist/detective, but it contains many examples of real-life magick and ritual practices. He also obtained the rights to Fortune's *The Esoteric Orders and Their Work*. Carl was hoping that someone at the Society of the Inner Light might be willing to write introductions for the new editions of these classic works he was planning, and soon he was put in touch with the society's secretary, Basil Wilby, who later (at Carl's urging) became an author in his own right by the name of Gareth Knight. Wilby, a.k.a. Gareth Knight, agreed to Carl's proposal and penned an essay titled "The Work of an American Occult Fraternity" that was included in Llewellyn's 1962 edition of *The Secrets of Dr. Taverner*. The book was a hit, and Llewellyn's edition proved to be the first of many American printings as the once-rare book grew in fame and popularity with its new widespread availability. Llewellyn's reprint of Fortune's *The Esoteric Orders and Their Work* also met with great response.

Other early releases from Llewellyn included a reprint of *Thought Dial* by Sydney Omarr (which included a dial with a spinning arrow that could be used for predictions), a reprint of *Heaven Knows What* by Grant Lewi, and *Basic Principles of Astrology: A Modern View of an Ancient Science* by Ruth Hale Oliver, Mary Glennon Harter, and Vernon Clarke. The cover illustrations for *Basic Principles of Astrology* as well as for *The Secrets of Dr. Taverner* reprint were created by acclaimed American artist and illustrator Hannes Bok.

In a further effort to expand the audience for his books, and to hopefully start building a community, Carl decided that he would also try his hand at publishing magazines. He wanted to create a culture and build upon the growing interest in occultism and astrology that was just beginning to bud in America. *New Dimensions* magazine launched its first issue in the spring of 1963. Basil Wilby/Gareth Knight was to be the editor and one of the main contributors, and the magazine would cover topics ranging from witchcraft to divination, presented with somewhat of a scholarly slant. The first issue contained an article on witchcraft by Patricia Crowther; a serialized, previously unpublished manuscript on ritual magick by the late Dion Fortune (by kind permission of the Society of the Inner Light); an article on effective magick by Margaret Bruce; fiction by astrologer Marc Edmund Jones; poetry, tarot, book reviews, and even cartoons. Gareth Knight wrote the book reviews under the pseudonym Thomas Connor, a name he came up with based on his pet conure that had come from the island of St. Thomas.

It was difficult to get new magazines placed in mainstream book outlets and on newsstands, so Carl offered *New Dimensions* through classified ads and specialty shops, offering single issues for just fifty cents. After only a handful of issues, however, Carl faced facts that his *New Dimensions* magazine was a flop, so he sold it to Gareth Knight, who teamed up with a publisher in England and continued it.[145]

Carl soon tried again with a monthly magazine that he called *MinuteScope*. Featuring articles and even artwork by Carl himself, *MinuteScope* was edgier and more accessible than *New Dimensions* had been. The inaugural issue in December of 1963 featured an auburn-haired young woman on the full-color cover dressed in a prim red dress, pointed black kitten heels, and a bright blue leather meditation mask that covered her face entirely. In its glossy pages readers could expect to find "news of the Unusual, the unexpected, the Bizarre," as well as astrological forecasts, information

---

145   Sutin, "Father of the New Age."

about psychic research, and a variety of articles on occult topics ranging from clairvoyance to astrological business forecasting.[146]

The second issue featured an article written by Carl about the witch's cradle, the sensory deprivation device used as an aid for prompting altered states of consciousness that he had written to Gerald Gardner about years prior. Carl wanted to address the topic from a place of experience, so he constructed one of the devices and rounded up a team of friends to take part in the experiments. The feature article included sketches of the witch's cradle that Carl had drawn himself based off the drawings and information he had obtained from Margaret Bruce with the help of Gardner. Artist Hannes Bok created the color illustrations of the witch's cradle for the magazine's cover.[147]

Carl didn't shy away from the controversy that such subjects as witch's cradles and sensory deprivation masks might inspire; in fact, he wanted to "stir the pot" and prompt his readers into a dialogue where they would become engaged in the topics covered and maybe even send in their own contributions of articles and illustrations. Magazine publishing greatly appealed to him as he could see the potential in having a regular, frequently published format with which to reach out to readers and in turn have them reach back out to him and to each other. He was really hoping to create a community where readers could interact, contribute, and mutually benefit.

Just as he had discovered with *New Dimensions*, however, Carl soon realized that the audience for *MinuteScope* was simply not large enough to justify the costs of printing and producing the magazine. After just a few issues, *MinuteScope* was discontinued. He didn't want to let it go, but it just didn't make sense from a business standpoint to continue it. "Still, magazine publishing is fun, and nothing quite serves particular special-interest communities

---

146 *MinuteScope*, December 1963–January 1964.

147 Cuyler W. Brooks, Jr., "The Hannes Bok Illustration Index," http:// fanac.org/Fannish_Reference_Works/NedBrooks/BOKINDEX.htm.

quite as well," Carl remarked. He hadn't given up entirely on the idea of magazines, however, and in future years he would launch several others that would meet with varying degrees of success.

At the beginning of 1964, Carl realized he had spread his finances a little too thin. He was financing everything, and he found that he simply couldn't afford to keep going the way he was, draining his own personal resources in order to back every project that sparked with special potential. He had decided to purchase a house that would double as a proper headquarters for his growing publishing enterprise, which had left him with a lot less to work with in terms of personal financial resources. There were simply too many worthy projects to be able to take on all of them, and some projects he had been planning had to be delayed or scrapped. Among them was a book on the Kabbalah that Gareth Knight had written at Carl's suggestion, as well as a tarot deck he had created with Dutch artist Sander Littel. Knight eventually found a publisher for those works, however, and the seeds that Carl had planted in the budding author bloomed to full fruition.

With the move to his new home and new headquarters, Carl decided to phase out the pharmaceuticals and food products that Chester-Kent had for so long been in the business of producing and officially shifted the company's focus to that of books. The Adlerika building in downtown Saint Paul was sold, and Carl soon set up the new Llewellyn headquarters in the old and spacious house he had purchased, which just so happened to have a reputation for being one of the most haunted dwellings in Minnesota.[148]

By the mid-sixties, the book business had begun to transform in a way that was beneficial to readers and publishers alike. In 1966 B. Dalton books led the way in creating a more aggressive bookselling culture, opening a chain of bookstores in regional shopping malls, suburban areas, and downtown business districts around

---

148 Kelly, "Angels' Voices."

the country.[149] B. Dalton was founded by a member of the family that owned Dayton's department stores, which were based in Minneapolis. Carl had already forged a good working relationship with Dayton's, so getting his books placed in the B. Dalton stores wasn't too hard of a sale. B. Dalton proved that there was a thriving market for books, which led to more individuals and companies deciding that opening a bookstore might be exactly what they wanted to do. Suddenly there were a lot more bookstores around, and many of those bookstores were now featuring Llewellyn titles right alongside the more traditional mainstream books. This helped Llewellyn's sales grow exponentially and further helped establish the credibility of their books as well as their subject areas as a whole.

Meanwhile, another transformation of culture was taking place across America: 1967 was deemed the Summer of Love, bringing thousands of adherents of the new hippie movement to San Francisco in search of new ways of living and loving. San Francisco was the home of the Grateful Dead, whose psychedelic, dynamic music seemed the perfect soundtrack for the changing times. The movement spread throughout the nation, gaining the attention of those who wanted to think differently and live independent of the shackles of conventional mainstream modes of being. Minds were open, and Llewellyn books provided a flood of interesting, alternative information with which to fuel and nurture the freethinking attitudes that had become increasingly apparent.[150]

The new culture of the "flower children" was widely publicized by the media, which helped spur public interest in topics like astrology even further. By 1968 astrology had become a phenomenon. As Carl put it,

> All of a sudden, everyone knew the sign he was born under and wanted to know more. A lot of publishers thought that initial fad interest would fall off, but I thought the volume would grow, and

149   Ibid.
150   Sutin, "Father of the New Age."

it has, and more so I think on the serious side than just the fad
aspect of it.[151]

Irma L. Norman, who was trustee-director of the First Temple of
Astrology in Los Angeles at the time, commented that astrology is
"spreading like wildfire in Southern California. People are discovering that it's based on natural laws; the whole universe is based
on natural laws." The temple, founded in 1907, had 300 students
and 20 instructors at the time, and in the foyer Llewellyn books,
including the *Moon Sign Book* and the *A to Z Horoscope Maker and
Delineator,* were offered for sale to students and visitors.

Carl answered the call for more astrology by releasing a string
of advanced titles on the subject, including a reprint of Ada Muir's
Pluto the Redeemer, Donald A. Bradley's *The Paradox Problem in
Astrology* and *Solar and Lunar Returns, The Lunation Cycle* by
Dane Ruhyar, and Grant Lewi's *Astrology for the Millions.* Lewi's
Heaven Knows What was so popular that it had been picked up by
a book club, giving Carl an idea for a whole new way in which his
books could be distributed to a larger audience of interested readers. To this day, book club sales of Llewellyn titles continue to be
an important element of the company's success.

With the popularity of astrology on the rise, Carl wanted to further open people up to other occult studies such as magick and
tarot. In 1968 Llewellyn released *Roll Away the Stone.* With a
lengthy introduction written by Israel Regardie, who had served as
Aleister Crowley's personal secretary, the hardcover book with a
black cloth cover and gilt lettering included the full texts of Crowley's *The Psychology of Hashish,* including *The Herb Dangerous* as
well as a translation of *The Poem of Hashish.* The book played a
large role in reintroducing the works of Aleister Crowley to a generation of Americans who had never heard of him or who thought
of him only as a crackpot with deviant leanings that may have
written some obscure poetry at one time or another. Today, how-

---

151   "Temple of the Moon," *Los Angeles Times,* September 24, 1967.

ever, Crowley's influence on the modern occult movement is both obvious and undeniable.

Soon, Israel Regardie's own books were released through Llewellyn, which also left a mark on the occult world that is still apparent today. In 1969 Carl published a reprint of Regardie's series of books outlining the complete curriculum of the magickal Order of the Golden Dawn. First published as a four-volume set in 1937 by Chicago's Aries Press, the books had become rare and difficult to obtain. Very few people had access to the Golden Dawn system. Unless you were ready to be initiated into the order, there simply wasn't an easy way to research their practices and learn about the Golden Dawn methods of magick. Carl changed that by making Regardie's magickal information readily available to everyone, bringing an end to the tide of elitism that had kept the occult "occult" for so long. The books were released in a handsome two-volume set of hardcovers titled *The Golden Dawn: An Account of the Teachings, Rites, and Ceremonies of the Order of the Golden Dawn.* The publisher was listed as the Weschcke family's Hazel Hills Corporation, with Llewellyn Publications listed as the distributor. The ad copy Carl wrote described the books as "the most comprehensive occult study course available," and at over 350,000 words in the complete manuscript, it's hard to argue that point. The books were sold for $25 a set, and today these first editions fetch upward of $200 from antiquarian book collectors.

In the same year that Regardie's Golden Dawn curriculum was released, Carl also published the first edition of Louis T. Culling's *The Complete Magick Curriculum of the Secret Order G.B.G. (The Great Brotherhood of God)* in both paperback and hardcover formats. A respected magician from the UK, Culling was a friend to Carl and was his elder. He had already published a few books through Samuel Weiser, Inc., at the time a very small and obscure publisher of esoterica that had naturally arisen out of Weiser's bookstore in New York City, the country's first-ever and most well-known occult bookstore of the day. Carl didn't think of Weiser as competition in any kind of negative sense, though they published in the same subject areas. He reasoned that the more people who were drawn to the occult world, the better it would be for all occult businesses and for the book trade as a whole.

Carl had expanded Llewellyn's list substantially since he had first purchased the company, but he continued dreaming up new ideas to increase his business and further his mission. He decided he might like to expand into tarot decks. He had actually been dreaming of it for years. Some years prior he had become aware of Aleister Crowley's *Thoth Tarot*, which Crowley had designed between the years of 1938 and 1943. The deck had never been printed professionally, and it was not readily available to the general public. Carl had contacted the Ordo Templi Orientis—Crowley's own magickal order—and had obtained permission to publish the deck. However, he wasn't certain whether or not he would be able to actually do it, as he had no way of knowing the quality of the original art.

There weren't any copies of the deck in existence that were of good-enough quality that Carl could simply have them reproduced, but he had learned that the original paintings by Lady Freida Harris that the cards had been based on were being stored in a vault at Lloyds Bank in London. Carl asked Gareth Knight, who was living in London, if he could check out the paintings in person to see if they had been preserved well enough to make a new printing of the tarot deck a viable possibility. Gareth went to Lloyds Bank with his friend Roma, and the two made the necessary arrangements to view the paintings. Gareth recalled,

> *Roma and I spent a fascinating couple of hours at Lloyds Bank in Piccadilly examining all 78 paintings (plus one for the back design), which were of considerable size, brought up from the vaults on trolleys by puzzled, sweating, and not best pleased officials.*

The paintings were indeed in good enough condition that a new *Thoth Tarot* could be created, yet Carl would have to sit on the project for several years before proceeding due to financial restraints. At last, in 1969 Aleister Crowley's *Thoth Tarot* was issued, packaged in a plain yet attractive white box featuring the OTO emblem and shiny gold lettering. The publication of the deck represented not only the first professional printing of Crowley's now-famous tarot, but also marked the first-ever tarot deck to be published by Llewellyn.

More titles by Ophiel had also been issued, including *The Art and Practice of Getting Material Things Through Creative Visualization*, *The Art and Practice of Clairvoyance*, and *The Art and Practice of the Occult*. There was a new divination system in the works as well, called *The Oracle of Fortuna*. Ophiel had also written a series of short vignettes, which Carl urged him to develop into correspondence courses on occult learning. These short vignettes were sold individually in sealed envelopes to make up the lessons in each course of study. Ophiel partnered with Carl for two of these correspondence course series: Ophiel's Sealed Lessons in Astral Projection and Ophiel's Sealed Lessons in Occult Power. Ophiel would send the manuscripts, written in green ink on yellow legal-sized paper, and Carl would type them up (or have them typed) and then print these manuscripts himself, rolling them out page by page on his old-fashioned tabletop printing press that he kept in his home. Though Carl contributed a fair portion of his own information to both of these correspondence courses and did all the editing, he let the full spotlight for the lessons shine upon Ophiel. To put it plainly, it was, after all, Ophiel's parade, and Carl didn't feel the need for any credit as it wasn't important to accomplishing the work at hand.

One of the manuscripts that was part of Ophiel's Sealed Lessons in Occult Power series was titled "The Thread: An Occult Vignette." Along with the manuscript—handwritten on his customary yellow paper with shining green ink—Ophiel included a personal note to Carl that read:

Please have the girls type this as soon as possible and let's get it on the road. More is coming. If they are not going to do it send it all back. Charge if you must but get it out![152]

Ophiel was planning more courses and more books, and Carl couldn't seem to get them out quickly enough for Ophiel's liking. He felt his message was important, and he didn't care for that message to be delayed. Whether or not his urgency was based on the fact that he didn't start writing and teaching until later in life or whether the urgency was based on the value he saw in his ideas or whether it was for some other reason entirely, the world will probably never know. Carl did his best to get the work out quickly, as he very much believed in the value of that work too, but with virtually no staff to speak of and limited resources of time and money, there were indeed the ordinary delays in publication that can crop up and usurp more ambitious intentions. Ophiel himself was convinced that there were forces at work actively delaying and thwarting his information—which he described as "occult dynamite"— from reaching the multitude of lives it was destined to touch. He felt that if Carl were trying hard enough, he could get Ophiel's books out more quickly, and he eventually took his work elsewhere.

Ophiel's books were picked up by Samuel Weiser, Inc., in the mid-seventies, but it wasn't long before Ophiel would become dissatisfied with them too. Ophiel issued his last book, *The Art and Practice of Contacting the Demiurge*, independently in a small print run of paperbacks that are extremely rare today, selling for hundreds of dollars. Although his ideas didn't spread as far as he would have liked during his lifetime, Ophiel's legacy of a practical, results-based approach to the occult lives on, as his books offer a multitude of teachings and techniques that are still valid and valuable for the modern student. There exist to this day groups

---

152   Edward Peach, letter to CLW accompanying "The Thread: An Occult Vignette," October 16, 1970.

of students and online learning communities dedicated to studying the works of Ophiel, which were first brought into the public awareness with the integral and catalytic help of Carl.

The demand for quality occult learning materials had grown exponentially since the start of the decade, and with that demand had opened a new wave of metaphysical supply shops around the country in which you could find an ample selection of Llewellyn books prominently lining the shelves. Their catalog had tremendously expanded, too, and by the end of the decade, Llewellyn was distributing over 10,000 different titles from publishers in the US, the UK, and India, which Carl sold directly to consumers and offered at wholesale prices to retailers around the country. The times had changed, and they were changing still, and Carl was ready to wholeheartedly embrace it.

Chapter 6

Life in a Haunted House

I n 1964, with Llewellyn quickly growing, Carl felt it was time to acquire more official premises for his publishing business. He had some money set aside from earnings and family trusts, so he decided to invest in some property of his own that could double as a home and office. He could have purchased any other home in the city, but what he chose was a crumbling mansion on Saint Paul's most prestigious avenue that just so happened to have a reputation for being the most haunted house in the town. Rumors of ghosts who roamed the mansion's cavernous halls had circulated for years in the community, which, for Carl, only added to the appeal. Built in 1883 and located just a few blocks away from the Saint Paul Cathedral, the mansion at 476 Summit Avenue was aging and dilapidated, remodeled and reworked by former owners for the sake of modernization and convenience, and too frequently at the expense of the home's original beauty. Even in its rundown state, however, the house was a stunning sight to behold.

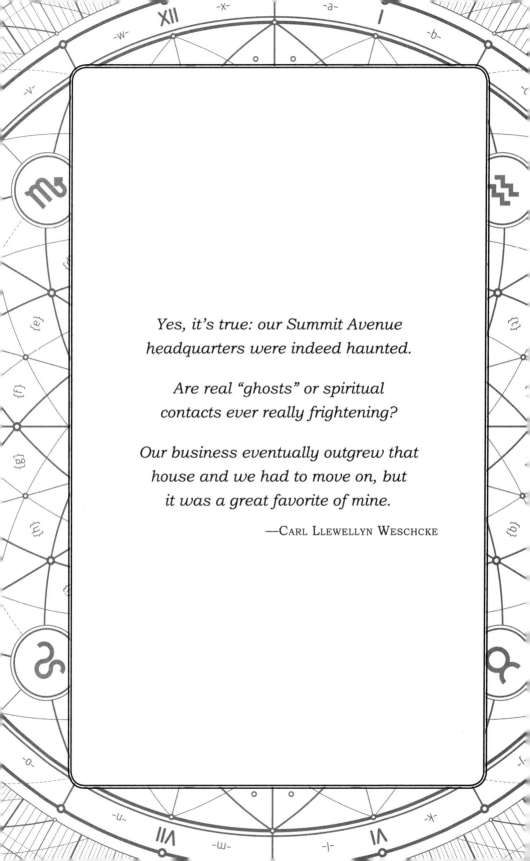

*Yes, it's true: our Summit Avenue
headquarters were indeed haunted.*

*Are real "ghosts" or spiritual
contacts ever really frightening?*

*Our business eventually outgrew that
house and we had to move on, but
it was a great favorite of mine.*

—Carl Llewellyn Weschcke

The mansion had been built by Chauncey Griggs, who served as a colonel for the Union in the Civil War and who later owned a large grocery firm in Saint Paul. He was also involved in lumber, coal, and banking. Griggs commissioned acclaimed architect Clarence Johnston to design his elaborate home right beside the future site of his best friend and business partner Addison Foster's equally grand home. Made in a Richardsonian Romanesque style and one of the first homes in Saint Paul to use Bayfield brownstone from Lake Superior, the sprawling mansion encompasses 16,534 square feet and includes nine fireplaces, wood-paneled walls, carved lintels and arches, slate-shingled gables, and a corner tower that is three stories tall. There is also a carriage house on the property that is itself larger than many family homes, with 2,954 square feet of space.[153]

The stateliness and grandeur of the historic home appealed greatly to Carl, and he saw beyond the needed repairs and restorations to a splendid house that had once hosted gatherings and banquets that were the talk of the town. When under the ownership of the Griggses, the mansion was the scene of a New Year's Eve party so spectacular that it gained a mention in the local paper. Describing the mansion as "splendidly planned for a reception," the reporter for the *Saint Paul Daily Globe* recounted the decorations of exotic tropical plants and flowers, giant Christmas trees, and fresh evergreens illuminated by the glow of gas lamps burning late into the night:

> *The long suite of rooms terminating in the dining-room presented an appearance not only beautiful in the decorations, but in the elegant costumes of the ladies and the animated conversation.*

153 Keith, "Chauncey and Martha Griggs House"; "Richardsonian Romanesque Saint Paul"; McClure, "Rooms to Spare"; Bear, "This Romanesque Pile"; United States Department of the Interior National Park Service, "National Register of Historic Places Inventory—nomination form 76001067, Griggs-Upham House 476 Summit Ave.," 11.

Dressed in gowns of silks, point lace, and richly embroidered velvets adorned with diamonds, roses, and pearls, the leading ladies of the Saint Paul social scene turned out in number for the Griggses' 1887 New Year's Eve bash.[154]

Less than seven years later the home would be the scene of a tragic and violent death, the first of several occurrences over the years that led many to believe the house may be haunted by lingering spirits. Mysterious footsteps, the cold touch of ghostly hands, an eerie presence that haunts the home's upper levels,[155] and even disembodied heads floating down the hallways[156] are among the many frightening phenomena that have been witnessed by residents and visitors alike.

Some potential house buyers would surely have been daunted by these rumors, but Carl was all the more intrigued. Without hesitation, he purchased the mansion from the Saint Paul School of Art, who had owned it for the previous twenty-five years. Carl explained:

> The director of the Art School—which previously occupied the residence—informed me of several instances of manifestation. It was the general belief of the faculty that two entities they named Martha and George occupied the house. I was thrilled![157]

While open-minded and enthusiastic about the possible presence of ghosts, Carl wasn't the type to simply believe without experiencing things for himself. He was eager to see if there was any truth behind the rumored hauntings. "Even before I moved in I would stop by to see how work was going on repairs and painting," Carl later recounted to a reporter from the *Saint Paul Pioneer Press*. "There was quite a bit of activity by whatever or whoever is

---

154   *Saint Paul Daily Globe*, "New Year's Reception."

155   "Saint Paul Haunted House, Griggs Mansion," Haunted Houses, accessed June 25, 2017, http://www.hauntedhouses.com/states /mn/griggs_mansion.htm.

156   Woltman, "Saint Paul's Haunted Past—and Present."

157   Night Sky, "Carl Llewellyn Weschcke."

in the house." A window on one of the upper floors kept opening, Carl would close it, and the next day he would find it open again; all the workmen would adamantly deny that they had had anything to do with it. After this occurred several times, the window was firmly nailed shut—"But it was open again when I made my next visit," Carl said.[158]

Unbothered by the ghostly happenings, Carl settled comfortably into the house with his three cats and continued renovations. The mansion would be not only home for Carl, but it would also serve as headquarters for Llewellyn. Some adjustments had to be made in order to make the house suitable for its purpose. "I had a 'Magick Room' in the basement—the original 'billiard's room,'" Carl explained. The floor was eventually adorned with a magick circle, painted in a geometric pattern of fiery oranges and reds.[159] Another renovation Carl made to the mansion was the addition of a library, installing enough shelving to house his ever-growing collection of metaphysical, philosophical, and occult books, which already at that time was pushing close to 10,000 volumes.[160]

For his sleeping quarters, Carl turned the traditional master bedroom into a mystical oasis. A reporter from the *Minneapolis Star* described the room as "walled in silver vinyl that casts other-worldly reflections of crimson, mauve, and vermillion from the stained-glass pendants overhead."[161] The metallic wallpaper was decorated with a pattern of human figures in strange positions. Many of the home's original features Carl left intact, including the carved marble mantelpiece depicting a motif of roosters that crowned one of the house's many magnificent fireplaces.

Carl had actually been planning the renovations for years before he acquired the house. He had taken night classes in oil painting there when the mansion was occupied by the Saint Paul School

---

158 Giese and Farmer, "What Haunts Summit Avenue Mansion?"

159 CLW email to Melanie Marquis, February 21, 2011.

160 Giese and Farmer, "What Haunts Summit Avenue Mansion?"

161 Klobuchar, "A Bulletin from Beyond."

of Art, and he could see the original beauty of the home hiding beneath the modern, low-quality modifications that the mansion had been subjected to over the decades. Carl appreciated the house, and he made it his goal to restore the home to its original character wherever it was practical to do so. "I intend to make it as authentic as possible," Carl told a reporter at the time, "but without the gingerbread and curly cues of the old days."[162]

He also didn't do a thing to dissuade the rumors of his house being haunted. Carl was no fool; he was keenly aware that a publisher of New Age and occult books that happened to be headquartered in the town's most infamous haunted mansion was a great draw for publicity. He wanted to make more people aware of Llewellyn Publications, and he wanted to show people that it was okay to believe in so-called supernatural things that were actually just as real as anything else. With these goals in mind, he stepped into the spotlight, opening his home to those who were curious to investigate the ghostly phenomenon that was said to occur there. He would talk to whomever visited not only about the ghosts, but also about his own beliefs in magick and other mystical phenomena. Fame was never something that motivated nor appealed to Carl, however. He became a public figure out of a passion to empower others to realize their maximum potentials, to open their minds to the world's many possibilities, and to the new worlds of mind, body, and spirit that Llewellyn books provided.

Of course, exposing one's occult leanings to public scrutiny tends to draw its critics, and sometimes those critics came marching right up to Carl's front door. One incident he recounted was particularly unpleasant:

> I once had a crazed theology student show up at the door pointing his finger at me and yelling "Thou shalt not suffer a witch to live!" I shouted some other Bible quote at him—I wish I could remember it because it totally deflated him. I shoved him off the

---

162 Lewis, "New Owner to Restore Ex-Gallery."

steps and closed the door. I believe that if I had showed any
fear, he would have barged on in.[163]

Even with occurrences like that going on, Carl didn't back away from media attention. When a group of reporters from the *Saint Paul Pioneer Press* wanted to investigate the rumored hauntings at the mansion, Carl invited them to spend the night in the house and see for themselves. On a cold night in February, the team of two reporters and one photographer stepped through the doors of the old haunted mansion. There was nothing overtly frightening that could be immediately detected, yet all three men experienced a strange feeling of uneasiness and sense of foreboding upon entering the home. The team had faced many dangerous situations in their time with bravery, but an unaccountable fear had fallen upon them nonetheless, and they were not able to shake it. This feeling intensified as they ascended the stairwell to the home's upper floors.[164]

The men were to be spending the night in a sprawling room on the third floor that had originally been a ballroom and had later been transformed into an art studio with the addition of an enormous skylight when the house was in the hands of the Saint Paul School of Art. Many students of the art school over the years had reported feeling a presence that seemed to look over their shoulders as they worked in the room, painting their latest creations.[165]

Carl left the lights on for the reporters and left them alone in the room, retiring to his sleeping quarters on a lower floor after a long and exhausting day. He had his own restroom, he told the reporters, and assured them that he would not need to leave his bedroom or come upstairs. The investigators were on their own, so they set up shop in the room and waited in silence.

---

163   CLW email to Melanie Marquis, January 1, 2013.

164   Giese and Farmer, "What Haunts Summit Avenue Mansion?"

165   "Saint Paul Haunted House, Griggs Mansion," Haunted Houses, accessed June 25, 2017, http://www.hauntedhouses.com/states /mn/griggs_mansion.htm.

Many hours passed without event, and yet that same unaccountable sense of fear and anticipation that had gripped the men's hearts ever since they had walked through the front door persisted. Soon, much to their dismay, there would be good and apparent reason for that fear.

One reporter explained:

> *Suddenly, at 1:20 a.m., outside our room but on our floor, there were at least five distinct thumps—like heavy footsteps. At 3:35 a.m. there was a creaking sound—like soft footsteps—on the stairs. We stared at each other in silence... At 3:40 a.m. reporter Giese walked to the top of the staircase... He returned to the room and said he had 'an almost overpowering urge' to step away from the stairs—a 'feeling' that there was 'something' on those stairs that was not Carl Weschcke or any of his cats. Minutes later, at 3:45 a.m., there was again the same squeaking sound on the stairs—a sound that might be made by feet starting up the stairs to our floor and then stopping.*

That was enough for the reporters. Around 4:00 a.m. they decided they had had all they could take:

> *We let ourselves out, locking the door behind us. We looked up at that hulking stone mansion. We were relieved to be outside it... We all agreed on one thing. There is no prize on earth that could get us to spend a single night alone in that great stone house that seems to speak in sounds we cannot explain or understand.*[166]

A noted medium named Roma Harris was also invited to investigate. She reportedly did not know anything of the house's history or rumored hauntings. "The house has a heaviness about it—like a ball and chain," the medium described. "There has been much sorrow here, a lot of suffering...things have been done that shouldn't have happened." She went on to describe several spirits that she sensed, including a young maid who had died, a uniformed sol-

---

166   Giese and Farmer, "What Haunts Summit Avenue Mansion?"

dier, and a former gardener she identified as Charles Wade.[167] While there seems to be no record of a Charles Wade having been employed at the residence, there was indeed a Charles Wack who was working as a vegetable gardener in Saint Paul in the late 1800s near the turn of the century.[168] The uniformed soldier that Roma described, dressed in blue trimmed with gold, seems to well match the appearance of the home's original owner, Colonel Chauncey Griggs.

And as for the maid? Rumors of a young maid who in 1915 had hung herself on the third-floor stairwell, pregnant and jilted by her lover the chauffeur, had persisted for decades. Her spirit is believed to account for the eerie presence that seems to linger on the home's staircases and upper floors.[169]

Could rumors have gotten crossed, however, and the truth of the story is that this woman was not a young maid, but actually a middle-aged cook named Therese Obermeyer? If not, this young maid was not the first death by hanging to have taken place in the Summit Avenue mansion. In 1893 the Summit house had been sold by the Griggses and was in the hands of Henry Pratt Upham, a local bank manager. The Uphams had owned the house for several years, using it as a home and as a gathering place for Saint Paul's social elites. For a while, the Uphams' home served as the clubhouse for the Nushka Club. Founded to promote interest in outdoor winter sports, over the years the club had morphed into a who's who social group of the wealthy that met at the Summit Avenue mansion for masquerade parties, dances, and more.[170]

167 Giese and Farmer, "What Haunts Summit Avenue Mansion?"

168 Wack, "Man Wanted."

169 CLW email to Melanie Marquis, December 4, 2011, and "Saint Paul Haunted House, Griggs Mansion," Haunted Houses, accessed June 25, 2017, http://www.hauntedhouses.com/states/mn/griggs_mansion.htm.

170 Rahm, "The Nushka Club."

The Uphams had several paid staff at the time, including a cook by the name of Therese Obermeyer. A news item in the *Saint Paul Globe* dated November 5, 1893, included the following report:

> *Therese Obermeyer, forty years of age and employed as cook at the residence of H. P. Upham, 476 Summit Avenue, committed suicide yesterday morning by hanging herself. The woman had been in the employ of the family for two years and was well liked. For some time past she has been very despondent owing to a misunderstanding with the man who has been paying her attentions with a view to matrimony. The trouble was over a difference in religious views, and this so prayed on her mind that she took her life.*[171]

The lady of the house, Mrs. Upham, discovered Therese suspended in one of the upper rooms, a shawl wrapped tightly around her neck.[172] While the article explains the suicide as being caused by torment over "a difference in religious views," there may be a little more to it than that. Curiously, a news item dated exactly one month before the suicide occurred reports a mysterious robbery at the Upham residence. Jewelry and money valued at $600 was stolen right from under the noses of the Uphams while the family was inside the home, leading the newspaper to label the perpetrator a "sneak thief—bad and bold." The article explains:

> *The family were at dinner at the time the robbery occurred and the movements of the thief were so quiet that it was nearly an hour after before the visit was discovered. The basement door which was always kept locked was found unlocked, and burnt matchsticks were discovered strewn across the floors of the upper rooms.*[173]

Could the "sneak thief" have been Therese's lover or perhaps even Therese herself? Could guilt over the robbery have been the cause of her suicide or did she know too much, and maybe

---

171 *Saint Paul Daily Globe*, "Took Her Own Life."

172 Ibid.

173 *Saint Paul Daily Globe*, "Jewelry and Cash Secured by a Sneak Thief."

it wasn't a suicide at all? An apparent suicide note written to Therese's brother was found on the scene, so the coroner deemed it unnecessary to call for an inquest.[174] Whether murder or suicide, Therese certainly died an unnatural and violent death at 476 Summit Avenue. Could her spirit have remained behind?

Those who believe the house is haunted point to the fact that the home has had numerous owners over the years, many leaving quickly and abruptly after hiring staff and sinking loads of money into decorations and renovations. Other owners took a more lighthearted approach, jokingly installing an "emergency kit" in the front hall that contained holy water, a stake and mallet, a wooden cross, and a supply of garlic—just in case.[175] Ghost stories do tend to take on a life of their own over time, and the truth often gets swept away in the tide of tall tales. For instance, one of the mansion's most notorious ghosts has been reported to haunt the library, flipping through books as he supposedly had loved to do before he died in the mansion ages ago. "All those bookcases were installed by me," Carl explained, "which puts the lie to the story about one ghost flicking through pages of books in the library. There was no library before my days."[176]

While feeling that many of the ghost stories were decidedly exaggerated, Carl did believe the house to be deserving of its haunted reputation, recounting that

> There were two entities that I think of as "psychic residues," including that of the maid who hanged herself on the third-floor stairwell. The other was the man who dressed in evening clothes—he always attended symphony and opera events formally dressed.[177]

A tall, thin apparition with a black suit and top hat, the latter ghost was believed to be the spirit of an artist who had been

---

174 Ibid.

175 McClure, "Rooms to Spare."

176 CLW email to Melanie Marquis, September 29, 2012.

177 Ibid.

employed by the Saint Paul School of Art when the art school was stationed at the Summit Avenue mansion. It was rumored that he had been fired amid false accusations, and out of depression and anguish had taken his own life. The first appearance of this sharp-dressed ghost was reported by Delmar Kolb, who was assistant director at the Saint Paul School of Art. At the time Kolb was living in a room on the home's basement level. In 1958 he told a local reporter of encountering the spirit of the man who had killed himself, explaining that

> even when I heard of his death, I didn't believe it—until one night, when I was sleeping in the house and felt a clammy hand on my forehead. Then I knew he was dead and those had been his hands—his telling me that he was really dead.

A few nights later, the ghost appeared to the man again, this time materializing at his bedside dressed in the fancy attire he favored for a night on the town.[178] Subsequent residents and visitors to the house have reported seeing a finely dressed gentleman who would vanish just as quickly as he had appeared. Carl, however, seems to be the last person to have sighted this spirit:

> He made one last appearance in the room I used as my office— dressed as usual, but what was interesting is that this was in full daylight with the sun coming in from huge west-facing windows at his back. He then just faded away, never to be seen again.[179]

Carl was careful to differentiate between what he considered to be "psychic residues"—what most people would think of as ghosts—and spiritual presences that were able to consciously communicate. While a psychic residue is much like an echo, an afterimage left behind, other presences are actually present in spirit. Carl described one such entity that became very special to him over the years:

---

178   Towne, "Spook Parade on Summit Avenue."

179   CLW email to Melanie Marquis, September 29, 2012.

There was another spiritual presence throughout my stay and who I believe is still with me. I call him "the ghost named George" and do feel I communicate with him. He's always helpful.[180]

When Carl first purchased the house, he was told of an entity known as George. Could this be the same George, or could "George" possibly be Llewellyn George, the original owner and founder of Llewellyn Publications?

Carl would neither confirm nor deny any suspicions regarding the true identity of George but merely reiterated that George always gave very helpful advice:

> *He's moved with us to every home since meeting him in the mansion on Summit Avenue. Maybe one of these days I will let George speak for himself in "Letters from a Ghost named George."* [181]

On another occasion, Carl elaborated:

> *Whether George is, in fact, a "ghost" or spirit of someone departed is not really important to me. George could as well be some kind of spirit guide or other entity, or some alter ego of my own, or my own Higher Self. But when I do write a question to George, I seem to get an answer.*[182]

Carl felt very energized in the home that he shared with "the ghost named George." Llewellyn was quickly growing under the guidance of Carl's entrepreneurial spirit and vision, and the Summit house proved to be the ideal place for the small publishing company to spread out her wings and take flight. Carl only had a small handful of employees at the time, and he managed many aspects of the business himself, often working eighteen-hour days:

> *Shipping, the active warehouse, and mailing list maintenance was in the basement, along with a small printing press upon which I cranked out mailing pieces and also Ophiel's Sealed*

---

180 Ibid.

181 CLW email to Melanie Marquis, December 4, 2011.

182 CLW email to Melanie Marquis, May 9, 2012.

Lessons in Occult Power. The old kitchen was the office (the pantry was my kitchen), and production and marketing was up on the third floor under a huge skylight. My office was wherever I was, and I was the sales force, the chief marketer, the publicist, and the chief writer for the annuals, for which I also did the typesetting and the artwork. And, I was also the editor for the books we did![183]

Carl was still involved in the civil rights movement at the time, too, working tirelessly for the NAACP as well as the ACLU.

Socializing was never a huge priority to Carl, but he did find pleasure in hosting the occasional extremely elaborate party or uniquely unforgettable get-together for his friends to enjoy. Halloween was a favorite holiday, with the Summit mansion being the site of one of the best parties in town. Carl's lifelong friend George Millard recollected:

Those parties at the Griggs mansion were some of the big events in Saint Paul...the Ophelia-type woman in the coffin just inside the front door as we entered...the costumes attendees wore... how long it lasted into the a.m.![184]

The Halloween party Carl held in 1966 was covered in the *Saint Paul Dispatch*, with the article featuring a photo of party guests dressed as members of the Addams family gathered around Ophelia in her coffin.[185]

One particularly vivid memory that Carl would always recall from his Halloween parties at the old haunted mansion occurred one night when the party seemed like it would never end. The party "just went on and on," Carl remembered, "and I just left them to see it to the end and went to bed alone about 2 a.m. I woke up to find a guy wearing a fur coat climbing into my bed!"[186]

---

183 CLW email to Melanie Marquis, February 21, 2011.

184 George Millard email to Sandra Weschcke, shared with Melanie Marquis, January 18, 2017.

185 *Saint Paul Dispatch*, "Week-End's Parties Spooky."

186 CLW email to Melanie Marquis, August 11, 2013.

Many of Carl's guests were magickally minded, as he often invited hypnotists, astrologists, palmists, psychics, tea-leaf readers, and other mystics to join him for an interesting evening of cocktails and conversation. Among the regular guests was Prince L. Bokovoy Jr., a Minneapolis graphologist known for his uncanny predictions and expert character insights. Also in frequent attendance was Ruth Gardner, author of *A Graphology Student's Workbook*, and Judy Boss, who wrote a book about her experiences with automatic writing as a means of communicating with the deceased.[187] Often, Carl would invite his authors to come visit and stay with him in the haunted mansion. On one occasion when Ophiel was visiting, Carl told him about the phenomenon of the windows on the upper floors continuing to periodically open themselves and commented that it had never happened on the lower floor. The next morning, the downstairs windows were found to all be open. "Even the ghosts liked Ophiel," joked a close friend of Carl's who was a frequent visitor to the home.

The Summit house soon became a place of personal development and growth, a place where magick happened and where connections were made. Carl simply had a way of inspiring those around him to do more, to be more—to explore and expand their abilities. Larry Wright, one of Carl's friends at the time, wrote a book called *Book of Legendary Spells*. In the acknowledgments, Larry—writing as Elbee—credits Carl for his success:

> The author gratefully acknowledges the unstinting help and advice of Mr. Carl L. Weschcke without whose assistance this book could hardly have been written. Together with his vast knowledge of all phases of the occult, he gave the author free access to his priceless library, one of the largest private collections of occult works in the United States.[188]

---

187   Klobuchar, "A Bulletin from the Beyond."

188   Elbee Wright, acknowledgments for *Book of Legendary Spells* (Minneapolis: Marlar Publishing Company, 1968).

Larry and his girlfriend Marlene were frequent guests at the Summit house, and Carl greatly enjoyed talking with the couple about magick, books, and more. "They were always together," Carl recalled fondly. "I have an immediate memory of the three of us sitting outside on the steps of my old stone mansion."[189]

Though Llewellyn would eventually move on to separate premises, the Summit Avenue mansion provided the perfect foundation and home base for Carl's early publishing endeavors. Around the mansion developed a community of like-minded seekers, just as Carl was bringing together an even larger community of seekers through Llewellyn Publications.

---

189   CLW email to Melanie Marquis, July 15, 2012.

From Ernest J. Weschcke, Carl's brother:

When I was living in La Crosse, Wisconsin, in the early 1960s, my first marriage was having some problems, so brother Carl invited me to come to his house on 476 Summit Avenue for a few weekends. He kind of took me under his wing and guided me through some tough times.

We went to the Old Gas Light—it was like a private Playboy's Club in Minneapolis by the University of Minnesota. We had some fun times there. Other times, we would just go out to dinner and talk. He was there to listen to problems and help me with some advice.

———————————

I believe that I did succeed in increasing a positive public awareness of Wicca, but it was also a period of personal growth. Wicca was new to me, and it reflected my values as to the reality of the magickal world that is always at hand.

Some credit us with starting the New Age in publishing, but it really was the times themselves. We were pioneers in this market, and we worked hard, and we believed—and still believe—in what we are doing.

Occultists see the Earth as a living entity; witches see the Earth as the Great Mother; scientists see the Earth as a life system. Our congregation is the coven, the family, the small group. Our chapel is the outdoors: the forest glade, the open prairie. Our teacher is the depths and heights of our own psyche—our Inner Self whom we contact by the methods and techniques of magick or psychotherapy. Of dogma we have none, but our "holy book" is the Book of Knowledge—all knowledge.

—CARL LLEWELLYN WESCHCKE

Chapter 7

1970s

I n less than a decade, Carl had transformed Llewellyn Publications from a small astrological mail-order publishing house into a rapidly growing publisher of a vast variety of books that was grossing more than $1,000,000 in sales annually.[190] Carl continued to seek out new distribution channels for his books, and while he had good success in getting bookstores and other retailers to carry the Llewellyn line, he realized that he could create more opportunity yet for his company by opening up a store himself.

The Gnostica Bookstore was opened at 1414 Laurel Avenue in downtown Minneapolis, offering classes through the Gnostica School of Self-Development as well as a vast array of books. The premises he chose would also provide more room for his publishing operations, so he was able to move the managerial aspects and mail-order components of Llewellyn Publications into the new space. The store would sell a vast array of books and occult products, as Carl firmly believed in variety. Whether or not it was a Llewellyn publication, if it was a good book, Carl wanted to help

---

190 Smith, "Space Feats Stimulate Occult."

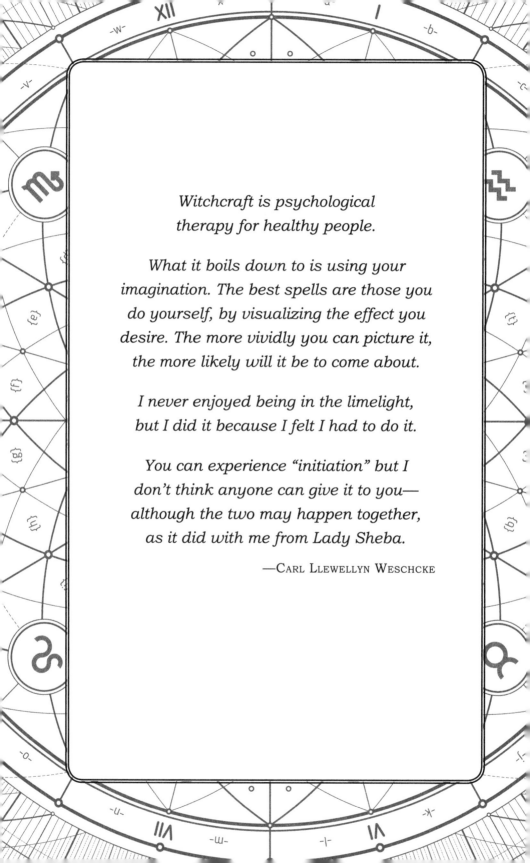

*Witchcraft is psychological
therapy for healthy people.*

*What it boils down to is using your
imagination. The best spells are those you
do yourself, by visualizing the effect you
desire. The more vividly you can picture it,
the more likely will it be to come about.*

*I never enjoyed being in the limelight,
but I did it because I felt I had to do it.*

*You can experience "initiation" but I
don't think anyone can give it to you—
although the two may happen together,
as it did with me from Lady Sheba.*

—CARL LLEWELLYN WESCHCKE

make it available to readers, and he made those products available at his bookstore as well as through the Llewellyn catalog. Carl Sr.'s book, *Growing Nuts in the North*, was featured in the Llewelyn catalog right alongside titles like *Weekend Warlock* and *History and Origin of Druidism*.[191] Carl was always on the lookout for interesting books that he could help get into the hands of more readers, whether it was through publishing the books himself or distributing books from other publishers. He even published a book about a well-publicized murder that had happened in Saint Paul, *The Carol Thompson Murder Case*. A Saint Paul socialite and mother of four, Thompson was murdered by her husband in 1963. The story was told by Donald John Giese, who incidentally was among the group of reporters that had braved a night in Carl's haunted Summit Avenue mansion years before.[192]

Soon, Carl was distributing books for nearly seventy different publishers, including Astrological Book Society of America, Life Resources Institute, Scope Reports, and Occult Sciences Book Club. To help keep up with all this exponential growth, Carl had a computer installed for Llewellyn in February 1970 to help with data collection and business forecasting. He was always enthusiastic to take advantage of new technologies, and it wasn't long before he was using an IBM computer to help with the typesetting for Llewellyn's rapidly expanding line of books.

Llewellyn's best-selling titles at the start of the seventies included *Astrology for the Millions* by Grant Lewi, *The Mystical Qabalah* by Dion Fortune, and *The Art and Practice of Getting Material Things Through Creative Visualization* by Ophiel.[193] Another title that proved popular was Llewellyn's 1970 release of *The Legend of Aleister Crowley*, a book that examined the press attacks on Crowley that had taken place in the 1920s. The book had been

---

191   Knoblauch, "Speaking of Occult..."
192   Schlaver, "The Carol Thompson Murder Case."
193   Pickwick Books advertisement, *Los Angeles Times*, May 10, 1970.

originally published in 1930 by London's Mandrake Press, and it was hard to come by in the United States prior to the Llewellyn reprint. Carl was excited about it, proclaiming it the "Book of the Week" at his bookstore and writing up some ad copy in his enthusiasm that described the book in rather sensationalist yet nevertheless irresistibly intriguing language:

> *Who and what is Aleister Crowley? Prophet of a new Aeon or the most evil man in the world? Here is the record of persecution, here is the man himself in his own words.*[194]

Llewellyn reprinted or distributed many of Crowley's works through the years, including *Diary of a Drug Fiend* and the last book Crowley wrote before his death in 1947, titled *Magick Without Tears*.

Llewellyn had something for everyone, and it seemed that nearly everyone was developing some kind of interest in astrology, magick, yoga, meditation, divination, or other occult studies intended to expand the mind. Astrology had found its way into the mainstream, and witches were starting to peek out from the shadows. Raymond Buckland had arrived in New York City several years prior and had set up a coven there where he began training people in Gardnerian Witchcraft, the religion created by Gerald Gardner that was known back then as simply "Wicca." Buckland had been initiated by Gardner himself in England and had been charged with the task of bringing the new Old Religion to the United States. There were also more magickal orders popping up in California, particularly in Southern California and in the San Francisco Bay area. While society at large may have generally frowned upon things like magick and witchcraft, those interested in the subjects had begun to discover one another, and they were getting together to practice, learn, and interact at Carl's Gnostica Bookstore and other places where occultists were given space to build community. Llewellyn books and the occult in general were gaining ground.

---

194   Gnostica Bookstore advertisement, *Minneapolis Star*, March 13, 1970.

Mainstream bookstores were devoting larger and larger sections of their shelving to occult books in order to meet the increased demand. One employee at the B. Dalton bookstore in Minneapolis shed some light on the overall atmosphere surrounding the occult at the time, commenting that although the store had greatly expanded their occult section in response to customer demand, the people who came in to buy these books usually acted rather self-conscious. "They act just like the ones who want to find pornography. It's never for themselves. It's always for relatives of friends," the employee said.[195] People were interested, they just weren't quite sure if they would be okay with their neighbors, friends, and family knowing they were interested. Astrology, yoga, and meditation were viewed as relatively innocuous, but there was still a tremendous amount of stigma and misunderstanding when it came to topics like magick and witchcraft.

A firm believer in the educational and transformative power of books, Carl continued to seek out innovative authors and manuscripts that he felt could have a broad or significant impact. He had a knack for spotting talent and recognizing genius, and was the first to publish many authors who have since become world renowned. As the oldest and largest independent occult book publisher in America, Llewellyn attracted many of the best talents, who would send Carl their manuscripts and hope for the best. One such author was the aforementioned Gardnerian witch Raymond Buckland. In 1970 Carl published Buckland's *Practical Candleburning: Spells and Rituals for Every Purpose*. While the book doesn't offer a complete system of witchcraft, it does offer a solid collection of real spells and rituals written by a real witch—which is easy to take for granted in today's world, but which didn't really exist at the time. Since its first publication the book has sold more than 300,000 copies and remains to this day among the titles on Llewellyn's "Ultimate Best Sellers" list. An ad that Carl wrote for Buckland's book was run in the *Minneapolis Star Tribune*:

195   Abbasi, "Study Group, Books, Even Classes."

Witchcraft: the "lost" art has been found! Look: Practical Candle
Burning—*by the director of the only witchcraft museum in the
US, Raymond Buckland. Exciting reading, even if you don't use
one of the many authentic "spells" listed. A different verse and
candles of different colors are used to create each mood. The
right atmosphere makes anything seem possible.*

For just $2.06, customers could have the book shipped right to
their door.[196]

The following year Carl published Buckland's *Witchcraft from the
Inside*, a book that illuminated in detail for the American public
for the first time ever the practices and beliefs of the modern witch
and the ins and outs of the new religion of Gardnerian Wicca. With
his books published by Llewellyn, Buckland was able to reach
new audiences of interested people all over the country eager to
find out what witchcraft was really all about. *Witchcraft from the
Inside* made it possible for people to learn about witchcraft independently. If you weren't in a coven, you could at least read about
the real-life practices of real-life modern witches.

Carl himself was getting very intrigued by witchcraft, and his
initial interest in the subject that had begun in his college days
was freshly renewed. Not only had Carl received a manuscript
out of the blue from this talented witch named Raymond Buckland, but he had also received a manuscript out of the blue from
a different kind of witch who went by the name of Lady Sheba. A
Kentucky-born witch who was about ten years Carl's elder, Lady
Sheba would prove to have a grand significance in the growth of
witchcraft in America as well as in the growth of Carl himself.

Lady Sheba, known in everyday life as Jessie Wicker Bell, sent
Carl a copy of her personal Book of Shadows to see if he would
be willing to publish it. She said that the Goddess had told her
to share it with the world. Carl was extremely impressed, and the
book was released in 1971, marking the first time that a com-

---

196   *Practical Candle Burning* advertisement, "Armchair Shopper,"
      Star Tribune, March 14, 1971.

plete Book of Shadows was published for the general public in the United States. A Book of Shadows is a compilation of all the teachings, spells, and rituals of a witches' coven or of an individual witch, and traditionally such books are kept very secret and copied only by hand and only by those who were initiated into the coven or who had the book passed down to them by a friend or relative. A professionally published Book of Shadows suddenly available in bookstores and occult shops across the country was something that had never been seen before, and while it excited many, it shocked and angered others.

Lady Sheba found herself the object of criticism from witches around the world who felt she was breaking oaths of secrecy by publishing the work or making claims that the text of the book wasn't original. Lady Sheba responded by stating that she had never claimed to have written the book—it was a Book of Shadows as it had been passed on to her, and she wasn't sure who the original author or authors were. She also emphasized that the time for secrecy had passed. Like Carl, Lady Sheba was a firm believer in sharing magickal information with others who might benefit from that knowledge.

Lady Sheba lived in Michigan at the time, so it wasn't long before she and Carl decided to meet in person. Carl learned a lot from Lady Sheba. They quickly became friends and practiced witchcraft together and with others within Carl's circle of free-thinkers. Soon he was initiated into Lady Sheba's coven of the American Order of the Brotherhood of the Wicca. When asked forty-three years later what it was like to be initiated by Lady Sheba, Carl still called it "the most powerful experience" he ever had: "I've been initiated into several magickal traditions, with nowhere the same power."[197]

After practicing what he learned from Lady Sheba and developing some practices of his own, Carl soon started his own coven, called Camelot Star of the North Coven, and served as high priest

---

197 CLW email to Melanie Marquis, September 10, 2013.

of the small group that met in the basement of his haunted Summit Avenue mansion. He designed an emblem for the coven that he called the "Star of the North" symbol and even compiled his own Book of Shadows of sorts, gathering notes, creating new rituals, and developing new practices that blended American Celtic and Gardnerian witchcraft traditions with high magick techniques and his own ideas. Carl was a thinker, and he put a great deal of effort into applying his mental and intuitive abilities to discern all he could about the inner meanings and inner workings of witchcraft and magick. He never thought he knew it all and was one of those rare people who truly is a lifelong student, forever striving to learn, develop, innovate, and improve. As high priest of Camelot Star of the North Coven, Carl initiated dozens of witches into the Craft.[198]

Wanting to do his part to raise awareness of the new religion of the Wicca, Carl would personally contact local reporters and invite them to attend rituals, visit his bookstore, review a Llewellyn book, or ask him any questions they might have about magick, witchcraft, and Wiccan belief. Publisher, bookstore proprietor, and business executive, Carl presented to the media a new idea of what a witch could be. He was successful and smart, perfectly respectable in appearance, and perfectly likable. He didn't fly around on a broom or hang out in the middle of a swamp stirring up toxic brews to clear up a warty green complexion. He presented himself as perfectly normal, and he presented himself as a witch. Carl is credited with being the first person in the Twin Cities to publicly declare that he was a witch, and he did this at a time when the word was seldom heard outside of fairy tales.[199]

In the summer of 1971 Carl had another magickal experience that proved to be profoundly significant. Through a mutual friend he met Sandra Heggum, the woman who would soon become his loving partner for life. A couple of months after their meeting, Carl

---

198   Kotula, "Witchcraft."

199   Morphew, "New Age Publishers."

hosted the first of many magickal festivals in Minneapolis, bringing together witches, druids, astrologers, and other magickally minded individuals to the Twin Cities for several days of workshops, banquets, and celebrations. In conjunction with the first festival, Carl put out a newsletter through his bookstore that he called *Gnostica News*. Soon, the newsletter developed into a full-fledged magazine by the name of *Gnostica* magazine.[200]

The magazine included news and information on witchcraft, magick, sex and the occult, music, pop culture, and more. "Recognizing every system of thought, it encompasses all phases of modern life—ecology, spiritual needs, para-sciences (astrology, ESP, palmistry, etc.), natural living, the predictive sciences, and current events," stated the *Gnostica* magazine advertising rates sheet.

Gnostica Bookstore employee Ron Wright served as the first editor of *Gnostica* magazine. Within a few years, Ron moved on, and Isaac Bonewits—druid and author of *Real Magick*—was hired to fill the position as editor. Carl helped arrange some media appearances for his new editor to promote the magazine, and Isaac appeared as a guest on Tom Snyder's popular television talk show *Tomorrow* singing the praises of *Gnostica* magazine.[201] In its prime, *Gnostica* magazine had as many as 60,000 monthly readers.[202] However, it seems not everyone was thrilled with the magazine. One ad for the publication advised, "*Gnostica* magazine is on your newsstand. Ask for it as they might try to hide it…If they won't sell it to you, call."[203] Around this same time Carl also had a magazine that he called *Astrology Now*, edited by acclaimed astrologer and opera singer Noel Tyl. The magazine discussed many aspects of astrology, with one issue focusing on how the new technology of computers could be used to help astrologers make more accurate predictions.

---

200 *Minneapolis Daily American*, "Witchcraft Isn't Devil Worship."
201 *Detroit Free Press*, "Tonight's Television Programs."
202 *The Baltimore Sun*, "Witchcraft."
203 Gnostica News advertisement, *Star Tribune*, May 16, 1976.

In October 1971, soon after Carl had hosted his first magickal festival, he was back in the spotlight as host and narrator of an hour-long television special about Halloween called *Night of the Black Cat*. Carl wrote much of the script himself and arranged for the camera crew to film an authentic witchcraft ritual as part of the program. To prepare for the special, Carl wrote to Lady Sheba for advice and input. On letterhead printed with runes and a magick symbol, Lady Sheba told Carl that the Halloween sabbat was the only time in which she uses black candles and the only time of year that witches are allowed to communicate with the dead.

TV Guide provided a listing for *Night of the Black Cat* hosted by "occult master Carl Weschcke":

> *Halloween as a celebration of life and death is examined with special emphasis on the black mass, witchcraft and crystal ball gazers.*[204]

Carl opened the program with the following:

> *Some call witchcraft the "old religion" and it is old...part of the traditional wisdom of nature...the intuitional knowledge of spontaneous psychological experience. But it is also new...as we shall see...for people today are studying not only witchcraft, but also astrology, tarot cards, and magick...all the occult sciences that concern themselves with the inner side of life.*

Later in the show, Carl explained one of the main rituals witches use to celebrate this sabbat:

> *Death is as much a part of life as is birth, and at Halloween, we offer food and drink to the ghosts of our ancestors out of respect and to remind us of our own time to depart this world for the next.*[205]

With factual information about witchcraft making its way to the masses, many people found Wicca to be the path that suited them best. Carl attributed the rise in witchcraft to being part of the

---

204 *TV Guide*, October 31, 1971.
205 CLW script for "Night of the Black Cat," October 1971.

"return-to-nature" movement that had people seeking out simpler lifestyles more in tune with the earth, while Raymond Buckland, whom the *Baltimore Sun* deemed the "Dean of American Witches," credited the easygoing, relaxed attitude of witchcraft, so often lacking in the organized mainstream religions.[206]

The sudden boom in the number of witches around the country was noticeable enough to draw a barrage of nationwide media attention. An article in the *Pittsburgh Press* proclaimed 1972 to be the "Year of the Witch" and named the Twin Cities as the center of the modern witchcraft revival. The article reported:

> *Practically any movement has a headquarters, and it's beginning to appear that the likely headquarters for followers of the occult is the unlikely city of Minneapolis. Normally, one would think that a far-out movement of this kind would have headquarters within commuting distance to San Francisco or Los Angeles. But a certain sign has appeared, designating Minneapolis as the predestined capital of sorcery. For reasons unknown even to those who specialize in divining the unknowable, a star, akin, they say, to the one over Bethlehem, has appeared over Minneapolis... Over the past several years, mystics in impressive numbers have been making pilgrimages to Minneapolis or settling there. The emigres have included a lama from Tibet, a holy man from India and a former Lutheran minister from Oregon, all of whom have found the city to be a promised land, spiritually and materially. The main force which serves to unite these disparate divines, giving them a sense of community and occasionally bankrolling their enterprises through hard times, is millionaire publisher of occult books and magazines, Carl Weschcke.*[207]

The star that's mentioned was seen by Lady Sheba, who witnessed the star and its streaming energies while on a visit to Carl's home.[208]

---

206 *The Baltimore Sun,* "Witchcraft."
207 Peterson, "The Year of the Witch."
208 Ibid.

It wasn't just witches who were drawn to the Twin Cities, either. Former Lutheran minister Vernon Harms, who led seventy of his followers from Oregon to Minneapolis, told a reporter,

> God brought us here. It was His wish for us to become cleansed and then be shown off to the rest of the world what clean living can do for mankind... If God pulls this off, He'll establish heaven right here.[209]

Jim Hague, who operated a retreat center called Harmony Hills, reportedly got the idea to move to Minneapolis from Christian evangelist Billy Graham: "Billy told me that people have a livelier spiritual response in the Twin Cities than in any other place in the world."[210] Carl explained it by saying that

> There's scientific basis to the Minneapolis magnetism which so many people feel. You can scoff at astrology, but we're all perfectly aware of the effect which the moon has on gravity because we see the tides.[211]

Built on Precambrian bedrock rich in iron ore, the land on which the Twin Cities reside is home to some of the oldest rock formations in the Midwest.

Carl was delighted to see more people taking an interest in spirituality. At Carl's encouragement, Lady Sheba expanded her Book of Shadows, and in 1972 *The Grimoire of Lady Sheba* was released. With the exposure from Llewellyn publishing and distributing her books, and with the controversy that ensued from a witch making long-held secrets public to the masses, Lady Sheba quickly became one of the most well-known witches in the country. Described by a local paper as "a plump, pleasant grandmother who is not amused if you ask her to turn you into a frog," Lady Sheba was the friendly, approachable witch who nevertheless radiated great power and authority. She declared, in fact, that she was no less than the

---

209   Peterson, "Witch Capital of the World."
210   Ibid.
211   Ibid.

Queen of Witches, appointed to the role by the "gracious Goddess" herself. She didn't seem very bothered by the criticism, and she made good use of her fame to try to clear up public misconceptions about witchcraft. "There are still prejudices and superstitions about what witchcraft is," she told a reporter in 1972. "Deliver us from such nonsense."[212]

Carl was also seizing every opportunity to educate the public about witchcraft. He was invited to present a lecture on magick, witchcraft, astrology, and occultism at the Rothwell Student Center on the University of Wisconsin campus at Superior. His lecture was titled "Occult Renaissance '72." Sponsored by the university, the lecture was free to attend and open to the public.

Carl was a powerful speaker. Reporter Mary Straub, who attended one of his presentations to the Aquarian Astrological Society, described what it was like to join Carl in a demonstration of the Middle Pillar ritual:

> Carl led his audience in a ritual designed to transform each of them into pillars of energy and inner strength. When his normally soft voice boomed in Hebrew chant, "EH HEH YEH," it surely vibrated not only his own energy centers, but the entire room and centers of everyone present. I couldn't help but think, "He must be an excellent singer."[213]

Carl, who always dreamed of being able to use the power of his voice to move people magickally, was surely flattered by the description.

Carl not only liked to educate, he also liked to provide opportunity. As his success grew, Carl was able to share that success by providing good jobs and orchestrating opportunities for his friends and others whose talents he believed in. By February 1972 the Llewellyn Publications team included twenty editors and artists and seventeen commissioned sales reps to help with all the

---

212 Smith, "Witches Meet in City."
213 Straub, "High Priest of the Occult."

tasks of the publishing business that Carl once had to carry out alone.[214] Through his publishing house as well as his bookstore and magick school, he was creating opportunities for the talented people around him to shine, offering them gigs as psychic readers, magickal studies teachers, authors, astrologers, and more. One newspaper reporter not only called Carl an "occult sage," but also named him "Jim Finks of the local witches," comparing him to the championship-winning, charismatic coach of the Minnesota Vikings.[215]

The "Year of the Witch" was an exciting year for Carl, and one in which he seemed to have a Midas touch, encountering success in his business life as well as in his spiritual life and personal life. On Winter Solstice 1972 Carl and Sandra got married, and before the next Winter Solstice they would have a beautiful baby boy.

Carl's family wasn't the only thing that was growing. The witch community in the Twin Cities continued to gain more members, and by December 1973 there were forty-six covens in Saint Paul alone.[216] Carl was always eager to spread the truth about witchcraft, and he had a way of explaining things in a down-to-earth style that everyday non-witches could find relatable. He described Wicca to a reporter in Tinley Park, Illinois, as simply "a religion that brings one closer to nature and into closer relationship with the inner rhythm of the world."[217]

He was also passionate in his quest to protect self-identified witches from prejudice and guard their civil rights. Even though he was never a fan of organized religion, he and Sandra founded the First Wiccan Church of Minnesota in 1973 to serve as a legal vehicle for religious protections for witches, if the need arose. Carl had received an honorary Doctor of Divinity degree from Universal Life Church the year prior. The church was officially registered "for

---

214   Peterson, "The Year of the Witch."

215   Klobuchar, "A Bulletin from the Beyond."

216   Lightman, "Filming *Isis* Among the Witches."

217   Straub, "High Priest of the Occult."

purposes of research into magick, parapsychology, and spiritual healing." Meetings were to take place at the Gnostica Bookstore. As Carl wrote,

> *Membership in the church also is intended to give an umbrella of protection to the people of the Wicca, for oftentimes law seems to overlook the Constitutional guarantees of religious freedom, except for those who belong to a religious corporation. For this reason, a membership card will be provided.*[218]

After a few years when other organizations had formed to serve a similar purpose, the church was dissolved. Carl explained,

> *I was always opposed to institutionalizing Wicca. What I really was saying with the First Wiccan Church was: "Hey, look, world! These aren't just strange people. They have a religion, and they deserve respect!"*[219]

Though short-lived, the church had helped to establish a precedent in Minnesota and served as an example and an inspiration for witches to seek and gain equal protection under the laws of religious freedom.[220]

Carl also participated in an occult studies program that was sponsored by the Richfield Community Library and Southdale-Hennepin Area Library. Consisting of a series of talks and discussions with question-and-answer sessions, other panelists included Ruth Gardner and Bob Griswald. Carl wrote a letter to the Richfield Community Library following the event:

> *I'm really pleased to know that the response to the program has been positive, and I'm particularly pleased that the library saw fit to respond to this interest in the occult—particularly in the face of "adversity" that I know greets such affairs.*[221]

---

218   CLW letter to Donald Ahern, August 14, 1973.

219   Kelly, "Angels' Voices."

220   "Witchcraft and Neo-Paganism," Encyclopedia.com, http://www
      .encyclopedia.com/religion/encyclopedias-almanacs-transcripts
      -and-maps/witchcraft-and-neo-paganism.

221   CLW letter to Richfield Community Library, March 1974.

The libraries had decided to offer the program in response to library patrons' increased interest in ESP, graphology, palmistry, tarot, and witchcraft.

Carl had become so well-known in the burgeoning world of witches that he was approached by filmmaker Maury Hurley, who wanted to film a movie about witches. "I wanted to do something that dealt with different kinds of perspectives, different kinds of realities, different kinds of mystical or religious beliefs," Hurley explained. The film was to be called *Isis*, and it was to be released by Woodbine Pictures, Hurley's own company that he owned with some friends. The budget was only $18,000, with Hurley and two of his friends using their own money that they made shooting commercials and industrial films to fund the project. "If we can pull it off for $18,000—which includes a sizable contingency—that in itself will be a remarkable experiment," commented Hurley. The film was to center around the story of a young woman who discovers witchcraft, then gets caught up in a classic battle of good versus evil, struggling to decide if she should team up with the "bad" witches or the "good" witches.[222]

Hurley consulted with Carl to find out more about witchcraft and maybe connect with some real witches through him who could act in the film. Upon meeting, Hurley realized Carl would be the perfect person to play the role of high priest of the witches' coven. Hurley commented on his choice, explaining,

> He's not an actor of course, but it would be difficult to find an actor to play the part as well as he does it. He has a great look about him—a great face, a great beard, and a great presence. His eyes are perfect and he has a magnificent bass voice.

Carl was cast as the "good" witch, while Granville Van Dusen was to play the "bad" witch. The starring role of the young woman witchcraft initiate in the film would be played by a local Minneapo-

---

222   Lightman, "Filming *Isis* Among the Witches."

lis actor named Mari Rovang. Astrologer Noel Tyl was also to have a role.[223]

The filming was shot at various locations including Carl's basement-level oval-shaped magick room in the Summit Avenue mansion. There was already a mirror-lined coffin with candles burning inside that Carl had made himself, and on the floor was a vibrantly colored magick circle. A Tiffany lamp hung from overhead, providing a ruddy, mystical glow. Hurley found the room to be the perfect setting for his film as-is, with no further props or adjustments needed. The movie would be made in a way that preserved the authenticity of the witch's practices as much as possible. Hurley explained,

> We don't have a traditional script, with specific scenes and a bunch of dialogue all lined out. That would be effective for most films, but not for this one. What we're trying to do is show things in such a way that one scene propels us into the next scene...It's a strange way to work, but judging from what we've seen to date, it's worth it.[224]

Scenes in the film included a traditional witchcraft initiation in which the initiate entered the circle skyclad (nude), her hands bound loosely behind her back with a silken cord. Carl called on a pantheon of gods and opened the circle. Herb Lightman, a reporter who had been brought along to witness the filming, commented at the time, "I can't shake the feeling that there are more entities in that room than I can see."

One of the actors gave the whole group a fright when she fainted during the filming of the initiation scene. Carl rushed to her side, rubbing her wrists and calling for water. The woman soon came to, reporting that she had heard voices and seen visions. Hurley asked Carl if they should still proceed with the scene they had planned to film the following night, which was to feature a "calling down

---

223   Clepper, "Movie Takes Advantage."
224   Lightman, "Filming *Isis* Among the Witches."

the moon" ceremony. Carl advised that their mistake had been in actually invoking the powers, who apparently didn't care for the unknown film crew invading the ritual space. Carl said the ritual could proceed as planned, only they wouldn't open the circle. Said Carl, "We were trying to be completely authentic, but we got more authenticity than we bargained for!"

The "calling down the moon" ceremony would be filmed at Hazel Hills, and Carl's mom greeted both film crew and witches with a tray of sandwiches and hot, freshly brewed coffee. The scene was to be filmed outside around a bonfire surrounded by torches, and it was absolutely freezing. Carl joked that maybe they were "indoor witches" after all. The wind was blowing strong, and propane tanks had to be buried in the frozen ground to fuel the torches in the chilly air. Resourceful camera operator Ned Judge made use of two Coleman lanterns and a bare quartz lamp with a makeshift aluminum foil reflector to provide extra lighting.[225]

When all was said and done, director Hurley called Carl a "remarkable actor."[226] The film was to debut with a series of local showings in the fall of 1974 that never happened. Woodbine Pictures was unable to get all the funds together that they needed to polish and promote the film. However, *Isis* remains listed under Maury Hurley's movie credits,[227] so it's possible that there is a reel of film somewhere out there in the world that will one day resurface and make Carl a movie star. *American Cinematographer* magazine did a long feature article about the film while it was still in the filming process, and Carl wrote to the magazine to thank them for their coverage. Carl wrote, "It really is a great adventure working with Maury Hurley—and who would have ever thought my picture would be in a movie magazine!"[228]

---

225   Lightman, "Filming *Isis* Among the Witches."

226   Clepper, "Movie Takes Advantage."

227   "*Isis* (1973)," BFI, http://www.bfi.org.uk/films-tv
-people/4ce2b72f36d9b.

228   CLW letter to *American Cinematographer* editor, January 25, 1974.

In the spring of 1974, soon after the filming of *Isis* was complete, Carl hosted a "WitchMeet" to bring together the seventy-three members of the American Witches Council that had formed at his larger Gnosticon festival the previous fall. The group represented many different traditions of witchcraft and magick, and together they agreed on a collective statement of belief that could be issued to the general public for purposes of showing what witches really believed. The statement was called "The Thirteen Principles of Wiccan Belief." Today, the document is often criticized for being too vague and not taking into account the diversity of witchcraft, but at the time the goal was to prevent misunderstandings that might arise from individual witches portraying the Craft to the media in erroneous and negative ways that could hurt the movement as a whole. The council was comprised of a diverse group of individuals representing a wide variety of spiritual paths, and each of the thirteen principles were adopted by a unanimous vote.

Several members of the American Witches Council joined with Carl and a handful of other innovative magickal people the following fall to found an organization they called the World Esoteric Assembly. The purposes of the organization were stated as

> providing access to the resources within the occult community, and accepting responsibility for stewardship to the biosphere, responsibility to those who come to us for guidance, and responsibility to the planet on which we live.

A network of ceremonial magicians, druids, witches, a chaos magician, and others, the World Esoteric Assembly was to be "not an authority but a collection of authorities," with each group and individual to remain autonomous. The benefit in working together would be to provide a structure to focus magickal power as a group on a worldwide basis toward common goals. In a flow of ideas, some of these goals are laid out in the group's founding documents:

> One of our aims is the evolution of humanity to higher levels; raising consciousness to a higher plane for the good of the species; to accelerate exquisitely the evolution of humanity toward

conscious participation in the communicating intelligences; rec-
ognizing that our responsibilities are greater than we have real-
ized.[229]

It's amazing that Carl was able to keep up with all he was doing. He had a young son, a wife, a publishing company, a bookstore, and a magick school. He had a family to love, festivals to orchestrate, businesses to run, executive roles to fill, cooperative networks to create. He had an endless flow of work to do, yet he still took the time to do what he could to boost public awareness of witchcraft and other alternative practices. In October 1974 alone, Carl had eight different speaking engagements that included talks for two high school classes and a business luncheon, plus two television interviews and an interview on a local radio station. He and his wife, Sandra, were also asked to produce an hour-long videotape for distribution on the University of Wisconsin campus. Carl hadn't sought out a single one of these engagements. They had all come to him, and he was seldom inclined to turn down a good opportunity, no matter how much work he had to do. Carl frequently worked twelve- and eighteen-hour days, and he would often sit up late through the night reading over new manuscripts that he had received. At age forty-four, Carl Weschcke was a driven man, to say the least.

He even made time to work on his own magickal development. He corresponded frequently with Osborne Phillips and Melita Denning of the Ordo Aurum Solis, an initiation order of the Ogdoadic tradition of Western mysticism. Carl would write to the couple, who lived in England at the time, often asking their advice and opinions on new rituals and techniques he was working to create. Carl became a member of the Ordo Aurum Solis, and by 1975 he was writing to his friends about starting an Aurum Solis group in the US. Denning and Phillips soon arrived in America to focus on

---

229   "World Esoteric Assembly," document accompanying "Founders of the World Esoteric Assembly," CLW personal files, September 18, 1974.

expanding the scope of their work. Years later Carl briefly became the seventh Grand Master of the tradition (typically a lifelong appointment) when Denning had decided to take a break from the role, but he graciously stepped aside when she changed her mind and asked to be reinstated. Jean-Louis de Biasi, tenth Grand Master of Ordo Aurum Solis, explains:

> *He was surprised because such a request is unusual in our tradition. Nobody can retake a lifetime consecration without the agreement of the one in charge. Carl has never been interested in honors. Being a Grand Master was an opportunity to share his expertise and not a way to express a will of power. Consequently, and as Carl told me later, it was not something difficult for him to resign as Grand Master. However, he has always been eager to follow the inner work of the order and its development in the world.*

Carl urged Denning and Phillips to share their magickal practices and knowledge of the Ordo Aurum Solis by writing books. They weren't sure they could do it but figured they would give it a try since Carl was so enthusiastic about the idea. Excerpts from their writings were first published in Carl's *Gnostica* magazine, and the encouragement was enough to set Denning and Phillips on their road to becoming successful authors. At Carl's request, the couple went on to write the five-volume Magical Philosophy series along with many other titles for Llewellyn Publications that are now considered classics in the Western magickal tradition. The Magical Philosophy series, which outlined the Hermetic and Theurgic traditions of the Ordo Aurum Solis, has had a long-reaching impact on modern occult study.

Whenever Carl had an idea in mind for a book that he was passionate about, it was difficult to dissuade him, and even magickal forces seemed to be at work to help make his dreams into reality. Judy Hipskind, the dean of Carl's magick school, recalled the memorable occasion that set her on the path to writing her first book, *Palmistry: The Whole View*:

> *Carl asked me to write a book when I first worked there, and*
> *I agreed, only in my mind I thought maybe in about ten years*
> *I would do it. Carl continued to press for a book from time to*
> *time, and I always said sure, but we never discussed a timeline.*
> *About two years into this process, Carl came to the area where I*
> *was working and flapped a piece of paper in my face. I had been*
> *writing a column for his magazine and we called the column*
> *"Palmistry Updated." Well, the piece of paper he had in his hand*
> *was a letter from the famous astrologer Sydney Omarr, order-*
> *ing a copy of my book, "Palmistry Updated." Carl wanted me to*
> *see the request with my own eyes. I have no idea how Sydney*
> *Omarr got the idea it was a book; maybe he thought the column*
> *was an excerpt from the "book." Carl said, "Now, if this doesn't*
> *make you write that book, nothing will." My response: "Okay, I'll*
> *do it. I resign." If I shocked him, he didn't react. He wanted that*
> *book done more than anything.*

Carl also offered encouragement to Israel Regardie, suggesting ideas for more books and articles that he might write for Llewellyn. One project that Regardie did at Carl's urging was editing Aleister Crowley's *Gems from the Equinox*, which outlined Crowley's ideas for how a magickal order should operate. Regardie wrote to Carl regarding the book:

> *I must confess to being quite impatient about its appearance. I*
> *feel that it, together with the Golden Dawn, will be the two big*
> *jobs of editorship that I have ever undertaken—and they will live*
> *long after I'm gone.*[230]

The Llewellyn staff had grown to nearly fifty employees, and with business still booming, they needed more space in which to work.[231] Carl purchased a five-story building in Saint Paul to house his bookstore as well as his publishing enterprise. Located at 213 East Fourth Street across from the Union Depot in Lowertown Saint Paul, the building had been home to the Minnesota

---

230   Israel Regardie letter to CLW, August 30, 1974.
231   St. George, "Wands and Witches."

Knitting Mills for the past twenty-two years.[232] The ground floor would be home to the Gnostica Bookstore, an herbal tea shop, a magick shop, and several other stalls of merchandise that the Weschckes referred to as "Gabriel's Arcade," naming it after their son. The other floors of the building would house Llewellyn's editorial offices, mail order department, and warehouse.

By the middle part of the decade, Llewellyn had about sixty titles on its list. An average of six books a year focused on the topic of witchcraft,[233] while other titles explored topics ranging from psychic self-defense to pyramid power. An article in the *Chicago Tribune* read:

> Llewellyn Publications in Saint Paul, Minnesota, may have the
> most unusual list of customers in the country—warlocks and
> witches; astrologers and palmists; occult experts; and true
> believers in parapsychology, divination, UFO's, the Tarot, and
> neo-paganism.[234]

Whether or not Llewellyn's customers were unusual, the fact that there was a tremendous number of them was undisputable.

Llewellyn's single biggest customer at the time was B. Dalton. With over two hundred stores across the country, B. Dalton provided excellent exposure and distribution for Llewellyn's line of books, which in turn prompted other booksellers to carry the Llewellyn line, as well. "Occult books no longer are confined to occult bookstores," Carl told a reporter. "In fact, we've been selling some titles lately to Methodist bookstores."[235] The biggest markets for Llewellyn books were on the East Coast and West Coast, though Texas and Florida also had a lot of occult book buyers. The

232 Minnesota Knitting Mills, "History," "Company History," accessed
     March 11, 2018, http://www.mnknit.com/history/.

233 *The Baltimore Sun,* "Witchcraft."

234 Knoblauch, "Signs of the Occult."

235 St. George, "Wands and Witches."

Moon Sign Book continued to be Llewellyn's best seller, with the 1976 edition selling more than 100,000 copies.[236]

Carl's wife, Sandra, was taking a more prominent role in managing Llewellyn and was soon officially filling the role of vice president. Acting as spokesperson for Llewellyn on many occasions, Sandra's aura of sensibility brought an air of normalcy and practicality to Llewellyn that it didn't have before in quite such large measure. In 1976 she told a reporter, "Our books are not far out. We publish quality books by authors who use different methods to achieve the same results."[237]

Llewellyn books were soon to get another boost that would push the company even further into the eyes of the mainstream. In 1977 Llewellyn struck a deal with Bantam Books, granting Bantam the rights to produce mass-market paperback editions of a dozen of Llewellyn's personal astrological guides and almanacs that had been authored by Marylee Bytheriver under Carl's direction. By the following year, Bantam had sold more than 1.5 million copies of Llewellyn's titles, so they sought to expand that list and began issuing mass-market editions of the *Moon Sign Book*, Grant Lewi's *Heaven Knows What*, and *Llewellyn's Astrology Calendar*. Carl told a reporter at the time,

> *We'd always had good trade distribution as a specialty publisher, but there are only 10,000 trade outlets in the country and only about 4,000 really sell books and we were selling to only about 2,000 of them. But the number of mass market outlets is over 100,000 and distribution of that size requires much more clout than we had. But Bantam has clout to the nth degree and their interest in us has allowed us to reach a much larger audience.*

A public relations representative from Bantam, Diane Perlberg, added that the collaboration was a win for their publishing house as well, saying:

---

236 Knoblauch, "Signs of the Occult."
237 Knoblauch, "Signs of the Occult."

Llewellyn has an awful lot of respectability in its field, and when we acquired Carl's line, we picked up the respectability he had built up and it added another dimension. So, it has been a hand-in-hand type of venture.[238]

The books with Bantam increased Carl's fame and further added to his reputation as an expert on astrology and other mystical topics. Wicca was becoming more and more well-known to the general public, and people were craving information. Carl soon found himself bombarded with an increasing number of requests for interviews by television shows, radio stations, newspapers, and magazines from around the country.

He was even invited to be a special guest at a Gloria Vanderbilt fashion show that Gloria herself attended. His fondness for predicting annual style trends based on astrological patterns and influences had earned him a reputation as an arbiter of fashion. Truth be told, Carl had always had an interest in cutting-edge designs, and he even had experience with shoemaking and dressmaking. In his college years Carl had been inspired to craft a pair of high-heeled pointe shoes for one of his girlfriends who had developed an interest in unique fashions. He had cut a pair of tiny toe shoes in half that he had found at a thrift store and spliced them together with a pair of high heels, whittling a new set of stiletto-style heels himself and attaching everything together with a bent metal bar. He wrapped the shoes in black tape and added eyelets and a bright red ribbon. He had also designed his and Sandra's wedding clothes and had them custom made to suit his exact specifications. He had designed and crafted numerous masks, robes, and other garments over the years as an occasional hobby. While his fame as an astrologer, witch, and publisher outshined his merits as a fashion baron, Carl's talents for trendspotting and predicting popular fashions hadn't gone unnoticed. Carl delightedly joined

---

238 Smith, "Saint Paul Book Firm's Success," and Walters, "Paperback Writers."

Gloria Vanderbilt for her fall fashion show held in Minneapolis at Orchestra Hall.[239] For just $2.50, Minneapolis's aspiring fashionistas were treated to a meet and greet with Gloria Vanderbilt and the other special guests including Carl, as well as a coffee buffet and a sneak peek at Vanderbilt's fall 1979 collection.[240]

While Carl had agreed to appear at the fashion show, it was one of the last major media appearances he did before attempting to take a major step back from all the media attention he'd been getting. Keeping up with all he was doing while trying to keep up with his rapidly growing son and business at the same time had become too much. He had accidentally grown much older somehow, and he found that he just didn't have as much energy as he had enjoyed in his youth.

Thanks largely to the growth of Llewellyn and to Carl's enormous efforts in educating the public about witchcraft and the occult, there were many others now who were stepping forward to declare themselves witches and correct misinformation about occult practices that were still circulating in the public spheres. While he did continue to make occasional media appearances and agree to interviews here and there, there wasn't as much pressure as there had been in the past, when Carl had felt like he needed to seek out such opportunities, when it had been essential to educate the public about the very existence of magick and witchcraft.

Carl explained:

> There was a lot of that public "service" work, and it eventually became too much to handle along with business and family, so I declined further invitations and requests; by then many other groups were organizing to give Wicca a positive public face, and I concentrated on the business side of publishing for the Pagan community.[241]

---

239   Mall Fashion Show advertisement, *Star Tribune*, August 20, 1979.

240   *Star Tribune*, "Dayton's Salutes the American Designers."

241   Night Sky, "Carl Llewellyn Weschcke."

People had become more aware, and Carl knew there were others to now share the cause. He was ready to shift from being a center of attention himself to being able to focus his attention more toward his family. The Weschckes had relocated out of the big haunted house and into a quieter family-style home in the suburbs.

Are You a Witch?

Compiled by "experts at the Gnostica school," this quiz was included with an article about the witchcraft boom of the seventies. A yes answer to more than five of the following questions indicates a "natural ability" in the magickal arts:

- Do you carry good luck charms?

- Have you ever experienced déjà vu, that feeling of having "been there before"?

- Have you ever used your psychic force alone to direct events (for example, successfully willing that someone say or do something you want)?

- Do you believe in the power of suggestion?

- Witchcraft is an old Earth Religion. Can you respect it as such?

- Do you keep a secret diary?

- Are you fascinated by the use of herbs and spices for cookery and in their old medicinal use?

- Do you believe in reincarnation?

- Do you talk to your plants, your cat or dog, and believe these and other things in your home have a secret language?

- Have others ever referred to you as a witch?

Chapter 8

Gnostica Bookstore

Carl's idea for a bookstore had blossomed naturally out of the growth of Llewellyn, and in turn, the bookstore helped Llewellyn to achieve even greater heights of success. Llewellyn was becoming known as a reliable source of information on a wide variety of occult subjects, and more and more people were turning to their books to learn more about astrology, psychic development, and more. By the end of the sixties, public interest in astrology, witchcraft, and other occult subjects was noticeably on the rise, and what was once restricted to the subcultures was beginning to make itself visible in the mainstream. Carl attributed much of the increased interest in occultism to "the decline in orthodox religion and the increasing demand of people for a philosophy in their personal lives." He also felt that the recent space mission that had brought humans to the moon had renewed the public fascination with outer space and spurred many people to take up the study of astrology.[242]

---

242 Smith, "Space Feats Stimulate Occult."

As Llewellyn's popularity grew, so too did the stock of books that must be stored, so Carl had decided that he needed to acquire another building. The building could serve a dual purpose, providing a place to keep the rapidly expanding stock of Llewellyn books and also offering a place to sell those books directly to the people who wanted them. He began to dream of opening a bookstore, and he started to look around for premises. A large old building on Laurel Avenue in downtown Minneapolis caught his eye.

Built around the turn of the century, the 13,000-square-foot brick and stucco dwelling had been the home of the Gill Brothers Mortuary for the previous sixty-nine years. The building was large enough to provide space for a bookstore and then some. As large as the Summit Avenue mansion was, the publication business had slowly begun to take over the house like a creeping vine that grows overnight and suddenly is all over the place. Carl wanted to be able to move some of the Llewellyn operations into a separate facility. He arranged to take a tour of the property.

Carl was enchanted with the high ceilings, long history, and somewhat creepy atmosphere of the former mortuary. He also liked the location. Close to three major downtown exits from the three freeways that entered the city, the building would be easy to access from the suburbs. It was only two blocks away from the main bus depot and only a block from the main public transit route that cut through the city. It was an easy walk from the main shopping district in downtown Minneapolis but not smack-dab in the middle of it. Carl explained:

> Just as we determined to serve the entire Twin Cities, we also recognized that today, astrology and the occult are objects of curiosity to many people, and we felt we couldn't afford to be in the main "walk-in" retail trade area and thus have to be in the position of answering hundreds of idle questioners. The location we have is just off the main shopping area—easily accessible, but not on "main street."

The building was purchased, and renovations were made. One of the renovations was a paint job for the outside walls of the vast building. Carl wanted his bookstore to stand out, so he asked the painters to cover over the existing creamy white paint with a darker tone. He was expecting a deep brown color, but he must have been looking at the color samples in dim lighting or else the painters got confused because there was a mix-up. When Carl arrived to see how the paint job was progressing, he discovered his bookstore had been painted with a lovely shade of deep purple. It definitely stood out, which was the original intention, so Carl decided to keep the odd paint job and consider it a lucky accident, adding a bright yellow moon to the side of the building for good measure. The new store would be called Gnostica Bookstore.

Carl derived the name from the word *gnosis*, meaning "knowledge," as he wanted the Gnostica Bookstore to be a place of wisdom. He knew from the start that his bookstore wouldn't be "only" a bookstore, and his vision included classes, lectures, and indeed a full program of occult learning made available to the student in a wide array of disciplines. He wanted it to be a place where people could get together and share ideas—a place where people could discover more about all they were meant to be. A page of personal notes that he penned around the time he opened the Gnostica shares more of Carl's vision:

> *I feel that the Gnostica Bookstore, being a place of knowledge and a place where all people interested in astrology and in the occult can come freely, meets the modern need of intelligent people seeking understanding. By encouraging people to come and meet socially and exchange ideas, to study together and work together informally, we offer a "place of knowledge" where each person can find his own way. Unlike fundamentalist religion, occultism does not look upon people as children that have to be guided and pushed through life, but instead recognizes each as a truly unique soul with a truly unique destiny. Those of us who accept reincarnation must recognize then that each person is the product of billions of years of evolution, and hence*

*is a very special person at the same time that he is a facet in
an evolving universe. This concept both gives perspective and
recognition to the serious student who seeks to make his life
meaningful.*[243]

To announce the grand opening of his new enterprise, Carl
sent out two direct mailings to Llewellyn's customer list of book
buyers who lived in the Saint Paul/Minneapolis area. The mailings announced the grand opening and extended an invitation to
attend the open house events that the Gnostica Bookstore would
be hosting each Sunday. Carl also printed up thousands of flyers
that he placed in local coffee shops, boutiques, theaters, and other
establishments. The flyer advertised that the Gnostica would have
more books than any other occult bookstore in America, and it
also mentioned that Ophiel and other special guests might soon
pay a visit to the new store. "The Gnostica will also specialize in
the unusual and unique gift items," the flyer read, "such as porcelain and pottery mugs, framed tiles and ashtrays in every sign of
the zodiac; plus incenses and crystal balls."

In January 1970 Gnostica Bookstore opened its doors in all its
purple glory and became the new headquarters and first retail out-
let of Llewellyn Publications. Carl wrote about the opening in an
article for *Publishers Weekly*:

> *We opened the Gnostica Bookstore at exactly 8:02 a.m. on Jan-
> uary 15, 1970. This time—while not exactly the best time astro-
> logically for starting a new venture—was chosen as the best
> time in terms of my own horoscope. I feel that any new venture
> has to be considered as a projection of the personal horoscope,
> only taking on an independent existence as the venture itself
> becomes independent. So the store was opened at an appropri-
> ate astrological time, and also with an appropriate magickal rit-
> ual—as befits an astrological and occult bookstore.*[244]

---

243   From CLW personal notes labeled "An Astrology/Occult Bookstore,"
       1970.
244   Weschcke, "Shop Ventures into Unknown."

Carl envisioned Gnostica Bookstore as a place where people could get together, where they could learn. One early advertisement for the store extended an invitation to "share your ideas and interests" and "meet new friends" at the Gnostica, where you would also find "spontaneous discussion groups" and "enlightenment entertainment."[245]

As the first bookstore in Minneapolis or Saint Paul to specialize in astrology and the occult, and the largest of such stores to exist anywhere in the country, the opening of the Gnostica Bookstore attracted the attentions of the mystically minded as well as the media. An article from the *Minneapolis Star Tribune* describes the cold air and heavy carpeting in the Gnostica store as being still "reminiscent of the mortuary it once was."[246]

With a heady smell of incense in the air and the mystical sounds of exotic music piping through the cavernous yet crowded room, stepping into Gnostica was like stepping into another world. There were over 100,000 books in stock, divided into numerous subcategories including numerology, astrology, noology, ghosts, ESP, tarot, yoga, and Zen. There were books on graphology, alchemy, clairvoyance, divination, dreams, I Ching, cartomancy, palmistry, and magick. There was even a small section featuring obscure titles in demonology and the dark arts for the handful of customers who were interested in such subjects.

Many of the books were Llewellyn publications, and others were titles that Carl had chosen to distribute in hopes of gaining a wider audience of people interested in occult philosophy. All the books available through the Llewellyn catalog were also made available in the bookstore, so it wasn't long before the store was stocking nearly every English-language magickal text that was currently in existence. Many Twin Cities residents were delighted. Suddenly, occult books that had been hard to come by for years, as well as

---

245 Gnostica Bookstore flyer, 1970.
246 Smith, "Space Feats Stimulate Occult."

exciting new titles, were readily available at a convenient location in the heart of downtown Minneapolis.

Even more interesting than the books, however, were the other products sold at Gnostica. From aluminum spirit trumpets to crescent moon necklaces and stiletto heels, Gnostica had it all. There was even a fireman's helmet with a large crystal mounted onto it that could be worn to boost one's psychic powers. One employee who had grown up in North Dakota liked to refer to these additional products as the "farm implements" line. The Aura Research Kit was among the more popular items sold at Gnostica. Consisting of a pair of goggles complete with "a full range of complementary filters, spare frames, and an instruction booklet," the device was intended to enhance a person's ability to "see" the aura and decipher meaning from variations in its appearance.[247]

The odd and enormous assortment of items coupled with the strange look of the high-ceilinged, aging building gave the Gnostica a unique mystique that couldn't be found anywhere else in the Twin Cities. When a writer for the *Minneapolis Star* visited the store to get his fortune told, he wasn't sure what he would find in the colorful building that he had always known as a mortuary. He wrote:

> *I'd been avoiding the Gnostica, what with its purple walls and generally mysterious reputation. I was uneasy walking among the books on witchcraft while I waited for the palm reader to finish with another client. A group of silent people who trooped up the basement stairs and out the front door aroused my curiosity, but I didn't feel it was right to ask what goes on in the basement of the Gnostica.*[248]

At a time when occult bookstores were still a rare commodity, the opening of Gnostica in Minneapolis proved to be a significant development for the city, providing a gathering place and common

---

247   Smith, "Space Feats Stimulate Occult."
248   Hodierne, "Seers Predict."

ground for the many magickal practitioners and students of the occult who had previously hidden in the shadows, unaware that they were not alone. "We delight the mystic, encourage the student, challenge the skeptic, and welcome the curious,"[249] read an ad for the Gnostica, and indeed they did. Customers of all ages flocked to the store not only for books and magickal supplies, but also for the sense of community found there. Each Sunday Gnostica Bookstore hosted an open house from 1:00 p.m. to 6:00 p.m. that was free to attend. Complimentary tea and fortune cookies were served while visitors made new friends and chatted with the staff about common interests not typically thought of as very common. There was usually some form of entertainment provided, such as free handwriting analysis, a yoga demonstration, or a free lecture on magickal philosophy. To advertise the Sunday social hours, Carl ran ads promising readers that Gnostica was the place to "meet and talk with interested people, consult the experts, open your mind."[250] People were invited to bring in the ad to receive a free psychic reading during the event.

The ads caught the attention of an extremely diverse and interesting crowd. Often the open house events would draw in as many as 500 potential customers. There was no cost to attend, the treats and the psychic readings were free, and there was no sales pressure, but the people who came to Carl's bookstore liked what they saw and they wanted it. Sunday quickly established itself as Gnostica's biggest sales day of the week.

From tarot and palmistry to astral projection and tantra, no subject was considered too "out there" or off-limits at Gnostica. It was a place where people could be themselves and become more than they were. Young adults proved to be the most serious students of the occult arts, leaning toward the more complex and scholarly books. "The little old ladies want their fortunes told and

---

249 Gnostica Bookstore advertisement, *Star Tribune*, March 19, 1978.
250 Gnostica Bookstore advertisement, *Star Tribune*, May 21, 1970.

take a lighter view of it,"[251] the forty-year-old Carl commented at the time. Whether they came in for the free treats or to learn some new tricks, the crowd that gathered at the bookstore grew larger and larger. Carl even hosted summer art shows to help draw customers into the store, giving local artists opportunities to show off their work.[252] Whether young or old, beginner or adept, everyone was treated as a friend at the Gnostica.

The community atmosphere lent itself perfectly to Carl's idea for a magick school, as people were organically coming together at the Gnostica to hear lectures, take classes, see demonstrations, share ideas, and generally learn and grow through interaction with one another as individuals. The Gnostica was already building a reputation as being a center of occult learning, and Carl wanted to take that a step further by opening up an official school. He would use the upper level of the bookstore for classroom space, and the school would be called the Gnostica School of Self-Development. There, students of all ages would be able to take classes in everything from astrology to Jungian symbolism.

Carl dreamed of using this school as a research center as well, much like he had dreamed of a decade prior. He wanted not only to share the knowledge that was to be found in occult studies; he also wanted to contribute to the growth of those studies and hoped that with a large group of students, they might together or individually discover new truths, techniques, and applications that could be of benefit to all. The Gnostica School brochure provided a mission statement that Carl wrote himself:

> *The Gnostica School of Self-Development offers the student instruction and practical application in all areas of esotericism in these categories: Astrology, Character Analysis and Occult Studies. All courses are taught without bias; no cults or "secret" teachings are promoted, no ethical or moral systems are imposed on the student. We are a School, not a Society. The Gnostica*

---

251 *Minneapolis Star*, "Ex-Occultist Turned Power Against Satan."
252 *Star Tribune*, "Summer Solstice Magical Arts Festival."

School also offers training in research techniques and applica-
tions of modern scientific equipment and methods to the exten-
sion of our knowledge in these areas. Our goal is an evolutionary
one—that as our students apply their learning, they will contrib-
ute to our ability to teach more; that as we grow as a school, we
can also grow as a research center, and as we expand our body
of students and faculty, we can offer more in the way of direct,
practical applications of these subject areas in helping people
meet specific problems.[253]

Classes offered that season included alchemy, astrology (including natal astrology, horary astrology, and mundane astrology),
astral projection, clairvoyance, extrasensory perception, graphology, I Ching, Jungian symbolism, the Kabbalah, meditation training, palmistry, ritual magick, witchcraft, world religions, yoga disciplines, yoga philosophy, and Zen. For this, Carl needed teachers,
so he sought out, magnetically attracted, and magickally mani-
fested a team of talented psychics, magick practitioners, diviners,
and other occult experts to join the staff of the Gnostica School.
He found a good supply of teachers without too much trouble, but
what he really needed next was a dean, someone who could offer
classes as well as act as administrator, organizer, and program
director for the school. He wanted to find a person with academic
credentials who also had strong occult leanings and an abundance
of natural talents. He needed to find exactly the right person, so
he put that thought out into the universe with every intention and
with full expectation that the person who should be his dean would
come to him.

It didn't take very long at all before Carl's wish was fulfilled. A
young woman named Judy Hipskind, who was on her way to a Led
Zeppelin concert, happened to pop into the Gnostica Bookstore
one day to check it out. It turned out that this young woman had
everything Carl had been hoping for in a dean. Judy was currently

---

253 Gnostica School of Self-Development brochure, Winter 1971,
     mission statement by Carl L. Weschcke, Director of Studies.

a professor of Spanish at a university in Wisconsin, and she was a very gifted palmist, graphologist, and a natural psychic. She was also extremely intelligent, kind, loving, and fun to be around. Carl offered her the position, and after some thought, Judy accepted. She put in her resignation at the university and took her post as the dean of the Gnostica School of Self-Development. In addition to administrative duties, she would also provide instruction in the art of palmistry.

By the spring of 1971, Carl's little magick school had over 100 students enrolled. Less than a year later, that number had climbed to 250. Classes were offered on divination, spirit communication, yoga, dream interpretation, and many other topics of interest. Special guests were often invited to present lectures and seminars at the school/bookstore. Among the guest teachers who offered lectures at Gnostica Bookstore or in conjunction with Carl's Gnosticon festivals over the years were Melita Denning and Osborne Phillips, Dr. Jonn Mumford, Lady Sheba, Selena Fox, Noel Tyl, Ophiel, Raymond Buckland, and many other talented individuals who had made a name for themselves in the arts of magick, yoga, witchcraft, astrology, and other occult philosophies. Denning and Phillips offered lectures on the Aurum Solis magickal tradition, including a class called "Foundation and Circle" that discussed the elementary bases of magickal practice.[254] Dr. Jonn Mumford taught a series on Kriya Yoga in which he thrilled the crowd by sticking a hatpin through his tongue without any sign of pain or injury.[255] Lady Sheba offered courses in witchcraft,[256] which quickly gained a throng of practitioners in the Twin Cities area.

In fact, some of the most popular classes regularly offered in the standard curriculum at the Gnostica School were the classes on

---

254 Gnostica Bookstore advertisement, *Star Tribune*, November 26, 1978.

255 *Minneapolis Star*, "Occult—Religion Outside the Church—Growing."

256 Gnostica Bookstore advertisement, *Minneapolis Star*, January 12, 1971.

beginning and advanced witchcraft. A reporter for the *Minneapolis Star* wrote,

> Weschcke said there is a tremendous current interest in witch-craft, which he described as a "nature religion" and not Satanism. He said he hopes to use the Gnostica school and bookstore in Minneapolis as models for developing similar enterprises in other cities.[257]

It was in the summer of 1971 that Carl met the love of his life, Sandra Heggum. Instantly hitting it off, Sandra soon started working as manager of Llewellyn Publications. It was an exciting time for Carl; he was filled to the brim and running over with love, life, energy, and inspiration.

That autumn, the Gnostica hosted the first of what would be several large festivals, bringing witches, magick practitioners, and other occultists together for several days of fun, learning, and plenty of opportunities to buy books.

Carl's hopes of inspiring others to follow his lead by opening their own magickal bookshops was coming to fruition, and it was doing so a little too close to his doorstep. By the end of 1972, there were three other occult bookstores thriving in the Twin Cities—The Tarot, Bell Book and Candle, and Sign of the Sixth House.[258] With other stores moving into the area and Llewellyn still growing, Carl soon decided to relocate to a more modern and efficient headquarters in Saint Paul that could better house his publishing business as well as his bookstore. He and Sandra had gotten married by this time, and Carl was ready to convert the Summit mansion to a home rather than the home/business it currently was. The former mortuary building, called an "oasis in downtown," was put up for sale in 1973,[259] and the move to 213 East Fourth Street in the Lowertown district of Saint Paul was soon made.

---

257 *Minneapolis Star*, "Occult—Religion Outside the Church—Growing."
258 Smith, "The Rise of the Occult."
259 Gnostica Bookstore advertisement, *Minneapolis Star*, February 5, 1973.

Gnostica Bookstore tried its best to get settled into its new home. When a community festival was taking place at nearby Mears Park, Gnostica Bookstore set up an "Astrology Alley" outside the shop where festival attendees could get free readings from a row of palmists, graphologists, astrologers, psychics, and tarot readers that lined the alleyway. The Gnostica also hosted an art exhibit and painting demonstration with free coffee and desserts inside the bookstore to coincide with the Mears Park festival. The open house social hours continued at the Saint Paul store every Sunday, along with the customary tea, fortune cookies, and free psychic readings.

The crowds at the new location never reached the proportions that they had in the larger, less conservative city of Minneapolis, however. As the decade came to an end, Llewellyn had once again expanded to the point of needing more space, but business at the Gnostica was still in a decline from its golden days. Carl kept the bookstore going as long as he could but eventually made the tough decision to close the store and focus solely on the publishing business.[260]

Reflected Carl,

> All that was a lot of fun, but as Llewellyn's publishing activities grew, it was harder to justify such diversity. We just didn't have the resources to do everything. Younger bodies can do a lot, but age slowly takes its toll and forces common sense. And, as Llewellyn grew, I could slow down.[261]

Carl didn't exactly slow down, but he did scale back the scope of his activities. He concentrated his attentions full-force on enjoying more time with his family and strategizing about new ways to further grow his publishing business.

---

260 Nelson, "A Supernatural Plan."
261 CLW email to Melanie Marquis, February 25, 2011.

Minnesota NAACP members picket outside of the St. Paul Woolworth's for integrated lunch counters in 1960.

Carl's NAACP lifetime membership plaque from September 1956.

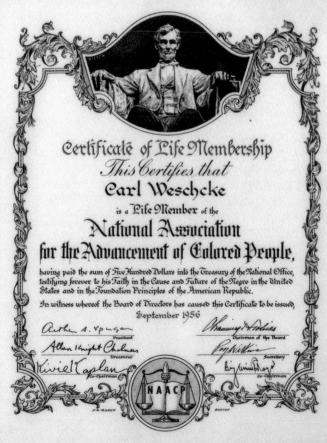

Certificate of Life Membership

This Certifies that

Carl Weschcke

is a Life Member of the

National Association

for the Advancement of Colored People,

having paid the sum of Five Hundred Dollars into the Treasury of the National Office, testifying forever to his Faith in the Cause and Future of the Negro in the United States and in the Foundation Principles of the American Republic.

In witness whereof the Board of Directors has caused this Certificate to be issued,

September 1956

President
Chairman of the Board
Treasurer
Secretary
Co-Chairman
Co-Chairman

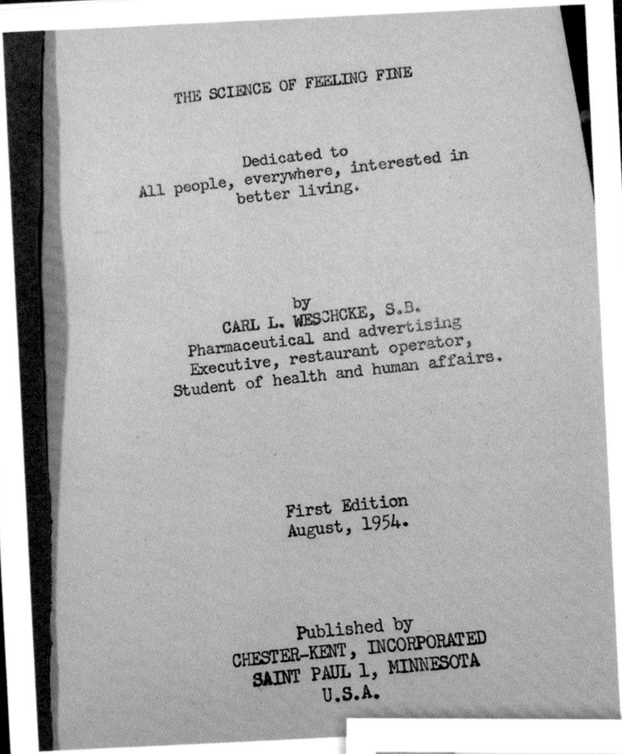

The first full book written and published by Carl before buying Llewellyn: *The Science of Feeling Fine* (Chester-Kent, 1954).

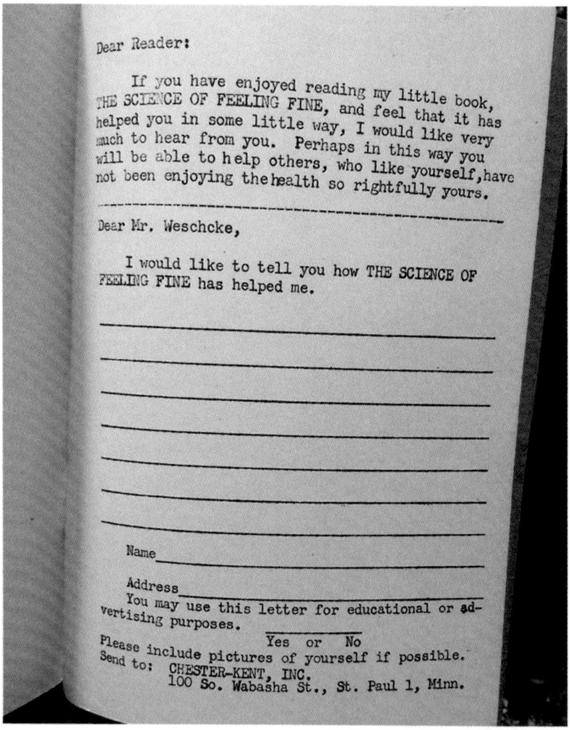

THE SCIENCE OF FEELING FINE

Dedicated to
All people, everywhere, interested in
better living.

by
CARL L. WESCHCKE, S.B.
Pharmaceutical and advertising
Executive, restaurant operator,
Student of health and human affairs.

First Edition
August, 1954.

Published by
CHESTER-KENT, INCORPORATED
SAINT PAUL 1, MINNESOTA
U.S.A.

The last page of *The Science of Feeling Fine* showing Carl's marketing skills, a precursor to today's "To Write to the Author" found in every Llewellyn book.

Dear Reader:

If you have enjoyed reading my little book,
THE SCIENCE OF FEELING FINE, and feel that it has
helped you in some little way, I would like very
much to hear from you. Perhaps in this way you
will be able to help others, who like yourself, have
not been enjoying the health so rightfully yours.

Dear Mr. Weschcke,

I would like to tell you how THE SCIENCE OF
FEELING FINE has helped me.

Name
Address
You may use this letter for educational or ad-
vertising purposes.
Yes or No
Please include pictures of yourself if possible.
Send to: CHESTER-KENT, INC.
100 So. Wabasha St., St. Paul 1, Minn.

A LLEWELLYN PUBLICATION

U.S.A PRICE 25¢
IN GREAT BRITAIN 2/-

MINUTE SCOPE

The Astrological Outlook for *News, Weather, Business & Markets*

What's happening in Psychic Research, the Occult Sciences, Astrology. News of the Unusual, the unexpected, the Bizarre. Reviews of new books, the cinema.

VOLUME I   Number I

DECEMBER 1963

(Nov./Dec. Double Issue)

CONTENTS

THE GIRL IN THE LEATHER MASK—CAN S
Sensory Deprivation & Extra Sensory Pe

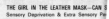

Carl's early forays into
magazine publishing.

U.S.A. Price 50¢
In Great Britain 3/6

Witchcraft Today
MAKING MAGIC WORK
Murder At Malden Manor
THE TAROT CARDS
Occult Experiences
...and more!

may
1963

NEW DIMENSIONS

A LLEWELLYN PUBLICATION

Carl, the young
businessman.

One of Carl's proudest moments was publishing
Aleister Crowley's *Thoth Tarot* in 1969.

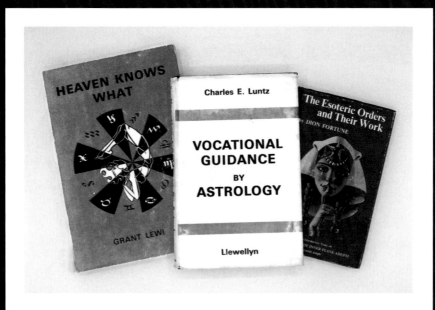

A sampling of early Llewellyn books published in 1962 after Carl purchased Llewellyn.

Carl resting at home
with his books nearby.

1964, when Carl purchased his St. Paul mansion.
(photo courtesy of the *Twin Citian* magazine)

Carl studying with his first cat, Dougie.

A happy, mischievous Carl.

Another first for Minneapolis

The Gnostica Bookstore

 1414 Laurel Avenue
Just off Hennepin at 14th

The GNOSTICA is the largest ASTROLOGY and OCCULT bookstore in America with over 100,000 volumes in NUMEROLOGY GRAPHOLOGY ESP YOGA ALCHEMY CLAIRVOYANCE DIVINATION DREAMS I CHING CARTOMANCY TAROT PALMISTRY and MAGICK.

SUPPLIES and GIFTS
LECTURES and CLASSES
OPEN TO THE PUBLIC

PHONE 612/339-2420

- EVERY SUNDAY 1-6
- TEA AND FORTUNE COOKIES
- SHARE YOUR IDEAS AND INTERESTS
- MEET NEW FRIENDS
- SPONTANEOUS DISCUSSION GROUPS
- ENLIGHTENMENT – ENTERTAINMENT

MONDAY THURSDAY FRIDAY 10-9
TUESDAY WEDNESDAY SATURDAY 10-6
SUNDAY 1-9

in this unique store!

- Browse among more than 100,00 volumes on Astrology, Magick, Witchcraft, Tarot, ancient religions, Yoga, all Occult Sciences
- Register for classes and free lectures
- Have your palm read, your handwriting analyzed, your I Ching oracle cast
- Discover many unusual gifts
Bring this ad for a free reading any Friday evening or Sunday.

The Gnostica Bookstore
1414 Laurel Avenue (off Hennepin at 14th)
M Th F 10-9   Sun 1-9   Tu W S 10-6

Print ads for Carl's pride and joy, his very own bookstore, Gnostica, which opened in the early 1970s.

Shoppers at Gnostica Bookstore.

The front of the Gnostica Bookstore building, which housed the bookstore, school, Llewellyn's business offices, shipping, and warehouse departments.

GNOSTICA
Summer Class Schedule

JULY 1971

1414 Laurel Avenue, Minneapolis
Phone 339-2420

Lectures were held in the basement, and regular classes on the first floor.

SPRING 1973 · "A Place of Knowledge"

Gnostica Bulletin
Voice of the Gnostica Bookstore · and Gnostica Study Center

NOEL TYL

(TOP LEFT) The witches silently assemble in the dimly-lit ritual room, located on the lower level of Carl Wheeler's home. It is an old room, filled with the trappings of witchcraft. The magic circle and pentagram are drawn on the carpet. Candles burn in a miniature coffin standing against the wall. (CENTER) Between scenes, Director Maury Hurley gives his "coven" instructions. Sky Schere with bare feet stands at the left. (RIGHT) The coven kneels, awaiting the "power" to attend. (CENTER) The naked witch, hands tied behind her back, begins the ritual. (LEFT) Witches chant around the hoodoo during "Calling Down of the Moon" ceremony.

Candid photographs taken during filming of "Calling Down of the Moon" ceremony show actual witches stripping to nude ceremonials. This is basically a Joyous ceremony, during which the coven sing, dance and dance around the fire. "Excites were fueled by propane tanks buried in the ground. Late cameras didn't like to observe. "In photograph at TOP CENTER, Real Judge holds his "homemade El Light," which consists of a bare quartz lamp hanging from a cord, battery-powered and backed up by a "reflector" made of cooked aluminum foil. It is amazingly efficient.

FILMING "ISIS" AMONG THE WITCHES
or "I DON' WANNA GET TURNED INTO NO FROG!"

Daredevil editor accompanies group of intrepid film-makers shooting a witchcraft movie and almost ends up green and bumpy

By HERB A. LIGHTMAN

"Witches?... In St. Paul, Minnesota? You gotta be kidding—"

"Honest Injun," says the voice on the other end of long distance. It's Maury Hurley, cameraman, editor, and if he succeeds—but then, old Maury would sound excited reading the telephone book. "There're covens and covens of witches in St. Paul—46, to be exact," he goes on. "It's got something to do with how the stars are arrayed. The main star is poised right over St. Paul—so all the witches flock there. It's practically the witch capital of the world!"

"So... must be green with envy," I crumble.

"Anyway, we're making this feature movie with a full cast of real live witches—and they're even going to let us film their secret rituals. We want you to come along."

He's just made me an offer I can't refuse! In the time that it takes me to pack my broomstick and bat wings, I'm on the plane and off to the Twin Cities. All witches aside, the main reason that I've dropped everything to go to that a couple of years ago I had a wild time with Maury and his zany crew while they were shagging snowmobiles around during the filming of their first feature—then called "STORM" (see 1972)—now I was much impressed with this group of turned-on dudes who would rather make movies than eat (and it sometimes comes to that).

Actually, they've got their own production company in Minneapolis, Stock-hoff-Mitchell Productions, which makes industrial films, documentaries, TV specials, and the like—but they dream of features, just as kids at Christmas have visions of sugar plums dancing through their tiny skulls. Having made one feature, they're now bitten by the bug. But when someone else's money to spend, this time it's their own money—$18,000 total budget.

A neat trick, if they can do it.

"Sure we can do it," says Maury Hurley. "In fact we have to do it. Pete Maury is nothing, if not positive. Three of us are taking some of the money we make in our other company, shooting industrials, and we're committing it to this project. If we can pull it off for $18,000—which includes a sizable cash deferral—we'll have a very workable experiment. It's a great way to make this movie, but you couldn't do it on any other kind of movie. We don't have to shoot on a steady schedule. We can work the shooting in between things we're doing in our other company. Not being locked in to our schedule, we can pour into it all of the creativity and work and time that's necessary—and still do it on our budget.

He tells me that the name of the film is "ISIS" and he wants me to—and I ask him how he happened to decide on a film about witchcraft.

"I wanted to do something that dealt with different kinds of realities, different kinds of planes of existence," he tells me. "At first I thought of doing something about Zen or Yoga, but I

Although he may not look like a witch, Carl Wheeler is the leader of a coven in St. Paul, Minnesota. He is also Marv Hurley's father-in-law. Here he is playing the leader of a no-account witch-coven called "ISIS", a Pola-Sky Production.

A 1973 article on the filming of the movie *Isis*, a fun experience for Carl. Although the film was never released, Carl discovered that he was a natural actor. (reprinted courtesy of *American Cinematographer* magazine)

Carl during a Pagan celebration at a local park in the early 1970s; Carl is between Sandra and Isaac Bonewits, with Noel Tyl standing behind them.

Carl and Sandra at their wedding, wearing lavender robes that Carl designed himself.

Carl and Sandra with her parents after the wedding ceremony.

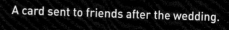

Come up and see me sometime...

...and meet the wife

Carl walking up the
grand staircase in the
St. Paul mansion.

Gnostica issue #49 featuring Sandra on the cover.

Gnostica 49

$2.00

Esoteric Knowledge for the New Age

JAN/FEB 1979

VOL 6 · NO 6

URI GELLER
Super Psychic or Poltergeist Victim?

Spirit Mediums
Fact or Fraud?

Chicano Witchcraft
For Money, Love

Nostradamus Predicted
Pope John-Paul I

You Are Psychic!
Learn to Use Your Psi Power

Magickal Tarot
Tool for Inner Develop
and Self Transformatio

Carl hard at work in his office in the St. Paul mansion with feline assistants, Isis and Dougie.

Sandra beaming with their infant son, Gabe.

Carl looks lovingly upon
their son, Gabe.

A sweet family photo of
Carl and Sandra with little Gabe.

A Weschcke family vacation out West.

A hungry Carl and Gabe at Thanksgiving at their modern home in Woodbury, MN.

On the way to another vacation, stopping by a park in southern Minnesota, where Carl got into tree hugging.

Carl makes plans for a magazine article with an employee.

Carl shows off one of his prize books, the classic *Llewellyn's New A to Z Horoscope Maker*.

Carl and Sandra taking a little tim for a vacation in England.

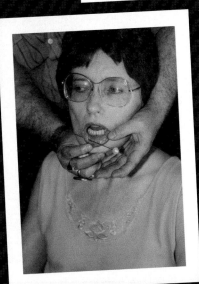

Jonn Mumford performed mantra anesthesia on Sandra. She said "the experience caused a tremendously powerful mood-altering release of energy."

Llewellyn moved from 213 East Fourth Street in St. Paul to 84 South Wabasha in St. Paul in 1988. Here is the whole crew at the Wabasha building!

*From Judy Hipskind Collins,
former dean of Gnostica School,
palm reader, psychic, and author:*

My birthday was approaching, and a group of my students and a fellow faculty member I was friends with had devised a plan to take me to Minneapolis for a Led Zeppelin concert. We set off on a cold April morning, taking the road that led north from La Crosse to Minneapolis. There were eight of us piled in a station wagon, all set to have a good time.

We got to Minneapolis with a whole afternoon to go before the Led Zeppelin concert, so we explored the West Bank—a really fun place with great hippie digs, with lots to see, and so much to do that our group went off in different directions. We made plans to meet a short while later for a meal.

A place called Jonah and the Whale, a leather goods store, seemed a good place to start our explorations. A few of us went in the door and were greeted by a friendly guy who had an Australian-sounding accent. This got my attention immediately because I was dating an Australian man at the time. When I asked this fellow if he was from Australia, he said no, he was an American who had lived in New Zealand, and that he intended to emigrate there. I spontaneously said, "Good luck with that. I know New Zealand is cracking down on emigration because my uncle is at the embassy in Wellington."

"Oh yeah?" he said. "I used to date a chick whose dad was at the embassy."

I got an uncanny feeling and asked him, "What was her name?"

"Jane Grove," he replied.

"That's my first cousin!"

He pointed to the hat he was wearing and said, "Oh yeah? She gave me this hat."

I had walked straight into a store in the magical state of Minnesota and met a man who had dated my cousin in New Zealand. We talked a bit more about my cousin and life in New Zealand. The atmosphere was alive and buzzing with some indefinable current. To gather my wits, I started looking around the store and noticed a sheet of mimeographed paper taped to the wall.

When I got close to the paper, I could not believe my eyes: that sheet of paper announced WORLD'S LARGEST OCCULT BOOKSTORE!—in capital letters, in that old-fashioned purplish-looking mimeograph ink. The print went on to describe what seemed a vast selection of books for sale on every topic dear to my heart, and many more subjects. I could not believe my luck! I just had to go see the store, and we asked for directions to the address on that paper. We decided we could just make a quick run and still be in time to meet up with the rest of our group. I felt the pressure of a limited amount of time to get this great adventure accomplished.

When we got to the Gnostica Bookstore, I was dumbfounded to see this long building painted a deep purple color with what looked like a big yellow banana near the rear of the building. That yellow banana was actually supposed to be the yellow Llewellyn moon logo.

We hurried inside. Oh my. What a place! Incense burning, people browsing among rows of tall metal shelves holding an astonishing array of books, mostly hardcover, if memory serves. The atmosphere was hushed and the excitement of discovery palpable, emanating from customers eagerly lifting books, gazing at titles, exploring pages. Over against the wall on a low table sat a big urn filled with Constant Comment black tea, Styrofoam cups, and a huge offering of fortune cookies. That just capped the atmosphere. Back then, that tea was about as exotic as you could get. This was adventure! This was discovery! No New Age banners, no proliferation of bright and jazzy paperbacks. Those would come in the future. Here you had a sense of being at a deep pool of knowledge, much like discovering an oasis in a desert.

As my eyes grew accustomed to the dim magical interior, I was aware of several tables lining the walls and people sitting at those small tables, talking in hushed tones with customers who listened intently to every word. These were readers! The exotic meter kicked up a notch. I scanned the row and saw a table without a customer at the moment. A sign on the table announced: "Prince Bokovoy, Graphology Readings." Graphology! I had never met another person who could analyze handwriting; I thought I had arrived in nirvana. All I wanted to do was to compare notes with him for a few minutes. I hurried up to the table, introduced myself, and said that I also was involved with handwriting, and could he please discuss a bit of what he knew with me?

He looked up at me, seemed to pause a second, as if considering something, then burst into a spirited tone, quite upbeat and pulsing with energy. He said no. *No???* I thought. *What do you mean no? I've come all this way and will probably never have a chance again to talk to someone in person about graphology, and you are telling me no?* But he sounded excited. What was going on? I tried again. "No," he said, "because you have to come meet the owner."

I protested, "We only have a few minutes here, and I need to talk to you."

"No, you don't. You need to meet the owner." He leapt up from the table and walked away. I followed him, insisting again that I just wanted to hear a few words from him about graphology. He kept walking and went up to a large, tall man standing on the opposite side of the room. I stopped in my tracks and he called over his shoulder, "You need to meet the owner."

And with that he pulled Carl forward and introduced us as if he'd known me a long time. And then he disappeared, melting into the shadows, as if he had been an apparition. I was left standing with Carl. We instantly made polite conversation. Carl asked where I was from. I told him I had come up with a group of friends from La Crosse, and that I taught Spanish at the university there. His energy seemed to go up a notch as well. I complimented all the book selection and told him about my interest in graphology, palmistry, and astrology. He pulled me out of the main aisle, deeper into the row of shelves, and asked if I would look at his palm. I did. And then we fell into a lively discussion about astrology. I remember him telling me he felt a person became more like his or her moon sign after the age of thirty.

We returned to the main aisle, and he looked at me and said, "You're the one. You are the one I asked the universe to send." I was totally nonplussed. He went on, "I'm opening a school, the Gnostica School for Self-Development. I sent out the intention for a person with academic credentials to come into the store. I need someone to be dean of my school. You are going to be that dean." He was quite insistent. I could not make much sense of it all in the moment. I knew I did not have a job beyond the current school year, set to end in six weeks, as I was filling in for a faculty member for a year. I did have plans to go to North Carolina and work with Dr. Rhine, the man who coined the term ESP. He had been one of my advisors on my college theology thesis, "The Role of ESP in the Noosphere of Teilhard de Chardin." Carl and I exchanged cards, and I had to leave the store quickly so I could meet the rest of my group on time.

Four days later a letter from Carl containing a formal job offer arrived in my mailbox at home in La Crosse. He wanted to make arrangements to meet again to discuss the role I might have at his school.

Saturday, six days after our initial meeting at the store, I found myself sitting in Carl's study at the Summit Avenue house, getting acquainted and learning more about his vision for the school. He had a curriculum in mind, ranging from astrology through yoga and including witchcraft. He had a woman in mind to teach that class, a fellow lined up to teach dream analysis, a woman to teach yoga, another fellow to teach astrology. Now he had me to teach palmistry, and later on, graphology as well. Ruth Gardner taught our early classes in graphology. He had several other teachers and classes in mind as possible additions to the school.

Work remained to be done, but Carl had made a good start and had the building ready to go. Gnostica School was the use he intended to make of that second floor in the purple book-store building.

His idea was to have a soft opening in June, get the classes in place, up and running, and a solid curriculum established after we saw the response to our initial offerings. The school would have an official opening in January 1971, along with a celebratory open house.

I was attracted to his vision, his enthusiasm for the school, and also his wider vision of becoming a center of knowledge to help usher in a New Age. A school seemed a very logical step, and certainly he had all the books any student would need right in the bookstore.

He carefully nurtured the bookstore, attracting more and more people with his Sunday gatherings. Many people came for the tea, the chance to meet others interested in this new world, and certainly for the readers. In 1970 this was all a novel concept. I'm certain Carl was the first to have a metaphysical bookshop on this scale, offering the amount of inventory he did and providing readers to further awaken everyone's interest. He really had a rapt audience for his ideas. He personally came to every Sunday open house and talked with as many people as possible. People sometimes lined up just to meet him. His charismatic ideas, his voice, his presence made it clear something very different and exciting was afoot, and people wanted to be part of it all. And always, the Sunday readings kept the mix of ideas going and showed participants just how this exciting knowledge could benefit them. This was exactly what Carl wanted—to introduce people to new ideas, tips for self-development from the books and the readers, so that we could all move forward into the New Age he envisioned.

The times were very exciting.

By September 1971 Carl and I and others had managed to present the first international festival featuring speakers from all over the world speaking on what we called "Aquarian" topics, drawing people from around the country and overseas. This convention drew a large group of Wiccan practitioners who became public on a larger stage than they ever had in the past, simply because Carl provided an attractive venue for them to do so.

Gnostica, a prime source of knowledge for a New Age, was now truly set up and functioning, as first envisioned and then carefully drawn into manifestation by Carl. I believe that electric current I felt in the leather goods store just after meeting a man who knew my cousin in New Zealand, and seeing the sign he posted leading to Carl's store, was none other than a manifestation of the power of Carl's intentions.

Carl loved to joke and tease…he laughed a lot, as I recall. Sometimes I couldn't get a straight answer out of him on nonsense kinds of things. For instance, the Gnostica building was long and stretched way back from the street. He was able to use the back part of that building for shipping, the front part for the retail operation, and the second story for the school. He had plenty of room. I remember below the Llewellyn logo, near the backside of the building, was an oblong sign that said "Deliver Flowers Here." I asked him what that sign was for. He never did tell me. His only reply was, "Someone might want to send us flowers."

In a very different way, I found out eventually what the sign was all about. On one of my first weekends reading at the store once I moved to Minnesota, I met a man whose name was Charlie Brown. Turned out he was the real Charlie Brown. He was in art school in Minneapolis with Charles Schultz and others who were eventually featured in the comic strip under different names. Well, Schultz told Charlie, "I have an idea (for a comic strip) and it involves sketching your face and using your name." Charlie gave him permission to do so.

While I was reading Charlie's hands, I happened to tell him how much I wished young people could have their hands read as a guidance tool in school or counseling. After our reading, he brought that back up, said "you've just talked to the right person," and proceeded to tell me he was supervisor at the Hennepin County Juvenile Detention Center and asked me if I would come volunteer there and read the kids' hands. I did so. We became friends and he early on told me who he was for real and shared eventually the story of all of his life with me.

We were very close friends until his death. But in the process of sharing traumatic moments of his life, he told me his father had committed suicide when Charlie was ten years old. He then told me that the day we met, when I was doing the reading for him, we were seated in the very spot where he had last seen his father's casket, and that he was so overcome by it all, he found it hard to speak…though he did. That is how I learned Carl's building had been a mortuary for years, and thus that sign about the flowers. The interesting thing is I have to wonder why the sign wasn't taken down or painted over. Needless to say I didn't ask Carl once I found out the significance of the sign.

Carl and I had so many long conversations, often while walking. He loved to take long walks, calling them "constitutionals." He often reflected on his family, his ancestors, but particularly his grandfather, during these walks. We ate a lot of meals together, too, and I remember one night we had blueberries for dessert. To this day, I remember him pronouncing, "Most people don't like blueberries, they just like the way the name sounds." I found it funny in the moment and still do. That was decades before we "discovered" antioxidants and blueberries became the go-to food for health-oriented types. Little did he know back then how popular blueberries would become.

So although I can't remember but the bare minimum of specific examples, I do want to stress how easily Carl laughed, joked, and teased in the early years. I think he became more of an "august" personality as he entered the world of Wicca, led groups, built and grew a company, and became a media presence with his looks so underscoring the gravitas of what he had to offer. And of course his voice, which was deep and resonant and rippled with sincerity as he promoted all he believed in.

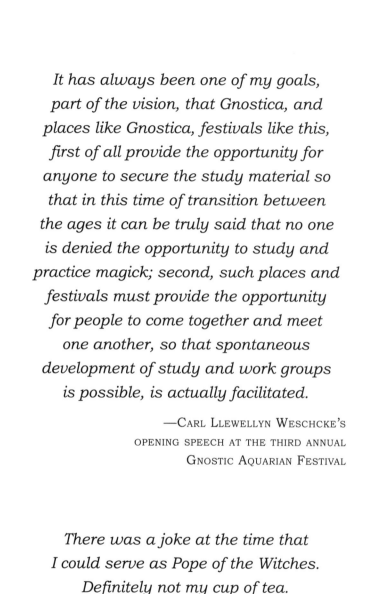

It has always been one of my goals, part of the vision, that Gnostica, and places like Gnostica, festivals like this, first of all provide the opportunity for anyone to secure the study material so that in this time of transition between the ages it can be truly said that no one is denied the opportunity to study and practice magick; second, such places and festivals must provide the opportunity for people to come together and meet one another, so that spontaneous development of study and work groups is possible, is actually facilitated.

—Carl Llewellyn Weschcke's
opening speech at the third annual
Gnostic Aquarian Festival

There was a joke at the time that I could serve as Pope of the Witches. Definitely not my cup of tea.

—Carl Llewellyn Weschcke

Chapter 9

Gnosticon Festivals

O ut of the community building at the Gnostica Bookstore and school came something even larger. A local hotel owner who was in the neighborhood had become fascinated with the constant flow of interesting-looking people heading in and out of the Gnostica. He spoke to Carl and gave him the idea to have a festival, something in the vein of a modern Woodstock for witches.[262] Naturally, Carl loved the idea, and he soon created advertisements for the event and set about inviting the greatest magickal teachers he could find to come speak at the festival. Respected magician and author Louis T. Culling of the Secret Order G.B.G. was to be among the esteemed guests. While the stated purpose of the festival was to celebrate the coming Age of Aquarius,[263] Carl also called the event "the first serious effort to make the dramatic increase in occult and astrological interests meaningful to the public."[264] The festival was named the Aquarian Festival of Astrology

---

262 Peterson, "The Year of the Witch."

263 *Morning News,* "Occult Fete Dawns Dimly."

264 *St. Cloud Times,* "Occult School Opens in Mpls."

and the Occult Sciences, and a date was set for early September 1971. Over 200 people came to the festival for seminars in ritual magick, hypnosis, astrology, past life regression, Chinese acupuncture, tarot, witchcraft, palmistry, and the I Ching.[265] The first large public gathering of magickal minds to be seen in America in modern times, the Aquarian Festival of Astrology and Occult Sciences helped inspire and set the standard for today's Pagan festivals and magickal conventions.

The first night of the festival included a full moon ritual led by Bruce LaHue, who was an employee at the Gnostica, and two companions including a former Playboy bunny from Detroit. Lady Sheba had originally been planning to lead the ritual, but she was ill, so Bruce and his friends agreed to fill in. The ritual was held in the parking lot of the Gnostica Bookstore, with a large group of festival attendees gathering around 9:00 p.m. Reporters from the *New York Times* and the *London Daily Express* were also on the scene. Brian Vine, representing the *London Daily Express*, commented to another reporter, "We British put the matches to the first witches and I thought I'd see what the current witches are up to."[266]

Under a cloudy sky that disappointingly obscured the moon completely, Bruce cast a circle with his magickal sword while his friends Betty and Clara lit candles and placed them around the space. A chalice was filled with red wine, and the ritual commenced. At one point when the ritualists were "drawing down the moon"—the practice of calling forth lunar energies through a combination of words, actions, and emotions, performed here publicly for the first time[267]—the clouds that had been filling the skies suddenly parted to reveal the brilliance of the shining full moon. The ritual participants didn't even notice, as their view was obscured by the surrounding buildings, but a newspaper photographer who

---

265   *St. Cloud Times,* "Occult School Opens in Mpls."

266   Smith, "Witches Stir Brew Under Full Moon."

267   Lady Sheba, *Witch,* 75.

was stationed on a nearby rooftop saw it all. Within just a few short moments, the clouds had closed back up again.[268]

The festival gained a fair amount of publicity, for no one was used to seeing witches practicing their craft openly in the heart of a bustling city. "Self-appointed witches are conducting public rituals, fully clothed for the TV cameras, that would have landed them and probably the onlookers, too, on the stake 300 years ago," reported the *New York Times*.[269]

Carl reflected,

> *I felt some ambivalence about all the publicity. On the one hand, I was proud that publications like* The New York Times *and* Playboy *chose to give it coverage. On the other hand, the attention we received was not as dignified as I would have preferred. The publicized circus atmosphere was not really that prevalent.*[270]

Taking part in a magick festival right out in the open was decidedly nonconformist, an act of defiance that was downright thrilling for those who had been craving an opportunity to connect and exchange ideas with so many others who shared their interests. Louis T. Culling, whom one reporter described as a "77-year-old gnome-like practitioner of occult magick," commented, "I'm so disenchanted with the status quo that if I could find anything better than occultism to revolt with, I'd try it, too." While reporters were taken aback by what they saw, Carl assured them there would be much more to come. "This is nothing but the birthpang in the coming occult renaissance,"[271] he stated, and it just so happened that he was absolutely right.

By the fall of 1972, when the second annual festival was to be held, there were an estimated 100,000 witches in the country, with dozens of covens in the Twin Cities area.[272] Carl had decided the

---

268   Smith, "Witches Stir Brew Under Full Moon."

269   Flint, "Mystic Sciences Booming."

270   Sutin, "Father of the New Age."

271   Flint, "Mystic Sciences Booming."

272   Smith, "Witches Meet in City."

name of the festival was a bit too long and cumbersome, so for the second annual event, he changed the name to the Gnostic Aquarian Festival.[273] The event was held at the Hyatt Lodge hotel in Minneapolis and the Gnostica Bookstore, and over 400 people, double the number from the year before, showed up to enjoy several days of classes, rituals, and demonstrations.[274] Lady Sheba was present, as was Judy Boss.[275] A temple dance led by an expert who had studied under a guru in India was also on the schedule.[276] The opening ritual in particular was a special event. With the night of the full moon falling on the Autumn Equinox for the first time in 500 years, participants had high expectations for a magickal experience. Lady Sheba conducted the ritual poolside at the Hyatt, her shining eyes and commanding presence captivating the crowd. It was a simple ritual involving a request for wisdom from the goddess Diana, a meditation, and the traditional sharing of cakes and wine.[277] A very skeptical Robert Anton Wilson, who was attending for the first time that year, said of the experience, "I got outside my usual rationalism and I'm not sure if I can ever get back in again."[278]

Out of the next year's festival came an unexpected development that has now become a part of American magickal history. The festival itself was outstanding, filled with interesting workshops and even more interesting people. Among the speakers were parapsychologist Jose Feola, astrologers Noel Tyl and Marc Edmund Jones, famous witches Lady Cybele and Lady Sheba, and Quantz Crawford, who claimed to be master of the "supernatural orgasm." P.E.I. (Isaac) Bonewits offered a talk on the hammer of

---

273   Gibson, "In the Light of the Full Moon."

274   Smith, "The Rise of the Occult."

275   Smith, "Housewife Says Dead Communicate Through Her."

276   Gibson, "In the Light of the Full Moon."

277   Smith, "Witches Meet in City."

278   Robert Anton Wilson, "The Witches are Coming." RAWilsonFans. org. Accessed October 5, 2017. http://rawilsonfans.org/1973/01/. Entertainment Gallery, January 1973.

Thor and also spoke about how witches and occultists had helped out behind the scenes in WWII, casting spells to bring down German aircraft, eliminating gestapo cells, and bringing on Hitler's downfall and death. There were twenty-five lectures offered daily,[279] and there was even an unscheduled and unauthorized "Dionysian nude frolic" that spontaneously occured in the hotel pool. "That was a shock to many persons and, I confess, to myself," Carl admitted.[280] To welcome all the presenters and special guests, Carl had hosted a special banquet at his Summit Avenue mansion. One guest described the living room decorated with black and gold, the shining black dinner plates, and the gold-plated cutlery that added to the mystical and lavish atmosphere of Carl's home.[281]

The festival—with its name transformed into simply "Gnosticon"—included a variety of magickal rituals and a multitude of workshops on yoga, sex magick, herbal healing, hypnosis for triggering psychic abilities, demonstrations of past life regression, and more; there were graphologists and tarot readers, aura readers and astrologers. It was what happened after hours during the days of the festival, however, that would be the best remembered throughout the years for its lasting and significant impact. Carl told a local reporter who had covered the festival about this most interesting development:

> One of the very important outcomes of the festival, to me, was the creation of a "council of American witches" that resulted from the 73 initiated witches who met nightly in private session. These represented a great many traditions who have never met together before and whose various traditions and rituals have remained secret and private each from the other for hundreds of years. We really had an ecumenical council that will result in increased communication and cooperation and a sharing of knowledge and practice in the years to come.

279   Richler, "Witches' Brew."

280   Sutin, "Father of the New Age."

281   Richler, "Witches' Brew."

The council included Ed Fitch, Isaac Bonewits, Lady Sheba, Herman Slater, Margot Adler, Oberon (Tim) Zell and Morning Glory, and a host of other witches representing Alexandrian, Gardnerian, Nemeton, Pagan Way, Church of All Worlds, ADF, and many other affiliated and non-affiliated witches of various stripes and types. The goal was to find common ground between their many diverse beliefs—to create, as Carl put it, "a list of principles to define, for the general public, the central belief system of Wicca."[282]

The Council of Witches didn't quite manage to work out all their differences before the Gnosticon festival had ended, so they decided to get back together in a few months to finish the work they had started. They reconvened at a spring WitchMeet where the group met its goal. It was at this same WitchMeet that Oberon (Tim) Zell and Morning Glory, whom he had met at a recent Gnosticon festival, were wed in a Pagan handfasting ceremony that included over 500 celebrants.

Later Gnosticon festivals were every bit as interesting, fun, and educational, each hour filled with workshops on astrology, graphology, magick, palmistry, psychic healing, reincarnation, parapsychology, philosophy, herb lore, and more. The fourth annual event brought in guest speakers Isaac Bonewits, author and co-founder of the ADF; Ruth Gardner, the handwriting analyst; Robert Anton Wilson, who went on to popularize Discordianism; Jack and Mary Rowan, the hypnotists; world-famous astrologer Noel Tyl; religious scholar and author J. Gordon Melton; paranormal researcher Richard Alan Miller; and Morning Glory and Oberon Zell—who, at that time, was known simply as Tim. Hourly lectures, nightly movies, a private club, and a "magical mystery astro-ball" were all on the agenda.[283] The ball was the big event, and Carl donned a golden eagle Horus mask in honor of the occasion.

---

282 Weschcke, "Witchcraft: The Fastest Growing Religion in America," undated, circa 1997–1998.

283 Classified ads, *Minneapolis Star Tribune*, September 15, 1974.

The fifth annual festival, Gnosticon 5, took place in the fall of 1975, soon after a group of 186 scientists who were "concerned about the increased acceptance of astrology in many parts of the world" had issued a statement in *Humanist* magazine decrying astrology and pronouncing that there was "no scientific foundation for its tenets." Carl countered the claims by pointing out that astrology was a valid system with millions of practitioners. Noel Tyl, who was offering astrology seminars at the festival, estimated that as many as 50 million Americans followed their horoscopes in the daily papers or otherwise employed astrology in their everyday lives. "People are feeling the need to find more personal meaning in their lives," explained Carl. "They want to recover an old relationship with the natural."[284]

The final Gnosticon festival to be held took place in 1976, and although it was the last, it was one of the best. Raymond Buckland offered classes on scrying, love magick, visualization, and candle magick,[285] Dr. Jonn Mumford presented workshops on kundalini and developing psycho-sexual power for spiritual illumination,[286] and Selena Fox, who had recently founded Circle Sanctuary, offered a talk as well as a musical performance with her then-partner Jim Alan.[287] There were also classes on biorhythms, witchcraft, palmistry, hypnosis, ritual, magick, and more.[288]

As productive as the festivals were for those who attended them, they weren't exactly profitable, and Carl always bankrolled the difference. But with a growing son as well as a growing publishing company both eager for more of his attention, he simply couldn't justify continuing the festivals any longer. Besides, he didn't really need to. By this time Carl's magick had worked, and others were getting inspired to follow his lead and start magickal gatherings of their own.

---

284 Clever, "Clustered Stargazers."
285 Classified ads, *Minneapolis Star Tribune*, June 27, 1976.
286 Classified ads, *Minneapolis Star Tribune*, June 24, 1976.
287 Selena Fox email to Melanie Marquis, October 5, 2017.
288 Knoblauch, "Signs of the Occult."

***From Selena Fox,
senior minister at Circle Sanctuary and
executive director of Lady Liberty League:***

I first connected with Carl Weschcke shortly after I founded Circle, now also known as Circle Sanctuary, at Samhain 1974. In those times before email and social media, our friendship began by postal mail correspondence. He and I shared the vision and goal of networking Pagan and other metaphysical and magical people together through publishing and events. We also envisioned and worked for equal rights for Witches, Wiccans, and Pagans in American society and beyond.

Carl invited me and my then-partner Jim Alan to be presenters at the very last Gnosticon conference he held. This event brought together Witches, Wizards, Wiccans, Pagans, Astrologers, Seers, and Magicians from many traditions. The final conference, Gnosticon 6, was held in Saint Paul, Minnesota, in 1976. It was there that Carl and I met face-to-face for the first time. I presented a talk, and Jim and I performed our own style of Pagan music at the conference and at the Gnostica Bookstore. One of my favorite memories of Gnosticon 6 is being at the magnificent private dinner for guest presenters that Carl and Sandra hosted. It was a wonderful evening. I enjoyed conversing and socializing with him and others there. He was a marvelous host and that event was a dynamic Aquarian Age version of ancient Pagan Greek Symposium traditions.

Carl was a visionary, publisher, teacher, and innovator. Carl embraced new technology as it emerged and incorporated it into his endeavors. In the 1970s as cassette tapes grew in popularity for audio recordings, Carl created a recording studio at Llewellyn headquarters and began producing cassette tapes. Among the first cassette tape recordings Carl produced was of songs and chants that Jim Alan and I had written and performed in the newly created Llewellyn recording studio.

Carl was a leader, activist, and social reformer, working for equality, freedom, justice, and wisdom in American society and the world. One of his most important contributions for the quest for equal rights and religious freedom for Pagans was helping to bring Pagan leaders together and craft the Thirteen Principles of Wiccan Belief and then working to have them and Witchcraft/Wicca included in a federal government diversity handbook, the first edition of the *US Army Chaplains Handbook* published in 1978.

When the Pentagon decided to do an update in 1983, Carl asked me to take on the revision, which I did. Although this handbook is no longer a current publication, this historic document has continued to be cited in Pagan civil rights cases and by researchers in the emerging academic field of Pagan Studies. It was among the documents submitted in Circle Sanctuary's federal lawsuit against the VA, the settlement of which in 2007 resulted in the US Department of Veterans Affairs finally adding the Pentacle to its list of emblems of belief that can be included on the grave markers the VA issues to honor deceased US military veterans.

I am thankful to have known Carl and collaborated with him over the years. May his legacy of good works continue to enrich this world and beyond.

The Council of American Witches

At the third annual Gnostic Aquarian Festival held in Minneapolis in September of 1973, a private WitchMeet was held each night. Though advertised as being for "initiated witches only," the meetings actually brought together dozens of people from varying traditions, not all of them witchcraft related. The meetings didn't start with the intention to form any sort of organized witch's council. Initially, the meetings were arranged to settle a dispute between Herman Slater and Gavin Frost.

Gavin Frost was of the belief that gay people could not be Wiccan, while Herman Slater felt that everyone should be welcomed into Wicca equally, regardless of sexual orientation. With the two not being able to settle their disagreement, and in the process pulling others into the fray, Carl suggested that they might find a solution to their problem in a more organized and civil manner. The nightly WitchMeets then morphed into the Council of American Witches, whose purpose had grown from settling the feud between Frost and Slater into a vision of finding a common ground on which all of those present, with their many different traditions of magick and witchcraft, could agree. Carl stayed up late that night creating the first draft of what would come to be known as the Thirteen Principles of Wiccan Belief.

It bears explaining that, while in today's understanding, the term "Wicca" applies to a very specific set of beliefs and practices in the Gardnerian witchcraft tradition, back then "Wicca" was used as an umbrella term, much like "Pagan" or even "occultist" or "New Ager" is used today. There was differentiation in practices, just as there is today, but there was also a feeling of unity, as those differences had not yet been picked apart and highlighted over the course of many years. Today, people can say whether they are Alexandrian Witches or ADF Druids or Hellenistic Polytheists or whatever else they might be. Back then, the only word people generally knew to describe their beliefs and practices was "Wiccan," and even when they did have a specific path by a specific name with which to identify, all those varied paths were still typically considered to fall under the category of "Wicca." It's kind of funny that in modern times, those unfamiliar with the many different varieties of Paganism often call it all "Wicca," much to the chagrin of the practitioner who is sitting there thinking, "I'm not a Wiccan, I'm a traditional witch! Geesh!"

In today's world, those present at the WitchMeet would certainly not all be labeled as Wiccan. There were Celtic Reconstructionists, members of the Church of All Worlds, and representatives from Pagan Way and House of Ravenwood. There were self-described Druids, unaffiliated wizards, solitary witches, an American Eclectic witch, and many, many others. There were seventy-three members of the council in total.

Finding common ground proved more difficult than expected. In addition to the battle between Slater and Frost, tempers were also rising toward Lady Sheba, who had declared to the crowd that as Queen of the Witches, the Goddess had taken her into the astral realms and showed her a "star of knowledge" hanging over Saint Paul that proclaimed it to be the center, the place where a great temple would be constructed in honor of the Goddess. There was bickering and disagreement, and tempers continued to flare. Lady Sheba was challenged by several people, among them Isaac Bonewits, who questioned on what authority she had gained the right to be Queen of the Witches. She responded that the Goddess had appointed her so, and that like it or not, respect it or not, the fact remained that she was queen. One of those present, George Lincoln, abruptly rose, pointed a finger at her, and shouted, "Lady Sheba, I challenge you! In the name of the Great White Brotherhood, do you stand in the light?" "Go into the astral and the Goddess will answer you thar [there]," she coolly responded in her southern drawl.[289]

---

289 Richler, "Witches Brew."

Despite the conflicts, good conversations were still had, and many of those present wanted to proceed with the plan to find some common principles they could use to help clear up misconceptions about what exactly a Wiccan was and was not. The festival ended before the task was complete, so the group decided that they would meet again at the WitchMeet to be held April 11–14, 1974.

When the spring WitchMeet rolled around and the council came together once again to try reaching some level of agreement, Carl thought it would be a good idea to establish a sense of order right from the start. He opened the meeting by suggesting that the council adopt the following rules:

> *The American Council of Witches has come together in WitchMeet for the purpose of cooperative learning, mutual work to solve problems facing us all as witches, and the joining together in unity for common goals while preserving individual coven and tradition autonomy…I also suggest that we continue the informality of organization established at the first WitchMeet and designate an unofficial chairman of the council to provide the necessary structure that any group requires to function with purpose, and a recording secretary. I also suggest that we agree that no public statements of principles or action will be issued except upon unanimous vote, but that the rules of operation of the WitchMeet be adopted by majority vote.*

The rules were adopted and the meeting proceeded. With all the strong and very different personalities present, it seemed difficult at first for anyone to agree on much of anything. As so often is the case, people were getting caught up by the details and struggling to see a bigger picture in which they could all be a part. The council had every reason to succeed, however, so they didn't give up. Wicca was just starting out, and there was a lot of false information about it swirling about in the media. There was also a concern about the possibility of individuals claiming authority and speaking for the Wicca in ways that were not at all accurate. At last, an agreement was reached.

Carl recalled the experience many, many years later:

> ... the original basis for the meeting of the group that became the council was an opportunity to reconcile differences between two different positions on gays in Wicca. By writing the "Principles of Wiccan Belief," I attempted and we succeeded in a firm foundation that led to the two leaders of the opposing factions—Herman Slater and Gavin Frost—shaking hands... Upon the adoption of the "Principles of Wiccan Belief" with very minimum changes from my first draft (prepared overnight), there was interest in turning the collective group assembled into a permanent body.
>
> Unfortunately, I was elected the chair—having hosted the meeting and chaired the discussion and adoption of the Principles. There was some dispute, never settled as I recall, about the name. I know that I proposed "The Council of American Witches" for the basic reason that I believed and still do that American Witches were building a non-European tradition and I wanted to avoid the perception that we were "beholden" to the British. There was concern that "CAW" would be confused with the Church of All Worlds, so the alternative American Council of Witches was proposed but I do not think it was adopted.
>
> I say it was unfortunate that I was elected as chairperson as I did not really have the time to devote to another organization beyond Llewellyn and Gnostica, and a new family along with obligations to manage my father's estate and all the problems associated with a small business in an industry that had never considered itself a business. I did my best as long as I could—getting the Principles published in the Army Chaplains Guide being a major accomplishment with the help of Rev. J. Gordon Melton, but after we had to give up sponsoring the annual Gnosticons as a loss leader we couldn't afford... I turned the updates for the Chaplains' Manual over to Selena Fox and let the organization die of inattention.[290]

---

290 CLW, "Comments on the Council of American Witches," September 20, 2006.

The Thirteen Principles of Wiccan Belief

The council agreed unanimously on the following statement and Thirteen Principles of Wiccan Belief:

The Council of American Witches finds it necessary to define Witchcraft in terms of the American experience and needs. We are not bound by traditions from other times and other cultures and owe no allegiance to any person or power greater than the Divinity manifest through our own being. As American Witches, we welcome and respect all life-affirming teachings and traditions, and seek to learn from all and to share our learning within our Council. It is in this spirit of welcome and cooperation that we adopt these few principles of Wiccan belief. In seeking to be inclusive, we do not wish to open ourselves to the destruction of our group by those on self-serving power trips, or to philosophies and practices contradictory to those principles. In seeking to exclude those whose ways are contradictory to ours, we do not wish to deny participation to any who are sincerely interested in our knowledge and beliefs, regardless of race, color, sex, age, national or cultural heritage, or sexual preference.

We therefore ask only that those who seek to identify with us accept those few basic principles:

We practice rites to attune ourselves with the natural rhythm of life forces marked by the phases of the Moon and the seasonal Quarters and cross-quarters.

We recognize that our intelligence gives us a unique responsibility toward our environment, we seek to live in harmony with Nature, in ecological balance, offering fulfillment to life and consciousness within an evolutionary concept.

We acknowledge a depth of power far greater than is apparent to the average person. Because it is far greater than ordinary, it is sometimes called 'supernatural,' but we see it as lying within that which is naturally potential to us all.

We conceive of the Creative Power in the Universe as manifesting through polarity—as masculine and feminine—and that this same Creative Power lives in all people and functions through the interaction of the masculine and feminine. We value neither above the other, knowing each to be supportive of the other. We value sexuality as pleasure, as the symbol and embodiment of Life, and as one of the sources of energies used in magickal practices and religious worship.

We recognize both outer and inner or psychological worlds—sometimes known as the Spiritual World, The Collective Unconscious, the Inner Planes, etc.—and we see in the interaction of these two dimensions the basis for paranormal phenomena and magickal exercises. We neglect neither dimension for the other, seeing both as necessary for our fulfillment.

We do not recognize any authoritarian hierarchy, but do honor those who teach, respect those who share their greater wisdom and knowledge, and acknowledge those who have courageously given of themselves in leadership.

We see religion, magick and wisdom-in-living as being united in the way one views the world and lives within it—a worldview and philosophy-of-life which we identify as Witchcraft, the Wiccan Way.

Calling oneself "Witch" does not make a Witch, but neither does heredity itself, or the collecting of titles, degrees and initiations. A Witch seeks to control the forces within him/herself that make life possible in order to live wisely and well, without harm to others and in harmony with Nature.

We acknowledge that it is the affirmation and fulfillment of life in a continuance of evolution and development of consciousness that gives meaning to the Universe we know and to our personal role within it.

Our only animosity toward Christianity or toward any other religion or philosophy-of-life is to the extent that its institutions have claimed to be "the one true, right and only way" and have sought to deny freedom to others, and to suppress other ways of religious practices and belief.

As American Witches, we are not threatened by debates on the history of the Craft, the origins of various terms, the legitimacy of various aspects of various traditions. We are concerned only with our present and future.

We do not accept the concept of "absolute evil" nor do we worship any entity known as Satan or the Devil, as defined by the Christian tradition. We do not seek our power through the suffering of others, nor do we accept the concept that personal benefits can only be derived through denial to another.

We seek within Nature for that which is contributory to our health and well-being.

The statement of beliefs was circulated in *Touchstone*, the newsletter Carl had developed for the council. The members of the group were to use it as a resource to protect from misunderstandings and help dispel sensationalist media portrayals of witchcraft.

Chapter 10

Carl the Astrologer

Carl did much over the years both behind the scenes and under the spotlight to advocate not only for a greater understanding of witchcraft and magick, but also for a practical and scientific approach to astrology that would be readily available to everyone. The *Minneapolis Star* called him a "super-astrologer,"[291] and he even appeared as an expert guest on the *Phil Donahue Show* to discuss his "no-nonsense approach to astrology and the influence of the stars on real life situations."[292]

As the main author of the *Moon Sign Book* and the *Astrological Calendar* for several years after purchasing Llewellyn, Carl wrote extensively about astrology. The *Astrological Calendar* even contained Carl's fashion predictions and recommendations for the coming year. Remember those spike heels, chain belts, and heavy jewelry of the mid to late seventies? Carl foresaw it all.[293]

---

291 Barbara Flanagan's column, *Minneapolis Star*, December 30, 1971.

292 *Baltimore Sun*, "TV Listings," July 29, 1979.

293 Barbara Flanagan's column, *Minneapolis Star*, December 30, 1971.

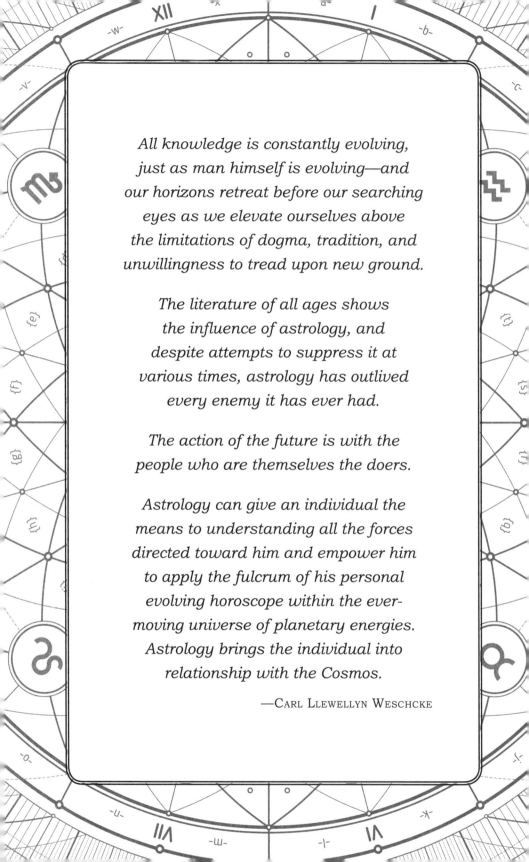

*All knowledge is constantly evolving,
just as man himself is evolving—and
our horizons retreat before our searching
eyes as we elevate ourselves above
the limitations of dogma, tradition, and
unwillingness to tread upon new ground.*

*The literature of all ages shows
the influence of astrology, and
despite attempts to suppress it at
various times, astrology has outlived
every enemy it has ever had.*

*The action of the future is with the
people who are themselves the doers.*

*Astrology can give an individual the
means to understanding all the forces
directed toward him and empower him
to apply the fulcrum of his personal
evolving horoscope within the ever-
moving universe of planetary energies.
Astrology brings the individual into
relationship with the Cosmos.*

—Carl Llewellyn Weschcke

Llewellyn was built on astrology books, and throughout the years this topic has remained an important mainstay of the company's publications. It was Llewellyn George's passion for astrology that first launched Llewellyn, and it was Carl Weschcke's passion for astrology and a host of other metaphysical and magickal topics that grew Llewellyn into what it is today. Carl valued astrology and recognized it as a real and ancient science yet to be fully understood or utilized to its maximum potential. Having employed astrology as a guide in his personal life as well as in his business endeavors, Carl knew firsthand the benefits astrology offered, and he wanted to help others become aware of and access these benefits, too, writing that

> It's "Nature's Own Clock"—the movement of the moon and of the sun and planets—that tells us how to live in tune with the pulse of all life on earth. At a fundamental level, in the electromagnetic and gravitational fields within which everything moves, everything is tied together![294]

With astrology today being thought of by many people as nothing more than those vague, true-for-everyone horoscopes you see on popular internet sites that aren't even based on accurate astrological data, it's easy to make the mistake of discounting it as a bunch of superstitious foolishness intended solely for entertainment. However, there is a real science to it. As Carl explained,

> Life energies, and the currents of gravity and magnetism, the flow of cosmic energies from the sun, and the high winds that control our weather, relate to the planetary movements just as do the ocean's tides to the moon's phases. It is knowledge of these patterns and relationships that enable us to forecast the trend of events, and that enable us to take our own positive actions to swim with the tides—not to sink against them.[295]

---

294 CLW, "Dear Friend," Gnostica Bookstore newsletter, January 1981.
295 Ibid.

He admired the analytic style of Dr. Carl G. Jung, who had examined the birth charts of many of his patients to see if, statistically, the astrological predictions given by the horoscope were in agreement with what he personally knew of each individual's personality and case history. Carl explained:

> His studies led him to the concept of synchronicity which recognizes that there are meaningful connections between events other than direct cause and effect. This concept provides a basis for our astrological philosophy, for it rests on the concept that the universe is an organic Whole, the parts of which necessarily move together sympathetically as well as affecting one another in the causal sense.[296]

Carl favored a scientific approach to astrology that was based on research, experimentation, and experience. Before an audience in Minneapolis in 1962, Carl said:

> Astrological theory must stand the test of internal logic and must be subject to verification from other disciplines. We know, through experience, that astrology is a real and valid science. But we should also know that—like any other science—we need to test, and to constantly weed out ideas and methods that are faulty and search and test new ideas and methods to increase the accuracy and application of astrology.[297]

Carl did indeed delight in putting the newest methods and technologies into action. Soon after acquiring Llewellyn, he recruited a government researcher who was involved with the space program to serve as Llewellyn's research director. This researcher, who preferred to use the pseudonym "Gary Duncan," was able to create for Llewellyn the first astrological ephemeris ever to be prepared using an electronic computer. The ephemeris provided precise information on planetary positions and other celestial occurrences for the

---

296   CLW, "Astrology and Research" speech given in Minneapolis,
      Minnesota, at an unknown event, November 20,1962.
297   Ibid.

years 1961–1970 and enabled more accurate astrological forecasting than had previously been available.[298]

The fact that astrology was relentlessly misunderstood and devalued was a problem that bothered Carl, and it was his sincere hope to find a way to reconnect the masses with the truth and benefits of real astrology. He delivered numerous talks on astrology to diverse audiences, and through Llewellyn he published countless books on the subject that found great success. Carl was especially proud of publishing Noel Tyl's *Principles and Practice of Astrology*. Released in 1970, the multi-volume series aimed to offer a comprehensive study course in modern astrology that was both in-depth and understandable. Carl had dreamt of publishing such a series for many years, and he had approached Noel with the concept. The books proved to be substantially influential, teaching generations of professional astrologers modern methods for casting horoscopes and making more accurate astrological predictions. Carl and Noel became good friends who shared a mutual respect and admiration for one another. Carl said of Noel that he was "a man I will call brother in this lifetime as once before."[299]

Throughout his long life, Carl continued to believe in the benefits of astrology and hoped that more people would learn enough about it to give it a chance and see for themselves the advantages astrological forecasting can bring:

> *I want to see a public understanding and appreciation of what astrology really is, and on all those applications that empower the individual. I want people to be inspired to learn enough astrology —aided by their computers (and iPhones)—to cast their own horoscopes and use those techniques for career guidance, business timing, gardening and horticulture, relationships, personal living, etc., and to understand and appreciate those larger dimensions of extreme weather forecasting, political astrology,*

298 CLW presentation to the Antique Society, circa 1961.
299 CLW, "Noel Tyl," circa 1970.

planetary cycles in relation to economic and cultural factors, and more.[300]

For well over a century, Llewellyn has been the world's premier source for astrology books, offering titles for every skill level from beginner to professional. Thanks to pioneers like Llewellyn George, authors like Noel Tyl, and publishers like Carl Weschcke, today anyone with an interest in astrology can find a plethora of study materials to learn all about it, as well as the courage to put it to the test.

---

300 CLW email to Melanie Marquis, September 28, 2009.

***From Noel Tyl, written for
Carl's memorial service:***

Believe it or not, I met my brother Carl in a haunted house…
right here in Saint Paul, Minnesota, in that great mansion on
Summit Avenue. The spirits were most benevolent that first
night as silver dollars found their way under the closed door
to my room.

That's my kind of publisher!

I was on a stopover between Seattle and my home at the
time, in Dusseldorf, Germany. Llewellyn was going to publish
my first manuscript and Carl wanted to meet me—this burly,
kindly man who right off the bat had greeted me in all serious-
ness as his long-lost brother. Throughout that entire weekend—the weekend that changed my life—I saw Carl Weschcke
working constantly in that funky publishing house in Minneapolis. Carl was happy, indeed, finally to have found his
lost brother. All the while he had an "I told you so" chuckle of
delight in his eyes.

That's my kind of publisher!

That was forty-five years ago. Forty-five years of his life lessons, reliable love, and business logistics that did change my
life. That first weekend saw the conception of a giant idea and
a flurry of activity: we were planning the twelve-volume modernization of astrology: *The Principles and Practice of Astrology*…all our conceptions were planned at that big breakfast-
lunch-and-dinner table under Carl's leadership. The volumes
were completed in record time—faster than one a month—as
if the volumes had already been written and needed only to be
retrieved from the collective unconscious. The astrology world
was compelled to recognize Carl and Llewellyn once again as
the worldwide leader of innovative and practical thought in
astrology. And this led to twenty-three more volumes written
or edited by yours truly.

In brotherly spirit, I could call Carl and tell him the idea for a new book, and he would immediately say, "When will I have it?" And the support didn't stop; it came in surprising ways. I remember mentioning to Carl that I so wished I had access to Simmonite's discovery work with solar arcs written around 1880. He said, as matter-of-factly as could be, "Oh, I have that book; a first edition, no less. I'll send it to you." (Carl's library was a wonder of his private world.) Now this is a precious book. It arrived not under guard nor by Brinks truck but in a simple mundane manila envelope! Carl trusted the universe. All would be well.

And let's remember that voice. I was an opera singer for twenty-six years, but even with all my training, Carl's rich, deep-in-the-woods voice was downright intimidating. Once I had a contract to sing with the Minnesota Symphony—an evening of Wagner—and I felt that the spirits might just rearrange things—give me a cold, for example—so that Carl could do a Wiccan poetry reading with symphonic accompaniment instead! His voice was a force of nature. I never heard Carl seriously criticize another author or practitioner. His spirit soared above all that. His respect for the endurance of ancient truths to make the future happen was constantly inspiring. I used to tease him about the "grandfather membership" clause offered way back when by the American Federation of Astrologers, making him a high-ranking member with those letters after his name! Carl teased in return, "Well, Noel, when are you going to write your first witchcraft book and start earning some real royalties?"

So my brother is gone...or is he just wrapped in a shining fog? We can talk to him anytime we wish and wait to hear back that glorious voice, that loving cheer, and that patient leadership. Thank you and bless you, dearest brother Carl. You are now in the Pantheon of the Famed.

That's my kind of publisher.

Chapter 11

A Love to Last a Lifetime

Before Carl met Sandra in 1971, he didn't really have marriage on his mind. Absorbed in work and the growth of his business, Carl was in many ways the appealing yet ever uncatchable bachelor. He loved intelligent, beautiful women and enjoyed dating whenever he could, but preferring to keep perpetually productive, as was his habit, he usually didn't have a whole lot of time for socializing. Sometimes his dates would find themselves at an NAACP banquet or other obligatory function that was already on the agenda. What he lacked in time, however, he made up for in romance, bringing flowers or other small gifts, writing love notes, and always striving to look his best if he were to be meeting with a special lady.

Conscientious, considerate, and having that sort of aura that lets one know that this is a person who can be trusted and relied upon, Carl was very attractive, not to mention the fact that he lived in a mansion and owned his own publishing company, to boot. He had the privilege of knowing a lot of intelligent, beautiful, and

*Sandra and I were married in a Wiccan
ceremony of my own creation—which
for our hundred-plus non-Wiccan
guests was seen mostly as fantasy.
But look how real Wiccan and Pagan
wedding rites have become.*

*Small things mean a lot more
than you ever imagine.*

*When Gabe was young, starting about
age five, we used to take two to four-week
summer driving vacations out west, mostly
staying for a time either in Santa Fe or
Tucson, and almost always going through
South Dakota's Black Hills and Badlands,
with a stop at the famous Wall Drug. Those
were the most enjoyable days of my life.*

*Can you define love? No.
You experience it…Love is experience.
I love, and I open myself to love.*

—Carl Llewellyn Weschcke

interesting women, and although he had fun with his dates, he hadn't yet met the one that he felt could truly be a life partner.

He was getting older, and although he was pretty much content being single, for a while he had been quietly considering the possibility that it might be time to pursue a more long-term, serious relationship. He wanted that deeper connection; he longed for a love that was truly cosmic. In the early sixties, soon after purchasing Llewellyn, he had examined the astrological birth charts of several of his favorite women friends to see if anything more serious was in the stars,[301] but it wasn't fated for the right partner to come along just yet. For many years, Carl contented himself with casual dating, putting the quest for epic love on the back burner and pretty much forgetting about it as he continued to work tirelessly to build the success of his publishing company.

One day, an old friend of Carl's arranged for him to have a blind date. On July 16, 1971, the two met for lunch at a Mexican restaurant, neither really knowing what to expect.[302] Her name was Sandra Heggum, and she was native to Minnesota, just as Carl was. She was ten years younger than him, smart, down to earth, and extremely beautiful, with a mane of long auburn hair and a sharp, inquisitive look in her eyes. Carl, with his well-trimmed beard, dark-framed glasses, and twinkling, soul-searching blue eyes, was instantly star-struck. The conversation remained casual, but the two immediately hit it off and sensed there might be something very special about their connection.

Sandra was feeling "the spark" and invited Carl to extend the date by going shopping with her, as he had mentioned that he loved fashion. He declined the invitation as he had to get back to work, but it wasn't long before he would ask her out again. "I thought he was fascinating!" Sandra recalled. "He was so charismatic. I

---

301 From CLW personal files circa 1962–1964.

302 Sandra K. Weschcke email to Melanie Marquis, July 3, 2017.

liked him right away."[303] Carl liked Sandra right away, too, and they quickly became frequent dating partners. Carl soon realized that Sandra's practical mind would be an asset to his publishing company, so he hired her to help manage his booming business. Sandra handled many of the managerial, marketing, and accounting aspects of Llewellyn from the Gnostica Bookstore building in downtown Minneapolis, while Carl continued to handle production, promotion, and purchasing from the Summit mansion in Saint Paul.[304]

Sandra proved a perfect balance for Carl and a wonderful addition to his life, not only in her value to Llewellyn, but more importantly on a personal level, providing Carl with a strong mind and caring soul with whom to share ideas and enjoy good times. Her sweetness and beauty were a constant source of inspiration, but to Carl her value stretched far beyond that. Practical and shrewd, discerning and thoughtful, Sandra didn't back down from telling Carl when she thought a particular idea he presented wasn't exactly the most sensible.

Having a commanding presence, Carl found that those around him tended to avoid telling him no about anything—not because he was ever mean or domineering, but simply because he always came across as so confident and enthusiastic, it was hard to resist hopping on board with whatever train of thought he was driving. "I'm who I am and no one really welcomes contradicting me,"[305] Carl explained. However, Carl didn't mind being contradicted; he rather enjoyed being challenged, as it gave him the opportunity to question his own conclusions and refine his thinking. He wanted a woman who would speak her mind, and Sandra is a woman who simply couldn't be any other way than direct, genuine, and honest. Carl was proving to be a good match for Sandra as well, introducing her to a mystical and magical way of life that her logical, down-

---

303 Sandra K. Weschcke personal interview with Melanie Marquis, January 2017.
304 CLW email to Melanie Marquis, July 15, 2012.
305 CLW email to Melanie Marquis, September 8. 2013.

to-earth mind had never before considered. Sandra embraced the new world that had become apparent to her with an open mind and a loving heart.

Having a professional working relationship as well as a more intimate friendship and undeniable mutual attraction, the two quickly grew very close. There was something extra special about this woman, and Carl could sense it. He was so intrigued that he decided to examine her birth chart, as he had done for special girl-friends past. The stars had yet to find him a suitable match, but he was hopeful that this lovely lady born under the sign of Cancer just might be the one. He asked Sandra to marry him, and luckily for Carl, both Sandra and the stars agreed. Their horoscopes indi-cated that theirs was a fortunate and formidable pairing.

Carl wanted to have a magickal wedding ceremony and realized that their marriage could also be a wonderful opportunity to help educate the public about alternative spirituality. Although inter-est in Wicca and witchcraft was quickly growing, there was still a long way to go. They decided to have a traditional Wiccan hand-fasting and invited a crowd of around 300 that included friends, family, Llewellyn employees, and a couple of reporters from the local papers. "I believe it is time for followers of the 'Old Religion' to come out of hiding and make themselves known. We have nothing to hide,"[306] Carl explained at the time. Reporter Don Ahern called the event the "first public witch wedding in recorded history."[307]

At a time when many traditional marriage ceremonies included expectations of servitude of the woman to the man, this wedding between two witches was decidedly different. "Weschcke explained that the 'Wiccas' view the man and woman joined in marriage as full partners, and there is no pledging to 'honor and obey,'" Don Ahern reported. "He said both the man and the woman enjoy equal status in the marriage and in the ceremony of marriage."[308]

---

306   Ahern, "Witch Wedding Public."
307   Ibid.
308   Ibid.

Carl handled all the wedding preparations, from the ceremony to the clothes to the decorations. He designed the wedding ritual and wrote the vows himself,[309] drawing on existing rituals in the American-Celtic Wiccan tradition and Pagan Way[310] practices for inspiration to create a new yet authentic marriage rite. "I prepared the rite after a great amount of 'psychic research,' i.e. meditation and inner planes contact," Carl explained in the notes to his wedding rite. "In the process of preparing this rite, I believe I have recovered from the past some things that were once a part of Wiccan practices."[311]

Carl wanted the wedding to truly honor the greatness and magick of his union with Sandra, and he put a tremendous amount of thought and effort into the planning and preparations. Carl even designed the couple's wedding attire, a lilac and violet hooded robe for himself and a matching lilac and violet robe with a lace over-robe for Sandra that highlighted the beauty of his bride-to-be. He chose these colors because he thought of them as very joyful, symbolic of their happy, loving, and passionate union.

The wedding took place on the Winter Solstice of 1972 at the Universalist Church in Minneapolis.[312] There, a crowd of celebrants that included over 100 non-Pagans gathered to witness the beginning of a marriage that would last a lifetime.[313] The wedding guests were a mix of witches, occultists, family, friends, employees, and other curious well-wishers eager to find out what Wicca and magick were really about. Universalist minister John Cummings was on hand to help officiate and witness the legal exchange of vows,[314] but Carl and Sandra themselves would take the leading

---

309 CLW email to Melanie Marquis, December 10, 2011.
310 Pagan Way was a neopagan training tradition and network created in 1970 by Thomas Giles, Ed Fitch, and Joseph B. Wilson.
311 Gnosticus, *A Wiccan Rite of Marriage.*
312 Ahern, "Witch Wedding Public."
313 CLW email to Melanie Marquis, December 10, 2011.
314 Ahern, "Witch Wedding Public."

role in the marriage ritual. Carl noted that "in the Wicca, every initiate is a priest or priestess—hence it is important that the Wiccan couple work together and take as active a role in the ritual as is possible!"[315] As a truly magical rite and not one that was merely just for show, the Weschcke wedding would involve the guests as active participants. Carl explained in the preliminaries to the ritual,

> Unlike a play where the actors and actresses project to the audience, we ask that you, the friends and loved ones, project to us. Live within us for the moment, nourish our ritual with your Spirit, feel for us the love that is the blessing we ask of you for this marriage.[316]

A special type of magick circle was cast, called the marriage circle. Measuring twelve feet in diameter, the circle was laid with flowers and pine boughs. A candle was placed at each of the cardinal directions, and on the altar was placed a gold candle to represent Carl and a silver candle to represent Sandra. Incense, water, salt, a scourge, a sword, and a cup of wine were also among the altar tools, along with custom-made crowns of silver and gold for the bride and groom. A wand that held the two wedding rings was placed front and center on the altar.

The ceremony began with a moment of meditation followed by the casting and consecration of the magick marriage circle. First, the incense on the altar was set ablaze to release a fragrant perfume, blending the elements of fire and air. Then, using the tip of the athame, the handle held jointly in their hands, Carl and Sandra together added three measures of salt to the water on the altar, combining the elements of water and earth. The athame still held jointly, the couple then walked the circumference of the circle, casting power through the blade as they went to form a protective and sacred space. The couple then sprinkled the salted water and

---

315 Gnosticus, *A Wiccan Rite of Marriage.*
316 Ibid.

wafted the smoldering incense at each of the cardinal points of the circle, thus consecrating the space with the power of the elements. They also consecrated each other, with the water as well as with the incense. Pentagrams were traced in the air at each direction as a means of salute and summons to the Divine. They called upon the Mighty Ones, the gods and the powers of Nature. They called upon beings of air, fire, water, and earth. They called upon the Goddess and God to bear witness and to bless their sacred rite.

The rings had been resting on the wand on the altar, and when it came time for their use, Carl and Sandra each held an end of the wand and placed their other hands upon the rings.

"Is it your wish, Sandra, to become one with this man?" the officiant asked.

"It is," replied Sandra.

"Is it your wish, Carl, to become one with this woman?"

"It is," replied Carl. As Carl slipped the ring onto Sandra's finger, he looked into her eyes and told her, "It is my wish to become one with you." As Sandra put the other band onto Carl's finger, she said the same to him. The vows were then exchanged, each speaking directly to the other, their hands clasped firmly together:

"I vow to love and honor you in our ways. I vow to devote myself to your well-being and happiness. I vow never to be unworthy of your love and respect for me and of our ways of loving and living, and our belief in Divine and Eternal Life. So I will it to be!"

The officiant then spoke, "Then as the Goddess, the God, and the Mighty Ones are witness to this rite, I now proclaim you to be of one body, of one soul, and of one spirit. I now proclaim you husband and wife!"

They kissed as a way to seal their union, then the ceremony continued with an enactment of the "Legend of the Goddess," a mystery rite from Lady Sheba's *Book of Shadows* that is utilized to teach the truths of life, death, love, and magick and how they are intertwined. After the mystery was enacted, the couple led a dance around the circle and soon invited the wedding guests to join in.

In lieu of a reception, the couple followed with what they preferred to call a celebration, the term "reception" being thought of as too formal and feeling that a wedding should be "a happy occasion, not a rigid one." Each guest had been asked to bring along a bottle of red country wine, and these were poured into a large cauldron. Flowers from the marriage circle were mixed with the wine, and Sandra and Carl were the first to taste it.

Sandra recalled fondly,

> *The wedding was perfect; it really was impressive. The only trouble was unfortunately we left the church in quite a mess because of our cauldrons of country wine (with flowers floating in the wine). I heard later that the church complained about it, but they never said anything to us. I don't remember any of that; I think I was in a storybook dream.*

Overlooking a little spilled wine here and there, the wedding had indeed turned out beautifully—so well, in fact, that the newlyweds decided that their marriage rite should be made available to everyone. Carl wrote in the notes to accompany the ritual that

> *Today many persons have come to want a marriage rite that is magickally meaningful. Many people today want personal religious experience that is both emotionally fulfilling and intellectually understandable, and that is also spiritually powerful. Many people today want direct contact with the Forces of the Inner Life—without mediation by a "third party." I prepared this marriage rite within the American-Celtic Wiccan Tradition as the marriage rite for Sandra and myself, and we wish to share it with any who desire to use it.*[317]

In 1972 Llewellyn Publications released *A Wiccan Rite of Marriage in the American Celtic Tradition for use by Covens and Individuals* as a 56-page softcover book with plastic comb binding. The author was listed as "Gnosticus"—Carl's magickal name.

---

317 Gnosticus, *A Wiccan Rite of Marriage.*

Sandra moved into the Summit Avenue mansion the day after the Thursday wedding, and the newlyweds were back at work the following Monday.[318] While Carl continued working from the Summit Avenue headquarters, Sandra continued to work at the Gnostica Bookstore building in downtown Minneapolis, from where she managed many important aspects of the publishing business. On the more conservative and practical side than Carl, she provided balance to her husband's sometimes overzealous ambition. If one of his ideas was a little too "out there," Sandra would gently nudge him back toward reality. And for a no-nonsense woman like Sandra, Carl's creativity, charisma, and sage-like mystique kept life fresh, fun, and exciting. They made a perfect team, and with the birth of their one and only child, whom they named Gabriel Llewellyn Weschcke, they soon made the perfect family.

Both Sandra and Carl devoted themselves to the happiness and care of their son, just as they continued to remain devoted to each other. It was no small task running a publishing company as well as a bookstore and occult learning center while raising a child, but they found ways to manage and make it work. Carl felt great pride in his son, and he often mentioned him in letters to friends and colleagues. Carl wrote to a friend,

> It is amazing to see how fast they learn things. The other evening he learned to climb stairs, and to go down stairs, and the transition from the first time to the second time to a third time was just amazing to witness. It was that same evening that he first started walking while pushing his giraffe on wheels ahead of him.[319]

The giraffe Carl mentions is one that he crafted himself out of wood in hopes of delighting his young son. In a letter to Israel Regardie several months later, Carl writes, "Gabriel is just beginning to really expand his vocabulary, and I'm really looking forward to seeing what his gymnastics lessons do."[320]

---

318   Sandra K. Weschcke email to Melanie Marquis, July 3, 2017.
319   CLW personal files, 1974.
320   Ibid.

Carl and Sandra truly enjoyed their little family, and they truly enjoyed each other, too. Despite whatever other pressures and responsibilities there might be, taking the time to make one another feel valued and loved was one thing that kept the Weschcke's union strong, vibrant, and passionate throughout the many years they would share together. Their schedules often clashed, each busy with various responsibilities and commitments, but Carl and Sandra made it a priority to spend time together as much as they possibly could. One tradition was to do their best to share at least one meal together each and every day. Even when lunch was something simple, like a grilled cheese sandwich, it was greatly appreciated, as was the opportunity to talk and hear about one another's day, to discuss any new ideas or concerns, to genuinely enjoy each other's company, and to generally reconnect. The love they shared overflowed to their son, and before they knew it Gabe was quickly transitioning from a baby into a spirited little boy.

Day to day life was hectic but happy, and holidays were simple but joyful affairs that usually centered around a big family dinner. One year, the Weschckes sent out a Yuletime greeting card to friends and family that featured a drawing of the couple peeking in on Gabe gazing in wonder at a small pile of presents waiting beneath the tree.[321] As busy as the Weschckes were with their booming businesses, their biggest priority and greatest joy was in helping their son to grow, play, learn, and dream, and they both took full advantage of every opportunity to do so.

Of course, raising a young child in a big, creepy mansion while at the same time being purveyors of occult books and magickal learning did have its challenges. Although in reality they held tightly to strong family values, the Weschckes didn't always exactly look like a traditional family to those on the outside of their world who weren't fortunate enough to know them very well personally. Sandra recalled one incident that occurred when Gabe was still

---

321 *Minneapolis Star*, "Celebrity Greetings."

very young. A new nanny had been hired, but after only being employed a short time, Sandra overheard the woman making a frantic phone call one night when they were entertaining some of the speakers for the Gnosticon festival. "They have a party going on and someone has brought a snake in the house!" the nanny stated with alarm in her voice. "There is a snake in the house! And a baby!"[322] Carolyn Clark, who was high priestess for the Church of All Worlds, had brought over one of the live snakes that she would be using in her workshop at the festival. Despite this perfectly logical explanation, that was it for this nanny. She could tell there was something unordinary about the Weschcke home—too unordinary, for her tastes—and she abruptly quit the job. Finding the whole incident quite silly, Sandra laughed it off and placed another "help wanted" ad in the local paper, mentioning their "lovely Saint Paul home" and their "very pleasant family."

Llewellyn was continuing to gain publicity and attention, and while it was one thing to have zealots banging on the front door to pronounce one a sinner when Carl had been single, the thought of stuff like that happening with his young son and wife in the house was enough to make him want to step back from the spotlight a bit, or at least live in a little less infamous dwelling. Llewellyn had grown right along with Gabe, and it was becoming increasingly impractical to have what was now a family home doubling as headquarters for a thriving book publishing business. Gabe was to be enrolled at the Saint Paul Academy, where Carl had gone as a lad, but the Weschckes wished to give their son the double benefit of a good education in the city together with a quieter life in the country. Carl had many fond memories of his own childhood explorations of the woods surrounding his grandfather's house and roaming around his father's orchards, and he wanted his son to have similar opportunities to explore nature. Even though the Summit

---

322   Sandra K. Weschcke personal interview with Melanie Marquis, January 2017.

Avenue mansion was well-loved and full of many joyful and unforgettable memories, the family decided it was time for a move.

"If that house had been in the country, we would have kept it," Carl explained. "I just did not want to raise Gabe in the city. We decided to move from Saint Paul to a nice home on a lake as a better environment for Gabe."[323] They chose a home surrounded with tall trees, and as the family settled in, the old mansion was put up for sale.

Moving out of the mansion proved to be quite a monumental transition. What fit in well in the antique hulk of a house didn't necessarily look so right in a modern family-style home. Many items were sold as the family downsized into a more practical dwelling in which to raise their son. A notice in the local newspaper for the Weschcke's moving sale illustrates the vast array of interesting items Carl had procured over the years as a bachelor living in the old haunted house, including listings for twelve matching fishbone, opal, and gold lampshades made by the acclaimed New York design firm Quezal, fourteen oriental rugs, a marble-top Victorian commode, thirty bookcases, several electric beds, an antique rowing machine, and even a chastity belt![324] After the Weschckes sold the mansion, it was converted by subsequent owners into several rental units,[325] a fact Carl found disappointing.

The new home proved to be lovely, though, and as Gabe grew older, the lake behind the house became a great source of family fun. The Weschckes owned a pontoon boat, and Carl loved to take Gabe and Sandra out on the lake for a cruise over the slowly rippling water. They also enjoyed many road trips together in the summertime when Gabe would be on break from his schooling, exploring the American landscape and making stops at national

---

323 CLW email to Melanie Marquis, September 28, 2012.

324 "Notice: Moving Sale for Carl L. Weschcke, 476 Summit Ave.," *Minnesota Star*, July 29, 1977.

325 *Villager*, "Rooms to Spare."

parks and monuments along the way.[326] New Mexico and Arizona were favorite destinations, with Carl sporting an old cowboy hat the whole time and a wide grin most of the time, and Gabe acting as official photographer, chronicling the family's adventures. When the trip was through, the family would put together a photo album complete with humorous captions to highlight the more memorable aspects of their journey.

Although there was always work to be done and more work after that in the Weschcke household, there was also a never-ending supply of love, happiness, closeness, and caring that brought luck and success not only to their marriage, but to all of the many endeavors they would enjoy together as a couple and as a family.

---

326   CLW email to Melanie Marquis, April 4, 2011.

From Sandra K. Weschcke:

I found my love for Carl early on, almost immediately, and it is still with me today, and it will never leave me. Carl had the most beautiful blue penetrating eyes that could focus on you in an intense, loving way; he was kind and considerate. Even in our relationship he thought about what would be best; his intellectual approach was always evident and his intellect was huge, most often used to help me as well as other people to reach their full potential.

We never had a personal argument; we had a few about the business side of the business, but that's all. As a Virgo he planned the best family vacations and had the most thorough itineraries, showing his family a real good time. He was fun as well as serious. He was afraid of heights but took us out west into the mountains to see our beautiful country in its raw beauty. He was a good and loving husband. He was a wonderful, caring father; he was so happy to have a son. He gave me what most of us strive for: a wonderful life.

From Gabe Llewellyn Weschcke:

I have many favorite memories of my dad. He was always fair, supportive, and funny, and would listen to what I had to say. We had an old Monopoly set from his childhood that we would play together. It was perfect except for one missing property card. We created a replacement card to fill the gap. He usually let me buy my favorite properties, Boardwalk and Park Place. They were the most expensive, so to me, of course, they were the most important. We enjoyed playing chess together too, although I didn't have the patience for it.

In the summer Dad and I would walk down the long dirt road we lived on to get the mail. Our dog, Charlie, would crisscross our path, following every scent. I would hunt for shiny rocks and anything else exciting. As a family we would take road trips out west every summer, usually ending up in New Mexico or Arizona. Mom would share the driving while Dad read manuscripts until I bugged him enough to play cards. Those are some of the best memories of my childhood.

———————————

What's in a Name?

A lot, according to Carl. Soon after he and Sandra had married, Carl had been thinking about the power that is in a name. He had recently acquired his magickal name of Gnosticus, which had given him cause to contemplate and consider the meaning and power of his "everyday" name that his parents had bestowed upon him. Born Carl Louis Weschcke, Carl didn't feel any particular attachment to his middle name. "It doesn't mean anything," Sandra recalled Carl saying at the time. "Louis" was indeed a family name, but then again so was "Carl" and so was "Weschcke"—not to mention the fact that you can find a "Carl Weschcke" in generation after generation of the Weschcke family line.

Carl wanted something more unique, something different, something more meaningful, powerful, and personal. If having a "magickal name" like Gnosticus could provide additional benefits within the circle, then wouldn't having a "magickal name" placed smack dab in the center of one's "everyday name" be likely to provide benefits, too? And so it was that Carl—being Carl—decided to improve his name. He followed through with the idea and soon had his name officially and legally changed to Carl Llewellyn Weschcke. When his son was born, Carl opted to share with his child this new meaningful and magickal middle name.

A Carl By Many Names

Who *was* Carl Llewellyn Weschcke? New Age visionary or person with the most difficult to spell last name in the world? These are the names that his critics have called him. These are the names with which his friends and fans have adorned him.

Compiled from media sources dating from the 1960s into the 2000s, the following is a list of just some of the many names that have been used to describe the man who changed his middle name to Llewellyn:

- Occult Master
- Father of the New Age
- Pope of the Witches
- High Priest of the Occult
- Well-Groomed Father Christmas
- Leading Purveyor of Witchcraft
- Bonafide Witch
- Warlock
- Businessman
- Great Bearded Sage
- One of Saint Paul's Earliest Witches
- Saint Paul's Most Well-Known Witch
- Builder of Bridges
- Expert Astrologer
- A Pioneer in Publishing and the Paranormal
- Public Enemy #1
- #2 in Command of White Witchcraft after Sybil Leek
- Bearded Bard of Astrology Publications
- Collector of Prodigious Quantities of Mystic Magic
- An Eclectic
- A Magick Man

Chapter 12

1980s

P ublic Enemy Number One." "Number two in command of white witchcraft after Sybil Leek." These were just a couple of the monikers Carl gained as a figurehead of the New Age in the eighties. Although he had stepped back from the spotlight— or at least had tried to—there was no denying that through his various endeavors, Carl was helping countless people explore their interests and expand their abilities in metaphysical and magickal subjects on a scale much larger than had ever been seen. Llewellyn brought books on subjects that were generally viewed as fringe phenomenon into a widening web of mainstream bookstores, making information that had been previously hard to come by readily available to the masses. Even though the metaphysical books were too often hidden in the darkest, most distant nook of the store, it was incredible for seekers of magickal knowledge to be able to buy books on the subject at the local mall, especially for those who were isolated in places where witchcraft was seen as an evil practice and magick overlooked as mere make-believe. For many, finding their first Llewellyn book was kind of like finding a friend, a

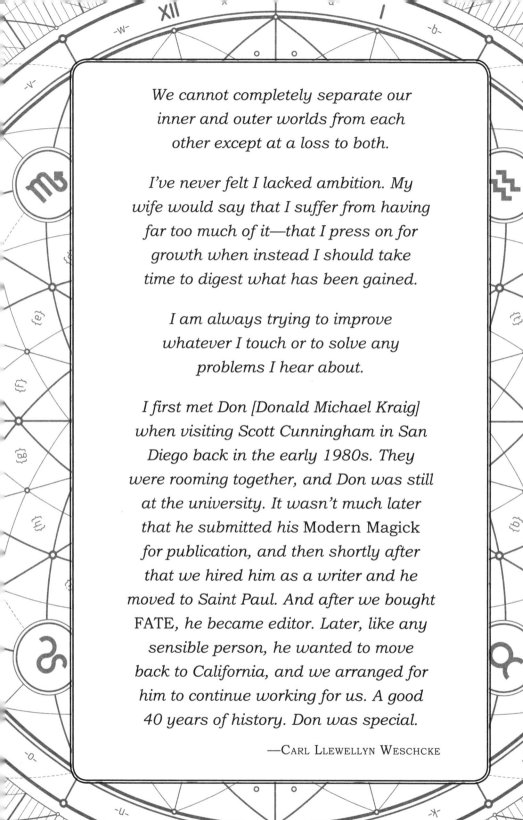

We cannot completely separate our inner and outer worlds from each other except at a loss to both.

I've never felt I lacked ambition. My wife would say that I suffer from having far too much of it—that I press on for growth when instead I should take time to digest what has been gained.

I am always trying to improve whatever I touch or to solve any problems I hear about.

I first met Don [Donald Michael Kraig] when visiting Scott Cunningham in San Diego back in the early 1980s. They were rooming together, and Don was still at the university. It wasn't much later that he submitted his Modern Magick *for publication, and then shortly after that we hired him as a writer and he moved to Saint Paul. And after we bought* FATE, *he became editor. Later, like any sensible person, he wanted to move back to California, and we arranged for him to continue working for us. A good 40 years of history. Don was special.*

—CARL LLEWELLYN WESCHCKE

long-awaited validation that you were not alone, that someone else believed in you, that your abilities were not just your imagination.

Although interest in subjects like astrology had expanded and become far more mainstream, many still opposed the spreading of occult knowledge. Jim Peters, music director of Saint Paul's Zion Christian Life Center, was among the most vocal. Peters and his family had been leading a crusade against rock music, and in the spring of 1980 they held a rally that drew over 1,000 people. In addition to warning of the "dangers" of rock and roll, Peters went on to caution the crowd about Proctor and Gamble, whose company logo he deemed to be "Satanic." Peters claimed that the Proctor and Gamble logo, featuring a man in the moon and thirteen stars, was not only associated with a thirteenth-century coven of witches, but also revealed support of Sun Myung Moon and the Unification Church. He drew similarly erroneous conclusions about the crescent moon adorning Carl's Gnostica Bookstore while it was still in operation in Saint Paul, speaking about it at rallies and seminars and causing widespread rumors that twisted the facts as well as the fiction. When a local newspaper ran an article about Peter's opposition to the Proctor and Gamble logo, the newspaper received numerous calls from readers reporting that the very same symbol could be found on the door of a "Satanist church" in the Twin Cities area. Aside from the fact that Gnostica Bookstore was clearly a bookstore and not a church, the only similarities between the Llewellyn logo and the Proctor and Gamble logo is that both symbols feature a moon, and neither was inspired by Satanism.

When questioned about the matter by a local reporter, Peters accusingly called Carl "number two in command of white witchcraft after Sybil Leek" and reiterated his beliefs that both the Gnostica crescent moon and the Proctor and Gamble logo were linked with the darkest of arts. Carl responded to Peter's comments by calmly explaining that he was "not a leader of witchcraft" and that to the best of his knowledge, witchcraft as a whole was "very fragmented, with no national leadership." He informed the reporter

Weschcke is an example of a person who, through unstinting dedication to what he believes is important, in the face of personal opposition and the lure of more lucrative fields of business, makes a valuable and difficult statement of individuality. Society is always enriched by such people.

—MATTHEW WOOD, AUTHOR OF
LLEWELLYN'S 1984 *SUN SIGN BOOK*, IN A
LETTER TO THE EDITOR, MAY 20, 1986,
STAR TRIBUNE "SENSITIVE PORTRAIT"

that Llewellyn's crescent moon logo had been in use since 1905, chosen as company symbol for the obvious reason of the *Moon Sign Book* being one of Llewellyn's signature publications.[327]

Carl wasn't too bothered by the criticism; he had books to publish, and some of those books would become Llewellyn's ultimate best sellers. In the early 1980s, Carl received an intriguing manuscript from a little-known writer by the name of Scott Cunningham. The manuscript was about magickal herbalism. Scott had years of real-life experience with the subject, and his writing style was straightforward, informative, and accessible. A contract was offered, and in 1982 Cunningham's *Magical Herbalism* was published, marking the beginning of Scott's very successful career as a Pagan book author and as a beloved and valued member of Carl's Llewellyn family. The two met in person soon after when Carl was traveling through California on a family road trip.

Scott had a small apartment in San Diego that he shared with his friend Donald Michael Kraig, a philosophy student at a local university and an aspiring stage magician and musician. The roommates shared an interest in magick and were mutual friends with both Raymond Buckland and Raven Grimassi. When Carl and his family stopped by to see how Scott was coming along on his latest manuscript and to say hello, Don joined them for lunch. Carl mentioned that perhaps Don could write a book sometime, too, and soon after, a manuscript entitled *Modern Magick* arrived at the Llewellyn headquarters. In 1988 the book was published, and it has since become one of the go-to titles for the practice of modern Western magick. Carl decided to have Don record some audio to go along with it, and the same year *Using Modern Magick* was released on cassette tape.

Both Scott and Don's interest in witchcraft and magick deepened, and soon they found themselves studying Aradian witchcraft with Raven Grimassi. In 1983, just a year after his first book for

---

327   Fuller, "Rumor Giving Company a Devil of a Time."

Llewellyn was published, Scott was diagnosed with lymphoma. He overcame the illness, however, and went on to write many titles that remain among Llewellyn's top sellers. *The Truth about Witchcraft Today*, released in 1988, has endured to this day as one of Llewellyn's best sellers, selling nearly a quarter million copies in its thirty years so far.

Scott's books brought validation to the solitary witch and opened the doorway to self-initiation. Most covens were found in the bigger cities, and for many people there wasn't much chance of joining up with one. This could leave the unaffiliated witch doubting whether or not they were as much of a "real" witch as someone who had "officially" been initiated into an "official" coven. Scott's books offered complete self-initiation rituals and spells for the solitary witch that were easy to understand yet full of depth, giving the solitary practitioner access to information and resources to help them practice and grow in their Craft without the need of a coven.

Just five years after *The Truth about Witchcraft Today* was released, Scott passed away following a series of infections arising as a result of HIV. Scott truly gave his heart to the world, pouring his efforts into sharing all he could of himself through his prolific writing, despite his personal suffering and obstacles. The love he felt for plants and for the earth and people is apparent in the words he left behind. Through his work, he removed a huge limit that had been fooling many people into thinking they were less; like Carl, Scott was a believer in helping people know that they were more.

Remarking on Scott's level of dedication, Carl recalled all the hours of typing and retyping that Scott put into his manuscripts before the days of computers, when such work had to be done on a mechanical machine. "I do believe the 'hard work' energy is magical and is still reflecting in the continuing sales of his books," Carl remarked.[328] Indeed, *Wicca: A Guide for the Solitary Practitioner* has sold well over 1,000,000 copies since its original publication in

---

328   CLW email to Melanie Marquis, September 11, 2011.

1988, enduring to this day as one of the most-recommended titles for new witches.

Carl was a pretty hardworking and dedicated individual himself, and his dedication to Llewellyn was reflected in his own personal magick practices. Among Carl's daily rituals was a visualization and meditation focused on the success of the company and the safety and well-being of the many individuals on whom that success depended. New book titles were placed on the altar, and Carl would energize them with his intention that they would meet with great success. He visualized Llewellyn's distribution network growing, seeing the energies he sent out in the world returning in the form of profits. Then, one by one, Carl would send blessings and protection to each of his employees and authors in turn, from Raymond Buckland and Lady Sheba to Scott Cunningham and Ed Fitch.[329]

He visualized himself and Llewellyn as one, imagining an eagle's giant wings spreading out widely to embrace his authors, his employees, his associates, his books, and even the Llewellyn headquarters itself. Carl thought of Llewellyn as an extension of himself, a part of his essence and purpose, and he felt a personal responsibility and genuine caring for the people who helped make all that great work possible.

One thing Carl did to benefit his employees as well as his customers was to always try to stay ahead of the technology curve, continuing to put the latest advances to use to better serve his customers and to make his employees' jobs easier and more efficient. One such technological wonder Carl obtained for the Llewellyn office was the DR-70 Astrology Minicomputer, first manufactured in 1978 by Digicomp.[330] No matter where they lived in the world,

---

329 From CLW personal files.

330 Green, "Computer Calculates Astrological Charts," and Computer History Museum, "Collections," "Artifact Details," "Digicomp DR-70 Astrology Minicomputer," http://www.computerhistory.org/collections/catalog/102746921.

readers could now easily obtain through Llewellyn a computer-generated detailed horoscope report that even included vocational guidance.

Improved technologies helped astrologers to be more accurate, and as a result, it was starting to be seen as a more credible science. Even President Ronald Reagan was regularly consulting with an astrologer, who used the same type of DR-70 Astrology Mini-computer used by Llewellyn to help the president predict the best times to fly, the best times to schedule press conferences, and the best times to sign treaties.[331] By the time Gabriel Weschcke was just eight years old, he took an interest in helping his parents at the Llewellyn offices and often pitched in by entering data into the DR-70 Astrology Minicomputer. Llewellyn's personalized horoscope service was in high demand. The DR-70 made possible more precise calculations of planetary positions and movements, which in turn allowed for more accurate astrological forecasting than had previously been available.

Llewellyn had also expanded their line of audiotapes, releasing a recording from Melita Denning and Osborne Phillips in 1981 titled *Llewellyn's Deep Mind Tape for Astral Projection.*

By utilizing the latest technologies and publishing books focused on the expansion of consciousness, Llewellyn gained a reputation for being revolutionary as well as evolutionary. Even Timothy Leary took notice. Former psychology professor at Harvard and self-proclaimed "evolutionary agent and cheerleader" for the "mind revolution," Leary was an outspoken advocate for psychedelics and an icon of the anti-establishment. He also happened to be friends with Steve Bucher, who was at the time serving as vice president of Llewellyn Publications. When Leary visited the Twin Cities in 1982, he met with local newspaper reporters at Bucher's house, where he was enjoying a casual breakfast. "In every city in the world"

---

331 Computer History Museum, "Digicomp DR-70 Astrology Minicomputer," http://www.computerhistory.org/collections /catalog/102746921

Leary commented, "there are large groups of people involved in communications, computers, the frontiers of science who are my friends. So when I come into town, it's an excuse for a party and to exchange important survival information: the best computers, best video, best drugs, best books." He generously added that "Saint Paul-Minneapolis has been promoted and is now number 3 in the hedonic age—the hedonic, aesthetic, erotic age," ranking just after Aspen and Beverly Hills, by Leary's estimations.[332]

Although the book business demanded a tremendous amount of time and attention, Carl put a lot of work and effort into other projects that would further provide for his family and contribute to the Weschcke legacy of innovation and ability. The Weschcke family owned forest land in northern Wisconsin, and in 1982 Carl and his younger brother Ernest dreamed up an idea for utilizing the land profitably yet sustainably.

Wood-burning furnaces in factories and homes were common, and with these furnaces came a host of problems. The wood was expensive, furnaces had to be manually fed, and they also created a great deal of pollution. Forever the improver, Carl realized there had to be a better way to do things. He and Ernest developed a way to compress sawdust and shavings from nearby sawmills into pellets that could be used as furnace fuel. Preserving trees by utilizing reclaimed materials, and producing about 50 percent less particulate pollution than coal, the pellet fuel offered a more environmentally friendly alternative to logs or coal. The wood pellets were also more convenient, as they could be fed into the furnace automatically, without requiring the human touch to stoke and feed the fire. The pellet fuel was much cheaper to produce than oil, natural gas, or electricity, and it could be sold for a lower price. If the supply of sawdust and scraps from the sawmills wasn't adequate for whatever reason, Carl and Ernest would do small cuttings and

---

332 Johnson, "Leary Taps Like Minds for Mission."

slashings from their own thickly forested acreage.[333] A large tract of the Weschcke's northern Wisconsin landholdings was sold to the state to be preserved as an addition to the Bibon Swamp Wildlife Area.[334]

The brothers opened business as the Forest Fuel Corporation, and soon their wood pellet fuel factory was up and running, with Ernest taking the lead as president and chairman. With wood stoves becoming more popular and similar pellet fuels being developed in other places, it seemed that fortune would favor the Forest Fuel corporation.

Plans for a second factory were even in the works at one point,[335] but the company struggled to gain profitability and the second factory was never opened. It was a disappointment that the business didn't succeed. But Carl always tried to embrace change, and if something didn't work out like he had hoped it would, it was never long before he was on to the next thing.

By the mid-eighties, Llewellyn was publishing its first crystal books. Among them was Phyllis Galde's *The Truth about Crystal Healing*, which she had written at Carl's encouragement and request. Carl reached out to rock and gem shops to market the new books on crystals, as there were not yet stores at the time devoted primarily to crystals. That was about to change. Soon, crystal shops were popping up in major cities across the country, and a new term to describe the "fad" phenomenon had been resurrected from decades before: New Age was once again a concept, only now the term meant crystals, meditation, yoga, and Zen. Somehow the original meaning of the term in reference to the dawning of the New Age of Aquarius, the age of enlightenment, had been reduced into a few practices that basically meant "metaphysical, but not witchcraft." No matter what people called it, plenty

---

333   Church, "Wood Pellet Firm."

334   *Stevens Point Journal*, "Big DNR Land Purchase Approved."

335   Church, "Wood Pellet Firm."

were buying into it. *Crystal Power* by Michael G. Smith was Llewellyn's top-selling title for 1988, outselling at the time even Raymond Buckland's *Complete Book of Witchcraft*, which was released two years prior in 1986 and remains to this day one of the best-selling and most respected witchcraft books of all time, with over a half million copies sold. Another crystal book called *Crystal Healing: The Next Step* had over 10,000 book orders prior to release, which was the largest number of preorders that Llewellyn had seen so far.[336] Where witchcraft had become the movement of the seventies, crystals and a modern perspective on New Age practices set the tone for the eighties.

The concept of chakras—a system of energy centers within the human body—also came onto the radar of more everyday Americans around this time, and Llewellyn had the books to learn all about it. One such book was the 1987 release of Anodea Judith's *Wheels of Life: A User's Guide to the Chakra System*. Sandra recalled how she and Carl had been on a business trip, and Carl had sat up late in their hotel room reading over a manuscript he had received for consideration from a prospective new author. Sandra had gone to sleep but was awoken several times in the night by Carl's unconscious exclamations of "This is good! This is really, really good!" Carl was right; *Wheels of Life* has become one of Llewellyn's top-selling books and is considered one of the best books for learning about the chakra system and how to work with it.

The eighties also saw some changes and expansions to the Llewellyn line of annuals. The *Sun Sign Book* was added in 1984; a few years earlier, in 1978, the *Planetary Daily Guide* that had been a part of the *Moon Sign Book* since its beginning was separated into its own annual called the *Daily Planetary Guide*.

Despite the popularity of his books, Carl found that he was still attracting the unwanted attentions of those who believed that his publishing company was a purveyor of evil. Andrew Olsen, a far

---

336   "BP Report," Knowledge Industry Publications.

right gubernatorial candidate for Minnesota, told his supporters that Carl Weschcke was nothing less than "Public Enemy Number One,"[337] and he vowed that if he were elected governor, the first thing he would do would be to "get rid of Llewellyn Publishing in Saint Paul, which is one of the leading purveyors of witchcraft and Satanism in this country."[338] Olsen never became governor, but business at Llewellyn continued to boom.

By the end of the decade, Llewellyn was publishing about three titles each month and generating more than 5 million dollars in sales each year.[339] B. Dalton alone accounted for more than $500,000 in annual sales.[340] Carl was also expanding his overseas markets, attending booksellers' conventions in America and Europe and forging connections with book distributors from around the world.[341]

Llewellyn's line of astrology books continued to do very well. With the greatest growth in serious-level astrology books intended for professionals, it wasn't unusual for a single title to sell more than 15,000 copies. Interest in tarot was also on the rise, and by that time Llewellyn had more than 100 decks in print. With the increase in inventory, the offices on Fourth Street became severely overburdened. Carl decided to acquire a larger space in a more modern building, and in 1989 Llewellyn was relocated into an old Coca-Cola bottling plant across the river from the old office.[342] Carl had actually dreamed of moving into the property for years, so it was especially nice to achieve this new milestone in Llewellyn history. Llewellyn quickly settled into the new space and was ready to head into the nineties at full force.

---

337   Skophammer, "Update: Carl Weschcke."
338   Byrne, "LaRouche Followers."
339   Skophammer, "Update: Carl Weschcke."
340   Sutin, "Father of the New Age."
341   Skophammer, "Update: Carl Weschcke."
342   Ibid.

From Anodea Judith:

Carl was like a spiritual father to me. I felt his wisdom, his love, and his incredible mind from all that he has studied over the years. Coming out to his home and seeing his library was very moving and inspiring to me. He was a pioneer and a creator of possibility.

He believed in me before anyone knew who I was and gave me my first chance, supporting my book *Wheels of Life*. Every time I saw him over the years, I felt great love. He made a difference in the world. We are all different because of him. He will be missed.

———————————

"Me and Carl" by Raymond Buckland:

My first contact with Carl was in 1969. At that time I had just written the book *Witchcraft from the Inside* and offered it to Llewellyn. Carl's interest at that time was in ceremonial magic rather than Witchcraft, however he was very interested in my book and wanted to publish it. This he did and this started a long relationship which lasted until his death in 2015. I became a fervent member of the "Llewellyn family," writing many books for them over the years.

Carl was an enthusiastic supporter of my work and was always ready with a suggestion for another book for me to write. In those early days I was living on Long Island, New York. I made the trip to Saint Paul a number of times, initially to Carl's beautiful home on Summit Avenue. I recall his marriage to Sandra and I remember a young Gabe running around the halls of the big house.

I was lucky enough to be invited to the Gnostica festivals that Carl held, there meeting many of the other Llewellyn authors, such as Brad Steiger (who remains a good friend) and astrologer Noel Tyl. With Llewellyn's later regular presence at the American Booksellers Association convention—which became Book Expo America—I was lucky enough to be frequently invited to appear at the booth, to read tarot cards, introduce new books, or similar. The high points of those gatherings were always the author dinners, which Carl sponsored. Everyone had to stand up, introduce him- or herself, and say a few words. It was a great way to meet new authors and to reconnect with old ones, and quickly became an excuse for stand-up comedy!

In the 1980s I was living in San Diego and frequently got together with a fellow San Diego resident and Llewellyn author, Scott Cunningham. One time Carl visited the city and took Scott and me out to dinner. Among the many things we discussed was the possibility of Llewellyn moving its headquarters to San Diego. Carl had been thinking about it and, of course, Scott and I tried to persuade him to do it. But it was not to be.

A book of mine, *Gypsy Love Magic*, was launched with a Gypsy costume party organized by Sandra. When my main Witchcraft book (generally known as "Big Blue") was published in 1986, the launch party was held at Carl and Sandra's home...a wonderful event, memories of which I will always cherish. This was all typical of the "family" atmosphere at Llewellyn, with Carl at the helm.

Both at the old Llewellyn dinners and overall with Llewellyn, Carl was very much the patriarch. He was the idea man, the person to go to with a problem, the confidante. I always very much enjoyed any time I spent with him. He was about four years my senior and in recent years we would tell each other that we would live to be over 100. Sadly, for Carl, this was also not to be (I still have hopes for myself!).

Carl was a very dear friend and I will miss him terribly. Happily there are many memories that will stay with me always.

———————————————

"Me and Ray" by Carl Weschcke:[343]

I've known Raymond Buckland for nearly a half century, and that's a long time. When you know someone that long, and particularly when he is both friend and—in this particular case—a working partner (which is the way I, as a publisher, work with an author), you know and care more about the person than his work.

Perhaps the fact that Ray and I are both Virgos and nearly the same age adds to the rapport that fifty years of friendship and association develops. When he sends me pictures of his office and workshop, I immediately identify with the efficient yet decorative layout and organization of his working equipment and materials. When we have discussed new publication projects, I appreciate the detail of his presentation and the examples of the proposed project. Ray is as much a craftsperson as he is a writer and researcher, and this shows up in the various oracles and card projects he has created over the years.

Ray is also an adventurer. That shows up in his flying. Ray doesn't fly an ordinary plane but has instead built his own "lite" aircraft that is little more than a hang glider with a motor. Flying such a contraption turns your body into part of the aircraft, and that means that every flight is a real adventure, for you are not separated from the element of air through which you are flying any more than a bird is separate from the air.

Ray has gone through the trauma of heart surgery, and that is a different kind of adventure. It's not one anyone seeks out, but the close encounter with mortality is transformative no matter your beliefs and other experiences.

---

343 Previously unpublished thoughts on Ray, October 18, 2006.

In addition to the many books on the Craft that most of you know about, Ray has written on other subjects and fiction as well. Fiction is different. Writing fiction, no matter the plot and the characters, always expresses the writer in new ways. All writing is an adventure in which the writer learns surprising things about the subject and about himself. I've always thought of it as "learning what you didn't know you knew," but fiction brings out an intimate encounter with yourself. Journaling does this too, but in a different way. With fiction writing you are employing your imagination in magickal ways—creating an alternate reality in ways similar to ritual.

As many readers know, the reality we create in our imagination is real, but different than the physical world in which we live—yet what is imagined sometimes appears in the physical world. All writing is transformative to the writer, and—hopefully—to the reader as well. We don't write only to inform, only to show "how it's done" or to just provide a collection of facts for reference.

A good writer provides his readers a transforming experience. In Ray's case, he has provided his readers with a great deal of information, much of it how-to and much of it factual reference material, but he has also provided his readers the kind of transformative experience that brings them into the magical dimensions he writes about.

That's my story about this man, Raymond Buckland, my friend, partner, and karmic brother. Reading Ray's books is to take a trip with him into new worlds of mind and spirit.

From Jean-Louis de Biasi:

In 2003 I became the tenth Grand Master of the Aurum Solis. Traditionally this function is a lifetime commitment. In a few words, I can say that the Aurum Solis is a Neoplatonist and Hermetic tradition coming from a long lineage called the Golden Chain. I knew that Carl had been the seventh Grand Master of this Order in 1987. This is very important because unlike other initiatic Orders, the Aurum Solis never split. This is a perfect example of unbroken lineage going from a Grand Master to the other. So immediately after my ritual consecration as Grand Master, I sent an email to Carl to respectfully introduce myself to him. A few days after, I received a very warm email from him sharing his views on this tradition. It was the beginning of a relationship that continued until his death. I met Carl and we had a regular correspondence by email and Skype. Carl was always informed of the internal life of the Order.

I had the privilege to have the foreword of my books written by Carl. It was always for him the opportunity to share his views on the subjects I was writing on: Freemasonry, the tarot, the Western Tradition, etc. It is worth reading them to understand Carl's beliefs in his late years.

In June 2010 we invited Carl to a congress of the Aurum Solis in Las Vegas. He participated in the congress through video conference. Attendees asked him questions and welcomed his insights on several essential subjects. During this event the Aurum Solis gave him solemnly a certificate of recognition for his amazing work.

During the years that followed, we shared a lot about spirituality, life, and politics. Through my words, you can easily understand that I have a great admiration for Carl. We can see a lot of people around us that are saying something and doing something else. Others are changing their views as they become famous, with less financial stress. I never saw such behaviors with Carl. He was always eager to find the best way to help people to develop their inner potential. He has been involved in the development of the human mind, magic, and spirituality all his life. According to Carl, knowledge and genuine initiations must be shared with the largest number of people possible. The number of emails I received from Carl talking about the urgency to help people to evolve are countless.

Even if I talked a lot with Carl about Freemasonry, he has never been initiated in this fraternity. Nevertheless, I strongly believe that Carl embodied the main principle of Freemasonry by being a real builder. Carl was someone always building something new, developing new ideas, talking about new books and projects. He was open to innovation and new technologies. He will always be for me a Grand Master and a builder talking about freedom and success while achieving a real "Great Work" in the alchemical meaning of this word.

Trade Shows

Carl found further exposure and opportunity for Llewellyn at booksellers' conventions and trade shows. Bringing together publishers, distributors, buyers, and others involved in the book trade, the conventions were a chance to network, shop for distributors, and form alliances. For Carl,

> *BEA and INATS use to be the highlight of the summer for me—to meet people, to celebrate our authors and products, to experience the action, and to see old friends.*

Llewellyn attended its first American Booksellers' Association Convention (now better known as BEA: BookExpo of America) in 1974. When Carl's sales manager informed him that the event was only for showing books and not for selling them, he wouldn't accept it. "That doesn't make sense to me," Carl told his sales manager. "I want to sell books." Selling books at the tradeshows simply wasn't done back then. Books were offered out for free as samples or merely put on display to pique interest. Carl wanted to do things differently. Carl recounted,

> *So we took book orders at the show, and everybody was aghast—except the booksellers. I had announced a special deal in advance: pre-paid orders would get a special discount. And B. Dalton came running over with their check! It was revolutionary! Dynamic! In three or four years, everybody was doing it.*[344]

The following year, Carl took Llewellyn overseas to the Frankfurt Book Fair, and soon he was making regular appearances at trade shows in Europe as well as in the US.

Llewellyn made its presence and its strength apparent in the world of books. Book conventions were generally rather dull and predictable, but Carl and his team preferred to shake things up. At one BEA convention held in DC in 1987, Carl and the rest of the Llewellyn crew donned green astronaut helmets in promotion of their new Star Wares astrology software and Matrix Astro Talk

---

344   Kelly, "Angels' Voices."

computers, drawing huge crowds of curious onlookers eager to find out what in the world they were up to.[345] At another BEA convention held in 2000 in Chicago, one reporter noted the "long, curling lines of people waiting to get their fortunes told by numerologists and aura, tarot card and palm readers at the Llewellyn Worldwide exhibit."[346] Unlike most other publishers at the book conventions, Llewellyn didn't just promote books, they also offered an experience.

At the International New Age Trade Show (better known as INATS), Llewellyn was known not only for bringing the best in books, but also for hosting the very best parties. While Carl wasn't much of a party animal himself, he took great pride and pleasure in orchestrating the most elaborate gatherings. One such party was Egyptian-themed, with Sandra and Carl and their guests donning ancient Egyptian-style costumes. Dancers provided entertainment, and the Weschckes were happy to enjoy their guests despite their exhaustion after a long day on their feet on the trade show floor. Creating opportunities for others to not only have a good time, but to also learn and network, was one of Carl's passions. He also enjoyed demonstrating the success and grandeur of Llewellyn Publications. "He was a showman," Sandra explained.

He also liked to show off his authors, and the trade shows provided a way to gain more prominence and exposure for Llewellyn's best writers. The trade shows also offered opportunities for those authors to connect one-on-one with Carl and other members of the Llewellyn team. Best-selling author Richard Webster recalled meeting Carl for the first time at a book convention overseas. Carl had invited Richard to share a drink of scotch, and Richard gratefully accepted. Feeling a little nervous and anxious to impress his publisher, Richard mentioned to Carl an idea he had for a book he wanted to write. Carl asked him how long it would take to complete

345 Wood, "Minnesota Booksellers Make Presence Felt."
346 Walsh, "BookExpo Covered Something for Everyone."

it, and Richard responded with what he thought was an overly ambitious underestimate of six months. Carl responded, "Can you do it in three?"

Carl simply had a presence, a way about him that strongly affected everyone around him and encouraged them to do their best. He also had a way of making others feel very welcome, whether it was at a convention, his home, a party, or the Llewellyn headquarters. Anna-Marie Ferguson, famed artist and creator of *Legend: The Arthurian Tarot* and *The Llewellyn Tarot*, recalled fond memories of meeting Carl and attending trade shows with him and his team:

> *A lasting impression of Carl came with my first visit to Minnesota in my early twenties. Carl gave me a tour of the Llewellyn building and introduced the staff. The last stop was the warehouse. What particularly impressed me was how pleased the warehouse staff were to see their boss. They came out from all corners and behind shelves with big smiles. "Hi Carl." "Hi Carl!" A sure sign of a good man and leader. It was a pleasure to walk down the aisles of trade fairs with Carl, for the same welcome would unfold as that first tour in the Llewellyn warehouse, with other publishing houses waving and calling out hello to Carl. My first trip down the aisle with Carl he wore a fedora hat, and given his trouble with his knees he also walked with a cane at the time, which actually added to his air of debonair.*

When Llewellyn first started going to the book conventions, the book industry wasn't really much of an industry. Many publishers were subsidized literary publishers, and Llewellyn helped lead the charge in transforming the book industry into a profit-based business. Carl recalled, "Publishing people were aghast at my actually selling books at the main convention, but they soon followed our path."[347] Today, Llewellyn continues to have a strong presence at numerous tradeshows and book industry events around the world.

---

347   CLW email to Melanie Marquis, February 21, 2011.

FATE

In 1988 Carl acquired *FATE* magazine, a Chicago-based publication dedicated to "true reports of the strange and unknown." The magazine had been around since 1948, published by Portland resident Ray Palmer and his associate Curtis Fuller. The idea for the magazine was inspired by a strange experience that had happened to a pilot named Kenneth Arnold in 1947.

Arnold had been flying near Mount Rainier, a glacier-capped peak rising 14,410 feet above the lush woodlands of Washington state, when he suddenly spotted something strange. Something was flying over the mountain, but it didn't look like any aircraft he had ever seen before. There were nine objects, all glowing with a bright, blue-white light, that appeared to be flying in a "V" formation over the mountain at extremely high speeds. An experienced pilot, Arnold estimated the flight speed to be about 1,700 mph—about three times the speed of today's commercial aircraft. A prospector who was working on a nearby mountain spotted the same objects around the same time that Arnold did, adding credibility to an otherwise unbelievable story. Arnold shared his experience with Ray Palmer and *FATE* magazine was born, featuring the pilot's UFO encounter as the cover story for the inaugural issue.[348] The story gained national attention, and is often credited with having sparked the UFO craze that continued into the decades that followed.[349]

FATE's pages were filled with articles examining paranormal phenomenon and first-hand stories of UFO encounters like Arnold's and other unexplainable mysterious experiences. Having been an avid reader of *FATE* himself, and an enthusiastic believer in the potential of the monthly magazine format, Carl was delighted to have the magazine under his charge. Circulation for

---

348 Peiken, "Addicted to *X-Files*?"

349 History.com, "Kenneth Arnold." http://www.history.com/topics /kenneth-arnold.

FATE was 100,000 a month at the time, a number that Carl hoped to increase by at least 150 percent within two years.[350]

"*FATE* not only tells you about what happens; it also explores the reality," Carl explained. "Phenomena happens, and it shakes up our belief system. We're always reshaping our perception of reality." Articles seen in the pages of *FATE* included tales of spontaneous human combustion, using computers to speak with the dead, levitation, psychic experiences, alien encounters, and more. Many of these topics were—and still are—thought of as "kooky," but Carl understood that there is often more to the strange than meets the eye, and that people are curious to know what that "more" is, explaining

> *The big message I want to get out is to be open-minded. I'm old enough to have gone through a time when most people thought of reality as a very limited thing. I remember my science teacher saying humans would never make it to the moon because the human body couldn't survive going up into space.*[351]

FATE addressed topics that others wouldn't, and it took those topics seriously. Although the subject matter was often unusual or controversial, the articles were well-researched, and readers who sent in personal experience stories were required to sign a notarized affidavit asserting the authenticity of their encounter.

Under Carl's charge, the magazine was eventually changed from a digest-sized publication into a full-size, full-length magazine format.[352] Phyllis Galde was soon hired as editor of the publication. Although Carl's goal of achieving a circulation of a quarter million was never to be met, *FATE* still made its impact on society and left the staff with some unforgettable memories. On one occasion, a man covered head to toe in red paint burst into the *FATE* offices with a garbage bag in his hand. He announced that the bag con-

---

350   Skophammer "Update: Carl Weschcke."

351   Peiken, "Addicted to *X-Files*?"

352   Forteana, "Fate," http://fortean.wikidot.com/fate.

tained a manuscript and asked if he could leave it there. The staff politely told him no, and fortunately he calmly left. "Some things are just so unexplainable, we don't even try," remarked associate editor Frank Spaeth.[353]

The impact of *FATE* magazine could also be witnessed in pop culture. The popular TV show *The X-Files*, for instance, was at one point suspected of getting ideas for its shows straight from the pages of *FATE*. One issue of the magazine featured a story on golems, for instance, and a couple of months later, golems were featured on an *X-Files* episode. Llewellyn's art director at the time, having heard a rumor that the *X-Files* creator was a *FATE* subscriber, became suspicious. He wrote to the show's producers on multiple occasions, asking for credit to be given to *FATE* for the story ideas. The letters were never answered, but *FATE* continued to inspire its readers nonetheless.

When *FATE* celebrated its fiftieth anniversary in the late '90s, Carl was asked how a magazine like *FATE* could survive that long. "No product, especially a magazine, can stay around for fifty years unless it meets a need," Carl said. "*FATE* recognizes that the impossible can be possible; we explore the unknown so that it can be known."[354]

Phyllis Galde had left her post as editor in 1994 in order to focus on her own publishing company, but in 1999 Carl persuaded her to come back and reclaim her old position in order to halt a decline in circulation. She did, and in fact she did so well in that position that she ended up buying the magazine from Carl just a couple of years later.[355] Today, *FATE* magazine has returned to its original digest size and is still running strong.

---

353 Peiken, "Addicted to *X-Files*?"

354 Forteana, "Fate," http://fortean.wikidot.com/fate.

355 Youngblood, "Determined to Succeed."

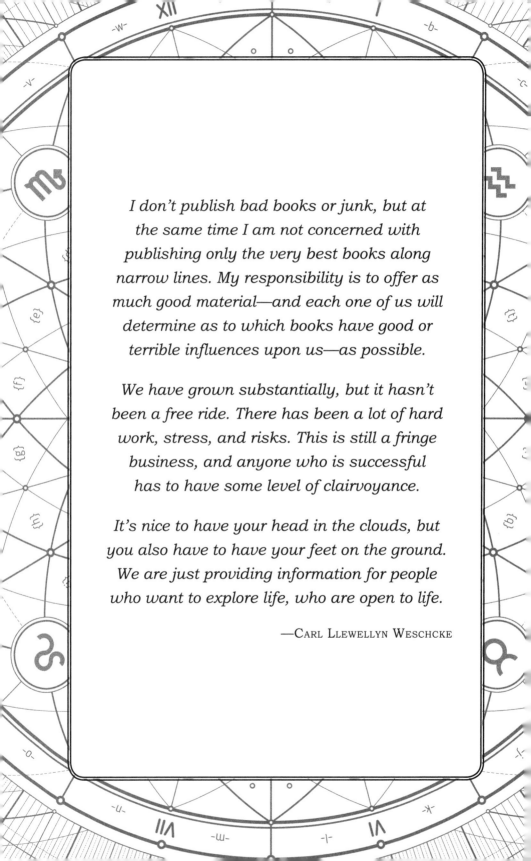

I don't publish bad books or junk, but at the same time I am not concerned with publishing only the very best books along narrow lines. My responsibility is to offer as much good material—and each one of us will determine as to which books have good or terrible influences upon us—as possible.

We have grown substantially, but it hasn't been a free ride. There has been a lot of hard work, stress, and risks. This is still a fringe business, and anyone who is successful has to have some level of clairvoyance.

It's nice to have your head in the clouds, but you also have to have your feet on the ground. We are just providing information for people who want to explore life, who are open to life.

—Carl Llewellyn Weschcke

Chapter 13

1990s

With the nineties came a whole new wave of modern witches. Movies like *Teen Witch* had helped pique fresh interest in a subject that had waned somewhat beneath the tide of materialism that had dominated the eighties. With the rise of the new "New Age" that had sprung out of the crystal craze, an invisible divide had formed between those who called themselves witches and those who simply enjoyed tarot cards, crystals, candles, herbs, and all the other things that witches often like. With witches being portrayed on TV by attractive, popular teens, witchcraft suddenly became more appealing, which translated into booming business for Llewellyn. More and more people were wanting to learn about witchcraft, just as they had twenty years prior in the seventies. And just like in the seventies, witchcraft still wasn't something that most people talked about openly.

"People are afraid to say what they believe," one anonymous witch told a newspaper reporter. "They're afraid to be true to their thoughts."[356] Decidedly, most witches were still "in hiding"

---

356 Penticuff, "For 'White Witch,' Craft Is About Love, Not Newts."

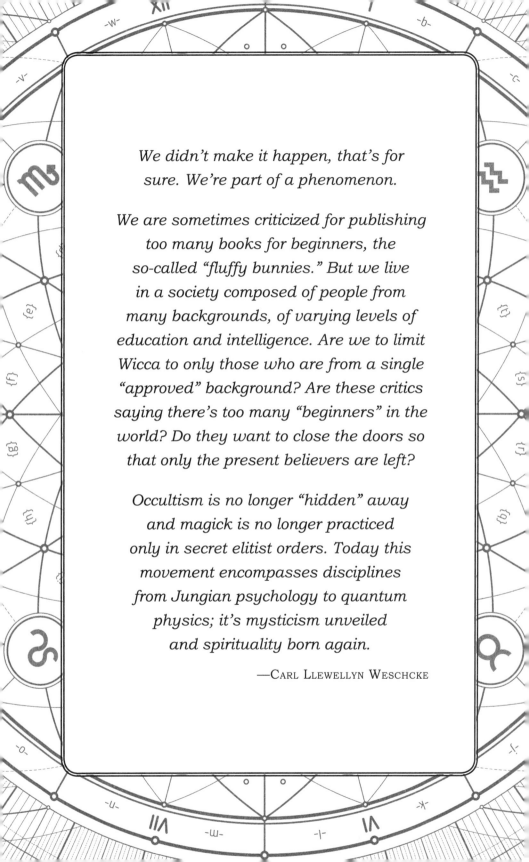

*We didn't make it happen, that's for
sure. We're part of a phenomenon.*

*We are sometimes criticized for publishing
too many books for beginners, the
so-called "fluffy bunnies." But we live
in a society composed of people from
many backgrounds, of varying levels of
education and intelligence. Are we to limit
Wicca to only those who are from a single
"approved" background? Are these critics
saying there's too many "beginners" in the
world? Do they want to close the doors so
that only the present believers are left?*

*Occultism is no longer "hidden" away
and magick is no longer practiced
only in secret elitist orders. Today this
movement encompasses disciplines
from Jungian psychology to quantum
physics; it's mysticism unveiled
and spirituality born again.*

—Carl Llewellyn Weschcke

in these days before the internet. If you didn't happen to already know that someone was a witch, it wasn't generally something you could ask about. For a generation of these closet-bound witches, Llewellyn books provided not only the information they needed to practice their craft, but also the reassurance that they were not alone in those practices. Even if you didn't personally know any other witches, the fact that so many witchcraft books existed, and the fact that you could buy those books from regular, everyday bookstores, was proof positive that there were indeed many other witches across the country and throughout the world.

Llewellyn's audience was rapidly growing, and so was their line of publications. Llewellyn had rung in the new decade with a brand-new annual added to its list: *The Magical Almanac*. Edited by Raymond Buckland, the book contained an assortment of everyday practical magick for everyday practical folks—some of whom might very well be witches. It remains one of Llewellyn's most popular almanacs.

Carl worked closely with many authors, suggesting books and sometimes whole series of books that they might write, and giving them the confidence, inspiration, and courage that they needed to do so.

One of Llewellyn's best-selling authors in the nineties was Ted Andrews. Born in Dayton, Ohio, in 1952, Ted had experienced clairvoyance as a child and often had dreams of animals and spirit guides. He grew up to become an animal keeper, with a deep love, respect, and understanding for all types of furry, scaly, and feathered friends. He published his first book with Llewellyn in 1989 called *Simplified Magic: A Beginner's Guide to New Age Qabala*. He quickly followed with many more titles, including books on the magick of images, names, dreams, and more. 1993 brought the release of the book that would prove to be Ted's best-selling title, *Animal Speak: The Spiritual and Magical Powers of Creatures Great and Small*. The book shows how to discover your spirit animal and learn to understand nature's signs. Between the time of the book's release and Ted's death from cancer in 2009, the book had sold more than 500,000 copies. By January 2018 the book had sold over 100,000 more.

Carl had decided that he wanted to be the leading source of mind, body, and spirit books not only for America, but for the whole world. In 1991, in reflection of this firm intention, he had changed the name of his company from Llewellyn Publications to Llewellyn Worldwide. Prior to this, Llewellyn had still technically been operating as a subsidiary of Chester-Kent, Inc. (the old family business name), but with the new moniker, Carl's publishing house was officially incorporated as Llewellyn Worldwide.

The name change was indeed a harbinger of what was to come. In 1994 Llewellyn introduced its first Spanish-language titles. It was a risk, but Carl was willing to take it in hopes of building up a global audience. Among the first publications was *Cómo Triunfar Sobre la Ansiedad y Los Problemas*, a Spanish-language edition of Guy Finley's popular self-help book *The Secret of Letting Go*. At first, Carl focused on selling the new Spanish language titles in Mexico and South America, but the US soon proved itself to be the biggest market for these newly translated titles. Although the book sales didn't come from where he thought they would come, Carl's gamble had paid off in a big way. The demand for Spanish- language occult books was so high in the US that major book retailers like Borders and Barnes and Noble kept Llewellyn's Spanish language line in stock,[357] offering books on a wide variety of subjects ranging from angels to feng shui. Within just a few years of launching the line, Llewellyn was publishing as many as ten Spanish-language titles each year.

The success of the Spanish-language titles as well as the increasing popularity of witchcraft boosted Llewellyn's profitability through the roof, and the publishing industry couldn't help but take notice. In November of 1994, with more than 7.4 million in

---

357   Kirch, "Llewellyn Looks to the Stars."

annual sales,[358] Llewellyn Worldwide was included in *Publishers Weekly* "Twelve on the Fast Track" list, a feature highlighting the year's best rapidly growing niche publishers.[359] This was a special honor for Carl, one of those "full circle" moments where you're able to see where you're at and look back and see exactly how far you have come. It's unlikely that Carl ever would have bought Llewellyn if he hadn't seen the notice advertising it for sale in an issue of *Publishers Weekly* so many years before, so it was a neat experience to have his publishing house honored in the very same publication that had started his journey. Llewellyn earned a spot on the list the next year, too, boasting a 51 percent sales increase for 1995.[360]

Much of those increased sales had come from witchcraft books. Nearly half of the Llewellyn list was comprised of witchcraft books, and these books were among their best-selling titles.[361] Llewellyn was proving that witchcraft was much more than a silly fad doomed to fade. Witchcraft was a serious study, and there were many serious students who wanted to learn about it.

The popularity of the New Age was also on the rise, and metaphysical shops were popping up all over the country. By 1997 there were over eight hundred such stores in the US. Carl added a new salesperson to focus solely on metaphysical shops, and as a result, Llewellyn's sales to these stores more than doubled.[362] Books on crystals, meditation, yoga, and Eastern mysticism were in high demand.

Carl had a knack for spotting trends, as well as a knack for experiencing fortuitously synchronistic flashes of inspiration. One such idea that came into being was the Tattwa cards. Carl worked in collaboration with Dr. Jonn Mumford to create something new

---

358   Penticuff, "For 'White Witch,' Craft Is About Love, Not Newts."

359   Wood, "1994."

360   Wood, "On Books."

361   Penticuff, "For 'White Witch,' Craft Is About Love, Not Newts."

362   CLW notes for *Ingram's Business Review*, 1997.

that he thought his readers would like—a set of cards based on the ancient Hindu system of Tattwas, which are said to be the five elements, or aspects, of Deity. Carl did most of the work on the cards, while Jonn worked on the accompanying book. *Magical Tattwas* was released in 1997, packaged as a book and deck set, which included the twenty-five colorful Tattwa cards of Carl's creation.

Seeing the success of so many metaphysical stores that had opened in recent years prompted Carl to get back into the shopkeeping business himself. He opened a Llewellyn kiosk at the Mall of America in Bloomington, Minnesota, that he called Moonspells. In addition to offering on-site horoscope casting, Moonspells kept about seventy-five different Llewellyn books and other products in stock. Carl's son, Gabe, had just graduated from Babson Business College, and he was in need of a summer job before continuing graduate studies in publishing at Pace University. Carl talked him into working at Moonspells, and Gabe spent many long hours at the kiosk that summer, casting horoscope charts, ringing up customers, and recommending books. The customers were great, but for some reason or other, the mall seemed to be playing Beach Boys music on repeat the whole summer long. It wasn't too unbearable, though. It was here at Moonspells that Gabe grew closer with his girlfriend, Michele, who also worked at the kiosk. It wasn't long before Gabe and Michele were married.

Carl dreamed of adding tarot readers and palmists at the Moonspells kiosk to provide more of a draw for potential customers, but the idea wasn't destined to pan out. Though the kiosk stayed busy, it didn't stay busy enough to make up for the high rent on the retail space. It simply wasn't financially viable or practical to keep it open, so the kiosk was closed before the idea of adding fortunetellers could be implemented.[363] Although brief, Llewellyn's presence at the Mall of America introduced scores of readers to their books and helped bring a new level of exposure and normalcy

---

363 Morphew, "Publisher Capitalizes on Interest."

that helped propel the company—and their subject areas—further into the mainstream.

By 1997 the humble mail-order publishing house founded by Llewellyn George was pumping out seventy-two new titles a year, three calendars, and five other annuals. Carl had teamed up with AirLift in the UK, Ingram's book distributors, and other companies to help him distribute his books worldwide. Llewellyn had expanded its line considerably, and Carl was looking for ways to expand it more. In addition to the mainstays of astrology, Wicca, and tarot, Llewellyn had come to be known as a leader in books on ceremonial magick, folk magick, healing and herbalism, parapsychology, UFOs, palmistry, Neopaganism, shamanism, yoga, Tantra, and more. Carl sought to broaden Llewellyn's offerings in the subjects of self-help, spirituality, Taoism, martial arts, Latin American religion and magick, African-based spirituality, and Celtic and North European systems. He had also expanded Llewellyn's divination line, publishing an average of four new tarot decks each year.[364] Many of these, like the Robin Wood Tarot published by Llewellyn in 1991, have since become fan favorites in the tarot community.

Like other Llewellyn products, Llewellyn's tarot decks found their way onto prominent display shelves and into storefront windows in metaphysical shops as well as mainstream bookstores across the country. The prominence and prevalence of Llewellyn helped bring a higher profile to tarot where it was finding increasing acceptance in the public view. "No longer confined to emporiums of the occult and mail-order catalogs, tarot cards are now prominently displayed in major chain bookstores," reported an article in the December 4, 1997, edition of the *Chicago Tribune*. A spokesperson for Llewellyn at the time explained that tarot was

---

364   CLW notes for Ingram's Business Review, 1997.

"no longer a niche market" like it had been in decades prior: "Tarot readers are the people next door."[365]

The growing popularity of tarot inspired Carl to seek out talented new artists to join his ever-growing Llewellyn family. When he learned about the work of artist Anna-Marie Ferguson, he was smitten. The artwork for Anna-Marie's *Legend: The Arthurian Tarot* was detailed and beautiful, and on a personal level, she made a strong impression on Carl and struck him as an absolutely brilliant individual. For all her sweet demeanor and mild manners, Anna-Marie was clearly destined for greatness, and Carl could see it clearly. He enthusiastically offered to publish her tarot deck but told her that she would need to write the companion book herself.

Having always fancied herself an artist and not a writer, Ferguson was hesitant to write the companion book for the deck, but Carl insisted that it absolutely had to be her, that she was the only person who could write it properly. Though uncertain she could do it, she complied with Carl's wishes—and naturally, Carl was right. Anna-Marie could indeed write; *Legend: The Arthurian Tarot* deck and its companion book, *A Keeper of Words*, was a hit. This title, as well as her *Llewellyn Tarot* that she created under Carl's vision and urging, continue to be popular amongst tarot readers and collectors decades later, and Anna-Marie has since become an award-winning artist of great acclaim.

From witchcraft-themed to multicultural, Llewellyn was publishing a wide variety of tarot decks in the nineties, and a wide variety of regular, everyday people were buying them. A 1996 article in the *Hartford Courant* reported that tarot card sales were at an all-time high. "America would seem to be on a kind of divination binge as the millennium draws to an end," wrote reporter Garret Condon.[366]

As mainstream as Llewellyn's tarots and books had become, however, they were still decidedly anti-establishment, and Carl

---

365 Lauerman, "Got a Problem?"

366 Condon, "The Future Market."

remained the figurehead and symbol of the revolutionary, non-conformist mindset that characterized Llewellyn's publications. Though he had tried repeatedly to step back from the spotlight, in 1996 Carl was still touted as "Saint Paul's best-known witch."[367] There were dozens of Pagan groups in the Twin Cities at the time, and the region was still known for having one of the highest concentrations of Pagans in the country. A 1996 poll of Minnesotans revealed that 24 percent of people in the state believed in witchcraft, a 10 percent increase in the number of believers when the poll was first conducted in 1987.[368]

With the increase in visible Pagans came a push for greater tolerance and equality toward witchcraft and other Pagan religions and practices. "Pagans are pushing for greater public acceptance, although they still experience considerable discrimination and fear of being known in public," one article reported.[369]

Naturally, Carl was never one to discriminate against Pagans. By 1997 Carl's staff had grown to a team of ninety, with many of those employees identifying as Pagans, Witches, occultists, diviners, herbalists, and astrologers. Proclaimed a reporter from the *Saint Paul Pioneer Press*,

> The people at Llewellyn Publications actually practice what they publish, and that could include anything from traditional Wiccan (witchcraft) ceremonies to ancient rituals of magic and divination.[370]

Carl explained his philosophy:

> We're unique in that we are a niche publisher deeply involved with the subject matter that we publish. Where possible, we continue to hire and train people who have New Age interests and skills. Yet, we never sacrifice good business practice and professional skills for the New Age belief system.[371]

---

367 Morphew, "Publisher Capitalizes on Interest."
368 Hogan, "Pagan's Progress."
369 Ibid.
370 Morphew, "New Age Publishers."
371 Ibid.

Carl went out of his way to create a family atmosphere and a culture of success at Llewellyn. Every Midsummer brought the annual employee picnic to the Weschcke home for a day of food, fun, and celebration. Carl liked to establish traditions, little rituals of sorts. He had employees feed each other cake and shower each other with money, envisioning a great future for Llewellyn and for themselves. Halloween brings costume contests, with each department vying for top honors. One year someone drove a real motorcycle into the Llewellyn offices as part of their costume! Yule brings a great party that always includes a toast to "Success! Success! Success!"—Carl's often-repeated mantra.

Carl always greeted and talked to those who worked for him, and he treated everyone as equals regardless of their position at the company. Carl would also take the time to send personalized notes of encouragement to employees, seeing interoffice memos as a wonderful opportunity. Carl explained,

> I use [memos] to develop vision and motivation in the people I've written them for. Written memos are much more magical than a phone call or a conversation. They're energy embodied in material form. And they're durable—you can refer back to them. Once you've read them, you can move on to using your own imagination.[372]

In 1998 Llewellyn issued its first-ever *Witches' Calendar*. The calendar featured important witch holidays, called sabbats, marked new moons and full moons, and even included a full copy of the Thirteen Principles of Wiccan Belief that had been drafted by Carl and his American Witches Council decades before. The first 25,000 copies of the calendar sold out in two weeks, and it quickly went back for a reprint.[373] The *Astrological Calendar* for 1998 was also a huge hit. Featuring paintings by UK artist Nigel Jackson as well as the usual horoscopes, planetary positions, and basic

---

372   Sutin, "Father of the New Age."
373   Llewellyn Worldwide press release, circa 1997–1998.

astrological information, the calendar had already sold more than 70,000 copies by the end of 1997.[374]

The year 1998 also brought the release of *Teen Witch: Wicca for a New Generation* by Silver RavenWolf. Offering young witches practical advice for taking a magickal approach to dealing with the demands of homework, parents, dating, and other issues relevant to teens, the book was an instant success, breaking the record for the highest number of pre-orders for any Llewellyn title to date. By the end of 1999, RavenWolf's book had sold more than 80,000 copies. The popularity of shows like *Charmed*, *Sabrina the Teenage Witch*, and *Buffy the Vampire Slayer* helped fuel the fire, as did the release of the Harry Potter book series and accompanying movies. More and more people were gaining access to the internet each day, which provided a source of information as well as a means of connection. Soon, everyone at least had a fantasy of what a real witch is, whether or not that fantasy had very much to do with the reality. A reverend from Atlanta hoped the rise in witchcraft practice was just a fad. "A lot of it's just people acting out, people riding the wave of something that's counterculture and crazy," said Reverend Rob Arp of the Mount Paran Church of God.[375]

As the decade drew to an end and the world prepared to enter into a new millennium, Llewellyn released a book about the predictions of Nostradamus written by an author named Stefan Paulus. Paulus was scheduled for a call-in interview on Ron Hunter's popular "Hunter into the Night Show" broadcast on WTIX-AM radio in New Orleans to talk about his book *Nostradamus 1999*. During the November 15 broadcast, the host had asked listeners to call in with any questions they had for Paulus, who would be joining them on the air in just a few minutes. The phone lines began lighting up within seconds, and about a minute and a half later, they all went out. The phone lines were all dead, and the host was left

---

374   Religion News Service, "Faith-Based Calendars."

375   *Atlanta Journal-Constitution*, "When an Old Religion Meets Pop Culture."

without the ability to take calls or phone his special guest. More than 30,000 listeners had simultaneously called in, which jammed the telephone lines and cut off phone service to a thirty-block area of New Orleans. A circuit overload had blown a transmitter.

Meanwhile, Paulus waited patiently by the phone, wondering why the station was not calling him for his interview at the planned time. As the minutes ticked by, Paulus decided to pick up the phone himself and call the station to see what was going on. He found, of course, that like everybody else, his call couldn't get through. When Paulus found out what had caused the phone outage, he commented,

> *I was in awe and shocked. I know the interest and the sale of the book has just been phenomenal since it was released, but to completely shut down phone service to part of a city is something perhaps even Nostradamus couldn't foresee! It's exciting to hear my research on the sixteenth-century prophet is impacting so many people.*[376]

Llewellyn would soon outgrow its space once more, and the mail order and shipping operations were moved into a separate warehouse in a nearby industrial park while the rest of the business remained at their headquarters in the old Coca-Cola building.[377] Carl was sad to see his team divided, commenting,

> *Of course, with computer and phone connections with the main office, everything was seamless—but still it was like a split in the family and we looked forward to eventually getting it all back together.*[378]

As the century drew to an end, Carl thoughtfully prepared and planned to take Llewellyn forward into 2000 and beyond.

---

376   Llewellyn Worldwide press release, 1998.
377   "Llewellyn Moves to a New Campus in Woodbury, Minnesota," March 1, 2005, https://www.llewellyn.com/about/event.php?id=715.
378   Llewellyn's Author Newsletter, November 2005.

From Silver RavenWolf:

Within every publisher is the soul of a writer. In an email to me in April of 2012, Carl wrote: "Hi Ho Silver! (an opening he used frequently in our correspondence, which made me laugh because I adored the Lone Ranger television series in the '50s) We're both writers at heart and I've waited all these years of building a business before I had my chance....and—hopefully—*Clairvoyance for Psychic Empowerment* (will be published) July 1, 2013—if I can just finish it all up by the end of this June."

Carl was one of the most amazing individuals I have ever met—always supportive, highly intelligent, and deeply caring of his family, friends, and employees. My experiences weren't just with Carl, but with Carl and Sandra as a strong and powerful team. Their conversations, alone or together, were always sound, thoughtful, and visionary. As an author and a person, I learned you could count on both Carl and Sandra to have your back when unusual circumstances (which sometimes happen in the world of words) occurred. And, when it is all said and done, it is the kind and courageous actions I remember, and how both individuals gave me (along with the family of Llewellyn employees) the opportunity to try to do my best. To me, there has been no greater gift in my life than the chance to live my passion. Thank you, Carl and Sandra.

From Calvin Green, Llewellyn employee:

When I think about Carl Weschcke, I only can say "Success! Success! Success!" This man I met and had a chance to be around, I never had a bad feeling around him. He always had a vibe that helped me understand that positive thought brings positive results. He never judged me by my size or the color of my skin. He had this attitude—the voice, the look that made you take notice—this attitude of just being a positive man.

"Success! Success! Success!"—It's not just about business, but it's about the content of our character. Carl Weschcke was a great man.

———————————

From Jean-Louis de Biasi:

Spiritual traditions and occult movements are not random manifestations of history. They are built by restless figures who have the strength and the will needed to move things. It is quite easy to talk, but really building something, developing original thoughts that can change people's lives, is rare. Carl Llewellyn Weschcke has been first a publisher but also an author, a magician, one of the founders of the New Age movement, and so much more.

In France I discovered Carl's work through the books published by Llewellyn Publications and the magazine sent all over the world. Back then, Wicca was considered in France as a dark and satanic movement. But the books coming from Llewellyn Publications, those from Scott Cunningham for example, were luminous and exciting. Every book was showing another reality of the occult world. France has always been conservative regarding its esoteric and occult organizations. Everything coming from abroad and more precisely from the United States was seen as exotic and superficial. These new movements were moved aside as proof of the lack of understanding of the Western Tradition. Some books about Qabalah were seen a little differently. However, everyone knew that most of this new and powerful energy was coming from one extraordinary man: Carl Llewellyn Weschcke.

He was the one driving these movements, finding the right authors fitting in his vision of the occult world, always several steps in front of everyone.

———————————

From Barbara Moore:

In 1997 Llewellyn hired me as a production assistant. I didn't want that specific job, but I very much wanted to be part of the company. I knew about Llewellyn because of my interest in tarot, but I had no idea of how important Llewellyn was (and still is) as a voice for knowledge, new ideas, alternate wisdoms, and things beyond visible or scientifically observable reality.

Carl was both a guiding and a driving force of Llewellyn. He was a visionary. Sometimes his visions or ideas thrilled me and sometimes—well, sometimes I just didn't get him. That is probably something that true visionaries deal with all their lives. Even if I didn't always understand him, he was always inspiring.

Because Carl was so knowledgeable and (at the time) very involved with the company, I always made sure I was very prepared for meetings so that I could answer any questions he had thoroughly and concisely. In that way, he helped push me to learn my subject matter and be the best I could be in my job.

As much as I appreciate Carl's leadership and knowledge, the more casual interactions we had will always be most precious to me. When I started at Llewellyn, Carl came into the office to work. Later, he began working from home but coming in for meetings. Sadly, toward the end of his life, he did not come to meetings, but he always sent his opinions about what we were discussing via email to be read aloud. He always had his hand in things.

After he started working at home, sometimes my partner (who also worked for the company) and I would go visit him at home during lunch. We'd bring lunch and eat together, talking about whatever topic interested him at the time and sometimes his past, which was fascinating. We usually brought him cake because he liked it but wasn't supposed to have it, or at least not much. The lunches, with the private chats and forbidden cake, were like sweet secrets that were only for us. I always left those lunches with my head spinning, full of ideas and possibilities and wonder.

Carl helped me to become a better editor and to have a mind open to wondrous potentials. Not many people get that from the head of the company they work for.

From Jonn Mumford:

In 1995, in collaboration with my good friend and publisher, Carl Llewellyn Weschcke, I began working on a book updating the original scrying cards based on the Tattwas as used by the Hermetic Order of the Golden Dawn founded 1887.

Carl had the copyright to addendums, provided by Israel Regardie, from the Hermetic Order of the Golden Dawn. These addendums were written instructions given to the members. From three of these manuscripts we were able to construct the system they used for clairvoyance, utilizing the Tattwa cards as known at that time.

Carl designed the cards and searched until he found a printer that could reproduce, to his genius idea, in fluorescent, luminescent colors never before used in printing.

The printer's first attempt at printing was a failure, as the complex inks required bled into each other. They called in an inorganic chemist to solve the problem, and the results were stunning!

The book was designed to update with everything I had learned from Ananda Ashram in South India and Bihar School of Yoga in the North so we could produce a system update for the twentieth and twenty-first century. I introduced into the manuscript a collection of original exercises never released before, using my knowledge of psychobiology combined with my Indian training regarding the Swara, or psychic flows. In 1996 I typed up the manuscript, sitting in Carl's Minnesota library. *Magical Tattwas* was published in 1997 with a set of twenty-five beautiful cards suitable for meditation, scrying, and divination.

Carl Llewellyn Weschcke was a master of ritual magic and knew well the power of imagination to release creative forces resulting in the observable crystallization, materialization, and actualization of desire through intention.

He was also a friend, patron, and mentor to me. He has given me a great deal, and my life would be less if he had not been such a pivotal part. *Magical Tattwas* would never have been born without his integral contribution, and to this day I miss this man who could come up with ten creative ideas every day—before breakfast!

From Cyndi Dale:

The first time I met Carl, I was nervous. I knew he was smart, intelligent, and all-seeing. What would I say? How would he perceive me? The fear cleared at my initial impression.

This is a soul that was present at the beginning of time. How fortunate we are that he walks amongst us, sharing the ancient truths he has carried forward.

Ever after, no matter what book I was working on for Llewellyn, I would shift into a state of gratitude for the knowing of this wise and bold soul. He isn't gone. A being as grand as him can never be really gone. I just hope I can catch ahold of the tiniest sparks of knowledge he is still sending our way.

———————

Carl bought *FATE Magazine* for Llewellyn in December 1988, publishing the best of the paranormal as well as subjects closer to Llewellyn's offerings.

Israel Regardie and Chic Cicero.

Sandra Tabatha Cicero and Israel Regardie.

Carl enjoying a beverage with Ray Buckland.

Occult luminaries Carl and Ray goofing around during a book show that featured one of Ray's gypsy magic books.

Carl with good friend, Llewellyn author, and former dean of Gnostica School Judy Hipskind Collins.

Carl in front of a hotel featuring Llewellyn for the American Booksellers Association's convention.

Llewellyn authors Richard Webster and Donald Michael Kraig—good ol' days with the good ol' boys.

Carl always worked hard representing Llewellyn at book shows.

Llewellyn authors Silver RavenWolf and Ted Andrews relaxing after a big day at a book show.

Carl with Anna-Marie Ferguson, a good friend and Llewellyn author and artist.

Carl celebrating with a group of Llewellyn authors: Edain McCoy, Richard Webster, and Joe Slate, who would be the co-author on most of the books Carl wrote in his later years.

Carl with Llewellyn author Konstantinos.

Family photo with Noel Tyl.

Carl with his employees during one of the famed Llewellyn Halloween parties.

Carl and Gabe.

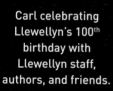

Carl celebrating
Llewellyn's 100th
birthday with
Llewellyn staff,
authors, and friends.

Carl and Sandra
pretending to relax.

Carl and Sandra on
vacation in California.

Carl, Sandra, and Gabe breaking ground in 2004 for the new Llewellyn building at 2143 Wooddale Drive in Woodbury, MN.

A beautiful portrait of Carl; it is this picture Sandra has hanging in her bedroom so she can talk to him every day, and it hangs in Llewellyn's main meeting room as well.

The Weschcke family: Carl and Sandra, Gabe and his wife Michele, and their daughters (L to R) Avery, Sydney, and Emily.

The crabapple trees starting to bloom at the building Llewellyn has called home since the summer of 2005; the company is still very happy here, surrounded by its lovely wooded campus.

Chapter 14

Llewellyn in the New Millennium

As the new century began, Llewellyn was already looking ahead to the future, planning new products, extending their networks, forging new beneficial alliances, and gearing up for the company's one-hundred-year anniversary. Carl wanted to do something special to celebrate this momentous occasion. Gabe was to begin working at Llewellyn that same year following his graduate program in publishing, which made the hundred-year celebration seem all the more significant. At Carl's suggestion, an expansive new section was added to the Llewellyn website highlighting the company's history. Carl provided much of that history himself, digging through decades-old files to find magazines, advertisements, and more from Llewellyn's earlier days.

Carl even took Llewellyn's birthday celebration to the Book Expo of America conference, bringing along a gigantic cake to be cut and shared right at the Llewellyn booth, where there were also free tarot readings, palm readings, and dream interpretations available. On hand to sign books and to join the celebration were Raymond

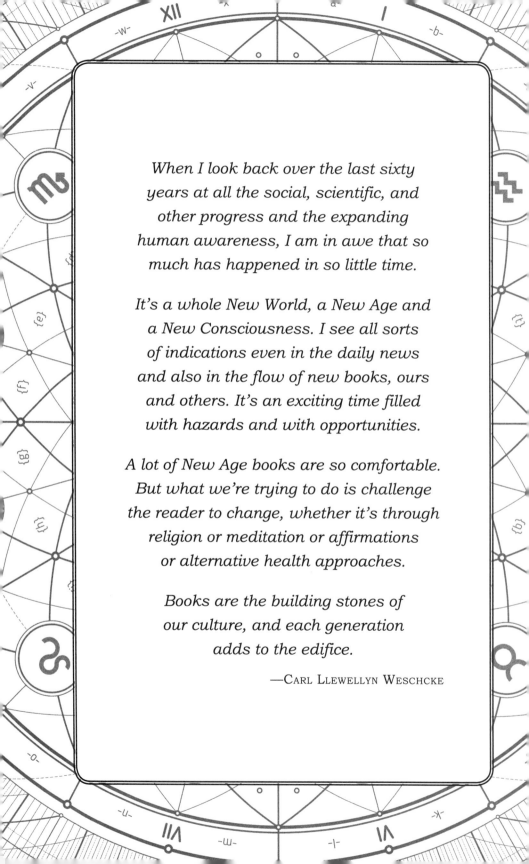

When I look back over the last sixty years at all the social, scientific, and other progress and the expanding human awareness, I am in awe that so much has happened in so little time.

It's a whole New World, a New Age and a New Consciousness. I see all sorts of indications even in the daily news and also in the flow of new books, ours and others. It's an exciting time filled with hazards and with opportunities.

A lot of New Age books are so comfortable. But what we're trying to do is challenge the reader to change, whether it's through religion or meditation or affirmations or alternative health approaches.

Books are the building stones of our culture, and each generation adds to the edifice.

—CARL LLEWELLYN WESCHCKE

Buckland, Dorothy Morrison, Silver RavenWolf, Karri Allrich, Konstantinos, Patricia Monaghan, Elaine Mercado, Dr. Joe Slate, and Richard Webster.[379] While the celebration was festive and Llewellyn indeed had a lot to celebrate, it was also a time of obstacles and uncertainty.

The start of the new millennium had brought challenges for the book industry. The rise of large chain bookstores and online retailers had forced many independent booksellers out of business,[380] and a nationwide recession in 2001 drove book sales down considerably. Even major publishers like Random House and Doubleday were forced to make cuts.[381] Llewellyn had a bit of an advantage over other publishers in that, while book sales overall were still lower than they once were, the number of people interested in books on magick and witchcraft continued to increase. By 2004 Llewellyn's gross sales were up to 16.5 million.[382]

A nationwide survey conducted in 2001 estimated that there were more than 433,000 self-identified Wiccans, Pagans, and Druids living in America,[383] though there were likely far more. The demand for books on witchcraft and Paganism was in no danger of ending, and by the middle of the decade, Llewellyn was publishing around 110 new books each year, along with fifteen different annuals, including several calendars and datebooks. They had over 600 books in print, with more than 100 tarot decks and kits as well as an ever-growing assortment of audio, video, and CD-ROMs.[384] Today Llewellyn has apps and websites instead of CD-ROMs and the cassette tapes of old, but the company's dedication to utilizing leading-edge technologies to better serve their readers remains unchanged.

---

379   *Publishers Weekly BEA Show Daily*, "What A Difference a Year Makes."

380   Wasserman, "The Amazon Effect."

381   Kirkpatrick, "Random House Begins Layoffs."

382   "Llewellyn Moves to a New Campus in Woodbury, Minnesota," March 1, 2005, https://www.llewellyn.com/about/event.php?id=715

383   Spencer Religious Groups, "Largest Religious Groups in the United States of America," Adherents.com, http://cdn.ca9.uscourts.gov /datastore/library/2013/02/26/Spencer_relGroups.pdf.

384   Kelly, "Angels' Voices."

Llewellyn brought competent editing and marketing to Pagan publishing, changing it forever.

—Jason Mankey, *Patheos*

The ascendance of his company has both mirrored and fueled the rise of New Age from an obscure fringe phenomenon to the remarkably mainstream movement it is today. And because of his influence, the Twin cities is one of the nations' major pagan population centers.

— Christopher Bahn, *The Rake*

Building for the Future

For quite some time, Llewellyn had been in need of more efficient, spacious, and modern headquarters, and Carl had been dreaming about such a place for even longer. The company was still split between their Saint Paul offices in the old Coca-Cola building fronting the Mississippi River and a large warehouse in an industrial park several miles away. Carl loved the old Coca-Cola building. He admired the old architecture and loved the riverfront location, but it just wasn't large enough to accommodate the rapid expansion of Llewellyn Publications. He may have found a way to make it work and stick with it, as he had been doing, but rumors had been circulating of developers planning to level the whole area. Carl and Sandra knew they would be forced to move out sooner or later, and they both agreed that sooner would be much more preferable than later.

Even though they were feeling the pressure to find a new space and to find it relatively fast, Carl took the time to find the perfect location for Llewellyn Worldwide. He first looked around for existing buildings that could be adapted, but he didn't find anything really suitable for his company's unique requirements. He decided it would be more effective to start from scratch and construct a new building that would fit the ideal of what he envisioned, so he set to work drawing up plans and designs for the new Llewellyn headquarters. "With input from all our staff, we began to design a floor plan that conformed to our workflow—acquisitions through to warehousing and shipment," Carl explained. Carl worked with an architect to develop and perfect the building plan, but few changes were made to the initial design that Carl and his team had created.

With the blueprints ready to go, now all Carl was lacking was a place to build. Again, he looked around the Saint Paul and Minneapolis area but didn't find exactly what he was looking for. A nearby suburb of Woodbury, however, seemed to have just the place, and the city was even willing to extend a tax break to Carl if he would relocate his thriving company there. The Weschckes made the purchase and construction soon began.

In July of 2005 Llewellyn moved into its new home in Woodbury. Carl, Sandra, Gabe, and a modest crowd of Llewellyn employees and friends were joined by the mayor of Woodbury for a ribbon-cutting ceremony to commemorate and celebrate the opening of a new era for Llewellyn and for Woodbury alike.

A vast stuccoed building covered with an array of multicolored Minnesota pebbles that slightly shimmer and sparkle in the rays of the sun, the Llewellyn headquarters welcomes its employees and guests through a celestial blue entryway, above which is painted a large Llewellyn crescent moon. "Now we have a superb and comfortable environment that is as enjoyable as it is efficient," Carl proudly announced in Llewellyn's Author Newsletter:

> Each department, and each person, is surrounded by the departments and people with whom they need to communicate for maximum creativity and efficiency. Every department has conference rooms, and our computer room, editorial library, and mail room are centrally located for the benefit of all.

There are even quiet spaces tucked about here and there in which employees can relax and gather their thoughts if they need a moment to de-stress throughout the workday.

Much of the surrounding 19 acres of woodland was left intact, preserved as wildlife habitat and enjoyed for its beauty and feeling of serenity that comes from wandering its hidden, narrow, winding paths that weave among tall old trees. Wild turkeys, a myriad of other birds, and even deer can be spotted in the Llewellyn woodlands.[385] In 2014 the vast lawn behind the warehouse was replanted with native prairie species, particularly those important to pollinators.

At 80,000 square feet, the building itself offers plenty of room for a spacious warehouse with floor to ceiling shelving stacked

---

385 CLW, Llewellyn's Author Newsletter, November 2005.

with boxes and boxes of books and more books. That wonderful "new book smell" of paper, ink, and binding glue permeates the air, giving the feel of being in an old library and in a mystical, magickal hall of knowledge all at once.

The new headquarters more than doubled Llewellyn's capacity, and the shipping department set an all-time record for the largest number of shipments in a thirty-day period just a month after they first made the move.[386] Carl was so excited for the new headquarters that to celebrate he even bought a new forklift for the warehouse, though he still hung on to the old forklift the company had been using for decades—suspected by one loyal employee to "probably be the oldest forklift in Minnesota" that's still in active use. "We've had that thing for years," commented longtime shipping department employee Calvin Green. "It has a steering wheel. They don't make them like that anymore. I think I might be the only one still here who can drive it, but it works! In fact, it works better than the new one sometimes, because the new one sometimes breaks."[387]

The mayor and the city of Woodbury welcomed Carl with open arms. "They're going to bring in good-paying jobs," said Mayor Bill Hargis, and indeed they did. Llewellyn continues to thrive in its Woodbury home with a staff of more than ninety employees.

Carl felt that the move to Woodbury represented "the opening of a new chapter" for Llewellyn, and he was feeling like the time had come for him to open up a new chapter for himself, as well. He found himself in the strange and unfortunate predicament once again of having accidentally grown much older through the years. With the increasing mobility issues and muscle pains that often come with older age, it had become more challenging and difficult for Carl to come into the office every day. He started working from home more often, but he would come visit headquarters as much

---

386 CLW, Llewellyn's Author Newsletter, November 2005.
387 Personal interview with Calvin Green, November 2017.

as he could. While he would still extend his hand and his heart in guidance of the company, Carl knew he could trust others to manage the day to day operations, and with Sandra at the helm and his son already showing himself to be clearly capable of carrying on his legacy, Carl knew he could take a step back and let others take the lead.

Bill Krause was hired as acquisitions manager and associate publisher, and he quickly proved to be a great asset to the company. Carl communicated often with Bill, discussing ideas for product development and strategic planning. Bill and Carl were not only publisher and chairman, but they also developed a lasting level of friendship and trust. The two men recognized in each other a high level of intelligence, and they appreciated that and made the most of it. Carl could churn out ideas by the baker's dozen, and Bill could pick out the best of the batch and suggest which ones he believed had the greatest risk of falling flat.

New imprints had been launched: Flux for young adult fiction and Midnight Ink for mysteries.[388] Both imprints published award-winning titles, including *Blue Is for Nightmares* by Laurie Stolarz. Stolarz's subsequent Blue Is for Nightmares series was hugely successful and helped to establish young adult fiction in the marketplace as its own unique genre. In addition to the new imprints, Llewellyn continued its tradition of publishing quality books on astrology, meditation, magick, Paganism, witchcraft, and other popular occult subjects of interest. Llewellyn George's *A to Z Horoscope Maker and Delineator*, originally published in 1910, was reissued as an expanded and revised edition. *Mapping Your Birthchart*, an astrology book that came packaged with a CD-ROM to allow readers to create their own horoscopes, was also launched to an enthusiastic response, with the first print run quickly selling out. The Spanish-language titles also continued to flourish, with an average of sixteen Spanish language titles published each

---

388 Nelson, "A Supernatural Plan."

year.[389] Llewellyn had also expanded its line of tarot, having forged at the start of the decade a mutually beneficial alliance with Lo Scarabeo, a tarot and oracle deck publisher based in Italy. Llewellyn's tarot specialist Barbara Moore explains:

> *In January 2000 Llewellyn partnered with Lo Scarabeo, an Italian tarot deck publisher. The main aspect of the partnership was that Llewellyn would be the exclusive distributor of Lo Scarabeo products in America and Canada. Such a relationship may seem cut and dry. Lo Scarabeo makes their decks; Llewellyn sells them. But our relationship is so much more than that. Mario, co-owner of Lo Scarabeo, comes to Llewellyn at least twice a year to discuss past sales, analyze successes, discern where things could be improved, and share future ideas... Several folks from Llewellyn attended Lo Scarabeo's thirtieth anniversary celebration held in Italy. After working with each other for nearly twenty years, we've all grown very close.*
>
> *We are united in our love of tarot and our desire to continually push the boundaries of what tarot was, is, and will become. Lo Scarabeo is one of the most creative and nimble companies in publishing. Our relationship is more than just business.*

The partnership made it possible for Lo Scarabeo to reach a much larger market, and it made it possible for Llewellyn to bring a much larger selection of tarot and oracle decks to its customers. Ever since Carl had acquired Llewellyn way back in 1961, the company has catered to a wide variety of interests, tastes, and abilities. Best-selling beginner-level books like Silver RavenWolf's *Solitary Witch*, which sold more than 65,000 copies in its first year alone, show up in Llewellyn catalogs and bookstores alongside more advanced and scholarly titles for experienced practitioners and researchers. No matter what the book is about or how well-known or as-yet-unknown is the author, every new Llewellyn title is given a half-page ad in the catalog when the book is released,

---

389 Kirch, "Llewellyn Looks to the Stars."

providing equal opportunity, potential, and platform for debut authors and best-selling authors alike.

While Llewellyn would receive criticism over the years for publishing books that some consider to be lacking in depth or too geared toward the beginner, the success of the titles with more mass-market appeal is what has enabled Llewellyn to take a chance on publishing the deeper-level, advanced, experimental, and controversial books that, by nature, have smaller audiences and much less market potential. Llewellyn's best sellers make it possible for the company to publish more new books and also maintain a strong backlist with hundreds of titles. Having been around for well over a century, Llewellyn has the tenacity, hope, and foresight of a seasoned warrior, having witnessed many backlist titles flounder for years, only to become suddenly popular much later. Sometimes a book won't do very well in its debut but over time will slowly accumulate impressive sales through its lasting and steady appeal. Sometimes books are written before the world is quite ready for them, but once the world becomes ready, there those books are, readily found on Llewellyn's list for a new generation of readers. It's always sad to see a good book go out of print, so Llewellyn strives to keep their titles in circulation for as long as is feasible.

While Llewellyn is now in the next town over from Saint Paul in the picturesque suburb of Woodbury, and although the Gnostica Bookstore and School of Self-Development have long since closed their doors, the Twin Cities continue to be a hub for the magickally minded. Many of the students who first learned from Carl or who first discovered their spiritual path through a Llewellyn book have gone on to start covens, groups, magick schools, Pagan festivals, and occult stores of their own, making the Minneapolis/Saint Paul area truly one of the biggest centers for occult learning, Paganism, New Age philosophy, and witchcraft in the country. In 2007 there were estimated to be at least 136 Wiccan or Pagan groups in the Twin Cities region.[390]

With so many Pagans and witches around, one might think that misconceptions about these practices and hostility toward those who practice them would be a relic of the past, yet prejudices ensue just as they have always ensued. With each victory won, a new battle often arises. As the new millenium found itself well underway, witches and other Pagans were fighting for equality, pushing for greater tolerance and demanding fair treatment and equal rights. Pagan Pride events and similar festivals sprang up not only around the country but around the world, bringing together all types of Pagans to show the general public what Paganism really is all about. Pagans also fought a battle with the US government, with Selena Fox of Circle Sanctuary leading the Lady Liberty League in a campaign of public education, letter writing, phone calls, and rallies that eventually accumulated in a win for witchcraft. The Veterans Administration had historically and repeatedly refused to honor the wishes of Pagan soldiers who requested that their graves be marked with a pentacle or other symbol befitting their religion. As part of the effort, the Thirteen Principles of Wiccan Belief that Carl had been so instrumental in creating decades before with the Council of American Witches was submitted by Selena Fox as supporting evidence to help Pagan veterans win their rights. Rallies were held all over the country, and in the spring of 2007, just before the case was slated to go to federal court, the Veterans Administration agreed to add the pentacle to its list of religious symbols that could be placed on soldiers' gravestones in federal military cemeteries.

Carrying on Llewellyn's tradition of activism and social awareness, Llewellyn's own acquisitions editor Elysia Gallo was part of a rally and ritual on the steps of the state capitol in favor of the Pagan vets. When the pentacle was officially approved, she told

---

390 Miller, "Circle of Hope."

a reporter, "Finally, Wicca and other forms of Neo-Paganism are being taken seriously as valid spiritual paths."[391]

Finally, indeed. Since its emergence in America beginning in earnest in the mid to late sixties, witchcraft and other paths of Paganism have met with a relentless wave of criticism, misrepresentation, and misunderstanding. The tireless efforts of Carl, Selena Fox, and many others throughout the decades to break down barriers and correct misconceptions regarding Pagan beliefs have resulted in a greater tolerance and basic common understanding of what Paganism and witchcraft is and what it is not. Regardless, the forces of ignorance are persistent, and every generation, every decade, seems to have its dictators who adamantly cling to misguided philosophies and outmoded ways of thinking and being that seek to suppress and limit opportunities for anyone who doesn't fit the current societal mold of convention. Government assurances can turn into empty promises, and minds can close just as easily as they can be opened. As Carl learned through his active involvement in the civil rights movement of the fifties and sixties for over a decade, the struggle for civil rights of any variety isn't something that's won and done; it's a constant and repeating battle that must be won again and again by each individual, by each generation. The groundwork laid by Carl and others who have stood up for equality and civil rights for not only Pagans but for all people everywhere is a win in our favor on which we can build and leap. It's the business and responsibility of anyone who truly believes in freedom and opportunity for all, to be ready to rebuild again and again what the inevitable wrecking ball of ignorance and oppression seeks to destroy.

The myriad of books that Carl has brought into the world over the years have helped generations of witches, Pagans, occultists, New Agers, and other freethinkers to find their voice so that they too can build upon what has been started, and, with luck, succeed

---

391   Miller, "Wiccans Celebrate Settlement."

in building something that's entirely new and improved. Carl never presented himself as having all the answers, and it was his dear and sincere hope that by inspiring and enabling others to learn all they could to become more than they ever thought possible, that those same educated and enlightened souls would be able to make giant evolutionary strides into the future and lend a hand to those in need of a little more lifting up. It was Carl's belief that ignorance and prejudice would one day die with the past, opening us up to a New Age where each one of us can live as we are truly meant to be, where human violence is a forgotten concept and discrimination is recognized as stupidity. Carl was about to embark on a new adventure that would offer him an abundance of opportunity to help manifest that vision by offering encouragement and wisdom for the generations to come.

From Najah Lightfoot:

When I set upon the path of the Craft and the Old Ways, I was alone. I had no community, teacher, or circle to follow and guide me. All I had was the trusted name of Llewellyn.

The Llewellyn publications became my family and trusted resource. All I read from the books and articles became my circle, my place where I went for knowledge and sanctuary. In short, if I read it in a Llewellyn publication, I trusted it. I knew if I followed the guidelines or instructions of what I was reading, magick would become real and the ways of the Divine Mysteries would open and reveal themselves to me.

While I absorbed every word on the page in the Llewellyn books, there was a small but burning dream, a secret desire, that maybe one day I too could write for them. Writing for Llewellyn would bring me full circle, from the lonely novice and seeker to one who could give back, especially to those alone on the path, whose only friends could be found in books.

My dream came true in May 2013 when I received my first writer's contract as a contributing author for *Llewellyn's 2015 Witches' Companion*. It was as if my soul had burst open. My heart was on fire, alive with joy and the prospect of what might lie ahead for me. I was touched beyond words. And to make things even sweeter, the contract arrived on my birthday.

I could never think about Llewellyn without my heart pumping love to Carl. He was like my godfather, my grand-daddy. I'd never met him, but he always felt close to me, like I could just reach out and talk to him. So one day I decided to send him an email. I wanted him to know how much Llewellyn meant to me and how thankful I was to be one of their contributing authors. I had no idea if he would actually see or read my email. I didn't even think about getting a response, as I knew he must be a very busy man. My intent was simply to say thank you.

You can imagine my surprise four days later when there was a response from him in my inbox.

Carl thanked me for writing him. His gratitude was overflowing to his family, his staffers, to all the authors and writers, as well as to all the customers and readers. He considered us all his family. He spoke of how "we are all members of a great community of people who believe in themselves and that they can make a better world for all."

His words have stayed in my heart. They flow within every page and spur me on as I now write my first book for Llewellyn's readership.

I keep Carl's email close by as well as his picture on a candle I created for him. He is always with me, gazing at me, spurring me on to do my best, encouraging me that our words are necessary and, most importantly, that they matter.

From Michael Night Sky:

Carl will always be an inspiration to me and my magickal studies, for the whole world of modern magick may not have been the same without Carl's contributions: his life's passion for book publishing and sharing occult knowledge, his belief that we are capable of making a better world for ourselves and each other.

How often do we get to forge friendships of substance in this lifetime? When we do, we cherish them, as we should. I am happy to say I made a friendship with Carl, my occult super-hero. I am sure each person who has admired Carl's work with Llewellyn Publications has a different opinion on what Carl's greatest works are. In my book, we would not have a New Age of modern magick and witchcraft without Carl's contributions to the arts. In simple words, he gave us books to read, yet on a deeper, more subtle level, he gave us magick to use. Carl was a great friend.

———————————

Chapter 15

Carl Never Retires

've got 10,000 books I haven't read. I've got books I'd like to write," Carl told a reporter in the months leading up to his official "retirement" from Llewellyn Worldwide in 2005. In truth, Carl had a book collection of over 25,000 volumes and was well aware of the unlikelihood of his ever getting around to reading them all. He had more book ideas swirling around in his head than there will ever be enough paper in the world to capture. Still, taking a step back from Llewellyn was a lot easier said than done.

For decades, Carl had found tremendous joy and passion in building up his publishing company. He was so used to working so hard for so long that now, when he was supposedly retiring at the age of seventy-five, he found it virtually impossible to stop. In spite of the repeated urgings of his family and friends who felt that he could stay healthier if he could only slow down, Carl just couldn't seem to help himself from doing as much as he was superhumanly capable of doing. On a questionnaire that he filled out in 2008 for his sixty-year high school reunion, Carl wrote:

> *I'm still working full-time, meaning seventy hours, more or less, weekly. As chairman of Llewellyn Worldwide I've shifted most*

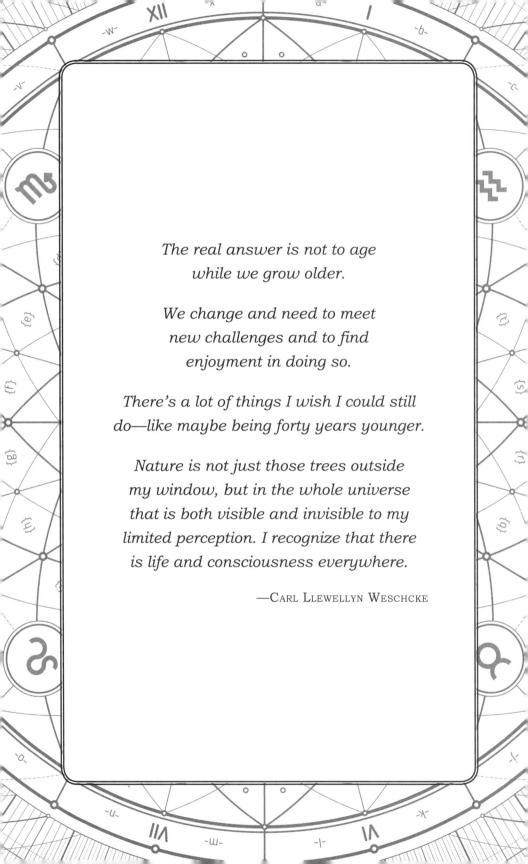

The real answer is not to age
while we grow older.

We change and need to meet
new challenges and to find
enjoyment in doing so.

There's a lot of things I wish I could still
do—like maybe being forty years younger.

Nature is not just those trees outside
my window, but in the whole universe
that is both visible and invisible to my
limited perception. I recognize that there
is life and consciousness everywhere.

—CARL LLEWELLYN WESCHCKE

of my work to writing—promotional articles, special advertising copy, and books. In addition, I work actively with our acquisitions department in planning and developing new book and product lines, working with particular authors on new projects, and otherwise foreseeing future trends and developing strategies to meeting new opportunities and challenges.

Even though he found plenty to do to be useful and stay busy, working from home was a huge change for Carl, who had always been so actively involved, going into the office daily and traveling frequently. "I do miss the conferences and trade shows," he admitted, "but after fifty years of pushing and leading, it is good to just write and think and study." He was extremely proud of his son, Gabriel, and after one occasion of seeing his son's business skills in action when he negotiated a partnership with IBS Bookmaster to help streamline operations and expand product lines, Carl remarked, "Gabe did a great job. It is so nice for me to sit back and see it all continuing—onward and upward!"[392]

While Carl was delighted to see his son carrying on his legacy so capably, and while he had every confidence in his wife, Sandra; his publisher, Bill Krause; and every other member of the Llewellyn crew, retiring from active duties was challenging. He had dedicated his life to the company and to its mission of expanding consciousness, and staying at home most of the time instead of getting out and about more regularly had the ready potential to become dull and depressing. He made the shift by recognizing his priorities and reinventing himself, appreciating and enjoying who he was and what he could do while continuing to strive to become something more.

Top on the list of priorities remained his wife and family. Every day, one of Carl's greatest pleasures was in spending time with Sandra, sharing breakfast and dinner together and talking about

---

392   CLW email to Melanie Marquis.

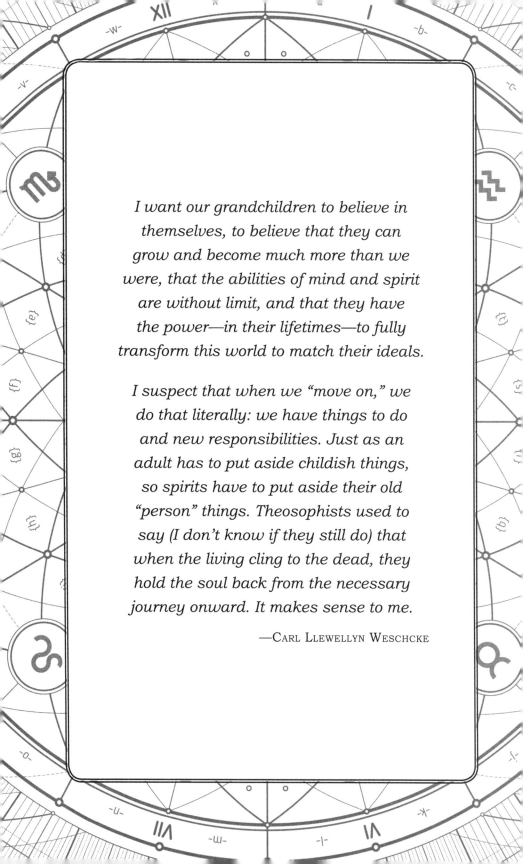

I want our grandchildren to believe in themselves, to believe that they can grow and become much more than we were, that the abilities of mind and spirit are without limit, and that they have the power—in their lifetimes—to fully transform this world to match their ideals.

I suspect that when we "move on," we do that literally: we have things to do and new responsibilities. Just as an adult has to put aside childish things, so spirits have to put aside their old "person" things. Theosophists used to say (I don't know if they still do) that when the living cling to the dead, they hold the soul back from the necessary journey onward. It makes sense to me.

—Carl Llewellyn Weschcke

their days. "She drives like a twenty-year-old and babies her cat," Carl remarked. "I am a lucky man."

Having watched his son grow up and carry on his publishing legacy was a true joy, and witnessing his grandchildren growing to be sensitive, smart, and thoughtful individuals under the loving care of their mother and father was something that truly filled his heart with love for them and a feeling of pride. Carl wasn't able to get around and travel anymore like he used to, but he could still look forward to visits with the grandchildren, who truly meant the world to him. He delighted in watching Sandra get down on the floor to play with the children, just as if she was a kid herself. His eldest granddaughter would often offer to help him to his chair, helping him up and down just like Sandra would. Carl found this incredibly sweet and caring, exemplifying her loving nature and natural instincts to be compassionate and helpful.

With all his great passion for books and all the other causes he championed in his life, all that was relatively insignificant when compared to his love for his family, to the simple joys of raising a child into a capable adult, watching grandchildren play, and sharing moments together with the love of your life. Carl walked his chosen paths in life with full gusto, but he was always mindful of the fact that the joy and meaning was in the journey and in the love he felt for those who chose to walk along with him in his life's adventures.

Carl also found pleasure in working on his psychic and magickal development. "There's a lot of things I want to practice that I only studied in the past,"[393] Carl said. Crystal gazing was among those practices, and he began a regular program to exercise and hone his abilities. He also practiced and experimented with lucid dreaming at the request of his pen pal and friend Stephen Brewster of Manchester, England. Stephen had first contacted Carl after discovering his profile on Facebook (which, incidentally, Carl referred

---

393   CLW email to Melanie Marquis, February 21, 2011.

Weschcke's wife, Sandra, receives far less credit than she deserves for the important part she has played in his life. It is hard to imagine the more mellowed, peaceful Carl Weschcke of later years without the woman who contributes so much to his life.

—LETTER TO THE EDITOR BY MATTHEW WOOD, *STAR TRIBUNE*, MAY 20, 1986 to as an "empire of nonsense"), with the idea in mind that he might ask Carl if he knew anything more about the mysterious writer Ophiel, of which very little could be found on the internet. Somehow or other, their emailed discussions morphed into lengthy conversations about magickal theories and psychic techniques, with Stephen eager to experiment and even adventure on the astral "inner planes" if Carl was willing. Carl liked his enthusiasm, and it pleased him to see a modern occultist who was actually interested in figuring out how things work and why, and who was willing to experiment and perhaps face failure for the cause of something cool and mystical possibly occurring. Whether or not any of Stephen and Carl's attempts to meet in the astral realm were successful will remain unknown, but the friendship was significant to Carl in that it allowed him a chance to talk about the ins and outs of one of his favorite topics: the expansion of human consciousness and how the mind might be utilized to the benefit of one's self and others. He enjoyed debating with Stephen about whether or not lucid dreaming had any advantages over astral projection or whether it was indeed a similar concept or something entirely different.

Although Carl didn't much care for precise definitions and categorizations of anything magickal or mystical, he did, however, consider himself to be a Wiccan at heart, which he thought of as a "true, modern Nature Religion."

> I practice Wicca as I look outside my office window and see the trees swaying in a gentle breeze, as I listen to the sound of the waterfall and the song of birds. I practice Wicca when I talk to my granddaughter, and when I recognize that I need to lose weight and do something about it. I am Wiccan in all that I try to do without benefit of seminary study or IRS approval. I am Wiccan every day of the week and every hour of the day. I am Wiccan because I seek to add beauty to my environment. I am Wiccan because I try to act with awareness and responsibility and knowledge in whatever I do.[394]

---

394 Night Sky, "Carl Llewellyn Weschcke."

From Stephen Brewster:

Some very brief background on me, as I am just a regular guy and not a big player in this whole story. I am a forty-five-year old male living in Manchester, UK. I'm just a quiet, modest, working-class guy and currently work in a food factory as a machine operator. As far as knowledge on occult/metaphysical/Wicca matters go, I am just a basic rank amateur. I should add that I am also a natural lucid dreamer and have been having lucid dreams since I was young, perhaps seven or eight years old. Lucid dreaming and astral projection have been a huge part of my life.

I first came across Ophiel's *The Art and Practice of Astral Projection* book when I was about seventeen or eighteen years old, and I couldn't put it down. With Ophiel's book, and others he wrote, I slowly learned about astral projection, kahunas, the occult, and first heard the name Carl Weschcke! He was for a long time just another name in a book for me, and it honestly didn't occur to me to personally write to him, since I wouldn't have even known what to say to him.

With the arrival of the internet, I slowly learned about computers and eventually joined an Ophiel online discussion group. I became an active member for many years whilst I searched for the "lost" Ophiel writings. Many of Ophiel's writings were issued in very small print runs on materials prone to deterioration, and there are still several works (including a series of cassette tapes) that have yet to turn up but which are known to exist because they are mentioned in other Ophiel writings. As was the experience of many other Ophiel students who had searched for these manuscripts, I too had discovered that it was and is often a long, hard slog finding them!

Sometime around the beginning of 2011, Carl Weschcke suddenly appeared on Facebook for only a very brief time. I contacted him and told him of my interest in Ophiel, whom Carl had known. I knew this from something Ophiel had written in his books. During our conversations I asked Carl if he had any of Ophiel's writings/materials that I could share with other Ophiel students. I wanted to make these rare teachings available to the benefit of anyone interested, just as Ophiel had intended and before they were potentially gone forever. Carl was really happy to help, digging through stacks of old files that had been packed up for years to unearth all he could find that he felt might be of use or interest.

We became online friends, and Carl, as I would call him after a while, gave me his email address. We would discuss Ophiel as well as other topics like the occult, lucid dreaming, astral projection, world events, family, food, and allsorts.

I honestly don't know why Carl took time to write to me when he was so busy and time was so valuable for him. But to Carl, the little guys, such as me, seemed to have the same worth as any top occult bigshot or important person. He sent me some of Ophiel's work, as I said, and he made special mention of the hard work his postroom staff had done to get them to me, and I asked Carl to thank them from me also. I've worked in a postroom myself and know it can feel like the lowest rung of the ladder so it was nice of Carl to recognise and appreciate the little guy, but as I say, that is the kind of man I found him to be! Lovely guy, as many who knew him will know. Shame I never got to physically meet him.

———————————

Carl had witnessed first-hand how the magickal and Pagan communities had grown over the years, how interest in occult subjects waxes and wanes but always endures. He had witnessed the development of a great diversity of magickal practices and spiritual disciplines. He experienced what it was like to be an occult seeker at a time when little information was available and most students had to practice alone. He had made space for these seekers to come together—around his books, his bookstore, his magick school, his magazines, and his festivals—and he had witnessed the formation of a grand magickal community. He experienced the rise of the internet and understood the significance and value of having this world wide web of limitless information and boundless opportunity for connection that we now have available. These developments excited him, and he forever hoped for greater growth, for the foundations laid in the past by himself and others to be a springboard into an even brighter, more expansive future.

When Paganism had first emerged, it was a thrilling time when people were excited to share ideas with others of "like mind," even if those "like minds" had vastly differing beliefs. It was a time of innovation, a time when individuals would take the tiniest seed of potential and nurture it into something new and tremendous. After decades of growth and development, after thousands upon thousands of occult books have been published and hundreds upon hundreds of magickal traditions have been established, it has become too easy for the everyday seeker to become complacent and leave the innovation to the established "experts." In a movement that has grown so large, the individual can forget that they are an essential part of it. One of Carl's core messages that he wanted to get across was that every individual matters and that evolution is the responsibility of every individual. Our potentials are without limit, but it's up to each of us to take our own steps forward.

Carl delighted in books that offered something new to say, that dared to try something different or that attempted to make sense of the how and why of magickal practice. He believed in books and felt that there will always be room for more books and for better and better books. He pushed his authors to be their best, to believe in themselves and share as much genuine, empowering information and personal insight as possible to deliver maximum benefits to their readers.

Carl decided he wanted to do some more writing himself, and he began to daydream about new book ideas and concepts. He had already been getting back into practice as a writer. In addition to writing the enlightening, inspiring, insightful, and often humorous introductory letters that welcome the readers to each month's issue of *Llewellyn's New Worlds* magazine and catalog, Carl had spent years adding detailed entries to the online Llewellyn Encyclopedia.

Containing a mixture of brief, straightforward definitions and thoughtful, information-packed lengthy essays and articles by multiple writers about an incredibly vast selection of terms and concepts relating to virtually any magickal, metaphysical, mystical, New Age, Pagan, or occult topic you can think of, the Llewellyn Encyclopedia is featured on the Llewellyn website. It provides a free and reliable resource and "starting point" for seekers needing more information to determine where their interests lie or who want to learn more about a particular subject area or double-check the accuracy of something they have read or heard that just doesn't seem to be quite right. The entries Carl wrote for the Llewellyn Encyclopedia are of the "lengthy" and "information-packed" variety, and all are filled with numerous gems of wisdom.

Carl had even toyed with the idea of writing some fiction, which he enjoyed indulging in occasionally but never had the opportunity or motivation to see any of these fantastical ideas through to a finished product. His passion was in empowering individuals through the extension of knowledge and the inspiration of innovative ideas and evolutionary concepts, and he found that the medium that suited him best for this purpose was writing nonfiction about magick, metaphysics, and spirituality.

Once he had started the flow of inspiration, it seemed that Carl couldn't stop writing, contributing literally hundreds (but probably thousands) of well-written, thought-provoking, informative articles and entries to the Llewellyn website, its publications, and its online encyclopedia. When Carl's close friend Dr. Joe Slate just happened to propose around this time that the two might write some books together, Carl jumped at the chance.

Carl had always dreamed of being a book author, ever since his college days when he started to compile notes for a book on Aleister Crowley that he never got around to writing. He had written and self-published his *Science of Feeling Fine* book before he was actually a publisher and still in his early twenties, and since then he had written countless articles, book introductions, newsletters, contributions for Llewellyn's almanacs, magazines, and more—yet somehow, he still didn't think of himself as a writer. He talked about how he "had always dreamed of being a writer" but had gotten sidetracked by becoming a publisher instead. Now it seemed that the opportunity had come and the time was right for Carl to write, and write he did.

Carl found that after all his years of living and learning and loving and experiencing, he had developed a head full of magickal information and spiritual learning, and he wanted to share all he could of what he knew. Carl's writing style somehow manages to be both academic and personal, down-to-earth and practical yet deeply complex and philosophical simultaneously.

His and Joe's first release was *Psychic Empowerment for Everyone*, a small guidebook that explored psychic empowerment techniques from both a practical and a scientific viewpoint. "It always amazes me to see my words in print. How do I know so much?" joked Carl after the book debuted. But he was soon back at it, proving that he had yet more to offer, and Carl and his co-author Joe set to work on a series of several new publications.

The books that Carl Llewellyn Weschcke and Dr. Joe H. Slate wrote together are absolutely enormous. All are several inches thick (with the exception of the first one) and containing an abundance of information and thought-provoking insights on so much more than you would ever expect to find. *The Llewellyn Complete Book of Psychic Empowerment*, for instance, addresses topics as far-ranging as remote viewing, psychokinesis, crystal gazing, sand reading, and self-hypnosis. *Clairvoyance for Psychic Empowerment*, released in 2013, weighs over two and a half pounds. "The only 'certainty' we have is that of continuing evolution," reads a line in the book. "We are here to grow, to become more than we are, and to realize the wholeness to which we are intended."

Together, Carl and Joe wrote eight books and produced several companion CDs. Stood side by side, the publications produced by Carl and Joe can easily fill well over a foot of shelf space. In addition to the books he wrote with Joe, Carl also produced a volume called *Dream ESP* based on the Taoist I Ching, as well as a newly revised edition of Louis T. Culling's *The Complete Magick Curriculum of the Secret Order G.B.G.* At an age when most individuals feel that it's too late for any kind of starting over, Carl proved that it's always possible to reinvent oneself. He had already lived a full life as a business executive, civil rights activist, and publisher, and now he had become still something more with his new career as an author.

Carl worked tirelessly on his writing, starting early in the morning and working till the evening with the exception of a brief lunch break somewhere in the middle. He kept extensive files of his research and pored over his manuscripts to find ways to improve and expand as he went along, double-checking charts and tables, compiling indexes, and writing glossaries. Few authors take so much time and effort with their manuscripts, but Carl knew that there is great value in what he called "that hard work energy." Carl believed there was magick in effort, saying:

I always worked hard as a publisher and a bookseller (and as an enlightened civil rights and civil liberties worker, a spokesman for astrology and Wicca, then as a husband and father), but I am working even harder as an author. It is, however, more challenging at my age than it was back in my twenties and thirties.[395]

Indeed, the years had taken their toll. Having struggled for some time with a rare condition that caused muscle pains and cramps, as well as having an ongoing heart and pulmonary condition, Carl found that staying active and mobile had become increasingly difficult. Experiencing the deterioration of his body, despite all his knowledge and practice of rejuvenation and healing techniques, was extremely frustrating for Carl and very difficult for those who loved him to witness. In 2011 Carl wrote,

I am constantly amazed, and frustrated, at what it means to be eighty years old in comparison to those old days when I could regularly work sixteen-hour days and still have time to mow the grass and enjoy a social life. It is frustrating to a man that I can't even help Sandra carry in groceries.

For a man who always did so much, it wasn't easy to do any less, so he poured his extra energy and focus into the books he was writing and in enjoying the company of those who were closest to him.

On November 7, 2015, with Sandra and Gabe by his side, Carl passed away at the age of eighty-five. He hadn't wanted to die so young. He had wanted to live to be 120—probably one of the few goals he had at which he wasn't able to succeed. In hopes of living longer, he had opted for a surgery that his doctor had recommended to correct a problem he was having, but complications had arisen and he wasn't able to heal as he had tried so hard to do. While he may have said he would have liked to live to be 120, it seems certain that if he had been given the choice, Carl would

---

395   CLW email to Melanie Marquis, November 26, 2011.

have gone on living forever so that he would never have to miss his friends or leave his family's side.

When news of Carl's passing spread, the impact he had made on the magickal world was highlighted by the outpouring of love and gratitude toward Carl from hundreds of personal friends and thousands of readers who had learned something meaningful from a Llewellyn book. The notice of Carl's death reached over half a million people on Facebook, with more than 24,000 people reacting to, commenting on, or sharing the post. One reader commented, "Back before the internet, if it hadn't been for Llewellyn, I'd have had almost no source of information on Wicca and Paganism." Llewellyn publisher Bill Krause commented, "Carl wanted people to attain their best self. Whether it was mental or physical, he was interested in people reaching their maximum potential." For the many who loved him or found inspiration in his work, the loss of Carl was hard to bear. "Do you know why this happened?" asked Carl's middle granddaughter in a letter she wrote to him following his death. "You will always be a part of this family," she wrote.

Carl will indeed remain a part of not only the Weschcke family, but also the Llewellyn family and legacy, his memory an ever-present guiding influence and source of inspiration. He still sits at the head of the table in Llewellyn's main conference room, gazing out with his wise, loving, soulful eyes from a picture that hangs behind an empty seat. With more than 2,000 titles in print in 2018 in all categories of mind, body, and spirit, Llewellyn continues to water the seeds planted by Llewellyn George and to propagate the hybrid crops and glorious fruits that flourished under Carl's stewardship. He left behind a legacy so large it cannot be measured, for what he left behind was knowledge and love, two forces whose power is both infinite and exponential.

"Become more than you are and all that you can be!" was one of Carl's favorite mottos and oft-repeated calls to action that he would mention in his writings and in letters and emails to his many correspondents. Carl Llewellyn Weschcke became more in this life, and in doing so he opened doorways and windows into "New Worlds of Mind, Body, and Spirit" that we are all invited to step forward through and see beyond so that we might gain the wisdom to become more, too.

He did all he did out of love, and love is the purest essence of ambition.

We know where we came from,
we know where we're at, and
we know where we're headed.

—SANDRA K. WESCHCKE [396]

396   Kirch, "Llewellyn Looks to the Stars."

From Kristoffer Hughes:

My introduction to Llewellyn Worldwide and to Carl was by means of Scott Cunningham's *Magical Herbalism*, a copy of which I had found in a secondhand bookshop near my home in Wales. Eventually I was to read Cunningham's biography *Whispers of the Moon*, which expressed the deep connection Carl and Cunningham had, and something about that depiction of those two men warmed my heart. I had only ever dreamed of writing a book adorned with that little crescent moon. Dreams are important, and there are times in life when they do come true—as did mine in 2011 when I joined the Llewellyn Worldwide family. A Welsh television production company was interested in my book and followed me to Minnesota to meet the Llewellyn team and Carl.

The memory of that day is as clear, crisp, and fresh as the snowy hills that surrounded the Weschcke homestead. Though in poor health, he had invited myself and the TV crew to meet him at his home and recount some history of Llewellyn Worldwide for the documentary. He seemed so familiar, as if I had met him a hundred times, and whilst frail there was a vibrancy about him, a fire that burned brightly in his eyes—he was everything I had imagined him to be, and perhaps more. He sat in a large leather chair at his table, surrounded by books, in a checked shirt, his white beard and hair gleaming in the winter light that flooded through the window behind him. I am rarely a man who is lost for words, but here I was stumped and gobsmacked. I felt quite in awe of him.

He asked me which author I favoured at the Llewellyn family, to which the answer was Scott Cunningham. His eyes lit brighter at that, and I saw so much love in them for a man long since departed from this world. Carl struck me as a man who loved deeply, who wore his heart upon his sleeve, and who inspired others with the brightness of fire that gleamed in his eyes. His voice was something that lifted my heart: deep, resonant, powerful, sagacious, and compelling, I could have sat at that table all day and listened to his stories and the divine rhythm of his voice. How fortunate that we recorded some of the time I spent with him, and I often look back at that video with great fondness.

What struck me the most was to be in the company of someone who had inspired countless individuals, not only to discover the arts of metaphysics and the New Age, but to be led to pen those books for themselves. I include myself as one of those inspired to sit and write. And in truth, Carl was a vital part of that journey. He was someone who literally changed the face of occulture forever, and he encouraged his authors—his children—to inspire, to reach out and continue to change the world. To have met him was and continues to be one of the highlights of my life.

What is remembered lives.

———————————

Carl's Calls to Action

It is everyone's responsibility to grow and gain wisdom. Stop depending only on others to tell you what's true, what's correct, how to vote, how to spend your money, where to live, where to travel, when to do this, when to do that, who to love, who to hate, and the whole litany of instructions others seek to impose on you. Wake up! You have only one true commandment to follow, and that is to grow and become more than you are.

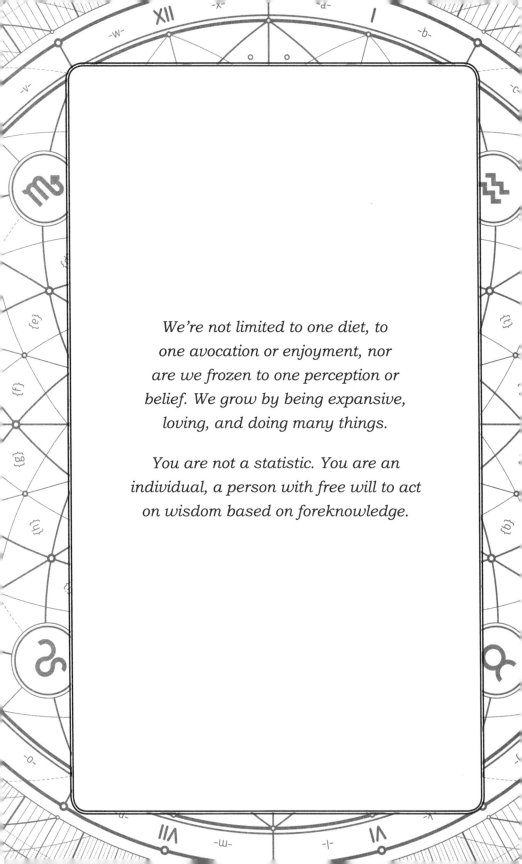

We're not limited to one diet, to one avocation or enjoyment, nor are we frozen to one perception or belief. We grow by being expansive, loving, and doing many things.

You are not a statistic. You are an individual, a person with free will to act on wisdom based on foreknowledge.

*Don't worship the past, and
realize that we are all on a journey
moving forward and upward.*

*I don't know God; I don't know the creator.
I don't even know what it really means.
But we're here. Now. The one thing I see is
that growth seems to be important. There
is evolution. So that must be the ultimate
meaning of existence: to grow. And there
must be a continual opportunity to grow.*

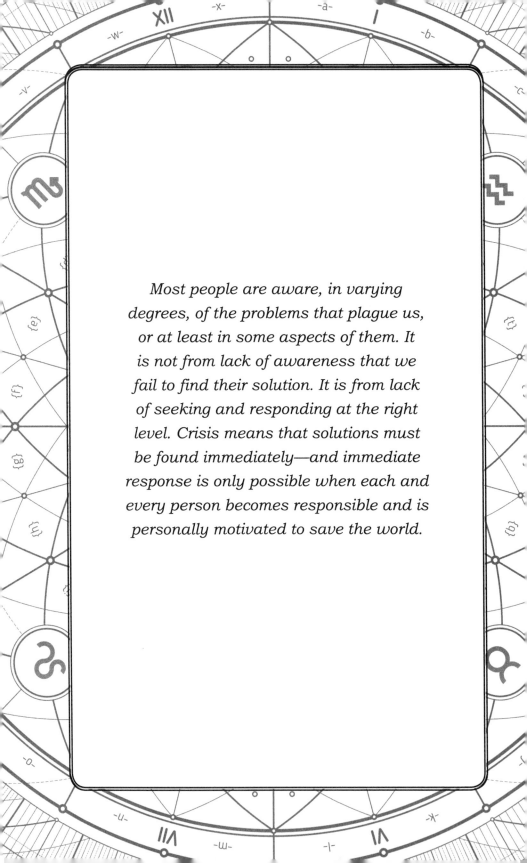

Most people are aware, in varying degrees, of the problems that plague us, or at least in some aspects of them. It is not from lack of awareness that we fail to find their solution. It is from lack of seeking and responding at the right level. Crisis means that solutions must be found immediately—and immediate response is only possible when each and every person becomes responsible and is personally motivated to save the world.

What we do today shapes tomorrow,
and it is within our power to make
tomorrow a brighter day. That
is what we are born to do.

It'll take love to bring us together, a
strong will to meet the challenge, and the
wisdom to put our knowledge to work.

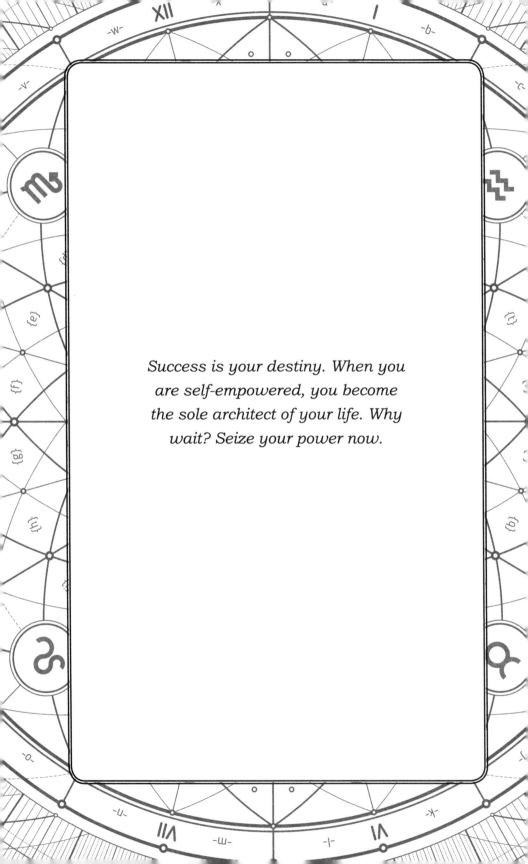

Success is your destiny. When you are self-empowered, you become the sole architect of your life. Why wait? Seize your power now.

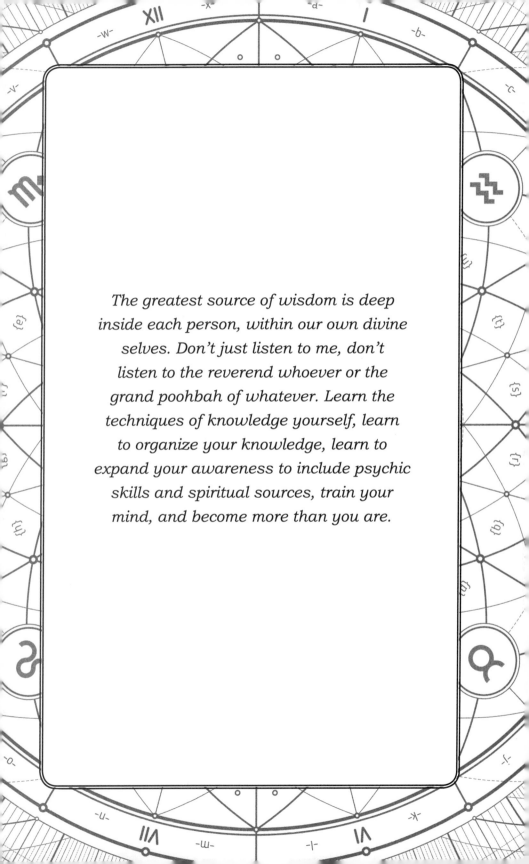

The greatest source of wisdom is deep inside each person, within our own divine selves. Don't just listen to me, don't listen to the reverend whoever or the grand poohbah of whatever. Learn the techniques of knowledge yourself, learn to organize your knowledge, learn to expand your awareness to include psychic skills and spiritual sources, train your mind, and become more than you are.

SANDRA'S FAVORITE PHOTOGRAPH OF CARL

Sweet Memories

Our first date was actually a blind date arranged by a mutual friend for lunch on July 16, 1971. It was too short but long enough to set a spark between us. Our second date was to Carl's friends' home on the St. Croix River, where we had a fine dinner and afterwards relaxed by the water on a hammock, and at that moment it seemed like a magical beginning for us. I had no experience with or thoughts about anything esoteric, but I had a huge open mind and was willing to listen.

When I first met Carl, he was newly excited about Wicca because he had recently met Lady Sheba, and while he understood Wicca and had studied it, I don't think he previously had been very interested in pursuing it to the level he did. Iø think he surprised himself as he recognized the power of the movement and the people; this was something new that people were just starting to grasp for themselves, and he felt the power himself. The initiation he received from Lady Sheba was very profound and had a strong effect on him, opening that special world to him. Thus for a while our lives revolved around Wiccan practices, rituals, and various meetings with other covens. We were active in the Craft up until about 1975, when it slowly became obvious that being active in the Craft and running a business with a young family was not possible. Another element was Carl's long-time commitment to the practice of magick. Even in the Wicca days we often worked within circles with various magical experiments Carl thought up.

Carl had a blast planning our marriage, and as you read in the book he even designed my wedding gown, he wrote the text for the ceremony, and he planned every aspect of the event. It was a beautiful, special Wiccan wedding attending by 300 friends, family, and Llewellyn staff (yes, by this time and ever since February 1, 1972, I worked at Llewellyn).

My best memory of when our son, Gabe, was born was right after his birth. Carl brought him to me and I got up on my knees in the bed and we had a big hug with baby between us. This emotional occasion was the beginning of our happy family life. Carl and I were very happy being the parents of a healthy baby—our perfect little boy.

You have read about the movie earlier in the book, but only I know about how powerful and natural Carl the actor was. His voice boomed out as he opened the circle to call out to the elements, his power radiated throughout the circle, his radiant personality dominated the scene. It was unforgettable.

By this time Carl was developing relationships with authors, and when I talk about family several authors come to mind because they hung around the house so much. The first was Noel Tyl, who moved here from Germany and bought a home across the street from us. During these pre-computer days Carl thought the ideal project for Noel would be to write a twelve-volume astrology how-to set of books called *The Principles and Practice of Astrology* for people to learn astrology. Noel wrote the series and it sold well for a long time. Already family and authors and Llewellyn were intertwined. I was not exempt from Carl's pushing, and since we didn't have a real sales force in those days, I visited the Borders/ Walden buyer and sold them the series. So, we had busy, happy dinners with ourselves, sometimes with authors or family or all mixed together.

Early Llewellyn author Jonn Mumford was very special in our lives. Jonn lived in Australia but spent many summers with us while he and Carl worked on *A Chakra & Kundalini Workbook,* as well as other projects relating to Tantra.

Our family spent the first three years in a big old mansion on Summit Avenue in St. Paul. The home lent itself to big parties, and we had impressive press parties and festival parties in our home, with our nanny watching Gabe. The parties accommodated up to one hundred people, they were catered, and they were exciting opportunities for us to grow Llewellyn through networking and author development. Later we moved to the country, to Woodbury, to a pretty house on a lake, where we had many fun family days with our son and dog on the water. This home lent itself to parties too, and we had large family reunions, author parties, and staff parties. Carl set the pace, he had a vision every time, nothing was done without a purpose but also always done in a warm and folksy manner. We were down to earth, sharing what we did and loved.

Llewellyn was Carl's heart, an extension of himself, a way for him to be who he was, to bring education and knowledge through the books he published and the authors who came to him, the authors he developed for all people interested in the magical arts. The book is all about this; I can only add something about Carl's passion for Llewellyn, which was so rich and alive and a part of him. Our lives revolved around Llewellyn. Our wonderful family vacations were built around book shows, so we went to the show and then had a family vacation in the show's geographic area. We especially liked it when the shows were held in California or Texas, as the Southwest was our favorite area. Carl loved the Southwest so much that he wanted us to move to Santa Fe, except that idea proved impractical for Llewellyn. Even so, the desert Southwest spoke to him.

Carl made meticulous plans for our family vacations out West. His itinerary was most Virgo-perfect. We had a station wagon–style vehicle that we would pack up with Gabe in the back with his toys (no seat belts in those days) and off we would go through South Dakota to visit the Black Hills and the Badlands, into Wyoming to visit Yellowstone, and on to Santa Fe, New Mexico (our favorite). Other years we visited the various canyon lands and explored Arizona, including Sedona. Except for at night when Carl stayed up late reading manuscripts, we were your typical American vacationing family. Carl always packed his computer (he had one of the very earliest ones) and a ton of work, but family took over. Alas, he never got all that work done, and the computer gathered dust.

Carl was so excited about our trade shows. He sent me and Noel Tyl to our very first show back in 1974 in Washington, DC. What a time that was! We had a very small booth with a homemade backdrop, and we were so inexperienced, but regardless it was a new beginning for Llewellyn and so exciting that Carl came with the following year to the show in NYC. We attended the show for many years until recently, when the show lost some of its luster.

Carl always told me he was an introvert, which I could never believe, so he explained that as a young man who wanted "to go places," he had pushed himself to be an extrovert. He was able to bridge both worlds, when you think about how at ease he was with people, and I don't think he ever felt emotionally drained from being with people—he may have gotten some good energy out of it. On the other hand, Carl was at his happiest when he was home at his computer. He always said there was a brain-to-fingers connection that enabled him to express himself easily and even enhance his thinking to a higher level.

I could tell you ten different ways about "that was Carl's first love" because he loved life so much and he wanted a long life so he could read all the books he wanted to read and study enough to learn everything and help everyone he possibly could through his publishing efforts. It could have been the study of magick principles, Llewellyn, Llewellyn authors, his own deep thinking, his creativity, his family (of course Gabe and I, but also his parents and siblings and his old school chums lovingly referred to as "the

Boys"). More than anything, Carl loved to develop authors. He had a gift of seeing potential in people and loved working with them to bring it out. Carl loved Llewellyn. Llewellyn truly was his heart.

Although Carl has departed from this earth, our relationship lives on through my conversation with him. I have his picture in my bedroom along with some of his precious mementos and his ashes. I have made a sacred altar for him, and I talk to him every day, many times a day. I believe he sometimes helps me find the best solution, and I am certain he is happy that I am at the office every day. Above all, it is a comfort to me to keep him in my life. My love for Carl will never end.

—*Sandra K. Weschcke*

Appendix

Carl's Natal Chart Analysis

The standout feature in Carl Weschcke's natal chart is his Cardinal Grand Cross, which features multiple conjunctions. Cardinal signs start each of our seasons, and in the natal chart they are the fuel behind any project or endeavor. We tend to think of squares as difficult, but just as gifts are bestowed upon us in the form of trines, squares and oppositions are challenges that the universe grants us in order for us to evolve to our highest spiritual forms. As we have seen, Carl turned any challenges he faced into opportunities.

This powerful Cardinal Grand Cross features a Mars in Cancer square to Uranus in Aries. This aspect causes a desire to break free of norms and to bring about intense and sudden changes. A Saturn square Uranus aspect challenged Carl to combine stability with growth and expansion. Uranus in Aries and the Moon in Aries in the first house make squares to Jupiter in Cancer in the fifth house. Jupiter square Uranus is one of the luckiest aspects in astrology, making the native excited for new horizons and adventures. He created new horizons through creative expansion. Mercury in Libra in the seventh house also forms squares to Mars in the fourth house and Jupiter in the fifth house, influencing quick, creative decisions, as well as bestowing great optimism and aspirations for those he knew professionally and personally. Mercury in Libra opposes Uranus in Aries. Uranus in Aries knows what it wants, and conjunct his moon in Aries, lends a brilliant mental and intellectual quality. Carl was an innovative, creative inventor and master occultist. Carl's mental vitality, passion, and energy is shown by Mercury in opposition to Uranus. While this aspect can, at times, lend anxiety or nervous tension, Carl channeled this potentially turbulent energy into inventiveness, novel ideas, and new projects. For sure, Carl was a brilliant pioneer. Mercury in Libra squares Saturn in Capricorn. This aspect makes the native highly intelligent and cautious, which nicely balances the harsher aspects involved in this Grand Cross. Mercury in Libra helped Carl to communicate in a delicate and efficient way with those he mentored. And finally, Mars in Cancer in the fourth house opposes Saturn in Capricorn in the tenth house. Carl viewed any obstacles as motivators for success. If there were only two ways to achieve a goal, by using his intense drive to succeed, he created a third way.

Saturn in the tenth house is noted for producing highly ambitious personalities, and Carl was certainly known for his determination and commitment to his career. Saturn, Capricorn, and the tenth house all represent the father. And Carl is known as the father, and pioneer, of the occult and of the mind, body, spirit community. Although natal Saturn is not conjunct his Midheaven on the tenth-house cusp in Sagittarius, his tenth-house placement of Saturn in Capricorn (its home sign and house) is much more powerful, as it indicates a person who will win positions of authority, achievement, and naturally handle power with grace. This is especially true given Saturn's involvement in the Cardinal Grand Cross. By way of Carl's natal Saturn placement, along with his Cardinal Grand Cross, it is no surprise that he rose to prominence, maintained success, and was seen as a mentor and father figure to so many.

Carl has a Pisces ascendant, and thus, Neptune is his chart ruler. Pisces and Neptune represent psychics, the occult, and astrology. It also gives the bearer a dreamy quality. Neptune, his chart ruler, falls into his sixth house of daily work. His daily work was his occult publishing house. His sixth-house cusp of daily work falls in Leo, and Leo is represented by the Sun. His Sun in Virgo falls on the descendant and in the seventh house of relationships. He gave back to his community and mentored others through his work. The lower octave of Neptune is Jupiter. His Jupiter in Cancer resides in his fifth house of creative manifestation, while the ruler of his Cancer fifth house, the moon, falls into his first house. He is the embodiment of his daily creative manifestations. As well, Jupiter is the ruler of Sagittarius, falling on his tenth-house cusp of career and worldly ambitions.

Also of note is Carl's Jupiter conjunction to Pluto. Wealth, sometimes extreme wealth, is a common manifestation of Jupiter in conjunction to Pluto. This powerful combination resides in his fifth house of creativity, and Carl literally built his creative empire from the ground up.

With his North Node in Aries in the first house, Carl was destined to be a pioneer of the occult. And with the North Node in conjunction to his Moon in Aries, Carl was very good at dealing with the public and working with women. This is especially important in the publishing industry. Uranus in the first house is conjunct his Moon in Aries. He felt perfectly comfortable as a free-thinking, unique soul.

If we carefully examine Carl's chart, we find a Grand Trine formation with Juno in Capricorn placed in the eleventh house of social welfare, trine his Sun in Virgo in the seventh house of the other, and trine Chiron (the wounded healer) in Taurus in the second house of values. Carl was president of the NAACP's Minnesota branch. He also served as the ACLU's vice president. This trine configuration shows that Carl had a natural propensity for serving the public and giving to others. Carl believed in reaching our fullest potential and giving others a platform to do the same.

Juno is placed in Capricorn in the eleventh house. With Juno in Capricorn, Carl's ideal partner was someone who could be not only his wife but his business partner; a person who is educated, practical, and possesses good business sense. Indeed, he found his ideal in his wife, Sandra. Carl's Venus sextile Saturn aspect mirrors this perfectly, as Carl took his commitments and obligations seriously. He had a practical approach to money and love that steadied them in the darkest of times.

With his angular Sun in Virgo, situated on the descendant and in the seventh house, Carl attracted business partners and friends who supported him in achieving his goals. Partnerships were very important to Carl. Combined with his Pisces ascendant, he gave off a magnanimous yet mysterious energy. When Carl entered a room, you knew it. Because his Sun is angular, it's easily one of the most powerful points in his chart. With the Sun and Mercury in the seventh house, Carl was a man who valued relationships and intellectual conversations with others, especially his immediate family. This is supported by his Venus in Scorpio conjunct the eighth-house cusp and trine to Mars in Cancer in the fourth. He was a solid defender of home and hearth who used his resources well. Not only was this true of his immediate family. Carl treated Llewellyn Publications as an extension of his home, and he treated his employees as family. Those with a seventh-house Sun give of themselves to the world. Carl's gift to the world was his service to publishing, his belief in the potential in others, and his dedication to building new horizons in mind, body, and spirit.

—Rose Wright

Bibliography

Abbasi, Susan. "Study Group, Books, Even Classes Offer Several Ways to Learn about the Occult." *Minneapolis Star.* February 26, 1970.

Ahern, Don. "Witch Wedding Public." Ridder News Service. June 1, 1973. Accessed July 2, 2017. https://www.llewellyn.com/about/event.php?id=231.

"American Civil Liberties Union of Minnesota (Saint Paul, Minn.): An Inventory of Its Records at the Minnesota Historical Society, Historical Note." Minnesota Historical Society Research Library. Accessed July 9, 2017. www.2.mnhs.org/library/findaids/00497.xml.

Armstrong, Robert. "Saint Paul Book Firm's Success Was Written in the Stars." *Minneapolis Star Tribune.* November 5, 1978.

Associated Press. "Home of NAACP Official Shot At." *Asbury Park Press* (Asbury Park, New Jersey). July 20, 1954.

———. "NAACP Lawyers Threatened in Louisiana: Disbarment Action Urged." *The Bee* (Danville, Virginia). September 25, 1954.

Atlanta Journal-Constitution/The Orlando Sentinel. "When an Old Religion Meets Pop Culture." November 13, 1999.

The Austin Daily Herald. "Human Rights Bills Have Hard Sledding." May 15, 1959.

Bahn, Christopher. "Hubert Humphrey Was a Vampire!" *The Rake.* March 29, 2005. http://rakemag.com/2003/10/hubert-humphrey-was -vampire/.

The Baltimore Sun. "Witchcraft." March 6, 1976.

Bear, Rob. "This Romanesque Pile Is the Most Haunted House in Saint Paul." *Curbed.* September 14, 2012. Accessed June 30, 2017. https://www.curbed.com/2012/9/14/10329170/this -romanesque-pile-is-the-most-haunted-house-in-st-paul.

Blodgett, Tim. "Saint Paul Holds Hearing on Open Occupancy." *Minneapolis Star Tribune.* May 23, 1959.

"BP Report: On the Business of Book Publishing." *Knowledge Industry Publications* (White Plains, NY), vol. 13, no. 30. July 27, 1988.

Byrne, Carol. "LaRouche Followers Set Sights on Control of State DFL Party." *Star Tribune.* March 22, 1986.

Bytheriver, Marylee. "Llewellyn George: A Biography," foreword to revised *A to Z Horoscope Maker and Delineator.* Llewellyn George. Woodbury: Llewellyn Worldwide, 2007.

Castner, Lynn S. "The Case for Commitment Law Reform," letter to the editor. *Minneapolis Star.* April 18, 1966.

"Celebrity Greetings." *Minneapolis Star.* December 22, 1977.

Cesnik, Jim. "Astrology Book Claims New Year Will Be Tense." *Minneapolis Sunday Tribune.* December 31, 1961.

Church, Frank. "Wood Pellet Firm Isn't Fired Up about Valley Site." *The Post-Crescent* (Appleton, Wisconsin). November 16, 1982.

Clepper, P. M. "Movie Takes Advantage of City's Reputation As a Witch Center." *Pioneer Press.* June 2, 1974.

Clever, Dick. "Clustered Stargazers Shrug Off Scientists' Attack on Astrology." *Minneapolis Star.* September 11, 1975.

Condon, Garret. "The Future Market." *Hartford Courant* (Hartford, Connecticut). March 5, 1996.

Detroit Free Press. "Soothsaying Auto Worker Flint's Presidential Hope." March 27, 1932.

Detroit Free Press. "Tonight's Television Programs." October 30, 1974.

Evening Telegram (Superior, Wisconsin). "Magic, Witchcraft and Astrology Lecture Topic." April 18, 1972.

Flint, Jerry M. "Mystic Sciences Booming." *New York Times.* September 14, 1971.

Ford, Marcia. "Religion Update: Finding Help on the Shelves." *Publishers Weekly.* May 23, 2005.

Forteana, "Fate," http://fortean.wikidot.com/fate.

Frost, Guy. "Ida Hulery Fletcher and the Portland School of Astrology." *Guy Frost Faerie Faith Papers.* New Age Movements, Occultism, and Spiritualism Research Library. Valdosta State University, Valdosta, GA.

Fuller, Jim. "Rumor Giving Company a Devil of a Time." *Star Tribune.* March 25, 1980.

Gag, Wanda. *Growing Pains: Diaries and Drawings for the Years 1908–1917.* Saint Paul: Minnesota Historical Society Press, 1984.

Gage, Amy. "Witchcraft in the 'burbs." *Star Tribune.* December 18, 2004.

Gibson, Richard. "In the Light of the Full Moon." *Minneapolis Star.* September 26, 1972.

Giese, Don, and Bill Farmer. "What Haunts Summit Avenue Mansion?" (Fourth in a series: "The Haunted Among Us.") *Saint Paul Pioneer Press.* February 26, 1969.

Gnosticus. *A Wiccan Rite of Marriage in the American Celtic Tradition, for use by Covens and Individuals.* Saint Paul: Llewellyn Publications, 1972.

Green, Susan. "Computer Calculates Astrological Charts." *The Burlington Free Press.* December 8, 1981.

Green, William D. "Race and Segregation in Saint Paul's Public Schools, 1846–1869." Minnesota Historical Society. collections/*Minnesota History Magazine* articles. Accessed May 13, 2017. http://collections.mnhs.org/MNHistoryMagazine /articles/55/v55i04p138-149.pdf.

The Greenville News (Greenville, South Carolina). "Timmerman Doesn't Believe Brownwell Will Investigate NAACP Subversive Charge." May 4, 1954.

The Guardian. "'The Most Impure Tale Ever Written': How *The 120 Days of Sodom* Became a Classic." October 7, 2016. Accessed July 14, 2017. https://www.theguardian.com/books/2016/oct/07 /marquis-de-sade-120-days-of-sodom-published-classic

Hodierne, Robert. "Seers Predict, Love, Fame, 6 Kids—and Sunday Rain." *Minneapolis Star.* August 4, 1972.

Hogan, Susan. "Pagan's Progress." *Star Tribune.* October 31, 1996.

Houck, Davis W. and David E. Dixon, editors. *Women and the Civil Rights Movement, 1954–1965.* Jackson: University Press of Mississippi, 2009.

Italie, Leanne. "Gay-themed Books Take Off with Youths." Associated Press. *The Desert Sun.* June 27, 2010.

Johnson, George X. "Leary Taps Like Minds for Mission." *Minneapolis Star.* February 18, 1982.

Keith, Christopher J. "Chauncey and Martha Griggs House 476 Summit Avenue." Saint Paul Historical Society. Accessed June 25, 2017. http://saintpaulhistorical.com/items/show/349

Kelly, Aidan. "Inventing Witchcraft: The Gardnerian Paper Trail." *Iron Mountain.* Summer 1984, 23.

Kelly, Patty. "Angels' Voices, Silver's Spells, Sticks, Stones, Roots, and Bones." *Twin Cities Business Monthly.* August 2004.

Kirch, Claire. "Llewellyn Looks to the Stars." *Publishers Weekly.* January 12, 2004.

Kirkpatrick, David D. "Random House Begins Layoffs as Executives Fear Long Sales Slump." *New York Times.* December 19, 2001. http://www.nytimes.com/2001/12/19/business /random-house-begins-layoffs-as-executives-fear -long-sales-slump.html

Klobuchar, Jim. "A Bulletin from the Beyond." *Minneapolis Star.* September 12, 1973.

Knoblauch, Mary. "Signs of the Occult Point to Saint Paul." *Chicago Tribune.* July 1, 1976.

Kotula, Denise. "Witchcraft: The Wiccan Faith." *Minnesota Daily.* October 31, 1979.

Lauerman, Connie. "Got a Problem? Pick a Card: Tarot Has Moved Out of the Occult Realm—to Become the Low-Cost 'Shrink in a Box.'" *Chicago Tribune.* December 4, 1997.

Lewis, Dorothy. "New Owner to Restore Ex-Gallery on Summit." Circa 1963.

Library of Congress. "NAACP: A Century in the Fight for Freedom." Accessed July 10, 2017. https://www.loc.gov/exhibits/naacp/the-civil-rights -era.html

Lightman, Herb A. "Filming Isis Among the Witches." *American Cinematographer*. December 1973, 1571.

"Little Italy: A Floodplain Neighborhood." National Park Service. Accessed July 10, 2017. https://www.nps.gov/miss/learn/education/upload/LittleItaly_30x40.pdf

"Llewellyn Moves to a New Campus in Woodbury, Minnesota." Llewellyn. March 1, 2005. https://www.llewellyn.com/about/event.php?id=715

Mankey, Jason. "25 Most Influential People in the Birth of Modern Paganism." *Patheos*. March 7, 2013.

Marks, Susan. "Civil Unrest on Plymouth Avenue, Minneapolis, 1967." MNOpedia. http://www.mnopedia.org/event/civil-unrest-plymouth-avenue-minneapolis-1967

Marquis, Melanie. "Interview with Carl Llewellyn Weschcke." *Tarot Reflections*. November 5, 2009. http://www.ata-tarot.com/reflections/11-05-09/interview_with_carl_llewell.html

McClure, Jane. "Rondo Neighborhood." Saint Paul Historical. Accessed July 7, 2017. http://saintpaulhistorical.com/items/show/160

———. "Rooms to Spare: City Allows Summit Mansion to Be Sold As Is, But Sets Six-Year Window to Reduce Living Units." *Villager*. June 9, 2010.

Mencken, H. L. "On Astrologer Llewellyn George." *Baltimore Evening Sun*. March 15, 1913.

Miller, Pamela. "Circle of Hope." *Star Tribune*. March 3, 2007.

———. "Wiccans Celebrate Settlement Allowing Symbol on Gravestones." *Star Tribune*. April 24, 2007.

Minneapolis Daily American. "Witchcraft Isn't Devil Worship." September 21, 1973.

Minneapolis Star. "Ex-Occultist Turned Power Against Satan." March 2, 1979.

———. "Federal Official, Freeman to Talk on Fair Housing." March 4, 1960.

———. "55% Prefer Owner's Rights in Housing Open Occupancy." March 16, 1958.

———. "Frank Farrell Named Head of State ACLU." January 15, 1963.

———. "Lord Asks Chance to Explain Rights Views." November 20, 1954.

———. "NAACP Group Will Present Awards to 11." May 22, 1964.

———. "NAACP Names Officers." December 10, 1956.

———. "Occult—Religion Outside the Church—Growing." March 13, 1971.

———. "Think Patient Home Prowler: Hospital Inmate Believed Victim of Householders Fire." August 30, 1933.

———. "Town Toppers." November 17, 1959.

Minneapolis Star Tribune. "Chairmen Named for NAACP Convention." January 27, 1959.

———. "Dealers Say Law Is Not Solution to Fair Housing." September 11, 1963.

———. "A Fair Housing Law." April 15, 1961.

———. "Fair Housing Will Be Topic of Conference." February 28, 1960.

———. "Horticultural Group Honors 9." October 15, 1956.

———. "Housing Group Names Drug Official to Board." October 10, 1959.

———. "NAACP Hails Those Who Picketed in the City."
February 29, 1960.

———. "State ACLU Elects Karlins as President." December
14, 1964.

———. "St. Paul Man Protests U.S. Seizure of Book."
February 1, 1959.

Morning News (Wilmington, Delaware). "Occult Fete Dawns
Dimly." September 7, 1971.

Morphew, Clark. "Publisher Capitalizes on Interest in
Nontraditional Belief." *News-Journal* (Mansfield, Ohio).
June 1, 1996.

———. "New Age Publishers Offering 'Tomorrow's Science
Today.'" *Saint Paul Pioneer Press.* July 22, 1990.

Nelson, Todd. "A Supernatural Plan." *Star Tribune.* October
24, 2011.

Newlund, Sam. "Passes Both Houses: Bill Will Rewrite
Commitment Law." *Minneapolis Star.* May 19, 1967.

The News-Palladium (Benton Harbor, Michigan). "Police
Probe Report Life of NAACP Chief Here Threatened."
October 28, 1954.

New Ulm Review. "Oldest Mayor in America." February 17,
1904.

Night Sky, Michael. "Carl Llewellyn Weschcke: Bringing
Magick to the Masses." *PanGaia* #50. Winter 2009, 17.

"Oklahoma City African Americans Sit-in for Integration,
1958–1964." Global Non-Violent Action Database.
Accessed July 9, 2017
nvdatabase.swarthmore.edu/content/oklahoma-city
-african-americans-sit-integration-1958-64

Ophiel. *Astral Light.* Volume 1, book 1. Undated, circa 1961–
1967.

———. *The Art and Practice of Astral Projection.* Saint Paul: Peach Publishing, 1961.

Orlando Sentinel. "Mixing Suits Threatened by NAACP." November 29, 1954.

Peiken, Matt. "Addicted to *X-Files?* Then Say Hello to *Fate.*" *Herald and Review* (Decatur, Illinois). April 23, 1998.

Penticuff, David. "For 'White Witch,' Craft Is About Love, Not Newts." *Muncie Evening Press* (Muncie, Indiana). October 31, 1994.

Peterson, Franklynn. "The Year of the Witch." *The Pittsburgh Press.* February 20, 1972.

———. "Witch Capital of the World." 1971 Sunday Group Feature. *Houston Chronicle.* January 2, 1972.

Pittsburgh Courier. "NAACP Faces Challenge as 'Leader' of Negroes," June 25, 1960.

Price, Ben. "Using Boycott, Anti-Negro Drive Rises in South." *Minneapolis Star.* November 26, 1954.

Publishers Weekly BEA Show Daily. "What a Difference a Year Makes." June 2, 2001.

Rahm, Virginia L. "The Nushka Club." *Minnesota History Magazine* 43 (Winter 1973): 303–307. Minnesota Historical Society Collections. Minnesota Historical Society. Accessed June 2, 2017. http://collections.mnhs.org/MNHistoryMagazine /articles/43/v43i08p303-307.pdf

Religion News Service. "Faith-Based Calendars Help Balance Time and Eternity." *Tampa Bay Times.* December 27, 1997.

"Richardsonian Romanesque Saint Paul Part III." Glessner House Museum. Accessed June 25, 2017. https://www.glessnerhouse.org/story-of-a-house/2014 /10/richardsonian-romanesque-st-paul-part.html

Richler, Mordecai. "Witches' Brew." *Playboy*. July 1974.

Saint Paul Daily Globe. "Jewelry and Cash Secured by a Sneak Thief—Bad and Bold." October 4, 1893.

———. "New Year's Reception." January 2, 1887.

———. "Took Her Own Life: Disagreement with Her Lover the Cause." November 5, 1893.

Saint Paul Dispatch. "Week-End's Parties Spooky." October 31, 1966.

"Saint Paul Haunted House, Griggs Mansion." Haunted Houses. Accessed June 25, 2017. http://www.hauntedhouses.com/states/mn /griggs_mansion.htm

Schlaver, Clarence O. "The Carol Thompson Murder Case." *Star Tribune*. January 27, 1970.

Shaver, John. "MCLU to Probe City, County Jails." *Minneapolis Star Tribune*. April 27, 1966.

Sheba, Lady. *Book of Shadows*. Saint Paul: Llewellyn Publications, 1971.

———. *Witch*. Saint Paul: Llewellyn Publications, 1973.

Skophammer, Roger. "Update: Carl Weschcke." *Star Tribune*. September 10, 1989.

Smith, Robert T. "Housewife Says Dead Communicate Through Her." *Minneapolis Star Tribune*. September 24, 1972.

———. "Space Feats Stimulate Occult." *Star Tribune*. July 29, 1970.

———. "Saint Paul Book Firm's Success was Written in the Stars." *Star Tribune*. November 5, 1978.

———. "The Rise of the Occult." *Star Tribune*. December 17, 1972.

———. "Witches Meet in City, but Frog Changes Unlikely." *Minneapolis Star Tribune.* September 23, 1972.

———. "Witches Stir Brew Under Full Moon." *Minneapolis Star Tribune.* September 6, 1971.

Star Tribune. "Dayton's Salutes the American Designers." August 19, 1979.

———. "Deputies Trail Society Bandit." December 3, 1935.

———. "Summer Solstice Magical Arts Festival." July 5, 1970.

St. Cloud Times (St. Cloud, Minnesota)."Occult School Opens in Mpls." September 4, 1971.

Stevens Point Journal. "Big DNR Land Purchase Approved." January 29, 1982.

St. George, Ozzie. "Wands and Witches in Downtown Saint Paul." *Saint Paul Pioneer Press.* September 16, 1975.

Straub, Mary. "High Priest of the Occult, Bonafide Witch." *Tinley Park Illinois.* September 1973.

Sutin, Lawrence. "Father of the New Age." *Minnesota Monthly.* May 1989.

Towne, Oliver. "Spook Parade on Summit Avenue." *Saint Paul Dispatch.* March 16, 1966.

United States Department of the Interior National Park Service. "National Register of Historic Places Inventory— nomination form 76001067, Griggs-Upham House 476 Summit Ave.," 11.

Wack, Charles. "Man Wanted." March 13, 1890. Accessed June 25, 2017. https://www.newspapers.com/image /81064665/?terms=charles%2Bwack

Walsh, Ray. "BookExpo Covered Something for Everyone." *Lansing State Journal* (Lansing, Michigan). June 11, 2000.

Walters, Ray. "Paperback Writers: Astrology's Star Authors Shine Brightly." *News Press* (Fort Myers, Florida). September 4, 1978.

Wasserman, Steve. "The Amazon Effect," *The Nation*. May 29, 2012. https://www.thenation.com/article/amazon-effect/

Wellcome, J. W. B. "The Pioneer Doctors of the Minnesota Valley, Second Paper, Dr. Carl Weschcke of New Ulm." *Northwestern Lancet*, volume 22.

Weschcke, Carl. *Growing Nuts in the North*. Saint Paul: Webb Publishing Company, 1953.

Weschcke, Carl Llewellyn. "Mrs. Penny's Spirit Rocking Chair." *Llewellyn Journal*. February 18, 2005.

———. "Myself at Babson." Academic paper, Babson College. October 1, 1948.

———. "A Really Scary Ghost Story." *Llewellyn Journal*. January 1, 2005.

———. *The Science of Feeling Fine*. Saint Paul: Chester-Kent, Inc., 1954.

———. "Shop Ventures into Unknown." *Publishers Weekly*. March 8, 1970.

———. "Table Tipping and Ouija." *Llewellyn Journal*. February 11, 2005.

———. "Telepathic Communication." *Llewellyn Journal*. January 1, 2005.

Wilson, Robert Anton. "The Witches Are Coming." Accessed October 5, 2017. http://rawilsonfans.org/1973/01/

"Witchcraft and Neo-Paganism." Encyclopedia.com. http://www.encyclopedia.com/religion/encyclopedias -almanacs-transcripts-and-maps/witchcraft-and -neo-paganism

Woltman, Nick. "Saint Paul's Haunted Past—and Present." *Pioneer Press*. TwinCities.com. Accessed June 30, 2017. http://www.twincities.com/2015/10/25/10-haunted -st-paul-sites-halloween/

Wood, Dave. "1994 Was a Year of Literary Occurrences Happy and Sad." *Star Tribune*. January 1, 1995.

———. "Minnesota Booksellers Make Presence Felt." *Star Tribune*. June 14, 1987.

———. "On Books." *Star Tribune*. March 3, 1996.

Wright, Elbee. Acknowledgments for *Book of Legendary Spells*. Minneapolis: Marlar Publishing Company, 1968.

Youngblood, Dick. "Determined to Succeed." *Star Tribune*. May 9, 2002.